New SAT Guide, 1st Edition

Resources & Explanations:

IVYGLOBAL.COM/STUDY

PASSWORD: greenbook

New SAT Guide, 1st Edition

This publication was written and edited by the team at Ivy Global.

Editor-in-Chief: Laurel Perkins

Producers: Lloyd Min and Junho Suh

Editing: Sacha Azor, Corwin Henville, Nathan Létourneau, and Kristin Rose

Writing: Sarah Atkins, Amanda Bakowski, Spencer Bass, Natalia Cole, Yvonne Greenen, Helen Huang, Keven Ji, James Levine, Lucy Liu, Casey O'Leary, Sarah Pike, Julia Romanski, and Martha Schabas

Formatting: Alexandra Candib, Elizabeth Cox, Keven Gungor, Lei Huang, and Yolanda Song

Proofreaders: Beini Chen, Caroline Incledon, Caroline Jo, Somin Lee, Amelia McLeod, and Michael Protacio

Marketing: Sabrina Bartlett, Shavumiyaa Chandrabalan, Lisa Faieta, Lana Lam, Howard Fung, and Kalden Tsung

Interns: Tyler Ishikawa, Justin Strauss, Andrew Wallace

About the Publisher

Ivy Global is a pioneering education company that delivers a wide range of educational services.

E-mail: publishing@ivyglobal.com

Website: http://www.ivyglobal.com

Contents

ESSAY

MATH

PRACTICE TESTS

Chapter 1
Introduction

SECTION 1
How to Use this Book

Welcome students and parents! This book is intended to help students prepare for the SAT, a test created and administered by the College Board.

Most colleges and universities in the United States require the SAT as part of the application process for admission. For many high school students, the SAT is a huge undertaking and a major source of anxiety. It is our goal to ease your concerns by demystifying the SAT and offering you tips, tricks, and plenty of practice to help you do your best. This book will help you turn this challenging admissions requirement into an opportunity to demonstrate to colleges that you can and will succeed.

In this book, we provide you with a comprehensive breakdown of the new SAT and proven test-taking strategies to approach the different sections and question types. This book contains chapters about the new SAT's Reading Test, Writing and Language Test, Essay Test, and Math Test, as well as multiple practice tests. Here is what's inside:

- 2 full-length practice tests at the end of the book
- 1 additional full-length test included as separate practice sections after each chapter
- More than 500 additional practice problems and drills
- Lists of SAT vocabulary, word roots, and recommended outside reading

The first key to succeeding on the SAT is to know the test, so we recommend familiarizing yourself with the structure, format, and timing of the test. Read through this book in order to gain an understanding of the inner workings of the exam. Chapters 2, 3, 4, and 5 discuss the Reading Test, Writing Test, Essay, and Math Test, respectively. These chapters provide specific information about the question types and content you will encounter in these sections of the SAT. They also provide helpful review of key English and Math concepts. Once you know what's what and you have honed your math, reading, and writing skills, test your skills with the practice exams at the end of this book in Chapter 6.

Also, check out our website for even more resources: http://ivyglobal.com/study. There, you'll find more resources to supplement the practice in our book, as well as information about upcoming tests, tutoring services and prep classes, and other tips to help you do your best.

Good luck studying!

SECTION 2
ABOUT THE SAT

- Part 1: What is the SAT?
- Part 2: The New SAT in Detail
- Part 3: Taking the SAT

WHAT IS THE SAT?
PART 1

INTRODUCTION

The SAT is a standardized examination designed to measure students' abilities in three areas: reading, writing, and mathematical reasoning. The SAT is written and administered by the College Board. Many American colleges and universities require SAT scores for admission and consider these scores an important factor in judging the quality of applicants.

Why do colleges care about the SAT? Because grading standards vary from one high school to another, it can be hard for colleges to know whether two applicants with the same grades are performing at the same level. Therefore, having everyone take the same standardized test gives schools another metric for judging your abilities against another student's.

Of course, SAT scores aren't the only things that colleges consider when assessing applicants. Your high school grades, course selection, extracurricular activities, recommendation letters, and application essays are all factors that colleges will use to decide whether you are a good fit for their school. However, in today's highly competitive admissions process, a solid SAT score may provide you with the extra edge needed to be successful.

WHAT'S NEW?

The College Board is implementing significant changes to the SAT that will take effect in the spring of 2016. The new SAT will include a Reading Test, a Writing Test, and a Math Test. Together, the Reading and Writing Test scores will contribute to an Evidence-Based Reading and Writing Area score from 200 to 800 points, and the Math Test score will contribute to a Math Area score from 200 to 800 points. Therefore, your total SAT score on the new exam will be between 400 and 1600. In comparison, the old SAT had a score range from 600 to 2400.

The new SAT will also include an optional Essay Test. The essay will be assigned a separate score that will not factor into your total scaled score for the SAT. Instead, you'll receive an essay score from 1-4 on three specific criteria: Reading, Analysis, and Writing.

The changes to the SAT extend beyond the new format and scoring. The content of the sections will also undergo important revisions. In the Reading and Writing Tests, you'll see a greater emphasis on assessing writing conventions and the author's command of evidence. You'll see passages from a wider range of disciplines, including excerpts from the "Founding Documents" and the "Great Global Conversation." You'll also see vocabulary that is less obscure and used more widely in college.

The Math Test will focus on the core math areas of algebra and data analysis, and will feature more questions drawn from real-life situations. On the optional Essay Test, you'll be given more time (50 minutes), and you'll be asked to demonstrate your ability to analyze data and explain an author's writing style.

The new SAT will also eliminate the guessing penalty. When answering multiple choice questions, you will no longer be deducted a 1/4 point for wrong answers. Also, the new exam offers only 4 answer choices (A to D), compared to 5 answer choices (A to E) for the old exam. You now have a better chance of guessing the right answer (1 in 4 chance) and also won't be penalized for it!

Here's a chart that summarizes some of the important differences between the old SAT and the new SAT:

The Old SAT vs. The New SAT		
Category	Old SAT	New SAT
Timing	• 3 hours 45 minutes	• 3 hours 50 minutes (including the optional 50 minute Essay)
Sections	• Critical Reading • Writing (includes the Essay) • Math	• Evidence-Based Reading and Writing • Math • Essay (optional and separate from the Writing Test)
Areas of Emphasis	• General reasoning skills • Challenging vocabulary used in limited contexts • Using logic to solve unfamiliar and abstract math problems	• Applying reasoning and knowledge to real-world situations • Using reading, writing, and math skills to analyze evidence • Vocabulary meaning and word choice in a greater range of contexts • Demonstrating core applied reasoning skills in algebra and data analysis
Question Types	• 161 multiple choice • 10 grid-in	• 141 multiple choice • 13 grid-in
Answer Choices	• 5 answer choices (A to E) for m/c questions	• 4 answer choices (A to D) for m/c questions
Penalty	• Guessing penalty: quarter-point deduction for wrong answers	• No penalty for wrong answers
Scoring	• Total scaled score from 600 to 2400, comprised of area scores from 200-800 in Critical Reading, Mathematics, and Writing • Essay score factored into Writing scaled score	• Total scaled score from 400 to 1600, comprised of area scores from 200-800 in Math and in Evidence-Based Reading and Writing • Essay score reported separately • Subscores and cross-test scores demonstrating skills in more specific areas

THE NEW SAT IN DETAIL
PART 2

The changes to the SAT might look complicated, but in the long run they're good news for students. The new scoring system will produce more subscores (the College Board calls them "Insight Scores"), which will paint a clearer picture of your abilities. The new emphasis in the content will more clearly reflect your readiness for college. With these changes, the College Board is trying to help you demonstrate your level of preparation, as well as help colleges understand your particular strengths more easily. Let's take a look in detail at what these changes entail.

THE FORMAT

The SAT is 3 hours long (plus 50 minutes for the optional Essay). It is composed of the following sections:

- 100-minute Evidence-based Reading and Writing section
  - Reading Test (65 minutes, 52 questions)
  - Writing and Language Test (35 minutes, 44 questions)

- 80-minute Math section
  - Calculator allowed section (55 minutes, 38 questions)
  - No-calculator allowed section (25 minutes, 20 questions)

- Optional Essay-writing section (50 minutes)

THE SCORING SYSTEM

The new SAT will have three **test scores** on a scale from 10 to 40. There will be one test score for each test: the Reading Test, the Writing Test, and the Math Test. The Reading Test score and the Writing and Language Test score will be added together and converted to a single **area score** in Evidence-Based Reading and Writing; there will also be an area score in Math based on the Math Test Score.

The area scores will be on a scale from 200 to 800. Added together, they will form the **composite score** for the whole test, on a scale from 400 to 1600. The Essay will be scored separately and will not affect your scores in other areas.

SAT Scoring	
Test Scores (10 to 40)	• Reading Test • Writing Test • Math Test
Area Scores (200 to 800)	• Evidence-Based Reading and Writing • Math
Composite Score (400 to 1600)	• Math (Area Score) + Evidence-Based Reading and Writing (Area Score)
Essay Scores (1 to 4)	• Reading • Analysis • Writing

The College Board will also be reporting new types of scores. **Cross-test scores** for **Analysis in Science** and **Analysis in History/Social Studies** will be based on performance on specific questions across different tests relating to specific types of content. For example, your cross-test score in Analysis in Science will be based on your performance on questions relating to science passages on the Reading Test as well as questions using scientific data on the Math Test. These scores will be on a scale from 10 to 40.

There will also be seven **subscores** based on particular question types within each test section. Subscores will be reported on a scale from 1 to 15. Four will be related to particular questions in the Reading and Writing Test: Words in Context, Command of Evidence, Expression of Ideas, and Standard English Conventions. The other three relate to specific types of questions on the Math Test: Heart of Algebra, Problem Solving and Data Analysis, and Passport to Advanced Math. You'll learn more about what these subscores are measuring in the chapters explaining what these questions are like.

As of our publication date, the College Board had not released detailed information on how these scores will be calculated.

TAKING THE SAT
PART 3

Now that we've covered the format and content of the new SAT, let's talk about how you go about taking the exam. The SAT is administered at standard testing dates and locations worldwide throughout the academic year. These standard dates fall in January, March, May, June, October, November, or December, but the March test date is only available in the United States. You can see the upcoming dates in your location on the College Board website: sat.collegeboard.org.

HOW DO I REGISTER?

The easiest way to sign up for the exam is on the College Board website: sat.collegeboard.org. You'll need to fill out a personal profile form and upload a recognizable photo which will be included on your admission ticket.

You can also register by mail. To do this, ask your school counselor for *The Student Registration Guide for the SAT and SAT Subject Tests*, which includes a registration form and a return envelope. You'll need to enclose a photo with this paper registration form.

When you register, you can sign up for your preferred date and location. However, testing centers often run out of room, so make sure you sign up early in order to reserve your place! There is also a cut-off for registrations a month before the test date, after which you'll need to contact the College Board to see if late registration or standby testing is an option.

The new SAT is scheduled to be first administered in the spring of 2016. If you are registered for an exam that will be administered before then, you will be writing the old SAT exam.

When Should I take the SAT?

Typically, students take the SAT during 11th grade or the beginning of 12th grade. However, you should plan to take the exam when you feel most prepared, keeping in mind when colleges will need your scores.

Almost all schools will accept scores through December of your 12th grade year. After December, it really depends on the school to which you are applying. If you are planning to apply Early Admissions to any school, you'll need to take the test by November of 12th grade at the very latest.

Can I Re-Take the SAT?

Yes! The College Board has no limits on how many times you can take the SAT. Many students take the exam two or three times to ensure their scores represent the best they can do. However, we don't recommend taking the exam more than two or three times because you'll get fatigued and your score will start to plateau. Prepare to do your best each time you take the test, and you shouldn't have to re-take it too many times.

How do I Send My Scores to Colleges?

When you sign up for the SAT, you can select which schools you'd like to receive your scores. You can also do this after taking the SAT by logging onto your account on the College Board website. If you have taken the SAT more than once, the College Board's "Score Choice" program allows you to choose which test results you would like to report to most schools. You can't "divide up" the scores of different tests—all sections of the SAT from a single test date must be sent together.

However, certain schools don't participate in the "Score Choice" program. These schools request that applicants send the results of every SAT test they have taken. Even so, most schools have a policy of only considering your highest scores. Some schools will take your best overall score from a single administration while others will mix and match your best scores for your entire test history. You can see how your prospective schools consider your scores by visiting their admissions websites.

How do I Improve My Score?

The key to raising SAT scores is a long-term strategy. Score improvement on the SAT occurs only after consistently practicing and learning concepts over a long period of time. Early on in your high school career, focus on building vocabulary and improving essay-writing skills. Read as much as you can beyond your school curriculum—materials like novels, biographies, and current-event magazines. Keep up with the math taught in your classes and ask questions if you need help.

In addition to keeping up with the fundamental concepts and skills tested on the SAT, you'll need to learn how to approach the specific types of questions included on the exam. In the next section, we'll talk about some general test-taking strategies that will help you tackle the format of the SAT as a whole. Then, you can work through Chapters 2-5 to learn specific strategies for the SAT Reading, Writing, Essay, and Math Tests. In Chapter 6, you'll be able to apply these strategies to 2 full-length practice tests.

With enough practice, you'll be prepared to score your personal best on test day! Let's get started.

Section 3
Approaching the SAT

In this section, we will help you prepare for the SAT with effective ways to approach studying and test taking. We will cover some tips to keep in mind before test day, essential strategies to employ on test day, and what to keep on your radar after you walk out of that test center.

TEST-TAKING STRATEGIES
PART 1

In addition to learning the material tested on the SAT, you'll also need to learn the best strategies for tackling the question types you'll see on the SAT. These strategies include knowing what you're going to see on the test, managing your time, guessing effectively, and entering your answers.

KNOW THE TEST

The first step in tackling the SAT test is to know the test. By knowing how much time you have for each section, the number of questions in each section, and the directions for each section, you will be ahead of the game. Knowing the test will help to eliminate surprises and reduce your anxiety on the day of the test.

It is important to remember that the SAT is not like a high school test. In high school, you encounter tests with a lot of different formats and scoring systems. Most of these tests are probably a maximum of one hour long. Your high school teachers also remind you to show your work on your tests and to explain your answers. Most teachers have a policy of "no work, no credit."

The SAT, however, is a **standardized exam**: every time you take the test, you'll see the same types of questions, number of questions, and time limits. This means that you can become very familiar with the format of the exam in advance. The scoring is also the same from exam to exam, and sections on the SAT are not weighted differently. Each question is worth the same number of points; questions that seem more difficult and those that seem easier have the same point value.

There is a set time limit. Even though the test is broken up into multiple sections, you do not have control over how to divide the total time among the individual sections. Unlike a normal hour-long high school test, the SAT runs between three and four hours long—so you'll need to practice building your stamina!

Finally, the scoring machine that grades your exam does not care that you penciled brilliant logic in the margins of the test booklet—the machine only looks at your answer choice. Your answer choice is either right or wrong; there is no partial credit.

While the SAT is not like a high school test, your high school background will help you on the SAT. The SAT tests reading, writing, and math skills, three areas which your teachers have been helping you to improve since elementary school. This book will help you review these fundamental skills while practicing strategies for the specific ways these skills are tested on the SAT.

MANAGE YOUR TIME

The SAT is like a running race. To be successful in a race, you must know the course—the distance, the start and end points, the terrain, the obstacles, and the water breaks. By looking at the race as a whole, you can plot out where the uphill, flat, and downhill sections are located so that you know where you will need to adjust your pace, gait, and energy exerted. Similarly, to do well on the SAT, you need to know the length of the test, the time allowed for each section, the question types, your personal strengths and weaknesses, and the snack/bathroom breaks.

You have 3 hours to complete the test and 154 questions to answer, each of which will require a different amount of time to read and solve. Remember that time between sections isn't transferable; you're given a set amount of time for each section and you can't proceed to the next section if you finish early. Time yourself when you practice, developing a sense of what "a quarter-of-the-way through" and "halfway through" feels like in each section. Finished early? Use that leftover time to go over your answers and make sure you entered them correctly.

It's important not to get too stuck on any single question and to move through the test at a steady pace. Don't waste 10 minutes on a question that stumps you, only to find that you do not have enough time to answer the things you know inside-out. Each question is only worth one point, regardless of its difficulty. If you are stuck on a problem, you should make your best guess and move on. Circle the problem in your question booklet or mark it on your scratch paper so you can look at it again if you have time.

As you practice for the SAT, you are bound to figure out the kinds of questions you are good at versus those that give you pause. Skim through each section and answer your strong suits first, then move on to the types of questions that you tend to find more difficult. Remember to make a guess and circle any questions you skip; you do not want to forget about them and leave them unanswered.

MAKE AN EDUCATED GUESS

Time management is key because you want to be able to answer as many questions as possible, especially since the College Board has eliminated the guessing penalty for the new SAT. You should try to answer every question because you have nothing to lose—just more points to gain! At the same time, you should strike a balance between quality and quantity. Budget your time so you can get to every question, but you also have the opportunity to read each question carefully and consider each answer choice.

If, after reading the question and each answer choice closely, you are still unsure of the answer, you should guess. This is where the next weapon in your SAT arsenal comes into play: **Process of Elimination**, or the system by which you'll narrow down your possible answer choices.

As you read through the answer choices, don't select an answer on your first read-through. For each option, choose to either "knock it out" if you know it is incorrect, or leave it open to reconsider later if it seems possible. Once you have assessed all of the answer choices, you can compare any that you left open and select the best one. In some cases you may even be able to knock out every answer except for one on your first read through the questions. In this case you will have found the correct answer!

Let's look at how this works with an example math problem:

If $y = x^2$ and $-1 < x < 1$, which of the following could be a possible value for y?

    (A) $-\dfrac{5}{4}$

    (B) $-\dfrac{1}{4}$

    (C) $\dfrac{1}{4}$

    (D) $\dfrac{5}{4}$

If you weren't sure how to answer this question, you could just plug in all of the answer choices for y in the equation and see which one works. However, if you think about the equation a bit, you'll see that there are some choices you can eliminate. The equation says that y is the square of x. Think about what happens when you square a positive or negative number—the result is always positive! Therefore, choices (A) and (B) are impossible—if x is a real number, then x^2 can't be a negative number. You can knock out (A) and (B) right away.

Now you're left with (C) and (D). If you're short on time, you could guess and you'd have a 50-50 chance of gaining a point. Or you could realize that because x is a fraction greater than -1 and less than 1, x^2 can't be greater than 1. This means that you can eliminate choice (D) as well, leaving you with the correct answer: (C).

WRITE AND BUBBLE CLEARLY

There are few things you can control on the SAT. You cannot decide what the essay prompt will be or what questions will be included. You cannot spend more time than the time allotted for each section. However, you *can* control what answers you put down. What you write in your answer sheet determines whether you'll get a point or not, so you don't want to make a mistake when it comes to bubbling your answers!

Remember to always mark your answer in your answer sheet. Even if you circle or designate the correct answer in the exam booklet itself, you will be awarded no credit unless the corresponding bubble on the answer sheet has been filled in. Make sure to fill in each bubble completely and to use the correct No. 2 pencil. Also, always make sure you are filling in the correct section of the answer sheet. Before beginning each section, double check that you are working on the corresponding section of the answer sheet.

When you write your essay, write as legibly as you can. Even though you're trying to write quickly, your readers need to be able to read your handwriting in order to give you points. Remember to write your essay only within the margins on the lined pages provided in your answer sheet—your readers won't be able to see anything you write outside of these margins! Don't write part of your essay in your test booklet.

While you are not given credit for any answers designated or work shown in the test booklet, you are not penalized either. If it helps to mark up reading passages or jot down notes, feel free to do so. Cross out answer choices when performing process of elimination. Use margins and blank space in the test booklet to work out math problems and outline your essay. Underline key words, phrases, or sections of reading passages. The test booklet is yours to use how you choose, so mark it up however you feel will help you do your best.

CREATE A STUDY SCHEDULE
PART 2

To prepare to do your best on test day, you'll need to organize your time leading up to the exam. First, you'll need to assess your strengths and weaknesses in order to figure out *what* to study. Then, you'll need to organize *how* you will study in order to make the best use of your time before you take your test.

IDENTIFY YOUR STRENGTHS AND WEAKNESSES

To determine your areas of strength and weakness and to get an idea of which concepts you need to review, work through some practice questions. You can try out the questions for the Reading, Writing, Essay, and Math tests in Chapters 2-5 of this book, or you can take one of the full-length practice tests in Chapter 6.

Then, check your answers against the correct answers. Write down how many questions you missed, and note the topics or types of questions you found most challenging. What was challenging for you? What did you feel good about? Did you get questions wrong because you made a careless error, or did you get questions wrong because you did not know how to solve them? Reflecting on these questions will help you determine your individual strengths and weaknesses, and will help you decide what to study before your test date.

PLAN YOUR STUDY TIME

After determining your areas of strength and weakness, create a study plan and schedule for your SAT preparation. Work backward from your test date until you arrive at your starting point for studying. The number of weeks you have until your exam will determine how much time you can (and should) devote to your preparation. Make sure you leave enough time to review and practice each concept you'd like to improve—remember, practice is the most important!

To begin, try using this sample study plan as a model for your own personalized study schedule.

Sample Study Plan

My test date is: _____.

I have _____ weeks to study. I will make an effort to study _____ minutes/hours each night, and I will set aside extra time on _____ to take timed sections.

I plan to take _____ full-length tests between now and my test date. I will study for _____ weeks and then take a practice test. My goal for this test is to improve my score in the following specific areas:

_____

_____

_____

_____

_____

If I do not make this goal, then I will spend more time studying.

Study Schedule			
Date	Plan of Study	Time Allotted	Goal Reached?
Jan 1	Review 10 vocabulary words and quadratic equations	1 hr	Yes, I know these 10 words and feel comfortable with quadratic equations.
Jan 3	Review the next 10 vocabulary words and parts of speech	1 hr	I know these 10 words, but I'm still a bit shaky on parts of speech. I'll review this again tomorrow and ask my English teacher for advice.

TEST DAY

After you've prepared by reviewing and practicing each area you need to improve, you're ready for test day! Here are some tips to make sure you can do your best when the big day comes.

BEFORE THE TEST

On the night before the test, study only lightly. Make a list of your three biggest fears and work on them, but don't try to learn anything new. Pick out what you are going to wear to the test—try wearing layers in case the exam room is hotter or colder than you expect. Organize everything you need to bring. Know where the test center is located and how long it will take to get there. Have a nutritious meal and get plenty of sleep!

On the morning of the exam, let your adrenaline kick in naturally. Eat a good breakfast and stay hydrated; your body needs fuel to endure the test. Allow enough time for traveling to the test center, and be sure to follow your admissions ticket for directions on how early you should arrive. Remember to bring the following items with you:

TEST DAY CHECKLIST

- [ ] Admission Ticket
- [ ] Approved Photo ID
- [ ] No. 2 pencils and erasers
- [ ] Calculator with new batteries and back-up batteries
- [ ] A watch
- [ ] Snack and water bottle
- [ ] I have directions to the test center and have instructions for finding the entrance.
- [ ] I am leaving at _____ am on test day. This allows time for delays.
- [ ] I have set my alarm.

You need to be on time, or you can't take the test!

During the Test

During the test, you cannot overestimate the importance of a positive outlook. You have spent months preparing for the SAT—now it is time to be confident in the work you have done and in the knowledge you have acquired. Stay confident—trust yourself, your abilities, and all of your preparation. Walk into the test room with every expectation that you will do well.

Stay focused. This is your time to show the College Board what you are capable of. Keep your mind on the task at hand, which should be nothing but the question in front of you. If you find your mind wandering, pull your focus back to the test. Don't look around the room to compare your progress to that of your neighbors. Everyone works at their own pace, and you have no idea which particular part of the section your neighbors are working on.

Remember the test-taking strategies that you've practiced. Read and think carefully. Be sure to read each question in its entirety, and to read and consider every answer choice. Work at a good, even pace, but be sure to work continuously. Keep an eye on your time throughout each section (and make sure your watch's time matches the proctor's clock). Frequently double check that you are bubbling answers in the correct section of your answer sheet.

Make educated guesses and remember to utilize process of elimination. Use your test booklet to cross out answers which you know are wrong, work out math problems in the margins and the free spaces, and annotate reading passages. Answer the easy questions first, and skip ones to which the answer is not immediately apparent. Be sure to mark questions that you skip so that you can quickly turn back to them after you finish all the other questions in the section.

Take a deep breath and remember: you are smart and accomplished! Believe in yourself and you will do just fine.

After the Test

First things first: give yourself a pat on the back! You have just completed a huge step in your educational career. Your score report should become available to you about two to four weeks after you take the test. This score report will contain your composite score, area scores, test scores, and all those subscores.

These scores are important because you will likely send them to colleges for consideration for admission. Remember to keep things in perspective. College applications will also entail submitting essays, recommendations from your teachers and guidance counselors, high school grades, descriptions of activities and sports in which you participate, and other components. Even if you feel that your SAT scores are not an accurate reflection of your abilities and capabilities, you have many other opportunities to shine in the other areas of your applications.

Remember, too, that you can retake the SAT. In fact, many students take the SAT two or three times. After you take the SAT the first time, you can pinpoint which areas you will need to practice more. Students often improve their scores after taking the test a second time.

Chapter 2
Reading

INTRODUCTION TO THE READING TEST

The SAT Reading Test is a test of advanced reading comprehension. You will be given a variety of different reading passages, and asked questions about each one. While the passages and questions will be new every time, the breakdown of the SAT Reading test as a whole will always be the same. By learning about it now, you can rest assured you will not encounter any surprises on test day!

THE BASICS

You'll have 65 minutes to complete the SAT Reading Test, which is comprised of 4 individual passages and 1 pair of passages. This pair will be made up of two shorter, related passages by different authors that address a similar topic or theme. You will learn more about paired passages in Sections 3 and 6. Each passage or pair will be between 500 and 750 words, for a total of 3250 words overall.

Each passage will have 10 or 11 questions, for a total of 52 questions for the entire section. There will also be 1 or 2 graphics in every SAT Reading Test, which correspond to specific passages. You will be asked a couple of questions about these graphics and how they relate to the passage.

SAT READING TEST BY THE NUMBERS

- 65 minutes to complete section
- 4 single passages and 1 paired passage
- 500-750 words per passage or pair
- 3250 words total
- 10-11 questions per passage for a total of 52
- 1-2 graphics per test

SCORING

You'll receive several different scores from your answers on the Reading Test.

You will receive an individual **test score** for Reading, which summarizes your performance on the Reading Test as a number from 10 to 40. You will also receive an **area score** for Evidence-Based Reading and Writing, which combines your scores from the Reading and Writing Tests. Your Evidence-Based Reading and Writing score will be a number between 200 and 800, making up half of your total Composite Score on your SAT.

Questions from the Reading Test will contribute to two **cross-test scores**, which evaluate your skills in Analysis in History/Social Studies and Analysis in Science by looking at your performance on questions across the SAT. Your answers on the Reading Test will also contribute to two of your **subscores** on the SAT: Command of Evidence and Relevant Words in Context.

PASSAGES

The passages you will encounter may include informative passages, persuasive passages, and narrative passages. The passages will contain all of the information needed to answer the questions on the test; you will never need to rely on any of your own prior knowledge about the material.

All passages in the SAT Reading Test will come from previously published sources, and may represent a variety of tones and styles. The chart below shows the specific breakdown of passage types that you will see in each Reading Test.

PASSAGE BREAKDOWN

Passage Type	Topics	Number of Passages
Literature	Classic and contemporary literature from the United States and around the world	1
History and Social Studies	Anthropology, communication studies, economics, education, geography, law, linguistics, political science, psychology, and sociology	1
Founding Document or Great Global Conversation	Historically important, foundational texts from the United States (Founding Documents), other historically and culturally important works dealing with issues at the heart of civic and political life (Great Global Conversation)	1
Science	Both basic concepts and recent developments in the natural sciences, including Earth science, biology, chemistry, and physics	2

The passages will not be presented in order of difficulty. You can choose to read them out of order, by tackling passages with familiar subjects first.

QUESTIONS

The questions associated with the passages will assess whether or not you understand information and ideas in the text, and are able to analyze the author's use of persuasive language and argument. You will also be tested on combining information from related pairs of passages, as well as from passages and their graphs.

The questions will be presented in a consistent order. However, they are not presented in order of difficulty. You will first be asked more general questions about central ideas, themes, point of view, and the overall text structure. This will be followed by more specific questions that may ask you for the meaning of a particular word or phrase, or to find the specific evidence that supports a claim. Many of these questions will have line references, which will point you to the material being discussed in the question.

You'll be asked a variety of questions for each passage, but the question types themselves will be repeated often. For example, you may be asked about the text structure of more than one passage on your test. There are also two question types that will appear with every passage. You will always be asked two Words in Context questions, and two Evidence questions for every passage or pair of passages. Both of these question types will be discussed further in Section 4.

The rest of this chapter will introduce you to all of these concepts in more detail, and we will teach you strategies to approach the passages and correctly answer questions. Reading comprehension is something you can improve with practice, so take your time to work through all of the lessons and exercises in this chapter.

Section 2
Approaching the Reading Test

To succeed on the SAT Reading Test you need strategies to help you both read passages and answer the questions that accompany them. In this section, you'll first learn what to look for in a passage, how to be an active reader, and how to better understand what you read by summarizing. You'll see how these techniques can be applied to a reading passage, and practice using them yourself.

Then, you'll learn how to read the questions and answer them efficiently and accurately. We'll also teach you strategies for guessing, so you earn as many points as possible on the SAT Reading Test. You'll practice with individual questions, and then have a chance to put everything you've learned into action with full-length practice passages at the end of the section.

READING A PASSAGE
PART 1

On the SAT Reading Test you will encounter different types of passages, just as you encounter various types of content in your everyday reading. While the different kinds of passages will be explored further in Section 3, the basic strategy for reading a passage will remain the same regardless of the content of the passage.

WHAT MAKES THE SAT DIFFERENT?

The SAT requires a different kind of reading than what you may do in your everyday life. Normally when you read, you are probably focused on the content of the text. You may read a newspaper to find out about world events, or you may read a textbook to learn new facts and theories.

You are less likely to be reading these texts and thinking consciously "I really like how the author organized her argument across three paragraphs," or "I see that she is supporting her point with this example. Interesting."

However, the techniques, evidence, and structure an author uses are all things you are likely to be asked about on the SAT Reading Test. Thus, when you read SAT passages you will need to understand their content and also *how* and *why* the author organized them in a certain way.

Questions on the SAT Reading Test will go beyond basic comprehension. The SAT will test if you understand how different parts of the passage relate to each other, how the author makes her point or persuades the reader, and the opinions of the author and other people discussed in the passage. If you are already looking for these things as you read, answering the questions will be faster and easier.

PLAN YOUR APPROACH

1. **Choose your order of passages.** The reading passages are not presented in order of difficulty, so you may choose to attempt them out of order. Tackle passages with familiar or interesting subjects first, as you will likely find these easier. If you do this, be sure to bubble in your answers on the correct part of your answer sheet!

2. **Read one at a time.** Read only one passage or pair of passages at a time, and try to answer all the related questions before moving on to the next passage. Switching between passages will make it harder to recall what you have read.

3. **Read the passage introductions.** Read any italicized information at the beginning of a passage. This can include details about the passage such as its author, intended audience, date, topic, and other important context to help you understand the passage.

4. **Read the passages in full.** Try to read the passage in full before looking at the questions. In this section you will learn what to look for in a passage so you'll be ready for the questions. Don't skim the questions before reading the passage, as you will have to re-read each one before you answer. It is more efficient to read the passage first, and refer back to it for guidance when answering the questions.

You may have heard you can avoid reading the full passage by reading just the lines each question asks about. However, not all questions will have line references that tell you what to read, and some questions will require you to read the entire passage and understand its structure. You will answer questions more accurately when you understand the whole passage.

One exception to this rule is if the five-minute warning has been called or you realize you do not have time to read another passage. In that case, you may look for a question that gives you a line reference, read that portion of the passage, and attempt the question.

Make sure to give yourself time to read the passage and not just skim it! You need to understand the passage to accurately answer questions. A good guideline is to split your time almost equally between reading a passage and answering its questions, with a bit more time devoted to the questions.

The chart below offers you some ideas for how to pace yourself. Remember that you have 65 minutes for the entire Reading Test.

Pacing Yourself			
Minutes Spent Answering Questions	Minutes Spent Reading	Total Minutes Per Passage	Reading Speed
8	5	13	Fast
7	6	13	Medium

MARK UP THE PASSAGE

On the SAT, you know you will be tested about the content you read, so you want to make an effort to understand it while you are reading it, rather than trying to make sense of the ideas only once you reach the questions. This means you need to be an **active reader** and interact with the passages to find and understand the information you will be tested on.

Specifically, the best way to be an active reader is to use your pencil to **mark up** the passage as you read by underlining text, and adding your own notes and symbols to highlight what is important. The goals of marking up the passage are to help you stay focused, understand what you read, and make it easy to find key ideas in the passage when you refer back to it.

Use your pencil as a guide to circle or underline two to three **main ideas** per paragraph. Main ideas are those that relate to the **5 w's:** "who," "what," "where," "when," and "why." Stay focused on the bigger picture by making sure the main points you identify help answer the following questions:

1. **Who** is involved in this passage? Look for the people being discussed (artists, scholars, scientists, politicians) or the characters in a literature passage, and think about who might be writing the passage.
2. **What** is being discussed in this passage? Are specific events, theories, or ideas discussed? Look for the major concepts in each section of the passage.
3. **Where** are the events in the passage taking place? This can mean a specific location (one science laboratory) or a general setting (schools in North America).
4. **When** are the events in the passage taking place? It is usually more important to know the order in which things occur than to know specific dates.

5. **Why** is the information in this passage important? How are the ideas in the passage connected, and what is the author's purpose for writing the passage?

You can skip over more specific details when identifying the main ideas of a paragraph or passage. Try to underline the key words in the passage such that if you were to read over just those words, you would have a good idea what the passage is about.

EXAMPLE PASSAGE

Let's look at the first few paragraphs from a reading passage and see how it might look if we mark it up using these ideas.

This passage is adapted from an article about an Italian Renaissance artist.

Tommaso Strinati clambers to the top of the rickety scaffold and laughs. "It's a good thing that all this Baroque
Line   work is so unimpressive," he says,
5   pointing at the clumsy trompe l'oeil painting covering the wall in front of him. "Otherwise, we might not have been allowed to scrape it off!"
A 28-year-old art historian, he is
10   standing 16 feet above the marble floor of San Pasquale Baylon chapel, a long-neglected nook of Santa Maria in Aracoeli, a Franciscan basilica in the center of Rome. Last year, Mr.
15   Strinati, who is still a graduate student, began studying the church's history. Records suggested that the Roman

artist Pietro Cavallini – a painter and mosaicist whose greatest works have
20   been destroyed – spent years decorating Aracoeli toward the end of the 13th century. Yet only one small Cavallini fresco, in the church's left transept, remained visible. Mr. Strinati
25   wondered: had other Cavallini frescoes been painted over with inferior work? And if so, could modern restorers uncover them?
"The answer to both questions was
30   yes," Mr. Strinati says. A close-up examination of the chapel's walls last summer revealed ghostly images lying beneath the surface. The entire chapel, it seemed, was a painted palimpsest.
35   And when a heavy altarpiece was removed from one wall, a remarkably tender portrait of the Madonna and Child was found hidden behind it.

Let's see how these key words helped us locate the 5 w's for this passage:

1. **Who** is involved in this passage? The passage is about the art historian Tommaso Strinati and the Roman artist Pietro Cavallini. We underlined their names in the first and second paragraphs.

2. **What** is being discussed in this passage? The passage is about how Strinati discovered Cavallini frescos that had been painted over. We underlined the information about Cavallini that Strinati gathered in the second paragraph, and also underlined that he wondered about work being painted over. Then we noted the

images beneath the surface and the hidden portrait in the third paragraph. These items proved Strinati's guess.

3. **Where** are the events in the passage taking place? We underlined Santa Maria in Aracoeli, the name of the basilica where Cavallini's art was found. The basilica is in Rome, which we also underlined.

4. **When** are the events in the passage taking place? We know that Cavallini painted the frescos at the end of the 13th century, as we underlined that information in the passage. The passage doesn't specifically tell us when Strinati made his discovery. But the passage is written in the present tense and modern English, so we can assume it was fairly recently.

5. **Why** is the information in this passage important? The information we underlined in the second paragraph shows a surprising contrast between ideas. If Cavallini spent years painting the basilica, why is there only one fresco? This sets up a bit of a mystery, which Strinati begins to solve in the third paragraph.

Though it can be tempting, don't go overboard with your active reading! Remember that the goals of marking up the passage are to help you stay focused, understand what you read, and make it easy to find key ideas in the passage. If you mark up your entire passage, nothing will stand out as important, and you won't be able to find anything. Your understanding will also be muddled, because you will be too focused on small details and not the bigger picture of what you have read.

EXERCISE ON MARKING UP A PASSAGE

Now that you've seen how to mark up a text, practice marking up the rest of the Cavallini passage below. This passage contains a lot of information, but not all of it contributes to the main ideas of the paragraph. Remember to stay focused on the 5 w's! When you are finished, compare your work with the fully marked-up version of this passage that follows.

Tommaso Strinati clambers to the top of the rickety scaffold and laughs. "It's a good thing that all this Baroque work is so unimpressive," he says, pointing at the clumsy trompe l'oeil painting covering the wall in front of him. "Otherwise, we might not have been allowed to scrape it off!"

A 28-year-old art historian, he is standing 16 feet above the marble floor of San Pasquale Baylon chapel, a long-neglected nook of Santa Maria in Aracoeli, a Franciscan basilica in the center of Rome. Last year, Mr. Strinati, who is still a graduate student, began studying the church's history. Records suggested that the Roman artist Pietro Cavallini – a painter and mosaicist whose greatest works have been destroyed – spent years decorating Aracoeli toward the end of the 13th century. Yet only one small Cavallini fresco, in the church's left transept, remained visible. Mr. Strinati wondered: had other Cavallini frescoes been painted over with inferior work? And if so, could modern restorers uncover them?

"The answer to both questions was yes," Mr. Strinati says. A close-up examination of the chapel's walls last summer revealed ghostly images lying beneath the surface. The entire chapel, it seemed, was a painted palimpsest. And when a heavy altarpiece was removed from one wall, a remarkably tender portrait of the Madonna and Child was found hidden behind it.

After months of careful paint-peeling, what has been uncovered are dazzling fragments of a late-medieval masterpiece completed shortly after 1285. Although the Aracoeli fresco is not signed, the figures strongly resemble those in a surviving Cavallini work, the resplendent "Last Judgment" fresco at nearby Santa Cecilia.

Mr. Strinati has grand ambitions for his discovery. He hopes that in a few years the fully restored fresco will not only rescue Cavallini's name from obscurity, but also upend the widespread notion that the first flowers of the Renaissance budded in Florence, not Rome. For the fresco's lifelike figures – in particular, an impish Christ child with charmingly flushed cheeks – suggest to Strinati that Cavallini may have anticipated some of the extraordinary naturalistic innovations that have long been credited to the Florentine artist Giotto.

Moreover, the Aracoeli fragments may provide a critical new clue in a decades-old battle concerning the "St. Francis Legend," the 1296 fresco cycle at Assisi, universally recognized as one of the foundations of the Renaissance. For centuries, the 28-scene cycle – which recounts the life of the saint with a narrative zest and compositional depth that leave the flat tableaus of the Byzantine era far behind – was attributed to Giotto. But since the 1930's, various scholars have questioned this judgment, claiming that the Assisi cycle doesn't resemble Giotto's other work. Now, the Aracoeli discovery is ammunition for Italian art historians who believe that Cavallini might actually be the primary creative force behind the "St. Francis Legend."

The growing debate about Cavallini's importance was the occasion for a symposium in Rome in November. *La Republicca*, an Italian daily, has cast the debate as "War Between Rome and Florence." Mr. Strinati is enjoying the ruckus. "I had a hunch that there was more Cavallini lurking around here," he says of the Aracoeli basilica. "But I didn't expect to find an exquisite work that could shake up the history of art."

Answer: Marking Up a Passage

Check how you did by comparing your marked-up passage to a fully marked-up version of the passage below. Don't worry if you did not underline your passage in exactly the same way. There can be more than one way to capture an idea. For example, in the fourth paragraph you may have underlined "shortly after 1285" rather than "late-medieval" to indicate when the Aracoeli fresco was painted. As long as you identified the same main ideas, you are on the right track.

Tommaso Strinati clambers to the top of the rickety scaffold and laughs. "It's a good thing that all this Baroque work is so unimpressive," he says, pointing at the clumsy trompe l'oeil painting covering the wall in front of him. "Otherwise, we might not have been allowed to scrape it off!"

A 28-year-old art historian, he is standing 16 feet above the marble floor of San Pasquale Baylon chapel, a long-neglected nook of Santa Maria in Aracoeli, a Franciscan basilica in the center of Rome. Last year, Mr. Strinati, who is still a graduate student, began studying the church's history. Records suggested that the Roman artist Pietro Cavallini – a painter and mosaicist whose greatest works have been destroyed – spent years decorating Aracoeli toward the end of the 13th century. Yet only one small Cavallini fresco, in the church's left transept, remained visible. Mr. Strinati wondered: had other Cavallini frescoes been painted over with inferior work? And if so, could modern restorers uncover them?

"The answer to both questions was yes," Mr. Strinati says. A close-up examination of the chapel's walls last summer revealed ghostly images lying beneath the surface. The entire chapel, it seemed, was a painted palimpsest. And when a heavy altarpiece was removed from one wall, a remarkably tender portrait of the Madonna and Child was found hidden behind it.

After months of careful paint-peeling, what has been uncovered are dazzling fragments of a late-medieval masterpiece completed shortly after 1285. Although the Aracoeli fresco is not signed, the figures strongly resemble those in a surviving Cavallini work, the resplendent "Last Judgment" fresco at nearby Santa Cecilia.

Mr. Strinati has grand ambitions for his discovery. He hopes that in a few years the fully restored fresco will not only rescue Cavallini's name from obscurity, but also upend the widespread notion that the first flowers of the Renaissance budded in Florence, not Rome. For the fresco's lifelike figures – in particular, an impish Christ child with charmingly flushed cheeks – suggest to Strinati that Cavallini may have anticipated some of the extraordinary naturalistic innovations that have long been credited to the Florentine artist Giotto.

Moreover, the Aracoeli fragments may provide a critical new clue in a decades-old battle concerning the "St. Francis Legend," the 1296 fresco cycle at Assisi, universally recognized as one of the foundations of the Renaissance. For centuries, the 28-scene cycle – which recounts the life of the saint with a narrative zest and compositional depth that leave the flat tableaus of the Byzantine era far behind – was attributed to Giotto. But since the 1930's, various scholars have questioned this judgment, claiming

that the Assisi cycle doesn't resemble
Giotto's other work. Now, the <u>Aracoeli</u>
<u>discovery is ammunition for Italian art</u>
80 <u>historians who</u> <u>believe that Cavallini</u>
might actually be the <u>primary creative</u>
<u>force</u> behind the "St. Francis Legend."
      <u>The growing debate</u> about
Cavallini's importance was the
85 occasion for a <u>symposium</u> in Rome in

November. *La Republicca*, an Italian
daily, has cast the debate as <u>"War</u>
<u>Between Rome and Florence."</u> Mr.
Strinati is enjoying the ruckus. "I had a
90 hunch that there was more Cavallini
lurking around here," he says of the
Aracoeli basilica. "But I didn't expect
to find an exquisite work that <u>could</u>
<u>shake up the history of art</u>."

SUMMARIZE

Another good way to be an active reader is to summarize as you read the passage.
Summarizing helps ensure that you understand what you read, and that you stay focused
throughout the passage rather than 'zoning out.' This way you can avoid the dreaded feeling
of finishing a passage and wondering what you just read!

Summarizing also makes long passages easier to manage. Breaking passages up into smaller
pieces is easier than trying to make sense of the entire passage all at the end.

As you read, make a summary after each paragraph. Use the words you have underlined to
help you. Your summaries should be short and snappy and cover only main ideas, not details
or specific examples. Try to keep your summaries three to six words long, like a newspaper
headline. Summarize in your own words. That ensures you have understood the paragraph,
and will be more likely to remember what your summary refers to.

EXAMPLE

Let's refer back to our passage about Cavallini, and see how we could summarize the main
ideas in the second paragraph.

      A 28-year-old art historian, he is
10 standing 16 feet above the marble floor
of San Pasquale Baylon chapel, a long-
neglected nook of Santa Maria in
Aracoeli, a Franciscan basilica in the
center of Rome. Last year, Mr.
15 Strinati, who is still a graduate student,
began studying the church's history.
Records suggested that the Roman
artist Pietro Cavallini – a painter and

mosaicist whose greatest works have
20 been destroyed – spent years
decorating Aracoeli toward the end of
the 13th century. Yet only one small
Cavallini fresco, in the church's left
transept, remained visible. Mr. Strinati
25 wondered: had other Cavallini frescoes
been painted over with inferior work?
And if so, could modern restorers
uncover them?

While there is a lot of information in this paragraph, the most important idea is about Cavallini's "missing" art. He reportedly spent a lot of time painting the basilica, so Strinati wonders why there is only one Cavallini fresco. To capture this we might write something as simple as "Seems could be more Cavallini." You might also choose to abbreviate the names of people mentioned in a passage using their initials or something else. So another summary for this paragraph might read "T.S. thinks hidden P.C. frescos."

EXERCISE ON SUMMARIZING

Now that you've seen how to make a good summary, you can practice with the rest of the Cavallini passage. Remember to keep your summaries short! The first three paragraphs have summaries.

#1 T.S. glad remove Baroque

    Tommaso Strinati clambers to the top of the rickety scaffold and laughs. "It's a good thing that all this Baroque work is so unimpressive," he says,
Line
5 pointing at the clumsy trompe l'oeil painting covering the wall in front of him. "Otherwise, we might not have been allowed to scrape it off!"

#2 T.S. thinks hidden P.C. frescos

    A 28-year-old art historian, he is
10 standing 16 feet above the marble floor of San Pasquale Baylon chapel, a long-neglected nook of Santa Maria in Aracoeli, a Franciscan basilica in the center of Rome. Last year, Mr.
15 Strinati, who is still a graduate student, began studying the church's history. Records suggested that the Roman artist Pietro Cavallini – a painter and mosaicist whose greatest works have
20 been destroyed – spent years decorating Aracoeli toward the end of the 13th century. Yet only one small Cavallini fresco, in the church's left transept, remained visible. Mr. Strinati
25 wondered: had other Cavallini frescoes been painted over with inferior work? And if so, could modern restorers uncover them?

"The answer to both questions was
30 yes," Mr. Strinati says. A close-up examination of the chapel's walls last summer revealed ghostly images lying beneath the surface. The entire chapel, it seemed, was a painted palimpsest.
35 And when a heavy altarpiece was removed from one wall, a remarkably tender portrait of the Madonna and Child was found hidden behind it.

#3. Found P.C. frescoes

    After months of careful paint-
40 peeling, what has been uncovered are dazzling fragments of a late-medieval masterpiece completed shortly after 1285. Although the Aracoeli fresco is not signed, the figures strongly
45 resemble those in a surviving Cavallini work, the resplendent "Last Judgment" fresco at nearby Santa Cecilia.

#4.

    Mr. Strinati has grand ambitions for his discovery. He hopes that in a
50 few years the fully restored fresco will not only rescue Cavallini's name from obscurity, but also upend the widespread notion that the first flowers of the Renaissance budded in Florence,
55 not Rome. For the fresco's lifelike figures – in particular, an impish

#5. Continued on next page...

#5.
Continued
...

Christ child with charmingly flushed cheeks – suggest to Strinati that Cavallini may have anticipated some

60 of the extraordinary naturalistic innovations that have long been credited to the Florentine artist Giotto.

Moreover, the Aracoeli fragments may provide a critical new clue in a

65 decades-old battle concerning the "St. Francis Legend, " the 1296 fresco cycle at Assisi, universally recognized as one of the foundations of the Renaissance. For centuries, the 28-

70 scene cycle – which recounts the life of the saint with a narrative zest and compositional depth that leave the flat tableaus of the Byzantine era far behind – was attributed to Giotto. But

75 since the 1930's, various scholars have

#6.

questioned this judgment, claiming that the Assisi cycle doesn't resemble Giotto's other work. Now, the Aracoeli discovery is ammunition for Italian art

80 historians who believe that Cavallini might actually be the primary creative force behind the "St. Francis Legend."

The growing debate about Cavallini's importance was the

85 occasion for a symposium in Rome in November. *La Republicca*, an Italian daily, has cast the debate as "War Between Rome and Florence." Mr. Strinati is enjoying the ruckus. "I had a

90 hunch that there was more Cavallini lurking around here," he says of the Aracoeli basilica. "But I didn't expect to find an exquisite work that could shake up the history of art."

#6. Continued...

#7.

Answer Key: Exercise on Summarizing

Paragraph 1: T.S. glad remove Baroque

Paragraph 2: T.S. thinks hidden P.C. frescos

Paragraph 3: Found P.C. frescoes

Paragraph 4: Resemble other P.C. work

Paragraph 5: P.C. maybe anticipated Giotto/Renaissance

Paragraph 6: P.C. maybe painted "St. F"

Paragraph 7: P.C. causing art history debates

PART 1 PRACTICE: READING A PASSAGE

Use your active reading techniques to read and mark up the following passage. Also write a short summary for every paragraph as you read. Use the answer key to check your work.

This passage is adapted from an article about workers in America.

The unemployment rate, the figure that dominates reporting on the economy, is the fraction of the labor force (those working or seeking work) that is unemployed. This rate has declined slowly since the end of the Great Recession. What hasn't recovered over that same period is the labor force participation rate, which today stands roughly where it did in 1977.

Labor force participation rates increased from the mid-1960s through the 1990s, driven by more women entering the workforce, baby boomers entering prime working years in the 1970s and 1980s, and increasing pay for skilled laborers. But over the past decade, these trends have leveled off. At the same time, the participation rate has fallen, particularly in the aftermath of the recession.

In one view, this decline is just a temporary, cyclical result of the Great Recession. If so, we should expect workers to come back as the economy continues to expand. Some research supports this view. A 2013 study by economists at the Federal Reserve Bank of San Francisco found that states with bigger declines in employment saw bigger declines in labor-force participation. It also found a positive relationship between these variables in past recessions and recoveries.

But structural changes are plainly at work too, based in part on slower-moving demographic factors. A 2012 study by economists at the Federal Reserve Bank of Chicago estimated that about one-quarter of the decline in labor-force participation since the start of the Great Recession can be traced to retirements. Other economists have attributed about half of the drop to the aging of baby boomers.

ANSWER KEY: READING A PASSAGE

Unemployment down; labor force same

The unemployment rate, the figure that dominates reporting on the economy, is the fraction of the labor force (those working or seeking work) that is unemployed. This rate has declined slowly since the end of the Great Recession. What hasn't recovered over that same period is the labor force participation rate, which today stands roughly where it did in 1977.

L.F. had increased, now

Labor force participation rates increased from the mid-1960s through the 1990s, driven by more women entering the workforce, baby boomers entering prime working years in the 1970s and 1980s, and increasing pay for skilled laborers. But over the past decade, these trends have leveled off. At the same time, the participation rate has fallen, particularly in the aftermath of the recession.

In one view, this decline is just a temporary, cyclical result of the Great Recession. If so, we should expect workers to come back as the economy continues to expand. Some research supports this view. A 2013 study by economists at the Federal Reserve Bank of San Francisco found that states with bigger declines in employment saw bigger declines in labor-force participation. It also found a positive relationship between these variables in past recessions and recoveries.

Could be recession (temporary)

But structural changes are plainly at work too, based in part on slower-moving demographic factors. A 2012 study by economists at the Federal Reserve Bank of Chicago estimated that about one-quarter of the decline in labor-force participation since the start of the Great Recession can be traced to retirements. Other economists have attributed about half of the drop to the aging of baby boomers.

Could be demographics (structural)

READING THE QUESTIONS
PART 2

Every question on the SAT Reading Test will be something you can answer based on the passage and no other outside information. Applying all the strategies you learned for understanding passages is the first step to answering questions quickly and correctly. Keep reading for more strategies to help you conquer reading questions.

REFER BACK TO THE PASSAGE

For every question, the correct answer will be based on something stated **explicitly** in the passage, or that can be **inferred** by reading between the lines of the text. Take advantage of the fact that the SAT Reading Test is an open-book test–you can refer back to the material you are being asked about!

Don't answer the questions by memory alone, and don't rely on your own knowledge or opinion of the subject, which might lead you to the wrong answer. You should always be able to support your answer choice with specific lines or words in the text, even if none are specified in the question.

Some questions use **line references** to indicate which part of the passage they are asking you about. When you are given a line reference, always return to the passage to review that line, as well as two to three lines before and after the one you are asked about. This helps you understand the context of the line in question, and there are often clues that will help you find the correct answer.

EXAMPLE

Let's see how this works with a line reference question from the Cavallini passage.

> The author mentions "an impish Christ child with charmingly flushed cheeks" (lines 56-58) in order to
>
> (A) provide an example of the fresco's lifelike figures.
> (B) describe Giotto's naturalistic style.
> (C) rescue Cavallini's name from obscurity.
> (D) suggest that it could help solve the "St. Francis Legend."

You may not remember this line from the passage, but if you refer back to the text you can easily answer this question. Here is the paragraph:

> Mr. Strinati has grand ambitions for his discovery. He hopes that in a
> 50 few years the fully restored fresco will not only rescue Cavallini's name from obscurity, but also upend the widespread notion that the first flowers of the Renaissance budded in Florence,
> 55 not Rome. For the fresco's lifelike figures – in particular, an impish Christ child with charmingly flushed cheeks – suggest to Strinati that Cavallini may have anticipated some
> 60 of the extraordinary naturalistic innovations that have long been credited to the Florentine artist Giotto.

If you read the lines referenced and skim the two lines above and below it, you learn that this fresco has particularly lifelike figures and is a good indicator of the naturalistic innovations in Cavallini's work. Thus, only answer choice (A) matches the passage.

The other answer choices are all ideas mentioned at different points of the passage, but not in reference to the painting of the child or in the lines you were asked about. Therefore, you know they do not match and you can eliminate them.

When you answer questions that do not provide line references, you should still refer back to the passage. Referring back to the passages helps you avoid answering questions based on your memory or outside knowledge, and ensures you have support for your answer. Because you will have marked up your passage, you will likely know where to find the evidence you need.

If a question asks you something general about the passage, you can refer back to the summaries you made while reading, and any notes you made in the margins. You can also double-check your answer choice against the passage to make sure it is a match.

PICK & SKIP

The questions for every passage will follow in roughly the same order. More general questions will appear first. They will ask you about the passage as a whole including its main ideas, point of view, and structure.

Next will be questions that ask about particular details, lines, or words. The order of these more specific questions will also match the order of the passage. For example, a question about line 20 will appear before a question about line 30.

However, just like the passages themselves, the questions will not necessarily be presented in order of difficulty. If you find more specific questions easier to answer, then you can attempt those first. If you do this, be sure to bubble in your answers on the correct part of your answer sheet! As you refer back to the text to answer these questions you may enrich your understanding of the passage, which may help you to find the correct answers when you tackle the more general questions.

You may also choose to skip over a question and come back to it later. If you read a question and do not understand what it is asking or feel stumped, it may be a good idea to circle it and move on. Then, once you have answered the other questions for the passage, go back to the question you circled and re-read it. Parts of the passage you revisited in answering other questions may have helped you understand the question, or you may have a better idea of where to look in the passage for the answer.

If you still cannot decide on an answer for the question, make a guess and move on. Remember that each question is only worth one point, no matter how difficult it is, so you can make best use of your time by attempting other questions that you are better able to answer.

PART 2 PRACTICE: READING THE QUESTIONS

1. How will you approach the passage below and its questions?

2. What is your strategy if you cannot answer a question?

3. Practice marking up this passage and making paragraph summaries the way you learned to earlier in this section.

In our fables of science and discovery, the crucial role of insight is a cherished theme. To these
Line
5   epiphanies, we owe the concept of alternating electrical current, the discovery of penicillin, and on a less lofty note, the invention of Post-its, ice-cream cones, and Velcro. The burst of mental clarity can be so powerful
10 that, as legend would have it, Archimedes jumped out of his tub and ran naked through the streets, shouting to his startled neighbors: "Eureka! I've got it."
15   In today's innovation economy, engineers, economists and policy makers are eager to foster creative thinking among knowledge workers. Until recently, these sorts of
20 revelations were too elusive for serious scientific study. Scholars suspect the story of Archimedes isn't even entirely true. Lately, though, researchers have been able to document the brain's
25 behavior during Eureka moments by recording brain-wave patterns and imaging the neural circuits that become active as volunteers struggle to solve anagrams, riddles and other
30 brain teasers.
    Following the brain as it rises to a mental challenge, scientists are seeking their own insights into these light-bulb flashes of understanding,
35 but they are as hard to define clinically as they are to study in a lab.
    To be sure, we've all had our "aha" moments. They materialize without warning, often through an unconscious
40 shift in mental perspective that can abruptly alter how we perceive a problem. "An 'aha' moment is any sudden comprehension that allows you to see something in a different light,"
45 says psychologist John Kounios at Drexel University in Philadelphia. "It could be the solution to a problem; it could be getting a joke; or suddenly recognizing a face. It could be
50 realizing that a friend of yours is not really a friend."
    These sudden insights, they found, are the culmination of an intense and complex series of brain states that
55 require more neural resources than methodical reasoning. People who solve problems through insight generate different patterns of brain waves than those who solve problems
60 analytically. "Your brain is really working quite hard before this moment of insight," says psychologist Mark Wheeler at the University of Pittsburgh. "There is a lot going on
65 behind the scenes."

4. Which of the following can be inferred from the passage about anagrams, riddles and other brain teasers?

(A) It is possible to experience insight while solving them

(B) They can only be solved through insight

(C) They are best solved by thinking analytically

(D) They are best solved in a lab setting

5. Where in the passage did you look for your answer to the previous question?

6. The purpose of the first paragraph (lines 1-14) is to

(A) highlight the inventions created through insight.

(B) introduce the general concept of insight.

(C) describe the story of Archimedes.

(D) explain the origin of the phrase "Eureka!"

7. Where did you look for your answer to the previous question?

8. As used in line 55, "resources" most nearly means

(A) capital.

(B) energy.

(C) resort.

(D) finances.

9. Where did you look for your answer to the previous question?

10. The author quotes John Kounios in order to

(A) prove that numerous scientists are studying insight.

(B) suggest that research on insight is very basic.

(C) offer a definition and examples of insight.

(D) demonstrate that people often do not recognize insight.

11. Where did you look for your answer to the previous question?

ANSWER KEY: READING THE QUESTIONS

1. As suggested in Part 2, the best way to tackle a passage is to read the entire passage first, and then move on to answer the questions.

2. As discussed in this section, a good way to deal with a question you are unsure about is to circle it and come back to it after answering all the other questions about the passage. If you still cannot answer it, you can make a guess.

3. Many possible answers; check your work with a trusted reader.

4. A

5. In the second paragraph

6. B

7. In the first paragraph and your summary of it

8. B

9. Line 55 and two lines above and below for context

10. C

11. In the fourth paragraph

SELECTING YOUR ANSWERS
PART 3

Because you have learned how to effectively read passages, you will already have a lot of information once you reach the questions. Be sure to refer back to the passage when selecting your answer choices, as the correct answer will always be supported by the passage. The answer could be supported by explicit information, or by inferences you need to make by 'reading between the lines' and by connecting different ideas that the author puts forward.

THINK FOR YOURSELF

One of the best ways to answer reading questions is by **thinking for yourself** rather than relying on the answer choices. Remember, three of the four answer choices will be incorrect, so you should not base your selection on what they say! The answer choices may all seem similar, or may seem persuasive even though they are incorrect.

Instead your answer should be based on the passage, which you know contains valid information. Because you have already done a lot of work to understand the passage, you will likely already be able to figure out how to answer a question without even looking at the answer choices.

Once you read a question, try to come up with your own answer based on the knowledge you gathered when you read the passage. You can refer back to your paragraph summaries, and to the words and ideas you circled and underlined. Then, phrase the answer choice in your own words as if it were a short answer or fill-in-the-blank question, rather than a multiple-choice question. Practice covering up the answer choices to be sure you are coming up with your own answer rather than using the given choices as a crutch.

Let's practice using this technique with a question about the Cavallini passage:

> The primary purpose of the passage is to
>
> (A) explain an exciting discovery.
> (B) describe Cavallini's artistic style.
> (C) emphasize the importance of art history.
> (D) discuss Giotto's role in the Renaissance.

Based on your summaries and marking of the passage, what do you think it was trying to do? The passage explained how Strinati correctly guessed that Cavallini's work was covered over in the basilica. It then discussed the lost frescos Strinati was able to reveal, and the potentially major implications of Cavallini's work for art history.

We might summarize that as "explaining big artistic finding." Now let's look for an answer choice that matches our prediction.

Does one answer choice jump out at you right away? Answer choice (A) is almost an exact match with what you predicted! The other options are definitely not focused on the main ideas and purpose of the passage, so you can be confident in ruling them out. Doing the mental work of answering the question in your own words pays off when you can make your choice and gain a point so quickly.

PROCESS OF ELIMINATION

Because there is only one correct answer for each question, it can be helpful to eliminate the choices you know are wrong. This is called the **process of elimination**, which you learned about in Chapter 1. Feel free to review that information to refresh your memory.

Make sure you only eliminate answer choices you are certain are wrong, either because they are directly contradicted by the passage, or because there is no information in the passage to support them. You can eliminate answers by crossing them out in your test booklet. If you end up knocking out every answer choice, then you have misunderstood something. Re-read the question carefully, and consider all the choices again while referring back to the passage.

Let's put this to use with a question from the Cavallini passage:

> Based on the passage, which choice best describes the relationship between the fresco cycle titled the "St. Francis Legend" and the artist Giotto?
>
> (A) The fresco cycle established Giotto as the founder of the Renaissance.
> (B) Cavallini was originally thought to be the fresco cycle's artist, but many art historians now believe it was Giotto.
> (C) Giotto was originally thought to be the fresco cycle's artist, but some art historians now believe it was Cavallini.
> (D) Giotto painted the fresco cycle to capture the story of his life with narrative zest.

Refer back to the sixth paragraph, which discusses the "St. Francis Legend," and compare it to the answer choices to see if they are supported. Here is the sixth paragraph:

> Moreover, the Aracoeli fragments may provide a critical new clue in a
> 65 decades-old battle concerning the "St. Francis Legend," the 1296 fresco cycle at Assisi, universally recognized as one of the foundations of the Renaissance. For centuries, the 28-
> 70 scene cycle – which recounts the life of the saint with a narrative zest and compositional depth that leave the flat tableaus of the Byzantine era far behind – was attributed to Giotto. But
> 75 since the 1930's, various scholars have questioned this judgment, claiming that the Assisi cycle doesn't resemble Giotto's other work. Now, the Aracoeli discovery is ammunition for Italian art
> 80 historians who believe that Cavallini might actually be the primary creative force behind the "St. Francis Legend."

Answer choice (A) goes too far, as the passage never states that Giotto was the founder of the Renaissance. It only states that the "St. Francis Legend" is a foundational piece of art in the Renaissance, which is not the same. You can knock it out.

Answer choice (B) contradicts the passage, which says, "For centuries, the 28-scene cycle … was attributed to Giotto." You can knock it out.

Answer choice (C) matches the passage, so we can keep it open for now.

Answer choice (D) contradicts the passage, as the paintings depict the life of St. Francis, not the life of Giotto. You can knock it out, and choose answer choice (C) as your correct response.

Even if the process of elimination cannot help you knock out all the wrong answers, it is always helpful to have fewer answer choices to consider. Be sure to use it whenever possible!

BEST CHOICES

Remember that every question has only one correct answer. For many questions it will be clear that only one answer relates to the passages, as the others are not mentioned in the passage, or contradict information given in the passage.

However, other questions may have more than one answer option that could potentially be true. Remember you are looking for the **best choice**, which means the answer that most directly and completely answers the question, and is most supported by the passage. The best way to ensure that you select the best answer choice is to make sure you can find a word, line, or selection of lines in the text that support your answer.

EXAMPLE

Here is another example question from the Cavallini passage:

The passage most strongly suggests that the Renaissance

(A) began in the 1930s.
(B) had roots in neither Rome nor Florence.
(C) began in numerous Italian cities simultaneously.
(D) featured naturalistic styles of painting.

First, use the process of elimination to knock out any answer choices you know are wrong. Both answer choice (A) and answer choice (B) contradict the passage, so you can eliminate them.

Answer choices (C) and (D) do not contradict the passage, so you can now consider each one more closely. Which answer choice has more support from the passage?

While answer choice (C) doesn't contradict the passage, there is nothing in the text to tell us about other places the Renaissance may have been starting. Remember you cannot use outside information to answer questions, or make assumptions. You must find support for your answers in the passage itself.

On the other hand, you can find specific evidence to support answer choice (D). Lines 55-62 talk about how Cavallini's lifelike figures are evidence that he "may have anticipated some of the extraordinary naturalistic innovations" of the Renaissance. Lines 36-37 also describes a Cavallini portrait as "remarkably tender." While answer choice (C) could potentially be true, answer choice (D) can be proven true by the passage, and is therefore the best choice for this question.

What should you do if it seems that you can support two separate answer choices with information from the passage? First, make sure that the evidence supports the answer choice in the way you think it does. For example, some answer choices may use the same words as the passage, but in a way that means something different than the original text.

Second, for questions that ask what you can infer about the passage by reading between the lines, be sure to look for the most likely, or plausible, conclusion you can reach. Try to make as few leaps between ideas as possible. If your answer choice feels like a stretch, requires making a lot of assumptions, or relies on information or ideas not found in the text, it is likely incorrect. Avoid using your outside knowledge and stick to what is on the page.

GUESSING

Starting in 2016, the SAT will no longer deduct a quarter point for each wrong answer choice. That means that there is no downside to guessing. You should always guess on any questions you cannot answer with certainty.

But how can you guess to maximize your chances of gaining a few extra points? First, try to attempt the question using the processes discussed above. Even if the question is difficult, do your best to use the process of elimination and get down to two or three answer choices, which will improve your odds of guessing correctly.

You can also make a guess at a question, circle it, and return to it later. Once you have attempted all the other questions for the passage you are working on, come back to the question and re-read it to clarify what it is asking. Then, try again to answer the question.

Eliminate any wrong answers, and see if you want to change the answer you originally guessed.

It is a good idea to choose a letter beforehand that you will always use when guessing. This will save you from spending time deciding what answer choice to pick, and makes it easier to bubble in guesses. For any questions you do not have time to answer, simply fill in your bubble sheet using your chosen answer choice. Make sure you have time to enter a guess for every question you do not attempt before the 65-minute section ends!

PART 3 PRACTICE: SELECTING YOUR ANSWERS

1. Select and write down the answer choice you will use while guessing:

2. Practice with using this letter any time you answer SAT questions, so you can guess quickly on any questions you cannot answer.

3. Practice marking up this passage and making paragraph summaries the way you learned earlier in this section.

After the AHA[1] advised the public to eat less saturated fat and switch to vegetable oils for a "healthy heart" in
Line 1961, Americans changed their diets.
5 Now these oils represent 7% to 8% of all calories in our diet, up from nearly zero in 1900, the biggest increase in consumption of any type of food over the past century.
10 This shift seemed like a good idea at the time, but it brought many potential health problems in its wake. In those early clinical trials, people on diets high in vegetable oil were found
15 to suffer higher rates not only of cancer but also of gallstones. And, strikingly, they were more likely to die from violent accidents and suicides. Alarmed by these findings, the
20 National Institutes of Health convened researchers several times in the early 1980s to try to explain these "side effects," but they couldn't. (Experts now speculate that certain
25 psychological problems might be related to changes in brain chemistry caused by diet, such as fatty-acid imbalances or the depletion of cholesterol.)
30 We've also known since the 1940s that when heated, vegetable oils create oxidation products that, in experiments on animals, lead to cirrhosis of the liver and early death. For these
35 reasons, some midcentury chemists warned against the consumption of these oils, but their concerns were allayed by a chemical fix: Oils could be rendered more stable through a
40 process called hydrogenation, which used a catalyst to turn them from oils into solids.
From the 1950s on, these hardened oils became the backbone of the entire
45 food industry, used in cakes, cookies, chips, breads, frostings, fillings, and

frozen and fried food. Unfortunately, hydrogenation also produced trans fats, which since the 1970s have been
50 suspected of interfering with basic cellular functioning and were recently condemned by the Food and Drug Administration for their ability to raise our levels of "bad" LDL cholesterol.
55 Yet paradoxically, the drive to get rid of trans fats has led some restaurants and food manufacturers to return to using regular liquid oils—with the same long-standing oxidation
60 problems. These dangers are especially acute in restaurant fryers, where the oils are heated to high temperatures over long periods.

[1]The American Heart Association

Write the answers to the following questions in your own words.

1. The primary purpose of the passage is to:

2. The stance the author takes in the passage is best described as:

3. In lines 43-47 what is the most likely reason the author lists the types of foods that use hydrogenated oils?

For the following questions:

- Note which answers you can eliminate using the process of elimination, and why you know they are wrong.
- Note why the answer you selected is the best one, using words and lines from the passage to support your answer choice.

4. The author of the passage would probably agree with which of the following statements?
   (A) While trans fats are unhealthy, they are preferable to saturated fats.
   (B) Using large amounts of vegetable oil is safe as long as it is not hydrogenated.
   (C) Americans' attempt to avoid saturated fats has had other unhealthy consequences.
   (D) The process of hydrogenation eliminates the only problem with vegetable oils.

Which answers could you eliminate, and why are they incorrect?

Why is your answer the best choice?

5. Which of the following situations is most analogous to the problem presented in the passage?

   (A) Drivers are advised to avoid a certain highway because it has a lot of traffic, but the other road they take is backed up because of an accident.

   (B) Doctors prescribe an effective medicine for an illness, but when they administer a new treatment it causes side effects.

   (C) Shoppers frequent a local grocer, but when it closes they are forced to buy food at a more expensive market.

   (D) Farmers have a problem with frequent pests, but when they use a new harvesting technique fewer crops are eaten by insects.

   Which answers can you eliminate, and why are they incorrect?

   Why is your answer the best choice?

6. It can reasonably be inferred from the passage that it is best to consume vegetable oils

   (A) in regular liquid form, in large quantities.

   (B) in regular liquid form, lightly heated.

   (C) in solid form after hydrogenation.

   (D) in small amounts or not at all.

   Which answers could you eliminate, and why are they incorrect?

   Why is your answer the best choice?

ANSWER KEY: SELECTING YOUR ANSWERS

1. Describe the problems created by eating more vegetable oils to avoid saturated fats.

2. A concerned expert, a worried scholar or another similar choice.

3. To demonstrate how widespread the use of hardened hydrogenated oils has become.

4. C

    Answer choices (B) and (D) contradict the passage. Answer choice (A) is not supported by the passage, as the author never directly compares trans and saturated fats.

    The majority of the passage discusses the problem with vegetable oils. Lines 10-12 sum it up nicely: "This shift seemed like a good idea at the time, but it brought many potential health problems in its wake."

5. A

    Answer choices (B) and (C) begin with positive situations, whereas the passage begins with saturated fat being undesirable. Answer choice (D) ends with a solution, whereas in the passage vegetable oil caused further problems.

    The first sentence of the passage states that Americans were told to avoid consuming saturated fats, and that eating vegetable oils would be better for them. This is similar to how the drivers are told to avoid the highway and take another. The passage then describes the many health problems with vegetable oils, similar to how the drivers ended up with another traffic problem when they took the alternate route.

6. D

    Answer choices (B) and (C) contradict the passage, as both of these forms have unhealthy side effects.

    Answer choice (A) is plausible, but answer choice (D) is better. While vegetable oils are safest in their liquid form, lines 13-16 tell us that "people on diets high in vegetable oil were found to suffer higher rates not only of cancer but also of gallstones." Thus, it would be safer not to consume much vegetable oil, even in its liquid form.

Questions 1-10 are based on the following passage.

On a wind-swept point of black lava jutting into the Pacific Ocean, a small band of scientists and
Line
5 entrepreneurs is generating electricity, raising lobsters and growing strawberries using cold water from the depths of the sea. Eventually, they say, they hope the techniques they are devising here may increase food
10 supplies and produce energy without pollution and without the use of fossil fuels. For now, however, "cold water is the resource we're selling," said Thomas H. Daniel, technical director
15 of the Natural Energy Laboratory of Hawaii, where the projects are under way.

That water, pumped from a depth of 2,000 feet, comes up at a nearly
20 constant temperature of 6 degrees Celsius, or 43 degrees Fahrenheit. It has a high concentration of nutrients like nitrates, phosphates and silicates that foster the growth of plants and
25 algae. And it is pure, having been out of contact with the surface for centuries as it drifted slowly along the bottom, and thus is free of the pathogens that carry diseases.
30 When the laboratory began the project about 10 years ago, scientists here were confident it would be possible to put the water to profitable use. While profits have so far been
35 elusive, the researchers have demonstrated the feasibility of several ideas, solved formidable engineering problems and produced a wealth of data.
40 The lab, which operates on a budget of $1.5 million a year and has a staff of 20, began by seeking to use the differences in temperature between surface and deep sea water to produce

45 electricity in a process called ocean thermal energy conversion. But it is the other projects developed on this 322-acre site that seem more promising today: growing lobsters in
50 half the time it takes in their natural habitat along the coast of Maine; raising flounder, sea urchins and salmon; distilling fresh water and cooling buildings and industrial plants.
55 Next to the energy lab is the Hawaii Ocean Science and Technology park, a 547-acre site set aside by the state for commercial development of the laboratory's
60 findings. Once a project developed at the lab becomes profitable, it must move out, either to the park or elsewhere. Aquaculture Enterprises has already moved to the park. The
65 company has been experimenting since 1987 with lobsters and has begun test sales locally. The lobsters are raised in shallow tanks under green tents that block the heat of the sun. They are
70 kept in separate pans so they will not eat each other.

Joseph Wilson, a partner in the enterprise, said that by mixing cold and warm sea water to maintain a
75 steady temperature of 22 degrees Celsius, researchers have eliminated the near-hibernation of the lobsters in winter. That has cut growing time to less than four years from the seven and
80 a half years it takes in nature. As they learn more about the lobsters' environment, nutrition and genetics, he said, "we think that could be cut again to 30 months." But the cold water also
85 finds uses on land. Run through pipes the energy laboratory has laid in strawberry, lettuce and flower beds, the cold water keeps the plants at the

cool temperature they like and causes
90 fresh water to condense on the pipes.
The fresh water drips from the pipes
to water the plants. "When we want
the strawberries to think it's winter,"
95 Mr. Daniel said, standing under a
tropical sun, "we just run the cold
water faster." Strawberries with five
times more sugar than those in nature
have been produced.

1. This passage is primarily concerned with

   (A) describing a new alternative source of energy.

   (B) advocating alternatives to fossil fuels.

   (C) discussing new applications of a natural resource.

   (D) explaining the challenges of food production.

2. The purpose of the second paragraph (lines 18-29) is to

   (A) describe the beneficial properties of cold ocean water.

   (B) explain how nitrates, phosphates and silicates foster plant and algae growth.

   (C) convey the author's interest in the numerous uses of cold ocean water.

   (D) explore the process used to move cold water up to the ocean surface.

3. Based on the passage, which choice best describes the relationship between the electricity and food production projects involving cold ocean water?

   (A) The food production projects are more successful than the electricity project.

   (B) The electricity project is more profitable than the food production projects.

   (C) The food production projects depend on the electricity projects.

   (D) The food production projects undermine the electricity projects.

4. Which choice provides the best evidence for the answer to the previous question?

   (A) Lines 7-12 ("Eventually … fossil fuels")

   (B) Lines 30-34 ("When … profitable use")

   (C) Lines 46-49 ("But it … today")

   (D) Lines 67-69 ("The lobsters … sun")

5. As used in line 90, "condense" most nearly means

   (A) compress.

   (B) squeeze.

   (C) form.

   (D) consolidate.

6. The attitude of the scientists interviewed in the passage toward their current agriculture projects could best be described as one of

   (A) optimism.

   (B) contempt.

   (C) skepticism.

   (D) disappointment.

7. Which choice provides the best evidence for the answer to the previous question?

   (A) Line 34-39 ("While profits … data")

   (B) Line 64-67 ("The company … locally")

   (C) Line 72-78 ("Joseph Wilson … winter")

   (D) Line 80-84 ("As they … months")

8. As used in line 38, "wealth" most nearly means

   (A) capital.

   (B) fortune.

   (C) means.

   (D) abundance.

9. According to the passage, the growing time for lobsters can be reduced by

   (A) eliminating cold temperatures to prevent their near-hibernation.

   (B) preventing them from eating one another.

   (C) running cool water over them at a faster rate.

   (D) providing them with a high concentration of nutrients like nitrates.

10. What is the most likely reason the author describes Mr. Daniel as "standing under a tropical sun" (lines 94-95)?

(A) To contrast the local weather with the cold conditions created for the strawberries

(B) To give the reader a sense of place through vivid description

(C) To suggest that tropical locations are the usual growing region for strawberries

(D) To suggest that the local weather could pose a threat to the success of the strawberry crop

Questions 11-21 are based on the following passage.

The following passage is adapted from Sir Arthur Conan Doyle's novel "A Study in Scarlet," published in 1887. It features the narrator, Dr. John Watson, describing the detective Sherlock Holmes.

His very person and appearance were such as to strike the attention of the most casual observer. In height he was rather over six feet, and so
5   excessively lean that he seemed to be considerably taller. His eyes were sharp and piercing, save during those intervals of torpor to which I have alluded; and his thin, hawk-like nose
10 gave his whole expression an air of alertness and decision. His chin, too, had the prominence and squareness which mark the man of determination. His hands were
15 invariably blotted with ink and stained with chemicals, yet he was possessed of extraordinary delicacy of touch, as I frequently had occasion to observe when I watched him
20 manipulating his fragile philosophical instruments.
The reader may set me down as a hopeless busybody, when I confess how much this man stimulated my
25 curiosity, and how often I endeavoured to break through the reticence which he showed on all that concerned himself. Before pronouncing judgment, however, be
30 it remembered, how objectless was my life, and how little there was to engage my attention. My health forbade me from venturing out unless the weather was exceptionally genial,
35 and I had no friends who would call upon me and break the monotony of my daily existence. Under these circumstances, I eagerly hailed the little mystery which hung around my
40 companion, and spent much of my time in endeavouring to unravel it.
He was not studying medicine. He had himself, in reply to a question, confirmed Stamford's opinion upon
45 that point. Neither did he appear to have pursued any course of reading which might fit him for a degree in science or any other recognized portal which would give him an entrance
50 into the learned world. Yet his zeal for certain studies was remarkable, and within eccentric limits his knowledge was so extraordinarily ample and minute that his
55 observations have fairly astounded me. Surely no man would work so hard or attain such precise information unless he had some definite end in view. Casual readers
60 are seldom remarkable for the

exactness of their learning. No man burdens his mind with small matters unless he has some very good reason for doing so.

His ignorance was as remarkable as his knowledge. Of contemporary literature, philosophy and politics he appeared to know next to nothing. Upon my quoting Thomas Carlyle, he inquired in the naivest way who he might be and what he had done. My surprise reached a climax, however, when I found incidentally that he was ignorant of the Copernican Theory and of the composition of the Solar System. That any civilized human being in this nineteenth century should not be aware that the earth travelled round the sun appeared to be to me such an extraordinary fact that I could hardly realize it.

"You appear to be astonished," he said, smiling at my expression of surprise. "Now that I do know it I shall do my best to forget it."

"To forget it!"

"You see," he explained, "I consider that a man's brain originally is like a little empty attic, and you have to stock it with such furniture as you choose. A fool takes in all the lumber of every sort that he comes across, so that the knowledge which might be useful to him gets crowded out, or at best is jumbled up with a lot of other things so that he has a difficulty in laying his hands upon it. Now the skillful workman is very careful indeed as to what he takes into his brain-attic. He will have nothing but the tools which may help him in doing his work, but of these he has a large assortment, and all in the most perfect order. It is a mistake to think that that little room has elastic walls and can distend to any extent. Depend upon it, there comes a time when for every addition of knowledge you forget something that you knew before. It is of the highest importance, therefore, not to have useless facts elbowing out the useful ones."

"But the Solar System!" I protested.

"What the deuce is it to me?" he interrupted impatiently; "you say that we go round the sun. If we went round the moon it would not make a pennyworth of difference to me or to my work."

11. Watson's attitude toward Sherlock in the passage is best described as one of

(A) impatience.

(B) disdain.

(C) adoration.

(D) fascination.

12. Which choice provides the best evidence for the answer to the previous question?

(A) Lines 22-28 ("The reader … himself")

(B) Lines 45-50 ("Neither … world")

(C) Lines 56-59 ("Surely … in view")

(D) Lines 76-81 ("That any … it")

13. The primary purpose of the first paragraph (lines 1-21) is to

   (A) provide a description of Sherlock.

   (B) explain why Watson is interested in Sherlock's strange mannerisms.

   (C) describe Sherlock's delicacy in using his instruments.

   (D) introduce the tools Sherlock uses to solve mysteries.

14. Watson sees a surprising contrast between

   (A) Sherlock's expertise in some subjects and unfamiliarity with others.

   (B) his impression of Sherlock and Sherlock's attitude toward him.

   (C) Sherlock's motivations and enthusiasm for learning.

   (D) his own intellect and that of Sherlock.

15. Which choice provides the best evidence for the answer to the previous question?

   (A) Lines 1-3 ("His … casual observer")

   (B) Lines 61-64 ("No … doing so")

   (C) Lines 65-66 ("His ignorance … knowledge")

   (D) Lines 69-71 ("Upon my … done")

16. As used in line 20, "manipulating" most nearly means

   (A) exploiting.

   (B) tricking.

   (C) tampering.

   (D) handling.

17. The second paragraph (lines 22-41) suggests that Watson feels his interest in Sherlock was

   (A) something for which he may be judged, but was understandable under the circumstances.

   (B) a normal reaction in which he eagerly indulged.

   (C) embarrassing, as it failed to break the monotony of his existence.

   (D) acceptable, as it allowed him to unravel the mystery surrounding the detective.

18. As used in line 29, "pronouncing" most nearly means

    (A) uttering.

    (B) passing.

    (C) reciting.

    (D) declaring.

19. It can reasonably be inferred from the passage that once Watson learns Sherlock is unfamiliar with the Solar System, he

    (A) mocks him for his lack of education.

    (B) explains the concept to him.

    (C) asks Sherlock about his opinion on human memory.

    (D) decides it is not as important as he originally thought.

20. Which hypothetical situation involves the same form of expertise demonstrated by Sherlock?

    (A) A librarian is familiar with all types of media, both modern and antiquated.

    (B) A highly accomplished classical musician can play few other types of music.

    (C) A carpenter works with numerous types of wood but prefers one.

    (D) A new art student has been studying theory but has not yet created anything.

21. According to the passage, Sherlock believes the brain is like an attic because

    (A) a room can only hold so many items, similar to how human memory is not unlimited.

    (B) the human brain cannot grow, similar to how the walls of a room cannot be extended.

    (C) you cannot store endless memories, similar to how a skillful workman carefully chooses his projects.

    (D) a cluttered mind makes it difficult to recall important information, similar to how a crowded room can become dangerous.

Answer Key

1. C (Determining central ideas and themes/summarizing)

2. A (Analyzing purpose)

3. A (Understanding relationships)

4. C (Citing textual evidence)

5. C (Interpreting words and phrases in context)

6. A (Determining central ideas and themes/summarizing)

7. D (Citing textual evidence)

8. D (Interpreting words and phrases in context)

9. A (Determining explicit meanings)

10. A (Analyzing purpose)

11. D (Determining central ideas and themes/Analyzing point of view)

12. A (Citing textual evidence)

13. A (Analyzing purpose)

14. A (Understanding relationships)

15. C (Citing textual evidence)

16. D (Interpreting words and phrases in context)

17. A (Analyzing point of view/analyzing word choice)

18. B (Interpreting words and phrases in context)

19. B (Determining implicit meaning)

20. B (Analogical reasoning)

21. A (Determining implicit meaning)

ACKNOWLEDGEMENTS FOR THIS SECTION

The passages in this section were adapted from the following sources:

Daniel Zalewski, "Under a Shroud of Kitsch May Lie A Master's Art." © 2001 by *The New York Times Company*. Originally published July 28, 2001.

Glenn Hubbard, "The Unemployment Puzzle: Where Have All the Workers Gone?" ©2014 by *Dow Jones & Company*. Originally published April 4, 2014.

Robert Lee Hotz, "A Wandering Mind Heads Straight Toward Insight." © 2009 by *Dow Jones & Company*. Originally published June 2009.

Nina Teicholz, "The Questionable Link Between Saturated Fat and Heart Disease." © 2014 by *Dow Jones & Company*. Originally published May 6, 2014.

Sir Arthur Conan Doyle, "A Study in Scarlet." Published 1887.

Richard Halloran, "Tapping Ocean's Cold For Crops." © 1990 by *The New York Times Company*. Originally published May 22, 1990.

SECTION 3
SAT PASSAGE TYPES

Now that we've outlined the basic strategies that you'll use to approach the Reading section, let's talk about the passages. In this section, we'll show you how to approach each type of SAT passage. You'll learn what types of passages you can expect to see, what to expect in each type of passage, and how to apply the skills we've already reviewed to each type of passage.

There are five passages in the Reading section. These passages fall into three domains: one passage will be in the Literature domain, two will be in the Science domain, and two will be in the Social Science domain.

There are also a couple of special passage types: passages with graphics (like charts, graphs, or diagrams), and paired passages. One of the two Science passages will include graphics, and one of the two Social Science passages will include graphics. One Science or Social Science passage will actually be a set of two short passages.

The active reading strategies that we showed you in the previous section can be used for all of these passages, but the way that you should best apply those skills will depend on the type of passage that you're reading. The SAT will generally ask questions which are appropriate for the type of passage that you're reading, so the types of details that you should pay the most attention to will depend on the type of passage that you're reading.

In this section we're going to highlight some important elements that you'll want to keep an eye out for in each type of passage. We'll also give you some tips for interpreting graphic elements and for "connecting the dots" between paired passages. Then, we'll give you a chance to practice your skills.

LITERATURE PASSAGES
PART 1

There is one Literature passage in the Reading section of the SAT. The Literature passage that you encounter on the SAT will usually be an excerpt from a novel or short story. Sometimes it will be taken from a recently published source, and other times it may be taken from an older source. Passages from older sources might contain some old phrases that you're not necessarily familiar with, but most of the language will be understandable to modern readers.

Literature passages will usually tell a story, or describe a scene, object, or character—often with an underlying message, that is implied rather than being stated directly. With Literature passages your goals are to follow the details of what is actually being described, to try to understand any underlying message of the passage, and to pay attention to how the author uses language and literary techniques to convey that message. The tips that follow will help you use your active reading skills to accomplish those goals.

You won't be tested on your knowledge about specific works of literature, but you will need to be comfortable reading various types of literature. The best way to increase your familiarity with literature is to read it; once you've done the practice exercises in this book, check out the Further Resources in Section 7 of this chapter for some recommended reading.

Literature passages will never include graphics, and will not be presented as paired passages.

IMPORTANT DETAILS IN LITERATURE PASSAGES

As we mentioned in Section 2, you should pay special attention to important details in a passage as you're reading it. Which details are the most important will depend largely on what type of passage you're reading. There are a couple of types of details in Literature passages that you should pay special attention to, because you're more likely to be asked questions about these types of details in Literature passages than in other types of passages.

FIGURATIVE LANGUAGE

Literature passages often contain **figurative language**, which is language that's used in some creative or unusual way. Figurative language often doesn't mean exactly what it says, but instead has a second meaning. The SAT will often ask you to interpret specific pieces of figurative language, or to analyze how they affect the passage or why the author chose to use them.

There are seven basic kinds of figurative language:

Types of Figurative Language		
Alliteration	Repeating the same sounds in several words.	Snakes slither slowly on slippery surfaces.
Hyperbole	Major exaggeration.	I ate about ten tons of candy last Hallowe'en.
Idioms	A phrase with a special meaning, besides what the words themselves mean (although it might also be literally true).	That's not exactly brain surgery.
Onomatopoeia	Words that sound like the things they describe.	Moo. Whoosh! Meow.
Personification	Language that ascribes human characteristics, like personality traits, intentions, or human-like actions, to non-human things.	As we approached the mouth of the cavern, it belched out a noxious breath, and its foul exhalation warned of a deadly distaste for intruders.
Metaphor	Language that uses one thing to represent another thing or an idea, especially when they aren't very much alike.	Luke was adrift on a sea of opportunities, with no current to direct his course.
Simile	Language that compares two things of different kinds, using the words "like" or "as."	With the children finally all away at school, Sally's home was as vast and empty as a starless sky.

Correctly identifying figurative language can give you a lot of insight into the meaning of a story.

Paying attention to hyperbole, idioms, metaphors, personification, and similes in a passage will help you to answer questions about the meaning of certain parts of a passage and questions about how language is used in the passage. You will need to understand these elements of a passage in order to understand the underlying message of the passage, and sometimes you will need to interpret them correctly just to follow the details of the story. Paying attention to alliteration and onomatopoeia can give you some information about the author's purpose, and how the author is using language to achieve her purpose. You usually won't need to identify these elements in order to understand the story, but you might be asked to analyze how they're being used in the passage—so pay attention to them, and to the effect that they have in the passage.

If there are lots of these elements in a passage, or in a particular part of a passage, then you don't necessarily need to underline every instance. Just make a note that there's a lot of figurative language in that part of the passage, or in the passage overall, and pay attention to how it's being used.

CHARACTERIZATION

The people in stories, plays, and novels are characters. The moments when the author gives you new information about the characters are called **characterization.**

Writers can use a number of techniques for characterization. Here are some of the big ones:

Techniques for Characterization		
Description	An author might use physical details to suggest something about the character's life or personality.	She wore an expensive business suit, diamond earrings, and an elegant gold watch.
Dialogue	The style or content of a character's speech can reveal what the character believes or how he feels.	He stammered, "W-would you, um, I mean, would you like to maybe, uh, go out with me sometime?"
Action	The way an author describes a character's actions can tell you more than just what the character is doing.	As the time drew closer to her audition, she reviewed her script over and over, biting her nails.
Internal Speech	An author might state or paraphrase a character's inner monologue to let the reader know what the character is thinking.	She smiled and thanked her boss, privately thinking that she was looking forward to the day she never had to see his smug face again.
Responses	The way other characters respond to someone can give you clues about that character's situation.	When he walked into the guidance counselor's office, the secretary raised an eyebrow and said, "Again?"

Paying attention to how the author uses these techniques will help you to answer questions about characters and their relationships, and about the author's purpose. Keep an eye out for characterization, and pay attention to how it shapes individual characters, their relationships to one another, and their role in the story.

SUMMARIZING A LITERATURE PASSAGE

Next, remember that you should make short notes in the margins to briefly summarize what the passage is about. These notes should include some information about the style and purpose of the passage.

THE STRUCTURE OF A LITERATURE PASSAGE

As you read the passage, you should pay attention to how it's structured, the focus of different parts of the passage, and how they fit together.

Some Literature passages will be mostly **narrative**, which means that they focus on telling a story. A narrative passage describes events that happen in a certain order.

Others will be mostly **descriptive**, which means that they focus on describing an important person, place, or thing in detail.

Many of the passages you encounter will mix some narrative and descriptive elements. In passages that mix narrative and descriptive elements, the two kinds of elements are usually intended to support one another. Descriptive elements in a narrative passage often provide additional details about an important figure in the story, while narrative elements in a descriptive passage often help characterize the subject that the passage is describing.

Sometimes it can be hard to say whether a passage is mainly narrative or mainly descriptive, so it's important to pay attention to the balance of narrative and descriptive elements in a passage, and how those elements relate to each other. Pay special attention to which styles are used at the beginning and end of the passage: narrative passages usually start with an initial event, and move to a final event or a moral, while descriptive passages usually begin and end with information about their subject.

Part 1 Practice: Literature Passages

Below is an example passage. Read the passage, paying special attention to the elements we have discussed, and then answer the accompanying practice questions.

We were planning supplies for our trip. George said:

"Begin with breakfast." (George is so practical.) "Now for breakfast we shall want a frying-pan"—(Harris said it was indigestible; but we merely urged him not to be a fool, and George went on)—"a tea-pot and a kettle, and an ethanol stove."

"No oil," said George, with a significant look; and Harris and I agreed. We had taken an oil-stove on a boat trip once, but "never again." It had been like living in an oil-shop that week. It oozed. I never saw another thing ooze like kerosene oil. We kept it in the nose of the boat, and, from there, it oozed down to the rudder, impregnating the whole boat and everything in it on its way, and it oozed over the river, and saturated the scenery and spoilt the atmosphere. Sometimes a westerly oily wind blew, and at other times an easterly oily wind, and sometimes it blew a northerly oily wind, and maybe a southerly oily wind; but whether it came for the Arctic snows, or was raised in the waste of the desert sands, it came alike to us laden with the fragrance of kerosene oil.

And that oil oozed up and ruined the sunset; and as for the moonbeams, they positively reeked of kerosene.

We tried to get away from it at Marlow. We left the boat by the bridge, and took a walk through the town to escape it, but it followed us. The whole town was full of oil. We passed through the church-yard, and it seemed as if the people had been buried in oil. The High Street stunk of oil; we wondered how people could live in it. And we walked miles upon miles out Birmingham way; but it was no use, the country was steeped in oil.

At the end of that trip we met together at midnight in a lonely field, under a blasted oak, and took an awful oath (we had been swearing for a whole week about the thing in an ordinary, middle-class way, but this was a swell affair)—an awful oath never to take kerosene oil with us in a boat again.

And so for this trip, we confined ourselves to an ethanol stove. Even that is bad enough. You get ethanol pie and ethanol cake. But ethanol is more wholesome than kerosene, and much less persistent.

Line 5, 10, 15, 20, 25, 30, 35, 40, 45, 50, 55, 60

1. The main purpose of this passage can best be described as

   (A) suggesting that planning an adventure might be more fun than going on one.

   (B) telling the story of how a group of friends learned from a past mistake.

   (C) describing the process of planning and preparing to go on a trip.

   (D) explaining why it is important to avoid using certain types of fuel in enclosed spaces.

2. Based on the passage, we can most reasonably infer that Harris, George, and the narrator are

   (A) recent acquaintances planning a trip to get to know one another.

   (B) travelling companions who first met during an unfortunate journey by boat.

   (C) seasoned adventurers who regularly travel great distances.

   (D) old friends planning a trip similar to one they had taken before.

3. The author's purpose in describing how the oil affected the sunset and moonbeams (lines 32-34) is mainly to

   (A) describe the widespread pollution that the boys encountered as they travelled down the river.

   (B) contrast the environment of the boat with the lonely field the boys would visit later.

   (C) suggest that the smell of kerosene was so overwhelming that it tainted every other experience.

   (D) relate the specific event which finally persuaded the boys never to bring kerosene again.

Answer Key

1. B
2. D
3. C

SCIENCE PASSAGES
PART 2

There are two Science passages in the Evidence-Based Reading section of the SAT. The Science passages you encounter on the SAT will usually come from magazines, newspapers, or non-fiction books on popular science. Science passages will always be from contemporary sources, which means they're current science. Science passages on the SAT will be about natural or physical sciences—physics, biology, astronomy, chemistry, or similar fields.

You won't be tested on your knowledge of science, but you will have to be comfortable reading passages which use scientific language. Check out the Further Resources in Section 7 of this chapter for some recommended reading in science.

One of the Science passages will include one or two graphics. We cover graphics in Part 4 of this chapter, and discuss them further in the Writing and Math chapters of this book. You'll need to use the skills discussed in this chapter, as well as those discussed later, to tackle science passages with graphs.

One of the Science passages might also be a set of paired passages. That means that it will actually consist of two short passages, presented together. We cover paired passages in Part 5, where we'll give you some examples and a chance to practice with paired passages. Part 3 is only going to deal with single Science passages, but again, you'll need the skills discussed here *and* in Part 5 to deal effectively with paired Science passages.

With Science passages, your goal is to identify the main topic or argument, and understand how the additional information and evidence provided explains the subject or supports that argument. The tips that follow will help you to accomplish that goal.

IMPORTANT DETAILS IN SCIENCE PASSAGES

Just like you did with Literature passages, you want to note important people, places, and things as they are introduced in a passage, or when you get new information about them. Science passages might also include figurative language, and narrative or descriptive elements similar to those that you had to keep an eye out for in Literature passages. But generally, these won't be as common or important in Science passages. Science passages will focus more on communicating specific facts, either to help the reader understand a broader topic or to build an argument in support of the author's opinion on a scientific issue.

You need to pay special attention to data and experimental evidence, and to the elements of the argument presented in a passage.

ELEMENTS OF AN ARGUMENT

Often, Science passages are going to be mainly about building an argument that shows, using evidence and logic, why the author believes that some basic idea is true.

Keep an eye out for all of the following elements of an argument in Science passages:

Elements of an Argument	
Thesis	The main idea that the author is defending with her argument. There may be a sentence near the beginning that clearly states the thesis, just as we will recommend that you use in your own writing. However, there may not; be careful not to assume that whatever idea is mentioned earliest is the thesis. Look instead for the idea that the passage as a whole supports.
Claims	Claims are statements that the author says are true, or that we know she wants us to believe are true based on the surrounding context.
Supporting Evidence	Supporting evidence is the information that authors provide to back up their claims. It can take the form of data from studies, quotes from experts, historical examples, or other claims or facts that you might already agree with.
Counterclaims and refutations	Counterclaims are claims that disagree with or contradict claims made elsewhere in the passage, and refutations are statements intended to disprove other statements.
Conclusion	Argumentative passages often end with a concluding statement that restates the thesis. This is more than just repetition; the concluding statement is usually stronger than the thesis statement, and often includes a summary of the evidence presented in the text.

Europa, a moon of Jupiter, is the place where we are most likely to find extraterrestrial life in our own solar system. Liquid water is widely considered to be one of the most important preconditions for life, and there are likely vast oceans of liquid water beneath Europa's surface. Certain organic chemicals are also considered necessary precursors for life, and we have reason to believe that natural processes on Europa's surface create them in abundance. Given that sunlight is the main source of energy for life on Earth, it may seem that Europa's thick icy crust, which prevents any sunlight from reaching the ocean, would make life on the moon impossible. But there is an alternative source of energy on Europa: tidal flexing, a process in which gravitational tugs cause Europa's oceans to slosh about, generating heat and energy. With its suitable environment, and sources of the chemicals and energy necessary for life, it would surprise me more to find that Europa was barren than to discover life beneath its crust.

This paragraph begins with a clear statement of the thesis. It proceeds to offer a couple of pieces of supporting evidence. Then it raises a counterclaim, but only for the purpose of refuting it. Finally, it concludes with a summary of the evidence and a restatement of the thesis.

READING ABOUT EXPERIMENTS

Science passages will often discuss specific experiments. Sometimes details about an experiment may be offered as supporting evidence, and other times an experiment may be the main subject of the passage. To be sure that you understand Science passages, you should make sure that you're familiar with some basic facts about how experiments are conducted and what they mean.

THE BASIC IDEA

Experiments measure one thing: the interaction between cause and effect. Experiments measure whether a change in one thing causes a change in another, and what kind of change occurs.

To start, experimenters identify the **variables**—things or circumstances which might change or can be changed—that might have some influence on the relationship they want to test. Some variables will be intentionally altered, and some will only be measured.

It's not all changing and measuring, though: the passage might also mention that researchers took steps to **control** some variables. That most frequently means that experimenters took steps to prevent that variable from changing, because they wanted to avoid accidentally measuring the effects of that variable.

"Control" can be a tricky word in Science passages, because in everyday language it just means to influence or determine how something operates, and not necessarily to keep something the same. Rarely, an author might use the word in its more everyday sense to talk about how scientists made changes to certain variables. Pay attention to context to work out which sense of the word is being used.

You can get a good idea of what any experiment is about by paying attention to just two pieces of information: which variables the experimenters *change*, and which they *measure*.

Experiments are designed to measure the effect of the variable that scientists change on the variable that they measure.

EXAMPLE

Using timed growth lights, experimenters provided 12 hours of light to plants in Group 1 and 4 hours of light to plants in Group 2. Experimenters controlled for the effects of nutrition and hydration by using identical soil sources and providing equal amounts of water and fertilizer to all plants. Growth was measured by periodically recording the height and leaf size of plants, and weighing the pots.

Here, the use of "controlled" is explaining how scientists prevented differences in nutrition or hydration.

By looking at which variable experimenters changed and which they measured we can conclude that the experiment was designed to measure the effect of the amount of light that plants receive on their growth. We can also tell that experimenters were *not* interested in measuring the effects of hydration or nutrition.

DRAWING CONCLUSIONS

Whether a passage describes an experiment in detail or only talks about the results of an experiment, there are some important things to keep in mind when drawing conclusions from experimental evidence.

Experiments themselves are **value neutral.** That means that they might show a particular effect, but don't tell you whether it's a *good* or *bad* effect. An experiment might show that plants grow more quickly with more light, but that doesn't imply that plants *deserve* to grow more quickly or that you *ought* to give them more light. The author of the passage might offer their own opinion on the matter, but don't be tempted to assume that an experiment shows whether something is good or bad.

Also keep in mind that experiments only demonstrate very specific relationships. You can make some inferences about what else an experiment *suggests*, and what other ideas an experiment *supports*, but don't be tempted to imagine that it *demonstrates* anything other than the very specific relationship that it was designed to test.

SUMMARIZING A SCIENCE PASSAGE

Just as Literature passages could be divided into two basic categories, narrative or descriptive, we can generally split Science passages into two broad categories as well. Being able to identify which type of passage you're reading will help you to answer questions about the main idea and about the author's purpose.

Explanatory passages will provide information about a topic. Their purpose is simply to inform the reader. These passages will not support any particular side of an issue, although they might describe the positions taken about the issue by other people.

Argumentative passages will take a certain position on an issue, and provide additional information as evidence to support that position. The purpose of an argumentative passage is to build support for the author's position using specific evidence and logical arguments. Argumentative passages will often contain **position statements**, statements in which an author explicitly tells you what their position is on some contentious issue.

Keep an eye out for position statements and pay attention to the balance of evidence to help you decide what type of passage you're reading. Knowing what type of passage you're reading will help you to answer questions about the author's purpose, or the main purpose of the passage. Be sure to also pay attention to the elements of specific paragraphs and to identify their purpose, as you might be asked about the purpose of only a part of the passage.

PART 2 PRACTICE: SCIENCE PASSAGES

Below is an example passage. Read the passage, paying special attention to the elements we have discussed, and then answer the accompanying practice questions.

The United States Fish and Wildlife Service says homeowners use up to 10 times more chemicals per acre than farmers do. Some of these
5 chemicals rub off on children or pets, but most are washed with rainwater into our streams, lakes and rivers or are absorbed into our groundwater. These are the sources of our drinking
10 water, and tests show these chemicals are indeed contaminating our water supply.

A study by the United States Geological Survey released in 1999
15 found at least one pesticide, and often more than one, in almost every stream and fish sample tested, and in about half of the samples drawn from wells throughout the country. These
20 pesticides are going from our lawns and gardens into our drinking water and into our bodies.

The amounts of these chemicals are small and often considered
25 "acceptable," but scientists now know that they have a cumulative effect. Many chemicals that we use very casually on our lawns cause long-term health problems in ways that have only
30 recently been understood. They "disrupt," or throw out of whack, the endocrine system, made up of glands and hormones that control almost every aspect of our bodies' functions.

35 In 2009 the Endocrine Society, a group of doctors, researchers and educators who specialize in diseases related to the hormonal system, published a scientific statement based
40 on 485 citations from research papers showing growing evidence that there are significant health threats caused by endocrine-disrupting substances in our environment. In terms of scientific
45 research, 2009 is relatively recent. Epidemiologic studies take decades, and developing a battery of reliable laboratory tests also takes many years. This means that there are more studies
50 implicating older chemicals, many of which are no longer sold because of known toxicities.

But many scientists expect similar chemicals now in widespread use to
55 cause the same problems. Endocrine disrupters are linked to an increased risk for breast and prostate cancer, thyroid abnormalities and infertility. The Endocrine Society paper and
60 others also present evidence that links exposure to chemical contaminants to diabetes and obesity.

These chemicals are not safe just because they are available in stores.
65 Regulations governing the sale of chemicals do not reflect this new scientific information, because scientists are only now working on

standardized tests both in laboratory
70 animals and cell cultures to evaluate
whether a chemical disrupts the
hormonal system, and if so, at what
level.

What we put on our lawns and
75 down our drains winds up in our
drinking water, and it is not removed
by water treatment. Bottled water is
not a solution because it comes from
the same sources and is susceptible to
80 the same contaminants. But if we don't
put these chemicals in our yards, they
won't be in our drinking water.

In the last decade or so, plenty of
homeowners have been rejecting the
85 emerald green lawn and planting with
species that do not demand chemicals
and constant watering. But not nearly
enough of us have taken that step. We
need to see a perfect lawn not as
90 enviable, but a sign of harm.

1. The main purpose of this passage is to

    (A) argue that we should change our lawn-care practices.

    (B) recommend the use of new types of lawn-care products.

    (C) propose that people should no longer cultivate lawns.

    (D) describe the effects that lawns have on society.

2. The author cites a study by the Endocrine Society to support the claim that

    (A) pesticides currently available in stores may be as harmful as those which are
        banned.

    (B) chemical contaminants have been found throughout our environment.

    (C) conducting studies and developing tests can take years.

    (D) chemical contaminants may be causing physical harm to humans.

3. Based on information in the passage, we can infer that the author believes that the
    evidence about the safety of chemicals in stores today

    (A) is adequate to prove that they cause harm to humans.

    (B) shows that government regulators are ignoring the scientific data.

    (C) is sufficient to justify concerns about their safety.

    (D) explains the prevalence of diabetes and obesity.

Answer Key

1. A
2. D
3. C

SOCIAL SCIENCE AND HISTORICAL PASSAGES
PART 3

There are two Social Science passages on the SAT. Social Science passages might include graphic elements, and might be presented as paired passages.

One of these passages will resemble a Science passage. It will probably come from a magazine, newspaper, or non-fiction book, and it will be from a contemporary source. However, it will be from a field in the social sciences rather than the natural or physical sciences. The social sciences include fields like economics, psychology, linguistics, and history. You can approach a Social Science passage on one of these subjects much like you would approach a Science passage.

The other one will be very different, and this type of passage will be the focus of this part of this section. On each SAT, there will be one Historical document that is drawn from either the Founding Documents of the United States or the Great Global Conversation.

Founding Documents are those documents that shaped the history of the United States. This category includes documents like the Declaration of Independence, the U.S. Constitution, or the Bill of Rights. The Great Global Conversation refers to the ongoing global conversation about civic life. This category could include a Winston Churchill speech, a passage from a work written by Nelson Mandela, a letter from Gandhi—or a wide variety of other historically important documents or speeches.

These historical documents frequently use dated language that might not be very familiar. They also address complex topics: the nature of liberty, the role of government, the relationship between individuals and society, and so on. They're not exactly light reading, but don't worry; with practice, you can develop all the skills that you need to tackle these challenging passages.

Active Reading with Historical Passages

As with literature and science passages, you want to pay attention to the important people, places, and things as they are introduced in a passage, and to the lines in which you get new information about them. You're also going to want to pay attention to claims and facts in the passage, as the author or speaker of the passage may be building an argument.

But in historical passages, you are going to want to pay special attention to the way that the speaker or author uses **rhetoric**, or language which is designed to have a persuasive effect on a listener or reader. The types of figurative language we discussed in Part 1 can all be used for rhetorical purposes, so look out for figurative language and pay attention to how it's being used.

In historical passages, you should also keep an eye out for all of the following elements:

Common Rhetorical Techniques		
Rhetorical Emphasis	There are several techniques that speakers and authors might use to add emphasis to a point. They might repeat an important phrase or word several times, use several words in a row that all mean roughly the same thing, ask questions which they themselves answer, or use unusual or repetitive sentence structures to emphasize important points.	Were the original documents provided? No. Were uncensored copies provided? No. Was any reasonable effort made to share key information about the contents of the documents? No. Each and every request for additional information was totally and completely ignored.
Juxtaposition	A speaker or writer might place two very different things close together in a passage or speech, or provide a real-world example of where two very different things meet. Juxtaposition is used in order to highlight the contrast between the things being compared.	In the shadow of scrap-heaps piled high with the discarded luxuries of the world's richest economies, there live and work some of the poorest people in the developing world.

Analogies	In addition to using devices like metaphors and similes, the speaker or author in a Historical passage might employ analogies to compare the relationships between different sorts of things. Unlike metaphors and similes, however, analogies are often used to imply that if the things being compared are alike in some ways, they may also be alike in other ways. Analogies can also be used to make complex ideas easier to understand.	The government is like a pair of work boots: it protects us from injury and discomfort, but only if it is properly fitted. A pair of work boots which is too large or too small may do more harm than good, and had better be replaced.

PERSUASIVE HISTORICAL PASSAGES

Historical passages may be argumentative or explanatory, but you might also see **persuasive** passages, in which the author or speaker attempts to persuade the reader or listener to agree with their position using techniques besides evidence and logical arguments. Persuasive passages might rely mainly on **appeals to emotion**, in which the author makes statements designed to make you *feel* that they are right, rather than providing evidence on which to build their argument.

You should pay attention mainly to identifying the thesis of the passage, and how each portion of the passage works to support that thesis—either by providing evidence, or by using rhetorical techniques that have a compelling emotional effect on the reader. Keep an eye out for metaphors, similes, and analogies, which will often play an important role in this type of passage. Examine how the author or speaker uses language to emphasize certain points, and how they use evidence and arguments to support them.

PART 3 PRACTICE: SOCIAL SCIENCE AND HISTORICAL PASSAGES

Below is an example passage. Read the passage, paying special attention to the elements we have discussed, and then answer the accompanying practice questions.

President John F. Kennedy was the first Catholic to be elected president of the United States. During the campaign for the presidency, Kennedy faced attacks over the positions of the Catholic Church, and charges that as president he would "take orders from the Pope." In this speech, Kennedy addresses the "religious issue."

While the so-called "religious issue" is necessarily and properly the chief topic here tonight, I want to
Line emphasize from the outset that I
5 believe that we have far more critical issues to face in the 1960 election: the spread of Communist influence, until it now festers 90 miles off the coast of Florida; the humiliating treatment
10 of our president and vice president by those who no longer respect our power; the hungry children I saw in West Virginia; the old people who cannot pay their doctors bills; the
15 families forced to give up their farms; an America with too many slums, with too few schools, and too late to the moon and outer space.

These are the real issues which
20 should decide this campaign. And they are not religious issues—for war and hunger and ignorance and despair know no religious barriers. But because I am a Catholic, and no
25 Catholic has ever been elected president, the real issues in this campaign have been obscured— perhaps deliberately, in some quarters less responsible than this.
30 So it is apparently necessary for me to state once again not what kind of church I believe in—for that should be important only to me—but what kind of America I believe
35 in.

I believe in an America where the separation of church and state is absolute, where no Catholic prelate would tell the president (should he be
40 Catholic) how to act, and no Protestant minister would tell his parishioners for whom to vote; where no church or church school is granted any public funds or political
45 preference; and where no man is denied public office merely because his religion differs from the president who might appoint him or the people who might elect him.
50 I believe in an America that is officially neither Catholic, Protestant nor Jewish; where no public official either requests or accepts instructions on public policy from the Pope, the
55 National Council of Churches or any other ecclesiastical source; where no religious body seeks to impose its will directly or indirectly upon the general populace or the public acts of
60 its officials; and where religious liberty is so indivisible that an act against one church is treated as an act against all.

For while this year it may be a
65 Catholic against whom the finger of suspicion is pointed, in other years it has been, and may someday be again, a Jew, or a Quaker, or a Unitarian, or a Baptist. It was Virginia's
70 harassment of Baptist preachers, for example, that helped lead to Jefferson's statute of religious freedom. Today I may be the victim, but tomorrow it may be you—until

75 the whole fabric of our harmonious society is ripped at a time of great national peril.

Finally, I believe in an America where religious intolerance will
80 someday end; where all men and all churches are treated as equal; where every man has the same right to attend or not to attend the church of his choice; where there is no Catholic
85 vote, no anti-Catholic vote, no bloc voting of any kind; and where Catholics, Protestants and Jews, at both the lay and the pastoral level, will refrain from those attitudes of
90 disdain and division which have so often marred their works in the past, and promote instead the American ideal of brotherhood.

That is the kind of America in
95 which I believe. And it represents the kind of presidency in which I believe: great office that must neither be humbled by making it the instrument of any one religious group, nor
100 tarnished by arbitrarily withholding its occupancy from the members of any one religious group.

I believe in a president whose views on religion are his own private
105 affair, neither imposed by him upon the nation, nor imposed by the nation upon him as a condition to holding that office.

1. Kennedy's main purpose in this passage is to

(A) urge Americans to reconsider their religious views, in light of the many issues facing society.

(B) argue against providing government funds to religious organizations.

(C) express his view that religion and politics should be strictly separated.

(D) suggest that since all churches are equal they deserve equal representation in government.

2. Kennedy's tone in lines 6-9 ("the spread … of Florida") suggests that he feels that "Communist influence" is

(A) slowly decaying until it finally disappears.

(B) an offensive problem about which too little has been done.

(C) an unpleasant but mostly harmless irritation.

(D) the cause of most of the other problems in the United States at that time.

3. Lines 73-77 ("Today I … national peril") are most likely intended to suggest that

(A) when you treat a religious group unfairly, they are likely to treat others unfairly in the future.

(B) people are most likely to discriminate on the basis of religion during times of crisis.

(C) religious diversity and political harmony cannot exist in the same society.

(D) religious discrimination could lead to divisions which harm all Americans.

ANSWER KEY

1. C
2. B
3. D

PASSAGES WITH GRAPHICS

PART 4

Two reading passages on the SAT will include graphic elements. One of the passages will be a Science passage, and the other will be a Social Science passage. There will be one or two graphic elements accompanying each passage. The graphics will contain additional information about the subject that the passage is explaining, and will always be closely related to the main topic of the passage.

The graphics might be used to represent statistical data—as in bar graphs or pie charts—but they might also be charts or diagrams showing physical relationships or other concepts, like compasses showing bearings, diagrams of technology or natural systems, or trees showing genealogy or evolutionary history.

Passages might refer to information in graphic elements as supporting evidence without describing the information from the graph, so you may need to understand how to correctly interpret the graphic in order to correctly understand the passage. You may also be asked questions that will require you to interpret information presented *only* in the graphic. That type of question will be addressed in detail in Section 6 of this chapter.

READING THE GRAPHICS

Common Elements in Graphics	
Title	The title of a graphical element usually tells you what the graphic is intended to show.
Legend	A legend is a guide to the graphic, that shows you what different shades, images, or patterns mean in the image. Always read legends carefully when they're available.
Caption	If there's a caption below the graphic, read it carefully. The captions often provide directions for how to properly read the graphic, and extra details about the information provided in the graph.
Labels	Be sure to read all of the labels in a graphic, and make sure that you understand which elements they refer to and what they say about them.

Units	Be sure you know what units a graphic is using for data. The number ten will mean something very different on a chart showing distances in feet than on one showing distance in *thousands* of feet.
References in the passage	If the passage refers to the graphic, or to information in the graphic, pay attention to which information the passage is referring to and how the author is using the information from the graphic in the passage.

Sometimes, a graphic might contain a lot of information. You don't need to commit the whole thing to memory: just try to understand the graphic's relationship to the passage, and look for the essential elements described above so that when you need to check the graphic to get a specific piece of information you'll be able to find it quickly.

More information about graphics is provided in Section 6 of this Chapter and in Chapters 3 and 5.

PART 4 PRACTICE: PASSAGES WITH GRAPHICS

Below is an example passage. Read the passage, paying special attention to the elements we have discussed, and then answer the accompanying practice questions.

The level of the most important heat-trapping gas in the atmosphere, carbon dioxide, has passed a long-feared milestone, scientists reported Friday, reaching a concentration not seen on the earth for millions of years.

Scientific instruments showed that the gas had reached an average daily level above 400 parts per million— just an odometer moment in one sense, but also a sobering reminder that decades of efforts to bring human-produced emissions under control are faltering.

"It symbolizes that so far we have failed miserably in tackling this problem," said Pieter P. Tans, who runs the monitoring program at the National Oceanic and Atmospheric Administration (NOAA) that reported the new reading.

Ralph Keeling, who runs another monitoring program at the Scripps Institution of Oceanography in San Diego, said a continuing rise could be catastrophic. "It means we are quickly losing the possibility of keeping the climate below what people thought were possibly tolerable thresholds," he said.

China is now the largest emitter, but Americans have been consuming fossil fuels extensively for far longer, and experts say the United States is more responsible than any other nation for the high level.

The new measurement came from analyzers atop Mauna Loa, the

volcano on the big island of Hawaii
that has long been ground zero for
monitoring the worldwide trend on
carbon dioxide, or CO_2. Devices
there sample clean, crisp air that has
blown thousands of miles across the
Pacific Ocean, producing a record of
rising carbon dioxide levels that has
been closely tracked for half a
century.

Carbon dioxide above 400 parts
per million was first seen in the Arctic
last year, and had also spiked above
that level in hourly readings at Mauna
Loa.

But the average reading for an
entire day surpassed that level at
Mauna Loa for the first time in the 24
hours that ended at 8 p.m. Eastern
Daylight Time on Thursday. The two
monitoring programs use slightly
different protocols; NOAA reported
an average for the period of 400.03
parts per million, while Scripps
reported 400.08.

Carbon dioxide rises and falls on a
seasonal cycle, and the level will dip
below 400 this summer as leaf growth
in the Northern Hemisphere pulls
about 10 billion tons of carbon out of
the air. But experts say that will be a
brief reprieve—the moment is
approaching when no measurement of
the ambient air anywhere on earth, in
any season, will produce a reading
below 400.

From studying air bubbles trapped
in Antarctic ice, scientists know that
going back 800,000 years, the carbon
dioxide level oscillated in a tight
band, from about 180 parts per
million in the depths of ice ages to
about 280 during the warm periods
between. The evidence shows that
global temperatures and CO_2 levels
are tightly linked.

For the entire period of human
civilization, roughly 8,000 years, the
carbon dioxide level was relatively
stable near that upper bound. But the
burning of fossil fuels has caused a 41
percent increase in the heat-trapping
gas since the Industrial Revolution, a
mere geological instant, and scientists
say the climate is beginning to react,
though they expect far larger changes
in the future.

Indirect measurements suggest
that the last time the carbon dioxide
level was this high was at least three
million years ago, during an epoch
called the Pliocene. Geological
research shows that the climate then
was far warmer than today, the
world's ice caps were smaller, and the
sea level might have been as much as
60 or 80 feet higher.

Countries have adopted an official
target to limit the damage from global
warming, with 450 parts per million
seen as the maximum level
compatible with that goal. "Unless
things slow down, we'll probably get
there in well under 25 years," Ralph
Keeling said.

Yet many countries, including
China and the United States, have
refused to adopt binding national
targets. Scientists say that unless far
greater efforts are made soon, the goal
of limiting the warming will become
impossible without severe economic
disruption.

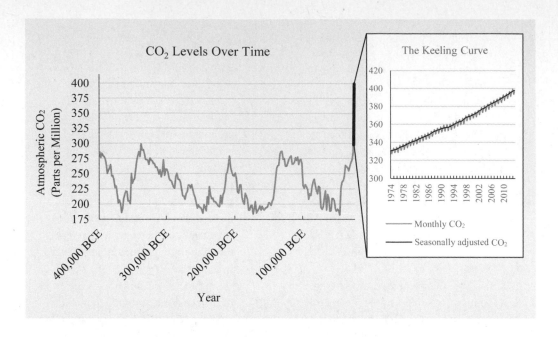

1. Based on information from the passage, we can conclude that during the winter

   (A) dropping temperatures will also cause a drop in carbon dioxide levels.

   (B) atmospheric sampling is less likely to produce accurate results.

   (C) atmospheric carbon dioxide levels are higher than at other times in the year.

   (D) scientists are able to sample air bubbles trapped in ice.

2. Based on information from the passage and graph, carbon dioxide levels

   (A) never reached 400 parts per million before the industrial revolution.

   (B) never reached levels as high as today in the preceding 400,000 years.

   (C) have been as high as 400,000 parts per million in the past.

   (D) are usually around 200 parts per million.

3. Information from the graph best supports which of the following statements?

   (A) From 1960 to 2010, carbon dioxide levels rose more slowly but to a higher point than at any other time in the past 400,000 years.

   (B) Seasonally adjusted carbon dioxide levels have been above 300 parts-per-million for more than 200,000 years.

   (C) Due to increasing carbon dioxide, sea levels in 2010 most likely rose to levels similar to those in the Pliocene.

   (D) Between 1960 and 2010, carbon dioxide levels sometimes dropped from month-to-month, but seasonally adjusted levels rose steadily.

ANSWER KEY

1. C
2. B
3. D

PAIRED PASSAGES
PART 5

One of the five sets of questions on the Reading section of the SAT will be about a set of two short passages, rather than one long one.

In many ways, this pair of passages can basically be treated as a single passage of a special type. Combined, the two passages in the pair are the same length as a single regular passage, have the same number of questions as a single regular passage, and—most importantly— are worth *the same number of points* as a single regular passage. Approach them as though they are just a special passage type that presents two points of view.

Each pair of passages will always be of the same type and about the same general subject. They might agree with one another, or they might disagree. They might just explore different aspects of the same subject, without directly agreeing or disagreeing with one another at all.

You should treat each of the two short passages the same way that you treat other passages of the same type. But remember to also pay attention to the relationship between the two passages.

LOOK FOR SIMILARITIES AND DIFFERENCES

Paired passages always have some similarities. There will also always be some differences between them. Look for similarities and differences in:

- **Main ideas:** Pay attention to the main idea in each passage, and consider how they compare. Do they agree? Disagree? Are they talking about *exactly* the same thing, or only related things?
- **Purpose:** Look for differences in the purpose of the passages. Is one author trying only to provide information about the subject, while the other is expressing an opinion?

- **Claims:** Pay attention to what the authors claim is true. See which claims the authors seem to agree about, which ones they disagree about, and which ones are addressed only by one author.

- **Style and Tone:** Pay attention to how the passages are alike or different in style and tone. Do they both contain dry, slightly boring exposition? Is one an exciting story about football, while another is an impassioned argument against allowing high-school students to play such a dangerous sport?

- **Focus:** Even if the passages are about the same main topic, they might address slightly different aspects of that topic. It might be that both passages are about tax policy, but one focuses on the effects of tax policy on the government's ability to raise revenues while the other focuses on the effects of tax policy on individuals and businesses.

SUMMARIZING PAIRED PASSAGES

When summarizing paired passages, start by jotting down summaries of each passage in the pair as you read them—just as you would with regular passages. Then, consider the relationship between the two passages, and think of a quick summary about how they relate to one another.

This summary won't usually be as simple as "Authors 1 and 2 agree" or "Authors 1 and 2 disagree." If that's all that comes to mind, you might want to think for just a moment longer; there's usually something more subtle going on. Consider the elements which are most different and most similar between the two passages, and make a note about them.

PART 5 PRACTICE: PAIRED PASSAGES

Below is an example passage. Read the passage, paying special attention to the elements we have discussed, then answer the accompanying practice questions.

The following passages discuss the length of work shifts for resident physicians in hospitals. Resident physicians are physicians who have graduated from a medical school, and are continuing their professional training by performing supervised work in a medical care facility.

Passage 1

At Brigham and Women's Hospital, we quantified the effects of work hours on medical error rates in a
Line group of first-year residents who
5 worked in intensive-care units under two sets of conditions: a traditional schedule with 24- to 30-hour shifts every other shift, and a schedule with 16-hour limits. On the former
10 schedule, the residents made 36% more serious medical errors than on the latter, and inadvertently fell asleep on duty twice as often on overnight duty. Longer shifts affect not just the
15 safety and health of patients but that of physicians as well. In surveys conducted by our group, residents working 24 or more hours in a row reported sticking themselves with
20 needles 60% more often, and had more than double the odds of having a car crash on the drive home from work as compared with shorter shifts. In a 2010 review of 23 studies on the effects of
25 reducing resident work hours, all but one showed an improvement or no change in patient care or resident sleep or quality of life. There were no objective data showing that shorter
30 work hours were worse for patients or physicians.

Despite the increasing emphasis on evidence-based decision making in medicine, these data have often been
35 met with a negative response. Those who oppose stricter work-hour limits say continuity of care demands long shifts. But even with 30-hour shifts, care of a patient eventually has to be
40 handed over to another team.

Medicine is also increasingly filled with specialists, a development requiring a team approach to deliver the best care. So we need to find better
45 ways for teams to communicate and to transfer information, rather than insist that doctors risk their own and their patients' health by working beyond their biological limits.
50 Doctors are not immune to biology. While we appreciate their dedication and sacrifice, we cannot allow them to harm others or themselves with the outdated and unnecessary "rite of
55 passage" of 24-hour shifts.

Passage 2

For a half-dozen years, the Accreditation Council for Graduate Medical Education has experimented with reduced work hours for
60 physicians-in-training. The current limit is no more than 80 hours per week. Now some want to reduce this even further.

I think we should challenge the
65 whole idea of having a central committee dictate work limitations for all residency programs.

Treating new physicians like shift workers is destroying the individual
70 patient-physician relationship. Having shorter shifts means more frequent "handoffs," which disrupts both education and patient care. Those who favor shorter shifts, and thus more

75 handoffs, may argue that quality of handoffs matters more than quantity. But quantity matters too. The shift-work culture means working until time is up, rather than until work is
80 done. The incentive is to leave problems for the next shift rather than to find and address them as early as possible.

Patients are now the collective
85 responsibility of the team, rather than primarily the responsibility of "their doctor." In the old system, the patient's doctor was expected to take care of anticipated problems as well

90 as possible before signing out. It is also more efficient for the doctor who already knows the patient to order the fever work-up, talk to the family, or assess progress and the potential need
95 for a change in the treatment.

In the old days, it was understood that residency would be grueling. A surgical residency was specifically compared with becoming a Marine.
100 The enemy was disease or death or human suffering, and the schedule of fighting was determined by the enemy, not by a central committee.

1. Both passages suggest which of the following is a main reason to be concerned about shift-length during residency?

(A) Freedom of choice for doctors

(B) The quality of medical care

(C) The safety of doctors

(D) Preserving traditional training methods

2. Which of the following forms of evidence is used in Passage 1, but NOT in Passage 2?

(A) Logical arguments

(B) Expert quotations

(C) Personal anecdotes

(D) Data from studies

3. The author of Passage 2 would most likely respond to the argument in lines 35-40 ("Those who … another team") by

(A) arguing that fewer hand-overs are still preferable, even if some are unavoidable.

(B) suggesting that doctors should continue to work until patients recover.

(C) pointing out that specialist training would not be possible with shorter shifts.

(D) proposing that we should develop a better system for hand-overs.

ANSWER KEY

1. B
2. D
3. A

ACKNOWLEDGEMENTS FOR THIS SECTION

The passages in this section were adapted from the following sources:

Adapted from Jerome K. Jerome, "Three Men in a Boat (to Say Nothing of the Dog)." Originally published 1889.

Adapted from Diane Lewis, "The Toxic Brew in Our Yards." © 2014 by *The New York Times Company*. Originally published May 10, 2014.

John F. Kennedy, Speech on His Religion, originally delivered to the Greater Houston Ministerial Association on September 12, 1960.

Adapted from Justin Gillis, "Heat-Trapping Gas Passes Milestone, Raising Fears." © 2013 by *The New York Times Company*. Originally published May 10, 2013.

Adapted from Steven W. Lockley, Jane Orient, "Should Medical Residents Be Required to Work Shorter Shifts?" © *Dow Jones & Company* 2013. Originally published February 18, 2013.

UNDERSTANDING THE FACTS

In this section you will learn about some common question types that you will find associated with every passage. These question types fall under the category of **Information and Ideas**, which means that they require you to understand the facts of the passage. This includes understanding specific lines from a passage, identifying main ideas, and analyzing how parts of the text relate to one another.

We'll describe each question type and the strategies for answering it, followed by practice exercises so you can try questions on your own. At the end of this section you will have a chance to apply what you've learned to full-length practice passages.

WORDS AND PHRASES IN CONTEXT
PART 1

Every passage or pair of passages will be accompanied by two **Words and Phrases in Context** questions. These questions will give you a word or phrase from the passage and ask you to select the answer choice that could best replace it. All of the answer choices will be valid synonyms of the word or phrase you are asked about, but only one will make sense in the original sentence.

EXAMPLE

Margaret runs a very successful business, yet still finds time to volunteer in the community.

As used in line 1, "runs" most nearly means

(A) operates.
(B) jogs.
(C) flees.
(D) functions.

This question is asking you to identify the word that could best replace "runs" in the original sentence. Notice that all of the answer choices are possible meanings of "runs"—your job is to find the meaning that is closest to what the author of the passage intended. Here are some strategies to help you identify this meaning.

THINK FOR YOURSELF

As you learned in Section 2, it is helpful to think for yourself when answering questions. You should use this approach for Words in Context questions. Refer back to the passage, and try thinking of a suitable word or phrase to replace the one you are asked about. Be sure to read the full sentence in which the word or phrase appears. You can also read a few lines above and below to help you understand the context in which the word or phrase is being used.

> Margaret runs a very successful business, yet still finds time to volunteer in the community.
>
> As used in line 1, "runs" most nearly means
>
> (A) operates.
> (B) jogs.
> (C) flees.
> (D) functions.

What is a word you can think of to define "runs" in this sentence? Perhaps something like "manages," as the sentence refers to a business that Margaret is in charge of. Now you can compare this idea to the answer choices.

The word "operates" is closest to your word "manages," and is the only answer that captures the right meaning for the sentence.

The second and third choices refer to the physical act of running or running away from something. The final choice refers to the way something works, as in "The car only runs/functions if it is filled with premium gas." Notice that these are all valid ways you can use the word "runs," but only the first answer would make sense in the original sentence.

PLUG IT IN

This example also demonstrates another important strategy for words in context questions. You can test each answer choice by plugging it back in to the original sentence to see if it fits. Remember that the correct answer must provide nearly the same meaning as the original word. Compare your choice to the original sentence and ensure it matches the context of the lines above and below in order to be sure of your answer.

If you weren't sure of your answer for the example question above, you could try plugging each answer choice into the original sentence to see which one makes sense:

- ✓ Margaret operates a very successful business …
- ✗ Margaret jogs a very successful business …
- ✗ Margaret flees a very successful business …
- ✗ Margaret functions a very successful business …

Only answer choice (A) makes sense when you plug it into the original sentence, so you know (A) must be the correct answer.

PART 1 PRACTICE: WORDS AND PHRASES IN CONTEXT

For each question below, choose the answer choice that most nearly means the same thing as the bolded word or phrase in each sentence.

1. We will **call upon** our citizens to act bravely in this time of need.
    (A) shout at
    (B) visit briefly
    (C) appeal to
    (D) cry for

2. Before they set out, Charu provided her companions with some **practical** advice about hiking in Death Valley.
    (A) functional
    (B) applied
    (C) useful
    (D) grounded

3. The most intriguing aspect of this new scholarship is its **synthesis** of modern and traditional techniques.
    (A) fusion
    (B) alloy
    (C) conflation
    (D) amalgamation

4. Hank was not used to being in the company of such **refined** individuals, and strove to choose his words and references carefully.
    (A) developed
    (B) unadultered
    (C) cultured
    (D) delicate

5. The doctor suggested an **aggressive** treatment plan upon learning of her patient's rare diagnosis.

(A) intensive

(B) violent

(C) militant

(D) enterprising

6. Today's economists are quick to point out that constant spending on consumer goods could leave you **saddled with** debt.

(A) burdened by

(B) packed with

(C) freighted by

(D) strained with

ANSWER KEY: PART 1 PRACTICE

1. C
2. C
3. A
4. C
5. A
6. A

EXPLICIT AND IMPLICIT MEANING
PART 2

All passages will usually have questions that ask you about specific ideas discussed in the text. These questions can come in two forms: Explicit Meaning and Implicit Meaning questions.

EXPLICIT MEANING

Explicit Meaning questions ask you about something stated more or less directly in the passage. To answer these questions, you will need to refer back to the text and read closely to understand what the author wrote. Use the process of elimination to knock out any answers that contradict what the author wrote, or any answers that are not directly stated in the passage. You are looking for ideas the author has stated directly. You do not need to interpret or analyze the words for any second meanings.

Remember the passage about the artist Cavallini from Section 2? Let's have a look at it again and see how an explicit meaning question about that passage would work.

Tommaso Strinati clambers to the top of the rickety scaffold and laughs. "It's a good thing that all this Baroque
Line work is so unimpressive," he says,
5 pointing at the clumsy trompe l'oeil painting covering the wall in front of him. "Otherwise, we might not have been allowed to scrape it off!"
  A 28-year-old art historian, he is
10 standing 16 feet above the marble floor of San Pasquale Baylon chapel, a long-neglected nook of Santa Maria in Aracoeli, a Franciscan basilica in the center of Rome. Last year, Mr.
15 Strinati, who is still a graduate student, began studying the church's history. Records suggested that the Roman artist Pietro Cavallini – a painter and mosaicist whose greatest works have
20 been destroyed – spent years decorating Aracoeli toward the end of the 13th century. Yet only one small Cavallini fresco, in the church's left transept, remained visible. Mr. Strinati
25 wondered: had other Cavallini frescoes been painted over with inferior work? And if so, could modern restorers uncover them?
  "The answer to both questions was
30 yes," Mr. Strinati says. A close-up examination of the chapel's walls last summer revealed ghostly images lying beneath the surface. The entire chapel, it seemed, was a painted palimpsest.
35 And when a heavy altarpiece was removed from one wall, a remarkably

tender portrait of the Madonna and Child was found hidden behind it.

After months of careful paint-peeling, what has been uncovered are dazzling fragments of a late-medieval masterpiece completed shortly after 1285. Although the Aracoeli fresco is not signed, the figures strongly resemble those in a surviving Cavallini work, the resplendent "Last Judgment" fresco at nearby Santa Cecilia.

Mr. Strinati has grand ambitions for his discovery. He hopes that in a few years the fully restored fresco will not only rescue Cavallini's name from obscurity, but also upend the widespread notion that the first flowers of the Renaissance budded in Florence, not Rome. For the fresco's lifelike figures – in particular, an impish Christ child with charmingly flushed cheeks – suggest to Strinati that Cavallini may have anticipated some of the extraordinary naturalistic innovations that have long been credited to the Florentine artist Giotto.

Moreover, the Aracoeli fragments may provide a critical new clue in a decades-old battle concerning the "St. Francis Legend," the 1296 fresco cycle at Assisi, universally recognized as one of the foundations of the Renaissance. For centuries, the 28-scene cycle – which recounts the life of the saint with a narrative zest and compositional depth that leave the flat tableaus of the Byzantine era far behind – was attributed to Giotto. But since the 1930's, various scholars have questioned this judgment, claiming that the Assisi cycle doesn't resemble Giotto's other work. Now, the Aracoeli discovery is ammunition for Italian art historians who believe that Cavallini might actually be the primary creative force behind the "St. Francis Legend."

The growing debate about Cavallini's importance was the occasion for a symposium in Rome in November. *La Republicca*, an Italian daily, has cast the debate as "War Between Rome and Florence." Mr. Strinati is enjoying the ruckus. "I had a hunch that there was more Cavallini lurking around here," he says of the Aracoeli basilica. "But I didn't expect to find an exquisite work that could shake up the history of art."

According to the passage

(A) Cavallini's work was widely known before the recent discovery of his frescos.
(B) prior to Strinati's discovery there was consensus about who painted the "St. Francis Legend."
(C) Cavallini painted frescos exclusively in Roman churches.
(D) not all of the work painted in Aracoeli after Cavallini's has been removed by Strinati.

To answer this question, see which choice is supported by information clearly stated in the text. Answer choice (A) directly contradicts the passage, as we're told that Mr. Strinati wants to "rescue Cavallini's name from obscurity" (lines 51-52). Answer choice (B) also contradicts the passage, as lines 75-78 state that "since the 1930's, various scholars have questioned" whether Giotto painted the "St. Francis Legend." Therefore, you can eliminate both (A) and (B).

Answer choice (C) is simply not supported by the passage. While the passage lists two churches in which Cavallini frescoes have been found, you are not given any other information about where else he may have painted. Remember that explicit meaning questions are asking about what is presented in the passage, so avoid making assumptions or guesses. You should eliminate answer choice (C).

You are left with answer choice (D), which matches exactly with information from the passage. In the first paragraph Strinati points to a "clumsy trompe l'oeil painting" in front of him while discussing unimpressive Baroque art. This is the type of art he was removing to reveal Cavallini's frescoes, so it must have been painted later. Because (D) is the only answer stated directly in the passage, it is the correct answer.

IMPLICIT MEANING

Implicit Meaning questions ask you about ideas that are presented more subtly in the text. For these questions you will need to read between the lines or combine clues from different parts of the text to understand what the author is suggesting. In some passages this may mean understanding literary devices such as metaphor. These concepts will be discussed further in Section 5.

Here are some ways that Implicit Meaning questions might be phrased:

- It can reasonably be inferred from the passage that …
- The passage most strongly suggests that …
- In lines 30-31 the phrase "better late than never" implies that …

Be careful not to take everything the author says too literally when answering implicit meaning questions. In real life you are probably good at picking up on implied meanings. For example, if your friend says she is "thrilled" to take out the trash but rolls her eyes as she says it, you know she is being sarcastic. Similarly, things like the tone and structure of a passage can help indicate what an author really means.

EXAMPLE

Let's look at another question about the Cavallini passage to see how Implicit Meaning questions work.

> The passage most strongly suggests that
>
> (A) Strinati believes Cavallini to be a superior artist to Giotto.
> (B) similarities between paintings can be used to determine who painted them.
> (C) Baroque artwork is considered less impressive than Renaissance pieces.
> (D) Renaissance frescoes were frequently painted over in Italian churches.

Which of these ideas are suggested by the passage? While answer choice (A) may be true, there is no information in the passage to support this idea. We know that Strinati thinks highly of Cavallini's work because of the adjectives he uses, like when he calls it "exquisite," at the end of the passage. However, he never compares Cavallini to Giotto.

Answer choices (C) and (D) are similarly not things that you could reasonably conclude on the basis of the passage. You are not given wider information about the Renaissance or about Baroque artwork in general; the passage only discusses the artwork at the Aracoeli basilica. While implied meaning questions require you to extrapolate slightly from the passage, you must still have evidence in the text to support your answer! Be careful of answers like these that are too broad.

Answer choice (B) can be supported by two different portions of the text. First, lines 69-78 indicate some historians believed Giotto had painted the "St. Francis Legend," but they began to question this because it does not resemble his other work. Lines 43-47 suggest that the Aracoeli frescoes are likely Cavallini's because they do resemble his other work. These both indicate that historians look at consistencies between paintings to help determine if the same person painted them. Therefore, (B) is the correct answer.

Part 2 Practice: Explicit and Implicit Meaning

Review the techniques we discussed in Section 2, and mark up and make summaries for this passage excerpt. Then, answer the Explicit and Implicit Meaning questions using the strategies you just learned.

This passage is adapted from an article about vaccinations.

Vaccination programs for children have prevented more than 100 million cases of serious contagious disease in
Line the United States since 1924,
5 according to a new study published in The *New England Journal of Medicine*. The research, led by scientists at the University of Pittsburgh's graduate school of public
10 health, analyzed public health reports going back to the 19th century. The reports covered 56 diseases, but the article in the journal focused on seven: polio, measles, rubella, mumps,
15 hepatitis A, diphtheria and pertussis, or whooping cough.

Researchers analyzed disease reports before and after the times when vaccines became commercially
20 available. Put simply, the estimates for prevented cases came from the falloff in disease reports after vaccines were licensed and widely available. The researchers projected the number of
25 cases that would have occurred had the pre-vaccination patterns continued as the nation's population increased.

The University of Pittsburgh researchers also looked at death rates,
30 but decided against including an estimate in the journal article, largely because death certificate data became more reliable and consistent only in the 1960s, the researchers said. But Dr.
35 Donald S. Burke, the dean of Pittsburgh's graduate school of public health and an author of the medical journal article, said that a reasonable projection of prevented deaths based
40 on known mortality rates in the disease categories would be three million to four million.

1. All of the following questions can be explicitly answered on the basis of the passage EXCEPT

    (A) How did researchers estimate the preventative impact of vaccinations?

    (B) Why did the researchers not include death rate estimates in the journal article?

    (C) What are some diseases for which vaccines became commercially available?

    (D) Why did death certificate data only become reliable in the 1960s?

2. Which of the following statements is true, according to the passage?

   (A) Childhood vaccination programs can be effective at preventing contagious disease.

   (B) Without the effect of successful vaccinations, the American population would have soared.

   (C) It is difficult for researchers to obtain reliable death certificate data.

   (D) Vaccinations for certain diseases are much more effective than vaccinations for other diseases.

3. It can reasonably be inferred from the passage that

   (A) most vaccines were very expensive when first introduced.

   (B) some vaccines became commercially available around the 1920s.

   (C) American public health reports only date back to the 19th century.

   (D) it is impossible to accurately predict the effect of disease on population growth.

4. The passage most strongly suggests that

   (A) the mortality rates for all diseases are well-known today.

   (B) scientists may choose not to publish all data estimates they make.

   (C) researchers always struggle to create accurate predictions when working with historical data.

   (D) the diseases the scientists focused on in their publication were those with the highest mortality rates.

Answers: Part 2 Practice

1. D
2. A
3. B
4. B

CENTRAL IDEAS AND RELATIONSHIPS
PART 3

There are several types of questions on the SAT Reading Test that require you to summarize ideas in the text, identify central ideas of the whole text, and examine relationships among these ideas. Be sure you are using the active reading and summarizing strategies discussed in Section 2 as you read each passage. Referring to the summaries you have already made will make these questions much easier!

SUMMARIZING

Summarizing questions ask you to identify a reasonable summary of specific parts of the passage. This will require you to paraphrase certain lines from the text, which means to provide a short, clear restatement of what you have read. The techniques you learned about summarizing in Section 2 will help you to paraphrase concisely and accurately, so review that section for guidance.

EXAMPLE

Moreover, the Aracoeli fragments may provide a critical new clue in a
65 decades-old battle concerning the "St. Francis Legend," the 1296 fresco cycle at Assisi, universally recognized as one of the foundations of the Renaissance. For centuries, the 28-
70 scene cycle – which recounts the life of the saint with a narrative zest and compositional depth that leave the flat tableaus of the Byzantine era far behind – was attributed to Giotto. But
75 since the 1930's, various scholars have questioned this judgment, claiming that the Assisi cycle doesn't resemble Giotto's other work. Now, the Aracoeli discovery is ammunition for Italian art
80 historians who believe that Cavallini

might actually be the primary creative force behind the "St. Francis Legend."

Which best summarizes lines 63-82?
(A) The Aracoeli discovery has contributed to the debate about who painted the "St. Francis Legend."
(B) The "St. Francis Legend" is important as an example of early Renaissance work.
(C) Many scholars doubt that Giotto was the artist responsible for the "St. Francis Legend."
(D) Cavallini was almost certainly the artist who painted the "St. Francis Legend."

Here only answer choice (A) provides an overall summary of the paragraph. Answer choices (B) and (C) are too narrowly focused, and answer choice (D) makes a judgment that goes beyond what can be supported by the passage.

If you are asked for a summary of a paragraph you can also refer to your notes and paragraph summaries. Then, compare your summary to the answer choices. Be sure you select an answer that is focused on the most important ideas of the paragraph. Make sure your answer contains ideas discussed within the paragraph in question rather than elsewhere in the passage, and make sure it is truly the focus of the paragraph and not merely a detail.

CENTRAL IDEAS

Determining Central Ideas and Themes questions ask you about the central ideas that are the focus of the text. We'll call these "Central Ideas" questions. To answer them, review the paragraph summaries you created to come up with an overall summary or to spot recurring themes in the passage. Then look for the answer choice that best matches your prediction.

You can also use the process of elimination to knock out incorrect answer choices. Check each option to be sure it meets the following two criteria: (1) it is true according to the passage and (2) it deals with most of the passage.

Making sure your answer is true according to the passage helps you knock out answer choices that mention new information or go beyond the passage. For example, just because a passage suggests that a new technology is a good idea does not mean that the author believes it is the best solution to a problem, unless that is stated in the text. Be wary of answer choices that include stronger opinions than the passage itself.

Ensuring your answer to a Central Ideas question deals with most of the passage helps you stay focused on the 'big picture' of the passage, rather than details. Just because something is mentioned in the passage does not necessarily mean it is a main idea! Look for ideas that are mentioned multiple times or are discussed in-depth across multiple lines and paragraphs.

IDENTIFYING CENTRAL IDEAS

Wrong Answers to Avoid	How to Avoid Them
Makes judgments or assertions that go beyond what is stated in the passage	Choose answers based only on what is stated in the passage
Mentions details that appear only briefly in the passage	Look for ideas discussed throughout the passage, or at least several paragraphs

EXAMPLE

With these ideas in mind, let's look at a Central Ideas question about the Cavallini passage.

> The events presented in the passage are best described as
>
> (A) a potential solution to the mystery of who painted a specific work of art.
> (B) one researcher's quest which is of little interest to other historians.
> (C) the painstaking removal of certain artwork to reveal more valuable pieces.
> (D) a new discovery with potentially major implications for art history.

Answer choice (A) demonstrates the second type of wrong answer in our chart, as it does not deal with the entire passage. While the mystery of who painted the "St. Francis Legend" is important, it is too specific to be considered the main idea of the passage as a whole. Rather, it serves as one example of how the discovery of Cavallini's work might impact art history in Italy. Answer choice (C) is also too narrow, because it only discusses events in the first few paragraphs of the passage.

Answer choice (B) demonstrates the first type of wrong answer in our chart, as it is not true according to the passage. Strinati's discovery and attempts to rescue Cavallini's work are described as having a big impact on other art historians and leading to many important debates. Therefore, they are of interest to other historians.

Answer choice (D) captures all of the main ideas of the passage. It first mentions discovery, which relates to the first half of the passage about Cavallini's hidden frescoes. It also notes how this will impact the art world, which is what author discusses in the final three paragraphs. You've found your answer!

RELATIONSHIPS

Some questions will also ask you to describe the ways parts of the passage relate to one another. Understanding Relationships questions will ask you to identify relationships between individuals, events, or ideas in a passage. We'll refer to these as "Relationship" questions. These relationships may be explicitly stated or may be implicit and require you to read between the lines.

To answer these questions, consider what elements you are asked about and put the relationship between them into your own words. As always, this ensures that you know what you are looking for and will be precise when selecting your answer.

To figure out the relationship between elements, look back to the passage. Where are the people or ideas mentioned, and what is said about them? You can also refer back to any important parts of the passage you marked up, or the summaries you made for each paragraph.

EXAMPLE

Let's look at an Understanding Relationships question about the Cavallini passage to practice these strategies.

> Based on the passage, which choice best describes the relationship between Cavallini and Giotto?
>
> (A) Giotto may have anticipated Cavallini's work.
> (B) Cavallini may have anticipated Giottos' work.
> (C) Giotto is a more contemporary artist than Cavallini.
> (D) Giotto is a less contemporary artist than Cavallini.

First, try to think of what you know about these two artists from the passage. You know that they worked around the same time period and have both been credited with the same work of art. New discoveries about Cavallini suggest he may have anticipated some of Giotto's techniques. Now see which answer choice best matches what you know.

You can knock out choices (C) and (D) because you know the artists painted around the same time. There is nothing in the passage to support answer (A). However, answer choice (B) matches what you know about the artists, and is the correct response!

Try another relationship question from this passage:

Based on the passage, which choice best describes the relationship between Florence's and Rome's role in the Renaissance?

(A) Florence is usually credited with following Rome in adopting Renaissance styles.
(B) Florence is usually credited with pioneering Renaissance styles that Rome adopted.
(C) Rome and Florence are credited with simultaneously launching Renaissance art.
(D) Florence is usually credited with abandoning Renaissance styles before Rome.

Here only answer choice (B) is supported by the passage. Remember that Strinati is trying to "upend the widespread notion that the first flowers of the Renaissance budded in Florence" (lines 52-54). Therefore, you can infer that it is generally believed that Florence started the Renaissance and other cities followed.

PART 3 PRACTICE: CENTRAL IDEAS AND RELATIONSHIPS

Review the techniques we discussed in Section 2, and mark up and make summaries for this passage excerpt. Then, answer the Summary, Central Ideas, and Relationships questions using the strategies you just learned.

The following passage is adapted from a 2009 article that discusses brain cells called neurons.

Neurons process and transmit information through electrical and chemical signals, and researchers have
Line discovered neurons that respond only
5 to certain famous figures.
    Probing deep into human brains, a team of scientists discovered a neuron roused only by Ronald Reagan, another cell smitten by the actress
10 Halle Berry and a third devoted solely to Mother Teresa. Testing other single human neurons, they located a brain cell that would rather watch an episode of "The Simpsons" than Madonna.
15   In one sense, these findings are merely noise. They arise from rare recordings of electrical activity in brain cells, collected by neuroscientists at the University of California, Los
20 Angeles, during a decade of experiments with patients awaiting brain surgery for severe epilepsy. These tingles of electricity, however, gave the researchers the opportunity to
25 locate neurons that help link our perceptions, memories and self-awareness.
    In their most recent work this year, the research team reported that a single
30 human neuron could recognize a personality through pictures, text or the sound of a name—no matter how that person was presented. In tests, one brain cell reacted only to Oprah
35 Winfrey; another just to Luke

Skywalker; a third singled out Argentine soccer star Diego Maradona.

Each neuron appeared to join
40 together pieces of sensory information into a single mental impression. The researchers believe these cells are evidence that it only takes a simple circuit of neurons to encode an idea,
45 perception or memory.

"These neurons will fire to the person no matter how you present them," says bioengineer Rodrigo Quian Quiroga at the U.K.'s University
50 of Leicester who studied the neurons with colleagues at UCLA and the California Institute of Technology. "All that we do, all that we think, all that we see is encoded by neurons.
55 How do the neurons in our brain create all our perceptions of the world, all our emotions, all our thinking?"

1. Which of the following best summarizes lines 28-45?

(A) Individual neurons combine information to identify personalities presented in different forms.

(B) Individual neurons combine different pieces of information using a simple circuit.

(C) Every neuron in the human brain is capable of identifying different celebrities.

(D) Famous personalities can be presented in a variety of ways and still be recognizable.

2. The passage primarily focuses on which of the following characteristics of neurons?

(A) Their ability to independently recognize people and personalities

(B) Their involvement in conditions like epilepsy

(C) Their ability to be recorded during rare forms of research

(D) Their profound effect on all human perceptions

3. Based on the passage, which choice best describes the relationship between neurons and celebrities?

(A) Every neuron can identify all celebrities

(B) Every neuron can identify one celebrity

(C) One celebrity is identified by one neuron

(D) All celebrities are identified by all neurons

ANSWERS: PART 3 PRACTICE

1. A
2. A
3. C

EVIDENCE IN A PASSAGE
PART 4

As we discussed in Section 2, you should always be able to support any answer you choose by referring to words or lines in the passage. On the redesigned SAT Reading Test, you will also gain points by referring back to the passage–there will be two **Citing Textual Evidence** questions for each passage that ask you to identify the support for your answer to another question. We'll refer to these as "Evidence" questions.

Evidence questions will list four different sentences from the passage, and ask which one provides the best evidence to support your answer to the previous question. You should be sure you have answered the previous question before you attempt an Evidence question. Evidence questions are always worded as follows:

> Which choice provides the best evidence for the answer to the previous question?

REFER BACK

Once you see that you are being asked an Evidence question, refer back to your answer to the previous question and remember why you selected it. Find the paragraph or lines that supported your choice. Then, look at each answer choice for the Evidence question. Look for the choice that is a match for the paragraph or lines you identified, or for a choice that could be another piece of evidence for your answer to the previous question. Be sure to read each section of lines you are given in their original context in the passage.

EXAMPLE

Tommaso Strinati clambers to the top of the rickety scaffold and laughs. "It's a good thing that all this Baroque

Line
work is so unimpressive," he says,
5 pointing at the clumsy trompe l'oeil painting covering the wall in front of him. "Otherwise, we might not have been allowed to scrape it off!"

A 28-year-old art historian, he is
10 standing 16 feet above the marble floor of San Pasquale Baylon chapel, a long-neglected nook of Santa Maria in Aracoeli, a Franciscan basilica in the center of Rome. Last year, Mr.
15 Strinati, who is still a graduate student, began studying the church's history.

Records suggested that the Roman artist Pietro Cavallini – a painter and mosaicist whose greatest works have been destroyed – spent years decorating Aracoeli toward the end of the 13th century. Yet only one small Cavallini fresco, in the church's left transept, remained visible. Mr. Strinati wondered: had other Cavallini frescoes been painted over with inferior work? And if so, could modern restorers uncover them?

"The answer to both questions was yes," Mr. Strinati says. A close-up examination of the chapel's walls last summer revealed ghostly images lying beneath the surface. The entire chapel, it seemed, was a painted palimpsest. And when a heavy altarpiece was removed from one wall, a remarkably tender portrait of the Madonna and Child was found hidden behind it.

After months of careful paint-peeling, what has been uncovered are dazzling fragments of a late-medieval masterpiece completed shortly after 1285. Although the Aracoeli fresco is not signed, the figures strongly resemble those in a surviving Cavallini work, the resplendent "Last Judgment" fresco at nearby Santa Cecilia.

Mr. Strinati has grand ambitions for his discovery. He hopes that in a few years the fully restored fresco will not only rescue Cavallini's name from obscurity, but also upend the widespread notion that the first flowers of the Renaissance budded in Florence, not Rome. For the fresco's lifelike figures – in particular, an impish Christ child with charmingly flushed cheeks – suggest to Strinati that Cavallini may have anticipated some of the extraordinary naturalistic innovations that have long been credited to the Florentine artist Giotto.

Moreover, the Aracoeli fragments may provide a critical new clue in a decades-old battle concerning the "St. Francis Legend," the 1296 fresco cycle at Assisi, universally recognized as one of the foundations of the Renaissance. For centuries, the 28-scene cycle – which recounts the life of the saint with a narrative zest and compositional depth that leave the flat tableaus of the Byzantine era far behind – was attributed to Giotto. But since the 1930's, various scholars have questioned this judgment, claiming that the Assisi cycle doesn't resemble Giotto's other work. Now, the Aracoeli discovery is ammunition for Italian art historians who believe that Cavallini might actually be the primary creative force behind the "St. Francis Legend."

The growing debate about Cavallini's importance was the occasion for a symposium in Rome in November. *La Republicca*, an Italian daily, has cast the debate as "War Between Rome and Florence." Mr. Strinati is enjoying the ruckus. "I had a hunch that there was more Cavallini lurking around here," he says of the Aracoeli basilica. "But I didn't expect to find an exquisite work that could shake up the history of art.'

The passage most strongly suggests that the discovery of Cavallini's work

(A) was a fortuitous accident.
(B) will impact art history broadly.
(C) is one of many discoveries in the Aracoeli basilica.
(D) was a shocking surprise for Tommasso Strinati.

Which choice provides the best evidence for the answer to the previous question?

(A) Lines 30-33 ("A close-up … surface")
(B) Lines 39-43 ("After months … 1285")
(C) Lines 69-74 ("For centuries … Giotto")
(D) Lines 83-86 ("The growing … November")

First select your answer to the implicit meaning question. Which one can you support with information from the passage? Answer choices (A) and (D) contradict the passage, as you are told that Strinati had a hunch that he would find more work by Cavallini, and worked purposively to uncover this work. Answer choice (C) could be true, but the passage never discusses other discoveries in the Aracoeli basilica, so you cannot support this answer.

Answer choice (B) is supported by the passage by several ideas, such as the reconsideration of the "St. Francis Legend," Mr. Strinati's "grand ambitions," and other lines in the final three paragraphs. Therefore, (B) is the correct answer.

With this answer in mind, look at the options for the Evidence question. Remember that you are looking for the lines that most strongly suggest that Cavallini's work will have an impact on art history. Here is the question again:

Which choice provides the best evidence for the answer to the previous question?

(A) "A close-up … surface"
(B) "After months … 1285"
(C) "For centuries … Giotto"
(D) "The growing … November"

Here, none of the answers mention the "St. Francis Legend," or quote Strinati. But remember that there can be lots of ways to support an answer choice! Answer choice (D) also suggests that the Cavallini discovery is making waves, as a symposium was held to discuss how important this discovery might be. (D) is the correct response.

The other answer choices do not relate to the impact of the Cavallini discovery. Answer choice (C) is about Giotto, not Cavallini, so you can eliminate it. Answer choices (A) and (B) relate to characteristics of the Cavallini discovery but don't address the impact or importance the discovery may have for art history. You can knock them out as well.

IF YOU GET STUCK

If you're having trouble with an Evidence question, keep in mind that the lines that best support a given answer choice could be anywhere in the passage. An argument made in the second paragraph may be backed up by data or reasoning in the third or fourth paragraph, rather than appearing immediately after the argument.

If none of the answer choices seem to support your previous answer, take another look at each option and see if they might work in a creative or unexpected way. If they still don't seem to work, review the previous question. It is possible your original answer choice was incorrect and therefore does not match with the lines given in the Evidence question! If you ever change your answer to a question that precedes an evidence question, be sure to redo the accompanying evidence question as well.

PART 4 PRACTICE: EVIDENCE IN A PASSAGE

Review the techniques we discussed in Section 2, and mark up and make summaries for this passage excerpt. Then, answer the questions using the evidence strategies you just learned.

Across Colombia—from the walled coastal city of Cartagena to the sugar-cane fields outside Cali—there's a
Line palpable feeling of flux, of a society
5 shaking off its solitude and stretching out. Crime and poverty persist, but a measure of peace is making it safer to travel and do business across the region. This calm is also allowing
10 Colombia to export greater supplies of oil, gas, sugar and cut flowers, boosting the pace of its economic growth. Last year alone, the country attracted nearly $16 billion in foreign
15 investments. Luxury malls and beach resorts are sprouting up to cater to the country's 36,000 high-net-worth individuals. Tourism campaigns cheekily play down Colombia's war-
20 torn reputation with slogans such as "The only risk is wanting to stay."
Similar wealth booms have recently helped transform China and Brazil into global art hubs, so it makes
25 sense to see international curators and dealers booking trips to Colombia now. New York's Museum of Modern Art, Houston's Museum of Fine Arts and London's Serpentine Galleries,
30 among others, have all recently sent delegations of curators and patrons to scout art in Colombia. Pablo León de la Barra, a curator for New York's

Solomon R. Guggenheim Museum,
35 was among the early explorers, and the art he's uncovered since is impressive, he says. "For some, art has become a way of working through the communal trauma, but the younger ones are
40 trying to use art as an instrument of usefulness for something else. There are many things at play, but one of them is a desire for normalization."
Whenever curators and collectors
45 start sniffing around a new region, dealers and auctioneers invariably follow, eager to pounce on whatever the tastemakers discover. (A similar phenomenon has lately pushed up
50 prices for China's Zeng Fanzhi and Brazil's Beatriz Milhazes.) In the past year, these market movers have begun championing a potential poster boy for Colombia's rise in Oscar Murillo, the
55 28-year-old son of Cali sugar-cane farmers who now lives in London. Three years ago, Murillo's frenetic paintings—often made with the help of relatives using dust and debris from his
60 studio floor—were selling for as little as $10,000 apiece.
But last fall, Phillips in New York auctioned off one of the artist's 2011 canvases, Untitled (Drawings Off the
65 Wall), for $401,000, or 10 times its high estimate.

1. The passage most strongly suggests that

   (A) most Colombian artists now earn high prices for their work.

   (B) Colombia was not always as stable a country as it is now.

   (C) Colombian art has a long history of engaging dangerous themes.

   (D) Colombian art will become less popular at the initial interest subsides.

2. Which choice provides the best evidence for the answer to the previous question?

   (A) Lines 6-9 ("Crime … the region")

   (B) Lines 13-15 ("Last … investments")

   (C) Lines 32-37 ("Pablo … he says")

   (D) Lines 44-48 ("Whenever … tastemakers discover")

3. Based on the passage, which choice best describes the relationship between national prosperity and art?

   (A) Increased wealth in a nation leads to higher prices on the work of its oldest artists.

   (B) When a nation becomes less prosperous, it uses art to work through the trauma.

   (C) Economic prosperity can attract art buyers and collectors to a previously overlooked country.

   (D) As a country grows wealthier, its artists feel more encouraged to create.

4. Which choice provides the best evidence for the answer to the previous question?

   (A) Lines 9-13 ("This calm … growth")

   (B) Lines 15-18 ("Luxury malls … individuals")

   (C) Lines 22-27 ("Similar wealth … now")

   (D) Lines 62-66 ("But last … estimate")

Answers: Part 4 Practice

1. B
2. A
3. C
4. C

ANALOGICAL REASONING
PART 5

Analogical Reasoning questions ask you to find an answer choice that is analogous to (the same as) an idea or relationship presented in the passage. An **analogy** is an extended comparison between two things or situations. For example, if a character in a literature passage lies to a friend about a surprise party for them, you would look for an answer choice that presents an analogy for that situation—such as another situation where someone is harmlessly deceived for their own benefit.

These questions can be phrased in a variety of ways:

- Which of the following situations is most analogous to the problem presented in the passage?
- Which hypothetical situation involves the same paradox discussed by the author?
- The principle illustrated in lines 16-19 ("By … life") is best conveyed by which additional example?

Your job is to identify the situation that follows a similar pattern as an idea or relationship from the passage. The content or topics of the answer choices do not matter. Just because a passage is about cancer research does not mean the right answer will also be about cancer research, or scientific research at all. It might be about music, or politics, or any other subject, as long as it illustrates the same idea or reasoning as the original passage.

USE YOUR OWN WORDS

To answer these questions refer back to the passage and re-state the idea, principle, or relationship you are asked about in your own words. Then look for an answer choice that matches your description.

EXAMPLE

A 28-year-old art historian, he is 10 standing 16 feet above the marble floor of San Pasquale Baylon chapel, a long-neglected nook of Santa Maria in Aracoeli, a Franciscan basilica in the center of Rome. Last year, Mr. 15 Strinati, who is still a graduate student, began studying the church's history. Records suggested that the Roman artist Pietro Cavallini – a painter and mosaicist whose greatest works have 20 been destroyed – spent years decorating Aracoeli toward the end of the 13th century. Yet only one small Cavallini fresco, in the church's left transept, remained visible. Mr. Strinati 25 wondered: had other Cavallini frescoes been painted over with inferior work?	And if so, could modern restorers uncover them? Which of the following situations is most analogous to the mystery presented in lines 17-24? (A) A muralist spent weeks sketching and eventually completed a beautiful design. (B) A lawmaker took less time than originally expected to draft a bill. (C) Dancers took a few minutes to practice but did not master new choreography. (D) A chef spent hours in the kitchen but prepared only a couple of dishes.

To answer this question, first put the "mystery" from the referenced lines into your own words. Cavallini spent years decorating Aracoeli, and yet there is very little art by him in the basilica. We would expect there to be a lot of Cavallini paintings in Aracoeli. You might phrase this "mystery" more generally as "spent lots of time but little to show for it" or "less work than expected."

Which answer choice best matches your description of these lines? Only answer choice (D) shows another scenario where someone produced "less work than expected." Notice that this answer choice does not need to be about art to be analogous to the idea from the passage.

Answer choice (A) is about art but does not match the passage, because here the amount of effort seems to match the output. Answer choice (C) also doesn't match the passage—it is not surprising that dancers did not improve during only a few minutes. Choice (B) is almost the opposite of the passage, as more work was accomplished than expected. Therefore, none of these situations would be a good analogy for the mystery in the passage.

PART 5 PRACTICE: ANALOGICAL REASONING

Answer the following analogical reasoning questions using the approach you have just learned.

> According to scientists the relationship between sugar and adult-onset diabetes is different from what the population generally believes it to be. In reality, eating a diet high in refined sugar can lead to excess weight, and being overweight can predispose individuals to adult-onset diabetes.

1. Which of the following situations is most analogous to the relationship between sugar and adult-onset diabetes?

    (A) Increased exercise can lead to both improved mood and lower cholesterol over time.

    (B) Studying leads to increased comprehension, and increased comprehension always ensures a higher grade.

    (C) Investment causes companies to grow rapidly, and expanding companies are more prone to mistakes.

    (D) Having a father who is colorblind can predispose a child to colorblindness.

> As a new yoga instructor, Juri faced a challenge: guiding her students into the right alignment in their poses. As creative as she was in her descriptions of each position, it seemed they did not help her students recreate them. One day she began adopting the poses herself at the front of the class, hoping she could better describe them by focusing on her own muscle movements. Instead, she looked up and saw her students perfectly copying her form on their own mats.

2. Which hypothetical situation involves the same approach ultimately used by the yoga instructor?

    (A) A rugby coach uses a video of professional games to explain a new strategy.

    (B) A swimming instructor jumps in the pool to demonstrate a stroke.

    (C) Violin teachers have their students sing a melody before they attempt to play it.

    (D) A writing instructor suggests a list of books to read for inspiration.

When the scandal came to light I must admit I was hardly surprised; the mayor did, after all, have a reputation for deception and bending the truth. In a way then, I felt the journalists were nearly equally to blame. After all, was it not their job to investigate the credibility of claims, especially those coming from such an untrustworthy figure? But instead of uncovering his secrets they had been busy propagating the mayor's lies.

3. The attitude displayed by the narrator towards the journalists is most similar to which example?

    (A) The advertisers who overlooked a key defect in a car they are promoting are nearly as responsible as the engineers who built it incorrectly.

    (B) Police officers who arrest criminals on the wrong charges should be reprimanded for their mistake.

    (C) It is not a driver's fault if she gets lost because the map she is using is outdated.

    (D) A mail officer who delivers a package to the wrong address is more responsible than the sender who miswrote the address.

Answer Key: Part 5 Practice

1. C
2. B
3. A

PRACTICE SET

The following passages have been designed to test the question types you learned about in this section. Review the techniques we discussed in Section 2, and mark up and make summaries for this passage. Then, answer the questions using the strategies you just learned.

Questions 1-9 are based on the following passage.

For hundreds of years, coffee has been one of the two or three most popular beverages on earth. But it's only recently that scientists are figuring out that the drink has notable health benefits. In one large-scale epidemiological study from last year, researchers primarily at the National Cancer Institute parsed health information from more than 400,000 volunteers, ages 50 to 71, who were free of major diseases at the study's start in 1995. By 2008, more than 50,000 of the participants had died. But men who reported drinking two or three cups of coffee a day were 10 percent less likely to have died than those who didn't drink coffee, while women drinking the same amount had 13 percent less risk of dying during the study. It's not clear exactly what coffee had to do with their longevity, but the correlation is striking.

Perhaps most consequential, animal experiments show that caffeine may reshape the biochemical environment inside our brains in ways that could stave off dementia. In a 2012 experiment at the University of Illinois at Urbana-Champaign, mice were briefly starved of oxygen, causing them to lose the ability to form memories. Half of the mice received a dose of caffeine that was the equivalent of several cups of coffee. After they were reoxygenated, the caffeinated mice regained their ability to form new memories 33 percent faster than the uncaffeinated. Close examination of the animals' brain tissue showed that the caffeine disrupted the action of adenosine, a substance inside cells that usually provides energy, but can become destructive if it leaks out when the cells are injured or under stress. The escaped adenosine can jump-start a biochemical cascade leading to inflammation, which can disrupt the function of neurons, and potentially contribute to neurodegeneration or, in other words, dementia.

In a 2012 study of humans, researchers from the University of South Florida and the University of Miami tested the blood levels of caffeine in older adults with mild cognitive impairment, or the first glimmer of serious forgetfulness, a common precursor of Alzheimer's disease, and then re-evaluated them two to four years later. Participants with little or no caffeine circulating in their bloodstreams were far more likely to have progressed to full-blown Alzheimer's than those whose blood indicated they'd had about three cups' worth of caffeine.

There's still much to be learned about the effects of coffee. "We don't know whether blocking the action of denosine is sufficient to prevent or lessen the effects of dementia," says Dr. Gregory G. Freund, a professor of pathology at the University of Illinois who led the 2012 study of mice. It is also unclear whether caffeine by itself provides the benefits associated with coffee drinking or if coffee contains other valuable ingredients. In a 2011 study by the same researchers at the University of South Florida, for instance, mice genetically bred to develop Alzheimer's and then given caffeine alone did not fare as well on memory tests as those provided with actual coffee. Nor is there any evidence that mixing caffeine with large amounts of sugar, as in energy drinks, is healthful. But a cup or three of coffee "has been popular for a long, long time," Dr. Freund says, "and there's probably good reasons for that."

1. The passage as a whole suggests that the author would most likely agree with which of the following?

(A) Current research does not yet show convincing health benefits of coffee.

(B) The historical popularity of coffee is enough to demonstrate that its health benefits are significant.

(C) It would be beneficial to conduct further research on the health benefits of coffee.

(D) Doctors must begin advising patients at risk for dementia to increase their coffee intake.

2. Which choice provides the best evidence for the answer to the previous question?

(A) Lines 24-28 ("Perhaps most … dementia")

(B) Lines 68-69 ("There's still … coffee")

(C) Lines 75-79 ("It is … ingredients")

(D) Lines 89-93 ("But … for that")

3. It can reasonably be inferred from the passage that

(A) serious forgetfulness is a major cause of Alzheimer's disease.

(B) the formation of memories requires oxygen.

(C) once it is better understood, coffee will provide a cure for Alzheimer's disease.

(D) coffee consumption will increase once its health benefits are publicized.

4. Based on the passage, which choice best describes the relationship between caffeine and coffee?

(A) Coffee is only healthful when it contains caffeine.

(B) Coffee may be healthier than isolated caffeine.

(C) Coffee may be less healthy than isolated caffeine.

(D) Coffee is most healthful when supplemented with additional caffeine.

5. Which choice provides the best evidence for the answer to the previous question?

(A) Lines 33-35 ("Half of … coffee")

(B) Lines 61-67 ("Participants with … caffeine")

(C) Lines 69-75 ("We don't … mice")

(D) Lines 79-86 ("In … actual coffee")

6. According to the "large-scale epidemiological study" (lines 6-7) cited in the passage, women participants who were coffee drinkers

(A) were more likely to drink two to three cups of coffee a day than men.

(B) were less likely to drink two to three cups of coffee a day than men.

(C) were less likely to die than women who did not drink coffee.

(D) were more likely to die than men who drank coffee.

7. Which of the following is most analogous to the effects of adenosine on the brain described in lines 42-45?

(A) Antibiotics are often helpful in fighting infections, but only if they are used consistently.

(B) Even a small amount of arsenic can be dangerous, but consuming large amounts is deadly.

(C) Humor gives an essay character, but can detract from the argument if used in the wrong context.

(D) Operating power tools is very risky, except when done by trained professionals.

8. As used in line 59, "precursor" most nearly means

(A) model.

(B) prototype.

(C) predecessor.

(D) harbinger.

9. As used in line 84, "fare" most nearly means

   (A) travel.

   (B) survive.

   (C) manage.

   (D) shift.

Questions 10-19 are based on the following passage.

Is a job applicant lying to you?
What about your boss, or an
entrepreneur who is promising to
double your investment? Most of us
are bad at spotting a lie, at least
consciously. New research, published
last month in Psychological Science,
suggests that we have good instincts
for judging liars, but that they are so
deeply buried that we can't get at
them.

This finding is the work of Leanne
ten Brinke, a forensic psychologist.
"Perhaps our own bodies know better
than our conscious minds who is
lying," explained Dr. ten Brinke, now
at the Haas School of Business at the
University of California, Berkeley.

It's well accepted that most of us
are no better than a flip of the coin at
seeing a lie. A classic experiment
involves showing study subjects
videotapes of people, some of whom
are lying, who say they did not steal
$100; the subjects correctly guess the
liars about half the time. Dr. ten
Brinke and her collaborators at Haas
built on that experiment, with a twist:
after the subjects watched the video
and made their conscious assessments
of who was lying, the researchers tried
to measure the subjects' unconscious
reactions.

To do so, the researchers flashed
images of someone already seen in the
videotape—but this time in
milliseconds, indiscernible

consciously. The subjects then
completed a word task that involved
placing "truth" words (like truthful,
honest, valid) and "lie" words
(dishonest, invalid, deceitful) into their
proper categories. When study subjects
were flashed a picture of a liar, they
were significantly slower to lump
words like truthful or honest into the
"truth" category, but faster to lump
words like deceitful into the "lie"
category. The opposite was true when
the subjects saw a truthful person. So,
in general, the same people seemed
better at detecting lies unconsciously
than consciously. By scientific
measures, the size of the effect was
decidedly non-trivial, but not
overwhelming.

There are many theories about why
the ability to pick out liars gets lost in
translation to consciousness. Dr. ten
Brinke speculated that we tell one
another little lies all the time—for
survival, reproductive strategy, and so
on—and that part of getting along
socially is being able to let those
harmless lies escape notice.

Is it possible to tap into the
unconscious ability? "It's the million-
dollar question," she said. The study
fits into a rich history of lie-detection
research, with some researchers saying
they can read lies in facial expressions,
and others arguing that liars just don't
give off enough clear signals to allow
detection. "The cues are so faint," said

75 Dr. Bella DePaulo, a visiting professor of psychology at University of California, Santa Barbara and an expert in the science of lie detection. She said that there was some evidence, 80 including her own research, that supported the idea of unconscious or indirect lie detecting, but she doubted that it would ever become a truly effective system. Dr. ten Brinke has 85 started a new experiment, one that she hopes will offer concrete tactics to help us identify liars. It entails measuring physiological symptoms like blood flow and perspiration in 90 study subjects who are listening to a liar. That, too, is a twist. The traditional lie-detector test makes similar measures of a person suspected of lying. Maybe the better detector will 95 be the person listening, at least if the conscious mind can be left out of it.

10. The passage serves mainly to

(A) discuss ongoing scientific research.

(B) resolve a longstanding debate.

(C) suggest a definitive solution to a problem.

(D) describe breakthroughs in treating a disease.

11. Based on the passage, which choice best describes the relationship between lying and detection?

(A) It is easiest to detect lies using the unconscious mind.

(B) We unconsciously detect lies more accurately than we're aware of.

(C) We can most accurately detect lies using the conscious mind.

(D) We can most accurately detect lies when the liar is unconscious of their lie.

12. The passage most strongly suggests that

(A) there is still no consensus on the best way to catch liars.

(B) in the future there will be methods to detect lies with very high accuracy.

(C) humans' accuracy in distinguishing lies from truth is improving.

(D) there are fewer studies about lying conducted now than in the past.

13. Which choice provides the best evidence for the answer to the previous question?

(A) Lines 50-53 ("So … than consciously")

(B) Lines 68-74 ("The study … detection")

(C) Lines 87-91 ("It entails … a liar")

(D) Lines 94-96 ("Maybe … of it")

14. The results of the "classic experiment" (lines 21-26) most strongly suggest that

   (A) people are more successful in guessing if someone is lying to them than in actively trying to figure it out.

   (B) making a random guess would be about as accurate as consciously trying to figure out if someone is lying.

   (C) people are such poor judges of lying they are better off guessing if they are being deceived.

   (D) most of the time people assume that they are not being lied to.

15. Which of the following experiments would be most similar to the experiment described in lines 34-43?

   (A) An image of a clean or messy place is flashed for a few milliseconds and subjects are asked to complete word sets with clean or messy sounding words.

   (B) An image of a person is flashed for a few milliseconds and subjects are asked to say whether they've met that person before.

   (C) Subjects are allowed to examine the face of a person and then guess whether they will be likely to lie in the future.

   (D) Subjects are asked to examine an image of a house and then match the image with the most accurate descriptive words.

16. According to Dr. ten Brinke, humans' inability to spot lies may

   (A) be remedied with her current techniques.

   (B) help us study the brain.

   (C) serve a social purpose.

   (D) be overcome through concentration.

17. Which choice provides the best evidence for the answer to the previous question?

   (A) Lines 6-11 ("New research … them")

   (B) Lines 21-26 ("A classic … time")

   (C) Lines 59-65 ("Dr. ten Brinke … escape notice")

   (D) Lines 84-87 ("Dr. ten Brinke … identify liars")

18. As used in line 45, "lump" most nearly means

(A) group.

(B) congregate.

(C) accumulate.

(D) trudge.

19. As used in line 86, "concrete" most nearly means

(A) specific.

(B) established.

(C) physical.

(D) realistic.

ANSWERS: PART 6 PRACTICE

1. C
2. B
3. B
4. B
5. D
6. C
7. C
8. D
9. C
10. A
11. B
12. A
13. B
14. B
15. A
16. C
17. C
18. A
19. A

Acknowledgements for this Section

The passages in this section were adapted from the following sources:

Daniel Zalewski, "Under a Shroud of Kitsch May Lie A Master's Art." © 2001 by *The New York Times Company*. Originally published July 28, 2001.

Steve Lohr, "The Vaccination Effect: 100 Million Cases of Contagious Disease Prevented." © 2013 by *The New York Times Company*. Originally published November 19, 2013.

Robert Lee Hotz, "A Neuron's Obsession Hints at Biology of Thought." © 2009 by *Dow Jones & Company*. Originally published October 9, 2009.

Kelly Crow, "Colombia's Art Scene Heats Up." © 2014 by *Dow Jones & Company*. Originally published June 26, 2014.

Gretchen Reynolds, "This Is Your Brain on Coffee." © 2013 by *The New York Times Company*. Originally published June 6, 2013.

Matt Ritchel, "The Search for Our Inner Lie Detectors." © 2014 by *The New York Times Company*. Originally published April 26, 2014.

PERSUASIVE LANGUAGE

Passages on the SAT Reading Test will use a variety of techniques, devices, and types of language to communicate ideas to the reader. The questions that test these techniques fall under a category that the College Board calls **Rhetoric**, which means persuasive language. This section will cover the type of questions you will be asked about persuasive language and how to answer them.

First, you'll learn how to analyze word choice as well as the overall structure of a text. Next, you'll learn how to decipher the point of view and purpose of a passage. Finally, you'll learn how to assess arguments made by the author. There will be practice exercises for you to try along the way, and two passages at the end of the section where you will put together everything you've learned.

ANALYZING WORD CHOICE
PART 1

Analyzing Word Choice questions ask you how specific words, phrases, or patterns shape the meaning and tone of the text. They will often require you to read between the lines and comprehend the passage beyond a literal understanding of what is being said.

RHETORICAL DEVICES

You may be asked what certain rhetorical devices are achieving in the text. Remember that **rhetorical devices** are tools that the author uses to convey her argument, such as repetition, metaphor, or simile. You can refer back to Section 3 for a review of these devices. However, you don't need to know the definitions of rhetorical devices in order to answer these questions. Instead, you'll need to know what impact rhetorical devices have on shaping the text.

For example, repetition is often used to make or emphasize a point. Metaphors and similes are often used to describe or explain an interesting concept. To understand specific metaphors and similes, think about what is being used as a comparison. For example, birds are free to fly wherever they like, so comparing something to a bird is often meant to indicate freedom. Referring to a caged animal might suggest the opposite. Be careful of choosing an answer that is too literal when answering questions about these devices.

Let's see what a Word Choice question might look like for the following paragraph, taken from John F. Kennedy's inaugural address.

> In the long history of the world, only a few generations have been granted the role of defending freedom in its hour of maximum danger. I do not shrink from this responsibility —I welcome it. I do not believe that any of us would exchange places with
>
> Line any other people or any other generation. The energy, the faith, the devotion which we bring
>
> 5 to this endeavor will light our country and all who serve it—and the glow from that fire can truly light the world.

The rhetorical effect of lines 4-6 is to

(A) argue for citizen involvement to bring electricity to other nations.
(B) suggest that the action of citizens can benefit their country and the world.
(C) persuade listeners that they must share their resources with others.
(D) imply that all Americans have benefited from the actions of previous generations.

Be wary of interpreting the images of light and fire literally; here, Kennedy is using a metaphor to make a point about the power of citizen action. This is clearer when you read the entire paragraph, so always be sure to read the lines surrounding a Word Choice question. Answer choice (B) demonstrates that the light represents how the actions of the listeners will benefit the United States and the rest of the world. Therefore, (B) is the correct answer.

Answer choices (A) and (C) incorrectly interpret the imagery too literally, so they can be knocked out. Answer choice (D) talks about action being taken, but the paragraph refers to the energy and faith of those listening, not of a previous generation.

TONE

Word Choice questions may also ask you to analyze how certain words or lines shape the tone of a text, or to describe the tone of a passage overall. **Tone** refers to the feeling or attitude the author demonstrates in his writing. You can determine the tone of a passage by paying attention to the words the author uses, and to how you feel as you read the passage. Adjectives in particular help shape the tone of a text, so look out for them as you read.

The following words may be used by the SAT to describe the tone of the passage, or the attitude of a character or someone mentioned in the text. Use a dictionary to look up any words you do not know.

Tone Words		
Positive	Neutral	Negative
Captivated	Academic	Apathetic
Effusive	Candid	Caustic
Enthusiastic	Contemplative	Condescending
Engaged	Detached	Contemptuous
Excited	Dispassionate	Cynical
Fascinated	Impartial	Derisive
Humorous	Judicious	Disparaging
Intrigued	Pragmatic	Flippant
Laudatory	Scholarly	Grudging
Reverent		Skeptical
Whimsical		Vindictive

When you answer a tone question, first think back to your impression of the passage, or the section you are asked about. How did it make you feel? Think of your own word to describe the tone of the text. If you cannot think of a specific word, try to think more generally about the tone. Was it strong or neutral? Positive or negative? Happy or sad? Then compare your prediction to the answer choices.

Let's look at a tone question about the excerpt from John F. Kennedy's speech to see how this works.

EXAMPLE

In the long history of the world, only a few generations have been granted the role of defending freedom in its hour of maximum danger. I do not shrink from this responsibility – I welcome it. I do not believe that any of us would exchange places with any other people or
Line any other generation. The energy, the faith, the devotion which we bring to this endeavor
5 will light our country and all who serve it – and the glow from that fire can truly light the world.

The tone of lines 4-6 is best described as

(A) uncertain.
(B) confident.
(C) biting.
(D) delicate.

How would you describe the tone of these lines? The word "devotion" demonstrates Kennedy's strong commitment, and stating, "the glow from that fire can truly light the world" suggests his conviction that things will move forward in a positive way. You might choose a word like "encouraging" or "optimistic" to describe this tone. Once you compare this word to the answer choices, (B) is the only option that is close to your prediction.

Answer choice (A) is nearly the opposite of what you are looking for. (C) is too negative to describe the lines in question, and (D) is a poor fit as Kennedy's words are quite decisive and bold.

PART 1 PRACTICE: ANALYZING WORD CHOICE

Review the techniques we discussed in Section 2, and mark up and make summaries for this passage excerpt. Then, answer the Analyzing Word Choice questions using the strategies you just learned.

Edna often wondered at one propensity which sometimes had inwardly disturbed her without causing any outward show or manifestation on her part. At a very early age—perhaps it was when she traversed the ocean of waving grass—she remembered that she
Line had been passionately enamored of a dignified and sad-eyed cavalry officer who visited
5 her father in Kentucky. She could not leave his presence when he was there, nor remove her eyes from his face, which was something like Napoleon's, with a lock of black hair falling across the forehead. But the cavalry officer melted imperceptibly out of her existence.
    At another time her affections were deeply engaged by a young gentleman who visited
10 a lady on a neighboring plantation. It was after they went to Mississippi to live. The young man was engaged to be married to the young lady, and they sometimes called upon Margaret, driving over of afternoons in a buggy. Edna was a little miss, just merging into her teens; and the realization that she herself was nothing, nothing, nothing to the engaged young man was a bitter affliction to her. But he, too, went the way of dreams.

1.   The main rhetorical effect of the repeated word in line 13 is to

(A) underscore how frequently Edna had felt ignored in her teens.

(B) suggest that Edna often had to remind herself of her proper place.

(C) emphasize how little Edna mattered to the young man.

(D) imply that Edna lacked self-confidence around the young man and Margaret.

2. The author's tone is best described as

   (A) apologetic.

   (B) mournful.

   (C) invigorated.

   (D) reflective.

Answers: Part 1 Practice

1. C
2. D

ANALYZING TEXT STRUCTURE
PART 2

Analyzing Text Structure questions ask you about the structure of the text as a whole, or about the relationship between the whole text and a specific part of the text, such as one sentence or paragraph.

USE YOUR SUMMARIES

Referring back to the summaries you made while reading can help you answer Analyzing Text Structure questions. Reading these summaries will help you understand how the paragraphs relate to one another, and can help you figure out the relationship between a specific part of the text and the whole.

To understand the structure of an entire passage, re-read all your summaries while staying focused on the "big picture" of the passage as a whole, rather than individual paragraphs. Look for where certain ideas were introduced or where the focus of the passage changed. Make a quick summary in your own words to describe the way the passage progresses, and then compare it to the answer choices.

EXAMPLE

Let's see how this works with a question about the overall structure of a passage. Remember the summaries you wrote for the Cavallini passage in Section 2? Here is the passage and the paragraph summaries again:

#1 T.S. glad remove Baroque

Tommaso Strinati clambers to the top of the rickety scaffold and laughs. "It's a good thing that all this Baroque
Line work is so unimpressive," he says,
5 pointing at the clumsy trompe l'oeil painting covering the wall in front of him. "Otherwise, we might not have been allowed to scrape it off!"

A 28-year-old art historian, he is
10 standing 16 feet above the marble floor of San Pasquale Baylon chapel, a long-neglected nook of Santa Maria in Aracoeli, a Franciscan basilica in the center of Rome. Last year, Mr.
15 Strinati, who is still a graduate student,

#2 Continued next page...

#2 T.S. thinks hidden P.C. frescos

began studying the church's history.
Records suggested that the Roman
artist Pietro Cavallini – a painter and
mosaicist whose greatest works have
20 been destroyed – spent years
decorating Aracoeli toward the end of
the 13th century. Yet only one small
Cavallini fresco, in the church's left
transept, remained visible. Mr. Strinati
25 wondered: had other Cavallini frescoes
been painted over with inferior work?
And if so, could modern restorers
uncover them?

#3. Found P.C. frescoes

"The answer to both questions was
30 yes," Mr. Strinati says. A close-up
examination of the chapel's walls last
summer revealed ghostly images lying
beneath the surface. The entire chapel,
it seemed, was a painted palimpsest.
35 And when a heavy altarpiece was
removed from one wall, a remarkably
tender portrait of the Madonna and
Child was found hidden behind it.

#4. Resemble other P.C.

After months of careful paint-
40 peeling, what has been uncovered are
dazzling fragments of a late-medieval
masterpiece completed shortly after
1285. Although the Aracoeli fresco is
not signed, the figures strongly
45 resemble those in a surviving Cavallini
work, the resplendent "Last Judgment"
fresco at nearby Santa Cecilia.

#5. P.C. maybe anticipated Giotto/ Renaissance

Mr. Strinati has grand ambitions
for his discovery. He hopes that in a
50 few years the fully restored fresco will
not only rescue Cavallini's name from
obscurity, but also upend the
widespread notion that the first flowers
of the Renaissance budded in Florence,
55 not Rome. For the fresco's lifelike
figures – in particular, an impish
Christ child with charmingly flushed
cheeks – suggest to Strinati that
Cavallini may have anticipated some
60 of the extraordinary naturalistic
innovations that have long been
credited to the Florentine artist Giotto.
Moreover, the Aracoeli fragments
may provide a critical new clue in a

#6. P.C. maybe painted "St. F"

65 decades-old battle concerning the "St.
Francis Legend," the 1296 fresco cycle
at Assisi, universally recognized as
one of the foundations of the
Renaissance. For centuries, the 28-
70 scene cycle – which recounts the life
of the saint with a narrative zest and
compositional depth that leave the flat
tableaus of the Byzantine era far
behind – was attributed to Giotto. But
75 since the 1930's, various scholars have
questioned this judgment, claiming
that the Assisi cycle doesn't resemble
Giotto's other work. Now, the Aracoeli
discovery is ammunition for Italian art
80 historians who believe that Cavallini
might actually be the primary creative
force behind the "St. Francis Legend."

#7. P.C. causing art history debates

The growing debate about
Cavallini's importance was the
85 occasion for a symposium in Rome in
November. *La Republicca*, an Italian
daily, has cast the debate as "War
Between Rome and Florence." Mr.
Strinati is enjoying the ruckus. "I had a
90 hunch that there was more Cavallini
lurking around here," he says of the
Aracoeli basilica. "But I didn't expect
to find an exquisite work that could
shake up the history of art."

Which of the following best describes
the structure of the passage as a
whole?

(A) The passage introduces a scholar,
and then focuses on a discovery
he has made.

(B) The passage introduces an artist,
and details a new discovery of
his art.

(C) The passage makes an argument
about an artist, then supports it
with historical evidence.

(D) The passage considers both sides
of an issue, yet reaches no
conclusion.

The summaries for the Cavallini passage show that the first paragraph is about Strinati, and the second and third paragraphs introduce the hidden Cavallini frescoes he discovered. The rest of the passage is focused on Cavallini's work and the impact it might have on theories of art history. Answer choice (A) matches this progression, as Strinati is an art historian, and the remainder of the passage discusses the Cavallini discovery. Therefore, answer (A) is correct.

Answer choice (B) is close, but the passage does not begin by introducing the reader to the artist Cavallini. Answer choice (C) is incorrect because the passage as a whole isn't focused on one argument about Cavallini. There are smaller arguments supported with historical evidence in individual paragraphs, such as the "St. Francis Legend" in paragraph 6. However, this does not represent the structure of the passage as a whole. Answer choice (D) is also incorrect, as the passage does not debate two sides of an issue throughout.

MARK UP THE STRUCTURE

To help you get a better sense of the structure of a passage, you can also build upon the techniques you learned in Section 2 and mark up additional items in your passage. You can look for transition words, evidence, and examples in the passage.

Marking up Passage Structure		
Concept	Importance	How to mark it in the passage
Transition words	Indicate a change in direction of author's reasoning or argument	Circle the word
Examples or evidence	Clarify concepts discussed by the author; can reveal how an author has supported his or her argument	Note "e.g." or "e.v." in the margin

Here are a few paragraphs from the Cavallini passage. We've marked up transition words, evidence, and examples to show you how this works.

> Moreover, the Aracoeli fragments may provide a critical new clue in a
> 65 decades-old battle concerning the "St. Francis Legend," the 1296 fresco cycle at Assisi, universally recognized as one of the foundations of the Renaissance. For centuries, the 28-
> 70 scene cycle – which recounts the life of the saint with a narrative zest and compositional depth that leave the flat tableaus of the Byzantine era far behind – was attributed to Giotto. But
> 75 since the 1930's, various scholars have questioned this judgment, claiming that the Assisi cycle doesn't resemble Giotto's other work. Now, the Aracoeli discovery is ammunition for Italian art
> 80 historians who believe that Cavallini might actually be the primary creative force behind the "St. Francis Legend." The growing debate about Cavallini's importance was the
> 85 occasion for a symposium in Rome in November. La Republicca, an Italian daily, has cast the debate as "War Between Rome and Florence." Mr. Strinati is enjoying the ruckus. "I had a
> 90 hunch that there was more Cavallini lurking around here," he says of the Aracoeli basilica. "But I didn't expect to find an exquisite work that could shake up the history of art."

e.v.   *eg*

By noting the transition words, you can see how parts of the paragraph relate to one another, and also how assertions are supported with evidence and examples. For example, lines 74 to 78 provide evidence against the previous assertion about Giotto. It also provides the reason for questioning whether he was the original artist of the "St. Francis Legend."

PART 2 PRACTICE: ANALYZING TEXT STRUCTURE

Review the techniques we discussed in Section 2, and mark up and make summaries for this passage excerpt. Then, answer the analyzing text structure questions using the strategies you just learned.

> How many times have you heard that we humans are "using up" the world's resources, "running out" of oil, "reaching the limits" of the atmosphere's capacity to cope with pollution or "approaching the carrying capacity" of the land's ability to
> Line support a greater population? The assumption behind all such statements is that there is
> 5   a fixed amount of stuff—metals, oil, clean air, land—and that we risk exhausting it through our consumption.
> "We are using 50% more resources than the Earth can sustainably produce, and

unless we change course, that number will grow fast—by 2030, even two planets will
not be enough," says Jim Leape, director general of the World Wide Fund for Nature
10   International (formerly the World Wildlife Fund).

But here's a peculiar feature of human history: We burst through such limits again
and again. After all, as a Saudi oil minister once said, the Stone Age didn't end for lack
of stone. Ecologists call this "niche construction"—that people (and indeed some other
animals) can create new opportunities for themselves by making their habitats more
15   productive in some way. Agriculture is the classic example of niche construction: We
stopped relying on nature's bounty and substituted an artificial and much larger bounty.

1. The general organization of the passage is best described by which of the
    following?

    (A) A problem is introduced but the evidence supporting it is questioned; the author
        concludes the problem is solvable.

    (B) A problem is introduced with evidence to support it; the author introduces a
        competing argument.

    (C) Evidence is introduced and a problem is identified; the author offers additional
        information.

    (D) A problem is introduced and a solution proposed; the author offers an
        alternative solution.

2. The author's statement at lines 11-12 serves primarily to

    (A) introduce evidence for his conclusion.

    (B) provide support for an earlier argument.

    (C) summarize the passage.

    (D) introduce his main argument.

3. The author discusses "niche construction" (line 13) in order to

    (A) help explain his claim that humans can overcome the limits of existing
        resources.

    (B) counter the argument that humans are rapidly consuming resources.

    (C) provide an example of how humans can reduce their usage of limited resources.

    (D) suggest that the earlier claim that certain resources are limited is false.

Answers: Part 2 Practice

1. B
2. D
3. A

POINT OF VIEW AND PURPOSE
PART 3

Just like all texts you read, the SAT Reading Test passages were written from a specific point of view and for a specific reason. You may be asked two different kinds of questions about this: Point of View questions and Analyzing Purpose questions.

POINT OF VIEW

Point of View questions ask you to determine the point of view or attitude of the author. This may involve determining what the author's attitude is towards a specific subject, or describing how the author approached writing the text overall. These questions can sometimes be similar to Word Choice questions about tone, which you learned about earlier in this section.

One good place to find the author's point of view or opinion is through certain adjectives she may use. Some adjectives simply describe a fact, like "the sky is blue." However, there are also adjectives that are not facts, but rather demonstrate how we feel about something, like declaring, "Brussels sprouts are delicious."

When you see adjectives that convey an opinion in the text, and they are not attributed to another person or character in the passage, you can assume they represent the point of view of the author. There may be passages with very few strong adjectives or statements by the author that indicate her opinion. In that case, do not make assumptions that go beyond what is stated in the passage. Be wary of answer choices that state the author's opinion too strongly, or use absolute language like "best" or "worst" that doesn't fit with the passage.

EXAMPLE

Let's look at a Point of View question to see how this works:

> Dr. Chabra has found a way to help serious athletes recover more quickly from the stiffness caused by heavy training. Like any new medical intervention, Dr. Chabra's novel approach to treating muscle soreness has been met with some skepticism and a lot
> *Line* of questions. Still, many of her colleagues praised the innovative treatment; they rightly
> 5 recognized the valuable impact it could have on athletic performance.
>
> The author's attitude toward Dr. Chabra's new treatment is best described as
>
> (A) uncertain.
> (B) relieved.
> (C) disparaging.
> (D) approving.

While the second sentence of this paragraph indicates that there has been some skepticism about Dr. Chabra's treatment, it does not appear to be the author's attitude. Instead, the author aligns herself with Dr. Chabra's colleagues who have praised the treatment, which indicates a positive attitude. The adjectives "innovative" and "valuable" are also very complimentary and suggest the author thinks highly of Dr. Chabra's discovery. Answer (D) is therefore the correct response.

Answer choices (A) and (C) do not work, as the author is neither uncertain nor disapproving towards Dr. Chabra. Answer choice (B) does not make sense in the context of the passage, as nothing indicates that the author was previously worried and then consoled once she learned of Dr. Chabra's discovery.

ANALYZING PURPOSE

Analyzing Purpose questions ask you about the purpose of either an entire passage or specific lines or paragraphs. To answer these questions you need to analyze what the author was trying to achieve with his writing.

For questions that ask you about the purpose of the passage as a whole, you will want to choose a "big-picture" answer. Ask yourself why the passage was written. Was it to persuade the reader of something, to argue against a previously held idea, or just to introduce a new concept? Describe the goal of the passage in your own words before looking at the answer choices.

EXAMPLE

Here's an example of an Analyzing Purpose question from the Cavallini passage that you already tackled in Section 2:

The primary purpose of the passage is to

(A) explain an exciting discovery.
(B) describe Cavallini's artistic style.
(C) emphasize the importance of art history.
(D) discuss Giotto's role in the Renaissance.

Here, answers (B) and (D) are too narrow, and answer choice (C) is not discussed at all in the passage. Therefore, (A) is the correct answer.

You may also be asked about the purpose of individual lines or paragraphs. Again, try to think of what the author is trying to achieve with the portions of text you are asked about. Is he introducing or summarizing concepts? Providing arguments or counterarguments? Presenting a contrast for emphasis? Review your summaries and notes on the passage to see how the section you are analyzing relates to other parts of the text.

Remember that you are being asked about the role of a certain part of the passage, and not just what it says. You may need to read critically to understand the author's intent or goal! Be sure to carefully analyze persuasive language, and look at the lines before and after the ones you are asked about for clues to the author's intent.

PART 3 PRACTICE: POINT OF VIEW AND PURPOSE

Review the techniques we discussed in Section 2, and mark up and make summaries for this passage excerpt. Then, answer the Point of View and Purpose questions using the strategies you just learned.

> Dinner done and we sitting with our feet upon the fender, I said to Herbert, "My dear Herbert, I have something very particular to tell you."
> "My dear Handel," he returned, "I shall esteem and respect your confidence."
>
> Line "It concerns myself, Herbert," said I, "and one other person."
> 5 Herbert crossed his feet, looked at the fire with his head on one side, and having looked at it in vain for some time, looked at me because I didn't go on.
> "Herbert," said I, laying my hand upon his knee, "I love—I adore—Estella."
> Instead of being transfixed, Herbert replied in an easy matter-of-course way, "Exactly. Well?"
> 10 "Well, Herbert? Is that all you say? Well?"
> "What next, I mean?" said Herbert. "Of course I know that."
> "How do you know it?" said I.
> "How do I know it, Handel? Why, from you."
> "I never told you."
> 15 "Told me! You have never told me when you have got your hair cut, but I have had senses to perceive it. You have always adored her, ever since I have known you. You brought your adoration and your portmanteau here together. Told me! Why, you have always told me all day long. When you told me your own story, you told me plainly that you began adoring her the first time you saw her, when you were very young indeed."

1. The primary purpose of lines 15-19 is to

    (A) explain how Herbert knows that Handel loves Estella.

    (B) introduce the fact that Handel has loved Estella for a long time.

    (C) highlight Herbert's keen powers of perception.

    (D) suggest that many people must be aware of Handel's love for Estella.

2. The passage serves mainly to

    (A) describe the relationship between one friend and another.

    (B) recount a conversation between two friends.

    (C) reveal a mysterious character's secret motives.

    (D) foreshadow an upcoming action in a story.

Answers: Part 3 Practice

1. A
2. B

ANALYZING ARGUMENTS

PART 4

Analyzing Arguments questions ask you to analyze the way the author of the passage makes and supports her arguments. You may be asked to identify claims or counterclaims in a passage, whether explicit or implicit. You may also be asked to assess an author's reasoning and evidence.

ANALYZING CLAIMS AND COUNTERCLAIMS

Analyzing Claims and Counterclaims questions, or "Claims" questions, ask you to locate arguments the author makes. An **argument** is an idea that the author believes is true or is trying to persuade the reader to believe, and it is usually supported by evidence.

To find an author's argument, look for what the passage is trying to persuade you to believe. This may be clearly stated as a thesis statement, or may require you to read between the lines. Look for statements that are not necessarily factual, that make judgments, or that suggest a particular course of action.

A **counterclaim** or counterargument is an argument that goes against a previous argument in the passage. A counterclaim may disprove another person's claim that was previously mentioned by the author. It could also offer an alternative to an argument made by the author, showing that he recognizes the limitations of his earlier claim. The author may then conclude with this new argument, or present evidence to refute it and stand by what he had originally stated.

If you have trouble identifying arguments, ask yourself what the author seems sure about, or what he is trying to persuade you to believe.

EXAMPLE

Let's practice answering a Claims question about the paragraph below, from a speech by Anna Howard Shaw. Focus on identifying her argument as you read.

> Now if we should take a vote and the men had to read their ballot in order to vote it, more women could vote than men. But when the government says not only that you must be twenty-one years of age, a resident of the community and native born or naturalized,
> *Line* those are qualifications, but when it says that an elector must be a male, that is not a
> 5 qualification for citizenship; that is an insurmountable barrier between one half of the people and the other half of the citizens and their rights as citizens. No such nation can call itself a Republic. It is only an aristocracy. That barrier must be removed before the government can become a Republic, and that is exactly what we are asking right now, that this great state of New York shall become in fact as it is in theory, a part of a
> 10 government of the people, by the people, and for the people.

In lines 6-10 the author argues that

(A) a Republic is the only acceptable form of government.
(B) only those who can read should be allowed to vote in a Republic.
(C) a true Republic must allow both women and men to vote.
(D) a Republic is necessary to allow women to vote.

In this paragraph, Shaw is speaking about Republics in order to make a point about women's right to vote. Her comments about women and men in the earlier lines of the paragraph help make this clear, even though the heart of the argument is in lines 6-10. When Shaw says, "That barrier must be removed," she is referring to the barrier between women and exercising their right to vote, as stated in lines 5-6. Only answer choice (C) sums up this argument.

You can knock out answer choice (A) as it is too strong; you only know that Shaw is in favor of a true Republic, but she doesn't say much about other forms of government. (B) refers to something mentioned in the first line, which is also not an argument but an observation. Answer choice (D) is almost the inverse of Shaw's argument—she never says that having a Republic is the only way to grant women the right to vote.

ANALYZING EVIDENCE

Analyzing Evidence questions will ask you about what kinds of evidence the author uses to support her arguments, or whether she fails to use any. There are many different ways that authors can support their arguments. Here are some possibilities:

Types of Support		
Type of Evidence	Definition	Example
Data or Quantitative Evidence	Uses statistics, percentages, or other kinds of numbers	We should be doing more to preserve wildlife habitats. There are thousands of species becoming extinct each year, often because of habitat destruction.
Expert Opinion	Relies on the opinion or ideas of scholars, researchers, or other people with expert knowledge on the topic	The proposal to teach astronomy to young students is a good one. Dr. Yaskin, an astronomy researcher, believes it will drastically increase interest in the field.
Personal Example	Uses a personal experience or situation encountered by the author	Tourists are often unaware of local etiquette in the places they visit. I witnessed this first-hand on a recent trip to Guatemala.
Comparison	Compares an idea being discussed to something else to clarify or make a point	This engineering project is a poor idea. Building new bridges in small cities with few cars is like buying designer running shoes for toddlers; it is better to wait until they are big enough to need them.
Appeal to Emotion	Creates feelings in the reader to persuade them of an argument	This policy cannot be maintained if we are to consider ourselves a just nation. After all, how dispirited would you feel if your property, acquired through hard work over time, was taken from you without explanation?

Some kinds of evidence are more common in certain contexts. For example, an argument about the increasing infection rates for a certain disease would be better proven by data than by a personal anecdote.

To answer Analyzing Evidence questions, first locate the author's argument, and then ask yourself what he did to prove it. Keep in mind an author may use multiple types of evidence, and it may appear either before or after the argument itself.

EXAMPLE

Let's look at an example from the Cavallini passage. The following is a portion of the passage.

Records suggested that the Roman artist Pietro Cavallini – a painter and mosaicist whose greatest works have
20 been destroyed – spent years decorating Aracoeli toward the end of the 13th century. Yet only one small Cavallini fresco, in the church's left transept, remained visible. Mr. Strinati
25 wondered: had other Cavallini frescoes been painted over with inferior work? And if so, could modern restorers uncover them?

"The answer to both questions was
30 yes," Mr. Strinati says. A close-up examination of the chapel's walls last summer revealed ghostly images lying beneath the surface. The entire chapel, it seemed, was a painted palimpsest.
35 And when a heavy altarpiece was removed from one wall, a remarkably tender portrait of the Madonna and Child was found hidden behind it.

After months of careful paint-
40 peeling, what has been uncovered are dazzling fragments of a late-medieval masterpiece completed shortly after 1285. Although the Aracoeli fresco is not signed, the figures strongly
45 resemble those in a surviving Cavallini work, the resplendent "Last Judgment" fresco at nearby Santa Cecilia.

Mr. Strinati has grand ambitions for his discovery. He hopes that in a
50 few years the fully restored fresco will not only rescue Cavallini's name from obscurity, but also upend the widespread notion that the first flowers of the Renaissance budded in Florence,
55 not Rome. For the fresco's lifelike figures – in particular, an impish Christ child with charmingly flushed cheeks – suggest to Strinati that Cavallini may have anticipated some
60 of the extraordinary naturalistic innovations that have long been credited to the Florentine artist Giotto.

The author provides what evidence to support the idea that Pietro Cavallini is the artist behind the recently uncovered Aracoeli frescoes?

(A) The figures in the Aracoeli frescoes are remarkably lifelike.
(B) The figures in the Aracoeli frescoes resemble those in a known Cavallini work.
(C) The Aracoeli frescoes had been painted over by another artist.
(D) Cavallini was both a painter and mosaicist.

While all of these answer choices describe lines from the passage, only answer choice (B) actually supports the idea that Cavallini painted the Aracoeli. The resemblance to other Cavallini works is mentioned in lines 43-47 to explain how we can deduce that Cavallini was the artist, even though the work is unsigned.

Assessing Reasoning

Assessing Reasoning questions ask you to analyze an author's reasoning to see if it makes sense, or ask you why an author used a certain type of reasoning. If you are asked why an author used a certain type of reasoning, you can use a similar approach as you learned for Purpose questions earlier in this section. Focus on what the author's overall goal or purpose is for the lines you are asked about, so you can determine how the reasoning the author uses lines up with what she is trying to prove.

To assess if an author's reasoning makes sense, look at whether the evidence she has given truly supports or matches up with the argument she is trying to make. This may require looking at evidence over more than one paragraph, and combining it in ways that allow you to draw new conclusions.

Example

Let's look again at an excerpt from the Cavallini passage.

> Mr. Strinati has grand ambitions for his discovery. He hopes that in a
> 50 few years the fully restored fresco will not only rescue Cavallini's name from obscurity, but also upend the widespread notion that the first flowers of the Renaissance budded in Florence,
> 55 not Rome. For the fresco's lifelike figures – in particular, an impish Christ child with charmingly flushed cheeks – suggest to Strinati that Cavallini may have anticipated some
> 60 of the extraordinary naturalistic innovations that have long been credited to the Florentine artist Giotto.
> Moreover, the Aracoeli fragments may provide a critical new clue in a
> 65 decades-old battle concerning the "St. Francis Legend," the 1296 fresco cycle at Assisi, universally recognized as one of the foundations of the Renaissance. For centuries, the 28-
> 70 scene cycle – which recounts the life of the saint with a narrative zest and compositional depth that leave the flat tableaus of the Byzantine era far behind – was attributed to Giotto. But
> 75 since the 1930's, various scholars have questioned this judgment, claiming that the Assisi cycle doesn't resemble Giotto's other work. Now, the Aracoeli discovery is ammunition for Italian art
> 80 historians who believe that Cavallini might actually be the primary creative force behind the "St. Francis Legend."

Consider the author's statement that the Aracoeli discovery may suggest Cavallini painted the "St. Francis Legend." Does this argument make sense?

It does if we consider information the author has introduced over the previous two paragraphs. The author states that Cavallini's work may have been done before some of Giotto's, and thus may have been important to the start of the Renaissance. The "St. Francis Legend" is also described as a foundation of the Renaissance, but doesn't look like Giotto's other work. It would therefore make sense that Cavallini, who was painting during the early Renaissance before Giotto and may have been one of its leaders, could be the artist behind the painting.

When answering Assessing Reasoning questions, think critically about whether the author has supported his point, and whether you are convinced by the type of evidence he used. You can also refer to the types of evidence discussed in Analyzing Evidence questions, to see if the type of evidence that the author used is appropriate to his argument.

PART 4 PRACTICE: ANALYZING ARGUMENTS

Review the techniques we discussed in Section 2, and mark up and make summaries for this passage excerpt. Then, answer the Analyzing Arguments questions using the strategies you just learned.

It's a painfully First World problem: Splitting dinner with friends, we do the dance of the seven credit
Line cards. No one, it seems, carries cash
5 anymore, so we blunder through the inconvenience that comes with our dependence on plastic. Just as often, I encounter a street vendor or taxi driver who can't handle my proffered card
10 and am left shaking out my pockets and purse.

When I returned to the United States after living in Nairobi on and off for two years, these
15 antiquated payment ordeals were especially frustrating. As I never tire of explaining to friends, in Kenya I could pay for nearly everything with a few taps on my cellphone.
20 Every few weeks, I'd pull cash out of my American bank account and hand it to a contemplative young man stationed outside my local greengrocer. I'd show him my ID and

25 type in a PIN, and he'd credit my phone number with an equivalent amount of digital currency. Through a service called M-Pesa, I could store my mobile money and then, for a small
30 fee, send it to any other phone number in the network, be it my cable company's, a taxi driver's, or a friend's. Payments from other M-Pesa users would be added to my digital
35 balance, which I could later withdraw in cash from my local agent.

For me, M-Pesa was convenient, often simpler than reaching for my credit card or counting out paper bills.
40 But for most Kenyans, the service has been life-changing. Kenya has one ATM for every 18,000 people—the U.S., by contrast, has one for every 740—and across sub-Saharan Africa,
45 more than 75 percent of the adult population had no bank account as of 2011. When Safaricom, the major Kenyan telecommunications firm,

launched M-Pesa in 2007, pesa—
50 Swahili for "money"—moved from
mattresses to mobile accounts virtually
overnight. Suddenly, payment and
collection of debts did not require
face-to-face interactions. Daylong
55 queues to pay electric- or water-utility
bills disappeared. By 2012, 86 percent
of Kenyan cellphone subscribers used
mobile money, and by 2013, M-Pesa's
transactions amounted to some $35
60 million daily. Annualized, that's more
than a quarter of Kenya's GDP.

M-Pesa isn't the first mobile-
money service. The Philippines has
had at least rudimentary mobile
65 money-transfer systems since 2001,
but nine years later, fewer than 10
percent of Filipino mobile users
without bank accounts actively used
them, while the long tail of mobile-
70 payment systems has already
transformed Africa. Parrot programs
like Paga, EcoCash, Splash Mobile
Money, Tigo Cash, Airtel Money,
Orange Money, and MTN Mobile
75 Money have sprung up in several
African countries. Even government
has elbowed its way in: the Rwanda
Revenue Authority has introduced a
service that allows citizens to declare
80 and pay taxes right from their
cellphones.

1. The author makes which of the following arguments?

    (A) Americans should begin implementing and using M-Pesa.

    (B) M-Pesa is more convenient than most forms of payment in the United States.

    (C) Making easy payments is now only a problem in the United States.

    (D) Mobile money was difficult to introduce in Kenya.

2. The author makes use of which of the following to support her argument?

    (A) Personal experiences

    (B) Expert opinion

    (C) Appeal to emotion

    (D) Extended analogy

3. What is the main evidence offered in this passage for the claim that M-Pesa "has been life-changing" (lines 40-41)?

    (A) The author's explanation of how M-Pesa works

    (B) The author's descriptions of common financial transactions in Kenya

    (C) The author's statistics about the use of mobile money services in the United States

    (D) The author's statistics about the use of M-Pesa in Kenya

4. In lines 62-71 what is the most likely reason the author discusses Filipino mobile money services?

(A) To suggest mobile money services do not work well in all types of economies

(B) To contrast the limited success of mobile money services in the Philippines with the huge impact of mobile money systems in African countries

(C) To acknowledge that M-Pesa was not the first mobile money service to be widely used

(D) To imply that mobile payment services will continue to spread to new places in the coming years

Answers: Part 4 Practice

1. B
2. A
3. D
4. B

PRACTICE SET

The following passages have been designed to test the question types you learned about in this section. Review the techniques we discussed in Section 2, and mark up and make summaries for this passage. Then, answer the questions using the strategies you just learned.

This passage is adapted from a speech delivered to the United States Senate by Senator Robert La Follette on October 6th, 1917, shortly after the US entered the First World War.

I think all men recognize that in time of war the citizen must surrender some rights for the common good that
Line he is entitled to enjoy in time of peace.
5 But the right to control their own Government according to constitutional forms is not one of the rights that the citizens of this country are called upon to surrender in time of
10 war.

Rather in time of war the citizen must be more alert to the preservation of his right to control his Government. He must be most watchful of the
15 encroachment of the military upon the civil power. He must beware of those precedents in support of arbitrary action by administrative officials, which excused on the plea of necessity
20 in war time, become the fixed rule when the necessity has passed and normal conditions have been restored.

More than all, the citizen and his representative in Congress in time of
25 war must maintain his right of free speech. More than in times of peace it is necessary that the channels for free public discussion of governmental policies shall be open and unclogged. I
30 believe that I am now touching upon the most important question in this

country today—and that is the right of the citizens of this country and their representatives in Congress to discuss
35 in an orderly way frankly and publicly and without fear, from the platform and through the press, every important phase of this war; its causes, the manner in which it should be
40 conducted, and the terms upon which peace should be made. The belief, which is becoming widespread in this land that this most fundamental right is being denied to the citizens of this
45 country, is a fact the tremendous significance of which those in authority have not yet begun to appreciate. I am contending for the great fundamental right of the
50 sovereign people of this country to make their voice heard and have that voice heeded upon the great questions arising out of this war, including not only how the war shall be prosecuted
55 but the conditions upon which it may be terminated with a due regard for the rights and the honor of this nation and the interests of humanity.

I am contending for this right
60 because the exercise of it is necessary to the welfare of this Government, to the successful conduct of this war, and to a peace that shall be enduring and for the best interest of this country.
65 Suppose success attends the attempt to stifle all discussion of the issues of this war, all discussion of the

terms upon which it should be concluded, all discussion of the
70 objects and purposes to be accomplished by it, and concede the demand of the war-mad press and war extremists that they monopolize the right of public utterance upon these
75 questions unchallenged, what would be the consequences to this country not only during the war but after the war?

Our Government, above all others,
80 is founded on the right of the people freely to discuss all matters pertaining to their Government, in war not less than in peace, for in this Government the people are the rulers in war no less
85 than in peace. Though the right of the people to express their will by ballot is suspended during the term of office of the elected official, nevertheless the duty of the official to obey the
90 popular will continues throughout this entire term of office. How can that popular will express itself between elections except by meetings, by speeches, by publications, by
95 petitions, and by addresses to the representatives of the people? Any man who seeks to set a limit upon those rights, whether in war or peace, aims a blow at the most vital part of
100 our Government. And then as the time for election approaches and the official is called to account for his stewardship the people must have the right to the freest possible discussion
105 of every question upon which their representative has acted, of the merits of every measure he has supported or opposed, of every vote he has cast and every speech that he has made. And
110 before this great fundamental right every other must, if necessary, give way, for in no other manner can representative government be preserved.

1. The main purpose of the passage can best be described as

(A) explaining the responsibilities of citizens.

(B) suggesting that people should be allowed to have new rights.

(C) advocating for the protection of traditional freedoms.

(D) seeking the middle ground between two extreme positions.

2. Which of the following best characterizes the overall structure of the passage?

(A) An idea is introduced and then supported with arguments.

(B) Competing claims are described, the first is criticized, and the second is praised.

(C) A claim is presented and its critics are attacked.

(D) A proposal is outlined, its impact is analyzed, and an alternative is proposed.

3. La Follette's tone throughout the passage can best be described as that of a

    (A) neutral observer.

    (B) reluctant supporter.

    (C) determined advocate.

    (D) unrelenting critic.

4. In this passage, La Follette argues that the public must be more protective of its right to free speech during wartime than in times of peace because

    (A) free public discussion is necessary to ensure that the war is conducted properly.

    (B) the military is more likely to violate speech rights than the civil government.

    (C) people's right to express their will through their vote is suspended during wartime.

    (D) government officials have not yet recognized the growing belief that certain rights are being ignored.

5. The first sentence of the passage (lines 1-4) serves to

    (A) establish the position that La Follette will proceed to argue against.

    (B) define a concept that will be crucial to La Follette's claim.

    (C) express a general idea that La Follette will describe in greater detail.

    (D) state a general principle to which La Follette will discuss an exception.

6. La Follette claims that the right to free speech

    (A) should only be maintained as long as a number of other rights are guaranteed as well.

    (B) is the most important right for the proper functioning of democratic government.

    (C) must sometimes be limited in order for other rights to be upheld.

    (D) is the only protection necessary in a free society.

7. Which choice provides the best evidence for the answer to the previous question?

(A) Lines 11-13 ("Rather ... Government")

(B) Lines 26-29 ("More than ... unclogged")

(C) Lines 91-96 ("How can ... people")

(D) Lines 109-114 ("And before ... preserved")

8. The list of activities included in lines 105-109 ("every question…has made") is most likely included to

(A) describe the important public work that is done by La Follete and other representatives.

(B) imply that La Follette's colleagues fear public discussion because they have acted improperly.

(C) emphasize the broad scope of the public's right to speak about their representatives.

(D) explain the limits of the public's right to speak about the government during wartime.

This passage, adapted from a short story first published in 1996, describes the narrator's first lesson with a new music instructor.

When I was seven, my father, who played the violin on Sundays with a nicely tortured flair which we
Line considered artistic, led me by the hand
5 down a long, unlit corridor in St. Luke's School basement, a sort of tunnel that ended in a room full of pianos. There many little girls and a single sad boy were playing truly
10 tortured scales and arpeggios in a mash of troubled sound. My father gave me over to Sister Olive Marie, who did look remarkably like an olive.

Her oily face gleamed as if it had
15 just been rolled out of a can and laid on the white plate of her broad, spotless wimple. She was a small, plump woman; her body and the small window of her face seemed to interpret
20 the entire alphabet of olive: her face was a sallow green olive placed upon

the jumbo ripe olive of her black habit. I trusted her instantly and smiled, glad to have my hand placed in the hand of
25 a woman who made sense, who provided the satisfaction of being what she was: an Olive who looked like an olive.

My father left me to discover the
30 piano with Sister Olive Marie so that one day I would join him in mutually tortured piano-violin duets for the edification of my mother and brother who sat at the table meditatively
35 spooning in the last of their pineapple sherbet until their part was called for: they put down their spoons and clapped while we bowed, while the sweet ice in their bowls melted, while
40 the music melted, and we all melted a little into each other for a moment.

But first Sister Olive must do her work. I was shown middle C, which Sister seemed to think terribly
45 important. I stared at middle C and then glanced away for a second. When

my eye returned, middle C was gone, its slim finger lost in the complicated grasp of the keyboard. Sister Olive
50 struck it again, finding it with laughable ease. She emphasized the importance of middle C, its central position, a sort of North Star of sound. I remember thinking, "Middle C is the
55 belly button of the piano," an insight whose originality and accuracy stunned me with pride. For the first time in my life I was astonished by metaphor. I hesitated to tell the kindly
60 Olive for some reason; apparently I understood a true metaphor is a risky business, revealing of the self. In fact, I have never, until this moment of writing it down, told my first
65 metaphor to anyone.

Sunlight flooded the room; the pianos, all black, gleamed. Sister Olive, dressed in the colors of the keyboard, gleamed; middle C
70 shimmered with meaning and I resolved never—never—to forget its location: it was the center of the world.

Then Sister Olive, who had had to
75 show me middle C twice but who seemed to have drawn no bad

conclusions about me anyway, got up and went to the windows on the opposite wall. She pulled the shades
80 down, one after the other. The sun was too bright, she said. She sneezed as she stood at the windows with the sun shedding its glare over her. She sneezed and sneezed, crazy little
85 convulsive sneezes, one after another, as helpless as if she had the hiccups.

"The sun makes me sneeze," she said when the fit was over and she was back at the piano. This was odd,
90 too odd to grasp in the mind. I associated sneezing with colds, and colds with rain, fog, snow and bad weather. The sun, however, had caused Sister Olive to sneeze in this
95 wild way, Sister Olive who gleamed benignly and who was so certain of the location of the center of the world. niverse wobbled a bit and became unreliable. Things were not, after all,
100 necessarily what they seemed. Appearance deceived: here was the sun acting totally out of character, hurling this woman into sneezes, a woman so mild that she was named,
105 so it seemed, for a bland object on a relish tray.

9. The main purpose of the passage can best be described as

(A) explaining the narrator's love for a particular instrument.

(B) providing a description of the narrator's family.

(C) arguing that the world is not always as it appears.

(D) sharing some memories from the narrator's childhood.

10. Which of the following best characterizes the overall structure of the passage?

(A) A story is told, using vivid descriptions of the setting and characters to illustrate the thoughts and memories of the narrator.

(B) A mysterious character's past is explored by recounting the events from the point of view of a child.

(C) A story is told as a series of separate events that are tied together in the end.

(D) A location is described and a story is told about the location to explain its importance in the life of the narrator.

11. Which of the following best describes the narrator's first impression of Sister Olive?

(A) She did not seem interesting because she resembled a dull food.

(B) She seemed trustworthy because her appearance matched her name.

(C) She seemed competent because she could quickly and easily identify middle C.

(D) She seemed reliable because the narrator's father left the narrator in her care.

12. The 3rd paragraph serves primarily to

(A) emphasize the musical skill of the narrator's father.

(B) introduce a new character.

(C) describe the goal of the narrator's current actions.

(D) speculate about the most likely outcome of current events.

13. The effect of the phrase "we all melted a little into each other" (lines 40-41) is mainly to

(A) suggest that when they performed music together her family members were equal in talent.

(B) show how the family was as sweet as the pineapple sherbet that was melting in their bowls.

(C) express that the musical performance brought the family closer together.

(D) provide a vivid description of the melting sound of the performance.

14. The narrator had been reluctant to tell anyone about her first metaphor because

    (A) she only realized that it was a metaphor once she was older.

    (B) she understood that a metaphor can expose a person's private thoughts and feelings.

    (C) she had used the metaphor to remember the place of middle C, and did not want to reveal her trick.

    (D) she has always preferred to express herself through her music.

15. Which choice provides the best evidence for the answer to the previous question?

    (A) Lines 1-8 ("When I … pianos")

    (B) Lines 23-28 ("I trusted … olive")

    (C) Lines 59-62 ("I hesitated … self")

    (D) Lines 74-79 ("Then Sister … wall")

16. What is the main rhetorical effect of the repetition of the word "sneezed" in lines 81-86?

    (A) To denote the exact number of occurrences of a particular action.

    (B) To subtly shift the meaning of the word in each iteration.

    (C) To imply that there was no discernible difference between a set of incidents.

    (D) To emphasize the frequency and extent of an action.

17. Why does the narrator come to believe that "things were not, after all, necessarily what they seemed" (lines 99-101)?

    (A) Because Sister Olive looked like an olive but was actually a regular person.

    (B) Because although Sister Olive was mild-mannered she had a wild sneezing fit.

    (C) Because middle C seemed to disappear when she briefly looked away.

    (D) Because sunshine was the opposite of bad weather, yet still made Sister Olive sneeze.

Answers: Practice Set

1. C
2. A
3. C
4. A
5. D
6. B
7. D
8. C
9. D
10. A
11. B
12. C
13. C
14. B
15. C
16. D
17. D

Acknowledgements for this Section

The passages in this section were adapted from the following sources:

John F. Kennedy, "Inaugural Address." January 20, 1961.

Daniel Zalewski, "Under a Shroud of Kitsch May Lie A Master's Art." © 2001 by *The New York Times Company*. Originally published July 28, 2001.

Kate Chopin, "*The Awakening and Selected Short Stories*."

Matt Ridley, "The World's Resources Aren't Running Out." © 2014 by *Dow Jones & Company*. Originally published April 25, 2014.

Charles Dickens, "*Great Expectations*."

Dayo Olopade, "Africa's Tech Edge." © 2014 *The Atlantic Monthly Group*. Originally published April 16, 2014.

Robert La Follette, "Senate Address on Free Speech in War Time." Delivered in the U.S. Senate Chamber in Washington D.C., October 6th, 1917.

Patricia Hampl, "*I Could Tell You Stories: Sojourns in the Land of Memory*," ©1999 by W.W. Norton. Originally published June 1999.

COMBINING IDEAS

This section on Combining Ideas covers **Synthesis questions**, which you will encounter in certain passages. To **synthesize** means to combine, and Synthesis questions ask you to integrate information from more than one source to discover new insights and arrive at an answer. These question types appear only when you are dealing with paired passages or passages with graphs.

In this section, you will learn how to tackle both paired passages and passages with graphs, and you will practice what you've learned with exercises along the way. There are also full-length passages for you to test your skills at the end of the section.

PAIRED PASSAGES

PART 1

As you may recall from Section 3, one of your passages on the SAT Reading Test will actually be a pair of two shorter, related passages. You may also remember that the best way to approach these passages is to read them one at a time, and answer any questions that ask about just one of the passages first. After you finish reading the second passage in a pair, pause to consider the relationship between the two passages. Review Section 3 for a refresher on these ideas.

FINDING REPEATED IDEAS

To figure out the relationship between two passages, pay attention to information that appears in both passages. In addition to your usual notes and markings on passages, you can note ideas or important words in the second passage that are repeated from the first passage. You can also note any contrasts or opposites that you find as you read the second passage in the same way. This will help you easily find these lines if you are asked about any of these concepts.

EXAMPLE

Let's see how this works with an example of two short passage excerpts:

Passage 1

Plastic pollution is the nexus of some of the <u>major environmental challenges</u> facing us today. <u>Discarded</u>
Line <u>plastic bags</u> float in the ocean, they
5 tumble in the desert, they are found in riverbeds and dams. <u>They kill off marine animals</u> that confuse the bags with plankton and jellyfish; they end up calcified in the <u>stomachs of animals</u>
10 <u>on land</u>.

But the <u>greatest damage is economic</u>—the cost of cleaning up all that waste. That's why <u>dozens of countries and cities</u> around the world,

15 including 47 municipalities in California alone, have adopted ordinances <u>banning plastic bags</u>.

Passage 2

Across the world, cities are joining the latest <u>environmental</u>
20 <u>fad—banning plastic grocery bags</u>. Activists think banning the bags is a simple and environmentally responsible approach.

Some ban supporters <u>claim plastics</u>
25 <u>harm human health</u>, even when studies from organizations like the Environmental Protection Agency, the

| Centers for Disease Control and Prevention, and Pacific Northwest | *30* | National Labs show these <u>claims are false or exaggerated.</u> |

Passage 1 shows the main ideas marked up using the 5 w's you learned about in Section 2. Passage 2 also has main ideas underlined in its second paragraph, as these are new ideas that are not related to Passage 1.

However, the ideas in the first paragraph of Passage 2 overlap with ideas from Passage 1, and we've underlined these overlapping ideas with a wavy line. The idea of "banning plastic grocery bags" is underlined because it is repeated from line 17 in Passage 1. The term "environmental fad" is underlined because it suggests the issue is not serious, which is the opposite of the idea of "major environmental challenges" (lines 2-3) in Passage 1.

By noting how the passages overlap, you can see how they fit together. You can tell that the author of Passage 2 disagrees with the author of Passage 1 that plastic bags are a major environmental issue. Passage 2 discusses other topics like human health that Passage 1 does not address.

APPROACHING THE QUESTIONS

Questions that ask you about both passages in a pair are **Analyzing Multiple Texts** questions. We will refer to these as "Multiple Texts" questions. These questions will require you to consider elements from both passages at once. This can mean comparing the information from the passages, as well as their structure, tone, or way of making an argument.

To answer these questions, look for the element you are asked about in each individual passage first. For example, if you are asked about bird flight patterns, identify what each passage says about that topic. If you are asked about something more general like tone, use your notes and summaries to determine the tone of each passage first. Then you can combine or compare these ideas to find your answer.

Let's see how this works with a question about the plastic bag passage excerpts from above. Read the longer excerpts of the passages below and mark up the repeated and contrasting ideas. Then attempt the question that follows.

Passage 1

Plastic pollution is the nexus of some of the major environmental challenges facing us today. Discarded plastic bags float in the ocean, they tumble in the desert, they are found in riverbeds and dams. They kill off marine animals that confuse the bags with plankton and jellyfish; they end up calcified in the stomachs of animals on land.

But the greatest damage is economic—the cost of cleaning up all that waste. That's why dozens of countries and cities around the world, including 47 municipalities in California alone, have adopted ordinances banning plastic bags. Communities don't have much of a choice if they leave things as they are: They either drown in plastic bags or spend millions of dollars to clean up the mess—tax dollars that should go toward infrastructure, education and libraries.

San Jose, Calif., reports that it costs about $1 million a year to repair recycling equipment jammed with plastic bags. San Francisco estimates that to clean up, recycle and landfill plastic bags costs as much as 17 cents a bag, or approximately $8.5 million a year.

Elsewhere in the world, Bangladesh banned plastic bags because they clog storm-drain systems and cause major flooding, which in turn has significant economic cost.

Ireland's PlasTax was prompted by the cost of litter. The United Arab Emirates plans to eliminate the use of conventional plastic bags by 2013.

Passage 2

Across the world, cities are joining the latest environmental fad—banning plastic grocery bags. Activists think banning the bags is a simple and environmentally responsible approach.

Some ban supporters claim plastics harm human health, even when studies from organizations like the Environmental Protection Agency, the Centers for Disease Control and Prevention, and Pacific Northwest National Labs show these claims are false or exaggerated.

Consider a study from the U.K. Environment Agency that found plastic grocery bags have the lowest environmental impact in "human toxicity" and "marine aquatic toxicity" as well as "global-warming potential" even after paper bags are used four times and reusable cotton bags are used 173 times. Why? Largely because paper and cotton bags come from crops that require fertilizer, pesticides, herbicides and the like.

Critics also say that ban opponents ignore the environmental impact of bags over the course of their lifetime. But many studies do just that. The U.K. Environment Agency's study, for instance, compared the energy expended in creating, using and disposing of plastic, paper and reusable bags to arrive at its figures. Consumers would have to use a cotton bag 173 times before they match the energy savings of one plastic bag, assuming 40% of bags are reused—a percentage that's actually lower than the rate in some cities.

Some critics say we need to ban bags because voluntary take-back programs don't work. But the point of the programs is simply to reuse bags, and consumers already reuse bags to hold garbage or pick up after pets. As for the idea that plastic bags cost consumers more, the reason grocery stores use plastic instead of paper or other bags is that they cost less and hold more. Reusable bags are even more expensive.

Passage 2 differs from Passage 1 in
that only Passage 2
(A) discusses the impact of
    alternative types of bags.
(B) mentions types of costs
    associated with plastic bags.
(C) uses quantitative information
    to support its claims.
(D) provides examples of places
    that have banned plastic
    bags.

To answer this question you can refer back to the things you underlined and noted in the passages. Pay particular attention to ideas that overlap between the two passages. This can help you select answer choice (A), as lines 76-81 describe a concept that is not repeated from Passage 1. (A) is the correct answer.

You can knock out answer choice (B), as cost appears in both passages, even though in different ways. Passage 1 discusses the cost of cleaning up bags, and Passage 2 discusses the cost to the consumer.

Answer choice (C) is incorrect, as both passages use numbers to bolster their arguments; you may have noted this in lines 25-32 and 76-81. You can knock out choice (D) because only Passage 1 lists places that have banned plastic bags, and the question is asking about an idea only present in Passage 2.

PART 1 PRACTICE: PAIRED PASSAGES

Review the techniques we discussed in Section 2 as well as the techniques above, and mark up and make summaries for these passage excerpts. Then, answer the Multiple Texts questions using the strategies you just learned.

Passage 1

There are a lot of problems with tenure for college professors, but they all lead to the biggest one: It isn't good
Line for students. That's because tenure, by
5   giving professors permanent jobs largely on the basis of the work they have published, has created and enforced a system that rewards research over teaching.
10   There is clear evidence that research is more highly valued than teaching throughout the higher-education system. According to a 2005 study published in the Journal of
15   Higher Education, the more time college professors spend in the

classroom, the less they get paid. This was true not only at large research universities, but also at small liberal-arts colleges. Professors have gotten the message, busily churning out research for a growing number of publications that in most cases are read by next to no one.

Meanwhile, much of the teaching is being done by the people at the bottom of the academic ladder, the adjuncts. They make up more than half of college faculty today, and their effect on student learning has been well documented: An increase in adjuncts on campus produces both lower graduation rates and more grade inflation.

Passage 2

Critics of tenure argue that the system rewards research, not teaching. But pay comparisons indicating that research is more highly valued can be faulty: Professors in some fields are simply paid more than those in other disciplines, regardless of the amount of research they do, and different fields lend themselves to different proportions of classroom and research time. So direct lines between pay and classroom time are difficult to draw. My best estimate is that only 10% of American colleges and universities have serious research expectations for tenure. And every institution needs the research that 10% of American faculty do if everyone's teaching is to stay up-to-date.

Tenure doesn't guarantee that every faculty member is courageous, but it protects those who are. Not every faculty member will speak out against bad plans proposed by powerful administrators, but tenure protects those who do from retaliation. Not every faculty member takes risks in challenging students, but many do. Tenure protects faculty from the ideological wrath of students, parents and politicians.

The tenure system even offers some protection to those who don't have tenure. It helps establish a campus climate in which free expression is both tolerated and valued. It establishes a system in which long-term, intellectually unconventional and innovative work can be rewarded. It guarantees colleges and universities a core of faculty members who have the kind of institutional commitment and memory that makes good decisions and successful collaboration possible. Multiyear contracts can't do the same. They provide repeated opportunities to get rid of those who rock the boat. Multiyear contracts can keep people intellectually cautious.

1. Which contrast best describes how the author of each passage views the link between research and tenure?

   (A) Passage 1 claims tenure appointment is based too heavily on research; Passage 2 argues they should be more tightly linked.

   (B) Passage 1 argues tenure appointment is based too heavily on research; Passage 2 questions the data used by Passage 1 to reach this conclusion.

   (C) Passage 1 argues that research should not influence tenure; Passage 2 suggests altering the requirements for obtaining tenure.

   (D) Passage 1 suggests that professors focus less on research; Passage 2 suggests that professors focus more on teaching.

2. Both passages make use of which of the following?

   (A) Personal observations

   (B) Hypothetical situations

   (C) Expert opinions

   (D) Quantitative information

3. Unlike Passage 2, Passage 1 focuses on

   (A) the way tenure is linked to faculty research.

   (B) how tenure impacts the work of professors.

   (C) how tenure affects student outcomes.

   (D) the argument that tenure is an outdated concept.

4. Which choice provides the best evidence for the answer to the previous question?

   (A) "There are … students" (lines 1-4)

   (B) "There is … system" (lines 10-13)

   (C) "Professors have … one" (lines 20-24)

   (D) "Meanwhile … adjuncts" (lines 25-27)

5. The author of Passage 2 would most likely respond to the claim that tenure "isn't good for students" (lines 3-4) by arguing that

(A) tenure produces more innovative research and teaching.

(B) tenure promotes the highest caliber of teaching.

(C) encouraging large amounts of research is a more important goal.

(D) there is cultural value in preserving the traditions behind tenure.

ANSWERS: PART 1 PRACTICE

1. B
2. D
3. C
4. A
5. A

PASSAGES WITH GRAPHS
PART 2

At least one passage on every SAT Reading test will be accompanied by a graph, table, chart, or other graphic that represents information related to the text of the passage. Questions about these graphics are called **Analyzing Quantitative Information questions**, but we will refer to them as "Graph questions." **Quantitative** means describing something based on amount or quantity, so you will be interpreting numbers and visual information instead of words.

Graph questions can ask you either to analyze the information in the graph independently, or to understand how it relates back to the passage. We'll take a look at both of these types of questions here.

ANALYZING GRAPHICS

To analyze a graphic, carefully review what is being measured and the units of measurement. You can underline or circle any items on the graph that you are asked about in the question.

If you are asked a more general question, such as "Which claim is supported by the graph?" then assess each answer choice against the information in the graphic to see which is in line with the data. Be careful not to make any assumptions about information that you are not given, or to assume that trends presented in the graphic will remain true for other scenarios.

Let's look at an example to see how this works.

EXAMPLE

Temperatures in Singapore

Month	Jan	Feb	Mar	Apr	May	Year
Record high °F	93.7	95.4	96.8	96.4	95.7	96.8
Average high °F	86.2	88.2	88.9	89.1	88.9	87.8

Which claim about Singapore's weather is supported by the graphic?

(A) January is on average the coldest month of the year in Singapore.
(B) There have been higher record temperatures in April than in March.
(C) March has a greater difference between average and record temperatures than does the yearly average.
(D) March has a smaller difference between average and record temperatures than does the yearly average.

Here only answer choice (D) is actually supported by the chart. Because the record high for March is the same as the record high for the year, you can easily compare them and see that there is a larger difference between the 96.8 and 87.8. Answer choice (C) gives the opposite answer, so you know it is incorrect.

You can also knock out answer choice (A) because even though January is the coldest month according to the chart, the chart does not include data for the entire year. Answer choice (B) is incorrect as it confuses average temperature for the record temperature; the record high for March is higher than for April.

RELATING GRAPHS TO PASSAGES

To relate a graphic back to information in the passage, look for lines in the passage that discuss the same subjects being measured and presented in the graphic. You may have marked up these lines as you first read the passage. Then, compare the information from the passage to what is presented in the graph. You can underline or circle the items on the graph that you are asked about or that are repeated from the passage.

The graphic may present slightly different information than the passage, and you may need to combine these two sources of information in order to reach a broader conclusion than what you could support from just one source on its own.

Let's look at an example of a passage excerpt and graphic to see how this works.

EXAMPLE

Gross domestic product (GDP) is the market value of all goods and services produced within a country in a year. GDP is an aggregate figure, which does not consider the differing sizes of nations. Therefore, GDP can be stated as GDP per capita,
Line in which the total GDP is divided by the resident population on a given date. GDP per
5 capita is not a measure of personal income, as it is measured by dividing the total amount of GDP equally among all citizens. However, a high GDP per capita is generally considered an indicator of the economic health of a nation and the living standards of its citizens generally.

GDP per capita (current USD)

Year	2008	2009	2010	2011	2012
United States	46,760	45,305	46,612	48,112	49,641
United Kingdom	43,147	35,331	36,238	38,974	39,090

It can reasonably be inferred from the passage and graphic that

(A) The United States produced more goods and services than the United Kingdom for all years measured.
(B) The United Kingdom produced more goods and services than the United States for all years measured.
(C) The United States likely experienced better economic health than the United Kingdom for all years measured.
(D) The United Kingdom had a lower GDP than the United States in 2008.

To answer this question you need to combine information given in the chart with information stated in the text of the passage. Only answer choice (C) is supported by information from both sources. The chart shows you that the United States had a higher GDP per capita, and the passage tells you this is usually "considered an indicator of the economic health of a nation" (line 7). By combining these pieces of information you can select this answer.

Answer choice (A) is contradicted by information in the passage, which clarifies that GDP per capita does not measure total goods and services, but divides that number by the number of total citizens. Without knowing the population of the two countries for the years measured, it is not possible to determine which country produced more goods and services. There is a similar issue with answer choice (B).

Answer choice (D) is incorrect as the chart only indicates GDP per capita, which is different from regular GDP as defined by the passage.

PART 2 PRACTICE: PASSAGES WITH GRAPHS

Review the techniques we discussed in Section 2, and mark up and make summaries for the passage excerpts. Then, answer the Graph questions using the strategies you just learned.

By 2040, the developing world will account for 65 percent of the world's energy consumption, according to a report released by the United States Energy Information Administration. That's up from 54 percent in 2010, and over the next three decades energy consumption is predicted to grow at a 2.2 percent annual clip in non-OECD (Organization for Economic Cooperation and Development) countries. OECD nations–including Europe, the US, Canada and Australia– in contrast, will see their energy use increase by just 0.5 percent a year, roughly in line with population growth.

Those numbers foreshadow a climate change catastrophe. Most of the growth in energy consumption will occur in countries like China and India that rely on carbon-polluting coal and other fossil fuels to generate electricity. But compounding the problem is that energy consumption per person is predicted to rise as well in the developing countries as they grow richer and their citizens covet cars, better climate control, and power-hogging devices. In the EIA forecasts, energy use per capita remains flat in OCED countries over the next 30 years but jumps 46 percent in the developing world.

Figure 1: World Energy Consumption, 1990-2040

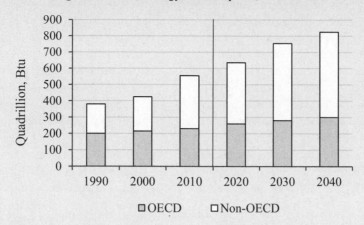

☐ OECD   ☐ Non-OECD

The British thermal unit (Btu) is a traditional measure of a unit of energy.

Adapted from US Energy Information Administration, "International Energy Outlook, 2013."

1. It can reasonably be inferred from the passage and graphic that

    (A) energy consumption per capita increased between 1990 and 2000.

    (B) energy consumption per capita decreased between 2000 and 2010.

    (C) consumption of fossil fuels in non-OECD countries will increase after 2010.

    (D) unless more renewable sources are found, OECD countries will reduce their energy consumption after 2010.

2. Which claim about energy consumption is supported by the graph?

    (A) Non-OECD countries had lower per capita energy use in 2000 than in 2010.

    (B) Non-OECD countries will consume double the energy in 2030 than they did in 2010.

    (C) OECD countries consumed the majority of the world's energy in 1990.

    (D) OECD countries consumed the majority of the world's energy in 2010.

According to the UN's population projections, the standard source for demographic estimates, there are around 600 million people aged 65 or older alive today. That is in itself remarkable; the author Fred Pearce claims it is possible that half of all the humans who have ever been over 65 are alive today. But as a share of the total population, at 8%, it is not that different to what it was a few decades ago.

By 2035, however, more than 1.1 billion people—13% of the population—will be above the age of 65. This is a natural corollary of the dropping birth rates that are slowing overall population growth; they mean there are proportionally fewer young people around. The "old-age dependency ratio"—the ratio of old people to those of working age—will grow even faster. In 2010 the world had 16 people aged 65 and over for every 100 adults between the ages of 25 and 64, almost the same ratio it had in 1980. By 2035 the UN expects that number to have risen to 26.

In rich countries it will be much higher. Japan will have 69 old people for every 100 of working age by 2035 (up from 43 in 2010), Germany 66 (from 38). Even America, which has a relatively high fertility rate, will see its old-age dependency rate rise by more than 70%, to 44. Developing countries, where today's ratio is much lower, will not see absolute levels rise that high; but the proportional growth will be higher. Over the same time period the old-age dependency rate in China will more than double from 15 to 36. Latin America will see a shift from 14 to 27.

The Big Shift

Old-age dependency, population aged 65 and over per 100 people aged 25-64

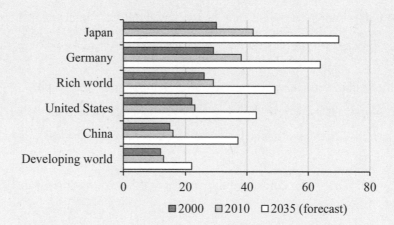

Adapted from "Age Invaders." ©2014 by The Economist.

3. It can reasonably be inferred from the passage and graphic that

   (A) Latin America will have a lower old-age dependency ratio than the rich world average in 2035.

   (B) Latin America had a lower old-age dependency ratio than the developing world average in 2000.

   (C) Japan will have 70 old people for every 100 of working age by 2040.

   (D) the United States will never have as high an old-age dependency ratio as Germany.

4. Which claim about old-age dependency is supported by the graph?

   (A) Japan has historically had a lower old-age dependency ratio than the United States.

   (B) The developing world will have a lower old-age dependency ratio than China in 2035.

   (C) The developing world had a higher old-age dependency ratio than China in 2010.

   (D) Germany's growing old-age dependency ratio is representative of rich countries overall.

Answers: Part 2 Practice

1. C
2. C
3. A
4. B

Practice Set

Part 3

The following passages have been designed to test the question types you learned about in this section. Review the techniques we discussed in Section 2, and mark up and make summaries for these passages. Then, answer the questions using the strategies you just learned.

Passage 1

Our nation's aging drinking-water systems will require staggering amounts of investment in the coming
Line decades—as much as $1 trillion over
5   the next 25 years, the American Water Works Association estimates. As things stand now, this burden will fall mostly on the public water utilities that serve about 80% of the U.S.
10   population.

But these bodies don't have the money to pay such bills. Many of them already have put off necessary improvements for years due to
15   insufficient public funding. And there is little chance of meaningful federal aid, given the national focus on debt reduction. The root of the problem is the artificially low rates the public
20   utilities have charged for years. These rates, kept low for political purposes, don't come close to supporting the long-range capital investment we would expect of any well-run
25   business.

Is privatization the solution in every case? Of course not. We must strive to find what works best for the customers in a specific situation.
30   Mismanagement is not a problem limited to private operators, just as good management is not intrinsic to public systems.

But private management can be
35   successful much more often than its critics would like to believe. Private-sector managers focus on the cost of service and return on capital. The new and innovative technologies in which
40   they invest may have a higher initial cost, but they offer savings, too, which can be shared with customers while improving service and quality.

Ultimately, the best water provider
45   is the one that is best able to deliver safe, reliable and accessible service. If the provider can also make a profit, that should be of less concern than its ability to deliver safe and affordable
50   drinking water.

Passage 2

Privatization is not the solution for deteriorating public water systems already feeling the double-pinch of dwindling local and federal funds.
55   Private companies that operate water systems have appalling track records of rate increases, poor system maintenance, faulty billing practices and other failures, sometimes even
60   jeopardizing the health and safety of local residents.

Some municipalities have taken their water systems back from private water providers. Indeed, some are
65   realizing what cities like New York, Baltimore and Boston realized a century ago—that water is best

controlled by an entity that is accountable to the public, not outside
70 shareholders.

Water service isn't a business enterprise; it's a basic human right, and what privatization proponents refer to as "political pressure" is
75 actually our democratic processes at work. Our elected leaders should absolutely respond to public concern about the affordability of their water service. The provision of water
80 service is a natural monopoly, and the public can exercise choice only at the ballot box through the election of the officials who oversee the service. How government-run utilities decide
85 to allocate costs among different users is a local decision that should be made in an open and democratic manner.

Rather than privatizing water
90 systems or asking household users to pay more, why not ask commercial and industrial water users to pay more for the services they profit from? We should also ask the federal government to establish a dedicated
95 source of federal funding in the form of a clean-water trust fund, similar to the program that provides funding for highways. This would provide a guaranteed source of funding for
100 replacing and maintaining public infrastructure systems, thereby alleviating communities of the burden of having to finance improvement projects on their own. When it comes
105 to efficiently and affordably providing water to our communities, public control trumps private profits.

1. Both passages are primarily concerned with the subject of

(A) how to charge individuals for drinking water.

(B) investing in new infrastructure for public water systems.

(C) privatizing public water systems.

(D) regulating American's drinking-water system.

2. Which of the following best describes the relationship between the two passages?

(A) Passage 2 advocates a different solution to the same problem discussed in Passage 1.

(B) Passage 2 provides a more detailed explanation for the situation described in Passage 1.

(C) Passage 2 offers alternative evidence in support of the argument made in Passage 1.

(D) Passage 2 focuses on a narrow aspect of the problem defined in Passage 1.

3. The authors of both passages agree that water service should be

   (A) priced to discourage excessive use.

   (B) financially profitable for operators.

   (C) priced differently for industrial use.

   (D) affordable for water consumers.

4. Unlike the author of Passage 2, the author of Passage 1

   (A) appeals to emotion by invoking the idea of human rights.

   (B) refers to the argument of the opposing side in order to refute it.

   (C) uses specific data to demonstrate the seriousness of the problem.

   (D) provides evidence to show that privatization of water services has been successful in the past.

5. The author of Passage 1 would most likely respond to Passage 2's claim that private water systems "have appalling track records of rate increases" (lines 56-57) by

   (A) demonstrating that rate increases best allow water providers to invest in future projects and other industries.

   (B) stating that public utility rates are too low and that raising them is necessary to ensure long-term sustainability.

   (C) explaining that high prices are, unfortunately, necessary due to dwindling federal aid for public works.

   (D) countering that political pressure will prevent prices from rising even if water companies are privatized.

6. What would the author of Passage 1 most likely think about the "clean-water trust fund" (line 96) proposed by the author of Passage 2?

   (A) That it is unlikely to be established while the federal government is trying to reduce its debt

   (B) That it would likely prohibit spending on vital technological development

   (C) That it is a good first step towards revitalizing struggling water systems and helping them to remain public

   (D) That it would be a risky investment because no similar fund has ever existed

7. Which best describes the difference between the main focus of Passage 1 and the main focus of Passage 2?

(A) Passage 1 is focused on how water utilities might turn a profit, while Passage 2 is focused on how citizens can campaign for better water use rates.

(B) Passage 1 is focused on how utilities fund infrastructure and innovation, while Passage 2 is focused on consumers' right to affordable water.

(C) Passage 1 is focused on the danger posed to water utilities by political corruption, while Passage 2 is focused on the maintenance of a free public debate over water use.

(D) Passage 1 is focused on the difficulties water utilities will face in the future, while Passage 2 is focused on the causes for these problems.

8. How would the author of Passage 2 would most likely respond to the assertion in Passage 1 that current rates for water service are too low to support necessary investments (lines 18-25)?

(A) By arguing that it is not necessary to invest additional funds in water services

(B) By suggesting that price increases should be avoided because they are undemocratic

(C) By observing that public utilities are able to invest in water services without raising rates

(D) By conceding that some price increases may be necessary, but should fall on commercial water users

Last year, Tim Hatton, an economist at the University of Essex in the U.K., rounded up data on the heights of European 21-year-olds dating from 1860 to about 1980. The results, published in the *Oxford Economic Papers*, were impressive: The average European man became about 11 centimeters taller between 1870 and 1970, gaining about a centimeter per decade. A mid-19th century British man stood just five feet, four inches tall, but he was five-foot-ten by 1980.

While about 80 percent of height is determined by genes, auxologists (those are height scientists) now believe that nutrition and sanitation determine much of the rest. As the New Yorker's Burkhard Bilger put it in 2004: "Height variations within a population are largely genetic, but height variations between populations are mostly environmental, anthropometric history suggests. If Joe is taller than Jack, it's probably because his parents are taller. But if the average Norwegian is taller than the average Nigerian it's because Norwegians live healthier lives."

Hatton and his colleagues, Roy E. Bailey from the University of Essex and Kris Inwood from the University of Guelph, created a database of 2,236 British soldiers who served in World War I, and then they looked up their birth records. The soldiers were relatively representative of the male population as a whole—about two-thirds of the 1890 British male birth cohort* enlisted. It turns out that subtle differences in their heights hinted at their origins.

The more kids there were in a household, the shorter they were. Not only because there was less food to go around, but also because it made it more likely that there were more people in each bedroom. "Crowding can help spread respiratory and gastrointestinal infections," Hatton said. "People sneezing on each other, that sort of thing."

People from industrial districts were shorter than those from agricultural areas. Regardless of income, the Dickensian living conditions of 19th century British cities suppressed height by about nine-tenths of an inch. On top of being hit with factory pollution, urban dwellers were packed into filthy, disease-ridden slums. As Kellow Chesney described in *The Victorian Underworld*, "Hideous slums, some of them acres wide, some no more than crannies of obscure misery, make up a substantial part of the metropolis … In big, once handsome houses, thirty or more people of all ages may inhabit a single room."

But as the 20th century wore on, that description became less and less apt. Tenements and slums were replaced with better housing; sewage systems and running water became standard. Women attended school in greater numbers and went from having five children, on average, to two. The 20th century was when Europeans achieved modernity, and as a result, it seems, they had to buy longer pants. "Together these developments help to explain the apparent puzzle of rapid improvement in average health status during a period of war and depression that predates the advent of universal health services," Hatton and his colleagues wrote.

For centuries, Americans were the NBA players of the world. We were two inches taller than the Red Coats we squared off against in the American Revolution. In 1850, Americans had about two and a half inches on people from every European country. But our stature plateaued after World War II, and since then, other countries shot past us. Now, the Dutch are the tallest, at an average of six feet for men and five-foot-seven for women. They've come a long way: In 1848, a quarter of Dutch men were rejected from military service because they didn't meet the five-foot-two height limit. "Today, fewer than one in 1,000 is that short," the Associated Press noted in 2006.

The Danes, Norwegians, and Germans stack up right under the Dutch. American men and women, meanwhile, measure just 5'9" and 5'4", respectively, barely edging out the Southern Europeans. John Komlos, an economic historian who has studied height extensively, thinks we Americans lost our height advantage because of poorer overall healthcare and nutrition compared to Europe. Our social shortcomings, he believes, are literally making us come up short.

"American children might consume more meals prepared outside of the home, more fast food rich in fat, high in energy density and low in essential micronutrients," he and co-author Benjamin E. Lauderdale of Princeton University wrote in 2006. "Furthermore, the European welfare states provide a more comprehensive social safety net including universal health care coverage."

A "birth cohort" is the group of people born during a specified period of time.

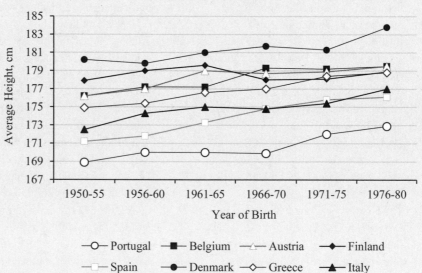

Evolution of Height
European Countries, Men

Country	Average Height of Birth Cohort, 1950-55 (cm)		Average Height of Birth Cohort, 1976-80 (cm)		Annual Growth Rate in Average Cohort Heights, %	
	Men	Women	Men	Women	Men	Women
Austria	176.3	165.6	179.6	167.1	0.07	0.04
Belgium	176.2	163.4	179.5	167.8	0.07	0.11
Denmark	180.3	167.2	183.7	168.6	0.07	0.03
Finland	177.8	164.3	178.7	165.9	0.02	0.04
Greece	174.7	163.3	178.6	165.9	0.09	0.06
Ireland	174.9	162.7	177.4	164.4	0.06	0.04
Italy	172.5	161.4	177.1	166.5	0.10	0.12
Portugal	168.8	158.9	172.9	162.5	0.10	0.09
Spain	171.3	160.4	176.1	165.5	0.11	0.12

Adapted from Jaume Garcia, Universitat Pompeu Fabra, "The Evolution of Adult Height in Europe: A Brief Note." (http://www.econ.upf.edu/docs/papers/downloads/1002.pdf)

9. According to the table, graph, and passage, which of the following groups had the lowest average height?

    (A) Women born in Denmark in 1950-55
    (B) Women born in Austria in 1976-80
    (C) Men born in Portugal in 1966-70
    (D) Men born in Greece in 1950-55

10. It can reasonably be inferred from the passage and the graph that

    (A) all Greek men are taller than Italian men.
    (B) a man born in Finland in 1968 is taller today than one born in 1964.
    (C) Danish people are the tallest people in the world.
    (D) conditions in Belgium are somewhat healthier than those in Portugal.

11. Based on the passage and the graph, in which pair of countries would you expect to find the most similar living conditions?

(A) Austria in 1976-80 and Belgium during the same period

(B) Belgium in 1976-80 and Spain during the same period

(C) Italy in 1950-55 and Spain in 1976-80

(D) Denmark in 1950-55 and Spain during the same period

12. Based on the passage and the table, which of the following statements is true?

(A) Women in Ireland gained an average of .04 centimeters in height between 1950 and 1980.

(B) Men in Spain got 11% taller between 1860 and 1980.

(C) Women in Greece got 0.06% taller each year, on average, between 1950 and 1980.

(D) Women born in Europe in 1960 were 1 cm taller than those born in 1950.

13. Based on information in the table, which of the following statements is true for every country included in the data presented?

(A) The tallest individual man in any birth cohort was no taller than 183.7 cm.

(B) The average height of the female birth cohort was lower but increased at a greater rate than the male birth cohort.

(C) Male birth cohorts had a higher average height and higher average increase in height than female birth cohorts between 1950 and 1980.

(D) Each male birth cohort had a higher average height than all female birth cohorts.

14. According to the graph, in which period's birth cohort did Belgian men first surpass Finnish men in height?

(A) 1956-60

(B) 1961-65

(C) 1966-70

(D) 1971-75

15. According to the table, which pair of groups saw the same annual increase in average height between 1950 and 1980?

(A) Italian men and Italian women

(B) Belgian women and Spanish men

(C) Finnish women and Greek women

(D) Greek men and Spanish men

ANSWERS: PRACTICE SET

1. C
2. A
3. D
4. C
5. B
6. A
7. B
8. D
9. B
10. D
11. A
12. C
13. D
14. C
15. B

Acknowledgements for this Section

The passages in this section were adapted from the following sources:

Daniela Dimitrova Russo, Todd Myers, "Should Cities Ban Plastic Bags?" © 2012 by *Dow Jones & Company.*

Naomi Schaefer Riley, Cary Nelson, "Should Tenure for College Professors Be Abolished?" © 2012 by *Dow Jones & Company.*

Todd Woody, "Here's Why Developing Countries Will Consume 65% of the World's Energy by 2040." © 2013 by *The Atlantic.*

"Age Invaders." © 2014 by *The Economist*

Richard G. Little, Wenonah Hauter, "Are We Better Off Privatizing Water?" © 2012 by *Dow Jones & Company.*

Olga Khazan, "How We Get Tall." © 2014 by *The Atlantic.*

READING AND VOCABULARY LISTS

The new SAT's Evidence-Based Reading and Writing Test assesses your ability to understand advanced reading material and advanced vocabulary. In this section, we've provided some reading and vocabulary lists that will help you prepare for this content. Working through this material will not only help you with your SAT score, but will also help you to become a better student in high school and in college. Best of luck studying!

READING LIST
PART 1

Below is a set of reading lists to help you prepare for the advanced reading material on the SAT. We have arranged these lists by grade level and subject, including literature, science, and social science. We've also included historical documents from two subject areas included on the SAT: the Founding Documents and the Great Global Conversation.

Look over the list and start with the books, magazines, and newspapers that most interest you. Make sure you are also familiar with documents from the Founding Documents and the Great Global Conversation, as many passages from the Reading Test will be taken from these areas. In addition to working through these lists, you can also build your reading skills by reading the first page of periodicals like *The New York Times* and *The Wall Street Journal* on a daily basis.

The more you can make reading an enjoyable part of your daily life, the more comfortable you will feel with the passages that you will see on the SAT.

LITERATURE

GRADE 9/10

Louisa May Alcott, *Little Women*

Maya Angelou, *I Know Why the Caged Bird Sings*

Piers Anthony, *Split Infinity*

Jane Austen, *Pride and Prejudice*

Francis Bok, *Escape from Slavery*

Ray Bradbury, *Fahrenheit 451*

Charlotte Brontë, *Jane Eyre*

Anthony Burgess, *A Clockwork Orange*

Paulo Coelho, *The Alchemist*

James F. Cooper, *The Last of the Mohicans*

Daniel Defoe, *Robinson Crusoe*

Charles Dickens, *A Tale of Two Cities*

> *David Copperfield*

> *Great Expectations*

> *Hard Times*

> *Oliver Twist*

Arthur Conan Doyle, *The Adventures of Sherlock Holmes*

Alexandre Dumas, *The Count of Monte Cristo*

George Eliot, *Silas Marner*

William Golding, *Lord of the Flies*

Hermann Hesse, *Siddhartha*

Victor Hugo, *Les Miserables*

Aldous Huxley, *Brave New World*

Ken Kesey, *One Flew Over the Cuckoo's Nest*

Sue Monk Kidd, *The Secret Life of Bees*

John Knowles, *A Separate Peace*

William Goldman, *The Princess Bride*

John H. Griffen, *Black Like Me*

John Hersey, *Hiroshima*

S.E. Hinton, *The Outsiders*

John Krakauer, *Into the Wild*

> *Into Thin Air*

Harper Lee, *To Kill a Mockingbird*

Lois Lowry, *The Giver*

Yann Martell, *The Life of Pi*

Frank McCourt, *Angela's Ashes*

Arthur Miller, *The Crucible*

George Orwell, *Animal Farm*

> *1984*

Reginald Rose, *Twelve Angry Men*

Edmond Rostand, *Cyrano de Bergerac*

J.D. Salinger, *Catcher in the Rye*

William Shakespeare, *Julius Caesar*

> *The Merchant of Venice*
> *Romeo and Juliet*
> *The Taming of the Shrew*
> *The Tempest*
> *Twelfth Night*

Mary Shelley, *Frankenstein*

Betty Smith, *A Tree Grows in Brooklyn*

John Steinbeck, *The Pearl*

Bram Stoker, *Dracula*

J.R.R. Tolkien, *The Hobbit*

Mark Twain, *The Prince and the Pauper*

Jules Verne, *20,000 Leagues Under the Sea*

John Wyndham, *The Chrysalids*

Paul Zindel, *The Pigman*

GRADE 11/12

Margaret Atwood, *The Handmaid's Tale*

Mark Bowden, *Blackhawk Down*

Emily Brontë, *Wuthering Heights*

Joseph Conrad, *Heart of Darkness*

Dante, *Inferno*

Barbara Ehrenreich, *Nickel and Dimed*

William Faulkner, *As I Lay Dying*

> *The Sound and the Fury*

F. Scott Fitzgerald, *The Great Gatsby*

Thomas Hardy, *Tess of the d'Urbervilles*

Ernest Hemingway, *The Sun Also Rises*

Joseph Heller, *Catch-22*

Hendry James, *The Portrait of a Lady*

> *The Wings of the Dove*

Sebastian Junger, *A Perfect Storm*

Sara Lawrence Lightfoot, *Balm in Gilead*

Ken Kesey, *Sometimes a Great Nation*

Niccolo Machiavelli, *The Prince*

Discourses on Livy

Gabriel Garcia Marquez, *Love in the Time of Cholera*

One Hundred Years of Solitude

Herman Melville, *Moby Dick*

Toni Morrison, *The Bluest Eye*

Alan Paton, *Cry, the Beloved Country*

Robert M. Pirsig, *Zen and the Art of Motorcycle Maintenance*

Sylvia Plath, *The Bell Jar*

Ayn Rand, *Anthem*

The Fountainhead

Erich M. Ramarque, *All Quiet on the Western Front*

Eric Schlosser, *Fast Food Nation*

William Shakespeare, *Hamlet*

King Lear

Macbeth

John Steinbeck, *The Acts of King Arthur and His Noble Knights*

The Grapes of Wrath

Of Mice and Men

Amy Tan, *The Joy Luck Club*

J.R.R. Tolkien, *The Fellowship of the Ring*

Alice Walker, *The Color Purple*

Edith Wharton, *The Age of Innocence*

T.H. White, *The Once and Future King*

Oscar Wilde, *The Picture of Dorian Gray*

Evelyn Waugh, *Brideshead Revisited*

Richard Wright, *Black Boy*

Virginia Woolf, *Mrs. Dalloway*

To the Lighthouse

MAGAZINES

The New York Times Magazine
The New Yorker

Science

Grade 9/10

Keith Devlin, *Life by the Numbers*

Dian Fossey, *Gorillas in the Mist*

Stephen Jay Gould, *Wonderful Life*
> *The Mismeasure of Man*

Joy Hakim, *The Story of Science*

Lawrence M. Krauss, *A Universe from Nothing*

Siddhartha Mukherjee, *The Emperor of All Maladies*

Nicholas Nicastro, *Circumference: Eratosthenes and the Ancient Quest to Measure the Globe*

Matt Ridley, *Genome: The Autobiography of a Species in 23 Chapters*

Oliver Sacks, *The Man Who Mistook his Wife for a Hat and Other Clinical Tales*
> *Musicophilia*

Carl Sagan, *Cosmos*

Rebecca Skloot, *The Immortal Life of Henrietta Lacks*

Jearl Walker, *The Flying Circus of Physics*

Grade 11/12

Bill Bryson, *A Short History of Nearly Everything*

Charles Darwin, *The Origin of Species*

Richard Dawkins, *The Selfish Gene*

James Gleick, *Chaos: The Making of New Science*

Brian Greene, *The Elegant Universe*

Stephen Hawking, *A Brief History of Time*
> *The Universe in a Nutshell*

Michio Kaku, *Hyperspace*

James Lovelock, *Gaia*

John Allen Paulos, *Innumeracy: Mathematical Illiteracy and its Consequences*

Neil DeGrasse Tyson, *Gravity in Reverse*

Edward O. Wilson, *The Diversity of Life*

MAGAZINES

National Geographic
New Scientist
Scientific American

SOCIAL SCIENCE

GRADE 9/10

Mark Abley, *Spoken Here*

Joan Dash, *The Longitude Prize*

Daniel L Everett, *Don't Sleep, There are Snakes: Life and Language in the Amazonian Jungle*

E.H. Gombrich, *The Story of Art*

Daniel Kahneman, *Thinking Fast and Slow*

Charles C. Mann, *1491: New Revelations of the Americas Before Columbus*
1493: Uncovering the New World Columbus Created

James Q. Wilson, *Bureaucracy: What Government Agencies Do and Why They Do It*

GRADE 11/12

Akhil Reed Amar, *America's Constitution: A Biography*

Julian Bell, *Mirror of the World: A New History of Art*

Jared Diamond, *Collapse: How Societies Choose to Fail or Succeed*
Guns, Germs, and Steel: The Fates of Human Societies

Malcolm Gladwell, *The Tipping Point*

George Lakoff, *Metaphors We Live By*

David McCullough, *1776*

James M. McPherson, *What They Fought For, 1861-1865*

Steven Pinker, *The Better Angels of Our Nature: Why Violence has Declined*
The Blank State: The Modern Denial of Human Nature

Robert B. Putman, *Bowling Alone*

Nate Silver, *The Signal and the Noise: Why So Many Predictions Fail – But Some Don't*

Timothy D. Wilson, *Strangers to Ourselves, Discovering the Adaptive Unconscious*

Howard Zinn, *A People's History of the United States*

MAGAZINES

The Atlantic

The Economist

National Geographic

Time Magazine

FOUNDING DOCUMENTS

GRADE 9/10

The Bill of Rights

The Constitution of the Iroquois Confederacy

Constitution for the United States

Declaration of the Rights of Man and the Citizen

United States Declaration of Independence

GRADE 11/12

Anti-Federalist Papers

Jonathan Elliot, *The Debates in the Several Conventions on the Adoption of the Federal Constitution*

James Madison, *Debates in the Federal Convention of 1787*

James Madison, Alexander Hamilton & John Jay, *The Federalist Papers*

GREAT GLOBAL CONVERSATIONS

GRADE 9/10

Ralph Waldo Emerson, *Society and Solitude*

Mohandas Gandhi, *Hind Swaraj or Indian Home Rule*

James Harrington, *Oceana*

Abraham Lincoln, *The Gettysburg Address*

Martin Luther King Jr., *Letter from Birmingham Jail*

Martin Luther King Jr. & Jesse Jackson, *Why We Can't Wait*

Suzanne McIntire (editor), *American Heritage Book of Great American Speeches for Young People*

John Stuart Mill, *On Liberty*

                              Considerations on Representative Government

Henry David Thoreau, *Walden*

Alex de Tocqueville, *Democracy in America*

Anna Quindlen, *A Quilt of a Country*

GRADE 11/12

Isaiah Berlin, *Four Essays on Liberty*

Edmund Burke, *Reflections on the Revolution in France*

Thomas Hobbes, *Leviathan*

John Locke, *Second Treatise of Civil Government*

Montesquieu, *The Spirit of the Laws*

Thomas Paine, *The Rights of Man*

                             Common Sense

Quercus (editor), *The Greatest American Speeches*

Jean-Jacques Rousseau, *Discourse on the Origin and Basis of Inequality Among Men*

                             The Social Contract

Willian Safire (editor), *Lend Me Your Ears: Great Speeches in History*

Elizabeth Cady Stanton, *The Woman's Bible*

Gregory Suriano (editor), *Great American Speeches*

Woodrow Wilson, *Congressional Government*

Max Weber, *Politics as a Vocation*

Mary Wollstonecraft, *A Vindication of the Rights of Women*

Malcolm X, *By Any Means Necessary*

NEWSPAPERS

The New York Times

The Wall Street Journal

SAT Vocabulary

Part 2

The new SAT's Evidence-Based Reading and Writing Test assesses your knowledge of college-level vocabulary—the kinds of words that you will need to know in order to understand academic writing about many different subjects. The vocabulary tested on the new SAT includes words that you are likely to see and use frequently in college courses, as well as words that have different meanings in different contexts.

Building your college-level vocabulary now will not only help you increase your score on the SAT, but also help you in your future studies. In this part, we've included a list of 250 college-level words, as well as lists of common word parts to help you learn new vocabulary.

Word Roots, Prefixes, and Suffixes

Many words can be broken into basic parts. **Roots** carry the basic meaning of a word, **prefixes** come before roots and alter their meaning, and **suffixes** come after roots and alter either their meaning or their part of speech. Because English is related to French, German, Spanish, Latin, and Greek, many of these word parts will look familiar if you speak one of those languages.

The lists below contain some of the most common roots, prefixes, and suffixes that make up English words. Start learning these basic parts to help you break down unfamiliar vocabulary and speed up your vocabulary building process for the SAT.

Common Roots		
ag, act	do	action, activity, agent
ambul	walk, move	ambulance, ambulatory, amble
ami, amo	love	amiable, amorous
anim	mind, soul, spirit	animal, animate, unanimous
anthro	human	anthropology, philanthropy
aud, audit	hear	audible, auditorium, audience

auto	self	automobile, autobiography, autograph
belli	war	belligerent, rebellious, bellicose
ben	good	benefactor, beneficial, benevolence
biblio	book	bibliography, Bible
bio	life	biography, biology
carn	flesh, meat	carnivore, carnal, incarnate
chron	time	chronic, chronology, synchronize
cid, cis	cut, kill	incision, homicide, insecticide
civi	citizen	civilization, civilian, civil
corp	body	corporation, corporeal, corpse
dem	people	democracy, demographic
dic, dict	speak	dictate, contradict, prediction, verdict
domin	master	dominant, domain, domineering
err	wander	error, erratic, errand
eu	good, beautiful	eulogize, euphoria, euphemism
fall, fals	deceive	fallacious, infallible, falsify
fid	faith	fidelity, confide, confidence
graph, gram	writing	grammar, telegram, graphite
loqu, locut	talk	soliloquy, loquacious, elocution
luc	light	elucidate, lucid, translucent
magn	great	magnify, magnate, magnanimous
mal	bad	malevolent, malediction, malicious
mori, mort	die	mortuary, immortal, moribund
morph	shape, form	amorphous, metamorphosis
nat	born	innate, natal, nativity
nom	name	misnomer, nominal
nov	new	novice, innovate, renovate, novelty
omni	all	omniscient, omnipotent, omnivorous
pac, pas, pax	peace	pacify, pacific, pacifist, passive
path, pass	disease, feeling	pathology, sympathetic, apathy, antipathy
phil	love	philanthropist, philosophy, philanderer
port	carry	portable, porter, transport, export
poten	able, powerful	potential, omnipotent, potentate, impotent

psych	mind	psyche, psychology, psychosis, psychopath
reg, rect	rule	regicide, regime, regent, insurrection
sacr, secr	holy	sacred, sacrilegious, sacrament, consecrate
scribe, script	write	scribe, describe, script
somn	sleep	insomnia, somnolent, somnambulist
spec, spic	see, look	spectators, spectacles, retrospect, conspicuous
tang, tact, ting	touch	tactile, tangent, contact, contingent
terr	land	terrain, terrestrial, subterranean
urb	city	urban, urbane, suburban
vac	empty	vacation, vacuous, evacuate, vacant
ver	truth	veracity, verify, veracious
verb	word	verbose, verbatim, proverb
viv, vit	alive	revival, vivacious, vitality

Common Prefixes		
ambi, amphi	both	ambidextrous, ambiguous, ambivalent
an, a	without	anarchy, anemia, amoral
anti	against	antibody, antipathy, antisocial
circum	around	circumnavigate, circumspect, circumscribe
co, col, com, con	with, together	coauthor, collaborate, composition, commerce
contra, contro	against	contradict, contravene, controversy
di, dif, dis	not, apart	digress, discord, differ, disparity
dia	through, across	diagonal, diameter, dialogue
dys	abnormal, bad	dysfunction, dyslexia, dystopia
e, ex, extra, extro	out, beyond	expel, excavate, eject, extrovert
in, il, im, ir (1)	not	inefficient, inarticulate, illegible, irrepressible
in, il, im, ir (2)	in, upon	invite, incite, impression, illuminate
inter	between, among	intervene, international, interjection, intercept
intra	within	intramural, introvert, intravenous
mis	bad, hatred	misdemeanor, mischance, misanthrope
mono	one	monarchy, monologue, monotheism
pan	all, every	panacea, panorama, pandemic
peri	around, near	perimeter, periphery, periscope

poly	many	polygon, polygamist, polyglot
post	after	postpone, posterity, postscript, posthumous
pre	before	preamble, prefix, premonition, prediction
pro	forward, for, before	propulsive, proponent, prologue, prophet
re, retro	again, back	reiterate, reimburse, react, retrogress
sub, suc, sup, sus	under, less	subway, subjugate, suppress
super, sur	over, above	superior, supernatural, supervise, surtax
syn, sym, syl , sys	with, together	symmetry, synchronize, synthesize, sympathize
trans	across	transfer, transport, transpose
un	not	unabridged, unkempt, unwitting

Common Suffixes		
able, ible	ADJ: capable of	edible, presentable, legible
ac, ic, ical	ADJ: like, related	cardiac, mythic, dramatic, musical
acious, icious	ADJ: full of	malicious, audacious
ant, ent	ADJ/N: full of	eloquent, verdant
ate	V: make, become	consecrate, enervate, eradicate
en	V: make, become	awaken, strengthen, soften
er (1)	ADJ: more	bigger, wiser, happier
er (2)	N: a person who does	teacher, baker, announcer
cy, ty, ity	N: state of being	democracy, accuracy, veracity
ful	ADJ: full of	respectful, cheerful, wonderful
fy	V: to make	magnify, petrify, beautify
ism	N: doctrine, belief	monotheism, fanaticism, egotism
ist	N: dealer, doer	fascist, realist, artist
ize, ise	V: make	victimize, rationalize, harmonize
logy	N: study of	biology, geology, neurology
oid	ADJ: resembling	ovoid, anthropoid, spheroid
ose, ous	ADJ: full of	verbose, lachrymose, nauseous, gaseous
osis	N: condition	psychosis, neurosis, hypnosis
tion, sion	N: state of being	exasperation, irritation, transition, concession
tude	N: state of	fortitude, beatitude, certitude

Vocabulary List

The vocabulary list below contains 250 words at the same difficulty level and of content areas that are most likely to appear on the SAT. Work your way through this list, using flashcards to learn words you don't know and looking up words that you're not sure how to use. To help you remember their meanings, see if you can break down any of these words into parts using the roots, prefixes, and suffixes charts above.

#	Word	Definition
1	accede	1. give in, agree to 2. take office
2	acclaim	praise
3	acquiesce	give in
4	affable (related: affability)	friendly
5	affected	1. influenced by something 2. artificial, trying to impress
6	affluent	wealthy
7	ailment	illness
8	ambivalence (related: ambivalent)	mixed feelings
9	amenable	1. cooperative, easily persuaded 2. receptive, responsive
10	animosity	hostility
11	anomalous (related: anomaly)	not normal, unusual
12	antecedent	what came before
13	antithesis	opposite
14	apathetic (related: apathy)	lacking interest
15	apparatus	device, equipment
16	arbitrary	random
17	archaic	old or old-fashioned
18	assail	attack
19	assuage	1. relieve, soothe 2. satisfy
20	atrophy	waste away
21	atypical	not normal
22	augment	enlarge, increase
23	auspicious	favorable, promising
24	aversion	dislike

25	banal	not original, common, boring
26	benevolent	generous
27	bog	marsh, swamp
28	buoyant	1. cheerful 2. floating 3. very active (in an economic context)
29	buttress	support
30	byzantine	excessively complex
31	cajole	persuade
32	callous	cruelly insensitive
33	capacity	ability
34	catalyst	something that triggers an event
35	caustic	1. bitter and sarcastic 2. acidic
36	cerebral	intellectual
37	charismatic	charming
38	circumscribe	restrict, limit
39	circumvent	overcome an obstacle
40	cite	1. quote as evidence 2. mention as an example
41	combustible	able to catch fire easily
42	compatible	1. able to co-exist peacefully, well-suited 2. consistent
43	compile	assemble, collect
44	comply	go along with rules
45	comprehensive	thorough
46	conducive	favorable to, likely to bring about a certain outcome
47	congenial	pleasant
48	conscientious	careful, hardworking
49	constraint	restriction, limitation
50	consummate	1. (verb) complete, make perfect 2. (adjective) highly skilled, perfect
51	contemporary	1. living or occurring at the same time 2. occurring in the present
52	contemptuous (related: contempt)	scornful, disrespectful
53	contingency	1. possibility 2. unforeseen event
54	convoluted	complicated, twisted
55	criterion	standard by which things are judged or measured
56	cursory	quick, hurried, not thorough
57	deficit	lack, shortage

58	definitive	absolute, authoritative
59	demure (related: demurral)	overly modest, shy
60	denounce	declare to be wrong, criticize
61	depose	1. remove from power 2. testify or give evidence (in a legal context)
62	deprecate (related: deprecating)	disapprove of, criticize
63	derivative	not original
64	derogatory (related: derogate)	insulting, disrespecting
65	destitute	poor
66	deter	prevent, discourage
67	detrimental	damaging, harmful
68	devoid	lacking
69	diligent (related: diligence)	hardworking
70	diplomatic	1. having to do with foreign relations 2. tactful, sensitive, polite
71	dire	urgent, dreadful
72	discount (verb)	1. reduce in price 2. ignore, disregard
73	discourse	discussion
74	discredit	harm someone's reputation
75	discrepancy	difference, mismatch
76	discriminating	selective, having refined taste
77	disseminate	scatter or spread widely
78	domestic	relating to the home or the home country
79	dominant	most important or powerful
80	dormant	not active
81	eclectic	from a variety of sources
82	efface (related: effacement)	erase
83	effervesce (related: effervescent)	bubble, fizz
84	eloquence (related: eloquent)	flowing and persuasive speech or writing
85	elude	escape from, avoid
86	embitter (related: embittered)	cause someone to feel bitter
87	empirical	based on observation and experimentation

88	encompass	include, surround
89	endorse	approve, support
90	enigma (related: enigmatic)	mystery
91	equanimity	calmness
92	equitable	fair, even-handed
93	erroneous	incorrect
94	evince	show clearly
95	exacting	demanding, having severe requirements
96	exasperate	annoy
97	excise	remove
98	explicit	fully expressed, leaving nothing implied
99	exploit	1. (verb) benefit unfairly from something 2. (noun) bold or heroic deed
100	facile	1. shallow, simplistic 2. effortless
101	facilitate	help, make easier
102	faction	a small group within a larger group
103	fallacy	mistaken belief, faulty reasoning
104	fastidious	careful, painstaking
105	fathom	1. (verb) understand 2. a unit of depth, usually measuring water
106	flag	1. (noun) symbol of a country or institution 2. (verb) point out, signal, draw attention to 3. (verb) become tired or weak
107	florid (related: floridity)	1. having a red or flushed face 2. flowery, elaborate
108	folly	foolishness
109	furtive	sneaky
110	generic	general, not specific
111	germinate	begin or cause to grow
112	glacial	1. icy, related to glaciers 2. cold, unfriendly 3. extremely slow
113	gravity	seriousness
114	hail	1. (noun) pellets of ice 2. (verb) rain down with force 3. (verb) signal, greet, call out 4. (verb) praise
115	harbor	1. (noun) safe place or shelter, particularly for boats 2. (verb) keep or hold in mind 3. (verb) give a home to, shelter, or hide someone
116	hedonist	someone driven by pleasure
117	heresy (related: heretic)	belief that goes against the established opinion

118	hierarchy	ranking, classification
119	hospitable	welcoming, friendly
120	hypothesis (related: hypothetical)	theory, guess
121	iconoclast (related: iconoclastic)	someone who attacks traditional beliefs
122	ideology	system of ideas, way of thinking
123	idiosyncrasy (related: idiosyncratic)	unique personal trait
124	impeccable	perfect, flawless
125	impetuous	impulsive, spontaneous
126	impetus	motivation
127	incarnate	1. possessing a concrete, material form 2. in the flesh
128	incontrovertible	definitive, unable to be denied
129	incorrigible	incapable of being corrected or improved
130	incredulous (related: incredulity)	disbelieving, skeptical
131	indiscriminate	unselective, random
132	indisposed	1. ill 2. unwilling
133	induce	1. bring about, cause 2. arrive at a conclusion by logical reasoning
134	inert (related: inertia)	not moving or active
135	inherent	innate, inborn, natural
136	inhibit (related: inhibiting)	hold back, restrain, prevent
137	innocuous	harmless
138	innovate (related: innovation, innovative)	make something new, change, create
139	insidious	sneaky, stealthy, treacherous
140	insular	1. related to or similar to an island 2. narrow-minded, isolated
141	integrity	1. honesty, dignity 2. completeness
142	inundate	flood, overwhelm
143	irony (related: ironic)	difference between what is expected and what actually happens
144	laborious	involving hard work
145	lofty	1. tall 2. majestic, noble 3. arrogant
146	lucid	clear, easily understood
147	lurid	sensational, shocking

148	malign (related: malignant)	1. (adjective) evil 2. (verb) criticize, speak ill of
149	mar	hurt someone's appearance
150	meander	wander
151	mercenary	1. (adjective) motivated by money 2. (noun) soldier hired to fight for a foreign country
152	mercurial	unpredictable, inconsistent
153	mitigate (related: mitigation)	make less serious, reduce
154	muted	quiet, soft
155	myopic	1. nearsighted 2. unimaginative
156	nebulous	vague, cloudy
157	nonchalance (related: nonchalant)	lack of concern
158	notorious (related: notoriety)	famous for something bad
159	novelty	1. newness, originality 2. a trinket or toy
160	odoriferous	having a strong or unpleasant smell
161	opaque (related: opacity)	1. not transparent 2. hard to understand
162	opportunist (related: opportunistic)	a person who takes advantage of opportunities, often unethically
163	orthodox	conservative, traditional
164	oversight	mistake
165	parochial	1. relating to church 2. narrow-minded, unsophisticated
166	particular (related: particularity)	1. specific, individual 2. fussy, demanding
167	partisan	1. supporter of a party or a cause 2. someone who is prejudiced towards a certain cause
168	patronize	1. support financially 2. act superior, look down on
169	peremptory	bossy, commanding
170	perennial	long-lasting, continual
171	perfidious	untrustworthy, disloyal
172	perverse	1. unacceptable, unreasonable 2. unnatural, abnormal
173	pigment	substance that gives color
174	plebeian	common citizen
175	poignant	emotionally touching
176	pragmatic (related: pragmatism, pragmatist)	practical
177	precipitate	cause a sudden outcome

178	precocious	having early development in maturity and intelligence
179	prescribe	1. recommend, advise 2. command
180	presumption	1. assumption, guess 2. boldness, disrespect
181	pretense	1. make-believe, fake 2. false claim
182	prevalent	widespread
183	proclivity	natural tendency
184	procure	get or provide
185	profane	1. not sacred or religious 2. showing disrespect for religion
186	prohibitive (related: prohibit, prohibition)	1. forbidding or restricting 2. excessively high in price
187	prolific	1. productive, creative, fertile 2. plentiful
188	prospective	likely or expected to become
189	quagmire	1. complex, difficult situation 2. bog or swamp
190	qualified	1. competent, able 2. limited
191	quash	1. reject 2. put down, suppress
192	radical	extreme
193	recourse	the act of turning to someone or something for assistance
194	rectify (related: rectitude)	put right, correct
195	regressive	backward-looking, becoming less advanced
196	rejuvenate	make young again
197	remission	reduction or decrease, particularly of a debt or medical symptoms
198	remote	distant, far
199	renounce	reject, abandon
200	repudiate	reject entirely, deny
201	repugnant	offensive, disgusting
202	resign (related: resignation, resigned)	1. give in, surrender 2. step down from a position
203	rhetoric (related: rhetorical, rhetorician)	persuasive speech or writing
204	rudimentary	1. basic 2. undeveloped, incomplete
205	sanction	1. (noun) penalty for disobeying a law 2. (verb) punish, impose a penalty 3. (verb) formally approve
206	sanguine	cheerfully confident, optimistic
207	satire (related: satirical, satirize)	sarcastic imitation

208	saturate	soak, make completely full
209	scintillating	lively, effervescent
210	scope	1. range 2. opportunity, possibility
211	sensational	amazing, shocking, scandalous
212	servile	submissive, overly willing to please
213	shopworn	worn out, trite
214	simile	comparison
215	solicitous (related: solicitousness)	expressing care or concern, often too much
216	sparse	lacking, rare
217	spate	outbreak of similar events happening one after another
218	spurn	reject, turn down
219	stagnant (related: stagnation)	not moving
220	stark (related: starkness)	harsh, plain
221	staunch	strong, loyal
222	stock (adjective)	standard, usual, automatic
223	strain	1. (verb) stress, force, make an excessive effort 2. (noun) excessive stress, effort, or force 3. (verb) separate solids from a liquid
224	stupefy	amaze
225	subjugate	conquer, dominate, control
226	subordinate	lower in rank, inferior
227	subservient	1. obedient, yielding 2. less important
228	subtle	not obvious
229	supine	1. lying on one's back 2. not resisting
230	susceptible	easily influenced or affected
231	sustain	1. strengthen, support 2. maintain, carry on 3. experience, suffer
232	synthesis	combination of elements or ideas
233	tangent (related: tangential)	1. different or irrelevant line of thought 2. a line that touches a curve at a point (in math)
234	tempestuous	stormy
235	tenacious (related: tenacity)	stubborn, determined
236	thrive	grow, develop, prosper
237	transcend	go beyond, rise above
238	trite	unoriginal, common

239	unorthodox	not traditional
240	unprecedented	without any previous example
241	usurp	seize power without authority
242	vicarious	felt indirectly by imagining someone else's experiences
243	vindicate (related: vindication)	clear someone of blame, prove to be right
244	virulent	1. poisonous 2. bitter, harsh, hostile
245	vitiate	spoil, destroy
246	vocation	career
247	vulnerable	susceptible, exposed
248	wane	lessen, become weaker
249	wary	cautious
250	wry	having a clever or grim sense of humor

SAT Reading Practice Test

Time – 65 minutes
52 Questions

Download and print an answer sheet available at ivyglobal.com/study.

Directions: For these questions, read the preceding passages and choose the best answer out of the choice provided. Be sure to fill in the respective circle on your answer sheet.

Questions 1-11 are based on the following passage.

The following passage is adapted from a book by W.E.B. Du Bois, who describes his experiences as a schoolmaster in a rural black community in Tennessee.

There came a day when all the teachers left the Institute, and began the hunt for schools. I learn from hearsay (for my mother was mortally afraid of firearms) that the hunting of
Line ducks and bears and men is wonderfully interesting, but I am
5 sure that the man who has never hunted a country school has something to learn of the pleasures of the chase. I see now the white, hot roads lazily rise and fall and wind before me under the burning July sun; I feel the deep weariness of heart and limb, as ten, eight, six miles stretch relentlessly ahead; I
10 feel my heart sink heavily as I hear again and again, "Got a teacher? Yes." So I walked on and on—horses were too expensive—until I had wandered beyond railways, beyond stage lines, to a land of "varmints" and rattlesnakes, where the coming of a stranger was an event, and men lived and
15 died in the shadow of one blue hill.

Sprinkled over hill and dale lay cabins and farmhouses, shut out from the world by the forests and the rolling hills toward the east. There I found at last a little school. Josie told me of it; she was a thin, homely girl of twenty, with a dark
20 brown face and thick, hard hair. I had crossed the stream at Watertown, and rested under the great willows; then I had gone to the little cabin in the lot where Josie was resting on her way to town. The gaunt farmer made me welcome, and Josie, hearing my errand, told me anxiously that they wanted
25 a school over the hill; that but once since the war had a teacher been there; that she herself longed to learn,—and thus she ran on, talking fast and loud, with much earnestness and energy.

The schoolhouse was a log hut, where Colonel Wheeler
30 used to shelter his corn. It sat in a lot behind a rail fence and thorn bushes. There was an entrance where a door once was,

and within, a massive rickety fireplace; great holes between the logs served as windows. Furniture was scarce. A pale blackboard crouched in the corner. My desk was made of
35 three boards, reinforced at critical points, and my chair, borrowed from the landlady, had to be returned every night. Seats for the children were rough plank benches without backs, and at times without legs. They had the one virtue of making naps dangerous—possibly fatal, for the floor was not
40 to be trusted.

It was a hot morning late in July when the school opened. I trembled when I heard the patter of little feet down the dusty road, and saw the growing row of solemn faces and bright eager eyes facing me.

45 There they sat, nearly thirty of them, on the rough benches, their faces shading from a pale cream to a deep brown, the little feet bare and swinging, the eyes full of expectation, with here and there a twinkle of mischief, and the hands grasping Webster's blue-back spelling-book. I
50 loved my school, and the fine faith the children had in my wisdom as their teacher was truly marvelous. We read and spelled together, wrote a little, picked flowers, sang, and listened to stories of the world beyond the hill. At times the school would dwindle away, and I would start out. I would
55 visit the Eddings, who lived in two very dirty rooms, and ask why little Lugene, whose flaming face seemed ever ablaze with the dark-red hair uncombed, was absent all last week, or why the unmistakable rags of Mack and Ed were so often missing. Then their father would tell me how the crops
60 needed the boys, and their mother would assure me that Lugene must mind the baby. "But we'll start them again next week." When the Lawrences stopped, I knew that the doubts of the old folks about book-learning had conquered again, and so, toiling up the hill, I put Cicero's "pro Archia Poeta"
65 into the simplest English, and usually convinced them—for a week or so.

GO ON TO THE NEXT PAGE ⟩

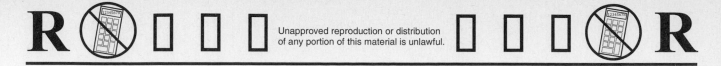
1. Which best describes Du Bois's attitude toward his work as a teacher?

    (A) He was relieved to have work despite the poor working conditions.
    (B) He was worried about living up to his students' expectations.
    (C) He was indifferent toward the simple activities he engaged in with his students.
    (D) He was proud of his school and felt respected by his students.

2. Which choice provides the best evidence for the answer to the previous question?

    (A) Lines 34-36 ("My … every night")
    (B) Lines 42-44 ("I trembled … me")
    (C) Lines 49-51 ("I loved … marvelous")
    (D) Lines 54-59 ("I would … missing")

3. Du Bois most likely discusses hunting (lines 2-6) in order to

    (A) suggest that hunting for schools is more dangerous than hunting game.
    (B) imply that he used similar techniques in finding a school as hunters use in hunting animals.
    (C) argue that he enjoyed finding a school more than he would have enjoyed hunting animals.
    (D) suggest that hunting for a school had its own unique challenges.

4. The rhetorical effect of lines 11-15 is to suggest that the places the narrator had reached

    (A) were small, contained communities.
    (B) were very dangerous.
    (C) had abnormally high death rates.
    (D) had never been visited by outsiders before.

5. As used in line 38, "virtue" most nearly means

    (A) bravery.
    (B) character.
    (C) decency.
    (D) benefit.

6. Du Bois's reaction to the "patter of little feet" (line 42) most strongly suggests that he felt a sense of

    (A) anxious anticipation.
    (B) unconstrained elation.
    (C) strong nostalgia.
    (D) unavoidable apathy.

7. The "errand" referred to in line 24 is best understood as

    (A) Du Bois's mission to find a new place of employment.
    (B) a search for materials to rebuild a local schoolhouse.
    (C) a message that Du Bois must deliver to the inhabitants of a small town.
    (D) a task that Josie offers to do for Du Bois.

8. The passage most strongly suggests that when students stopped attending school Du Bois was

    (A) relieved that he would have fewer pupils.
    (B) compelled to ensure they returned.
    (C) indifferent about their absence.
    (D) angry that they did not value their education.

9. Which choice provides the best evidence for the answer to the previous question?

    (A) Lines 51-53 ("We read … hill")
    (B) Lines 53-54 ("At times … start out")
    (C) Lines 59-61 ("Then … the baby")
    (D) Lines 62-66 ("When … or so")

GO ON TO THE NEXT PAGE

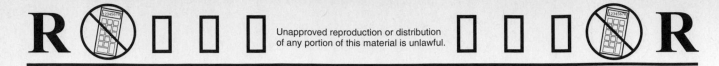

10. As used in line 64, "toiling" most nearly means

(A) endeavoring.
(B) sweating.
(C) working.
(D) plodding.

11. It can reasonably be inferred from the passage that Cicero's "pro Archia Poeta" (line 64) is

(A) a Latin treatise about farming.
(B) a short story about life in a small community.
(C) a homework assignment that Du Bois's students had not completed.
(D) a text that argues for the benefits of education.

GO ON TO THE NEXT PAGE

Questions 12-22 are based on the following passage.

The following is an excerpt from a speech given by Franklin D. Roosevelt in 1936. He was campaigning for a second term as President after winning the previous election in 1932.

On the eve of a national election, it is well for us to stop for a moment and analyze calmly and without prejudice the effect on our Nation of a victory by either of the major

Line 5 political parties. The problem of the electorate is far deeper, far more than the continuance in the Presidency of any individual. For the greater issue goes beyond units of humanity—it goes to humanity itself.

In 1932 the issue was the *restoration* of American democracy; and the American people were in a mood to win.
10 They did win. In 1936 the issue is the preservation of their victory. Again they are in a mood to win. Again they will win.

More than four years ago in accepting the Democratic nomination in Chicago, I said: "Give me your help not to win
15 votes alone, but to win in this crusade to restore America to its own people." The banners of that crusade still fly in the van of a Nation that is on the march.

It is needless to repeat the details of the program which this Administration has been hammering out on the anvils of
20 experience. No amount of misrepresentation or statistical contortion can conceal or blur or smear that record. Neither the attacks of unscrupulous enemies nor the exaggerations of over-zealous friends will serve to mislead the American people.

25 What was our hope in 1932? Above all other things the American people wanted peace. They wanted peace of mind instead of gnawing fear.

First, they sought escape from the personal terror which had stalked them for three years. They wanted the peace that
30 comes from security in their homes: safety for their savings, permanence in their jobs, a fair profit from their enterprise.

Next, they wanted peace in the community, the peace that springs from the ability to meet the needs of community life: schools, playgrounds, parks, sanitation, highways—those
35 things which are expected of solvent local government. They sought escape from disintegration and bankruptcy in local and state affairs. They also sought peace within the Nation: protection of their currency, fairer wages, the ending of long hours of toil, the abolition of child labor, the elimination of
40 wild-cat speculation, the safety of their children from kidnappers.

And, finally, they sought peace with other Nations—peace in a world of unrest. The Nation knows that I hate war, and I know that the Nation hates war.
45 I submit to you a record of peace; and on that record a well-founded expectation for future peace—peace for the individual, peace for the community, peace for the Nation, and peace with the world.

Tonight I call the roll—the roll of honor of those who
50 stood with us in 1932 and still stand with us today. Written on it are the names of millions who never had a chance—men at starvation wages, women in sweatshops, children at looms. Written on it are the names of farmers whose acres yielded only bitterness, business men whose books were
55 portents of disaster, homeowners who were faced with eviction, frugal citizens whose savings were insecure.

Written there in large letters are the names of countless other Americans of all parties and all faiths, Americans who had eyes to see and hearts to understand, whose consciences
60 were burdened because too many of their fellows were burdened, who looked on these things four years ago and said, "This can be changed. We will change it."

We still lead that army in 1936. They stood with us then because in 1932 they believed. They stand with us today
65 because in 1936 they know. And with them stand millions of new recruits who have come to know. Their hopes have become our record.

We have not come this far without a struggle and I assure you we cannot go further without a struggle. For twelve
70 years this Nation was afflicted with hear-nothing, see-nothing, do-nothing Government. The Nation looked to Government but the Government looked away. Powerful influences strive today to restore that kind of Government with its doctrine that that Government is best which is most
75 indifferent.

For nearly four years you have had an Administration which instead of twirling its thumbs has rolled up its sleeves. We will keep our sleeves rolled up.

GO ON TO THE NEXT PAGE

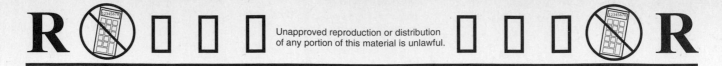

12. Based on the passage, which choice best describes how Roosevelt feels about his previous term as president?

    (A) His term was productive, and his record speaks for itself.
    (B) His term was productive, but his friends have overstated his success.
    (C) His term was a struggle that produced few good results.
    (D) His term has resulted in a deeply divided electorate.

13. Which choice provides the best evidence for the answer to the previous question?

    (A) Lines 20-21 ("No amount … record")
    (B) Lines 35-37 ("They sought … affairs")
    (C) Lines 49-50 ("Tonight … us today")
    (D) Lines 68-69 ("We have … struggle")

14. Based on the passage, which choice best describes the relationship between Roosevelt's previous term and what he plans to undertake if elected again?

    (A) He will build upon his previous successes by continuing to pursue the same goals.
    (B) He will learn from his failures and implement very different policies.
    (C) He will learn from his failures and help the struggling Americans he previously ignored.
    (D) He will alter his policies slightly based on the criticisms of voters.

15. In this speech, Roosevelt does which of the following to promote his administration?

    (A) Contrasts his administration's hard work with the indifference of the previous administration
    (B) Lists the shortcomings of the opposition party
    (C) Compares himself and his administration favorably to other leaders
    (D) Offers statistics to demonstrate the effectiveness of his policies

16. Which choice provides the best evidence for the answer to the previous question?

    (A) Lines 4-6 ("The problem … individual")
    (B) Lines 21-24 ("Neither … American people")
    (C) Lines 29-31 ("They wanted … enterprise")
    (D) Lines 76-77 ("For nearly … sleeves")

17. The main rhetorical effect of the repeated words in lines (8-12) is to

    (A) emphasize that Americans will succeed as they have before.
    (B) highlight that America's mood has changed.
    (C) suggest that Roosevelt will pursue only one goal if re-elected.
    (D) persuade listeners that the issues facing Americans are different than they were in 1932.

18. In line 25, what is the most likely reason that Roosevelt asks a question?

    (A) So he can answer it and demonstrate that he achieved what Americans hoped for
    (B) So he can answer it and argue that Americans' goals can only be accomplish if he is re-elected
    (C) To force the opposition to answer, and admit that they were ignorant of Americans' hopes
    (D) To encourage Americans to reflect on what they wanted in the past

19. As used in line 33, "springs" most nearly means

    (A) leaps.
    (B) vaults.
    (C) arises.
    (D) bounds.

20. The "army" mentioned in line 63 most likely refers to

    (A) the United States Army.
    (B) Roosevelt's opposition in the election.
    (C) new voters Roosevelt hopes to recruit.
    (D) individuals who support Roosevelt's administration.

21. It can reasonably be inferred from the passage that the phrase "farmers whose acres yielded only bitterness" (lines 53-54) most likely refers to farmers

    (A) whose crops had failed and therefore had nothing to harvest.
    (B) who opposed the agriculture policies of the previous administration.
    (C) who opposed Roosevelt's agriculture policies.
    (D) whose crops were too bitter to eat or sell.

GO ON TO THE NEXT PAGE

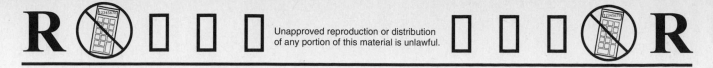
22. As used in line 75, "indifferent" most nearly means

    (A) impartial.

    (B) apathetic.

    (C) dispassionate.

    (D) objective.

GO ON TO THE NEXT PAGE

Questions 23-32 are based on the following passage.

Passage 1

We live in an amazing time. Very shortly, any individual will be able to know the sequence of his or her whole genome: This is the genetic recipe that guides the creation and functioning of our bodies. It's just a piece of what makes us unique individuals, but it's a critical piece.

What's to be gained from learning things about our bodies and our health that might scare us, but that we might not do anything about? There are four important ways a healthy person can medically benefit from obtaining his or her whole genome sequence.

Thousands of DNA combinations have been identified as indicators of susceptibility to specific diseases. Some argue that you might go through life worrying needlessly about a disease that never appears. On the other hand, spotting those DNA variants and recognizing whether you are at risk can lead directly to early diagnoses and preventive strategies.

Couples planning families can find out when they carry genetic risks for severe disorders and so make more informed choices: to have a baby together and hope for the best, for example, or to adopt. Doctors can better determine what drugs will be most effective for a patient, at what dose, and what drugs to avoid. Genome sequencing also can help in the diagnosis of illnesses yet to be identified.

Genome sequencing isn't perfect. There are mistakes. But not many. We can currently expect one misread bit of DNA among hundreds of thousands. Other common preventive medical procedures aren't free from errors either: Mammography and Pap smears have high overdiagnosis rates, and PSA testing (prostate specific antigen) is unreliable, yet we typically accept these problems. Moreover, continuing research will certainly identify more of the inaccurate and "missing" bits, leading to better clinical interpretations.

There are limits. Despite the incredible science behind sequencing, we won't be able to predict every possible condition in one's lifetime. Behaviors, environment and other factors are involved. But there are already individuals who have had a whole genome sequenced, and who learned the pharmacological, environmental, medical, or behavioral changes they could make to "compensate" for their genome.

There is no gene for compliance; it can require difficult changes to improve one's health. But for many people, that genome sequence may provide the crucial first step to move from "knowing thyself" to "helping thyself."

Passage 2

Most of us agree that in a few years, affordable genomic and epigenomic analyses of healthy individuals will allow for more individually tailored disease prevention and pharmaceutical treatment. But some serious challenges remain before this can be done safely.

One problem is that medically dangerous genetic mutations are quite rare in healthy individuals, but finding them today would still be enormously expensive. This year an entire genome will cost somewhere around $5,000 to be sequenced, analyzed with bioinformatics and interpreted. And while there is much to find in each genome that can reflect subtle health risks or aid in reproductive planning, we currently estimate that less than 2% of healthy people will have a dangerous and well-recognized DNA mutation that might cause a doctor to initiate surveillance or treatment. That means spending $250,000 to find even one such individual.

Finding well-recognized disease mutations in healthy people is just the tip of the genomic iceberg. We all have unique or novel mutations in disease-associated genes. I have 14 such mutations in my own genome! But the smartest geneticists in the world cannot always agree as to whether a novel mutation is dangerous. If a healthy person without family history has a novel mutation in a cancer predisposition gene, should we take X-rays every year for the cancer that might never appear? Should we do the same for their parents, brothers, sisters and children that carry the same mutation?

Perhaps we all underestimated how complicated it would be to move genomic knowledge into the practice of medicine and public health. Now is the time to make sure we get this right through rigorous basic and clinical studies that define which mutations are dangerous, and distinguish useful from unnecessary interventions. Soon, genomic insights will give us early warnings about life-threatening illnesses that we may be able to prevent. Soon, standards will be available to guide doctors about which findings are meaningful and which are not. Soon, there may be evidence to support the benefits of screening healthy individuals. But not today.

GO ON TO THE NEXT PAGE

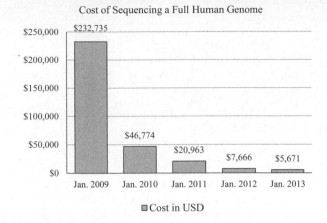

Cost of Sequencing a Full Human Genome

Adapted from Atul J. Butte and Robert Green, "Should Healthy People Have Their Genomes Sequenced At This Time?" ©2013 by The Wall Street Journal.

23. Both passages are primarily concerned with the issue of

(A) creating new genome sequencing techniques.

(B) reducing the existing risks of genome sequencing.

(C) whether genome sequencing is ready for widespread use.

(D) the costs currently associated with genome sequencing.

24. The author of Passage 1 can best be described as

(A) an excited proponent of a new technology who still recognizes its potential limitations.

(B) a skeptical critic of a new technology who is unconvinced by existing evidence supporting it.

(C) a biased advocate of a new technology who ignores counterarguments from opponents.

(D) a neutral scholar researching a debate over a new technology.

25. Which choice provides the best evidence for the answer to the previous question?

(A) Lines 6-8 ("What's … anything about")

(B) Lines 11-12 ("Thousands of … diseases")

(C) Lines 20-22 ("Doctors … to avoid")

(D) Lines 34-36 ("Despite … lifetime")

26. The author of Passage 1 does which of the following to suggest that genome sequencing is already accurate enough to be used, even though it sometimes produces errors?

(A) Notes that we accept errors in other common preventive tests

(B) Discusses the impossibility of error-free tests

(C) Argues that genome sequencing will lead to overdiagnosis

(D) States that less than 2% of healthy people will have a well-recognized DNA mutation

27. The author of Passage 1 would most likely agree with the author of Passage 2 about which of the following?

(A) Healthy individuals should not have their genomes sequenced.

(B) Genome sequencing will be more reliable in the future than it is now.

(C) Genome sequencing is currently too expensive to be useful.

(D) There is not enough consensus about which DNA mutations are dangerous.

28. Which choice provides the best evidence for the answer to the previous question?

(A) Lines 12-14 ("Some argue … appears")

(B) Lines 22-23 ("Genome sequencing … identified")

(C) Lines 31-33 ("Moreover … interpretations")

(D) Lines 41-42 ("There is … health")

29. As used in line 56, "reflect" most nearly means

(A) reconsider.

(B) reveal.

(C) mirror.

(D) imitate.

GO ON TO THE NEXT PAGE ⇒

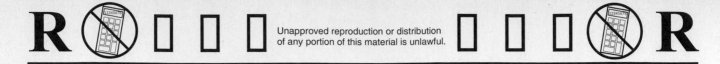
30. The author of Passage 2 most likely mentions that his own genome has mutations (lines 64-65) in order to

(A) emphasize how common mutations are.

(B) prove that most genetic mutations are harmless.

(C) give examples of well-recognized gene mutations.

(D) urge readers to have their genome sequenced.

31. As used in line 67, "novel" most nearly means

(A) innovative.

(B) unconventional.

(C) new.

(D) fresh.

32. The main rhetorical effect of the repeated words in lines 78 to 82 is to

(A) emphasize that the major benefits of genome sequencing have yet to be realized.

(B) imply that further research needs to be undertaken as quickly as possible.

(C) suggest that readers should sequence their genomes immediately.

(D) indicate that the author is concerned about new developments in genome sequencing.

GO ON TO THE NEXT PAGE

Questions 33-42 are based on the following passage

The following passage discusses the famous playwright William Shakespeare's acting career, which was based at the Globe Theatre in London during the late 1500s.

From beginning to end of a Globe performance, playgoers of all classes criticized freely and loudly. They volunteered advice, often hissed, and occasionally hurled an
Line
5 orange or two. When Hamlet admonishes Polonius of the players, "After your death you were better / have a bad epitaph than an ill report while you live," the same warning might have been applied to an actor of his audience. A poor player did not last long and tended to make a loud exit.

That Shakespeare endured the judgment of such
10 audiences for more than 15 years, the better half of his adult life, must attest to his skills as an actor. But his achievement is even more impressive if we consider the fact that performance, in the Elizabethan age, precluded anything resembling an official script. Plays were constantly evolving,
15 not only in response to critical reception but merely to meet the demands of a given moment. If a featured player departed or a fresh face joined the company, if the troupe traveled to a smaller venue or some circumstance limited stage time, if a command performance by the Queen saw the Master of
20 Revels strike obscene material, if costumes or props or even a player were for whatever reason unavailable—in all cases, the actors adapted, or they didn't eat.

For Shakespeare's readers, the benefit of such shifting demands is a surfeit of dialogue that a single performance
25 could never accommodate, in addition to delightful variants across the Quartos and Folios. For the actors, however, the experience must have been hellish, particularly given the fact that the Globe was not a Broadway playhouse but a repertory theater, and members of the ensemble typically performed
30 six different shows a week. Supporting actors often played multiple roles in a single performance, while a leading man like Edward Alleyn could expect to deliver more than 4,000 lines of verse each and every week.

As a matter of reputation, Shakespeare the actor fell
35 somewhere between these poles. While there is no indication that he was ever a box-office draw—that responsibility was left to the clownish antics of Will Kemp and the brooding heroics of Richard Burbage—he was always classed among the principal players of the company that eventually became
40 The King's Men, so named for their final patron. Apparently, the royal affinity suited Shakespeare, for he was said to favor "kingly parts," with legend having Hamlet's father as his farewell role.

If, as it seems, Shakespeare never stole the show, that's
45 its own compliment. To appear before a familiar crowd every day and to succeed without that success constantly reminding everyone that you, the actor, are busy playing a role— indeed, to leave the audience with no other impression than that demanded by inhabiting a fiction—this is the subtle craft
50 of the character actor, an art of remarkable modesty and extraordinary self-restraint. "[L]et your own discretion / be your tutor," Hamlet warns the players:

"Suit the action to the word, the word to the action; with this special observance, that you o'erstep not the modesty of
55 nature. For anything so overdone is from the purpose of playing."

33. Which one of the following best describes the organization of the passage?

(A) The author discusses the conditions facing all Elizabethan actors, then explores Shakespeare's acting style within these conditions.
(B) The author describes why Globe actors were critiqued, then lists the criticisms of Shakespeare's acting.
(C) The author explains the challenges of acting in Shakespeare's era, then discusses the star actors of the day.
(D) The author explores Shakespeare's acting style, then describes the lives of other Elizabethan actors.

34. The author makes use of which of the following to convey his point?

(A) Hypothetical scenarios
(B) Research data
(C) Historical facts
(D) Personal anecdotes

35. Which choice provides the best evidence for the answer to the previous question?

(A) Lines 23-26 ("For … Folios")
(B) Lines 30-33 ("Supporting … week")
(C) Lines 44-45 ("If … compliment")
(D) Lines 53-55 ("'Suit … nature'")

GO ON TO THE NEXT PAGE

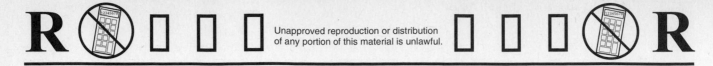
36. It can be reasonably inferred from the passage that Elizabethan audiences were generally

(A) comprised of poor citizens.
(B) large and reserved.
(C) easily entertained.
(D) boisterous and opinionated.

37. Which choice provides the best evidence for the answer to the previous question?

(A) Lines 2-4 ("They volunteered … two")
(B) Lines 7-8 ("A poor … exit")
(C) Lines 9-11 ("That Shakespeare … actor")
(D) Lines 14-16 ("Plays were … moment")

38. Based on the passage, the author would most likely praise which kind of actor?

(A) An actor who is modest about his or her success
(B) An actor who is classed among the principal players of his or her company
(C) An actor who is famous for his or her clownish antics
(D) An actor who is so convincing the audience forgets he or she is acting

39. As used in line 11, "attest" most nearly means

(A) authenticate.
(B) swear.
(C) witness.
(D) testify.

40. As used in line 20, "strike" most nearly means

(A) delete.
(B) hit.
(C) proceed.
(D) inflict.

41. The author refers to Will Kemp and Richard Burbage (lines 37-38) primarily to

(A) suggest that they were better actors than Shakespeare.
(B) list the members of The King's Men.
(C) provide examples of actors who played "kingly parts."
(D) contrast their popularity with Shakespeare's.

42. In lines 53-56 what is the most likely reason that the author quotes Hamlet?

(A) To provide evidence that Shakespeare was a character actor
(B) To demonstrate that Shakespeare hated overly dramatic performances
(C) To illustrate how Elizabethans were renowned for their subtle performances
(D) To support the argument that restraint can be valuable in acting

GO ON TO THE NEXT PAGE

Questions 43-52 are based on the following passage.

The following passage is adapted from an article about the future of food crops and the climate.

For decades, scientists believed that the human dependence on fossil fuels, for all the problems it was expected to cause, would offer one enormous benefit. Carbon
Line
5 dioxide, the main gas released by combustion, is also the primary fuel for the growth of plants. They draw it out of the air and, using the energy from sunlight, convert the carbon into energy-dense compounds like glucose. All human and animal life runs on these compounds.

Humans have already raised the level of carbon dioxide
10 in the atmosphere by 40 percent since the Industrial Revolution, and are on course to double or triple it over the coming century. Studies have long suggested that the extra gas would supercharge the world's food crops, and might be especially helpful in years when the weather is difficult.

15 But many of those studies were done in artificial conditions, like greenhouses or special growth chambers. For the past decade, scientists at the University of Illinois have been putting the "CO2 fertilization effect" to a real-world test in the two most important crops grown in the United
20 States.

They started by planting soybeans in a field, then sprayed extra carbon dioxide from a giant tank. Based on the earlier research, they hoped the gas might bump yields as much as 30 percent under optimal growing conditions. But when they
25 harvested their soybeans, they got a rude surprise: the bump was only half as large. "When we measured the yields, it was like, wait a minute—this is not what we expected," said Elizabeth A. Ainsworth, a Department of Agriculture researcher who played a leading role in the work. When they
30 grew the soybeans in the sort of conditions expected to prevail in a future climate, with high temperatures or low water, the extra carbon dioxide could not fully offset the yield decline caused by those factors.

They also ran tests using corn, America's single most
35 valuable crop and the basis for its meat production and its biofuel industry. While that crop was already known to be less responsive to carbon dioxide, a yield bump was still expected—especially during droughts. The Illinois researchers got no bump.

40 Their work has contributed to a broader body of research suggesting that extra carbon dioxide does act as plant fertilizer, but that the benefits are less than previously believed—and probably less than needed to avert food shortages. "One of the things that we're starting to believe is
45 that the positives of CO2 are unlikely to outweigh the

negatives of the other factors," said Andrew D. B. Leakey, another of the Illinois researchers.

Other recent evidence suggests that longstanding assumptions about food production on a warming planet may
50 have been too optimistic. Two economists, Wolfram Schlenker of Columbia University and Michael J. Roberts of North Carolina State University, have pioneered ways to compare crop yields and natural temperature variability at a fine scale. Their work shows that when crops are subjected to
55 temperatures above a certain threshold—about 84 degrees for corn and 86 degrees for soybeans—yields fall sharply. This line of research suggests that in the type of climate predicted for the United States by the end of the century, with more scorching days in the growing season, yields of
60 today's crop varieties could fall by 30 percent or more.

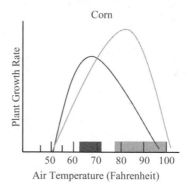

Corn

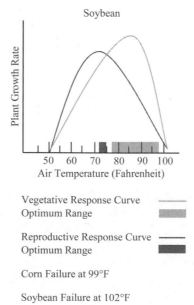

Soybean

Vegetative Response Curve
Optimum Range

Reproductive Response Curve
Optimum Range

Corn Failure at 99°F

Soybean Failure at 102°F

Adapted from 2009 report of the US Global Change Research Program, "Global Climate Change Impact in the United States." Agricultural Research Service, USDA.

GO ON TO THE NEXT PAGE ➤

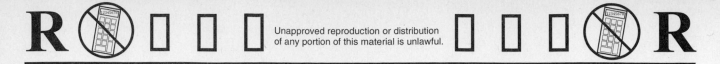
43. The primary purpose of the passage is to

   (A) convince readers to change their behavior in response to new scientific evidence.
   (B) explain how new evidence challenges what scientists previously believed.
   (C) describe the latest experiments being conducted in a certain scientific field.
   (D) summarize the challenges facing farmers in the future.

44. The passage most strongly suggests that scientists

   (A) previously ignored the potentially harmful effects of fossil fuel consumption.
   (B) had expected to observe at least one benefit from fossil fuel consumption.
   (C) underestimated the benefits of carbon dioxide for crops.
   (D) only began studying the effect of carbon dioxide on crops in the last decade.

45. Which choice provides the best evidence for the answer to the previous question?

   (A) Lines 1-3 ("For decades ... benefit")
   (B) Lines 21-22 ("They started ... tank")
   (C) Lines 40-44 ("Their work ... shortages")
   (D) Lines 48-50 ("Other ... too optimistic")

46. Based on the passage, which choice best describes the relationship between older studies about carbon dioxide's fertilizer effect and newer ones conducted by the Illinois researchers?

   (A) The newer studies completely confirm the findings of the older studies.
   (B) The newer studies support the basic findings of previous studies, but show a more modest effect.
   (C) The newer studies totally refute the findings of the older studies.
   (D) The newer studies partially refute the findings of the older studies by showing a much stronger effect.

47. Which choice provides the best evidence for the answer to the previous question?

   (A) Lines 16-20 ("For ... United States")
   (B) Lines 24-26 ("But when ... as large")
   (C) Lines 36-38 ("While ... during droughts")
   (D) Lines 54-56 ("Their ... fall sharply")

48. As used in line 25, "rude " most nearly means

   (A) vulgar.
   (B) inconsiderate.
   (C) unrefined.
   (D) grave.

49. As used in line 43, "avert" most nearly means

   (A) prevent.
   (B) turn away.
   (C) frustrate.
   (D) help.

50. Lines 44-47 serve primarily to

   (A) summarize the techniques used by the Illinois researchers.
   (B) suggest that there is consensus about the future increase in extreme weather.
   (C) describe the Illinois researchers' predictions for the future based on their research.
   (D) provide reasons to support undertaking further crop research.

51. It can reasonably be inferred from the passage and graphic that

   (A) soybeans and corn grow best at very different temperatures.
   (B) constant high temperatures could make it impossible to grow soybeans and corn.
   (C) soybean and corn yields could be increased by very low temperatures.
   (D) soybean and corn yields could be increased by very high temperatures.

52. Which claim about crop growth and temperature is supported by the graphic?

   (A) Soybeans but not corn can grow at 50 degrees.
   (B) Corn but not soybeans can grow at 70 degrees.
   (C) Neither corn nor soybeans can grow at 50 degrees.
   (D) Neither corn nor soybeans can grow at 70 degrees.

STOP

If you complete the problem set before time elapses, you may review your responses for this section.

Do not view or begin working on any other sections.

ACKNOWLEDGEMENTS FOR THIS SECTION

The passages in this section were adapted from the following sources:

W.E.B. Du Bois, "A Negro Schoolmaster in the New South." Originally published in *The Atlantic Monthly*, January 1899.

Franklin D. Roosevelt, Campaign Address at Madison Square Garden, New York City. "We Have Only Just Begun to Fight." October 31, 1936.

Atul J. Butte & Robert Green, "Should Healthy People Have Their Genome Sequenced At This Time?" © 2013 by *Dow Jones & Company*. Originally published February 13, 2013.

John Paul Rollet, "Was Shakespeare a Good Actor?" © 2014 by *The Atlantic Monthly Group*. Originally published April 23, 2014.

Justin Gillis, "A Warming Planet Struggles to Feed Itself." © 2011 by *The New York Times Company*. Originally published June 4, 2014

ANSWER KEY

1. D		27. B	
2. C		28. C	
3. D		29. B	
4. A		30. A	
5. D		31. C	
6. A		32. A	
7. A		33. A	
8. B		34. C	
9. B		35. B	
10. D		36. D	
11. D		37. A	
12. A		38. D	
13. A		39. D	
14. A		40. A	
15. A		41. D	
16. D		42. D	
17. A		43. B	
18. A		44. B	
19. C		45. A	
20. D		46. B	
21. A		47. B	
22. B		48. D	
23. C		49. A	
24. A		50. C	
25. D		51. B	
26. A		52. C	

Full explanations available at ivyglobal.com/study.

Chapter 3
Writing

INTRODUCTION TO THE WRITING TEST

Successful writers spend a great deal of time reading and revising their work. Writers are always looking to make their writing clear and effective while following the standard rules of written English. On the Writing and Language Test, you will be asked to revise and edit text from a range of content areas. Your job is to decide whether passages can be improved by making changes to the words, punctuation, or sentence order.

The questions in this section will test your knowledge of grammar rules and of the elements of effective writing. Parts of the passages will contain errors in grammar. You will be asked to correct errors in sentence structure, usage, and punctuation, which we'll discuss in Section 3. Other parts of the passages need to be revised to better express the ideas of the author. This will involve improving the development and organization of the passage as well as correcting errors in language use, which we'll discuss in Section 4.

First, let's go over some basic facts about the Writing Test.

THE BASICS

The SAT Writing Test is made up of four passages and 44 multiple choice questions. You will have 35 minutes to read the passages and answer the questions in this section. This means that you will have on average less than nine minutes to read each passage and answer the 10-12 questions that follow.

This may seem scary because nine minutes is not very much time! However, the passages are not long, so you should not need to spend more than a few minutes reading the passage.

In Section 2, we will discuss some strategies for reading the passages effectively and approaching the questions within the time limit.

SCORING

The questions on the Writing test contribute to several different scores on the SAT.

First, you will receive a test score for Writing, which only takes into account your answers to the questions on the Writing Test itself. Your Writing Test score will be reported as a number between 10 and 40. You will also receive an area score for Evidence-Based Reading and Writing, which combines your scores from the Reading and Writing Tests. Your Evidence-Based Reading and Writing score will be reported as a number between 200 and 800, and will be half of your total Composite Score on your SAT.

Additionally, your answers to selected questions from the Writing Test will contribute to two cross-test scores, which combine scores across all tests on the SAT to assess your skills in Analysis in History/Social Studies and Analysis in Science. The Writing Test will also contribute to four subscores on the SAT: Command of Evidence, Relevant Words in Context, Expression of Ideas, and Standard English Conventions.

THE PASSAGES

As we just saw, the Writing Test will ask you to read four passages and answer accompanying questions. These passages may be similar to essays you have read in the classroom and are typically four to five paragraphs long. The topics of the passages always include careers, social studies, the humanities, and science.

- The **career passages** usually present new trends or debates in major fields of work, such as health care, technology, or business.
- **Social studies passages** discuss figures, movements, or events from history as well as topics in the social sciences. These social science topics might be drawn from anthropology, psychology, sociology, or linguistics, as well as economics, education, geography, law, or political science.
- **Humanities passages** consider topics in the arts and letters, including figures and trends in fine art, music, dance, poetry, and prose.

- **Science passages** examine ideas, inventions, and discoveries in the natural sciences, which include earth science, biology, chemistry, and physics.

The passages will be 400-450 words in length, broken up into paragraphs. At least one passage will also contain an informational graphic. The graphic may be a table, graph, or chart that conveys information that is related to the passage topic. We will discuss how to approach questions on the graphics in Section 4.

THE QUESTIONS

Unlike on the Reading Test, the passages on the Writing and Language Test contain errors. The questions in this section ask you to revise an underlined portion of the passage in order to make it better.

Here is an example of what a question might look like:

(A) NO CHANGE
(B) resentful
(C) insidious
(D) odious

The first answer choice (NO CHANGE) indicates that the underlined portion of the passage shouldn't be changed. The second, third, and fourth answer choices provide different versions of the underlined portion of the passage. This question is asking you to select the best option for the underlined portion of the sentence, either by replacing it with one of the different versions provided, or by leaving it as it is.

Some questions may ask about one word in the passage, while other questions involve many words or many sentences within a paragraph. Sometimes, questions will ask more specific questions about what needs to be changed in the corresponding section. No matter what the question looks like, it should always be your goal to select the *best* option.

Here is an excerpt from a sample passage along with a guide for locating questions within the passage. Take a look at the way the text and questions will appear on the exam.

Passage Excerpt

The city of Athens, one of the two main actors in the Peloponnesian War, **1** experiencing a "golden age" prior to the war. Athens' access to the Aegean Sea allowed for trade routes to develop, bringing goods, language, and culture to Athenian society. The trade routes **2** ensured that essential grain and wheat were imported while native fields cultivated more specialized crops, such as olives and grapes. At the beginning of the Peloponnesian War, Athenian power was rooted in the nation's ability to defeat **3** enemies at sea. Its power also came from transporting necessary supplies to Athens through the sea trade.

[1] Athens' primary strategy was to avoid land battles and instead rely on this sea power. [2] This strategy served them well during the first half of the war. [3] However, sea power alone was not enough to secure Athens' victory. [4] During the second half of the war, Athens made a series of poor **4** strategic decisions, and Sparta was able to gain naval power and expertise. [5] When a plague broke out in Athens, Sparta had already developed a comparable navy. [6] Sparta was able to threaten and attack the supply of grain and silver **5** going into the port at the city of Amphipolis, delivering a final blow to the Athenian war fund. **6**

How to Read It

Numbers with a square gray background tell you which section that question is referring to in the passage. To answer question 1, you need to look for the underlined section next to the number **1**

The underlined portions of the passage are the sections that you need to revise. In question 2, you need to determine which word fits best in the space where "ensured" is now.

Numbers in [brackets] tell you the sentence number within a paragraph.

If there's no underlined section following a number in a gray box, read the question carefully: it should tell you which part of the passage it's asking about. If it says "here" or "at this location," it's referring to the spot where the number occurs in the passage.

In question 6, you need to determine where sentence 3 should be placed in the paragraph. To find sentence 3, look for the sentence labeled [3] rather than counting them yourself. Answer options may include "where it is now," and phrases like "between sentence 1 and sentence 2" Always use the numbers in brackets when determining which sentences the answer choices refer to.

Questions	How to Read Them

1. (A) NO CHANGE
   (B) were experiencing
   (C) had experienced
   (D) to experience

Looking at question 1, you might be puzzled at first — it doesn't appear that there is any question! When no text appears next to the question number, you should assume the question is asking, "What is the best version of the underlined portion?" Just go back to the passage, look for the **1**, and compare the underlined portion with the answers.

2. (A) NO CHANGE
   (B) protected
   (C) committed
   (D) dissipated

Question 2 also has no "question" attached to it, so again you can assume we are looking for the best version of the underlined section. Here, you want to look for the **2** and compare the underlined portion with the alternative answers.

3. Which most effectively combines the sentences at the underlined portion?
   (A) enemies at sea and to transport
   (B) enemies at sea; it power also came from
   (C) enemies at sea, transporting
   (D) enemies at sea and transportation of

In question 3, you are asked a specific question about the best way to combine two sentences. Again, look for the **3** and compare the underlined portion with the alternative answers.

We haven't reviewed all the rules you would want to know to answer the previous questions, but it is important that you feel comfortable reading the passage and locating questions within it. In case you were wondering, here are the answers:

1. C
2. A
3. A

In the next section, we will introduce some basic strategies you can use to master the Writing Test. We will then discuss some important writing concepts in Sections 3 and 4. Section 3 will present the basic rules of English grammar and apply those rules to identify grammar errors. After mastering grammar, we will move on to discuss effective writing in Section 4. By the end of this chapter, you will be able to correctly revise passages so that they follow the rules of English grammar and effectively express the author's ideas.

SECTION 2
APPROACHING THE WRITING TEST

In Section 1, you saw what the passages and questions on the Writing Test look like. Now, we will discuss some strategies you can use to tackle these passages and questions.

In this section, you'll learn how to read the passages in the most efficient way. Then, you'll learn how to work through the questions and choose the best answer. There are a few different kinds of questions on the Writing Test, so we will discuss how to deal with these using context clues and elimination. We'll also review general strategies for completing the Writing Test, including guessing and time management.

READING THE PASSAGES

On the SAT Writing Test, you will read and revise four passages using your knowledge of grammar and style. While you will read more about grammar and style later in this chapter, you should begin by learning general strategies for reading the passages effectively.

1. **Read passages out of order.** Like the reading passages, the writing passages are not given in order of difficulty, so you can choose the order in which you approach them. It can be helpful to try passages that are familiar or interesting to you first. For example, if you love science but can't stand history, you should tackle the science passage first and save the social studies passage for later. If you do this, remember to bubble in your answers on the correct part of your answer sheet!

2. **Read the whole passage.** The passages on the Writing Test are not as long as those on the Reading Test, so you should not try to "skim" the passages. On the Writing Test, every sentence is important! Even if sentences don't have underlined portions, they may give you valuable information that you will use to answer the questions.

3. **Work on one passage at a time**. Make sure you attempt all questions for a passage before moving on. It is easiest to answer the questions while the passage is fresh in your mind. If you're not sure about a question, circle it in your test booklet and enter a guess on your answer sheet. That way, you can easily go back to the question if you have extra time to check your answers.

You should give yourself enough time to read the passage and answer the questions before moving on to the next passage. Since the passages are shorter than those on the Reading Test, you should plan to spend more time answering the questions than reading the passage.

The following chart offers you some ideas for pacing yourself. Remember that you have 35 minutes for the entire Writing Test.

Pacing Yourself			
Minutes Spent Answering Questions	Minutes Spent Reading	Total Minutes Per Passage	Reading Speed
6.5	2	8.5	Fast
5.5	3	8.5	Medium

If you follow the timing on this chart, you will have a minute left to check over your answers!

NO OUTSIDE KNOWLEDGE REQUIRED

No matter what type of passage you are reading, you may see technical language you don't know. Don't be afraid! The Writing Test does not require any outside information about the topics in the passages. However, you will be expected to use the information the author gives you to decide whether an argument is logical, whether more facts are needed, and whether the ideas and grammar are sound.

Especially on the social studies and science sections, authors may use technical language about an invention or discovery. Often, the author will provide definitions for such terms. For example, the author might tell you that an echocardiogram creates images of the heart. If the author doesn't tell you this, don't worry about not knowing what echocardiograms do. All you need to know is how the word is used in the context of the passage. For example, the author might use the word in a list to describe examples of modern medical advances.

ACTIVE READING

One of your best tools to tackle passages is **active reading,** or using your pencil to mark up the passage. If you haven't already read Chapter 2, take a look at Chapter 2 Section 2 for a thorough discussion of active reading.

Some questions on the Writing Test will ask you about the main point, examples, or errors in the passage. To read actively, you should focus on identifying a main point or conclusion (if there is one) and any examples. Because many of the questions will ask you about errors in expression or grammar, you may also want to mark up places where you know a sentence could sound better.

Some passages will be missing information or have sentences that are in the wrong place in the paragraph. These parts of the passage might sound a little funny to you, so don't be surprised if this happens. If you can identify these types of errors while you're reading, selecting the correct answer choice will be much easier!

You should also identify words or phrases that are commonly confused or written incorrectly. We will go over some of these words and phrases in Section 3 of this chapter.

ANTICIPATE

In the Writing Test, questions frequently ask you to improve sentences, often by removing errors. When you encounter an underlined portion of a sentence, think to yourself: does this sound right? If not, you can **anticipate** what the answer choice is by coming up with your own correct answer and matching it to a given answer choice.

Some errors can be fixed in more than one way, so don't worry if your exact answer isn't there! If you can recognize the error, you can anticipate the *types* of answers that would correct the error.

EXAMPLE

As you are reading a passage, you come across this sentence:

> The goals of the movement were to improve access to education, obtain adequate
> **1** representation, and strengthening community partnerships.

Since a portion of the sentence is underlined, it contains a possible error. When you read the sentence, did you notice that "strengthening" sounded different than "improve" and "obtain"? Maybe you thought of changing "strengthening" to "strengthen." If not, don't worry – you will learn about spotting errors in lists in Section 4. If you did notice that something was strange and changed it to something else in your head, you were using anticipation.

When you read a sentence and notice that something sounds wrong, you can save time by identifying the error and trying to fix it in your head. This way, when you see the answer choices, you can more easily decide on the one that corrects the error.

PART 1 PRACTICE: READING THE PASSAGES

1. On the Writing Test, you will be given four passages. Which passage should you read first?

2. What should you do if you come across some technical terminology in a passage?

3. Practice marking up this passage by locating the main point.

> The city of Athens, one of the two main actors in the Peloponnesian War, underline experiencing a "golden age" prior to the war. Athens' access to the Aegean Sea allowed for trade routes to develop, bringing goods, language, and culture to Athenian society. The trade routes ensured that essential grain and wheat were imported while native fields cultivated more specialized crops, such as olives and grapes. At the beginning of the Peloponnesian War, Athenian power was rooted in the nation's sea power.

4. Can you anticipate revisions for the underlined portion?

Answer Key: Reading the Passages

1. You should first read the passage that either is the most interesting to you or addresses a topic you are already familiar with.

2. Look for context clues to help you determine the meaning, and don't worry about bringing in any outside knowledge. Remember, you only need to know how the author is using the word in the passage.

3. The main point of the passage is: "At the beginning of the Peloponnesian War, Athenian power was rooted in the nation's sea power."

4. The verb form of <u>experiencing</u> makes this sentence incomplete. You could anticipate a revision like "was experiencing."

READING THE QUESTIONS
PART 2

While you are reading the passages, you will come across underlined portions with question numbers next to them. As we saw in Section 1, these numbers signal that the question will ask you to revise the underlined section. You might need to revise words, phrases, or whole sentences in the passage. Depending on what part of the passage the question is asking about, you may want to pick certain questions or skip others.

PICK & SKIP

You do not have to answer the questions in the order that they appear. The most efficient way to go through each passage is to answer some questions as soon as you read them and save others until you have finished the paragraph or passage.

Most questions about parts of speech, punctuation, and sentence combination can be answered right after you read the appropriate sentence. When a word or short phrase is underlined in a sentence, you may be able to correct it as you read it. Try to anticipate the correct answer and then compare it to the available revisions.

However, for other questions you'll need to read other sentences in the paragraph to make your answer choice. For example, you may be asked to select the best version of a word to match the author's tone. You may also be asked to add, delete, or move sentences within a paragraph. Wait to answer these questions until after you have read the whole paragraph.

Finally, some questions are related to the passage as a whole. For example, a question may ask you to insert new information to support the passage's main idea or additional evidence to support a conclusion. Wait to answer these questions until after you have read the whole passage.

[1] Some positive psychologists suggest that happier people become more successful. [2] **1** <u>They suggest</u> that happiness creates success in a number of ways. [3] First, positive mood helps us to develop positive perceptions of ourselves and others. [4] **2** <u>Additionally</u>, experimental research has shown happier people are better at resolving conflict, engage in more social behavior, and have more energy than their unhappier peers. [5] Happier people have higher pain thresholds, a lower risk of cardiovascular disease, and lower blood pressure. [6] There are also health benefits to being happy. **3**

1 The underlined portion in question 1 is at the start of a sentence and has to do with grammar. We can tackle this question right away.

2 The underlined portion in question 2 is a single word, but it signals a transition. This means you should look at the sentences before and after this word in order to make your answer choice.

3. For the sake of the cohesion of this paragraph, sentence 6 should be
   (A) where it is now.
   (B) placed before sentence 5.
   (C) placed after sentence 2.
   (D) deleted.

3 Question 3 asks where sentence 6 should be placed in the paragraph. You need to read the entire paragraph to answer this question.

USE CONTEXT

Questions that require information from a whole paragraph or the whole passage are often more challenging and time-consuming to answer than those which require you to read only a single sentence. While it may seem tedious to read through many paragraphs to answer questions about one part of a sentence, the test writers have actually crafted the test in this way to help you! Full paragraphs give you access to examples of the author's style and clues to the meaning and usage of words.

In other words, full paragraphs allow you to use other sentences in the paragraph to help you answer questions. When you use other sentences in this way, you are relying on **context.** When you look at sentences in context, think about not only that sentence but also the ones before and after it. Context will help you to determine the author's tone and intention, the logical order of the passage, the style of writing and evidence, and the appropriate usage of words or phrases.

EXAMPLE

• As president, he was [1] <u>a garrulous</u> orator. He always struck the right balance between fluid and forceful expression, and his speeches were enjoyable and appropriate.

1. (A) NO CHANGE

    (B) a verbose

    (C) an eloquent

    (D) a bombastic

To answer this question, you need to use context clues to help you. If you only read the first sentence, every answer choice could be correct! To get the context, you need to read the next sentence as well. The second sentence tells you that the president had "fluid and forceful expression," and his speeches were "enjoyable and appropriate."

Now you can tell that garrulous is not the right word because it means extremely talkative, and you want something that means fluid, forceful, enjoyable, and appropriate. Looking at the answer choices, you can see that "eloquent" is the best answer choice because its definition includes our context clues.

You will not only be asked if certain *words* are used correctly in context, but also if entire *sentences* make sense based on their place in the passage. You may be asked to move a sentence to another location or add new information to support an idea—things that you can only do if you have a good understanding of the passage as a whole!

PART 2 PRACTICE: READING THE QUESTIONS

Read the passage below and answer the questions that follow.

[1] Athens' primary strategy was to avoid land battles and instead rely on this sea power. [2] This strategy served them well during the first half of the war. [3] **1** Finally, sea power alone was not enough to secure Athens' victory. [4] During the second half of the war, Athens made a series of poor **2** strategic decisions, Sparta was able to gain naval power and expertise. [5] When a plague broke out in Athens, Sparta had already developed a comparable navy. [6] Sparta was able to threaten and attack the supply of grain and silver going into the port at the city of Amphipolis, delivering a final blow to the Athenian war fund. **3**

1. (A) NO CHANGE
   (B) However
   (C) Additionally
   (D) to experience

1a. Should you answer this question right away?

1b. What context clues should you use?

2. (A) NO CHANGE
   (B) strategic decisions and yet Sparta was also able to gain
   (C) strategic decisions, gaining for Sparta
   (D) strategic decisions, while Sparta was able to gain

2a. Should you answer this question right away?

3. For the sake of the cohesion of this paragraph, sentence 6 should be

    (A) where it is now.

    (B) before sentence 1.

    (C) after sentence 3.

    (D) after sentence 4.

3a. When should you approach this question about cohesion of the passage as a whole?

ANSWER KEY: READING THE QUESTIONS

1. B

1a. You should answer this question after looking at the sentences before and after it since it uses a signal word.

1b. You can use the context clues "during the first half of the war" from sentence 2 and "alone was not enough" from sentence 3 to determine that you need a word that signals change.

2. D

2a. You should answer this question right away since it involves revising an individual sentence.

3. A

3a. You should answer this question after reading and referring back to the whole paragraph.

ANSWERING THE QUESTIONS
PART 3

You should use the approaches we just discussed to read the passages and the questions effectively. Once you have read the passage and the questions, you will be ready to choose an answer. When choosing the best answer, you can also use the strategies presented below, including checking your answer, choosing (A) appropriately, and guessing wisely.

PROCESS OF ELIMINATION

In Part 1, you learned that anticipating answers can help you save time and select the correct answer. Even if you can't tell right away if there is an error in an underlined section or anticipate what the correct version would be, you can still use the **process of elimination** to select the right answer.

You learned about the process of elimination in Chapter 1. Remember, the process of elimination involves "knocking out" answer choices that you know are incorrect so that you can compare those you have left to select the best answer.

On the Writing Test, you can use elimination in two ways. First, you should eliminate answer choices that don't correct the error in the underlined section. Then, you should eliminate answer choices that correct the error but introduce new errors. Because the correct answer has to be the *best* version of the underlined portion, any answers that have grammatical or stylistic errors cannot be the correct choice and should be eliminated.

Let's see how process of elimination can be used to choose the correct answer in the example below:

> The Iron Age and the Middle Ages bookend the classical cultures of Greece and Rome. For over a thousand years, Greek and Roman societies were the center of achievement in the <u>Mediterranean, in fact, the political, philosophical, and scientific</u> roots of our own modern society were formed from Greek and Roman culture.
>
> (A) NO CHANGE
> (B) Mediterranean. In fact, the political philosophical and scientific
> (C) Mediterranean, in fact, the political philosophical and scientific
> (D) Mediterranean. In fact, the political, philosophical, and scientific

In this example, the original sentence is a run-on sentence, which needs to be divided into two separate sentences (you can read more about run-on sentences in Section 3). First, eliminate any choices that don't correct this error. You can eliminate choices (A) and (C) because neither of those choices correct the run-on sentence. Only choices (B) and (D) split it into two separate sentences.

You're left with two possible choices that correct the run-on sentence: choices (B) and (D). Now, check to see whether one of these choices introduces new errors. Choice (B) corrects the run-on sentence by adding a period to separate the underlined portion into two sentences. However, choice (B) also takes away the commas between "political, philosophical, and scientific," which the sentences needs. Therefore, you can eliminate choice (B) because it introduces a new error.

You are now only left with choice (D), which is the correct answer! Choice (D) corrects the original error by separating the sentences without adding any new errors.

CHECK YOUR ANSWER

Once you select an answer, you should go back to the passage and test your choice. Replace the underlined section with the answer you chose and re-read the new sentence. Doing this will ensure that the sentence is now the best version. Remember, the best version of a sentence or paragraph will correct any original errors and avoid any new errors. Check each of your answers before marking them on your answer sheet.

EXAMPLE

> Amelia Earhart was a female aviation pioneer. <u>She set numerous aviation records, she</u> was not able to be located after her plane failed to reach its destination.
>
> **(A)** NO CHANGE
> (B) Having set numerous aviation records, she and her partner
> (C) After setting numerous aviation records, she
> (D) She set numerous aviation records and then she

In the original passage, the second sentence is incorrect because it connects two independent sentences, or sentences that can stand by themselves. We will discuss this topic in detail in Section 3.

To revise the sentence, you will need to change the underlined portion to include a dependent phrase, or a phrase that could not stand by itself as a sentence. Choice (B) does this by changing the beginning phrase to "Having set numerous aviation records," so you may be tempted to choose this answer. Remember to plug it back into the sentence! When you do so, it reads:

"<u>Having set numerous aviation records, she and her partner</u> was not able to be located after her plane failed to reach its destination."

You have now introduced a *new* error in the second half of the sentence. It is incorrect to say "she and her partner was not able to be located" because "she and her partner" is a plural subject and "was not able" is a singular verb. Therefore, choice (B) cannot be the answer.

The correct answer is choice (C) which makes the appropriate revision and does not introduce any new errors. Remember you should always check your answer by inserting it into the complete sentence to check that it is correct in context.

CHOOSING "NO CHANGE"

Much of this chapter will be focused on how to spot and correct errors in the passages on the Writing Test. However, some portions of the passages will need no correction. In these cases, the correct answer will be (A) NO CHANGE.

When questions have (A) NO CHANGE as a possible answer, you should not be afraid to pick it! Many students are hesitant to pick (A) because it seems "too easy." However, there *are* portions of the passage that are already in their best form. Remember to read the underlined portion using context and anticipation and go through the answer choices using the process of elimination. If you do this and still think that the portion is best unchanged, then it probably is! Go ahead and bubble in (A) NO CHANGE as your answer.

EXAMPLE

He was nearly forty years younger, yet his writing <u>was stronger and more popular than his mentor's writing.</u>

(A) NO CHANGE
(B) was stronger and more popular than his mentor.
(C) was stronger and more popular then his mentor's writing.
(D) was more stronger and more popular than his mentor's writing.

This sentence doesn't have any grammatical or stylistic errors, so the original version is correct. However, you also want to check the other answer choices to make sure that (A) is the best answer before you select it. Answer choices (B), (C), and (D) all contain grammatical errors, so they cannot be the correct answer. Therefore, you would choose (A) NO CHANGE.

You may find that (A) is the answer for more than one question in a single passage. Again, don't second-guess your answer just because you think there isn't an error. Follow the strategies above and feel confident in your choice!

GUESSING

In Chapter 1, you learned that there is no penalty to guessing on the new SAT, so you should always guess if you don't know the correct answer. On the Writing Test, you can improve your chances of guessing correctly by using the process of elimination. You are much more likely to guess correctly when choosing between two answer choices than among four!

If you get to the end of a passage and are unsure about one or more questions, make a temporary guess on the answer sheet, and circle the question in your test booklet. Once you have completed all of the passages, you can use any remaining time to go back to your circled questions. See if you can eliminate any more answers and make a better guess. However, make sure you always bubble in your guesses on your answer sheet—you don't want to run out of time and leave a question blank!

PART 3 PRACTICE: ANSWERING THE QUESTIONS

Read the passage below and attempt the questions that follow. For each question, note what answers you were able to eliminate and why. Also use process of elimination for guessing and choosing (A) NO CHANGE. Be sure to check your answer by inserting it back into the sentence.

According to Greek mythology, the Fates had the power to decide a person's destiny. They controlled each person's "thread of life." Clotho was the spinner of the thread, **1** she chose when people were born. Lachesis was the measurer, who chose a person's "lot" in life. **2** With her iconic measuring rod, Lachesis measured the thread of life. Atropos was responsible for cutting the thread of life, choosing the time of a person's death.

The Fates were **3** independent to the other gods and goddesses, controlling mortal threads of life without **4** interference. The Fates are often described as stern and severe. They are usually depicted holding representative items, such as a spindle, staff, or cutting shears. The Fates are referenced in several ancient works, **5** including the *Iliad* and the *Odyssey*, which are works of Homer.

1.   (A) NO CHANGE

    (B) she chooses

    (C) who chose

    (D) also choosing too

Which answers could you eliminate, and why are they incorrect?

2.   (A) NO CHANGE

    (B) With her iconic measuring rod, they

    (C) Her measuring rod was iconic, Lachesis

    (D) Having measured the thread of life with her iconic rod, Lachesis

Which answers could you eliminate, and why are they incorrect?

3.   (A) NO CHANGE

    (B) independent of

    (C) independent with

    (D) having independence from

Which answers could you eliminate, and why are they incorrect?

4.   In context, this word would be best replaced with

    (A) NO CHANGE

    (B) certainty

    (C) aggression

    (D) autonomy

Which answers could you eliminate, and why are they incorrect?

5.   (A) NO CHANGE

    (B) such as the *Iliad* and the *Odyssey*, which are two works of Homer.

    (C) including Homer's the *Iliad* and the *Odyssey*.

    (D) including these two works of Homer: the *Iliad* and the *Odyssey*.

Which answers could you eliminate, and why are they incorrect?

ANSWER KEY: ANSWERING THE QUESTIONS

1. C

   The underlined portion needs to be changed to a dependent clause. You can also get a hint from the sentence that comes after it; the two sentences share the same style. Answer choice (A) and (B) do not make the phrase dependent. Answer choice (D) is redundant.

2. A

   The first portion of the sentence is a modifier, so it gives you information about whatever word comes after the comma. The phrase is modifying "Lachesis," so you can eliminate answer choice (B). Answer choice (C) changes the modifier from dependent to independent. Answer choice (D) is redundant when read with the complete sentence.

3. B

   This question involves an idiom, or a phrase particular to the English language. The correct idiom is "independent of," so answer choices (A), (C), and (D) can be eliminated.

4. A

   To answer this question, you need to look at context, or the surrounding sentence or sentences. The sentence notes that the Fates act "independently." If the Fates act independently, would they control the threads of life without interference? Yes. Even if you didn't know what interference meant, you could use elimination. Certainty means confidence. They would not act without certainty, so you can eliminate (B). Aggression involves angry feelings or acts, so you can eliminate (C). They *might* act without aggression, but this has nothing to do with being independent. Autonomy means "freedom." This is the exact opposite of what we want. If the Fates are independent, they would act *with* freedom, not without. You can also eliminate (D).

5. C

   This question requires you to choose the most concise version. Answer choices (A), (B), and (D) all make the sentence too wordy and redundant.

SECTION 3
SAT GRAMMAR

Before we can talk about grammar questions you'll have to tackle on the SAT, we're going to go through a quick review of basic grammar concepts. Don't be scared by the technical names for these concepts—the SAT won't test you on any technical grammar terms! However, knowing these concepts will help you to understand and correct the grammar errors in SAT questions. In this section, you will review parts of speech and sentence structure, as well as common grammar errors that you might see on the Writing and Language Test.

PARTS OF SPEECH

PART 1

Parts of speech are the types of words you see in sentences. The part of speech tells you what a word is and what it does. In order to learn rules for words and sentences, you need to know how to identify what part of speech you're working with.

NOUNS AND PRONOUNS

Nouns are words that refer to people, places, things, or ideas. In the following sentences, nouns are underlined.

- <u>Friday</u> is usually my favorite <u>day</u> of the <u>week.</u>
- My <u>dog</u> ate my <u>shoes</u> this <u>morning</u>.
- I put on my furry <u>slippers</u>.
- The whole <u>class</u> laughed.
- <u>Ms. Samuels</u> liked my <u>humor</u>!

Nouns can be **concrete** (things you can see and interact with, like shoes and slippers) or **abstract** (ideas or concepts, like "Friday" and "humor"). Some nouns (like "class") refer to whole groups or categories of objects. Others (like "Ms. Samuels") refer to just one specific object. Nouns of this last type are called **proper nouns** and are always capitalized.

Possessive nouns show ownership. Instead of saying, "the sweater that Cindy owns," we say, "Cindy's sweater." Most singular nouns become possessive by adding an apostrophe (') and an "s" to the end of the word, even if the word already ends in "s." For plural nouns that end in "s," you only need to add an apostrophe to show possession. If a plural noun doesn't end in "s," go ahead and add both the apostrophe and the "s."

- The coach's stopwatch
- The boss's desk
- The dogs' leashes
- The children's toys

Sometimes nouns will be replaced by **pronouns**. In the following sentences, pronouns are underlined.

- My sisters don't like to watch TV, but <u>they</u> love when my parents take <u>them</u> to the movies.
- Maybe <u>they</u> will take <u>me</u> too!
- <u>We</u> should see the scary movie.

The noun that a pronoun replaces is called its **antecedent**. The antecedent has to be somewhere close to the pronoun so it can give us the context we need to understand who or what a pronoun is talking about. In the first example sentence above, "sisters" is the antecedent of "they."

In the following sentences, pronoun/antecedent pairs are underlined.

- <u>Marcus</u> never tries any food that <u>he</u> thinks <u>he</u> won't like.
- <u>Claire and Jordan</u> are very adventurous, so <u>they</u> try new food often.

VERBS

Verbs are words that refer to actions or states of being. In the following sentences, verbs are underlined.

- I <u>learned</u> new Spanish words in class, but I <u>forgot</u> them all by the next day.
- I <u>became</u> embarrassed when I <u>couldn't</u> even <u>remember</u> how to <u>say</u> my name!
- Kat always <u>laughs</u> way too hard at her own jokes.
- Brianna, on the other hand, <u>is</u> actually funny.

The two main types of verbs are **action verbs** (words for actions, like "learned," "laughs," or "say") and **linking verbs** (words for states of being, like "is," "became," or "could").

ADJECTIVES AND ADVERBS

Adjectives are words that describe or give more information about nouns—in technical terms, they "modify" nouns. In the following sentences, adjectives are underlined.

- The food in the <u>new</u> cafeteria is very <u>flavorful</u>.

- They only serve <u>raw</u>, <u>organic</u>, and <u>vegan</u> foods.

Adjectives usually come before the nouns they modify or are connected to them by linking verbs. Adjectives should not be confused with **adverbs**, which describe or give more information about adjectives, verbs, or other adverbs. In the following sentences, adverbs are underlined.

- I can run <u>pretty</u> <u>quickly</u> when I put my mind to it.
- My first race went <u>well</u>, but I could have done <u>better</u>.
- Sophia and I went to the play, but it <u>clearly</u> wasn't a date.
- We <u>always</u> see the school plays <u>together</u>.

As you can see, some adverbs end in the suffix "-ly," although many do not. Adverbs usually answer questions about the adjective or verb, like "where?", "why?", "when?", "to what extent?", "in what way?", or "how?".

PART 1 PRACTICE: PARTS OF SPEECH

For questions 1-4, identify the nouns and pronouns in each sentence.

1. If you don't use a clean bandage, that cut will definitely get infected.
2. Vegetarians don't eat meat; vegans also avoid eggs, dairy, and even honey.
3. I can see that this situation is going to become a problem.
4. Michael and Stacey were disappointed when they discovered the mall had closed.

For questions 5-9, identify the verb(s) in each sentence.

5. My dog chases cars for miles if no one stops her.
6. I would certainly know about that.
7. That safari was such a fun adventure!
8. Most people spit out their gum after it loses its flavor.
9. Elisa seems pretty upset, but she won't talk about it.

For questions 10-15, complete parts A and B.

Part A: Identify the adjectives and/or adverbs in each sentence.

Part B: Identify the noun modified by an adjective, or the verb or adjective modified by an adverb.

10. "That floppy hat suits you!" she said sarcastically.

    (A) Adjectives and/or adverbs:

    (B) Words modified:

11. Rory never eats dinner before 8 PM, even if he is incredibly hungry.

    (A) Adjectives and/or adverbs:

    (B) Words modified:

12. I sneezed so hard that I thought I would break a rib.

    (A) Adjectives and/or adverbs:

    (B) Words modified:

13. Lola was astonished the first time she saw a giraffe.

    (A) Adjectives and/or adverbs:

    (B) Words modified:

14. Today's lesson was extremely hard, but I almost understand it.

    (A) Adjectives and/or adverbs:

    (B) Words modified:

15. The disgust that Emilia felt when she found a fly in her smoothie was obvious.

    (A) Adjectives and/or adverbs:

    (B) Words modified:

Answer Key: Parts of Speech

1. *Nouns*: (1) bandage, (2) cut. *Pronoun*: you.

2. *Nouns*: (1) vegetarians, (2) meat, (3) vegans, (4) eggs, (5) dairy, (6) honey.

3. *Nouns*: (1) situation, (2) problem. *Pronoun*: I.

4. *Nouns*: (1) Michael, (2) Stacey, (3) mall. *Pronoun*: they.

5. *Verbs*: (1) chases, (2) stops.

6. *Verb*: (1) would, (2) know.

7. *Verb*: was.

8. *Verbs*: (1) spit, (2) loses.

9. *Verbs*: (1) seems, (2) won't, (3) talk.

10. (A) *Adjective*: floppy, *Adverb*: sarcastically

    (B) "floppy" modifies the noun "hat"; "sarcastically" modifies the verb "said."

11. (A) *Adjective*: hungry, *Adverbs*: (1) never, (2) incredibly

    (B) "hungry" modifies the pronoun "he"; "never" modifies the verb "eats;" "incredibly" modifies the adjective "hungry."

12. (A) *Adverbs*: (1) so, (2) hard

    (B) "so" modifies the adverb "hard"; "hard" modifies the verb "sneezed."

13. (A) *Adjectives*: (1) astonished, (2) first

    (B) "astonished" modifies the noun "Lola"; "first" modifies the noun "time."

14. (A) *Adjective:* hard, *Adverbs*: (1) extremely, (2) almost

    (B) "hard" modifies the noun "lesson"; "extremely" modifies the adjective "hard"; "almost" modifies the verb "understand."

15. (A) *Adjective*: obvious

    (B) "obvious" modifies the noun "disgust."

SENTENCES
PART 2

SUBJECTS AND OBJECTS

Sentences are groups of words linked together to express a complete thought. Every sentence must contain a subject and a verb. The subject is the noun or pronoun that the sentence is about. Frequently, the subject performs the action of the verb. In the following sentences, subjects are underlined, and their verbs are marked in italics.

- <u>Sam</u> *argues* with her boyfriend all the time.
- The <u>world</u> *exists*.
- <u>I</u> *eat* slowly.

Some sentences also contain **objects**. Objects are nouns or pronouns that the sentence's action affects. In the following sentences, objects are underlined.

- I eat <u>cherries</u> every day during the summer.
- Aviva often loses her <u>homework</u> right before it's due.
- He threw <u>me</u> into the lake.

All the objects above are **direct objects**, which means that they directly receive the action of the verb. What do I eat? I eat cherries. What does Aviva lose? Aviva loses homework.

Some sentences contain **indirect objects** as well. These are additional nouns and pronouns that are indirectly affected by the action of the verb. In the following sentences, indirect objects are underlined.

- My sister accidentally gave <u>me</u> food poisoning at Thanksgiving last year.

- Jason's teammates never pass <u>him</u> the ball.

- Have you read your <u>niece</u> her bedtime story yet?

In each of these sentences, both an indirect and a direct object are present. You can tell the two apart by asking yourself which object the verb is actually being done *to*. For example, in the last sentence, even though "niece" comes right after the verb, it is not the direct object. This is because the niece is not what you are reading—you're reading a story! The bedtime story is the direct object, and your niece, *to whom* the bedtime story is being read, must be the indirect object.

Most pronouns in English change form to reflect their role as a subject or object. We call this a change in **pronoun case.** In the following sentences, different forms of the same pronoun are underlined.

- Colin owes a lot of people money, but <u>he</u> knows no one will ask <u>him</u> for it.

- <u>I</u> demanded that my sister give <u>me</u> a great Christmas present after our Thanksgiving fiasco.

Here is a table that shows how pronouns change depending on their position in the sentence as a subject or object:

Subject	Object
I	Me
You	You
She	Her
He	Him
It	It
We	Us
They	Them
Who	Whom

You might find it hard to decide when to use "who" and "whom," since most people use "who" for both subjects and objects in casual, spoken English. In the formal grammar and writing tested on the SAT, however, the distinction between "who" and "whom" is important. "Who" is a subject pronoun, while "whom" is an object pronoun, as in the following examples:

- <u>Who</u> wants to go see a movie?
- Peter, <u>who</u> always asks me to buy his ticket, wants to come along.
- With <u>whom</u> do you want to go, then?

Because "who" and "whom" often appear in questions, you can decide which form you should use by imagining the answer to the question. Here is an example:

For <u>who/whom</u> did you buy that present?

How would you answer this question? You could say something like:

I bought the present for <u>her</u>.

You would use the object pronoun "her" in the answer, which means that in the question, you need to use the object pronoun "whom."

✓ For whom did you buy that present?

Another way you could figure this out is by noting that the pronoun comes after a **preposition**. Prepositions are words like "after," "in," "on," "during," "by," "for," "with," "of," and so on, that usually express relationships in space and time between words. We call any noun or pronoun that comes after a preposition an **object of the preposition**. Pronouns in this position are always in the object case. It is important to note that an object of a preposition can *never* be the subject of a sentence.

VERB FEATURES

Verbs also change their form depending on their context. First, verbs have to agree with their subjects in **number**. Singular subjects require singular verbs, and plural subjects require plural verbs, as in the following examples:

- Most <u>students live</u> together in the dorms. (plural)
- <u>He lives</u> alone in an apartment, though. (singular)

Verbs also change to show their **tense**. This feature of a verb tells us when an action takes place. You must be careful to make sure that verbs in SAT questions are in the right tense. Here are some examples of the most commonly tested tenses on the SAT.

The **present tense** is used to talk about actions that are currently happening, that happen generally or regularly, or that happen in literature.

- He <u>cries</u> every time he <u>goes</u> to a sad movie. (regularly)
- In Oscar Wilde's novel, Dorian Gray <u>descends</u> into a life of sin. (literature)

The **past tense** is used to talk about events that occurred and were completed in the past. It is often formed by adding "–d" or "–ed" to the end of a verb, but some English verbs form their past tense in different ways.

- I <u>unzipped</u> my backpack to find it full of eggs.
- She <u>ran</u> as fast as she could.

The **imperfect past tense** is used to talk about continuous or ongoing actions in the past. It is formed by adding "was" or "were" to the –ing form of a verb.

- When I ran past, you <u>were walking</u> pretty slowly.
- She <u>was looking</u> intently at the paintings.

You can use the imperfect and regular past tenses together to talk about events in the past. This means that both events happened at the same time, or one event interrupted the other.

- We <u>were going</u> to the bookstore when the bicycle <u>hit</u> us.
- My leg <u>cramped</u> while I <u>was swimming</u>.

The **present perfect tense** is used to talk about actions that occurred in the past, but are continuing in the present. It is formed by adding "has" or "have" to a special form of the verb called the **past participle**.

- Lucy <u>has played</u> the cello for years.
- Tomás and David <u>have eaten</u> way too many chicken nuggets.

The past participle is sometimes different from the regular past tense form of a verb. For example, the perfect past tense of "to go" is "have gone," never "have went."

The **remote past** or **perfect past tense** is used to talk about past events that took place before some other event or point in time that is already in the past. It is formed by adding "had" to the past participle.

- The movie bored me because I <u>had seen</u> it twice already.
- You weren't interested in the gossip because you <u>had</u> already <u>heard</u> the truth.

The **future tense** is used to talk about events that will happen in the future. It is formed by adding "will" or "shall" to the verb.

- We <u>will talk</u> about this later.
- Tomorrow I <u>shall be</u> in Aruba.

You may also want to talk about the future but from a time in the past. For example, you can discuss beliefs or thoughts about the future that you had at a previous time. When talking about hypothetical events or future events from a past perspective, use "would" rather than "will."

- Medieval warriors believed they <u>would</u> win if their faith were strong enough.
- I thought that she <u>would</u> get the best score in the class.

Take a look at the timelines below if you get confused about what verb tense to use:

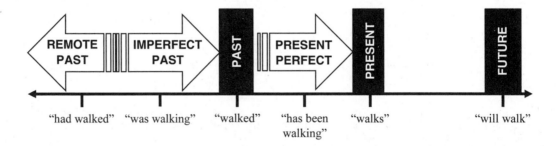

Finally, verbs also vary in **voice**. When a verb's voice changes, the entire sentence gets rearranged. When a sentence is in the **active voice**, the subject is the "doer" of the sentence's action:

✓ My brother ate the cookies.

In this sentence, the subject (my brother) performs the action (eating), and the object (the cookies) receives that action. However, this order gets flipped when we put the sentence in the passive voice. In the **passive voice**, the subject doesn't actually perform the action.

> ✗   The cookies were eaten by my brother.

Now the cookies are the subject of the sentence, even though they aren't performing the "eating"—my brother is the one who is eating. This rearrangement is written in the passive voice. The passive voice may sound more awkward to your ear than the active voice. In general, the SAT will want you to change sentences from the passive voice to the active voice.

CLAUSES

All sentences are made up of **clauses**. A clause is any group of words that contains both a subject and a verb. You might notice that this sounds quite similar to our definition of a sentence from earlier. Some clauses can actually stand on their own as complete sentences. These are called **independent clauses**. However, some clauses cannot stand alone. These are called **dependent clauses**.

EXAMPLE

Here is a dependent clause:

> ✗   Because I run every day.

You may have a gut feeling that something is missing here, like you have been left hanging. Dependent clauses often "feel" incomplete in this way, because they are not full sentences. You can complete them by attaching them to an independent clause:

> ✓   I'm healthy as a horse because I run every day.

Dependent clauses can be quite long, but this doesn't make them any more able to stand on their own as a sentence.

EXAMPLE

> ✗ Though I met up with friends, read a good book, played the guitar, and went dancing.

There is a lot going on in this clause, but it is still not a complete sentence. You can finish it with the addition of a short independent clause:

> ✓ Though I met up with friends, read a good book, played the guitar, and went dancing, I'm still bored.

In sentences with multiple clauses, we use words called **conjunctions** to connect clauses to one another and to show how they are related. In the examples above, we used conjunctions to link an independent clause to a dependent clause. The kind of conjunction that can do this is a **subordinating conjunction.** Subordinating conjunctions make any clause that starts with them dependent. You can see some examples of these words in the following table.

Subordinating Conjunctions	
After	Rather than
Although	Since
As	So that
As if	Than
As long as	That
As though	Though
Because	Unless
Before	Until
Even if	When
Even though	Whenever
If	Where
If only	Whereas
In order that	Wherever
Now that	While

Conjunctions express the kind of relationship that exists between two ideas. For example, in the first sentence above, the use of "because" tells us that there is a cause-and-effect relationship between the two ideas. Running every day is *causing* the speaker to be healthy as a horse. Some questions on the SAT will ask you to combine two sentences, or a sentence and an incomplete sentence, by finding the right subordinating conjunction to link them. To do this, you need to understand the logical relationship between the two ideas and choose the conjunction that expresses it best.

You can also join two related clauses into one sentence with a **coordinating conjunction**. These words can express the relationship between two independent clauses. Here are the coordinating conjunctions:

Coordinating Conjunctions	
For	Or
And	Yet
Nor	So
But	

One way to remember these conjunctions is with the mnemonic FANBOYS (**F**or **A**nd **N**or **B**ut **O**r **Y**et **S**o). In the following sentences, coordinating conjunctions are underlined.

- It's snowing really hard outside, <u>so</u> my driving lesson is cancelled.
- I'm a great dancer, <u>but</u> I don't like going to parties.

Some conjunctions come in pairs, and you have to use both conjunctions together in different places in a sentence. These conjunction pairs include:

Conjunction Pairs	
Both…and	Either…or
Neither…nor	Not only…but also

Here are some examples:

- <u>Neither</u> my mother <u>nor</u> my father wants me to go to the party.
- <u>Either</u> my cat is angry at me, <u>or</u> she is not feeling well.
- <u>Not only</u> do we have to swim ten laps, <u>but</u> we <u>also</u> have to do thirty sit-ups.

The last way you can join two related clauses together is through proper punctuation. One of the punctuation marks that you can use by itself to join together independent clauses is a **semicolon** (;). Here are some examples of semicolons used properly.

- She will definitely win the election for student council president; she has a very bright future.
- My cat is too fat to jump; my dog is too jumpy to train.

You can also use a **colon** (:) to join independent clauses, but only when they're directly related. Here are some examples of colons used correctly.

- I can't come to the party: I have to finish an important project.
- Winter is Casey's favorite season: he loves the sight of fresh snow on the ground.

Though you can't use **commas** (,) alone to join two independent clauses, you can use them along with a conjunction. If you look back at all of the examples of sentences with conjunctions, you'll see that they're used together with a comma.

Commas have some other uses as well. First, you can use commas to set off introductory or transitional words at the start of a sentence. These words, such as "however," "instead," "as a result," and so on, are like conjunctions because they convey the relationship between two ideas. However, they are not used in quite the same way. They typically appear at the beginnings of sentences or after semicolons. Here are some examples:

- I like to eat French fries as much as the next girl. <u>However</u>, I don't eat burgers.
- I declined his invitation to the party; <u>instead</u>, I'm going to go to a movie with some friends.

Commas are also used to separate words in a list of three or more items, as in these sentences:

- Her volunteer trip took her to Guatemala, Honduras, and El Salvador.
- If you are eating spaghetti tonight, you need to start browning the beef, chopping the vegetables, and boiling the water.
- Albert Camus, Jean-Paul Sartre, and Simone de Beauvoir were three famous authors.

Commas can also be used to set off information that is not vital to the meaning of a sentence. Here is an example:

- My brother, who can barely run around the block, definitely won't be running a marathon next week.

If you remove the clause between the commas, the sentence still makes sense; it's just lost some detail.

- My brother definitely won't be running a marathon next week.

PART 2 PRACTICE: SENTENCES

For questions 1-3, identify the subject, verb, and object(s) in each sentence. If there are two objects, specify which is direct and which is indirect.

1. Without thinking, he told Amanda his secret.
2. Rebecca gave me more unsolicited advice.
3. You're baking him muffins for his birthday?

For questions 4-6, choose the correct form for the pronoun in each sentence.

4. **Him/He** and Eva have been dating for almost a year.
5. Between you and **I/me**, this class is pretty much a joke.
6. **Who/Whom** do you work for?

For questions 7-9, place the given verb in the correct form in the blank.

7. Emma and Mina, neither of whom is a student, _____ to the university library all the time. (to go)
8. Because I _____ the book long before the movie came out, I wasn't interested in seeing it. (to read)
9. While I _____ TV, the phone _____ twice. (to watch, to ring)

For questions 10-12, join the two sentences into one grammatically correct, complete sentence using a conjunction. Adjust punctuation as necessary.

10. Laura is lactose intolerant. She avoids dairy products as much as possible.
11. Camels are herbivores. That won't stop them from biting you.
12. I am going to a fancy dinner. I have to change into nicer clothes than these.

For questions 13-15, add correct punctuation within each sentence as necessary.

13. Kate is really good at math however she tends to get anxious about tests.
14. Bronson who is vegetarian likes to sneak a little bacon now and again.
15. Rahul lifts weights runs and does yoga to stay in shape.

Answer Key: Sentences

1. *Subject:* he. *Verb:* told *Indirect Object:* Amanda. *Direct Object:* secret.

2. *Subject:* Rebecca. *Verb:* gave *Indirect Object:* me. *Direct Object:* advice.

3. *Subject:* you. *Verb:* baking *Indirect Object:* him. *Direct Object:* muffins.

4. He

5. me

6. Whom

7. go

8. had read

9. was watching, rang

Questions 10-15 have multiple possible answers. Here are some possibilities:

10. Laura is lactose intolerant and avoids dairy products as much as possible.

    (or) Laura is lactose intolerant, so she avoids dairy products as much as possible.

11. Camels are herbivores, but that won't stop them from biting you.

12. I am going to a fancy dinner, so I have to change into nicer clothes than this.

13. Kate is really good at math; however, she tends to get anxious about tests.

14. Bronson, who is vegetarian, likes to sneak a little bacon now and again.

15. Rahul lifts weights, runs, and does yoga to stay in shape.

COMMON GRAMMAR ERRORS
PART 3

Now that we've gone through the building blocks of grammar that you'll need to approach the SAT, let's take a look at some of the specific kinds of errors the SAT will ask you to correct. We'll begin with some of the more straightforward error types that the SAT will include in its Writing and Language Test passages. Though the SAT will try to trick you by disguising these errors, most of them will be fairly easy to spot once you know what to look for! Many of them will sound wrong to your ear, or they would if you spoke them out loud. Let's look at some of these errors now.

COMPLETE SENTENCES AND THEIR BOUNDARIES

Earlier, we talked about various types of clauses and how you can use and combine them. Some of the errors you'll have to correct on the SAT will ask you to rearrange or combine clauses in order to fix a sentence that is incorrectly structured.

You may encounter sentence fragments on the SAT. A **fragment** is a set of words or clause that cannot stand on its own, but that a writer has tried to use as a complete sentence.

EXAMPLE

> ✗ Emma didn't show up until 9 PM. Even though she said she'd arrive at 7.

Although the second "sentence" has a subject and a verb, it is not complete. You can see that it is a dependent clause. To fix this problem, you can attach it to the first sentence with a comma.

> ✓ Emma didn't show up until 9 PM, even though she said she'd arrive at 7.

Sometimes phrases will occur as fragments as well. A **phrase** isn't even a clause—it doesn't have both a subject and a verb.

> ✗ She said she got stuck in traffic, but tried her hardest to get there. Driving like a maniac and weaving in and out of traffic.

You'll notice that the second "sentence" here doesn't have a subject. In general, if you see a "sentence" whose verbs are all in "-ing" form, chances are there is a problem with it. To fix the sentence in this example, you have a couple of options. Attaching it to the main sentence with a comma makes it clear that Emma was the one driving like a maniac and weaving in and out of traffic:

> ✓ She said she got stuck in traffic but tried her hardest to get there, driving like a maniac and weaving in and out of traffic.

You can also resolve it by making the fragment into a stand-alone sentence:

> ✓ She said she got stuck in traffic but tried her hardest to get there. She drove like a maniac and weaved in and out of traffic.

The second sentence now has a subject ("she") and two verbs that agree with it ("drove" and "weaved"). Both are appropriately in the past tense, since the narrator is describing a completed past event.

Some sentences you encounter on the SAT will be kind of like the opposite of a fragment—they'll try to pack *too much* into one sentence. These include **run-on sentences**, which occur when two independent clauses are mashed together without proper conjunctions or punctuation.

EXAMPLE

> ✗ My cat is very mischievous she likes to climb where she's not supposed to be.
> ✗ My cat is very mischievous, she likes to climb where she's not supposed to be.

These sentences are both wrong because they combine two independent clauses in an inappropriate way. With no punctuation, the sentence is a run-on. With just a comma, it is a **comma splice**. In either case, the SAT will ask you to correct the mistake. Look for multiple-choice options that accomplish the following changes.

You can break a run-on into two sentences:

> ✓ My cat is very mischievous. She likes to climb where she's not supposed to be.

You can also split it up with a semicolon:

> ✓ My cat is very mischievous; she likes to climb where she's not supposed to be.

You can also make one of the clauses into a dependent clause:

> ✓ Because my cat is very mischievous, she likes to climb where she's not supposed to be.

Be especially careful with introductory and transitional words. As you may recall from Part 2, some words, like "however," "consequently," "nevertheless," and so on, must be placed at or near the beginning of a sentence.

EXAMPLE

> ✗ I needed to get a 97 on the exam to pass the course, consequently, I studied for weeks.

This is a comma splice. A new independent clause begins between the words "course" and "consequently," so you must split this sentence with a period or semicolon.

> ✓   I needed to get a 97 on the exam to pass the course; consequently, I studied for weeks.

Verb and Pronoun Shifts

As we discussed briefly in Part 2, some words in English change their form depending on certain factors. We will pay particular attention here to verbs and pronouns. When verbs or pronouns change their form because of other words in the sentence, this is called **agreement**. Some questions on the Writing and Language Test will test your ability to tell if verbs and pronouns are agreeing with other words as they should.

Subject-verb agreement is one of the forms of agreement the SAT will test. As the name implies, verbs must always agree with their subjects. Luckily, in English, this process is fairly simple. As we discussed in Part 2, verbs only have to agree with their subjects in number.

Most verbs do not change form in the present tense, except when the subject could be replaced with the pronouns "he," "she," or "it." For example, see these present-tense forms of the verb "to dance":

To dance (present tense)	
Singular	Plural
I dance	We dance
You dance	You dance
He/she/it dances	They dance

When speaking and writing in English, most native speakers are unlikely to make mistakes with subject-verb agreement. However, the SAT will sometimes try to trick you by putting a lot of extra words between the subject and verb, making it unclear what the actual subject is. You must be a sleuth and find the verb's true subject!

Example

> ?   The artist in the studio by the warehouse full of robots <u>draw/draws</u> all day.

Reading this sentence quickly, you might see the noun "robots" next to the verb "draw(s)" and assume that "robots" is the subject, making the verb "draw." However, the correct verb is actually "draws." You can solve this question by asking yourself: "What noun is actually *doing* the verb here?" In this sentence, who was drawing? The *artist* was. Artist is singular, so the correct verb is "draws."

> ✓ The artist in the studio by the warehouse full of robots <u>draws</u> all day.

The SAT may also try to trick you with subjects that are ambiguously singular or plural. This can happen when parts of the subject are connected by "and" or "or."

Subjects with "and" are always plural.

> ✓ The bowl and the spoon <u>are</u> in the cabinet.

When the subject uses "or," the verb agrees with the *closer* word.

EXAMPLE

> ? Brian or his colleagues <u>is bringing/are bringing</u> donuts.

Since the subject is "Brian or his colleagues," the verb has to agree with the closer part of the subject. In this case, that's "colleagues."

> ✓ Brian or his colleagues are bringing donuts.

Certain pronouns can also make it difficult to figure out whether the subject is singular or plural.

EXAMPLE

> ? Neither of my sisters <u>is/are</u> good at sports.
> ? Each of the princes <u>has/have</u> a chance to take the throne.

In these cases, it may be tempting to use the plural verb form, especially if you think that the plural nouns ("sisters" or "princes") are the subjects. However, those plural nouns are both objects of the preposition "of," which means that they can't be the subjects. The true subjects here are the pronouns "neither" and "each," which are both singular.

✓ <u>Neither</u> of my sisters <u>is</u> good at sports.

✓ <u>Each</u> of the princes <u>has</u> a chance to take the throne.

Here are some other pronouns that are always singular:

Singular Pronouns	
Either	<u>Either</u> of those gifts <u>is</u> a good choice.
Someone	I hope <u>someone</u> <u>brings</u> the cake!
Anyone	If <u>anyone</u> <u>speaks,</u> we will lose the game.
Somebody	<u>Somebody</u> always <u>forgets</u> to close the garage.
Nobody	By the time I got there, <u>nobody</u> <u>was</u> awake.
Everything	<u>Everything</u> in the kitchen <u>seems</u> clean.
Anybody	Let me know if <u>anybody</u> <u>finds</u> my keys.
Everyone	<u>Everyone</u> in my town <u>loves</u> football.

You will also need to watch out for **pronoun agreement**. Pronouns need to have the same number and gender as the nouns they are referring to (their antecedents). The SAT may try to trick you by changing a pronoun inappropriately or by making it unclear what noun it is referring to.

Avoid changing the pronoun you are using partway through the sentence:

✗ If <u>one</u> changes pronouns midsentence, <u>you</u> are doing it wrong.

If you start a sentence with one pronoun, stick with it all the way through.

✓ If <u>you</u> change pronouns midsentence, <u>you</u> are doing it wrong.

Similarly, if you are using one pronoun to refer to something in one sentence, do not change to a different pronoun in the next sentence.

> ✗   If <u>a doctor</u> prescribes too many antibiotics, <u>he or she</u> risks creating antibiotic-resistant strains of bacteria. However, <u>they</u> must also consider the welfare of patients in the here and now.

Instead, use the same pronoun in both sentences:

> ✓   If a doctor prescribes too many antibiotics, <u>he or she</u> risks creating antibiotic-resistant strains of bacteria. However, <u>he or she</u> must also consider the welfare of patients in the here and now.

Note that the correct sentence uses "he or she" as the pronoun. This is because the pronoun is replacing "a doctor," which is a singular noun. The plural pronoun "they" should be used only to replace plural nouns.

If it is unclear what the pronoun is referring to, then you need to fix the sentence:

> ✗   Carlos and Michael were neck-and-neck at the end of the race, but, in the end, he finished first.

Who is "he?" That pronoun could refer to Carlos, Michael, or some other guy who beat them both! Choose multiple-choice options that eliminate these kinds of unclear situations.

Last but not least, watch out for pronouns that are far away from the nouns they are referring to.

EXAMPLE

> ?   The best part of living in a major urban center, like New York or Los Angeles, is that <u>they have/it has</u> a lot of concerts, art exhibitions, and other cultural events to enjoy.

Reading this sentence quickly, you might see multiple cities mentioned ("New York or Los Angeles") and think the pronoun and verb should be plural ("they have"). However, try removing the part of the sentence that is set off between two commas. As we discussed in Part 2, material set off by commas in this way is often additional information that can be removed. You are left with:

> ? The best part of living in a major urban center is that <u>they have/it has</u> a lot of concerts, art exhibitions, and other cultural events to enjoy.

The pronoun refers to the "(urban) center," which is singular! This means the pronoun and its verb should also be singular.

> ✓ The best part of living in a major urban center, like New York or Los Angeles, is that <u>it has</u> a lot of concerts, art exhibitions, and other cultural events to enjoy.

TENSE, VOICE, AND MOOD SHIFTS

In Part 2, we talked about verb tense and voice. Some of the questions on the SAT will ask you to find the correct version of a verb based on its place in the sentence. As you've seen, many sentences involve more than one clause. Clauses presented one after another form a **sequence**, and the verbs in these sequences have to be in the correct tense and voice.

EXAMPLE

Verb tenses reflect changes in time:

> ✓ Patty <u>will begin</u> high school thirty years after her mother <u>graduated</u> from college.

Many tense mistakes involve the past tenses:

> ✗ When the doctor <u>opened</u> the kit, he found that many vials <u>spilled</u>.

If one of the events happened before the other one—it's farther in the past—then you can use the remote past tense to help make the order of events more clear. In this sentence, the spilling happened before the doctor opened the kit, so you should use the remote past tense of "spilled":

> ✓ When the doctor <u>opened</u> the kit, he found that many vials <u>had spilled</u>.

You should also watch out for verb tense in conditional sentences. **Conditional sentences** have a "condition" clause that starts with "if" or "when," connected to a "result" clause that gives the result of the condition. You use conditional sentences to talk about imaginary or possible situations.

If the result clause has "will," the condition clause should use the present tense of the verb.

> ✓ If she <u>trains</u> rigorously, she will be able to run the marathon.

If the result clause has "would," the condition clause should use the past tense of the verb.

> ✓ If she <u>trained</u> rigorously, she would be able to run the marathon.

What if the imaginary part has already happened? If the result clause has "would have," use the remote past tense of the verb:

> ✓ If she <u>had trained</u> rigorously, she would have been able to run the marathon.

EXAMPLE

Let's take a look at another example:

> ✗ If you <u>study</u> more, you <u>would get</u> better grades.
>
> ✓ If you <u>studied</u> more, you <u>would get</u> better grades.
>
> ✓ If you <u>had studied</u> more, you <u>would have gotten</u> better grades.

In Part 2, you also learned about the voice of a verb. You may remember that the active voice is usually preferable. However, the most important thing is to keep the voice of your verbs the same within a sentence—that is, use a **consistent voice**:

> ✗ The clown <u>makes</u> balloon animals for adults, and children <u>are entertained</u> by him.

This sentence uses both the active voice ("makes") and the passive voice ("are entertained"). Shifting voice in a sentence can be confusing. Be sure to keep the voice of verbs the same.

> ✓ The clown <u>makes</u> balloon animals for adults, and he <u>entertains</u> the children.

Another feature of verbs that can shift is the mood. The **mood** tells you if a sentence is a statement, question, command, suggestion, or desire. Just like voice, mood needs to be consistent within a sentence or group of sentences:

> ✗ Bring in the groceries. After that, <u>you should walk</u> the dog.

If the first sentence is a command, the second sentence should also be command.

> ✓ Bring in the groceries. After that, <u>walk</u> the dog.

PART 3 PRACTICE: COMMON GRAMMAR ERRORS

For questions 1-3, rewrite the sentences by joining fragments or splitting run-ons.

1. The dentist was a true perfectionist. Cleaning each tooth with equal care.
2. Derek went to the baseball game, my dad watched my ballet recital.
3. Sometimes we celebrate birthdays in the office, how many paper plates are left?

For questions 4-7, choose the correct form for the verb in each sentence.

4. Either of the costumes **is/are** appropriate.
5. The mammals, including the zebras and the elephant, **requires/require** more food.
6. The director or the actors **is/are** planning the cast party.
7. The first of the finishers **wins/win** a special prize.

For questions 8-11, choose the correct form for the pronoun in each sentence.

8. Even though I will likely win this debate, which involves writing, reading, and acting skills, I am still anxious about **it/them**.
9. Each of the designers has **his or her/their** own logo.
10. At summer camp, **one/you** will choose your own meals.
11. The plane, which was the size of two football fields and had **its/their** wing remodeled, just took off.

For questions 12-16, choose the correct form of the verb in each sentence.

12. Just after Julie had finished the test, she **plans/planned/will plan** her vacation.
13. If she **trains/trained** her dog, she would have a cleaner house.
14. When the bridge closed last week, our commute **was/had been/will be** disrupted.
15. Because we had already eaten breakfast, Charlie **was/is being/will be** forced to eat alone.
16. I would have come sooner if I **knew/had known.**

Answer Key: Common Grammar Errors

Here are some possible solutions, although other options may be correct:

1. The dentist was a true **perfectionist, cleaning** each tooth with equal care.

2. Derek went to the baseball game. My dad watched my ballet recital.

   (or) Derek went to the baseball game, **while** my dad watched my ballet recital.

3. Sometimes we celebrate birthdays in the office. **How** many paper plates are left?

4. Either of the costumes **is** appropriate.

5. The mammals, including the zebras and the elephant, **require** more food.

6. The director or the actors **are** planning the cast party.

7. The first of the finishers **wins** a special prize.

8. Even though I will likely win this debate, which involves writing, reading, and acting skills, I am still anxious about **it**.

9. Each of the designers has **his or her** own logo.

10. At summer camp, **you** will choose your own meals.

11. The plane, which was the size of two football fields and had **its** wing remodeled, just took off.

12. Just after Julie had finished the test, she **planned** her vacation.

13. If she **trained** her dog, she would have a cleaner house.

14. When the bridge closed last week, our commute **was** disrupted.

15. Because we had already eaten breakfast, Charlie **was** forced to eat alone.

16. I would have come sooner if I **had known.**

HARDER GRAMMAR ERRORS

The errors discussed in this part may be a little more difficult for you to spot. In fact, some of them may not sound wrong when you read through them in your head! Nevertheless, our tips will help you detect and correct these errors when you see them on the SAT.

PARALLEL STRUCTURE

Some sentences in the Writing and Language Test passages will be missing parallel structure. **Parallel structure** is a way of constructing a sentence so that different parts of the sentence all have the same grammatical structure. Parallel structure makes long sentences easy to read and gives them a natural flow. On SAT questions, you will sometimes be asked to change a part of a sentence to fix a broken parallel structure. Let's take a look at some examples.

EXAMPLE

> ✓ After a long day, I like listening to music, reading, and talking with friends.

This sentence has three elements listed in a series: "listening to music," "reading," and "talking with friends." Each of these elements is an "-ing" form of a verb: "listening," "reading," and "talking." Because they are all in the same form, this sentence has parallel structure. Here is the same sentence with its parallel structure broken:

> ✗ After a long day, I like listening to music, reading, and to talk with friends.

Now the three elements in the list are in different forms. "Listening" and "reading" are in "-ing" forms, but "to talk" is not. To answer parallel structure questions, you will need to identify the odd man out and find the multiple choice option that puts all the elements in the same form. Let's look at another example:

> ✗ Whether you fight with Ron or giving him the silent treatment, you're going to have to resolve the argument eventually.

This example is a little less obvious than the last one we looked at. What elements are being listed here? If you're not sure, try looking for key words like "and" or "or" that suggest that things are being put together or compared. Here, we find that our options for how to deal with Ron are being contrasted: we can "fight" or "giving him the silent treatment." You may already see the problem: "fight" is a present-tense verb, while "giving" is an "-ing" form. To fix this sentence, let's bring them in line with each other.

> ✓ Whether you fight with Ron or give him the silent treatment, you're going to have to resolve the argument eventually.

This is better! Now both elements being compared are present-tense verbs. Let's try out one more example:

> ✗ Discipline is necessary for anyone who wants to train for a marathon; being motivated is also a requirement.

Where's the parallelism here? This sentence probably doesn't sound obviously wrong at first. Let's look more closely at this sentence's structure. The sentence is made up of two independent clauses joined by a semicolon. The first clause is "discipline is necessary." This has the structure "[noun] is [adjective]." The second clause is "being motivated is also a requirement." This has the structure "[-ing form] is [noun]." We need to put these clauses in the same form.

> ✓ Discipline is necessary for anyone who wants to train for a marathon; motivation is also required.

That's more like it. Now both clauses are in the form "[noun] is [adjective]." There are other ways you could fix this parallelism, but this one is probably the best and most concise.

MISPLACED MODIFIERS

The SAT will also ask you to move or revise misplaced modifiers. **Misplaced modifiers** are phrases or clauses that are separated from the words they are meant to describe, creating ambiguities or mistaken meanings. Let's take a look at an example:

EXAMPLE

> ✗ While biking to work this morning, an odd thought struck Alanna.

What this sentence *means* to say is that Alanna was the one biking to work, but the misplaced modifier "While biking to work this morning" creates the impression that the "odd thought" was actually biking. We know this can't be true, so it must be a misplaced modifier!

We have a couple of options for how to fix misplaced modifiers. The general rule is that we need to reorder the sentence so that the modifier is as close as possible to the word it's meant to modify.

> ✓ While biking to work this morning, Alanna was struck by an odd thought.
> ✓ An odd thought struck Alanna while she was biking to work this morning.

In either case, we've put the modifier as close as possible to "Alanna," the noun it modifies. You'll notice that for these types of questions, you'll often need to change more than just a word or two. Often, entire clauses or the sentence as a whole will need to be reorganized or rewritten.

Usually, these modifying phrases will contain verbs in their "-ing" or "-ed" forms. Here's an example of a misplaced modifier sentence with an "-ed" form verb:

> ✗ Seasoned with many spices, Sam's mouth burned when he ate a bite of the curry.

This sentence makes it sound like Sam's mouth was seasoned with many spices, which is not too likely. The modifier is meant to refer to the hot curry, so we'll need to rearrange the sentence to reflect that.

> ✓ Sam's mouth burned when he ate a bite of the curry, which was seasoned with many spices.
>
> ✓ Seasoned with many spices, the curry burned Sam's mouth when he ate a bite of it.

You have multiple options when fixing a misplaced modifier, depending on how much you want to change the sentence. Some multiple-choice options on the SAT will make relatively minor changes, whereas others will overhaul the sentence. Make sure that the answer you choose doesn't introduce any new mistakes.

LOGICAL COMPARISON ERRORS

Errors in logical comparison can be some of the trickiest mistakes to spot on the SAT. **Logical comparison errors** occur when two unlike elements of a sentence are compared.

EXAMPLE

> ✗ Picasso's paintings are even stranger than Dali.

Though it seems like this sentence is just comparing two artists, it actually compares two unlike things: "Picasso's paintings" (the artworks) and "Dali" (the person). While the artwork might indeed be stranger than the person, we need to compare paintings to paintings.

> ✓ Picasso's paintings are even stranger than Dali's paintings.

We can also write this more concisely:

> ✓ Picasso's paintings are even stranger than Dali<u>'s.</u>

EXAMPLE

Let's take a look at another example:

> ✗ France's poets challenged artistic conventions, unlike writing anywhere else.

This sentence also compares two unlike things: "France's poets" (the people) and "writing" (the activity). This mistake can also be corrected with a minor change.

> ✓ France's poets challenged artistic conventions, unlike <u>those</u> writing anywhere else.

The pronoun "those" indicates that we are comparing France's poets to poets elsewhere. This makes the comparison logical.

CONFUSED WORDS AND IDIOMS

It is well known that English is a difficult language to master. In fact, many English words are confused even by native speakers. Sometimes this is because two words that sound or are spelled the same have different meanings. Other times, two similar sounding words are simply misused.

The table below shows commonly misused words:

	Definition	Correct Usage
Accept vs. Except	**Accept** – to receive or take as payment **Except** – with the exclusion of	We **accept** credit cards for purchases **except** those under five dollars.
Affect vs. Effect	**Affect** (verb) – to influence or change; the object is the thing that is changed. **Affect** (noun) – emotion or feeling **Effect** (noun) – a result **Effect** (verb) – to cause a change; the object is the change.	The rain did not **affect** our crop yield. This was not the expected **effect.** Bill sought to **effect** changes in environmental policy. Laura claimed indifference, but displayed an excited **affect.**
Allude vs. Elude	**Allude** – reference something indirectly. **Elude** – to escape.	In *The Aeneid,* Vergil **alludes** to events in Roman history. In it, Aeneas **eludes** the Cyclops.
Complement vs. Compliment	**Complement** – to complete, make perfect **Compliment** – to give praise	The red sash **complements** the rest of my outfit. I got many **compliments** on it today.
Counsel vs. Council	**Counsel** (verb) – to advise **Counsel** (noun) – advice **Council** – an assembly or meeting	The **council** meets every day. Their job is to **counsel** the king on matters of the State.
Elicit vs. Illicit	**Elicit** – to bring out **Illicit** – not allowed by law	We **elicited** a confession quickly. He was very open about his **illicit** behavior.
Emigrate vs. Immigrate	**Emigrate** – to leave and move to another place **Immigrate** – to come to a country to live there	Programs are available for skilled workers to **emigrate** from Asia. Many have thus **immigrated** to the U.S.
Eminent vs. Imminent	**Eminent** – standing out, prominent **Imminent** – about to take place	Dark, **eminent** clouds filled the sky. A storm was **imminent**.
Gracious vs. Gratuitous	**Gracious** – pleasantly kind, courteous **Gratuitous** – without reason or payment	Molly was a **gracious** host at the party, even when a guest began yelling **gratuitous** insults.
Infirmary vs. Infirmity	**Infirmary** – a place for care of the sick **Infirmity** – disability or weakness	The **infirmities** she was suffering from only increased as she aged in the **infirmary.**
Lose vs. Loose	**Lose** – become unable to find, misplace **Loose** – free, not bound together	I **will lose** my keys if they are tied on with a **loose** knot.
Precede vs. Proceed	**Precede** – to come before **Proceed** – to move forward	A loud noise **preceded** the fireworks. The officers told us to **proceed** with caution.

Principle vs. Principal	**Principle** – a rule or fact **Principal** (noun) – chief official **Principal** (adjective) – most important	Always use the **principle**: "Ask before taking." This is the **principal** way we keep track of items.
Reluctant vs. Reticent	**Reluctant** – feeling hesitation **Reticent** – reserved, silent	A **reticent** person, Jonah was **reluctant** to speak in public.
Respectful vs. Respective	**Respectful** – showing respect or admiration for **Respective** – relating separately	The guests were **respectful** of the rules she had set. They stayed at their **respective** tables.
Than vs. Then	**Than** – a conjunction used to compare **Then** – next or soon after	I told her I liked peas more **than** candy. **Then** she really thought I was lying!
Too vs. To	**Too** – in addition, also, or excessively **To** – a preposition used to show direction toward a point	Please drive **to** the market this afternoon. Make sure you bring the coupons, **too**: you don't want to spend **too** much.
Weather vs. Whether	**Weather** – temperature and conditions **Whether** – which of the two	I can't decide **whether** to go to the park or the gym. I suppose it depends on the **weather.**

There are also some words that are commonly confused but have specific grammatical rules that you can try to remember:

	Rule	Correct Usage
Among vs. Between	Use **between** only for relationships of two. Use **among** for relationships of more than two.	It was hard to choose **between** the red and pink scarves. **Among** the four gloves, the white ones were best.
Less vs. Fewer	Use **fewer** for people or things you can count. Use **less** for things that can't be counted or don't have a plural.	**Fewer** people are opening their own businesses these days. Unfortunately, this means **less** money is being spent locally.
Its vs. It's	**Its** is the possessive form of "it." **It's** means "it is."	**It's** hard to tell when the baby will start crying. **Its** arched brows make it always appear upset!
Their vs. They're	**Their** is the possessive form of "they." **They're** means "they are."	The team practiced all year, and **their** hard work paid off. **They're** going to the championship.
Whose vs. Who's	**Whose** is the possessive form of "who." **Who's** means "who is."	**Who's** going to the store with me? Judy is. Now **whose** car should we take?

Your vs. You're	**Your** is the possessive form of "you." **You're** means "you are."	**You're** too talented to give up acting. Plus, **your** voice is incredible!
Who vs. Whom vs. Which	**Who** and **whom** both refer to people; who is used as subject pronoun, and whom is used as an object pronoun. **Which** refers to things or groups.	**Who** brought the salad? To **whom** should I return the bowl? The bowl, **which** has a beautiful pattern on the inside, looks like it might be expensive.

Another challenging aspect of mastering English grammar is the use of idioms. Idioms are groups of words that have a meaning other than their literal meaning depending on their usage. For example, "put up with" and "do a favor" are idioms.

Idioms, or common expressions, are especially tough to approach because often they don't fit with the rules of our usual grammar. Some idioms involve using different prepositions with the same verb. For example, you would:

- Agree **on** a plan
- Agree **with** a person
- Agree **to** a proposal

Incorrect idioms can appear on the SAT Writing and Language Test. In order to correct them, you should get comfortable with the correct usage of some common idioms with prepositions:

Some Common Idioms			
Able to	Conscious of	Escape from	Opposed to
Believe in	Consists of	Excuse for	Preoccupied with
Blamed for	Depends on	Hope for	Protect from
Capable of	Differ from	Identical to	Recover from
Compared to	Discriminate against	Method of	Relevant to
Comply with	Equivalent to	Object to	Succeed in

PART 4 PRACTICE: HARDER GRAMMAR ERRORS

For questions 1-5, choose the portion of the sentence that contains an error, and re-write the sentence to correct the error.

1. Whether he was running the bases or swam in the pool, Mark was always the fastest athlete on the team.

2. Margie's cookies are better than Ted.

3. At Advanced Learning, we look for students who are bright, dedicated, and have motivation.

4. One requirement of the job is being a team player. Another is resilience.

5. She found France's food healthier than Portugal.

For questions 6-8, rewrite the sentence to correct misplaced modifiers.

6. Having searched through every aisle, the milk could not be found.

7. Running through the woods, the rock tripped Liza.

8. After attending one session, all future sessions were cancelled.

For questions 9-15, choose the correct form for the word in each sentence.

9. In the game show, contestants choose **between/among** three doors.

10. There were too many balloons for such a small party. Their presence seemed **gracious/gratuitous.**

11. When I called the company, the message said **their/they're** representatives were all on hold.

12. The bright red door was one of the **principle/principal** reasons we selected this house.

13. Pasta differs **with/from** rice in both its consistency and taste.

14. Luckily we were not **affected/effected** by the power outages caused by the storm.

15. The pirate promised them great suffering if they did not comply **to/with** his demands.

ANSWER KEY: HARDER GRAMMAR ERRORS

1. Whether he was running the bases or ~~swam~~ **swimming** in the pool, Mark was always the fastest athlete on the team. (Parallel Structure)

2. Margie's cookies are better than ~~Ted~~ **Ted's cookies.** (Logical Comparison)

3. At Advanced Learning, we look for students who are bright, dedicated, and ~~have motivation~~ **motivated.** (Parallel Structure)

4. One requirement of the job is being a team player. Another is ~~resilience~~ **being resilient.** (Parallel Structure)

5. She found France's food healthier than ~~Portugal~~ **Portugal's food.** (Logical Comparison)

Questions 6-8 have many possible solutions. Here are some possibilities:

6. Having searched through every aisle, **I/he/she** could not find the milk.

7. Running through the woods, Liza tripped on a rock.

8. After attending one session, **I/he/she** cancelled all future sessions.

Here are the correct forms for words in problems 9-15:

9. In the game show, contestants choose **among** three doors.

10. There were too many balloons for such a small party. Their presence seemed **gratuitous.**

11. When I called the company, the message said **their** representatives were all on hold.

12. The bright red door was one of the **principal** reasons we selected this house.

13. Pasta differs **from** rice in both its consistency and taste.

14. Luckily we were not **affected** by the power outages caused by the storm.

15. The pirate promised them great suffering if they did not comply **with** his demands.

SECTION REVIEW

PART 5

The chart below reviews all of the grammar terms we discussed in this section. Before you move on to the practice set in Part 6, make sure that you understand all of the terms in this chart. If you need to look up a term again, we've provided the part of this section where each term is discussed.

Grammar Terms		
Term	Examples	Location
Part of Speech	Noun, pronoun, verb, adjective, adverb	Part 1
Noun	Seagulls like to eat bread.	Part 1
Concrete Noun	I baked too many cookies.	Part 1
Abstract Noun	The soldiers showed great bravery.	Part 1
Proper Noun	Florida is warm all year round.	Part 1
Possessive Noun	Can I go to Mark's house?	Part 1
Pronoun	They brought flowers from the garden.	Part 1
Subject Pronoun	We saw Anisha at the party.	Part 1
Object Pronoun	Anisha saw us, too.	Part 1
Antecedent	My sister says she is scared of heights.	Part 1
Verb	She designs wedding gowns.	Part 1
Action Verb	We drive to New York every year.	Part 1
Linking Verb	Mona is a wonderful actress.	Part 1
Adjective	Jorge is a good actor.	Part 1
Adverb	Jorge performed well.	Part 1
Direct Object	Please hand Liam the pencil.	Part 2
Indirect Object	Please hand Liam the pencil.	Part 2
Preposition	The bat is still in the cave.	Part 2
Object of the Preposition	The bat is still in the cave.	Part 2
Present Tense	The band plays only cover songs.	Part 2
Past Tense	We clapped when the curtain closed.	Part 2
Imperfect Past Tense	The journalist was searching for a story.	Part 2
Present Perfect Tense	Michael has played tennis for years.	Part 2

Remote Past Tense	I wasn't hungry because I <u>had eaten</u> earlier.	Part 2
Past Participle	They have already <u>gone</u> to the store.	Part 2
Future Tense	The President <u>will speak</u> at noon.	Part 2
Active Voice	The chemicals <u>reacted</u> immediately.	Part 2
Passive Voice	She <u>was discovered</u> by the detective.	Part 2
Independent Clause	Pigs can fly	Part 2
Dependent Clause	When pigs can fly	Part 2
Conjunction	We bought ham <u>and</u> cheese.	Part 2
Subordinating Conjunction	<u>Even though</u> she lost, we had a party.	Part 2
Coordinating Conjunction	She practices a lot, <u>but</u> she never gets better.	Part 2
Conjunction Pairs	<u>Neither</u> my sister <u>nor</u> my brother found out.	Part 2
Fragment	Although he said he would.	Part 3
Phrase	Feeling happy.	Part 3
Run-on	You should take an umbrella it's raining.	Part 3
Comma Splice	I am a calm person, I am not when I fly.	Part 3
Subject-Verb Agreement	<u>Quinn and her sister are</u> at the pool.	Part 3
Pronoun Agreement	<u>Each student</u> should say <u>his or her</u> name.	Part 3
Conditional Sentence	If you study hard, you will succeed!	Part 3
Parallel Structure	We enjoy jogging, hiking, and swimming.	Part 4
Misplaced Modifier	Rushing to work, a bicycle hit Ron.	Part 4
Logical Comparison	Timmy's bike is faster than Donald's bike.	Part 4
Idiom	The Senator is <u>opposed to</u> the bill.	Part 4

PRACTICE SET

PART 6

For questions 1-30, choose the best version of the underlined portion of the sentence. Some sentences may not require a change. If a sentence is correct as written, mark it as (A) NO CHANGE.

1. The other writers and me went to lunch to celebrate the launch of our new book.

   (A) NO CHANGE

   (B) Me and the other writers

   (C) The other writers and I

   (D) I and the others who were writing

2. I would have arrived at work on time if I was waking up earlier.

   (A) NO CHANGE

   (B) will wake up earlier.

   (C) wake up earlier.

   (D) had woken up earlier.

3. When one is preparing to apply to college, you should get started early.

   (A) NO CHANGE

   (B) college, one should

   (C) college, you shall

   (D) college; you should

4. Without pencils, erasers, or calculators, neither Karl or Desmond could complete the exam.

   (A) NO CHANGE

   (B) neither Karl or Desmond couldn't complete

   (C) neither Karl or Desmond had completed

   (D) neither Karl nor Desmond could complete

5. The votes suggest that the crowd <u>likes Donna's pies more than Theresa</u>.

(A) NO CHANGE

(B) like Donna's pies more than Theresa.

(C) like Donna's pies more than Theresa's pies.

(D) likes Donna's pies more than Theresa's pies.

6. Mr. and Mrs. Piston came to my <u>recital, and they brought</u> flowers.

(A) NO CHANGE

(B) recital and they bring

(C) recital; bringing

(D) recital that brought

7. Although Evan usually hates <u>vegetables, he didn't object with</u> a salad for lunch.

(A) NO CHANGE

(B) vegetables; he didn't object to

(C) vegetables, he didn't object to

(D) vegetables he didn't object to

8. All of the band members <u>except the singer is joining us</u> for dinner after the show.

(A) NO CHANGE

(B) accept the singer is joining us

(C) accept the singer are joining us

(D) except the singer are joining us

9. When I entered the room, I <u>noticed there was an argument beginning among</u> the caterer and the event planner.

(A) NO CHANGE

(B) noticed there was an argument beginning between

(C) was noticing there was an argument beginning among

(D) was noticing there was an argument beginning between

10. Everyone <u>likes to play</u> Monopoly.

(A) NO CHANGE

(B) like to play

(C) liking to play

(D) to like playing

11. The movie features a superhero <u>who's superpowers include healing, flying, and reading minds</u>.

(A) NO CHANGE

(B) who's superpowers include healing, flying, and the ability to read minds.

(C) whose superpowers include healing, flying, and reading minds.

(D) whose superpowers include healing, flying, and the ability to read minds

12. Sometimes you are presented with a difficult <u>decision; one must start over or attempt</u> to correct the mistake.

(A) NO CHANGE

(B) decision, one must start over or attempt

(C) decision; you must start over or attempt

(D) decision; you must start over nor attempt

13. She wanted to go to <u>the movies the theater was closed</u> for renovation.

(A) NO CHANGE

(B) the movies, but the theater was closed

(C) the movies: the theater was closed

(D) the movies, the closed theater

14. <u>Oprah Winfrey, a popular talk show host</u> who has numerous television shows.

(A) NO CHANGE

(B) Oprah Winfrey, who is a popular talk show host

(C) Oprah Winfrey is a popular talk show host

(D) Oprah Winfrey a popular talk show host

15. Walking to the store, <u>the rain soaked Yasmine</u>.

(A) NO CHANGE

(B) store, the rain has soaked Yasmine.

(C) store, Yasmine soaked the rain.

(D) store, Yasmine was soaked by the rain.

16. <u>If anyone needs me,</u> I will be at the library!

    (A) NO CHANGE

    (B) If anyone need me,

    (C) If anyone needs I

    (D) If anyone need I

17. I want to attend Mariah's graduation <u>party, I promised</u> I would babysit for my neighbors this weekend.

    (A) NO CHANGE

    (B) party however I promised

    (C) party but however I promised

    (D) party; however, I promised

18. It's easier to learn to play an instrument <u>than teaching someone else how to play.</u>

    (A) NO CHANGE

    (B) than teaching someone else playing.

    (C) than to teach someone else how to play.

    (D) than to teach someone else playing.

19. She told me to <u>preheat the oven, stir the mix, and</u> grease the pan.

    (A) NO CHANGE

    (B) preheat the oven; stir the mix; and

    (C) preheat the oven, stirring the mix, and

    (D) preheat the oven and stir in the mix and

20. I brought the football for Bobby. <u>For who did you bring</u> the Frisbee?

    (A) NO CHANGE

    (B) For whom did you bring

    (C) For whom did you brought

    (D) For who have you brought

21. <u>Someone in the stands blows</u> a whistle every time the pitcher winds up.

    (A) NO CHANGE

    (B) Someone in the stands blow

    (C) Someone in the stands blowing

    (D) Someone in the stands, blowing

22. We can judge the quality of an invention by <u>its affect on society</u>.

    (A) NO CHANGE

    (B) by it's affect on society

    (C) by its effect towards society

    (D) by its effect on society

23. Also added to the timeline <u>were a project involving</u> renovations of sidewalks throughout the city.

    (A) NO CHANGE

    (B) was a project involving

    (C) was a project that was involving

    (D) were a project that was involving

24. While some think it is only a mythical object, the Holy Grail <u>has fascinated historians because of it's lasting</u> presence in art and literature.

    (A) NO CHANGE

    (B) has fascinated historians because of its

    (C) have fascinated historians because of it's

    (D) have fascinated historians because of its

25. Although Tiffany's ideas were promising, a complete <u>solution alluded her.</u>

    (A) NO CHANGE

    (B) solution alluded to her.

    (C) solution eluded her.

    (D) solution eluded from her.

26. <u>Since he is too tired to attend</u> the meeting, the other members gave his presentation.

(A) NO CHANGE

(B) Since he is too tired attending

(C) Since he was too tired attending

(D) Since he was too tired to attend

27. Tara wasn't used to receiving <u>compliments on her clothes; she</u> never considered herself especially stylish.

(A) NO CHANGE

(B) compliments on her clothes, she never

(C) complements on her clothes; she never

(D) complements on her clothes, she never

28. After hours of needless arguing, <u>the friends agreed with</u> a plan for the surprise party.

(A) NO CHANGE

(B) the friends agreeing with

(C) the friends agreed on

(D) the friends had agreed on

29. Every one of the volunteers <u>collect money for charity</u> throughout the year.

(A) NO CHANGE

(B) collects money for charity

(C) collect money, for charity

(D) collects money, for charity

30. If a teacher makes a mistake, <u>they should correct</u> it immediately.

(A) NO CHANGE

(B) they should have corrected

(C) he or she should correct

(D) he or she should have corrected

ANSWER KEY: PRACTICE SET

1. C
2. D
3. B
4. D
5. D
6. A
7. C
8. D
9. B
10. A
11. C
12. C
13. B
14. C
15. D
16. A
17. D
18. C
19. A
20. B
21. A
22. D
23. B
24. B
25. C
26. D
27. A
28. C
29. B
30. C

SECTION 4
EXPRESSING IDEAS

Now that we have reviewed some common concepts of grammar you will encounter on the SAT, let's take a look at the other concepts you will need to know. On the Writing Test, you will also revise the passages so that each sentence best expresses the ideas of the author. For example, passages will include errors in word usage or ordering of evidence. In this section, we will review the development of ideas, graphical representation of evidence, logical organization of ideas, and effective use of language.

DEVELOPMENT OF IDEAS
PART 1

To get his or her point across, the author needs to use proper development of ideas. This includes presenting an inclusive main point, relevant supporting information, and accurate graphical interpretations. Effective development is key to any passage; questions of this type require you to use both reading and editing skills.

PASSAGE STYLES

The author may develop his or her ideas differently depending on the style of her passage. Therefore, it will be helpful for you to understand and identify the different styles an author may use. Each passage might be informative, argumentative, or narrative in style.

Informative passages focus on presenting accurate information to the reader. Passages of this style may include summaries of data, research, or instructions. **Argumentative passages** involve the author taking a position and backing up this claim with evidence or logic. Passages of this style will try to convince the reader of the truth of an argument and will present facts as evidence.

Narrative passages present an experience and use periods of time to tell a story. Passages of this style may include autobiographical, biographical, or fictional writing, and often incorporate **anecdotes**, short and amusing or interesting stories about an incident or person.

Here is a summary of these passage styles:

Passage Styles		
Style	Goal	Examples
Informative	Give accurate information	Research, summaries, instructions
Argumentative	Persuade the reader	Opinions, debates, editorials
Narrative	Tell a story	Biographies, fiction, anecdotes

MAIN POINT

Every passage and paragraph should have a main point. The **main point** is the central idea, claim, or counterclaim that the author is trying to get across. The College Board calls the main point of a passage the "**proposition**."

Some questions will ask you to edit the sentence that contains the main point so that it better represents the central idea of the author. However, some passages or paragraphs are missing a main point altogether. In these passages, one of the questions will likely ask you to choose the best version of the main point from four options not seen in the passage.

Main points should:

✓ Express the core idea of the author

✓ Summarize the conclusion drawn from the information in the passage or paragraph

✓ Do so clearly and concisely

✓ Maintain the tone of the author and style of the passage

✓ Present new information that is not mentioned anywhere else in the passage

EXAMPLE

> After publishing *The Catcher in the Rye,* J.D. Salinger faced much unwanted attention and public scrutiny. The media was too harsh in questioning and commenting on his work and personal life. He also became tied up in unfair legal battles which further exposed aspects of his personal life. Over time, Salinger became more withdrawn from society and published less frequently.

Now, imagine you are asked to come up with a main point for this paragraph. Who is the passage about? What conclusion does the information support? Does the author give opinions, facts, or both?

The paragraph is about J.D. Salinger. The author mentions "unwanted attention" that Salinger received and gives examples of some problems he faced because of this attention. The main point of this paragraph might sound something like, "The attention from J.D. Salinger's success led to great personal and professional suffering."

SUPPORT AND FOCUS

In any passage, the main point is not enough to make a paragraph complete. Each paragraph will have **supporting information** that strengthens the main point. In some questions, you will be asked to support claims with additional evidence. Often, this means adding relevant information to strengthen a claim or clarify a point. Here are some types of support.

Types of Support		
Type	Explanation	Example
Facts	True and declarative statements	The first president of the United States was George Washington.
Statistics	Facts presented in numerical form	About 71% of the Earth's surface is covered with water.
Examples	Illustrations of the point the author is trying to make	Jack often gets into trouble. He was grounded just last week!
Opinions	Views of the author or an expert, not necessarily using facts	New York City is too crowded to be enjoyable.
Anecdotes	Personal stories or memories	Even though it was small, our family's lake house was my favorite place.

The style of writing often determines what type of evidence the author will use. Since argumentative passages use facts as evidence to back up their opinions, they may need statistical and factual evidence to support a claim. Informative passages often require the addition of definitions or explanations to increase clarity. Narrative style passages sometimes need an added anecdote or example to effectively portray a character or scene.

In these questions, the key idea is *relevant* information. Most of the answer choices will provide new facts, but the correct answer choice will contain evidence that best supports the sentence or sentences before it.

Sometimes a paragraph will contain an error in the development of evidence. For example, a sentence may be included that provides irrelevant facts or evidence that goes against the main point or goal of the passage. This type of sentence takes away from the **focus** of the paragraph, or its central point. In order to correct this error, you should choose to delete the sentence that provides irrelevant information.

Let's look at an example to see how adding, deleting, or revising sentences can help develop the author's ideas:

> [1] The Roman economy was the glue that held the empire together. [2] The economy allowed for the movement of people and goods, the primary drivers of success. [3] The Roman economy can be seen as both sophisticated and primitive. [4] However, they were limited by the slow modes of transportation available in a time before gasoline.

You may have noticed that something seems to be missing between sentences three and four. In sentence three, we are told that the Roman economy was "both sophisticated and primitive." However, sentence four only discusses a "primitive" aspect of the economy. So in this case, the best version of this paragraph would include a sentence that discusses a "sophisticated" aspect of the economy, such as:

> The Romans were able to move huge quantities of goods remarkable distances.

PART 1 PRACTICE: DEVELOPMENT OF IDEAS

Read the passage excerpt below and answer the questions that follow.

> Have you ever heard that elephants never forget? Well, elephants aren't the only animals with exceptional memories. When compared with other bird species, the Clark's Nutcracker has been determined to have remarkable memory skills. Scientists have studied the Clark's Nutcracker and found that they perform better on memory tasks and have larger hippocampi, regions of the brain that are associated with memory. Why does the Clark's Nutcracker have such a good memory? **1** It seems that Clark's Nutcrackers have developed exceptional memory skills in order to survive in their environment.
> [1] The environment of Clark's Nutcrackers forces them to store seeds away for the winter months. [2] Clark's Nutcrackers mainly live in mountains and rely on seeds of pines as their primary food source. [3] Nutcrackers typically nest in the early spring. [4] Clark's Nutcrackers collect and store large amounts of seeds in the ground during the growing season. [5] They then recover them with incredible accuracy when winter arrives. **2** [6] Without these stored supplies - and the memories of where they are located - the nutcrackers wouldn't survive. **3**

1. Which choice most effectively establishes the main point of the passage?

   (A) NO CHANGE

   (B) Not only do Clark's Nutcrackers have better memories, they also have larger brain structures that support memory.

   (C) Years of practice on experimental memory tasks have allowed the Clark's Nutcracker to develop their exceptional memories.

   (D) Scientists argue that the memory of the nutcrackers affects their ability to reproduce.

   What clues from the passage helped you determine the best main point?

2. Which choice, inserted here, most effectively adds support for the statement in sentence 5?

   (A) Winter temperatures can drop below freezing on the mountainside.

   (B) Nutcrackers also collect peanuts as a potential food source.

   (C) Typically, the Nutcrackers recover over 70% of their stored pine seeds.

   (D) Nutcrackers usually leave about ten seeds at each storage site.

   What type of support (fact, statistic, example, opinion, anecdote) is your answer?

3. To improve the focus of this paragraph, which sentence should be deleted?

   (A) Sentence 1

   (B) Sentence 3

   (C) Sentence 5

   (D) Sentence 6

ANSWERS: DEVELOPMENT OF IDEAS

1. A

    Paragraph 1 introduces the topic of the passage – memory in Clark's Nutcrackers. Paragraph 2 discusses how and why the nutcrackers have developed this memory to store seeds. Additionally, paragraph 1 asks the question, "Why does the Clark's Nutcracker have such a good memory?" The main point should answer this question.

2. C

    The correct answer (C) is a statistic. (A), (B), and (D) are facts, but they do not provide relevant support for the "accuracy" mentioned in sentence 5.

3. B

    The correct answer is (B). Information about when the nutcrackers nest isn't relevant to the main point of the paragraph, which is to explain how the nutcrackers' environment forced them to develop exceptional memories in order to survive. (A), (C), and (D) all serve to develop the idea that the environment of Clark's Nutcrackers helped force them to develop memories by showing the need to store food in order to survive, and showing how their memories help them to recover their stored food.

GRAPHICS
PART 2

Some passages will include **graphical representations** of evidence, which may include graphs, charts, tables, or other types of graphics. When passages contain a graphic, it will be your job to choose the answer that best translates the graphic into text. You can use the following checklist of questions to make sure you're properly reading a graph, chart, or table on the Writing Test.

✓ *What are the titles?*

   Titles tell you what the graphic is talking about. Titles may tell you who the data is about, what was measured, or when the data was collected. Sometimes titles will have subtitles that tell you more detailed information about the graphic or tell you what a portion of a table represents. Be sure to read the titles first to make sure you know what the graphic is about.

✓ *On a graph, what are the axes?*

   The two major vertical and horizontal lines on a graph are its **axes**. Axes tell you what two things the graph is measuring—the **variables**. Axes may represent time, quantities, prices, or numbers of people. After looking at the title, make sure to find the axes and locate what is being measured in the graph.

✓ *What are the units?*

   Units tell you how the graphic is measuring the variables. They are usually located next to or underneath titles or axes. We use units for numbers (hundreds, thousands, or millions), but also for things like temperature (Fahrenheit or Celsius). You shouldn't assume that units will be in the most common form, so always check what units the graphic is using. The units used in the graphic must be the same as in the correct answer choice. If not, you should check to make sure they were converted correctly.

   To represent large numbers without cluttering a graphic, authors may use different units to show the same information. For example, if the data is in thousands, the author may use the unit "thousands" to show that without changing the numbers on the graphic itself. In this case, "1" would really mean "1,000."

✓ *Is there a legend?*

Some graphs and charts have a legend. The **legend** tells you what different colors, shadings, shapes, or lines represent. Legends are often located on the bottom or side of the graphic. You should locate the legend before you look at the data so that you have an idea of what different designs represent.

SAMPLE GRAPHIC

Let's use the checklist on the following sample graphic:

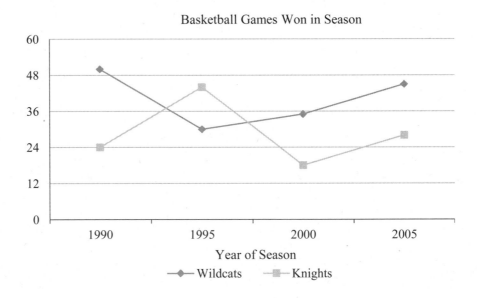

Basketball Games Won in Season

✓ *What are the titles?*

On this graph, the title is located at the top: "Basketball Games Won in Season." This lets you know we're looking at numbers of basketball games won.

✓ *On a graph, what are the axes?*

The horizontal (bottom) axis shows the years 1990, 1995, 2000, and 2005. This tells you that any data that is above that point can be matched with the given year. The vertical (side) axis has the numbers from zero to sixty. You can tell from the title that these numbers represent the number of games won.

✓ *What are the units?*

On the horizontal axis, the units are in years. You know this because of the label "Year of Season" below the axis. On the vertical axis, we are not given a unit label, so you can assume these are regular numbers.

✓ *Is there a legend?*

On this graph, the legend is located at the bottom. The legend tells you that the darker line represents the Wildcats and that the lighter line represents the Knights.

Once you know what the graphic is showing, you can use it to choose the correct answer choice. Questions on graphics will ask you to select the choice that contains accurate data based on the given graphic. This may seem simple enough, but graphics can be tricky! Often, graphics contain a lot more information than you need and can be easily misinterpreted. Let's discuss some common misinterpretations of graphics that you'll want to avoid.

TOTALS AND PARTS

Charts and tables will sometimes give you information about many groups. For example, pie charts may break up one large group into many subgroups and present numerical information about the subgroups. Tables may also present information about large groups and smaller subgroups or totals and parts. It is important to notice what the groups represent in a table.

EXAMPLE

Number of Families		
1 or more children	2 or more children	3 or more children
35,218	20,069	7,122

In this chart, you can see the title "Number of families" in the first row. In the second row, you can see the groups about which the chart is giving information. At first glance, you may assume that 35,218 families have one child, 20,069 have two children, and 7,122 have three children. However, the titles include "or more." That means that families in the "1 or more children" group can have one, two, three, or more children! Likewise, the second group can have two, three, or more children.

Based on the table, the statement below would be correct.

✓ According to census reports, the number of families with at least two children was 20,069.

However, the statement below would be incorrect:

✗ According to census reports, the number of families with exactly two children exceeded 20,000.

The title "2 or more children" explains that the number of families in this category is 20,069, but remember that means the families could be made up of two, three, or more children. This table does not list the number of families that only have two children.

EXAMPLE

Graphs can also use totals and parts. The graph below shows months within seasons:

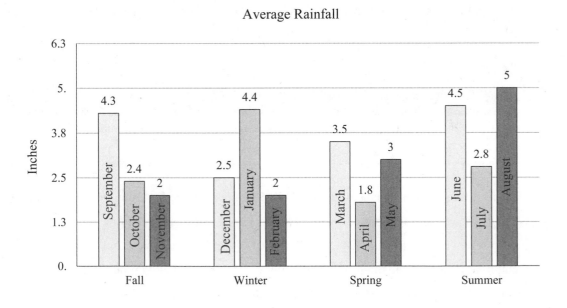

Based on the graph, the statement below would be correct.

✓   In the summer, July is the driest month.

However, the statement below would be incorrect:

✗   July is the driest month of the year.

NUMBERS AND PERCENTAGES

In the graphs above, the author used numbers as the main variable. You saw fifty baseball games won, 7,122 families, and four inches of rainfall. Numbers in graphics are usually straightforward, but there are a few things you want to remember:

- In graphics that represent increases or decreases, you cannot make assumptions about the totals. For example, if a graph shows that a kindergarten class increased its enrollment by five students, you cannot assume anything about the total enrollment after the increase unless you are given more information.
- When two variables increase in number, you cannot assume they are related or that one causes the other. For example, a graph may show that both test scores and candy bars sold in the cafeteria increased by fifty this month. You cannot assume that eating candy bars caused the higher test scores (even though you might want to!).

Sometimes the author will show information using percentages. **Percentages** are another way to write fractions, or parts of a whole. In graphs, percentages are often used to show changes, like increases or decreases. There are a few important things you want to remember about percentages:

- Percentages and numbers are different. Percentages represent a part of a total, but the total does not have to be one hundred. You know that having 10% is not the same as having ten, but this can be easily misinterpreted on graphs.
- In graphics that represent percentage increases or decreases, you cannot make assumptions about the numbers or totals without additional information.

- Large percentages do not always mean large numbers. For example, 90% may seem like a large percentage, but 90% of 10 is only 9. Likewise, large numbers do not always mean large percentages. For example, 800 may seem like a large number, but 800 is only 1% of 80,000.

Remember that if the units on an axis or in a title are percentages, you should keep this fact in mind when looking at your answer choices.

EXAMPLE

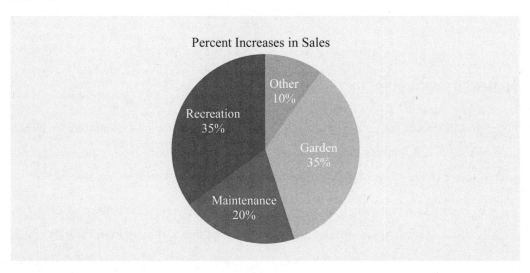

In this graph, you can tell from the title that the numbers in the graph represent *percentages*. Additionally, the title includes "increases." This means that the numbers in the graph represent the percent *increases* in sales, not the percent of the total sales.

Based on the graph, the statement below would be correct.

> ✓ Recreation and Garden supplies saw the largest increases in sales.

However, we don't have enough information to know whether the statement below is correct:

> ✘ Recreation and Garden supplies made up the largest portion of total sales.

Even though you will encounter only one graphic on the Writing Test, you will see graphics used throughout the SAT. Remember to use the checklist when reading graphics and pay close attention to graphics that use parts and percentages.

PART 2 PRACTICE: GRAPHICS

Using information from each graph, decide whether each statement that follows is true or false. If there is not enough information to know whether the statement is true, mark it as false.

Percent (%) of Students Using School-Provided Transportation		
	In 1977	In 2007
Richter School County	50	70
Grade 3	30	5
Grade 5	35	10
Grade 8	53	80
Grade 11	70	20

1. True or False: Only five students from grade 3 used school-provided transportation in 2007.

2. True or False: The number of students at Richter County School using school-provided transportation increased from 1977 to 2007.

3. True or False: The percentage of Grade 5 students using school-provided transportation decreased from 1977 to 2007.

4. True or False: More students from Grade 8 than Grade 5 used school-provided transportation in 1977.

Servings per Day

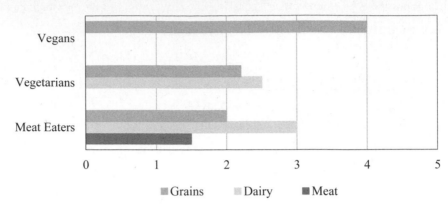

5. True or False: On average, meat eaters consume more servings of dairy per day than vegetarians do.

6. True or False: The average meat eater consumes 6.5 servings of food per day.

7. True or False: On average, vegans consume more grains per day than either meat eaters or vegetarians.

Seasonal Ticket Sales, and Breakdown of Fall/Winter Ticket Sales

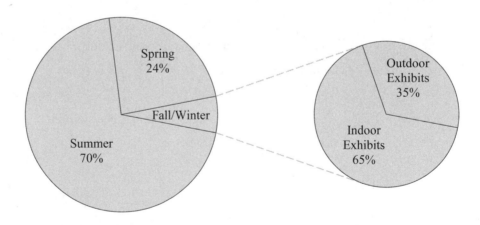

8. True or False: 30% of ticket sales occurred in seasons other than summer.

9. True or False: Based on the graph, we can determine that 65% of all ticket sales were for indoor exhibits.

10. True or False: During fall and winter, 35% of ticket sales were for outdoor exhibits.

ANSWERS: GRAPHICS

1. False – According to the title, the numbers in the chart represent percentages.

2. False – Remember, an increase in percentage doesn't always mean an increase in number.

3. True – The percentage dropped from 35% to 10%.

4. False – Although a larger percentage of grade 8 students than grade 5 students used public transportation, you cannot make any assumptions about the number of students.

5. True – Meat eaters consume an average of 3 servings of dairy each day, which is greater than the 2.5 servings of dairy consumed each day by vegetarians.

6. False – The total of meat, dairy, and grains totals 6.5 servings, but this does not include other food groups like fruits and vegetables!

7. True – Vegans consume 4 servings, while vegetarians consume 2.2 servings and meat eaters consume 2 servings.

8. True – Since 70% of sales occurred in summer, 30% occurred in other seasons.

9. False – We can only see that during the fall and winter 65% of ticket sales were for indoor exhibits. We don't have that information for the whole year.

10. True – During the fall and winter, 35% of ticket sales were for outdoor exhibits.

ORGANIZING IDEAS

Another important way an author expresses his ideas is through proper organization of ideas. Once the author develops a main point and gathers supporting information, the author must organize these pieces so that the paragraphs make sense to the reader.

LOGICAL ORDER

Within a paragraph, sentences should be organized in a logical order. When sentences are given in a logical order, they help the reader follow the author's train of thought. When sentences are presented out of order, the thoughts seem jumbled, and it can be hard to figure out what the author is trying to say.

On the Writing Test, you will be asked to revise, add, or remove sentences to improve the logical order of the paragraph. Sometimes you will be asked to move a sentence to another location in the paragraph in order to "improve the cohesion" or "improve the organization" of the paragraph.

In order to answer these questions, you should first identify what the sentence is *doing* in the paragraph. Is it a main point, evidence, example, or conclusion? Once you know what the sentence is doing, you will be able to determine the best location for it within the paragraph.

Often, the first sentence in a paragraph states the main point of that paragraph. Authors usually present supporting evidence after their main point so that the reader can use the supporting evidence to better understand the main point. If you see a main point floating in the middle of a paragraph, you should move it to the beginning of the paragraph.

> [1] Workplace wellness initiatives include health screenings and health education, along with changes to the workplace environment to facilitate healthy behavior. [2] Some even offer discounted gym memberships and access to programs to assist those who want to quit smoking. [3] Consequently, these wellness initiatives have been shown to reduce sick days and disability by 25%. [4] Corporate initiatives for workplace wellness promote fitness and healthy lifestyles among their employees in many ways. [5] They have also been shown to reduce costs. **1**
>
> 1. For the sake of the cohesion of this paragraph, sentence 4 should be placed
>   (A) where it is now
>   (B) before sentence 1
>   (C) after sentence 2
>   (D) after sentence 5

This question is asking about sentence 4: "Corporate initiatives for workplace wellness promote fitness and healthy lifestyles among their employees in many ways." What is this sentence doing in the paragraph? It is a general statement that is supported by the facts and examples contained in the other sentences. This type of sentence is a main point, and should be placed at the beginning of the paragraph. The correct answer is (B).

You may also have noticed that sentence 4 breaks up two sentences that should be linked (sentences 3 and 5). Sentence 3 notes that the programs reduce sick days and disability, while sentence 5 states that they also reduce cost. Sentence 5 adds on to the idea in sentence 3, so sentence 4 is disrupting the connection! If you see a sentence that breaks an important link, you should move that sentence to another location in the paragraph.

In "Support and Focus," you learned that many sentences in a paragraph add support for the main point through the use of facts, statistics, examples, opinions, and anecdotes. Since these sentences add support, you should place them closest to the idea they are supporting. Take the following sentences:

> ✗ For example, he played the piano, wrote poetry, and played quarterback. He was a modern "Renaissance man," known for excelling at many different things.

As they are now, the sentences above do not have a logical order. The first sentence begins with "For example," so you know that this sentence will be acting as an example. However, an example should come *after* the idea it is trying to support! We should rearrange these sentences so they read:

> ✓ He was a modern "Renaissance man," known for excelling at many different things. For example, he played the piano, wrote poetry, and played quarterback.

When you answer questions about logical order or cohesion, make sure that you test your choice by placing it back in the paragraph. Before you bubble in your answer, re-read the paragraph with the sentence in its new location. Correct answers may involve keeping the sentence where it is, moving it to a new location, or deleting it altogether.

SIGNAL WORDS

Authors use signal words and phrases to improve the logical order of sentences in a paragraph. **Signal words and phrases** connect information in a paragraph. These include words that signal continuations, examples, changes, and conclusions. In the example above, you saw the signal phrase "for example." Signal words and phrases not only tell you where sentences in a paragraph should go, but can also be useful tools to revise sentences to improve the logical order.

Common Signal Words	
Type of Signal Word	Examples
Continuations	Moreover, also, additionally, similarly, furthermore, next
Examples	For example, much like, specifically, for instance
Change	While, in spite of, yet, however, although
Conclusion	As a result, finally, therefore, consequently, hence

On the Writing Test, you will be asked to revise misused signal words. You may also need to add signal words or phrases to existing sentences to create transitions or improve the flow of the paragraph. In order to choose the best signal word or phrase, identify what the sentence is doing and refer to the chart above.

If a sentence is a conclusion, then the best signal word or phrase would come from the "conclusion" category. If a sentence begins a counterargument, then the best signal word or phrase would come from the "change" category. If the signal word is used as a transition, you should read the sentences before and after it to check for the type of transition that is taking place.

EXAMPLE

What emotion are you feeling right now? The answer to this question may not be so easy. There are over five hundred words in the English language used to describe emotions. Some have tried to categorize emotions into distinct groups. For example, Paul Ekman defined the six "basic emotions" as happiness, sadness, anger, fear, surprise, and disgust. **1** However, others suggest that emotions are not distinct, but rather that they fall on a spectrum. So perhaps you are somewhere between happy and surprised or between angry and afraid.

1. (A) NO CHANGE
   (B) In conclusion
   (C) For example
   (D) Furthermore

To determine what signal word best begins this sentence, you should identify what is happening between this sentence and the sentences before and after it. The previous sentence gives Paul Ekman's distinct categories of emotions. The sentence in the question notes that "others suggest" emotions are not distinct. Since the author is describing two different viewpoints on emotions, he or she needs to use a "change" word to transition. "However" is an appropriate word to indicate a shift or change, so (A) NO CHANGE is the correct answer. "In conclusion" signals a conclusion, "for example" signals an example, and "furthermore" signals a continuing thought, so these cannot be correct answer choices.

PART 3 PRACTICE: ORGANIZING IDEAS

For questions 1-5, identify whether each word signals continuation, example, change, or conclusion.

1. For instance

2. Furthermore

3. However

4. Although

5. Hence

For questions 6-7, read the passage below and answer the questions that follow.

[1] While many people think that sign language is an artificial means of communication, linguists have found compelling evidence that sign language is partially innate. [2] Some researchers have studied deaf children and compared those children who were exposed to sign language instruction and those who weren't. [3] They found that even without instruction, the children developed pointing and gestures that were very similar to those common to various sign languages. [4] Sometimes these gestures were even complex. [5] The children lacking instruction shared other similarities with the children who had received instruction. [6] <u>As a result,</u> the children relaxed their hands between "sentences," signaling an intuitive break in thought. [7]

6. (A) NO CHANGE

   (B) However,

   (C) Likewise,

   (D) For example,

7. For the sake of cohesion of this paragraph, sentence 4 should be placed

   (A) where it is now

   (B) after sentence 1

   (C) after sentence 5

   (D) after sentence 6

Answers: Organizing Ideas

1. Example
2. Continuation
3. Change
4. Change
5. Conclusion
6. D
7. A

EFFECTIVE LANGUAGE USE
PART 4

Have you ever read something that was difficult to understand because it was too wordy or vague? These types of mistakes occur when authors use ineffective language, like including too many words or using unclear phrases. While the order of sentences within a paragraph can help an author express her ideas, so can the proper use of words and phrases.

On the Writing Test, you will be asked to revise the language the author uses to more effectively convey his or her ideas. You can do this by making sentences precise and concise, while matching the style and tone of the passage.

PRECISION

Some questions on the Writing Test will ask you to choose which word or phrase best completes a sentence. To do so, you should first check for the most precise word. Choosing the most **precise** word means choosing the one that is most appropriate in the context of the paragraph. Your goal should always be to choose the right word for what the author means to say.

There are two main ways that the SAT will test your ability to choose an appropriate word. The first is to fill the answer choices with words that have similar meanings. However, one of these words will make more sense than the others in the context of the passage. The second way the SAT tests for appropriate word choice is by using commonly confused or misused words, which we discussed in Section 3.

Sometimes you can identify the error immediately and anticipate a better word to use. Other times, you may need to compare all the answer choices. When this is the case, you should first determine how the answer choices are different and then identify which answer completes the sentence correctly.

I was so distracted by the delicious smell wafting from the tray that I forget to put on an oven mitt. The result was my first—and very painful—burn. The skin surrounding the area was red and tender to the touch. I immediately covered it with a bandage so that I would not further **1** <u>provoke</u> the burn.

1. (A) NO CHANGE
   (B) frustrate
   (C) alleviate
   (D) aggravate

Using the context of the paragraph, you can tell that the burn is painful, red, and tender. In the final sentence, the author uses the word "further" to suggest that the bandage is being used to prevent more pain, redness, and tenderness. In order words, the bandage will prevent it from becoming more irritated. You want to choose an answer that means something like "irritate" or "make worse."

The correct answer is (D) aggravate, which means "to make worse or more serious." However, aggravate can also mean to annoy. "Provoke" and "frustrate" are synonyms of aggravate, but don't fit in the sentence. The author wouldn't "provoke" the burn, nor would he or she "frustrate" the burn. "Alleviate" means "to ease or improve," so it is an antonym of aggravate.

CONCISION

Other questions will require you to make the author's phrases or sentences more concise. **Concise** phrases and sentences give a lot of information in the fewest words possible.

The most concise option is not always the shortest. Sometimes when you make a sentence too short, you lose words that add meaning to the sentence. A concise answer will give all the same information as the original, just in fewer words. There are many ways you can make a sentence more concise.

In the passages on the Writing Test, some sentences will include words that don't make the sentence any better or add any more information. We call these "empty" words. By cutting these empty words out, the sentences will be clearer and more concise.

   ✗   He is <u>a man who is always busy</u>. He often switches <u>in a hasty manner</u> from one task to the next.

   ✓   He is <u>always busy</u>. He often switches <u>hastily</u> from one task to the next.

The first sentence has the words, "a man who is." These words are empty because we can eliminate them and still keep the meaning of the sentence the same. In the second sentence, "in a hasty manner" can be more concisely written using the adverb "hastily."

Many phrases can be cut down and still have the same meaning.

Cutting Empty Words	
Original	More Concise
At all times	Always
At the present time	Currently
At this point in time	Now
For the purpose of	For
The question as to whether	Whether
Used for the purpose of	Used for
Due to the fact that	Because
Because of the fact that	Because
The reason why is that	Because

You also want to cut out words or phrases that are repetitive. Just like empty words, phrases that repeat something the author already said make the sentence less concise.

EXAMPLE

   ✗   Novice drivers <u>who don't have much experience driving</u> are more likely to be involved in car accidents.

   ✓   Novice drivers are more likely to be involved in car accidents.

In the first sentence, "who don't have much experience driving" is unnecessary because you already know they are "novice drivers." Since "novice" means "lacking experience," the author does not need to repeat this using a phrase.

One final way you will be asked to make passages more concise is by combining sentences. When you combine sentences, make sure to use adequate punctuation and conjunctions to avoid comma splices and run-on sentences.

EXAMPLE

✘ Certain dog breeds have been bred as herding dogs. These breeds include sheepdogs and collies.

✓ Certain dog breeds, such as sheepdogs and collies, have been bred as herding dogs.

When you combine two short sentences using a phrase, you can keep the meaning the same but express an idea more concisely. Often, the correct answer will combine the two sentences by turning one sentence into a modifier or dependent phrase.

STYLE

An author can also express his or her ideas effectively using proper style. **Style** involves the words, phrases, and information the author chooses to include depending on the purpose of the passage. Style can refer to the way the author writes a sentence, a group of sentences, or the passage as a whole.

You have learned that each passage is a specific type: argumentative, narrative, or informative. Each of these types has a specific purpose. Argumentative passages try to persuade, narrative passages tell a story, and informative passages give the reader new knowledge. The author should try to match the style of the passage to the intended purpose.

You can use the chart below to identify the elements of style that each type of passage should use:

Passage Type	Style
Argumentative	Presents opinions and facts, includes analysis of evidence, can include more forceful language
Informative	Presents facts but not opinions, avoids casual language, often includes definitions
Narrative	More casual in style, uses descriptive language, often in first person voice, can include dialogue or quotations

No matter what type of passage you are reading, it should follow the rules of development, organization, and language use that we have outlined in this section. Any errors in development or organization can also damage the author's writing style.

TONE

Authors also develop a specific **tone**, or attitude, throughout the passage. For example, an author can have an authoritative tone if she is writing as an expert, or a disapproving tone if she is arguing against a proposition. You may be familiar with some common tones authors can take when writing, and identifying the tone of a passage is discussed further in Chapter 2.

On the Writing Test, you will not be asked to identify a word that describes the author's tone. Instead, you'll be asked to revise sentences or phrases so that they match the tone of the rest of the passage. To do this, you should pay attention to the tone the author adopts while you are reading the whole passage.

You may be able to spot places in the passage where the tone does not match. If you are given the opportunity to revise a section to better match the tone of the passage, choose the answer that continues the author's attitude. Ask yourself, does this fit in with the rest of the passage? Would the author express this thought in this way?

EXAMPLE

One of Jane Goodall's first observations about chimpanzees was that they possessed the ability to make and use tools. Previously, many scientists assumed only humans had this capability. Goodall observed chimpanzees creating rods out of grass; the chimpanzees would then use these rods to collect termites from a termite hole and lick the termites from the rod. **1** Chimpanzees are obviously as intelligent as humans.

1. Which choice is most consistent with the rest of the paragraph?
   (A) NO CHANGE
   (B) Those scientists who originally disagreed were not as observant as Goodall.
   (C) She determined that chimpanzees possess similar tool-making abilities to humans.
   (D) I will always admire Jane Goodall for her work in expanding our knowledge of chimpanzee abilities.

This paragraph is describing a discovery Jane Goodall made while living with chimpanzees. The paragraph primarily gives facts and uses descriptions because it is meant to inform and entertain the reader. It can be classified as an informative passage.

The final sentence of the paragraph breaks the tone by introducing an opinion. The word "obviously" is too strong, and the use of an opinion is not consistent with the rest of the paragraph. The sentence in answer (B) also introduces an opinion, so it does not match the tone either. Answer (C) continues the same tone by introducing a new fact about Goodall's conclusion from her discovery. Answer choice (D) switches to first person, while the paragraph is written in third person. Therefore, (C) is the correct answer.

Remember, when revising the passages, the correct answer will always be the *best* version of the section. Therefore, you need to think about how any changes will affect the development, organization, and language of the passage.

Part 4 Practice: Effective Language Use

Read the passage below and answer the questions that follow.

> Imagine you're doing your favorite activity. You might be playing baseball, piano, or chess. You might be painting, singing, or dancing. When you do this activity, do you lose track of time? Do you fail to notice that you're tired? If this happens to you, you are probably experiencing what is called "flow."
>
> You experience flow when you are completely involved in an activity. During flow, you are challenged but still have a pleasant experience. Flow involves intense and focused concentration on an activity. However, **3** <u>due to the fact that</u> this activity is rewarding, you may feel like time is flying or forget other worries. In order to continue to experience flow, you must **4** <u>unceasingly</u> seek new challenges. For example, if you achieve flow through sports, you should practice a few times every week and regularly establish new goals.

1. How would you describe the author's style?

2. How would you describe the author's tone?

3. (A) NO CHANGE

    (B) since you may feel like

    (C) because of the fact that

    (D) because

4. In context, this word would best be replaced with

    (A) NO CHANGE

    (B) consistently

    (C) seldom

    (D) incessantly

4a. What context clues did you use to make your choice?

Answers: Effective Language Use

1. The author's style is casual. The author uses questions and engages the audience by using "you" as the subject of many sentences.

2. The author's tone is friendly and informative, but not authoritative.

3. D

4. B

4a. In the next sentence, the author gives an example. The author states that to achieve flow you should practice "a few times every week." This would be described as consistently, not unceasingly, seldom, or incessantly.

PRACTICE SET
PART 5

Below are four passage excerpts and accompanying questions. Choose the answer that best completes or revises the portion of the text in question.

Questions 1-4 refer to the following passage.

The Liberty Bell

Recognizable by the large crack down its side, Philadelphia's Liberty Bell is a symbol of freedom and patriotism. However, both its name and famous cracked side **1** were added much later to the bell after many years. Originally called the "State House bell," the Liberty Bell was given its current name when it was **2** adopted as a symbol of the abolitionist movement. The origin of the crack on the side of the bell, **3** consequently, remains a mystery. By 1846, a thin crack developed along the side of the bell. It was **4** repaired in 1846. The bell cracked again and has not been rung since.

1. (A) NO CHANGE
   (B) were added to the bell.
   (C) were late additions to the bell.
   (D) were late additions to the bell, added after many years.

2. (A) NO CHANGE
   (B) encompassed
   (C) authenticated
   (D) corroborated

3. (A) NO CHANGE
   (B) however,
   (C) for example,
   (D) also,

4. Which choice most effectively combines the sentences at the underlined portion?

    (A) repaired in 1846, the bell cracked again

    (B) repaired in 1846, and then also the bell cracked again

    (C) repaired in 1846, cracking again

    (D) repaired in 1846, but the bell cracked again

Questions 5-10 refer to the following passage.

An Exploration of Aztec Society

[1] Aztec society was broken down into many levels. [2] The most basic unit was the family. [3] Every child went to school, creating **5** a unanimous education system in Aztec society. [4] The next level was a larger group **6** to which families belonged. [5] It was called the "calpulli." [6] Calpullis were fairly independent. **7** [7] Many calpullis made up a city-state.

8 At the bottom of the hierarchy were slaves. In Aztec society, no one was born into slavery. Rather, individuals became **9** slaves in order that they might pay for debts or as punishment for crimes. The class of the common people was the "macehualtin," which included warriors and craftsmen. The noble class was called the "pipiltin." Chosen from the pipiltin, a king ruled each city-state. Many Aztecs lived their entire lives as members of only one social class. **10** Unfortunately, there was the opportunity for social mobility through engaging in the priesthood or military service.

5. (A) NO CHANGE

    (B) an endemic

    (C) a universal

    (D) an insidious

6. Which choice most effectively combines the sentences at the underlined portion?

    (A) to which families belonged, called the "calpulli."

    (B) which families belonged to, calling it the "calpulli."

    (C) to which families belonged, and they called it the "calpulli."

    (D) to which families belonged; furthermore, it was called the "calpulli."

7. Which choice, inserted here, most effectively adds support for the statement in sentence 6?

(A) Families in calpullis were often related to each other.

(B) Calpullis were similar to tribes or clans in other societies.

(C) Calpulli means "large house" in Nahua, the language of the Aztecs.

(D) Calpullis had a chief, ran a local school, and controlled the use of land.

8. Which sentence, inserted here, would most effectively establish the main topic of the second paragraph?

(A) Aztec society was one of the first to introduce a child-centered social structure.

(B) Aztec society was also composed of different social classes.

(C) Aztec society highly valued priests and kings.

(D) Social mobility was an important goal of most Aztec men and women.

9. (A) NO CHANGE

(B) slaves to pay

(C) slaves because of their having to pay

(D) slaves for payment of

10. Which choice is most consistent with the tone of the rest of the passage?

(A) NO CHANGE

(B) Specifically

(C) However

(D) I think

Questions 11-15 refer to the following passage.

Real Life Robots

Robots don't only exist in sci-fi flicks. Robotics is a growing and advancing field of technology. Used in the automotive, manufacturing, and even medical industries, robots have proved ⑪ invaluable. ⑫ It has been said that robots can do work more efficiently than humans can. Some argue that increased reliance on robotics robs hardworking humans of jobs. However, ⑬ robots can take over assignments. Manpower can be shifted and used to improve overall processes.

 [1] One of the most important developments in the field of robotics was the creation of the robotic arm. [2] Because of its design, the robotic arm can move precisely but also hold and

transport great amounts of weight. [3] **14** For example, robotic arms are used to carefully construct a microchip as well as to move heavy auto parts on assembly lines. [4] Over time, the robotic arm has also become both more complex and more versatile, leading to its use in many industries. [5] Robots are able to complete routine activities, like vacuuming and removing garbage, without human assistance. **15**

11. (A) NO CHANGE

    (B) inestimable

    (C) infinite

    (D) esoteric

12. Which choice most improves the cohesion of the paragraph?

    (A) NO CHANGE

    (B) I think that the best thing about robots is that robots can do work more efficiently than humans can.

    (C) One reason robots are so useful is because they can do work more efficiently than humans can.

    (D) Robots can do work more efficiently than humans, many scientists have stated.

13. Which choice most effectively combines the sentences at the underlined portion?

    (A) NO CHANGE

    (B) when robots take over assignments, manpower can be shifted and used

    (C) as robots take over assignments, they then also shift manpower and use it

    (D) robots can take over assignments, this change leads to shifting manpower and using it

14. (A) NO CHANGE

    (B) In spite of this

    (C) Surprisingly

    (D) Often

15. To improve the focus of the paragraph, sentence 5 should be

    (A) where it is now

    (B) placed after sentence 2

    (C) placed before sentence 4

    (D) deleted

Questions 16-20 refer to the following passage.

Your Brain on Marketing

Every year, companies spend millions of dollars on marketing campaigns, securing commercial spots during the Super Bowl and hiring celebrities to endorse their products. [16] What are the effects on our brains? The answer is simple: marketing efforts are incredibly effective. Recently, scientists have become increasingly [17] interested in how marketing affects the psychology and also neurology of people.

One study by Hilke Plassman and colleagues presented a finding that would certainly be of interest to advertisers: changes in perceived value, but not actual quality, can have [18] inadequate effects on how much we like a product. In their experiment, they gave participants wines to taste and then asked them to rate how much they liked the wine and how "intense" they would rate the wine. The researchers manipulated the perceived value by changing the prices of bottles of wine. Each wine was presented twice, once with a lower price ($5 or $10) and once with a higher price ($45 or $90). The participants, [19] however, thought they were tasting a different wine each time. The results of the study indicated that [20] people would spend more on Wine 2 than Wine 1, and they also rated Wine 2 as more intense than Wine 1. Brain imaging also showed that higher prices brought about greater activity in the areas of the brain that indicate pleasantness.

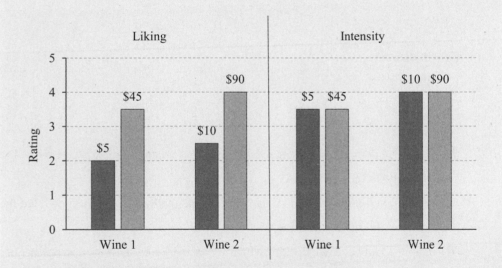

Participant Wine Ratings

Adapted from Plassman et al. Marketing actions can modulate neural representations of experienced pleasantness. ©2008 by Proceedings of the National Academy of Science

16. Which choice best improves the cohesion of the paragraph?

    (A) NO CHANGE

    (B) Why are celebrities more effective marketers than unknown actors?

    (C) Why spend so much time and effort on marketing?

    (D) What makes some marketing campaigns better than others?

17. (A) NO CHANGE

    (B) interested in the psychological and neurological effects of marketing.

    (C) interested in the effects of marketing on the psychology of people and neurology of people

    (D) interested in the psychological effects of marketing and the neurological effects too.

18. (A) NO CHANGE

    (B) vivid

    (C) dramatic

    (D) incomplete

19. (A) NO CHANGE

    (B) for example

    (C) finally

    (D) next

20. Which choice completes the sentence with accurate data based on the graph?

    (A) NO CHANGE

    (B) people liked each wine more the second time they tasted it, but they rated the intensity the same each time.

    (C) people liked each wine more when it was marketed as more expensive, but price did not have an effect on how intense they rated it.

    (D) the more intense the wine was, the higher the overall price.

Answer Key: Practice Set

1. C
2. A
3. B
4. D
5. C
6. A
7. D
8. B
9. B
10. C
11. A
12. C
13. B
14. A
15. D
16. C
17. B
18. C
19. A
20. C

SAT Writing Practice Test

Time – 35 minutes
44 Questions

Download and print an answer sheet available at ivyglobal.com/study.

Directions: For these questions, determine the solution to each question presented and choose the best answer choice of those provided. Be sure to fill in the respective circle on your answer sheet.

Questions 1-11 are based on the following passage.

Conflict and Cooperation: The Robber's Cave

In the 1950s, social scientists were fascinated with group interactions. During this time, many psychologists studied belonging, cooperation, and **1** conflict. They hoped to better understand the sources of prejudice and war. Specifically, they wanted to know what circumstances bring about conflict or cooperation among groups and if it is possible to reproduce these effects in experiments. One such scientist was Muzafer Sherif, who became interested in group interactions after witnessing a violent invasion in his homeland. In 1954, Sherif published his landmark study on group relationships, "The Robber's Cave" experiment.

Sherif's experiment was original in a number of ways. Sherif used a real world setting by placing twelve-year-old boys at a camp into two groups, the "eagles" and the "rattlers." The experiment had three stages. In stage one, the researchers separated the groups, and **2** they enjoyed the first days at the camp. In stage two, the boys were asked to engage in an athletic **3** tournament, it consisted of activities like baseball and tug of war. This competition led to increased hostility and an **4** ascension in physical and emotional conflict. In stage three, the researchers introduced problems for the boys at the camp. **5** For example, the boys were told that the camp's water supply was blocked and that the boys needed to repair it together. The goal of this phase was to encourage cooperation **6** among the two groups to solve the problem. Throughout the experiment, the boys were asked questions about members of their own group, the "ingroup," and members of the other group, the "outgroup."

The researchers observed changes in the boys' feelings and behavior as the stages progressed. In stage two, the boys developed negative stereotypes of the outgroup and were unlikely to choose friends from among **7** it's members. During the competitions, the boys showed unfriendly and aggressive behavior. Yet after the cooperation in stage three, the boys reported fewer negative feelings towards the outgroup and **8** were observed cooperating with each other more frequently. The researchers also found that **9** friendships with members of the outgroup increased for both groups between stages two and three.

[1] From this experiment, Sherif was able to determine that competition **10** tends to fuel conflict, and he also determined that working towards a common goal tends to increase cooperation. [2] This common goal also serves to reduce negative stereotypes and increase friendships between groups. [3] Other scientists used similar situations to bring out cooperation and conflict and witnessed the same effect. [4] Sherif concluded that while tension arises when groups form and compete, this tension can be relieved when a common goal is introduced. **11**

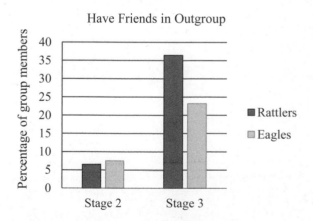

Have Friends in Outgroup

Adapted from Sherif et al. "Intergroup Conflict and Cooperation: The Robbers Cave Experiment." 1954.

GO ON TO THE NEXT PAGE

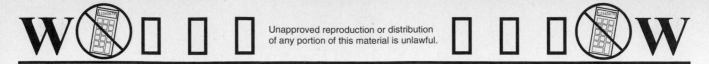
1. Which choice most effectively combines the sentences at the underlined portion?

   (A) conflict, and they hoped to better understand
   (B) conflict, hoping to reach a better understanding
   (C) conflict to better understand
   (D) conflict, understanding

2. (A) NO CHANGE
   (B) they all
   (C) them
   (D) the boys

3. (A) NO CHANGE
   (B) tournament, consisting of activities
   (C) tournament; consisting of activities
   (D) tournament, of which it consisted of activities

4. (A) NO CHANGE
   (B) arising
   (C) expansion
   (D) increase

5. (A) NO CHANGE
   (B) Successively,
   (C) Finally,
   (D) Yet,

6. (A) NO CHANGE
   (B) concerning
   (C) between
   (D) through

7. (A) NO CHANGE
   (B) its members
   (C) their members
   (D) there members

8. (A) NO CHANGE
   (B) were observed to be cooperating with each other
   (C) was cooperating with each other
   (D) cooperated with each other

9. Which choice completes the sentence with accurate data based on the graph?

   (A) NO CHANGE
   (B) friendships with members of the outgroup decreased for Eagles after stage three
   (C) after both stages, more Rattlers than Eagles had friendships with members of the outgroup
   (D) at least twenty Rattlers developed friendships with the outgroup after stage two

10. (A) NO CHANGE
    (B) tends to fuel conflict, also determining that a common goal
    (C) tending to fuel conflict and that working towards a common goal
    (D) tends to fuel conflict, and a common goal

11. For the sake of the cohesion of this paragraph, sentence 3 should be

    (A) Where it is now
    (B) Placed before sentence 1
    (C) Placed after sentence 1
    (D) Deleted

GO ON TO THE NEXT PAGE

Questions 12-22 are based on the following passage.

Jerome Robbins: Broadway and Beyond

Although Jerome Robbins began his career as a chorus dancer, today he is known as one of the most inventive choreographers in ballet and Broadway. **12** His Broadway shows are still performed around the world. They have remained some of the most beloved and acclaimed productions. Dancers and audiences alike **13** appreciates Robbins' works because of their engaging and dramatic style. During his career, Jerome Robbins created hundreds of theatrical masterpieces and captured the essence of American drama and dance in his work.

In 1940, Robbins joined the American Ballet Theatre and performed there for four years. In 1944, he began choreographing ballets, which he continued to do throughout his career. Robbins was inspired by the American **14** way of life, and he also liked to create pieces that highlighted the vitality and diversity of American culture. His first work, *Fancy Free*, was a jazz-inspired ballet about American sailors **15** who enjoy an evening on the town. At its premiere, *Fancy Free* received twenty-two curtain calls. Later that year, Robbins turned his ballet sensation into a musical, *On the Town*. Seamlessly transitioning between ballet and Broadway, **16** storytelling in any form was Robbins' gift. In the 1950s, Robbins created some of his most famous Broadway shows, including *The Pajama Game*, and choreographed dances for Rodgers and Hammerstein.

[1] In 1957, Robbins choreographed and directed *West Side Story*, which **17** will become an iconic American musical. [2] Inspired by Shakespeare's *Romeo and Juliet*, *West Side Story* explores the conflicts between ethnic groups in New York City and the trials of young love. [3] However, some critics found the elements of dance to be even more compelling than the story itself. [4] Following the success of *West Side Story*, Robbins produced two more Broadway triumphs, *Gypsy* and *Fiddler on the Roof*. [5] He became renowned for **18** exploring the limits of dance, music, and drama and also further experimenting with their boundaries themselves. [6] During this time, Robbins received numerous honors for his work, including five Tony Awards. **19**

Robbins also took some of his works from the stage to the screen. In 1956, he was asked to recreate his dances for the film *The King and I*. In 1961, he co-directed the film version of *West Side Story*, for which he won two Academy Awards. **20** While Robbins' Broadway shows continue to be produced around the world, his expansion into film **21** condensed his artistic legacy.

Throughout a career lasting more than fifty years, Jerome Robbins created innovative and iconic **22** works, in ballet, theater, and film. With the widespread success of *West Side Story* both on stage and on screen, Robbins showed that he truly was a master of the dramatic arts.

12. Which choice most effectively combines the sentences at the underlined portion?

   (A) His Broadway shows are still performed around the world remaining
   (B) Although his Broadway shows are still performed around the world, they remain
   (C) His Broadway shows are still performed around the world, and they have also remained
   (D) His Broadway shows are still performed around the world and remain

13. (A) NO CHANGE
   (B) appreciate
   (C) to appreciate
   (D) appreciating

14. (A) NO CHANGE
   (B) way of life; many of his pieces highlighted
   (C) way of life, liking to create pieces that highlighted
   (D) way of life, he liked to create pieces that highlighted

15. (A) NO CHANGE
   (B) who enjoys
   (C) which enjoy
   (D) whom enjoy

16. (A) NO CHANGE
   (B) storytelling in any form was a gift of Robbins.
   (C) Robbins had a gift for storytelling in any form.
   (D) any form of storytelling was Robbins' gift.

17. (A) NO CHANGE
   (B) have become
   (C) becomes
   (D) would become

GO ON TO THE NEXT PAGE

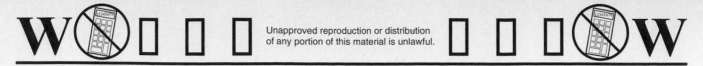

18. (A) NO CHANGE
    (B) exploring and experimenting with the boundaries of dance, music, and drama.
    (C) his exploration of dance, music, and drama and his experimentation with their boundaries.
    (D) both exploring the limits of dance, music, and drama and also experimenting with their boundaries.

19. Which choice, inserted between sentences 2 and 3, would most improve the cohesion of the paragraph?

    (A) NO CHANGE
    (B) The music was composed by Leonard Bernstein and the lyrics were written by Stephen Sondheim.
    (C) The show received praise for its endearing characters and gripping plot.
    (D) The dance scenes involved both upbeat group numbers and moving duets.

20. (A) NO CHANGE
    (B) Finally,
    (C) Because
    (D) Likewise,

21. (A) NO CHANGE
    (B) settled
    (C) solidified
    (D) toughened

22. (A) NO CHANGE
    (B) works; in ballet, theater, and film
    (C) works: in ballet, theater, and film
    (D) works in ballet, theater, and film

GO ON TO THE NEXT PAGE

Questions 23-33 are based on the following passage.

Physician Self-Referral

To combat the high costs of a medical education and increased reliance on technology, physicians sometimes establish themselves as investors in medical facilities **[23]** <u>to whom</u> they can refer patients. This arrangement is known as "physician self-referral." Traditionally, the American health care system has given physicians great professional freedom, and we have placed our health in the hands of physicians with the trust that they will act ethically and **[24]** <u>thinking about our most important interests.</u> **[25]** <u>However, health care costs are consuming more of the federal budget than ever before. Regulation aimed at</u> cutting costs will become increasingly important.

[26] The physician self-referral system creates incentives for doctors to provide unnecessary health care. In a self-referral arrangement, a physician invests money in another medical facility, such as an imaging center. The physician **[27]** <u>will have made</u> a profit when the imaging center does well. This encourages the physician to increase not only the number of patients he or she refers but also **[28]** <u>ordering more tests for each patient</u>. For example, the physician may suggest an imaging procedure, such as an MRI, be conducted before completing a simpler, more cost effective test. This phenomenon has been documented in studies showing that self-referring physicians order more unnecessary tests. **[29]** <u>Therefore</u>, it is clear that the financial incentives created by self-referrals result in excessive use of expensive medical services.

A physician's financial interest should never be placed above a patient's interest. Physicians typically know a great deal more about medicine **[30]** <u>then their patients</u>. Because of this, patients are inclined to trust the suggestions of their physician. In self-referral arrangements, physicians are able to take advantage **[31]** <u>of this asymmetry, they may suggest</u> unnecessary tests that are costly or painful. While many physicians who invest in medical facilities are likely able to uphold their **[32]** <u>virtuous</u> duty, regulation of physician self-referral is necessary as a protective measure for all patients.

[1] Some argue that self-referrals don't need to be placed under regulatory control. [2] After all, if we trust physicians with our health, why shouldn't we trust them with their own investments? [3] Further, physicians have specialized knowledge of medical services, so they might even seem like the "best" investors. **[33]** [4] But surely these benefits do not outweigh the risk of a corrupting influence on medical

practice, and so we must conclude that regulation of self-referral is essential for maintaining standards of practice.

23. (A) NO CHANGE
    (B) to which
    (C) to who
    (D) towards whom

24. (A) NO CHANGE
    (B) with our best interests in their minds
    (C) in our best interest
    (D) in order to preserve our interests

25. Which choice most effectively combines the sentences at the underlined portion?

    (A) However, as healthcare costs consume more of the federal budget than ever before, regulation aimed at
    (B) However, even though healthcare costs are consuming more of the federal budget than ever before, regulation aimed at
    (C) But now we must consider that healthcare costs are consuming more of the federal budget than ever before, so regulation aimed at
    (D) However, healthcare costs are consuming more of the federal budget than ever before, even though regulation aimed at

26. Which sentence, inserted here, would most effectively establish the main topic of the passage?

    (A) Ethical concerns have also become a factor in many regulatory debates.
    (B) Medical school costs have more than doubled in the last fifty years.
    (C) Such cost containment can be achieved in a variety of ways.
    (D) Regulation of self-referral arrangements has become necessary to reduce excessive use of services and maintain patient safety.

27. (A) NO CHANGE
    (B) makes
    (C) made
    (D) had made

GO ON TO THE NEXT PAGE

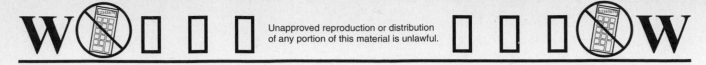

28. (A) NO CHANGE
    (B) to order more tests for each patient
    (C) the number of tests ordered for each patient.
    (D) to increase the number of tests per patient

29. (A) NO CHANGE
    (B) Surprisingly
    (C) Nevertheless
    (D) However

30. (A) NO CHANGE
    (B) than their patients know
    (C) than that of their patients
    (D) compared to the knowledge of their patients

31. (A) NO CHANGE
    (B) of this asymmetry and may suggest
    (C) of this asymmetry, but they may suggest
    (D) of this asymmetry; suggesting

32. In context, this word would be best replaced with

    (A) NO CHANGE
    (B) earnest
    (C) ethical
    (D) dispassionate

33. Which choice, inserted here, most effectively adds
    support for the statement in sentence 3?

    (A) Nurses also have specialized knowledge of medical
        services.
    (B) Most physicians choose to save their income over
        time.
    (C) Many physicians are involved in charities outside
        of their practice.
    (D) First-hand knowledge of medical practices allows
        physicians to invest in the most needed facilities.

GO ON TO THE NEXT PAGE

Questions 34-44 are based on the following passage.

Submarine Volcanoes

Volcanic eruptions are remarkable and dangerous natural events. While most well-known eruptions have come from volcanoes on land, volcanoes are also common structures on the ocean floor. These underwater volcanoes, called submarine volcanoes, are often submerged beneath more than 8,500 feet of water but produce about three quarters of the total volcanic output on Earth. [34] Even though they are mostly hidden, submarine volcanoes are part of an interesting and productive system.

Before they were able to detect submarine volcanoes, oceanographers were aware that underwater eruptions were occurring. In the 1990s, scientists created a new system to measure the small earthquakes that accompany underwater eruptions. On land, scientists are able to measure vibrations of the earth's surface. To measure underwater [35] earthquakes, however, it is more practical to listen to the acoustic waves travelling through the water. To see and explore the submarine volcanoes, oceanographers have utilized new aquatic technology that can handle the extreme heat and pressure around deep-sea volcanoes. For example, scientists use remotely operated vehicles to capture images and video of volcanic structures, underwater eruptions, and the marine life [36] dwelling in the volcanoes surrounding areas.

[37] Using these techniques, the effects of submarine volcanic eruptions have been observed by scientists. Over time, these eruptions have shaped the sea floor. Like land eruptions, underwater eruptions eject lava, a type of molten rock. However, underwater lava behaves differently [38] than terrestrial eruptions. After an eruption, water rushes over [39] the lava, so that it then receives 250 times the pressure of the atmosphere. Underwater, lava typically forms "pillows," whereas lava forms hard blocks on land. These pillows of lava [40] creates the edges of oceanic plates. Because lava cools and solidifies quickly underwater, some lava turns into volcanic glass. Lava from underwater eruptions also supplies heat and chemicals to unique volcanic ecosystems.

[1] Underwater volcanic ecosystems often form around thermal vents, openings in the earth's surface that release water heated by volcanic activity. [2] At these vents, water comes in and [41] proceeds to mix with natural chemicals, minerals, and bacteria before exiting the vents at high temperatures. [3] These ecosystems are home to an abundance of marine life, [42] including mussels, giant clams, and other organisms, that thrive in warm conditions. [4] The unique environment around thermal vents has allowed for an ecosystem of organisms that are able to live without energy from sunlight. [43]

While the recent explorations of submarine volcanoes have given scientists insight into underwater eruptions, [44] it is absolutely necessary that more continues to be learned. New technologies may allow scientists to capture and measure eruptions of submarine volcanoes, as well as to study the marine life thriving in volcanic ecosystems.

34. Which choice most effectively establishes the main point of the passage?

   (A) NO CHANGE
   (B) Many varieties of marine life, from bacteria to crabs and clams, thrive around submarine volcanoes.
   (C) There are several major distinctions between land and submarine volcanoes.
   (D) Because submarine volcanoes are more productive than land volcanoes, scientists should devote more time and resources to research in this field.

35. (A) NO CHANGE
   (B) earthquakes, it is consequently more practical to
   (C) earthquakes, it is however more practical to
   (D) earthquakes, however, scientists

36. (A) NO CHANGE
   (B) dwelling in volcanoes' surrounding areas.
   (C) that dwell in volcanoes surrounding areas.
   (D) that dwell in volcanoes surrounding areas.

37. (A) NO CHANGE
   (B) Using these techniques, the effects of submarine volcanic eruptions were observed by scientists.
   (C) The effects of submarine volcanic eruptions, observed by scientists using these techniques.
   (D) Using these techniques, scientists have observed the effects of submarine volcanic eruptions.

38. (A) NO CHANGE
   (B) than the behavior of terrestrial lava.
   (C) than does terrestrial lava.
   (D) than does the shaping of land.

GO ON TO THE NEXT PAGE

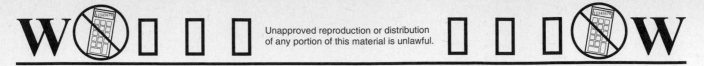
39. (A) NO CHANGE
    (B) the lava with
    (C) the lava, having received
    (D) the lava, and then with

40. (A) NO CHANGE
    (B) create the edges
    (C) creating the edges
    (D) to create the edges

41. (A) NO CHANGE
    (B) precedes
    (C) proposes
    (D) purports

42. (A) NO CHANGE
    (B) including mussels, giant clams, and other organisms, thriving in warm conditions.
    (C) including mussels, giant clams, and other organisms – to thrive in warm conditions.
    (D) including mussels, giant clams, and other organisms that thrive in warm conditions.

43. Which choice, inserted here, most effectively adds support for the statement in sentence 4?

    (A) In fact, some companies are looking to collect the valuable minerals from the floor of the thermal vents.
    (B) Bacteria use the chemicals from the vents to produce organic material, supplying the necessary energy for other organisms to survive.
    (C) The chemicals present in the water at thermal vents usually come to the ocean through rain, rivers, or groundwater.
    (D) The water from the thermal vents range in temperature from 60 to 400°C.

44. Which choice is most consistent with the rest of the passage?

    (A) NO CHANGE
    (B) we should still be learning more.
    (C) there is still more to learn.
    (D) scientists necessarily need to learn more.

STOP

If you complete the problem set before time elapses, you may review your responses for this section.

Do not view or begin working on any other sections.

Answer Key

1.	C	23.	B
2.	D	24.	C
3.	B	25.	A
4.	D	26.	D
5.	A	27.	B
6.	C	28.	C
7.	B	29.	A
8.	D	30.	B
9.	A	31.	B
10.	D	32.	C
11.	D	33.	D
12.	D	34.	A
13.	B	35.	D
14.	B	36.	B
15.	A	37.	D
16.	C	38.	C
17.	D	39.	B
18.	B	40.	B
19.	C	41.	A
20.	A	42.	D
21.	C	43.	B
22.	D	44.	C

Full explanations available at ivyglobal.com/study.

Chapter 4
Essay

INTRODUCTION TO THE SAT ESSAY

There are some major changes to the redesigned SAT, including that fact that the Essay portion is now optional. This means that you can now choose whether or not you want to write the Essay based on whether the schools you are applying to require it. Your essay score will not enter into your final numerical score for the SAT; instead, it will be reported separately.

During the essay portion of the SAT, you get to demonstrate your ability to comprehend source material, analyze an argument, and write effectively. You can think of the Essay section as the part of the test where you get to write your own answer.

You may already be familiar with essay prompts from the old SAT. The old SAT essay prompt asked you to generate your own argument and evidence in response to a fairly general and subjective question. The new SAT essay prompt is very different. Here is a list of the changes made to the SAT essay prompt and what that means for your own preparation:

- **New format:** You now get twice as much time to write the Essay—50 minutes instead of 25 minutes. You also get twice as much space to write your essay, with four available answer pages. This allows you to write more as well as have more time for revisions.

- **New prompt style:** While the old SAT essay prompt asked you wide-reaching, subjective questions, the new SAT essay prompt asks you to read and analyze a provided passage. The prompt itself is nearly the same on every exam—it is the passage that varies from test to test.

ESSAY SCORING

While the old SAT was scored using a very general holistic rubric, the new SAT essay is evaluated based on three specific criteria: Reading, Analysis, and Writing. Each of these criteria will be scored on a scale of 1-4. Below is a breakdown of what each of these criteria means and what the College Board expects to see in your essay.

- **Reading:** The College Board wants to see evidence in your essay that you read and understood the passage. There is a very simple way to demonstrate this: quote the passage. The best way to prove that you understood all the nuances of the passages is to use pieces of it effectively in your essay. We'll show you how to do this in Section 3.

- **Analysis:** The College Board wants to see that you can analyze the elements of someone else's argument and use this analysis to craft an argument of your own. You can achieve this by coming up with interesting, supportable claims and selecting strong, relevant evidence to support them. We will also be showing you how to do this in Section 3.

- **Writing:** The College Board wants to see evidence that you can not only come up with a good analysis, but that you can also effectively convey it to your reader. The scorers are evaluating your ability to come up with a coherent organization, use varied sentence structures, and employ good word choice and tone. You have likely learned many of these things in school, but we'll still do some practice in the coming sections to reinforce them.

SAMPLE ESSAY PROMPT

Here is a sample essay prompt so you can see the components of the new SAT essay.

This is the standard prompt introduction, which will always be the same.

As you read the next passage, consider how Yvon Chouinard uses

- evidence, such as facts or examples, to support claims.
- reasoning to develop ideas and to connect claims and evidence.
- stylistic or persuasive elements, such as word choice or appeals to emotion, to add power to the ideas expressed.

Adapted from "Tear Down 'Deadbeat' Dams" by Yvon Chouinard. ©2014 by the New York Times Company. Originally published May 7, 2014.

Of the more than 80,000 dams listed by the federal government, more than 26,000 pose high or significant safety hazards. Many no longer serve any real purpose. All have limited life spans. Only about 1,750 produce hydropower, according to the National Hydropower Association.

In many cases, the benefits that dams have historically provided—for water use, flood control and electricity—can now be met more effectively without continuing to choke entire watersheds.

Dams degrade water quality, block the movement of nutrients and sediment, destroy fish and wildlife habitats, damage coastal estuaries and in some cases rob surrounding forests of nitrogen. Reservoirs can also be significant sources of greenhouse gas emissions.

Put simply, many dams have high environmental costs that outweigh their value. Removing them is the only sensible answer. And taking them down can often make economic sense as well. The River Alliance of Wisconsin estimates that removing dams in that state is three to five times less expensive than repairing them.

The message has been slowly spreading around the country. More and more communities and states have reclaimed rivers lost to jackhammers and concrete. Last year, 51 dams in 18 states were taken down, restoring more than 500 miles of streams, according to the group American Rivers. Nearly 850 have been removed in the last 20 years, and nearly 1,150 since 1912.

But the work is far from done. I was disappointed to see the Energy Department release a report last week on the potential to develop new "sustainable" hydroelectric dams on rivers and streams across the country. The report follows President Obama's signing of two laws last year to encourage small hydro projects and revive nonproducing dams.

New dams are a bad idea. We've glorified them for decades, but our pride in building these engineering marvels has often blinded us to the environmental damage they cause. The consequences run the length of the river and beyond. Our many complex attempts to work around these obstacles would make Rube Goldberg proud. Interventions like fish elevators and trap-and-haul programs that truck fish around impoundments don't lead to true recovery for wild fish populations or reverse the other environmental problems caused by blocking a river's flow.

But we do know that removing dams brings streams and rivers back to life and replenishes our degraded aquifers.

A case in point is the Elwha River on the Olympic Peninsula in Washington, where two hydroelectric dams built early in the last century exacted huge environmental costs but were no longer important as power generators. Salmon runs that once reached about 400,000 fish a year dropped to fewer than 3,000. A year after the Elwha Dam was removed, Chinook salmon returned to the river in numbers not seen in decades, with three-quarters of them observed spawning upstream of the former dam site. Today, the river runs free from its headwaters in Olympic National Park to the Strait of Juan de Fuca, and a terrible wrong imposed on the salmon-dependent Lower Elwha Klallam tribe has been righted.

This is the passage you need to read and analyze in your essay.

President Obama should learn from that example. Most urgently, he should turn his attention to the Snake River in eastern Washington, where four dams along its lower reaches provide marginal (and replaceable) electricity generation that is outweighed by the opportunities for the revival of endangered salmon populations, plus the jobs and communities a healthy salmon fishery would support. Those deadbeat dams should be taken down and added to the list of dams in the process of being removed along the White Salmon River in Washington, the Penobscot in Maine and the Klamath in southern Oregon.

I've been working to take down dams for most of my life. The idea, once considered crazy, is gaining momentum. We should seize it and push for the removal of the many dams with high costs and low or zero value. The environmental impacts are too enormous.

Time and again, I've witnessed the celebration that comes with the removal of an unnecessary dam. After a river is restored and the fish have returned you never hear a single person say, "Gee, I wish we had our dam back."

These are the specific instructions for what your essay should accomplish.

Assignment: Write an essay in which you explain how Yvon Chouinard builds an argument to persuade his audience that obsolete dams should be removed. In your essay, analyze how Chouinard uses one or more of the features listed in the box above (or features of your own choice) to strengthen the logic and persuasiveness of his argument. Be sure that your analysis focuses on the most relevant features of the passage.

Your essay should not explain whether you agree with Chouinard's claims, but rather explain how Chouinard builds an argument to persuade his audience.

Pretty different, huh? Don't worry, these changes are actually to your advantage. While the old SAT essays asked you to generate all of your evidence on your own, now all of the evidence is right in front of you. You just have to learn how to use it, and that's what this chapter is all about.

In this chapter, we will cover:

- what the College Board looks for in a good essay;
- how to analyze someone else's argument;
- how to use your time wisely;
- and finally, how to put this all together to write a great essay.

So let's get started!

APPROACHING THE ESSAY

SAT Essay Basics
Part 1

In this part, we'll cover some essay writing basics and give you some tips that will help you to write a strong essay. Some of our tips will be very familiar, because writing an SAT essay has a lot in common with some of the writing assignments you may have received in school. But some of our tips will be quite different from what you normally use in school—these tips are specific to the SAT and what the College Board is looking for in an essay. We'll point these tips out and explain why it's so important that you follow them.

Use the Answer Sheet

Recall that you'll be given four lined pages in your answer sheet to write your essay. Don't write outside the space provided. The instructions on your exam booklet will also tell you this, but it is important enough to emphasize here. The only portion of your essay that the grader will see is what you write in the designated section of the exam booklet. Don't try to squeeze anything into the margins; your grader will never see it. For notes, use the space in your test booklet rather than your exam booklet.

Write neatly. We know, we know: you have heard this one before, but writing neatly is particularly important on the SAT. Unlike the other computer-graded sections of the SAT, the essay has to be read by another human being, which makes the legibility of your writing very important. Ensure that your grader sees the greatness of your essay by writing neatly and legibly.

Write as Much as Possible

Aim for the greatest amount of writing possible. One of the first things your grader will see is how much space your essay takes up on the answer pages provided. Filling up as much of the answer pages as possible tells your grader that you have taken the time to write a thorough, well-argued essay. You have plenty of space to write; use as much of it as possible to develop your argument.

Write six full paragraphs. You have a full fifty minutes to write; that's plenty of time to outline and write a six-paragraph essay. Six paragraphs will give you enough space to write an introduction, conclusion, several body paragraphs, and possibly even a counterargument. Writing six paragraphs will also properly break up four pages of writing. You want to give your grader a good structure so they can easily follow your argument: one long run-on paragraph can be difficult to follow, and so can too many short paragraphs.

BE EXPLICIT

State your argument as clearly as possible. Emphasize your main point in the first and last sentence of every paragraph. It's easy to think that the main point of your argument is abundantly clear throughout your essay. Of course it's clear to you—you're in the middle of writing it! Your grader is going to need a little more help following your argument, however. Help them out by re-emphasizing your main point at the beginning and end of every paragraph.

Refer back to the provided text. One of the purposes of the revised SAT essay structure is to test your ability to read as well as write. There is no better way to demonstrate that you properly understood the passage than by quoting it throughout your analysis. Having the passage right in front of you provides you with abundant evidence to use in your essay—take advantage of it!

REVISE

Clean up your spelling and grammar. Graders can penalize you for grammatical and spelling errors, particularly if it makes your essay difficult to read. So take the extra time the new SAT provides to read over your essay and fix any spelling or grammatical mistakes you may have made.

Revise, revise, revise. Besides giving you more time to write, the College Board has another purpose in giving you fifty minutes to complete the Essay: revision. Fifty minutes gives you plenty of time to go back and read over your essay after you've finished writing. It's easy to make silly mistakes when you're hurrying to write your argument down on paper. Take a few minutes at the end of the section to slow down and fix those mistakes. They're easy to fix as long as you have a good eraser!

Now that we've gone over some of the more basic essay-writing tips, it's time to delve into a more detailed explanation of how to write a good essay. Let's begin with the foundation of your essay: its structure.

STRUCTURING AN ESSAY
PART 2

Think of your essay as a house. If you want your house to remain standing, you have to build it using a good structure. Your essay works the same way. The best way to showcase your argument is to frame it with a good external and internal structure. This section will show you the best ways to structure your essay on the SAT.

EXTERNAL STRUCTURE

There are two types of structures that make up your essay. First is the **external** or overall structure. Think of this as the frame of the house. The frame of a house is what holds the house up. The external structure of your essay does the same thing. The proper arrangement of your introduction, body paragraphs, and conclusion provides the foundation for your argument. Without it, your grader will not be able to follow your argument and all of your wonderful analysis will be lost.

Below is a map of what the overall structure of your essay should look like, and estimates of how much time you should spend on each section. This is probably similar to the format you learned in school. The College Board is not looking for anything fancy; they just want you to make your argument in a clear and straightforward manner.

Analyze Passage (*10 minutes*)

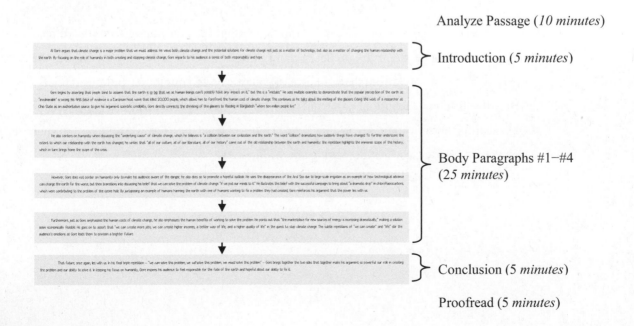

Introduction (*5 minutes*)

Body Paragraphs #1–#4 (*25 minutes*)

Conclusion (*5 minutes*)

Proofread (*5 minutes*)

INTERNAL STRUCTURE

Now we will address the other type of structure found in your essay: the internal structure. Going back to our house analogy, the **internal structure** is like the support beams of the house; they aren't quite as prominent as the frame of the house, but they are just as integral to holding up the structure. The internal structure of your individual paragraphs functions exactly the same way.

We will now walk through the internal structure of each type of paragraph in your essay: introduction, body paragraph, and conclusion.

INTRODUCTION

The introductory paragraph of your essay is the first one that your grader will read and thus sets the tone for the rest of your essay. You know the saying, "You only get one chance to make a first impression?" The same thing applies to your introduction; it's hard to structure a good, coherent essay if the introduction doesn't make any sense.

The best way to make your introduction clear is to keep it brief and straightforward. You may have learned the "funneling" technique for writing introductions in school, where you start with a broad statement and eventually work your way down to your thesis statement. Do *not* use this technique on the SAT. You don't have the time to write such a long introduction, and your goal should be getting to your point as quickly as possible so you can spend the bulk of your time focusing on your body paragraphs.

Start with a brief statement or two relevant to the prompt, demonstrating that you've read the passage and understood the author's claim. Then move directly to your **thesis**, the sentence where you will lay out the argument of your essay. In your thesis, be sure to briefly describe the different supporting arguments you will be making. This will make it easier for your grader to follow your essay as they read. Think of your thesis as a road map for your essay; you don't want your grader taking any wrong turns.

Body Paragraphs

After the introduction comes the meat of your essay: the body paragraphs. In your body paragraphs, you will elaborate on the different arguments that you mentioned in your thesis statement and link them together to create your overall analysis.

Each body paragraph is like a mini-essay, in a way. Each paragraph should start with a **topic sentence**. A topic sentence is like a mini-thesis statement: it states what the rest of the paragraph is going to be about.

Following the topic sentence should be 3-4 **supporting sentences**. In these sentences, you should analyze evidence you have found in the passage and explain how it supports the argument you made in your topic sentence.

Finally, following these supporting sentences, you should have a **concluding sentence**. This sentence should summarize the point you have made in your body paragraph so that you leave the reader with a solid foundation for going on to your next point.

It's also important to use **transitions** in your essay. Transitions are words or phrases that link your ideas together. They help your reader follow your argument and keep your writing from seeming choppy. The most common place for transitions is in your topic sentences. In the following sentences, the words in italics are examples of transitions:

- *However*, the author does not rely on personal experience alone.
- The author *also* builds her argument by using scientific evidence.
- *Furthermore*, the author uses vivid language to appeal to her readers' emotions as well as their intellect.

Conclusion

Your conclusion sums up the argument you have been making throughout your entire essay so that your grader knows exactly what your argument is. Therefore, it is very important that your conclusion be clear and, like your introduction, brief. Resist the urge to add new arguments in your conclusion; instead, just restate the arguments you have already made.

The first sentence of your conclusion should rephrase the thesis statement you wrote in your introduction. Don't rewrite it word for word (your grader will notice), but generally restate the ideas present in the thesis. The purpose of this sentence is to show how you have proven the arguments of your thesis statement.

Following this restatement of purpose, you should try to answer the "so what?" question. Your teachers may have asked you this question before at the end of a writing assignment. The point of asking this question is to make you think about the importance or implications of your argument. In other words, why should anyone care about what you've just written? Does it make you think about the author's claim in a different way? Or does it perhaps reveal some flaws in the author's argument?

You now know how to structure your essay; in terms of our house analogy, both the external and internal structures have been built. Now it's time to fill that house. In the next section, you will learn how to analyze another person's argument. You will use this analysis to "fill up" your essay.

PRACTICE SET

Read the sample introduction below. Then, identify the different elements that make it effective at introducing the writer's claims. Ask a trusted reader to check your work.

In "Tear Down 'Deadbeat' Dams," Yvon Chouinard makes a compelling argument for why the United States government should remove ineffective, environmentally harmful dams. Four distinct features make Chouinard's argument so compelling: his use of impressively large statistics, his employment of specific examples, his telling of personal anecdotes, and the logical organization of his argument. These features in combination make Chouinard's essay very convincing.

1. How does the writer demonstrate that she has read the passage and understood the author's claim?

2. What is the writer's thesis statement?

3. How does the writer describe the supporting arguments that she will be making in the essay?

Read the sample body paragraph below. Then, identify the components that make it effective at conveying its topic. Ask a trusted reader to check your work.

One feature of Chouinard's essay that makes it convincing is the effective use of evidence, particularly undeniably large numbers. For example, in the very first paragraph, Chouinard cites that "[o]f the more than 80,000 dams listed by the federal government, more than 26,000 pose high or significant safety hazards." Safety hazards numbering in the tens of thousands are difficult to ignore. Chouinard utilizes large-number statistics later when describing the example of the Elwha River: "Salmon runs that once reached about 400,000 fish a year dropped to fewer than 3,000." Again, a 397,000 drop in salmon in a single river makes a fairly compelling case for dam removal. Chouinard's skillful employment of large, eye-grabbing statistics gives his obscure topic more force and makes his argument more powerful.

4. What is the writer's topic sentence?

5. How does the writer analyze evidence from the passage in order to support the argument in her topic sentence?

6. What is the writer's concluding sentence?

Read the sample conclusion below. Then, identify the components that make it effective at summarizing the writer's argument. Ask a trusted reader to check your work.

> Chouinard utilizes many strategies to make his argument convincing, among them eye-grabbing statistics, specific examples, personal anecdotes, and logical organization. Together these strategies form a compelling claim for dam removal. Using these strategies is especially important in promoting a relatively low-profile environmental cause such as this.

7. How does the writer re-state the ideas present in her thesis?

8. How does the writer explain the importance or implications of her argument?

ANALYZING AN ARGUMENT

The Essay is not just a test of your writing ability—it's also a test of your reading ability. The assignment doesn't ask you to write about the *topic* presented in the provided passage; instead, you need to write about how the author builds his *argument* in the passage. That means you can't write a great essay without solidly understanding and analyzing the passage first.

The first step to writing your essay is to read the prompt carefully. Use **active reading** to mark up the provided passage. This way, you can easily refer back to the techniques the author uses to construct his or her argument. Those techniques are what the bulk of your essay should be about. For more information on active reading, see Chapter 2.

Of course, you want to be smart about what you're paying attention to. In this section, we're going to go over three different areas you can examine when you're looking for ways to analyze the author's argument: language, organization, and evidence. We'll discuss how to write about these areas, as well as how to fully support your claims so that your essay is both insightful and thorough.

LANGUAGE

PART 1

Authors choose every word carefully. The decision to use a certain word or phrase can tell you more than just the information the author is trying to get across. It can convey the author's opinion or add layers of emotion to what could have been just a statement of fact.

This might sound complicated, but you choose your words instinctively all the time. You use different vocabulary around your teachers than you do around your friends, or even around different groups of friends.

EXAMPLE

> After sleeping through his alarm, Carlos *ran* all the way to school.
> After sleeping through his alarm, Carlos *sprinted* all the way to school.

The information in these sentences is the same: Carlos slept through his alarm and headed to school quickly. The difference is in the language. By using "sprinted," the second sentence implies that Carlos was not only running, but running as fast as he could. This conveys a sense of urgency in Carlos's mission to get to school on time. If Carlos slips in the door just past the first bell, he might choose to use "sprinted" to persuade his teacher that he tried his best and wasn't just slacking—so maybe she could cut him a break this one time!

Now, the author of the passage probably won't be talking about a teenager who's late for class, but the same principles will apply. When you see a word that sticks out to you, ask yourself: how does this enrich what the author is trying to say? What does this word add that a different word would have lacked?

CONNOTATIONS

It can be useful to think about a word's **connotations**—ideas that might not be part of its dictionary definition, but are implied when people use that particular word. For example, you could describe your uncle who collects lizards as "eccentric" or "weird." Both of these words mean he's not what most people would consider normal, but "eccentric" has a neutral or even positive connotation, whereas "weird" has a negative connotation. An eccentric uncle is someone you hope adds excitement to a family reunion; a weird uncle is one you might hope stays home.

To identify the connotations of a word, think about how you usually hear people use it. A word that people generally use to describe something they don't like has a negative connotation; a word that people use for something they like has a positive connotation. If an author has chosen a word with a negative connotation, she is trying to paint what she's describing in a negative light.

RHETORICAL DEVICES

A **rhetorical device** is a tool the author uses to persuade the reader to agree with their argument. Rhetorical devices aren't just about the literal meaning of the words; they're about how those words are used to make an argument more vivid or appeal to the reader's emotions.

For example, an author who is concerned about losses in the bee population could just write, "Bees are dying in North America, South America, and Europe." However, she might also choose to write: "Bees are dying in North America. They're dying in South America. They're dying in Europe." That author would be using **repetition** to make her point more dramatic and persuade her reader to care.

That same author might also use rhetorical devices to explain why we should care about bees. She could say, for example, "Bees are as important to the planet as bones are to the human body." That would be a **simile**, a comparison of two unlike things using the words "like" or "as." In this case, comparing bees to human bones emphasizes how necessary bees are. Without bones, the human body would collapse, so she's implying that without bees, the planet would collapse.

A simile is an example of **figurative language**, or language used in a creative or interesting way. Figurative language is a common rhetorical device for authors who want to spice up their arguments and make them more compelling. You can learn more about specific types of figurative language in Chapter 2.

Remember that it is not enough just to identify tools the author uses. You must also pinpoint where the author uses these tools *and* state clearly how those tools contribute to the author's argument.

EXAMPLE

> Our nation's trees are crying out for relief from air pollution.

Trees don't cry; by giving a human characteristic to something that is not human, this sentence is using **personification**. However, your grader will not be impressed if you only write, "The author uses personification." You must be specific about where the author uses it, what it accomplishes, and, if possible, how it contributes to the overall argument: "The author states that our nation's trees are 'crying,' thus using personification to rouse the reader's sympathy. This gives emotional weight to her argument that we must work to end air pollution soon."

EXAMPLE

Suppose that in a passage arguing that it is important to preserve playgrounds, an author writes:

> Neglected playgrounds become dangerous playgrounds, and for most parents the risks posed by a dangerous playground are worse than no playground at all. Do we want future generations to grow up without memories of going down slides or playing on the swings?

The second sentence is a **rhetorical question**—not a question the author thinks needs to be answered, but a question used to make a point. Once again, it's not enough to write, "The author uses a rhetorical question," or even "The author uses a rhetorical question to support his point." A better claim to make about this would be: "By posing a rhetorical question about 'future generations,' the author invites the reader to imagine those generations growing up without safe playgrounds."

PART 1 PRACTICE: LANGUAGE

In the selection below, we've underlined writing choices you could talk about to analyze how the author uses language to add weight to his argument—that we should remove dams instead of building new ones. Choose four of these words or phrases and write a couple sentences explaining why the author has made these particular language choices. Remember to quote from the text and connect your examples to the author's purpose. Have a trusted reader check your work.

Adapted from "Tear Down 'Deadbeat' Dams" by Yvon Chouinard. © 2014 by the New York Times Company. Originally published May 7, 2014.

New dams are a bad idea. We've glorified them for decades, but our pride in building these engineering marvels has often blinded us to the environmental damage they cause. The consequences run the length of the river and beyond. Our many complex attempts to work around these obstacles would make Rube Goldberg proud. Interventions like fish elevators and trap-and-haul programs that truck fish around impoundments don't lead to true recovery for wild fish populations or reverse the other environmental problems caused by blocking a river's flow.

But we do know that removing dams brings streams and rivers back to life and replenishes our degraded aquifers.

1. The first word or phrase I am analyzing:

   Why has the author chosen this word or phrase to use?

2. The second word or phrase I am analyzing:

   Why has the author chosen this word or phrase to use?

3. The third word or phrase I am analyzing:

   Why has the author chosen this word or phrase to use?

4. The fourth word or phrase I am analyzing:

   Why has the author chosen this word or phrase to use?

EVIDENCE

PART 2

The author of the provided passage will use different kinds of evidence to support the point being made. In this part, we'll take a look at some of the evidence that an author might decide to use.

PERSONAL EVIDENCE

Sometimes evidence will be based on personal experience: a conversation the author has had, or an event she's witnessed, which relates to the topic at hand. For example, an author might choose to open an article about the use of technology among teens by talking about her kids who spend all of dinner hunched over their smartphones. A college professor writing about the attitudes of current undergraduates might list some examples of comments her students have made in her classes. An author vouching for the benefits of reading fiction might discuss her own experiences with fiction and how it's improved her life.

Personal evidence often makes a topic more immediate for a reader. It can illustrate what a large issue looks like in someone's day-to-day life. Authors sometimes also use it to make themselves seem relatable and therefore trustworthy. For example, in the passage we've been using, Yvon Chouinard writes, "Time and again, I've witnessed the celebration that comes with the removal of an unnecessary dam." This enables the reader to attach a specific image to a larger situation.

DATA AND ITS SOURCES

Other times evidence will be in the form of data, or facts collected by researchers to provide information about a group or issue. This kind of evidence is often presented numerically, as in the statement "80% of all statistics are totally made up." Other times, instead of giving a specific number, the author will summarize the data with a word or phrase such as "most" or "fewer than half."

Authors will typically give a citation for supporting evidence in the form of data. Sometimes this will be broad, as in the phrase "studies show…." Other times, however, they will specify the organization or people who collected the data by name. This is especially common if the data comes from an authoritative source, or a source which the reader has good reason to believe will provide accurate information. Drawing on an authoritative source lends the author credibility; using data from an authoritative source suggests both that it must be true and that the author is knowledgeable.

There are a variety of authoritative sources. Governmental organizations are a common one, whether named specifically (such as the Bureau of Labor Statistics) or just referred to as "the federal government." Authors also use professional bodies such as the American Medical Association, and international organizations such as the World Health Organization. If you're not sure what type of organization the author is naming, that's okay—just be sure to specify that it is an authoritative source.

A source might also be authoritative because of where it was first presented, such as in a reputable publication like the *New England Journal of Medicine*. You can also look for the names of universities, which usually signal an authoritative source. They might show up in citing data ("Researchers at Howard University have found…") or in providing individual expert testimony ("Henry Louis Gates, a professor at Harvard University…").

A source's expertise might also be established through other means. Someone might have written a book related to the subject ("Michelle Alexander, whose recently published *The New Jim Crow: Mass Incarceration in the Age of Colorblindness* deals with this topic…"). An expert might also have won a distinguished prize in his field ("Steven Chu, who received the 1997 Nobel Prize in Physics…"). Someone also might just have an extremely respected position that automatically lends her authority ("Supreme Court Justice Sonia Sotomayor has stated…").

WRITING ABOUT EVIDENCE

Writing about evidence means looking at a different set of elements than when you're writing about language. So far, we've given you an overview of what to look out for when you're hunting for the author's use of evidence. However, just like we discussed above, identifying these elements is only the first step. It's crucial that when you bring up evidence in your essay, you spell out how the author uses it to support her broader argument.

> Recently, researchers at the University of Pennsylvania have found that sleep deprivation causes permanent brain damage in mice. This should give us pause as we contemplate the trade-offs of encouraging young people to achieve success at the expense of resting their bodies.

You could write, "The author uses an authoritative source to show that sleep deprivation causes brain damage in mice," and it would be accurate. However, it would not be sufficient, because the mice aren't central to the author's main point: the author is using this evidence to discuss the effects of sleep deprivation on *people*. A better way to discuss this would be, "The author cites research on mice from The University of Pennsylvania, an authoritative source which gives scientific credibility to her argument that we should be concerned about the physical dangers of sleep deprivation in people."

The key thing to notice is that we made the link between what the author did—use an authoritative source—and *why the author did it*: to support the passage's broader argument. Don't assume this connection is obvious to your reader; while it may be, you need to prove that *you* see that connection, too.

Part 2 Practice: Evidence

As you read the following selection, look for different ways the author uses evidence to support his argument that old dams should be torn down and new dams should not be built. Identify four pieces of evidence along with their sources, and describe how this evidence supports the author's argument. Have a trusted reader check your work.

> *Adapted from "Tear Down 'Deadbeat' Dams" by Yvon Chouinard. ©2014 by the New York Times Company. Originally published May 7, 2014.*
>
> Of the more than 80,000 dams listed by the federal government, more than 26,000 pose high or significant safety hazards. Many no longer serve any real purpose. All have limited life spans. Only about 1,750 produce hydropower, according to the National Hydropower Association.
>
> Last year, 51 dams in 18 states were taken down, restoring more than 500 miles of streams, according to the group American Rivers. Nearly 850 have been removed in the last 20 years, and nearly 1,150 since 1912.
>
> A case in point is the Elwha River on

the Olympic Peninsula in Washington, where two hydroelectric dams built early in the last century exacted huge environmental costs but were no longer important as power generators. Salmon runs that once reached about 400,000 fish a year dropped to fewer than 3,000. A year after the Elwha Dam was removed, Chinook salmon returned to the river in numbers not seen in decades, with three-quarters of them observed spawning upstream of the former dam site.

Time and again, I've witnessed the celebration that comes with the removal of an unnecessary dam. After a river is restored and the fish have returned you never hear a single person say, "Gee, I wish we had our dam back."

1. The first piece of evidence I am analyzing:

   Its source:

   How it supports the author's argument:

2. The second piece of evidence I am analyzing:

   Its source:

   How it supports the author's argument:

3. The third piece of evidence I am analyzing:

   Its source:

   How it supports the author's argument:

4. The fourth piece of evidence I am analyzing:

   Its source:

   How it supports the author's argument:

ORGANIZATION AND REASONING
PART 3

How authors choose to organize their arguments can be just as important as the language and facts they use to make them. The authors of the essay passages recognize the importance of a logically organized and coherent argument, and they use organization to give their argument the most emphasis possible. We are now going to show you how to recognize these methods and how to write about them effectively.

LOGICAL STRUCTURE

Picking out the logical structure of a piece of writing might sound difficult, but in fact our brains do it subconsciously all the time. We are geared to find patterns in everything around us in order to make sense of it.

EXAMPLE

- Annie put a bandage on her scrapes.
- Annie fought with her mother about wearing knee pads while skating.
- Annie skated over some gravel and fell.
- Annie ignored her mother and went skating without knee pads.

On the first reading, these sentences don't make any sense at all, right? The events are out of order, and our brains pick up on that immediately. We might even try to start reorganizing the sentences without thinking about it (the correct order is 2, 4, 3, 1).

We apply this instinct to find patterns in pretty much everything we see, including writing. In fact, the SAT also tests this skill in the Writing Test, using multiple choice questions that ask you to select the best order from a choice of four options. On the Essay, you'll be recognizing the organization on your own, rather than picking it up from a line-up of potential options, and you'll be writing about how that organization helps (or hurts) the author's argument.

Tracking the Author's Argument

The easiest way to think about organization and logical reasoning is to think about how the author moves from one point to another. As you read the following selection, let's track the different ways the author uses evidence to support his argument that we should remove obsolete dams.

Adapted from "Tear Down 'Deadbeat' Dams" by Yvon Chouinard, 2014, The New York Times Company.

Of the more than 80,000 dams listed by the federal government, more than 26,000 pose high or significant safety hazards. Many no longer serve any real purpose. All have limited life spans. Only about 1,750 produce hydropower, according to the National Hydropower Association.

The author begins his argument with several statements about the negative effects of dams. This establishes the harm posed by dams, setting up the author to propose a solution.

In many cases, the benefits that dams have historically provided—for water use, flood control and electricity—can <u>now</u> be met more effectively without continuing to choke entire watersheds.

The author further establishes his argument by showing how dams are no longer useful.

"Now" is a word that can signal a logical contrast (i.e. while something was like this then, now it is different).

Put simply, many dams have high environmental costs that outweigh their value. Removing them is the only sensible answer. And taking them down can often make economic sense as well. The River Alliance of Wisconsin estimates that removing dams in that state is three to five times less expensive than repairing them.

The author summarizes his prior points and shapes them into a coherent thesis statement. He also provides his solution: remove the deadbeat dams.

The message has been slowly spreading around the country. More and more communities and states have reclaimed rivers lost to jackhammers and concrete. Last year, 51 dams in 18 states were taken down, restoring more than 500 miles of streams, according to the group American Rivers. Nearly 850 have been removed in the last 20 years, and nearly 1,150 since 1912.

The author broadens his argument from a personal opinion to a national "message," giving his argument greater clout.

<u>But</u> the work is far from done. I was

"But" is another organizational signpost that signals a logical turn.

disappointed to see the Energy Department release a report last week on the potential to develop new "sustainable" hydroelectric dams on rivers and streams across the country. The report follows President Obama's signing of two laws last year to encourage small hydro projects and revive nonproducing dams.

New dams are a bad idea. We've glorified them for decades, but our pride in building these engineering marvels has often blinded us to the environmental damage they cause. The consequences run the length of the river and beyond. Our many complex attempts to work around these obstacles would make Rube Goldberg proud. Interventions like fish elevators and trap-and-haul programs that truck fish around impoundments don't lead to true recovery for wild fish populations or reverse the other environmental problems caused by blocking a river's flow.

But we do know that removing dams brings streams and rivers back to life and replenishes our degraded aquifers.

A case in point is the Elwha River on the Olympic Peninsula in Washington, where two hydroelectric dams built early in the last century exacted huge environmental costs but were no longer important as power generators. Today, the river runs free from its headwaters in Olympic National Park to the Strait of Juan de Fuca, and a terrible wrong imposed on the salmon-dependent Lower Elwha Klallam tribe has been righted.

I've been working to take down dams for most of my life. The idea, once considered crazy, is gaining momentum. We should seize it and push for the removal of the many dams with high costs and low or zero value. The environmental impacts are too enormous.

The author maintains the urgency of his argument by pointing out that there is still much work to be done in removing dams.

The author moves to another point in his argument about dams: we shouldn't build any new ones. This both reinforces the points the author made earlier in the passage and allows him to introduce new evidence against dams.

After showing how bad dams are, the author shows us the other side of his argument—the many benefits of dam removal.

The author supports this logical turn with a specific example about the Elwha River. Again, the author uses a now/then contrast to illustrate the benefits of removing dams.

The author brings the argument back to his personal perspective, using his authority as a life-long fighter of dams to make his argument even more credible.

The author summarizes his prior points and shapes them into a coherent thesis statement. He also provides his solution: remove the deadbeat dams.

> Time and again, I've witnessed the celebration that comes with the removal of an unnecessary dam. After a river is restored and the fish have returned you never hear a single person say, "Gee, I wish we had our dam back."

The author concludes the passage with a statement that reinforces the apparent obviousness of his argument—who would ever want a dam back when its removal clearly provided so much good?

Not too bad, right? Following an author's argument is much like reading a roadmap: once you get used to the signs, it's easy to follow. But identifying the author's organizational and logical methods is only half of the job. You also need to be able to write about them effectively.

WRITING ABOUT STRUCTURE

After you have tracked the author's main argument through the passage, you'll need to figure out how to write about that structure. The easiest way to do this is to ask the question "Why?" Why does the author move from a certain point to another? Why does she use a certain kind of logical reasoning to connect these points? Answering these "why" questions will enable you to write about how these organizational decisions on the author's part did or did not aid her argument.

EXAMPLE

Take the first organizational turn we noticed in our example passage:

> In many cases, the benefits that dams have historically provided—for water uses, flood control and electricity—can now be met more effectively without continuing to choke watersheds.

We identified that the author places a turn in the middle of the sentence. The author acknowledges why we have built dams in the past, but then points out their current ineffectiveness. Why does the author do this? There are a few things we could write about to answer that question:

- First, acknowledging the past benefits of dams makes the author's argument seem more balanced and fair.
- Second, showing that these benefits can be provided by other more efficient mechanisms makes dams seem unnecessary.

- Third, showing that these other methods are more environmentally friendly makes dams seem unnecessary *and* bad.

And just like that, we have a paragraph's worth of writing about one small part of the passage's logical organization.

PART 3 PRACTICE: ORGANIZATION AND REASONING

Now it's your turn. Below are some more organizational and logical turns from the "'Deadbeat' Dams" passage. Explain why the author included these turns and how they help or hurt his argument. Have a trusted reader check your work.

> And taking them down can often make economic sense as well. The River Alliance of Wisconsin estimates that removing dams in that state is three to five times less expensive than repairing them.

1. Why did the author include this turn?

2. How does it help or hurt his argument?

> New dams are a bad idea. We've glorified them for decades, but our pride in building these engineering marvels has often blinded us to the environmental damage they cause.

3. Why did the author include this turn?

4. How does it help or hurt his argument?

PUTTING IT TOGETHER
PART 4

Now that we've gone over how to analyze an author's language, evidence, and organization, it's time to put them all together. In the sample passage below, we've marked up the full prompt text we've been using with the kinds of observations you might use in your essay.

SAMPLE PASSAGE ANALYSIS

As you read the passage below, consider how Yvon Chouinard uses

- evidence, such as facts or examples, to support claims.
- reasoning to develop ideas and to connect claims and evidence.
- stylistic or persuasive elements, such as word choice or appeals to emotion, to add power to the ideas expressed.

Adapted from "Tear Down 'Deadbeat' Dams" by Yvon Chouinard, 2014, The New York Times Company.

Of the more than 80,000 dams listed by the federal government, more than 26,000 pose high or significant safety hazards. Many no longer serve any real purpose. All have limited life spans. Only about 1,750 produce hydropower, according to the National Hydropower Association.

In many cases, the benefits that dams have historically provided — for water use, flood control and electricity — can now be met more effectively without continuing to choke entire watersheds.

Dams degrade water quality, block the movement of nutrients and sediment, destroy fish and wildlife habitats, damage coastal estuaries and in some cases rob

(1) Yvon Chouinard uses evidence from an authoritative source (the federal government) to support his claim that dams pose serious dangers. Placing this statistic in the first sentence adds urgency to his pleas.

(2) The author uses evidence from another authoritative source (the National Hydropower Association) to show that many more dams pose serious hazards than produce hydropower, suggesting that the dangers outweigh the benefits.

(3) The author acknowledges that dams "originally provided" specific benefits and suggests that there are now better ways of meeting these needs without negative consequences. The author demonstrates that he is knowledgeable about several sides of the issue.

(4) Vivid word choices such as "degrade" and "destroy" dramatize the effect of dams on the environment. The word "rob" heightens their menace, implying that dams are stealing nitrogen that rightly belongs to forests.

surrounding forests of nitrogen. Reservoirs can also be significant sources of greenhouse gas emissions.

Put simply, many dams have high environmental costs that outweigh their value. Removing them is the only sensible answer. And taking them down can often make economic sense as well. The River Alliance of Wisconsin estimates that removing dams in that state is three to five times less expensive than repairing them.

The message has been slowly spreading around the country. More and more communities and states have reclaimed rivers lost to jackhammers and concrete. Last year, 51 dams in 18 states were taken down, restoring more than 500 miles of streams, according to the group American Rivers. Nearly 850 have been removed in the last 20 years, and nearly 1,150 since 1912.

But the work is far from done. I was disappointed to see the Energy Department release a report last week on the potential to develop new "sustainable" hydroelectric dams on rivers and streams across the country. The report follows President Obama's signing of two laws last year to encourage small hydro projects and revive nonproducing dams.

New dams are a bad idea. We've glorified them for decades, but our pride in building these engineering marvels has often blinded us to the environmental damage they cause. The consequences run the length of the river and beyond. Our many complex attempts to work around these obstacles would make Rube Goldberg proud. Interventions like fish elevators and trap-and-haul programs that truck fish around impoundments don't

(5) After listing concrete examples of the damage caused by dams, the author summarizes his point that dams are harmful and not worth the environmental cost, and then concisely states his solution.

(6) The author uses statistics from another authoritative source (the River Alliance of Wisconsin) to support his claim that removing dams makes economic sense as well.

(7) By claiming that his solution is increasing in popularity, the author portrays his argument as viable, since communities and states have already adopted it.

(8) Careful word choice makes his cause seem righteous. Saying communities have "reclaimed" rivers that were "lost" positions dams as an injustice to the communities and environment.

(9) The author uses specific statistics as evidence to back up his claim that the removal of dams is already in process.

(10) The author clarifies that although his plan for dam removal is in some ways already in motion, the situation is still urgent.

(11) Referring to a specific event from as recently as a week ago makes the subject seem very timely.

(12) The author suggests that the appeal of new dams lies in our pride in building them rather than in anything they actually accomplish.

(13) Rube Goldberg was a cartoonist famous for drawings of gadgets that performed simple tasks in extremely complicated ways. By saying that our attempts to minimize the damage of dams would "make Rube Goldberg proud," the author is implying that we are doing many unnecessarily complicated things while overlooking the obvious solution.

(14) The author elaborates on the comparison he just made by naming some of those unnecessarily complicated interventions and stating that they are not effective.

lead to true recovery for wild fish populations or reverse the other environmental problems caused by blocking a river's flow.

But we do know that removing dams brings streams and rivers back to life and replenishes our degraded aquifers.

A case in point is the Elwha River on the Olympic Peninsula in Washington, where two hydroelectric dams built early in the last century exacted huge environmental costs but were no longer important as power generators. Salmon runs that once reached about 400,000 fish a year dropped to fewer than 3,000. A year after the Elwha Dam was removed, Chinook salmon returned to the river in numbers not seen in decades, with three-quarters of them observed spawning upstream of the former dam site. Today, the river runs free from its headwaters in Olympic National Park to the Strait of Juan de Fuca, and a terrible wrong imposed on the salmon-dependent Lower Elwha Klallam tribe has been righted.

President Obama should learn from that example. Most urgently, he should turn his attention to the Snake River in eastern Washington, where four dams along its lower reaches provide marginal (and replaceable) electricity generation that is outweighed by the opportunities for the revival of endangered salmon populations, plus the jobs and communities a healthy salmon fisher would support. Those deadbeat dams should be taken down and added to the list of dams in the process of being removed along the White Salmon River in Washington, the Penobscot in Maine and the Klamath in southern Oregon.

I've been working to take down dams for most of my life. The idea, once

(15) The author positions removing dams as the obvious solution being overlooked even though we already know that it is the one guaranteed solution.

(16) This specific example of the dams on the Elwha River underscores his points with vivid descriptions. The descriptions reinforce the idea of dams being obsolete, because these dams were no longer producing significant amounts of power. The descriptions also emphasize the harmfulness of dams, because of the large drop in salmon population. Finally, this case study also exemplifies the author's point that removing dams is an easy, obvious solution, since it only took a year after their removal to see dramatic positive results.

(17) The author portrays the dams as a terrible injustice to the environment—this time especially to a particular local tribe—and says the removal of these dams is necessary to restoring justice.

(18) Invoking the most powerful official in the country (President Obama) makes it clear that this is a national issue, lending the argument urgency and importance because of its national scope.

(19) The author makes clear that removing the dams in question would benefit both salmon (who would see their numbers replenished) and humans (who would see job creation opportunities).

(20) The author uses specific examples to restate his point that removing dams is something more and more communities are already choosing to do.

(21) By stating he has been active in this cause for a long time, the author grants himself the legitimacy of a firsthand witness to support his claim that the idea of taking down dams is gaining support.

considered crazy, is gaining momentum. We should seize it and push for the removal of the many dams with high costs and low or zero value. The environmental impacts are too enormous.

Time and again, I've witnessed the celebration that comes with the removal of an unnecessary dam. After a river is restored and the fish have returned you never hear a single person say, "Gee, I wish we had our dam back."

(22) After several specific, concrete examples, the author summarizes his argument again for emphasis.

(23) The author ends the article by using his personal experience to position himself as a legitimate authority on the benefits of removing dams. A colloquial expression ("gee") gives it a personal feel.

We've annotated this text to illustrate the kinds of choices you should look out for when you read the prompt you're given. You can see that we don't focus on just one kind of tool. Instead, we look at different tools the author wields from a variety of angles. It's important to show that you can recognize a diverse set of strategies.

However, finding these strategies is only the first step. If you were to read our notes like an essay, it would be a mess: totally disorganized, hard to follow, and lacking a clear thesis. In order to turn your thoughts into an essay, you'll need to identify the passage's overarching themes. Then you'll use those to organize your essay.

IDENTIFY THEMES

For the sample text that we've provided, you could pull out the following three themes. Pay attention to the way the author uses multiple strategies to develop each one.

Theme 1: Dams pose a crisis that is both serious and urgent. This is the problem the author is trying to demonstrate.

- He uses authoritative sources to provide evidence that dams are harmful, including the federal government and the National Hydropower Association. Statistics support his claims that dams are dangerous. The example of the Snake River makes it easier for readers to visualize the damage dams cause. In addition, he highlights different *kinds* of harm that dams cause, including depleting the salmon population, destroying wildlife habitats, and hurting the Lower Elwha Klallam tribe.

- He chooses strong words to bring the tragedy to life. Dams don't just block watersheds, they *choke* them. The word "choke" suggests violence. The salmon population in the Elwha River didn't just decrease, it *dropped*. The word "dropped" makes it sound drastic and shocking.

- He emphasizes that this is a problem right *now*. The Energy Department report from the previous week shows that the fight is far from over. By naming President Obama, he implies this issue that must be dealt with immediately, not in the future.

Theme 2: Removing dams is the most logical solution. This is what the author is trying to persuade his audience to believe.

- He identifies several benefits of dam removal. He uses the Elwha River example to show how removing a dam can revive the local salmon population, which benefits the environment. He points out that more salmon would provide job opportunities for local residents, which benefits the community. He uses an authoritative source to show that removing harmful dams is cheaper than fixing them, which benefits the economy.

- He addresses counterarguments that others might make, suggesting that there are no downsides to his plan. He states that there are better ways to accomplish what dams provide. He points out that we could find a way to replace the electricity generated by the dams on Snake River. He also claims that he has never seen anyone regret that a dam has been taken down.

- He argues that removing dams is becoming more popular. This suggests that its effects are positive enough to win people over to his side. He admits that the idea was "once considered crazy," which implies it has become common for people to change their minds about it.

Theme 3: Unnecessary dams are an injustice that must be corrected. This theme is crucial for taking our analysis to the next level. The previous two themes lay out the facts of the author's argument: what is happening (dams pose a crisis) and what we should do about it (tear them down). This theme is about why his argument matters—basically, why we should care. Here, he appeals to the reader's emotions and sense of justice.

- He uses language to frame the damage dams cause in moral terms. Dams "rob" forests of nitrogen, making them sound criminal. When communities take dams down, they "reclaim" rivers once "lost," suggesting that they have restored the natural order of things.

- He explicitly states that the loss of the salmon population of the Elwha River was a "terrible wrong" done to the Lower Elwha Klallam tribe, which was "righted" by removing the dam.

- He refers to dams which are deeply harmful and marginally beneficial as "deadbeat dams," using an adjective with a connotation that suggests a moral failing.

Notice that the author does not lay out these themes in order, detailing one in full and then abandoning it for the next. Instead, he weaves them together throughout the essay. By the time he gets to the example of the Elwha River, he can use it to make all of these ideas come together. This is important to watch out for as you plan your essay—remember that you might be drawing from different parts of the passage to fully support one of your points.

PART 4 PRACTICE: PUTTING IT TOGETHER

We've gone over how to structure your essay so that it's clear and easy to read. We've also given you the tools you need to analyze the different ways an author builds his argument, and write about it so that your own argument will be compelling. Now it's time to put these skills to work. Set a timer for fifty minutes and write the essay we've been working on in this chapter. We've provided the prompt again below. Have a trusted reader check your work.

As you read the passage below, consider how Yvon Chouinard uses

- evidence, such as facts or examples, to support claims.

- reasoning to develop ideas and to connect claims and evidence.

- stylistic or persuasive elements, such as word choice or appeals to emotion, to add power to the ideas expressed.

Adapted from "Tear Down 'Deadbeat' Dams" by Yvon Chouinard, 2014, The New York Times Company

Of the more than 80,000 dams listed by the federal government, more than 26,000 pose high or significant safety hazards. Many no longer serve any real purpose. All have limited life spans. Only about 1,750 produce hydropower, according to the National Hydropower Association.

In many cases, the benefits that dams have historically provided — for water use, flood control and electricity — can now be met more effectively without continuing to choke entire watersheds.

Dams degrade water quality, block the movement of nutrients and sediment, destroy fish and wildlife habitats, damage coastal estuaries and in some cases rob surrounding forests of nitrogen. Reservoirs can also be significant sources of greenhouse gas emissions.

Put simply, many dams have high environmental costs that outweigh their value. Removing them is the only sensible answer. And taking them down can often make economic sense as well. The River Alliance of Wisconsin estimates that removing dams in that state is three to five times less expensive than repairing them.

The message has been slowly spreading around the country. More and more communities and states have reclaimed rivers lost to jackhammers and concrete. Last year, 51 dams in 18 states were taken down, restoring more than 500 miles of streams, according to the group American Rivers. Nearly 850 have been removed in the last 20 years, and nearly 1,150 since 1912.

But the work is far from done. I was disappointed to see the Energy Department release a report last week on the potential to develop new "sustainable" hydroelectric dams on rivers and streams across the country.

The report follows President Obama's signing of two laws last year to encourage small hydro projects and revive nonproducing dams.

New dams are a bad idea. We've glorified them for decades, but our pride in building these engineering marvels has often blinded us to the environmental damage they cause. The consequences run the length of the river and beyond.

Our many complex attempts to work around these obstacles would make Rube Goldberg proud. Interventions like fish elevators and trap-and-haul programs that truck fish around impoundments don't lead to true recovery for wild fish populations or reverse the other environmental problems caused by blocking a river's flow.

But we do know that removing dams brings streams and rivers back to life and replenishes our degraded aquifers.

A case in point is the Elwha River on the Olympic Peninsula in Washington, where two hydroelectric dams built early in the last century exacted huge environmental costs but were no longer important as power generators. Salmon runs that once reached about 400,000 fish a year dropped to fewer than 3,000. A year after the Elwha Dam was removed, Chinook salmon returned to the river in numbers not seen in decades, with three-quarters of them observed spawning upstream of the former dam site. Today, the river runs free from its headwaters in Olympic National Park to the Strait of Juan de Fuca, and a terrible wrong imposed on the salmon-dependent Lower Elwha Klallam tribe has been righted.

President Obama should learn from that example. Most urgently, he should turn his attention to the Snake River in eastern Washington, where four dams along its lower reaches provide marginal (and replaceable) electricity generation that is outweighed by the opportunities for the revival of endangered salmon populations, plus the jobs and communities a healthy salmon fishery would support. Those deadbeat dams should be taken down and added to the list of dams in the process of being removed along the White Salmon River in Washington, the Penobscot in Maine and the Klamath in southern Oregon. I've been working to take down dams for most of my life. The idea, once considered crazy, is gaining momentum. We should seize it and push for the removal of the many dams with high costs and low or zero value. The environmental impacts are too enormous.

Time and again, I've witnessed the celebration that comes with the removal of an unnecessary dam. After a river is restored and the fish have returned you never hear a single person say, "Gee, I wish we had our dam back."

Assignment: Write an essay in which you explain how Yvon Chouinard builds an argument to persuade his audience that obsolete dams should be removed. In your essay, analyze how Chouinard uses one or more of the features listed in the box above (or features of your own choice) to strengthen the logic and persuasiveness of his argument. Be sure that your analysis focuses on the most relevant features of the passage.

Your essay should not explain whether you agree with Chouinard's claims, but rather explain how Chouinard builds an argument to persuade his audience.

ESSAY RUBRIC AND EXAMPLES

The new Essay will be graded on three different areas: Reading, Analysis, and Writing. Earlier, we went over what graders will be looking for in each of those areas. Now we'll see what that might actually look like in your essay.

THE COLLEGE BOARD'S RUBRIC

PART 1

First, we will look at what the College Board wants in the context of its new rubric. In this section, you'll see some examples of what the College Board is looking for in each of its grading criteria—Reading, Analysis, and Writing. We'll use examples from the previous annotated passage that we just reviewed, "Tear Down 'Deadbeat' Dams," by Yvon Chouinard.

READING

In the Reading domain, your graders are evaluating you on how well you show that you understand the prompt passage, including its main argument and the important details. Here are some examples of what they'll be looking for.

What College Board Wants	Good Example	Bad Example
Get the main idea. Even though the prompt gives you a version of the main idea of the passage, the College Board wants to see that you get it on your own.	In this passage, Yvon Chouinard argues that dams have a negative impact on the environment and generally should be removed.	In this passage, Yvon Chouinard talks about his own personal agenda that has something to do with dams.
Use the evidence. Refer back to the passage, either by quoting it directly or paraphrasing.	Chouinard supports his claim with statistics, such as the fact that "[o]f the more than 80,000 dams listed by the federal government, more than 26,000 pose high or significant safety hazards."	Chouinard talks about how lots of dams are doing bad things.
Use the evidence correctly. Use the evidence accurately, both by citing it correctly and by using it in the same spirit as the author.	Chouinard supports his claim with statistics, such as the fact that "[o]f the more than 80,000 dams listed by the federal government, more than 26,000 pose high or significant safety hazards."	Chouinard doesn't cite good facts to support his argument. For example, he states that only 20,000 of the more than 80,000 dams listed by the federal government pose significant safety hazards, which is not that many.

ANALYSIS

In the Analysis domain, your graders are deciding whether you understand the assignment. They want you to analyze an author's argument, not to give your own opinion. These are some things the graders will be looking at to determine your score.

What College Board Wants	Good Example	Bad Example
Analyze, don't respond to the passage. Your job is to analyze the author's argument, *not* respond to it with your own opinions.	Chouinard utilizes a combination of statistical evidence, personal examples, and appeals to authority to make the argument that harmful dams should be removed.	Chouinard really doesn't know what he's talking about; in my opinion, dams are super helpful.
Pick good elements to write about. Read the passage and identify what tools the author uses to make his/her argument.	Chouinard's use of strong numerical evidence shores up his argument and makes the issue seem more important and urgent.	Chouinard writes really well and thus makes a good argument.
Pick the right support for those elements. Pick the strongest, most relevant parts of the passage to support your claims.	For example, Chouinard uses statistics about the decreasing number of salmon in the Elwha River (400,000 down to fewer than 3,000) to demonstrate the negative effects dams have on wildlife.	Chouinard cites lots of statistics to support his argument. For example, he states once a dam is taken down, "you never hear a single person say, 'Gee, I wish we had our dam back.'" That's some strong statistical evidence.

WRITING

In the Writing domain, your graders are evaluating how well you structure your essay, as well as your use of language. Here are some things you should keep in mind.

What College Board Wants	Good Example	Bad Example
Make a claim. When you write an essay, you have to have some sort of claim or argument. This claim should go into a clear, concise thesis statement.	Chouinard uses statistical evidence, personal examples, and appeals to authority to build his argument that removing harmful dams is necessary to restore justice.	This is an interesting article about dams.
Organize your argument. Your reader won't be able to appreciate the greatness of your analysis if they can't properly follow your argument.	See Section 2, Part 2 earlier in this chapter.	See Section 2, Part 2 earlier in this chapter.
Switch up your sentences. Don't just use simple sentences—mix it up!	Though some of Chouinard's evidence comes in the form of personal anecdotes, much of it comes from authoritative sources. This combination of evidence makes his argument more well-rounded as well as easier to read.	Chouinard is a good writer. He makes good points. He uses good evidence.
Choose smart words. Try to include higher caliber words in your sentences. However, never use words whose meanings you don't entirely understand. This can actually hurt your essay.	Chouinard appeals to the federal government when he directly addresses President Obama.	Chouinard pretends he's talking to President Obama to make a point.
Use an academic tone. For an academic essay like this, you should always use a formal tone—avoid slang or informal language.	Although Chouinard can be didactic at times, overall he effectively argues for the removal of dams.	Even though this guy is pretty boring sometimes, you can really understand where he's coming from.
Use good grammar. Use good grammar and spelling. Be sure to read over your essay at least once after you've finished writing to catch any mistakes.	Chouinard argues that there are many reasons to close down deadbeat dams.	Chouinard argues "there are many reasons closing down Deadbeat Dams"

SAMPLE ESSAYS
PART 2

Now let's look at some sample student writing and see how the College Board's criteria apply to full-length essays. We have provided examples of four essays in response to the prompt below. The four sample essays demonstrate Reading, Analysis, and Writing scores of 1, 2, 3, and 4.

ESSAY PROMPT

As you read the passage below, consider how Al Gore uses

- evidence, such as facts or examples, to support claims.
- reasoning to develop ideas and to connect claims and evidence.
- stylistic or persuasive elements, such as word choice or appeals to emotion, to add power to the ideas expressed.

Adapted from former Vice President Al Gore's 2004 speech "The Climate Emergency," collected in Red, White, Blue, and Green: Politics and the Environment in the 2004 Election (2004), edited by members of Yale School of Forestry & Environmental Studies, James R. Lyons, Heather S. Kaplan, Fred Strebeigh, and Kathleen E. Campbell.

The environment is often felt to be relatively invulnerable because the earth is so big. People tend to assume that the earth is so big that we as human beings can't possibly have any impact on it. That is a mistake.

In Europe during the summer of 2003, we experienced an extreme heat wave that killed an estimated 20,000 people, and many predict such events will be much more commonplace as a result of increasing temperatures. The anomaly was extreme, particularly in France, with consequences that were well reported in the press. Year-to-year, decade-to-decade there's variation, but the overall upward trend worldwide since the American Civil War is really clear and really obvious, at least to me.

If you look at the glaciers around the world, you see that many are melting away. A friend of mine named Lonnie Thompson of Ohio State studies glaciers, and he reports that 15 to 20 years from now there will be no more snows of Kilimanjaro. This shrinking of glaciers is happening all around the world, including Latin America, China, and the U.S. In our own Glacier National Park, all of the glaciers are predicted to be gone within 15 to 20 years.

An area of Bangladesh is due to be flooded where ten million people live. A large area of Florida is due to be flooded. The Florida Keys are very much at risk. The Everglades are at risk.

The trend is very clear. What's behind it all? I've come to believe that global warming, the disappearance of the ocean fisheries, the destruction of the rain forests, the stratospheric ozone depletion problem, the extinction crisis, all of these are really symptoms of an underlying cause. The underlying cause is a collision between our civilization and the earth. The relationship between the human species and our planet has been completely changed. All of our culture, all of our literature, all of our history, everything we've learned, was premised on one relationship between the earth and us, and now we have a different one.

Think about the subsistence that we have always drawn from the earth. The plow was a great advance, as was irrigation. But then we began to get more powerful with these tools. At the Aral Sea in Russia, something as simple as irrigation on a large scale led to the virtual disappearance of the fourth largest inland body of water in the world. We're changing the surface of the earth, and technology sometimes seems to dwarf our human scale. We now have to try to change this pattern.

There's another assumption that needs to be questioned. In contrast to the idea that the earth is so big that we can't have any impact on it, there are others who assume that the climate change problem is so big we can't solve it. I, however, believe that we can if we put our minds to it. We had a problem with the ozone hole, a big global problem that seemed too big to solve. In response, we had political leadership and the world passed a treaty outlawing chlorofluorocarbons, the chemicals that caused this problem. The United States led the way, and we brought about a dramatic drop in CFCs and are now in the process of solving that problem. We now have the ability to buy hybrid cars like the Toyota Prius and the marketplace for new sources of energy is increasing dramatically. We're also seeing new efficiencies with energy savings. If we have political leadership and the collective political will to say it is important to solve this problem, we can not only solve it, we can create more jobs, we can create higher incomes, a better way of life, and a higher quality of life by solving the problem.

Everything we have ever known—and Carl Sagan made a beautiful long statement about this—all the wars, all the heartbreak, all the romance, every triumph, every mistake, everything we've ever known is contained in this small planet. If we keep the right perspective and keep our eyes on the prize, we *can* solve this problem, we *will* solve this problem, we *must* solve this problem. It really is up to you.

Assignment: Write an essay in which you explain how Al Gore builds an argument to persuade his audience that climate change is a serious problem we must address. In your essay, analyze how Gore uses one or more of the features listed in the box above (or features of your own choice) to strengthen the logic and persuasiveness of his argument. Be sure that your analysis focuses on the most relevant features of the passage.

Your essay should not explain whether you agree with Gore's claims, but rather explain how Gore builds an argument to persuade his audience.

Sample Essay #1

I agree with Al Gore that it's a good trend to help the environment. Earth is the only planet we have, its our responsibility to keep it safe. Otherwise who will?! Like he says in the time of the Civil War, they didn't know about pollution but now it's different. We now have the ability to buy hybrid cars or recycle your plastic to help the environment. no excuses. Two thousand people died in Europe because of global warming. It's time to shape up, America!! These days, there's to much technology and there messing up the oceans. Like I saw on the news that turtles are dying because people don't recycle plastic. Like Al says, we gotta stop asuming that nature is going to be OK when really we're the one's who are hurting nature. But I think things are getting better, you know? You see people now they are really working hard to make a differrence. Helping animals and planting trees. Green technology too. Scientists are figuring out important stuff that will help. I believe that in the end, we will be able to save the planet.

Score Breakdown: Essay #1

Reading Score: 1. The writer does not demonstrate that he comprehends Gore's main argument (that climate change is a serious problem we must address).

The writer does not demonstrate an understanding of important details or how they relate to the main idea. Although he highlights Gore's reference to the Civil War, this is not a substantial piece of evidence for Gore's argument. Meanwhile, the writer ignores other details that are more relevant to the central idea of the passage. Furthermore, the writer introduces errors not present in the source text. For example, he states that the number of people who died in the European heat wave was two thousand, when the passage says 20,000, or twenty thousand.

The writer does not use textual evidence to support his assertions. The only direct quote from the essay—"We now have the ability to buy hybrid cars"—is not presented as a quotation from the passage.

Analysis Score: 1. The writer does not attempt to analyze how Gore constructs his argument. Instead, the writer gives his own opinion about Gore's argument, which is not the assignment at hand.

Furthermore, the writer does not engage with Gore's use of the features highlighted by the prompt, or with the passage itself. Instead, the writer brings in his own evidence, such as something he saw on the news, rather than analyzing Gore's use of evidence. He also makes claims that do not relate to the passage itself. For example, he says scientists are making important discoveries, but no information in the passage supports that.

Writing Score: 1. The writer demonstrates little mastery of language and minimal organization.

The tone and style are too casual for an academic essay. Exclamations, rhetorical questions, and the informal use of the second-person point of view are inappropriate for formal writing. The word choice is often vague ("figuring out stuff") and full of clichés. There are also substantial errors in grammar and usage, including sentence fragments, run-on sentences, and homophone confusion. Sentences are generally simple, with little variation.

This essay also lacks a clear structure. Although the writer makes a central claim in his first sentence, the rest of the essay does not focus on that claim. Ideas are not separated into paragraphs, and the flow from sentence to sentence is unclear. The essay is also too short to develop a meaningful argument.

SAMPLE ESSAY #2

Al Gore says that we need to take better care of the earth. If we don't, things will get worse, and things are already pretty bad. "In Europe during the summer of 2003, we experienced an extreme heat wave that killed an estimated 20,000 people, and many predict such events will be much more commonplace as a result of increasing temperatures." The earth is in bad shape, we need to fix it.

One example Al Gore uses is the glaciers. The glaciers is melting, according to his friend Lonnie, and that's a big problem. If there are no more glaciers, that will mean we no longer have Glacier National Park. This is a big problem. "The trend is very clear." Rain forests are being destroyed, fisheries are disappearing from the oceans. This situation could be deadly.

Things are basically different than they've ever been before. Humans used to be farmers, so they didn't need technology. Now we have made enormous technological advances, but their bad for the planet. All the machines that we use are causing global warming.

But don't worry, there is some hope. We can still stop this menace if we get to work right now. There is other new technology that is making things better. For example, the Toyota Prius is a hybrid car which is are better for the environment. The United States is striving to improve and lead the way. Right now. We need politicians to step up. "If we have political leadership and the collective political will to say it is important to solve this problem," we can get it done. Al Gore thinks that we can solve the problem and have "a higher quality of life by solving the problem." This means that things can only get better for us from hear on out, if we listen to what he says. We made this problem, but we can fix it.

SCORE BREAKDOWN: ESSAY #2

Reading Score: 2. The writer demonstrates limited comprehension of the source text's central ideas.

The writer understands Gore's central argument—that we need to address a serious environmental problem—but she does not grasp the nuances of his argument about the relationship between humans and technology. Furthermore, she does not connect important details to how he uses them. For example, she highlights his example of glaciers melting, but does not link it to the mass flooding of areas where many people live, which is what makes this example significant in context.

Although the writer does not make any overt errors in referring to the passage, her discussion is not always precise. She does quote from the source text, but she does not provide context for the quotes, or explain why they are important. She also makes some unsupported claims.

Analysis Score: 2. The writer shows that she understands she is supposed to write about the passage, not the topic. However, her analysis lacks depth, and she often writes as if she is discussing her own opinion rather than Gore's argument.

The writer summarizes her perception of Gore's thesis, but she does not examine how he builds his argument. She discusses some of the most relevant features of Gore's argument (such as his example of the heat wave), but misses others (such as the changing relationship between humans and the planet). When she does talk about his evidence, she does not always do so effectively, and she does not analyze his reasoning or stylistic elements at all.

The writer does provide evidence for some of her claims, such as when she supports the statement that the earth is in bad shape by talking about the glaciers melting. However, other claims are both broad and not supported by the text.

Writing Score: 2. The writer demonstrates limited mastery of language and organization.

The tone in this essay is not conversational. However, the style is quite simple, and occasionally too casual for formal writing. Sentences vary in structure, but only slightly. There are also some errors in grammar and usage, including run-on sentences.

The writer does make a central claim—"The earth is in bad shape, and we need to fix it"—but it is not focused on the passage, which is what an essay's thesis should focus on. There is a clear series of ideas in the essay, but they are not well connected; the ideas do not build upon each other, and there is only one clear transition. Furthermore, although the essay is structured in distinct paragraphs that each have a clear topic, the sentences within those paragraphs are not clearly ordered to develop a point.

SAMPLE ESSAY #3

In Al Gore's speech, he describes some of the major issues that our environment is facing today. He says that although humanity has caused these problems, we also have the power to fix them. Gore uses strong evidence and persuasion to make his message seem urgent and important.

One of the most important ways that Gore builds his argument is the evidence he uses. He mentions an "extreme heat wave" in Europe that resulted in 20,000 deaths, which was "well reported in the press." This example of the consequences of raising temperatures makes the crisis seem massive. He also mentions a researcher at Ohio State who studies glaciers, using an authoritative source for his claim that the glaciers are melting at an alarming rate and will be gone "within 15 to 20 years." He explains that one of the issues with glaciers melting is mass flooding, such as in a part of Bangladesh "where ten million people live." Gore uses evidence to show that if we do not do something about climate change, many people will die.

The way he structures his argument is important to his message. First, he uses evidence to show that we are in a serious crisis. Then he explains why he thinks we have wound up here, because "the relationship between the human species and our planet has been completely changed." Modern technology, which has caused the problem, "sometimes seems to dwarf our human scale," which is why the crisis is so big that it can seem hopeless. After Gore makes the problem seem huge, he switches to a hopeful note, writing that although some people think we can't solve the problem, "I, however, believe that we can."

Another thing that makes his argument feel more emotional is the rhetorical tools that he uses. He uses repetition, which has a dramatic affect. He repeats "at risk" to describe the

Florida Keys and the Everglades, which really drives the risk home. Then he uses more repetition in the phrase, "we can solve this problem, we will solve this problem, we must solve this problem." He is driving his point home again, but this time what he is driving home is hope.

Ultimately, Gore is able to make his speech inspirational for the reader rather than depressing, because of how he builds his speech from the dire reports of a European heat wave to encouraging the reader to "keep our eyes on the prize." He gives a lot of bad news, but he makes the reader feel like all is not lost. After all, as he says, "It really is up to you."

SCORE BREAKDOWN: ESSAY #3

Reading Score: 3. The writer understands Gore's main argument, and clearly states it in his first paragraph.

The writer uses evidence from the text to support his claims. When he uses direct quotes, he provides enough context for them to make sense, and he explains why they are relevant to his argument. He focuses on details that are important for conveying the central ideas of the passage, and records them accurately.

To get a 4, the writer would have needed to discuss the more subtle aspects of Gore's argument, such as the way he connects the changing relationship of humans and the earth to both the problem and its solution.

Analysis Score: 3. The writer fulfills the assignment by focusing on how Gore builds his argument, not on the topic of the passage.

The writer analyzes the role that evidence plays in Gore's argument. He also analyzes how both the organization of the passage and certain stylistic choices make Gore's argument more compelling. Furthermore, he carefully chooses things to focus on which are significant in the passage. The writer develops his claims and supports them using evidence from the text.

To get a 4, the writer would have needed to fully develop his analysis more consistently. For example, his third paragraph would have been better if he had explained how the transition he identifies contributes to Gore's argument.

Writing Score: 3. The writer demonstrates adequate mastery of language and organization.

The writer has a central claim, which he states in his introduction and develops through the whole essay. He effectively organizes his essay into paragraphs with topic sentences and a clear focus on a single point. They are in a logical order and the writer uses transitions to make his argument easier to follow.

The tone and style are consistent and appropriately academic. The writer uses both simple and slightly more complicated sentences. He also chooses words that will communicate his meaning precisely. While there are a few mistakes, the essay demonstrates adequate proficiency in grammar and usage.

To get a 4, the writer would have needed to use greater variation in sentence structure and less repetitive language for a more sophisticated tone. He also could have used more transitions within paragraphs to develop his arguments more clearly.

STUDENT SAMPLE ESSAY #4

Al Gore argues that climate change is a major problem that we must address. He views both climate change and the potential solutions for climate change not just as a matter of technology, but also as a matter of changing the human relationship with the earth. By focusing on the role of humanity in both creating and stopping climate change, Gore imparts to his audience a sense of both responsibility and hope.

Gore begins by asserting that "people tend to assume that the earth is so big that we as human beings can't possibly have any impact on it," but this is a "mistake." He uses multiple examples to demonstrate that the popular perception of the earth as "invulnerable" is wrong. His first piece of evidence is a European heat wave that killed 20,000 people, which allows him to foreground the human cost of climate change. This continues as he talks about the melting of the glaciers. Citing the work of a researcher at Ohio State as an authoritative source to give his argument scientific credibility, Gore directly connects the shrinking of the glaciers to flooding in Bangladesh "where ten million people live." Once more, he emphasizes the human cost of climate change as he is establishing the severity of the crisis.

He also centers on humanity when discussing the "underlying cause" of climate change, which he believes is "a collision between our civilization and the earth." The word "collision" dramatizes how suddenly things have changed. To further underscore the extent to which our relationship with the earth has changed, he writes that "all of our culture, all of our literature, all of our history" came out of the old relationship between the earth and humanity; the repetition highlights the immense scope of this history, which in turn brings home the scope of the crisis.

However, Gore does not center on humanity only to make his audience aware of the danger; he also does so to promote a hopeful outlook. He uses the disappearance of the Aral Sea due to large-scale irrigation as an example of how technological advance can change the earth for the worse, but then transitions into discussing his belief that we can solve the problem of climate change "if we put our minds to it." He illustrates this belief with the successful campaign to bring about "a dramatic drop" in chlorofluorocarbons, which were contributing to the problem of the ozone hole. By juxtaposing an example of humans harming the earth with one of humans working to fix a problem they had created, Gore reinforces his argument that the power lies with us.

Furthermore, just as Gore emphasized the human costs of climate change, he also emphasizes the human benefits of working to solve the problem. He points out that "the marketplace for new sources of energy is increasing dramatically," making a solution seem economically feasible. He goes on to assert that "we can create more jobs, we can create higher incomes, a better way of life, and a higher quality of life" in the quest to stop climate change. The subtle repetitions of "we can create" and "life" stir the audience's emotions as Gore leads them to envision a brighter future.

That future, once again, lies with us. In his final triple repetition—"we *can* solve this problem, we *will* solve this problem, we *must* solve this problem"—Gore brings together the two sides that together make his argument so powerful: our role in creating the problem and our ability to solve it. In keeping his focus on humanity, Gore inspires his audience to feel responsible for the fate of the earth and hopeful about our ability to fix it.

Score Breakdown: Essay #4

Reading Score: 4. The writer demonstrates a clear and nuanced understanding of different aspects of Gore's argument, and states them in her introduction.

The writer focuses on details relevant to the passage and highlights their importance to Gore's argument. She consistently uses evidence from the text to support her claims. She also provides both context and explanation for the quotes she uses.

Analysis Score: 4. The writer clearly understands the assignment, structuring her essay entirely around her own analysis of Gore's speech. Her thesis is both specific and clear.

The writer analyzes the role that evidence plays in Gore's argument in ways that are relevant to her own thesis about his speech. She also analyzes both organizational choices and stylistic tools for how they contribute to the aspect of Gore's argument she has chosen to focus on. She develops each of her claims using evidence from the text.

Writing Score: 4. The writer demonstrates exceptional mastery of language and strong organization.

The writer states her central claim clearly in her introduction, and develops it throughout the essay. Her essay is effectively organized, with focused paragraphs in a logical order so that each one builds on the point the previous one made. At the end of each paragraph, she makes its relationship to her main argument clear. She also uses transitions to make her argument easy to follow.

The tone is consistent and academic. The style is sophisticated, employing a variety of sentence structures and vocabulary that allows her to be specific and concise. She demonstrates full proficiency in grammar and usage.

SECTION 5

SAMPLE SAT ESSAY PROMPTS

Here are five essay prompts to practice the strategies you learned in this chapter. Answer each prompt within a 50-minute time limit, and ask a trusted reader to check your work. In the chart below, we've also given you a checklist of questions you can ask yourself as you're reviewing your work.

Criteria	Checklist
Reading	✓ Did I show that I understand the passage's argument? (Remember that the prompt summarizes it for you!) ✓ Did I connect important details to the main idea? ✓ Did I use evidence from the text to support my claims?
Analysis	✓ Is my essay about the passage, *not* about the topic of the passage? ✓ Did I analyze the author's use of evidence, reasoning, and style, using specific examples from the text? ✓ Did I explain how my examples were relevant to my argument?
Writing	✓ Do I have a clear thesis statement? ✓ Do my paragraphs have topic sentences and transitions? ✓ Are my sentences grammatically correct?

ESSAY PROMPT #1
PART 1

As you read the passage below, consider how Rodrigo A. Medellín, Don J. Melnick, and Mary C. Pearl use

- evidence, such as facts or examples, to support claims.
- reasoning to develop ideas and to connect claims and evidence.
- stylistic or persuasive elements, such as word choice or appeals to emotion, to add power to the ideas expressed.

Adapted from Rodrigo A. Medellín, Don J. Melnick, and Mary C. Pearl, "Protect Our Bats." © 2014 by the New York Times Company. Originally published May 11, 2014.

Disease and heedless management of wind turbines are killing North America's bats, with potentially devastating consequences for agriculture and human health.

We have yet to find a cure for the disease known as white-nose syndrome, which has decimated populations of hibernating, cave-dwelling bats in the Northeast. But we can reduce the turbine threat significantly without dismantling them or shutting them down.

White-nose syndrome (also known as W.N.S.) was first documented in February 2006 in upstate New York, where it may have been carried from Europe to a bat cave on an explorer's hiking boot. In Europe, bats appear to be immune. But in North America, bats are highly susceptible to the cold-loving fungus that appears in winter on the muzzle and other body parts during hibernation, irritating them awake at a time when there is no food. They end up burning precious stores of energy and starve to death.

The consequences have been catastrophic. A 2011 study of 42 sites across five Eastern states found that after 2006 the populations of tri-colored and Indiana bats declined by more than 70 percent, and little brown bats by more than 90 percent. The population of the northern long-eared bat, once common, has declined by an estimated 99 percent and prompted a proposal from the United States Fish and Wildlife Service to list it as an endangered species. Other species of hibernating cave-dwelling bats have declined precipitously as well.

Whether these bats will recover or go extinct is unclear. Meanwhile, W.N.S. continues to spread rapidly. On the back of this year's extremely cold winter, it moved into Michigan and Wisconsin. It is now confirmed in 23 states and five Canadian provinces.

Tree-dwelling bats don't seem to be affected by W.N.S., since they don't hibernate in caves. But wind farms are killing them. Wind turbines nationwide are estimated to kill between 600,000 and 900,000 bats a year, according to a recent study in the journal *BioScience*. About half of those lost to turbines are hoary bats, which migrate long distances seasonally throughout North America. Eastern red and silver-haired bats, commonly seen in Central Park in New York City hunting insects at night, are also being killed by turbines by the tens of thousands.

We can't afford to lose these creatures. In the Northeast, all of our native bat species eat insects. One little brown bat can eat 1,000 mosquitoes in an hour, reducing the potential for mosquito-borne diseases. A colony of 150 big brown bats can protect crops from up to 33 million rootworms over a growing season. The Mexican free-tailed bats of Bracken Cave in south-central Texas consume about 250 tons of insects every summer night. The natural pest control provided by that species across eight Texas counties has been valued at nearly $750,000 as it protects the $6 million summer cotton crop. Nationwide, the value of bats as pest controllers is estimated to be at least $3.7 billion and possibly much more.

Today, genetic engineering may seem to provide an effective way to protect crops from insects, but pests have already developed resistance to some of these products. Insects also readily evolve resistance to chemical insecticides, and increased use of these chemicals would come at a great cost to human health. But

bats have shared the night skies with insects for at least 50 million years, and they know how to hunt and eat them.

Fortunately, we can reduce the mortality caused by wind farms, which are often located on windy routes favored by some migratory bats. Wind turbines usually switch on automatically at wind speeds of about 8 to 9 miles per hour, speeds at which insects and bats are active. But if, during times of peak bat activity, energy companies recalibrated their turbines to start at a wind speed of about 11 miles per hour, which is too windy for insects and bats to fly, turbine-related deaths could be reduced by 44 to 93 percent, according to a 2010 study published in the journal *Frontiers in Ecology and the Environment*. The effect on power output would be negligible—less than 1 percent annually.

Threats to bats also threaten us. We should step up research on the prevention and cure of white-nose syndrome. And we should require energy companies to take steps to protect bats from collisions with wind turbines. It is foolish to spend enormous sums to create pesticides and transgenic crops to fight insects, while investing little to protect bats, our most efficient insect fighters.

Assignment: Write an essay in which you explain how Rodrigo A. Medellín, Don J. Melnick, and Mary C. Pearl build an argument to persuade their audience that we need to protect North America's bat population. In your essay, analyze how the authors use one or more of the features listed in the box above (or features of your own choice) to strengthen the logic and persuasiveness of their argument. Be sure that your analysis focuses on the most relevant features of the passage.

Your essay should not explain whether you agree with Medellín, Melnick, and Pearl's claims, but rather explain how the authors build an argument to persuade their audience.

ESSAY PROMPT #2

PART 2

As you read the passage below, consider how Timothy D. Wilson uses

- evidence, such as facts or examples, to support claims.
- reasoning to develop ideas and to connect claims and evidence.
- stylistic or persuasive elements, such as word choice or appeals to emotion, to add power to the ideas expressed.

Adapted from Timothy D. Wilson, "Stop Bullying The 'Soft' Sciences." © 2012 by the Los Angeles Times. Originally published July 12, 2012.

Once, during a meeting at my university, a biologist mentioned that he was the only faculty member present from a science department. When I corrected him, noting that I was from the Department of Psychology, he waved his hand dismissively, as if I were a Little Leaguer telling a member of the New York Yankees that I too played baseball.

There has long been snobbery in the sciences, with the "hard" ones (physics, chemistry, biology) considering themselves to be more legitimate than the "soft" ones (psychology, sociology). It is thus no surprise that many members of the general public feel the same way. But of late, skepticism about the rigors of social science has reached absurd heights.

The U.S. House of Representatives recently voted to eliminate funding for political science research through the National Science Foundation. In the wake of that action, an opinion writer for the Washington Post suggested that the House didn't go far enough. The NSF should not fund any research in the social sciences, wrote Charles Lane, because "unlike

hypotheses in the hard sciences, hypotheses about society usually can't be proven or disproven by experimentation."

This is news to me and the many other social scientists who have spent their careers doing carefully controlled experiments on human behavior, inside and outside the laboratory. What makes the criticism so galling is that those who voice it, or members of their families, have undoubtedly benefited from research in the disciplines they dismiss.

Most of us know someone who has suffered from depression and sought psychotherapy. He or she probably benefited from therapies such as cognitive behavioral therapy that have been shown to work in randomized clinical trials.

Ever hear of stereotype threat? It is the double jeopardy that people face when they are at risk of confirming a negative stereotype of their group. When African American students take a difficult test, for example, they are concerned not only about how well they will do but also about the possibility that performing poorly will reflect badly on their entire group. This added worry has been shown time and again, in carefully controlled experiments, to lower academic performance. But fortunately, experiments have also showed promising ways to reduce this threat. One intervention, for example, conducted in a middle school, reduced the achievement gap by 40%.

If you know someone who was unlucky enough to be arrested for a crime he didn't commit, he may have benefited from social psychological experiments that have resulted in fairer lineups and interrogations, making it less likely that innocent people are convicted.

An often-overlooked advantage of the experimental method is that it can demonstrate what doesn't work. Consider three popular programs that research psychologists have debunked: Critical Incident Stress Debriefing, used to prevent post-traumatic stress disorders in first responders and others who have witnessed horrific events; the D.A.R.E. anti-drug program, used in many schools throughout America; and Scared Straight programs designed to prevent at-risk teens from engaging in criminal behavior.

All three of these programs have been shown, with well-designed experimental studies, to be ineffective or, in some cases, to make matters worse. And as a result, the programs have become less popular or have changed their methods. By discovering what doesn't work, social scientists have saved the public billions of dollars.

To be fair to the critics, social scientists have not always taken advantage of the experimental method as much as they could. Too often, for example, educational programs have been implemented widely without being adequately tested. But increasingly, educational researchers are employing better methodologies. For example, in a recent study, researchers randomly assigned teachers to a program called My Teaching Partner, which is designed to improve teaching skills, or to a control group. Students taught by the teachers who participated in the program did significantly better on achievement tests than did students taught by teachers in the control group.

Are the social sciences perfect? Of course not. Human behavior is complex, and it is not possible to conduct experiments to test all aspects of what people do or why. There are entire disciplines devoted to the experimental study of human behavior, however, in tightly controlled, ethically acceptable ways. Many people benefit from the results, including those who, in their ignorance, believe that science is limited to the study of molecules.

Assignment: Write an essay in which you explain how Timothy D. Wilson builds an argument to persuade his audience that the "soft" sciences are real sciences and should be funded. In your essay, analyze how Wilson uses one or more of the features listed in the box above (or features of your own choice) to strengthen the logic and persuasiveness of his argument. Be sure that your analysis focuses on the most relevant features of the passage.

Your essay should not explain whether you agree with Wilson's claims, but rather explain how Wilson builds an argument to persuade his audience.

ESSAY PROMPT #3

PART 3

As you read the passage below, consider how Tom Vanderbilt uses

- evidence, such as facts or examples, to support claims.
- reasoning to develop ideas and to connect claims and evidence.
- stylistic or persuasive elements, such as word choice or appeals to emotion, to add power to the ideas expressed.

Adapted from Tom Vanderbilt, "When Pedestrians Get Mixed Signals." © 2014 by the New York Times Company. Originally published February 1, 2014.

Let's put aside the tired trope that no one walks in Los Angeles—Ray Bradbury nailed that one with his 1951 short story "The Pedestrian," about a man picked up by the police for the suspicious activity of walking. In fact, Los Angeles has many places that are quite pleasant for walking.

Take the Silver Lake neighborhood: It does not even rank among the city's top 20 "most walkable" areas, according to the website Walk Score, yet still wins 75 points ("most errands can be accomplished on foot")—a number that puts many American cities to shame. In 2012, the city hired its first "pedestrian coordinators."

But then came the surest indication of a walking resurgence in Los Angeles: It suddenly had a pedestrian problem. As *The Los Angeles Times* reported, the Police Department was targeting people for a variety of pedestrian violations in downtown Los Angeles. "We're heavily enforcing pedestrian violations because they're impeding traffic and causing too many accidents and deaths," said Lt. Lydia Leos of the Los Angeles Police Department.

Thus a familiar pattern reasserts itself: The best way to reduce pedestrian deaths is to issue tickets to pedestrians. A similar dynamic can be seen in recent weeks after a spate of pedestrian deaths in New York City, where Mayor Bill de Blasio has endorsed more aggressive enforcement by the New York Police Department against jaywalkers. Enforcement against jaywalking varies between states, but it is an infraction in most, even a misdemeanor in some.

But neither enforcement nor education has the effect we like to think it does on safety. Decades of graphic teenage driving safety films did not bring down teenage driving deaths; what did was limiting the age and conditions under which teenagers could begin to drive. Similarly, all the "awareness campaigns" on seatbelt usage have had a fraction of the impact of simply installing that annoying chime that impels drivers to buckle up.

If tough love will not make pedestrians safer, what will? The answer is: better walking infrastructure, slower car speeds and more pedestrians. But it's easier to write off the problem as one of jaywalkers.

Nowadays, the word connotes an amorphous urban nuisance. In fact, the term once referred to country bumpkins ("jays"), who came to the city and perambulated in a way that amused and exasperated savvy urban bipeds. As the historian Peter Norton has documented, the word was then overhauled in the early part of the 20th century. A coalition of pro-automobile interests Mr. Norton calls "motordom" succeeded in shifting the focus of street safety from curbing the actions of rogue drivers to curbing rogue walkers. The pedestrian pushback was shortlived: An attempt to popularize the term "jay driver" was left behind in a cloud of exhaust.

Sure, we may call an errant driver, per the comedian George Carlin, an "idiot" or a "maniac," but there is no word to tar an entire class of negligent motorists. This is because of the extent to which driving has been normalized for most Americans: We constantly see the world through what has been called the "windshield view."

Those humans in Los Angeles who began walking a second or two after the light was blinking were, after all, violating the "Vehicle Code." Note that cars, apparently, do not violate a "Human Code."

As for pedestrian safety, which is the typical stated purpose of jaywalking crackdowns, more pedestrians generally are killed in urban areas by cars violating their right of way than are rogue pedestrians violating vehicles' right of way. Then there are those people struck on sidewalks, even inside restaurants. What do we call that? Jay-living?

Pedestrians, who lack air bags and side-impact crash protection, are largely rational creatures. Studies have shown that when you shorten the wait to cross a street, fewer people will cross against the light. When you tell people how long they must wait to cross, fewer people will cross against the signal.

When you actually give people a signal, more will cross with it. As the field of behavioral economics has been discovering, rather than penalizing people for opting out of the system, a more effective approach is to make it easier to opt in.

The Los Angeles Police Department may be patrolling on foot in downtown Los Angeles, but it is still looking through the windshield.

Assignment: Write an essay in which you explain how Tom Vanderbilt builds an argument to persuade his audience that penalizing jaywalking will not increase pedestrian safety. In your essay, analyze how Vanderbilt uses one or more of the features listed in the box above (or features of your own choice) to strengthen the logic and persuasiveness of his argument. Be sure that your analysis focuses on the most relevant features of the passage.

Your essay should not explain whether you agree with Vanderbilt's claims, but rather explain how Vanderbilt builds an argument to persuade his audience.

ESSAY PROMPT #4

PART 4

As you read the passage below, consider how Alfie Kohn uses

- evidence, such as facts or examples, to support claims.
- reasoning to develop ideas and to connect claims and evidence.
- stylistic or persuasive elements, such as word choice or appeals to emotion, to add power to the ideas expressed.

Adapted from Alfie Kohn, "Do Our Kids Get Off Too Easy?" © 2014 by the New York Times Company. Originally published May 3, 2014.

The conventional wisdom these days is that kids come by everything too easily— stickers, praise, A's, trophies. It's outrageous, we're told, that all kids on the field may get a thanks-for-playing token, in contrast to the good old days, when recognition was reserved for the conquering heroes.

Most of all, it's assumed that the best way to get children ready for the miserable "real world" that awaits them is to make sure they have plenty of miserable experiences while they're young. Conversely, if they're spared any unhappiness, they'll be ill-prepared. This is precisely the logic employed not so long ago to frame bullying as a rite of passage that kids were expected to deal with on their own, without assistance from "overprotective" adults.

In any case, no one ever explains the mechanism by which the silence of a long drive home without a trophy is supposed to teach resilience. Nor are we told whether there's any support for this theory of inoculation by immersion. Have social scientists shown that those who are spared,

say, the rigors of dodge ball (which turns children into human targets) or class rank (which pits students against one another) will wind up unprepared for adulthood?

Not that I can find. In fact, studies of those who attended the sort of nontraditional schools that afford an unusual amount of autonomy and nurturing suggest that the great majority seemed capable of navigating the transition to traditional colleges and workplaces.

But when you point out the absence of logic or evidence, it soon becomes clear that trophy rage is less about prediction— what will happen to kids later—than ideology —how they ought to be treated now. Fury over the possibility that kids will get off too easy or feel too good about themselves seems to rest on three underlying values.

The first is deprivation: Kids shouldn't be spared struggle and sacrifice, regardless of the effects. The second value is scarcity: the belief that excellence, by definition, is something that not everyone can attain. No matter how well a group of students performs, only a few should get A's. Otherwise we're sanctioning "grade inflation" and mediocrity. To have high standards, there must always be losers.

But it's the third conviction that really ties everything together: an endorsement of conditionality. Children ought never to receive something desirable—a sum of money, a trophy, a commendation—unless they've done enough to merit it. They shouldn't even be allowed to feel good about themselves without being able to point to tangible accomplishments. In this view, we have a moral obligation to reward the deserving and, equally important, make sure the undeserving go conspicuously unrewarded. Hence the anger over participation trophies. The losers mustn't receive something that even looks like a reward.

A commitment to conditionality lives at the intersection of economics and theology. It's where lectures about the law of the marketplace meet sermons about what we must do to earn our way into heaven. Here, almost every human interaction, even among family members, is regarded as a kind of transaction.

Interestingly, no research that I know of has ever shown that unconditionality is harmful in terms of future achievement, psychological health or anything else. In fact, studies generally show exactly the opposite. One of the most destructive ways to raise a child is with "conditional regard."

Over the last decade or so, two Israeli researchers, Avi Assor and Guy Roth, and their colleagues in the United States and Belgium, have conducted a series of experiments whose consistent finding is that when children feel their parents' affection varies depending on the extent to which they are well behaved, self-controlled or impressive at school or sports, this promotes "the development of a fragile, contingent and unstable sense of self."

Other researchers, meanwhile, have shown that high self-esteem is beneficial, but that even more desirable is unconditional self-esteem: a solid core of belief in yourself, an abiding sense that you're competent and worthwhile—even when you screw up or fall short. In other words, the very unconditionality that seems to fuel attacks on participation trophies and the whole "self-esteem movement" turns out to be a defining feature of psychological health. It's precisely what we should be helping our children to acquire.

Assignment: Write an essay in which you explain how Alfie Kohn builds an argument to persuade his audience that parents should show unconditional acceptance for their children. In your essay, analyze how Kohn uses one or more of the features listed in the box above (or features of your own choice) to strengthen the logic and persuasiveness of his argument. Be sure that your analysis focuses on the most relevant features of the passage.

Your essay should not explain whether you agree with Kohn's claims, but rather explain how Kohn builds an argument to persuade his audience.

ESSAY PROMPT #5

PART 5

As you read the passage below, consider how Lindsey Lusher Shute and Benjamin Shute use

- evidence, such as facts or examples, to support claims.
- reasoning to develop ideas and to connect claims and evidence.
- stylistic or persuasive elements, such as word choice or appeals to emotion, to add power to the ideas expressed.

Adapted from Lindsey Lusher Shute and Benjamin Shute, "Keep Farmland for Farmers." © 2013 by the New York Times Company. Originally published September 20, 2013.

When we went looking in upstate New York for a home for our farm, we feared competition from deep-pocketed developers, a new subdivision or a big-box store. These turned out to be the least of our problems. Though the farms best suited for our vegetables were protected from development by conservation easements, we discovered that we couldn't compete, because conserved farmland is open to all buyers—millionaires included.

Few bankers farm; long days with little pay lack appeal. A new report by the National Young Farmers Coalition, a group we helped start, reveals that one-quarter of the land trusts that oversee these conservation easements have seen protected land go out of production. Why? A nonfarmer had bought it.

Still, tax incentives in New York encourage nonfarmers to rent their land to farmers, so you would think suitable land would be easy to find. Most landlords, however, offer only short-term leases. They want peace and quiet; they don't

want vegetable or livestock operations that bring traffic, workers, noise and fences. But long-term land tenure is essential for vegetable and livestock growers, who need years to build soil fertility, improve pasture and add infrastructure. Only farms that grow low-value animal feed crops like hay, corn or beans are attracted to one-year leases.

Once well-off city residents who are looking for second homes buy the land, farmer ownership is over. After they've added an air-conditioned home, a heated pool and an asphalt drive, the value increases so much that no working farmer can afford it. The farm, and its capacity to feed a community, is lost.

Thankfully, there is a solution. The Vermont Land Trust and the State of Massachsuetts are keeping farmland in the hands of farmers through stricter conservation easements that limit who can own it, which keeps farms affordable and deters farm sales to nonfarmers.

In the next 20 years, 70 percent of the nation's farmland will change hands. Farmers do not live forever, and most farm kids do not choose to carry on the family business. An eager generation of young Americans is motivated to farm but, like us, they need land and few will be able to secure it without help.

The federal government and states spend hundreds of millions of dollars on farmland conservation each year, which can do much more than protect pastoral views for the wealthy. Those dollars must also be used to shore up rural economies and national food security with productive farms.

Eighty percent of us live in or near cities. It's critical that farms ring those cities, and that farmers in the ring be protected. The United States Department of Agriculture spends money to preserve farms, but matching funds are required, and there aren't enough.

Smart, self-interested cities would be wise to do their part. New York City needs to think about the land beyond the boroughs. The need is well documented: a recent study identified 614 vital unprotected farms in the Hudson Valley. New York City invested in the protection of its watershed in the Catskills; it needs to do the same with farmland to assure fresh food. It must come up with the money and leadership to help regional land trusts protect farms.

As water resources dwindle in the West, and as transportation and fuel costs climb and research shows that fresh, clean food is the key to a healthy life, isn't it the job of every city and town to secure the land and the farmers necessary to grow the food they need? Locking up land for farmers is the first step.

We started our Hearty Roots Community Farm nine years ago but quickly realized that we needed more stability than we were getting with the 20 acres we had rented in Dutchess County. After a grueling four-year search, a land trust came to our aid: with help from Scenic Hudson, we were able to buy a 70-acre farm in Clermont, a town of 2,000 people, just five miles north of where we'd been renting.

This land is protected only by a traditional conservation easement, but because it never made the transition to an estate and the previous landowner felt strongly that it be sold to a farmer, we got lucky. But what happens after us? We want to pass our stewardship of this land on to future farmers. We are now working with the land trust to tighten our easement and make sure that on our land, an American farm family will always have a chance to succeed.

Assignment: Write an essay in which you explain how Lindsey Lusher Shute and Benjamin Shute build an argument to persuade their audience that the government should make it easier for farmland to stay with farmers. In your essay, analyze how Shute and Shute use one or more of the features listed in the box above (or features of your own choice) to strengthen the logic and persuasiveness of their argument. Be sure that your analysis focuses on the most relevant features of the passage.

Your essay should not explain whether you agree with Shute and Shute's claims, but rather explain how Shute and Shute build an argument to persuade their audience.

Chapter 5
Math

INTRODUCTION TO THE MATH TEST

The new SAT Math Test will test certain topics in math as well as your ability to use reasoning and critical thinking to solve real-world problems. These concepts and skills provide the foundations for the math you will learn in college and use in everyday life. The SAT groups these concepts into four major areas that you will see on the Math Test: Heart of Algebra, Problem Solving and Data Analysis, Passport to Advanced Math, and Additional Topics in Math.

In this chapter, we will review all of the topics that you may see on the Math Test. We will also practice strategies for solving different types of questions and for tackling difficult or unfamiliar problems. But first, let's look at the format of the Math Test.

THE BASICS

The SAT Math Test includes two sections and a total of 58 questions. You can use your calculator on only one of the sections:

Section	Number of Questions	Amount of Time
Calculator Section	38 questions	55 minutes
No-Calculator Section	20 questions	25 minutes

In the Calculator Section, you'll have about 1.5 minutes to answer each question. In the No-Calculator Section, you'll have 1.25 minutes to answer each question. This might not seem like a lot of time, but reviewing and practicing the concepts in this chapter will help you apply your knowledge quickly and efficiently on test day! We'll talk about time management and other test-taking strategies in Section 2 of this chapter.

TOPICS

There are four main content areas covered by the Math Test. Here is a breakdown of the topics and number of questions in each content area:

Content Area	Topics Covered	Number of Questions Calculator	Number of Questions No-Calculator
Heart of Algebra	Fundamental concepts in algebra involving linear equations and inequalities	11	8
Problem Solving and Data Analysis	Interpreting qualitative and quantitative data, analyzing relationships	17	0
Passport to Advanced Math	More advanced concepts in algebra, including quadratic and higher-order equations	7	9
Additional Topics in Math	Geometry, trigonometry, complex numbers	3	3
Total		**38**	**20**

Questions on each of the four main content areas will be spread evenly throughout each section of the Math Test. In Section 3, we'll review some of the more fundamental math skills that apply to all of these topics. Then, in Sections 4-7, we'll cover the topics in each of these content areas in depth.

QUESTIONS

Both sections on the Math Test will have two types of questions: multiple choice questions and student-produced responses. In total, you will see 45 multiple choice questions and 13 student-produced responses on the Math Test.

Each section will start with the multiple choice questions, then progress to the student-produced responses.

Within each section, the multiple choice questions will be ordered by difficulty, and so will the student-produced responses. For example, in the Calculator Section, you will see 30 multiple choice questions ordered from easy to difficult, then 8 student-produced responses. The No-Calculator Section has 15 multiple choice questions and 5 student-produced responses.

Some of the questions will include real-world contexts in areas such as science and social studies. These questions will require you to apply reasoning and critical thinking skills to analyze situations, create mathematical models, and find relevant solutions. You will also see graphs, charts, and diagrams in some of the problems and answer choices.

SCORING

Each question is worth one point. The number of points you receive on each section will contribute to your raw score, which will be scaled to give you your final math score from 200-800. The Calculator Section has twice the weight of the No-Calculator Section in determining your score. Here is a chart that shows the scoring breakdown for each question type:

Section	Problem Type	Points	Percentage of Math Score	
Calculator	Multiple Choice	30	52%	66%
	Student-Produced Responses	8	14%	
No-Calculator	Multiple Choice	15	26%	34%
	Student-Produced Responses	5	8%	
Total		**58**	**100%**	**100%**

In the next section, we will discuss the different question types on the Math Test and learn strategies for approaching and solving each type of question. The rest of the chapter provides an in-depth review of the topics covered on the Math Test. To practice applying your knowledge, make sure to do the practice exercises for each section and the full practice Math Test at the end of the chapter. Let's get started!

SECTION 2
APPROACHING THE MATH TEST

To succeed on the SAT Math Test, you need to know specific math concepts and math skills. The good news is that the redesigned SAT Math Test evaluates math skills that you have learned in your high school classes. You just need to learn which skills the SAT tests, and what strategies you can use to apply your knowledge during the test.

In this section, you will learn about approaching problems, entering your answers, and using problem-solving strategies for the Math Test. You'll see how these techniques can be applied to sample math questions and practice using them.

Once you have mastered these strategies, you'll be ready to review the math concepts on the exam. All of these concepts are covered in Sections 3-7 of this chapter. If you feel comfortable with some or all of the material, you can complete the practice sets at the end of each section to determine which topics you should review.

PLAN YOUR APPROACH

PART 1

When you take the SAT Math Test, you can reduce your stress by planning ahead. Know what the directions say, how you will approach each question, and how to pace yourself. We'll go through these steps with an example below.

KNOW THE DIRECTIONS

You will be given directions and reference information at the beginning of each math section of the SAT. The directions contain important information about the types of questions you will see and how much time you have to complete them. Make sure to read the directions before starting the problems so you know what to expect in each section.

The "Notes" box at the beginning of each math section will look similar to the one below. This box will tell you whether you can use a calculator on that section. It also gives you information about the figures and functions you will see and use on the test.

Notes	1.	You may use a calculator on this section.
	2.	When a problem includes a figure, the figure is meant to be a helpful resource for solving that problem. If a problem does not state that its figure is NOT drawn to scale, you may assume the figure provides a correct representation of the information in the problem.
	3.	The domain of any function f is the set of all real numbers x for which $f(x)$ is a real number, unless otherwise stated.

The Reference box contains important formulas and facts. To use this information to your advantage, be familiar with what formulas are provided. Use this reference information when practicing for the SAT. Remember that this information is only helpful if you know how to use it to solve problems.

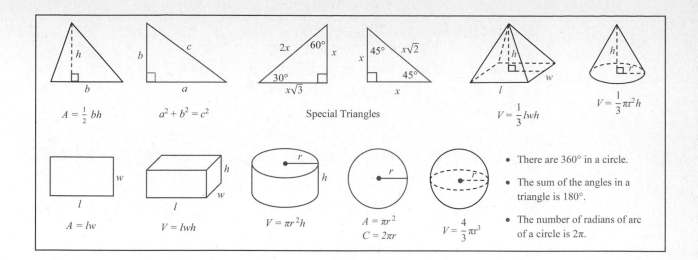

$A = \frac{1}{2}bh$ $a^2 + b^2 = c^2$ Special Triangles $V = \frac{1}{3}lwh$ $V = \frac{1}{3}\pi r^2 h$

$A = lw$ $V = lwh$ $V = \pi r^2 h$ $A = \pi r^2$ $C = 2\pi r$ $V = \frac{4}{3}\pi r^3$

- There are 360° in a circle.
- The sum of the angles in a triangle is 180°.
- The number of radians of arc of a circle is 2π.

READ THE QUESTION CAREFULLY

Read through the whole question. Don't assume you understand the question just by reading the first few words! Reading the whole question will help you avoid making assumptions that can lead to careless errors.

If you see unfamiliar or difficult-looking material, stay calm and keep reading until the end of the question. There might be more information in the question that will help you figure out the solution. If you still think a question is too difficult after you have finished reading the whole thing, you should make your best guess, circle it in your question booklet, and come back to it if you have time. Don't get anxious that you couldn't find the correct answer to a question.

EXAMPLE

The width of a rectangular field is one-quarter of its length. If the length is 16, what is the perimeter of the field?

(A) 4

(B) 24

(C) 36

(D) 40

UNDERLINE KEY WORDS

Underline or circle any information given in the question that will help you solve it. Our example question should now look something like this:

The <u>width</u> of a <u>rectangular</u> field is <u>one-quarter its length</u>. If the <u>length is 16</u>, what is the <u>perimeter</u> of the field?

IDENTIFY WHAT THE QUESTION IS ASKING

Ask yourself, "What is the question asking me to solve?" This is especially important for word problems. Sometimes the wording of a question can be confusing, so make it simpler for yourself and summarize in your own words what the question is asking for. Pay close attention to the key words you have underlined, and take a moment to remember their meanings as you summarize the question.

In our example question, you are being asked to find the perimeter of the rectangle. Put this in your own words: the perimeter is the length of the outline of the rectangle.

DRAW A CHART OR DIAGRAM

Charts and diagrams are great tools to help you visualize the problem and organize your information. In our example question, you might try drawing a quick sketch of a rectangle. Fill in any information given in the question:

$$\text{width} = \frac{1}{4} \text{ length}$$

length = 16

Come up With a Strategy

Strategize the best way to solve the question. Sometimes finding the answer requires some thought if there are multiple steps involved. Think about all of the information provided in the question and how it is related. Think about where you have seen this type of question before, and what methods you have used to solve similar types of questions. If there is a formula you know that could help, write it down.

Here's a strategy we could use to solve our example question.

- *We know*: length = 16
  - width = $\frac{1}{4}$ of length = $\frac{1}{4} \times 16 = \frac{16}{4} = 4$
- *We want*: the perimeter of the whole rectangle
- *Our strategy*: we can use a formula that relates a rectangle's perimeter to its length and width
  - perimeter = (2 × length) + (2 × width)

We can now plug in the values and solve:

$$\text{perimeter} = (2 \times 16) + (2 \times 4) = 32 + 8 = 40$$

Is our solution one of the answer choices? It is indeed! The answer is (D) 40.

Check Your Answer

Always check your work to make sure that you picked the best answer among all of the answer choices. Double-check your arithmetic to make sure that you didn't make any careless errors.

Check that you solved for what the question was asking. For example, if the question asked you to solve for a perimeter, make sure you didn't solve for area.

Try to determine whether or not your answer seems reasonable based on context. For example, if the length of one side of the rectangle is 16, the perimeter of the whole rectangle has to be greater than twice the length, or 32. Answers (A) and (B) in the example are less than 32, so they are unreasonable.

Finally, check that you bubbled in the answer on your answer sheet correctly. It would be a shame to have solved the question correctly and not get credit! Take a look at Part 2 to learn how to enter your answers correctly.

PACE YOURSELF

Remember that you will be answering questions under a time limit, and you need to leave yourself enough time to attempt every question on the test. One way to save time during the test is to be familiar with the format and instructions before the test day. Be aware of the number and types of sections that you will see. Before starting a section, look at the number of questions you will be answering and the time you have to answer them.

Here is a chart showing how many minutes you should average per question on each section of the Math Test. The questions in the multiple choice section are ordered from easy to difficult. Plan to spend less time on the early questions so that you have enough time for the more challenging ones at the end of the section.

Pacing on the Math Test			
Section	Total Time	Total Questions	Time Per Question
Calculator Section	55 minutes	38 questions	1.4 minutes per question
No-Calculator Section	25 minutes	20 questions	1.25 minutes per question

Finally, remember that every question is worth the same number of points. If you get stuck on any problem, make a guess and return to that question if you have time at the end. You don't lose points for guessing, so you should never leave a question blank. In Part 3, we'll talk about some strategies for guessing efficiently on the SAT Math Test.

ENTERING YOUR ANSWERS

PART 2

As we saw in Section 1, questions on the Math Test come in two types: regular multiple-choice questions and student-produced responses. The **multiple-choice questions** ask you to choose an answer from four possible choices, but the **student-produced responses** require you to come up with your own answer and enter it into a special grid.

For both question types, you'll need to bubble in your answer on your answer sheet. For a review of how to bubble in your answers to multiple-choice questions, see Chapter 1. Here, we'll discuss how to "grid in" your answers for the student-produced responses. The gridding process can be confusing, so you should practice thoroughly before the test day. This will help you avoid mistakes, save time, and build confidence.

GRIDDING IN

You will see directions for gridding answers immediately before the grid-in problems. To save time during the test, practice gridding answers before the test. This way, you can skip the directions for gridding answers and have more time to work on the problems.

You will enter your answers to student-produced responses in a grid like the one shown here. The grid has four columns, and in each column you can enter a digit from 0-9, a decimal point, or a fraction bar (/). This way, you can enter any value between 0 and 9,999.

The machine will score the bubbles you fill in on the grid. Make sure to fill in bubbles completely and mark no more than one circle in any column. Completely erase any stray marks in the grid.

Answers written in the boxes above the grid are *not* scored. You can write your answer into those boxes as a guide when you bubble in your answers, and it is a good idea to use the boxes to avoid bubbling errors. However, remember that you always need to bubble your answers as well!

PLACEMENT

You can start your answer in any column as long as you can fit in the whole answer. You may leave columns blank if the answer is fewer than four characters. For example, 64 can be gridded in the three ways shown below; all are correct.

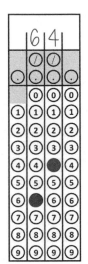 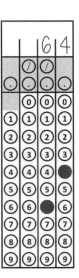

SIGNS

There is no negative sign in the grid, so all answers will be positive numbers or zero. If you get a negative number for an answer, either you have made a mistake or there are other possible answers. Check your work and rework the problem if necessary.

FRACTIONS AND DECIMALS

Grid-in responses may contain fractions or decimals. You can write these answers in either fraction or decimal form as long as you follow the rules below.

You can grid proper and improper fractions, but *not* mixed numbers. If the answer is a mixed number, you must convert it to an improper fraction or a decimal. For example, the answer $4\frac{1}{5}$ must be gridded as 21/5 or 4.2 as shown in the following grids.

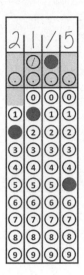 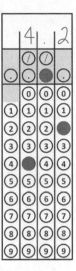

If you grid the answer as the mixed number 41/5 like the example below, the machine will read it as $\frac{41}{5}$, which is incorrect.

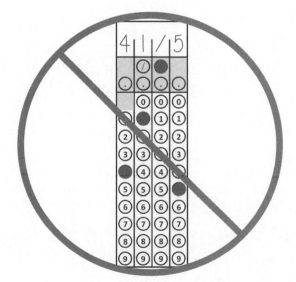

Some answers will not fit in the grid as a fraction and must be converted to a decimal. For example, $\frac{1}{100}$ must be gridded as .01 because 1/100 will not fit.

Decimals must be as accurate as possible. If a decimal is longer than four characters, grid the first four characters (including the decimal point) or it may be marked incorrect. For example, $\frac{4}{7}$ should be written as .571 with no zero before the decimal point. (Note that the first column does not have a bubble for zero.) The response .57 may be scored as incorrect because it is less accurate than .571.

You do not have to follow rounding rules when shortening your answer. If you round, do so at the last digit that you can fit in the grid. 8.127 can be bubbled as 8.12 or 8.13, but not as 8.1, which is less accurate.

Fractions may be left unreduced as long as they fit in the grid. If an answer was $\frac{3}{4}$, you could grid it as 3/4, 6/8, 9/12, or as a decimal.

MULTIPLE CORRECT ANSWERS

Some grid-in problems have more than one correct answer. In those cases, you may grid in any of the possible answers as long as it fits in the grid. There may also be multiple methods to arrive at a correct answer.

PROBLEM SOLVING STRATEGIES
PART 3

In Chapter 1, we reviewed general strategies that you can use on all parts of the SAT. In this section, we will learn strategies that apply specifically to mathematics questions. These strategies will help you use your time and resources, like your calculator and the testing materials, to answer questions quickly and to reduce your chance of making mistakes. You will also learn how to approach and answer questions that you do not know how to solve.

USE YOUR CALCULATOR

The Math Test is divided into a Calculator Section and a No-Calculator Section. Every math problem on the SAT can be solved without a calculator, but when you're allowed to use a calculator, it can help you save time and avoid errors.

You must provide your own calculator. A scientific or graphing calculator is recommended. You cannot use calculators with keypads, styluses, touchscreens, internet access, cellular access, or power cords. You also cannot use calculators that can play or record audio, video, or images. Your calculator can't make noise, and you can't use a laptop, tablet, or phone as a calculator. For a list of acceptable calculators, see ivyglobal.com/study/links/#calculator.

Make sure to practice using the calculator that you plan to bring to the SAT so you are familiar with it during the test. Before the test, make sure your calculator is working properly and has fresh batteries. Consider bringing a spare set of batteries or a back-up calculator.

Don't rely too much on your calculator when you take the test. On some problems, using a calculator can slow you down. When starting a problem, think about how you will solve it and whether you need to use a calculator. Look for ways to simplify the problem that will make the calculation easier, such as factoring.

Write down calculations and scratch work in the test booklet. This will help you avoid calculator errors and makes it easier to check your work and find errors. Also, remember that every problem can be solved without a calculator. If you find yourself doing complicated or tedious calculations, there is likely a simpler method to find the answer.

LOOK FOR SHORTCUTS

None of the problems should require time-consuming calculations. If your solution strategy is long or complicated, look for a simpler method or a trick to solve the problem more quickly. Also double-check to make sure you are solving for the correct variable or value.

There are often multiple ways to solve a problem, so look for shortcuts or tricks that will save you time and unnecessary work. When possible, simplify equations and expressions.

EXAMPLE

$$\frac{10x}{y} \times \frac{3}{4} \times \frac{2}{5} \times \frac{1}{6} =$$

(A) $\frac{x}{3y}$

(B) $\frac{x}{2y}$

(C) $\frac{x}{y}$

(D) $\frac{2x}{y}$

You could solve this problem by finding the product of all the terms. However, this is not the best approach. Instead, try to cancel as many factors as possible. The 3×2 in the numerator cancels the 6 in the denominator. You can rewrite the 4×5 in the denominator as 2×10 and cancel that 10 with the 10 in the numerator.

$$\frac{10x}{y} \times \frac{\cancel{3}\cancel{2}}{\underset{2\times10}{\cancel{4}\cancel{5}}}^{6} \times \frac{1}{6} = \frac{\cancel{10} \times \cancel{6} \times x}{2 \times \cancel{10} \times \cancel{6} \times y} = \frac{x}{2y}$$

Now you are left with $\frac{x}{2y}$, which gives you the correct answer, (B).

This approach reduces the chance of making an arithmetic or calculator error. In fact, it eliminates the need to use a calculator at all. If this question were on the no-calculator section, this approach is faster and safer than multiplying all the factors out by hand.

ELIMINATE AND GUESS

If you aren't sure how to solve a problem, you can make your best guess or even find the right answer through elimination. Determine which of the answer choices are incorrect and cross them out in your test booklet. Consider what you know about the correct solution and eliminate answer choices that are impossible. Does the answer have to be positive or negative? Odd or even? Does it have to be within a certain range of values?

EXAMPLE

Which of the following fractions is less than $\frac{1}{3}$?

(A) $\frac{4}{18}$

(B) $\frac{4}{12}$

(C) $\frac{3}{3}$

(D) $\frac{12}{9}$

Even if you are not sure how to solve this problem, you can still eliminate some of the wrong answer choices. You know that $\frac{1}{3}$ is less than 1. Remember that an "improper fraction" has a numerator that is greater than its denominator, and any improper fraction is greater than 1. Because answer (D) is an improper fraction, it must be greater than 1, so it can't be less than $\frac{1}{3}$. You can eliminate this choice right away.

You might also remember that a fraction with the same numerator and denominator is always equal to 1. Answer (C) has the same numerator and denominator, so it must be equal to 1 and can't be less than $\frac{1}{3}$. You can also eliminate answer (C).

If you don't know how to proceed with the arithmetic, you can guess between (A) and (B) and you will have pretty good odds of getting the correct answer. Or, you can look at answer (B) and reduce $\frac{4}{12}$ to $\frac{1}{3}$. Because the question is asking for a fraction that is less than $\frac{1}{3}$, (B) can't be the correct answer. You are left with only one possible answer: (A).

Remember that there is no longer a guessing penalty on the SAT, so you should *always* guess if you are unsure of an answer. Try to eliminate as many answer choices as possible before guessing. Then, make your best guess and move on so you have time to answer all of the questions in the section.

PLUG IN ANSWER CHOICES

Sometimes it is easier or faster to find the correct answer by plugging the answer choices into the problem. This can save you from doing long or complicated calculations.

When you use this strategy, it is best to start with choice (B) or (C). Most answer choices are listed in increasing or decreasing numerical order. If you start with (B) or (C), you may be able to eliminate multiple answers based on the result. For example, if the answers increase in value from (A) to (D) and you determine that choice (C) is too small, you can eliminate choices (A), (B), and (C).

EXAMPLE

$$\frac{9}{4x} = \frac{3}{8}$$

What is the value of x?

(A) 2
(B) 4
(C) 6
(D) 8

To solve by testing answer choices, start with (B) or (C). If you start with (B), $\frac{9}{4x} = \frac{9}{16}$.

This does not reduce to $\frac{3}{8}$, so (B) is not the right answer. However, you can use this to eliminate more than one answer choice. $\frac{9}{16}$ is greater than $\frac{3}{8}$, so you know that 4 is too small a value of x. Therefore, you can also eliminate any other values smaller than 4, such as answer choice (A).

Next, try (C). $\frac{9}{4x} = \frac{9}{24}$, which can be reduced to $\frac{3}{8}$, so (C) is the correct answer.

You can also use different strategies when plugging in answer choices. For example, if one or more of the answer choices is significantly easier to plug into the problem, consider starting with that one. Or if you are asked to find the largest (or smallest) value that satisfies a condition, start with the largest (or smallest) answer choice.

EXAMPLE

What is the largest integer, x, for which $\frac{66}{5x - 4}$ is an integer greater than 1?

(A) 1

(B) 2

(C) 3

(D) 4

Since you are looking for the largest possible value of x, start with answer choice (D). $\frac{66}{5(4) - 4} = \frac{66}{16}$, which is not an integer. Your next choice, (C), is $\frac{66}{5(3) - 4} = \frac{66}{11} = 6$, which is an integer, so (C) is the correct answer. Even though (A) and (B) also produce integers, you can stop after (C) because it is the largest value of x that satisfies the conditions.

REPLACE VARIABLES WITH NUMBERS

If you are more comfortable working with numbers than variables, you can replace variables in a problem with easy-to-use numbers. To avoid mistakes, make sure to write down which variables you are replacing with which numbers.

EXAMPLE

In y years, Alex will be three times the age of his sister Nancy. Currently Alex is a years old and Nancy is n years old. Which of the following expressions is equal to y?

(A) $\dfrac{a-3n}{2}$

(B) $\dfrac{a+3n}{2}$

(C) $a-3n$

(D) $a+3n$

You can solve this problem numerically instead of symbolically by substituting numbers that are easy to use. First, think of a possible set of ages where Alex is three times as old as Nancy. For example, you could say that Adam is 6 and Nancy is 2. To get a value for a and n, pick a number for y, such as $y = 1$. Since Adam will be 6 in $y = 1$ years, his current age, a, is $6 - 1 = 5$. Similarly, Nancy's current age, n, is $2 - 1 = 1$.

Next, substitute these values for a and n into the answer choices:

(A) $\dfrac{5-3(1)}{2} = 1$

(B) $\dfrac{5+3(1)}{2} = 4$

(C) $5 - 3(1) = 2$

(D) $5 + 3(1) = 8$

Since you defined y as 1, answer choice (A) is correct.

It is important to check all the answer choices when you substitute numbers. Certain number substitutions, especially 1, may give the "correct" solution for more than one answer choice. In that case, you'll need to pick some different numbers to test out, or you'll need to try a different method to solve the problem.

Use Figures

Any figure provided in the Math Test will be accurate unless noted otherwise. If an angle looks like a right angle, you can assume that it is one. It is safe to assume other features like parallel or perpendicular lines and relative angles or lengths. Charts, graphs, and gridded figures are always accurate.

Although you are not allowed to use a ruler, you can measure lengths by using the side of your answer sheet. Place the corner of the sheet at one point and mark the distance to another point. This strategy may help you eliminate answer choices or check your answer, although there will always be a way to solve these problems without measuring lengths.

Some figures may not show all of the lines that you need to solve the problem. You should add any necessary lines as accurately as possible.

Example

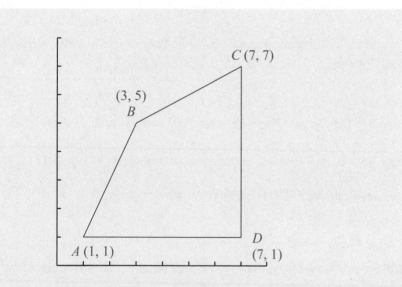

What is the area of quadrilateral *ABCD*?

(A) 18

(B) 24

(C) 30

(D) 36

Since quadrilateral *ABCD* is irregular, you cannot easily find the area. However, if you draw a line between *B* and *D*, you will have two triangles whose areas you can calculate:

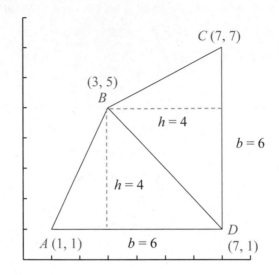

Define the base of triangle *ABD* to be $\overline{AD}$ and the base of triangle *BCD* to be $\overline{CD}$. The height of each triangle is the line segment from the base to the opposite vertex, perpendicular to the base. The bases and heights are labelled in the diagram.

We can use the formula $A = \frac{1}{2}bh$ to find the areas of each of these triangles. The area of triangle *ABD* is $\frac{1}{2}(6)(4) = 12$, and the area of triangle *BCD* is $\frac{1}{2}(6)(4) = 12$. Therefore, the area of quadrilateral *ABCD* is 24, which is answer choice (B).

If a figure is not provided for a geometry problem, draw a diagram. Figures may also be helpful for solving other types of problems. You might draw a number line, graph, or quick sketch of a situation. Keep your diagrams simple and accurate.

EXAMPLE

A square and a rectangle have the same perimeter. The square has a length and width of 4 and the rectangle has a length of 5. What is the area of the rectangle?

(A) 3

(B) 6

(C) 15

(D) 30

First, draw a diagram of the square and rectangle:

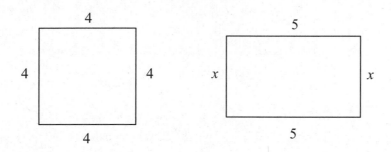

Since the perimeter of the square is $4 \times 4 = 16$, the perimeter of the rectangle is also 16. The perimeter is $2 \times 5 + 2x$, so you can set this expression equal to 16 and solve for x:

$$2 \times 5 + 2x = 16$$

$$10 + 2x = 16$$

$$2x = 6$$

$$x = 3$$

Remember that you are solving for the area, not x! From the diagram, you can calculate the area as $3 \times 5 = 15$, so (C) is the correct answer.

To check this answer, you can use the figures you drew. The area of the rectangle is close to the area of the square. None of the other answer choices are close to 15.

PAY ATTENTION TO UNITS AND VARIABLES

When choosing an answer, double check that it is in the correct units. The answer may have different units than the given data. Circle or underline any units given in the problem and the units of the answer. Problems involving units will almost always have answer choices that are correct for different units.

EXAMPLE

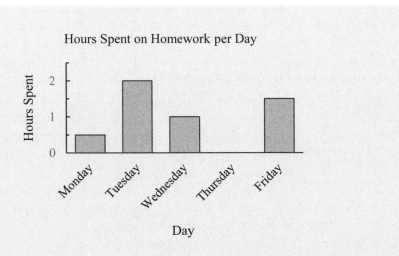

The chart above shows the amount of time Jenny spent on homework in one week. On average, how many minutes per day did Jenny spend on homework?

(A)   1

(B) 1.25

(C)   60

(D)   75

Notice that the units of the graph are hours, but the answer must be in minutes. First, find the average number of hours Jenny spends. We take the average by adding together her hours for each day and then dividing by the number of days:

$$\frac{.5 + 2 + 1 + 0 + 1.5}{5} = 1$$

Jenny spends an average of 1 hour per day, but you need to convert this into minutes. There are 60 minutes in 1 hour, so answer choice (C) is correct.

CHECK YOUR ANSWERS

Before starting to work on a problem, make sure you know what the problem is asking. On problems that take multiple steps, double check that your final solution is the answer to the problem, not an intermediate step.

Watch out for answer choices that are factors, multiples, or other variations of your answer. You may have forgotten a final step or gone too far in your calculation.

EXAMPLE

An isosceles triangle has a perimeter of 16. Two legs have length L and the other leg has a length of 6. What is the area of the triangle?

(A) 4

(B) 5

(C) 6

(D) 12

First, draw a diagram of the triangle:

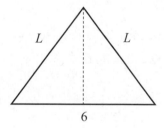

Next, find the value of L using the equation for the perimeter:

$$2L + 6 = 16$$
$$2L = 10$$
$$L = 5$$

Notice that answer choice (B) is 5, but that is *not* the answer to the question, which asks for area, not L.

To find the area, we must find the height shown by the dashed line. Notice that if we divide the triangle into two halves at the dashed line, it becomes two right triangles. We know that L, the hypotenuse, is 5, and the base of each new triangle is $6 \div 2 = 3$.

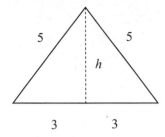

We can use the Pythagorean Theorem to find the height, which we've labelled h:

$$3^2 + h^2 = 5^2$$

$$9 + h^2 = 25$$

$$h^2 = 16$$

$$h = 4$$

Be careful – this is another intermediate solution! Now we can find the area of the original triangle using our values for base and height:

$$A = \frac{1}{2} bh$$

$$A = \frac{1}{2}(6)(4) = 12$$

(D) 12 is the correct answer.

If you have extra time at the end of a section, double-check your answers, especially for grid-in problems. Try to use a different process to find the answer to avoid making the same mistake twice. Write out your calculations when solving problems to make it easier to find your mistakes. Remember to always guess on problems that you cannot solve.

PART 3 PRACTICE: PROBLEM SOLVING STRATEGIES

For questions 1-3, cross out answer choices that are definitely wrong without fully solving the question. Briefly note why you eliminated certain choices. Finally, solve the problem.

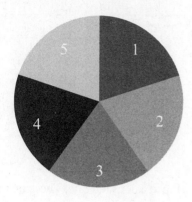

1. The spinner above has five equal sections, each with a number. What is the probability of spinning a 3 or a 5?

   (A) $\frac{1}{5}$ Eliminate?   If so, why?

   (B) $\frac{2}{5}$ Eliminate?   If so, why?

   (C) $\frac{1}{2}$ Eliminate?   If so, why?

   (D) $\frac{3}{5}$ Eliminate?   If so, why?

2. Matt has an average of 83% on four math tests. What score would he have to average on his next two tests in order to have an 85% average on all six tests?

   (A) 85%   Eliminate?   If so, why?
   (B) 87%   Eliminate?   If so, why?
   (C) 89%   Eliminate?   If so, why?
   (D) 91%   Eliminate?   If so, why?

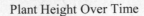

Plant Height Over Time

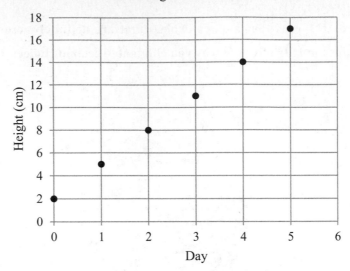

3. A young plant is growing at a constant rate. The graph shows the height of the plant over time. What is the relationship between d (the day) and H (the height)?

(A) $H = 3d$ Eliminate?   If so, why?

(B) $H = -3d + 2$ Eliminate?   If so, why?

(C) $H = 2d + 3$ Eliminate?   If so, why?

(D) $H = 3d + 2$ Eliminate?   If so, why?

For each of the following questions, plug in answer choices to select your answer.

4. If a box of pencils is divided equally among 6 people, there will be 3 pencils left over. If the pencils are divided equally among 4 people, there will be 1 pencil left over. Which of the following could be a possible number of pencils in the box?

(A) 23

(B) 33

(C) 43

(D) 53

5. The perimeter of a rectangle is twice its area. Which of the following are possible dimensions of the rectangle?

    (A) 1 by 6
    (B) 3 by 12
    (C) 4 by 4
    (D) 2 by 2

6. Carla has completed 12 of the 47 problems in her math worksheet. If she wants to finish the worksheet in the next seven minutes, how many problems does she need to complete per minute?

    (A) 5
    (B) 6
    (C) 7
    (D) 10

For each question below, pick a number that will simplify the question. Then, use this number to solve the question.

7. At a school barbecue, $\frac{6}{10}$ of the students ate a hamburger and $\frac{4}{10}$ ate a hot dog. There are twice as many hot dogs in a box as hamburgers. If the students ate 4 boxes of hot dogs, how many boxes of hamburgers did they eat?

8. Rectangle A is 9 times longer than Rectangle B. The width of Rectangle A is $\frac{1}{3}$ the width of Rectangle B. The area of Rectangle A is how many times greater than the area of Rectangle B?

9. From 2000 to 2001, the population of fish in a pond grew by 10%. From 2001 to 2002, the population of fish declined by 5%. By what percent did the population of fish rise from 2000 to 2002?

10. If a certain maple tree grew by 3 feet and then doubled in height, it would be the same height as a certain red oak. What is the relationship between the height of the maple tree (m) and the height of the red oak (r)?

Answer Key: Problem Solving Strategies

1. **B**

   In this case, all three of the other answer choices can be immediately eliminated. (A) is wrong because that's the probability of spinning one particular number, like 3 or 5. The probability of spinning a 3 OR a 5 must be greater than the probability of spinning just a 3 or spinning just a 5. (C) can be eliminated because the spinner is divided into sections of $\frac{1}{5}$ each, and it is impossible to make $\frac{1}{2}$ with whole sections of the spinner. (D) can also be eliminated because that corresponds to 3 slices— that's actually the probability of spinning a 1, 2, or 4.

2. **C**

   Eliminate (A) since Matt has to do better than his goal average on the final two tests in order to reach that average. (B) is a little trickier to eliminate, but you can eliminate it if you notice that the difference between 83% and 85% and between 85% and 87% is the same. Since the 83% average is from four tests and he only has two more tests to boost his average, he has to do better than an 87% on his remaining two tests in order to swing his average to an 85%. Neither (C) nor (D) is easily eliminated, but with only two to choose from you have less of a chance of making a mistake.

3. **D**

   (A) can be eliminated since that line would cross the origin, and the graph does not. (B) can be eliminated since the slope of the graph is positive. (C) is wrong since the y-intercept of that line would be 3 and the slope of that line would be 2. Since those values don't match the graph we see, we eliminate that answer choice.

4. **B**

   Divide each answer choice by 6 and 4 and note the remainders.

5. **D**

   Each answer choice gives a pair of side lengths: a by b. We know that Area $= ab$ and Perimeter $= 2(a+b)$. Since we're looking for the rectangle where Perimeter $= 2 \times$ Area, we're looking for the dimensions for which $ab = a + b$. Plug in all of the answer choice values into this equation, and the only one that works is (D).

6. A

   If you plug in (C), Carla would have completed 61 problems after 7 minutes. That's too many, so try (B). (B) leaves us with 54 problems in total, which is still too many, so pick (A), 5, the only smaller value.

7. 12

   Assume there were 100 students in total, so 60 students ate hamburgers and 40 students ate hot dogs. Since 4 boxes of hot dogs fed 40 students, there were 10 hot dogs per box. That means there were 5 hamburgers per box, so 12 boxes were required to feed 60 students.

8. 3

   Assume that Rectangle B has a length of 1 and a width of 3, then figure out the length and width of Rectangle A. When you compare the two areas, Rectangle A is 3 times the size of Rectangle B.

9. 4.5%

   Assume there were 100 fish in 2000. That means there were 110 fish in 2001 and 104.5 fish in 2002. It's kind of weird to think of half a fish, but we can still tell that the percent increase was 4.5%.

10. $2(m + 3) = r$

    Say the maple tree started out at 5 feet. The red oak is then 16 feet tall. If you aren't able to immediately translate into algebra, try a few more values to get a feel for it and you should get $2(m + 3) = r$.

FUNDAMENTAL MATH REVIEW

In this section, we will review the basic arithmetic that you will need to know for the Math Test. When you are confident with these basic math concepts, the SAT Math material becomes a lot easier. The concepts we will review in this section are:

- Properties of Integers
- Factors and Multiples
- Operations
- Fractions
- Ratios, Percentages, Proportions, and Rates
- Exponents and Radicals
- Scientific Notation

INTEGERS
PART 1

Integers are positive and negative whole numbers, such as –2, –1, 0, 1, 2, etc. Fractions and decimals are not integers. **Zero** is an integer, but it is neither positive nor negative.

Here is a chart that summarizes types of integers:

Integer Properties		
Word	Definition	Examples
Positive	Greater than zero	2, 7, 23, 400
Negative	Less than zero	–2, –7, –23, –400
Even	Divisible by two	4, 18, 2002, 0
Odd	Not evenly divisible by two	3, 7, 15, 2001
Prime	Only divisible by itself and 1	2, 3, 5, 7, 11, 19, 23
Composite	Divisible by numbers other than itself and 1	4, 12, 15, 20, 21
Consecutive	Follow each other in numerical order	2, 3, 4, 5, 6

FACTORS AND MULTIPLES

A **factor** of a number is a positive integer that divides that number evenly. For example, the factors of 12 are 1, 2, 3, 4, 6, and 12. When you divide 12 by any other integer, the result is not a whole number. For example, $12 \div 5 = 2.4$. Since 2.4 is not a whole number, 5 is not a factor of 12.

Multiples of a number are the product of that number and any positive integer. For example, some multiples of 3 are 6 and 21 because $3 \times 2 = 6$ and $3 \times 7 = 21$.

Factoring or **factorization** is the process of writing a number as a product of its **prime factors**—the factors that are prime numbers. To factor a number, first divide it by any prime factor. Keep dividing the remainder by prime numbers until the remainder is a prime. Keep track of each factor, even if you divide by the same factor twice.

To factor 12, you can first divide by the prime factor 2: $12 \div 2 = 6$. Divide 6 by another prime factor, such as 2, to get 3. Since the remainder, 3, is a prime number, the prime factors of 12 are 2, 2, and 3.

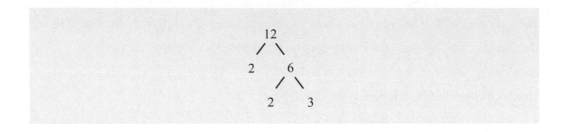

You can start the process with any prime factor, and the factoring will turn out the same.

You can find all the factors of a number by multiplying the prime factors by each other. For example, if you multiply the two factors of 2 together, you get 4, which is a factor of 12. Similarly, $2 \times 3 = 6$, so 6 is also a factor of 12.

Here is a chart that summarizes some types of factors and multiples:

Types of Factors and Multiples		
Word	Definition	Example
Common factors	Factors that two or more numbers share	6 and 15 have the common factors 1 and 3
Common multiples	Multiples that two or more numbers share	Some common multiples of 9 and 12 are 36, 108, and 216
Greatest common factor (GCF)	The largest common factor of two or more numbers	3 is the greatest common factor of 6 and 15
Least common multiple (LCM)	The smallest common multiple of two or more numbers	36 is the least common multiple of 9 and 12

One way to find the GCF and the LCM of two numbers is to organize their prime factors in a Venn diagram like the one below. First, factor each number. Then, write the shared prime factors in the middle of the Venn diagram. Write the remaining prime factors of each number in the correct side of the diagram. The circle under each number contains all the prime factors of that number.

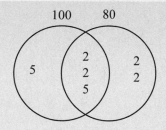

- The factorization of 100 is 2 × 2 × 5 × 5.

- The factorization of 80 is 2 × 2 × 2 × 2 × 5.

- The shared prime factors are 2, 2, and 5.

- The GCF is the product of shared factors: 2 × 2 × 5 = 20.

- The LCM is the product of all the factors in the diagram. Only count the shared factors once: 5 × 2 × 2 × 5 × 2 × 2 = 400.

OPERATIONS
PART 2

The four main operations in arithmetic are addition, subtraction, multiplication, and division.

Operations			
Operation	Name of Result	Words	Numbers
Addition	Sum	The sum of 3 and 4 is 7.	$3 + 4 = 7$
Subtraction	Difference	The difference between 5 and 2 is 3.	$5 - 2 = 3$
Multiplication	Product	The product of 6 and 4 is 24.	$6 \times 4 = 24$
Division	Quotient	The quotient of 40 divided by 5 is 8.	$40 \div 5 = 8$

If you perform operations with odd or even numbers, you can predict whether the result will be odd or even:

- even + even = even
- odd + odd = even
- even + odd = odd

- even × even = even
- odd × odd = odd
- even × odd = even

Here are some properties you should know for addition and multiplication:

- Associative Property: $(a + b) + c = a + (b + c)$ and $a(bc) = (ab)c$
- Commutative Property: $a + b = b + a$ and $ab = ba$
- Distributive Property: $a(b + c) = ab + ac$

And here are some properties you should know for subtraction and division:

- Subtracting a number is the same as adding its opposite: $a - b = a + (-b)$
- Adding a number to its opposite will give you zero: $a + (-a) = 0$
- Dividing by a number is the same as multiplying by its reciprocal: $a \div b = a \times \frac{1}{b}$
- Multiplying a number by its reciprocal will give you 1: $a \times \frac{1}{a} = 1$
- You can't divide any number by zero: $a \div 0$ is undefined

Order of Operations

The **order of operations** is the order that you must follow when carrying out multiple operations:

- **Parentheses:** Do any operations in parentheses first, following the order of operations within the parentheses.
- **Exponents:** Next, evaluate all exponents.
- **Multiplication** and **Division:** Multiply and divide from left to right.
- **Addition** and **Subtraction:** Add and subtract from left to right.

You can remember the order of operations with the mnemonic "**Please Excuse My Dear Aunt Sally**" or the acronym PEMDAS.

Example

Let's see how we'd use the order of operations to solve this calculation:

$$18 \div 3^2 \times 2 - 5 \ =$$

There are no parentheses in this expression, so move on to the next step and address exponents:

$$18 \div \mathbf{3^2} \times 2 - 5 \ = \ 18 \div \mathbf{9} \times 2 - 5$$

Next, address multiplication and division, working left to right:

$$\mathbf{18 \div 9} \times 2 - 5 \ = \ \mathbf{2} \times 2 - 5 \ = \ 4 - 5$$

Lastly, address addition and subtraction:

$$\mathbf{4 - 5} \ = \ -1$$

You have found your answer.

FRACTIONS

PART 3

A fraction can be thought of in two ways. First, it is another way to represent division. When we write $\frac{3}{4}$, we mean three divided by four. But more importantly, fractions are used to express parts of a whole.

A fraction often takes the form $\frac{a}{b}$. The number on top, a, is the **numerator,** and the number on the bottom, b, is the **denominator**. Here are some properties of numerators and denominators:

- If $a < b$, then $\frac{a}{b} < 1$.   This is called a **proper fraction**.

- If $a > b$, then $\frac{a}{b} > 1$.   This is called an **improper fraction**.

- If $a = b$, then $\frac{a}{b} = 1$.

You can compare two fractions by comparing their numerators and denominators:

- If two fractions have the same *denominator*, the fraction with the larger numerator is the larger fraction: $\frac{6}{7} > \frac{3}{7}$

- If two fractions have the same *numerator*, the fraction with the smaller denominator is the larger fraction: $\frac{5}{3} > \frac{5}{7}$

Mixed numbers are improper fractions written as an integer and a fraction. A mixed number is a sum of the integer and the fraction, *not* the product:

$$2\frac{1}{4} = 2 + \frac{1}{4}$$

$$2\frac{1}{4} \neq 2 \times \frac{1}{4}$$

A **rational number** is a number that can be expressed as a fraction of integers. Some examples include $-\frac{2}{3}$, $5\frac{1}{4}$, and 7. All of these can be expressed as a fraction of integers: $5\frac{1}{4}$ can be written as $\frac{21}{4}$, and 7 can be written as $\frac{7}{1}$.

Irrational numbers cannot be represented as a fraction of integers and will be expressed as a decimal or a symbol. Some examples include π, 81.52602934…, and any other non-repeating, infinite decimal.

EQUIVALENT FRACTIONS

A fraction can be written different ways and still represent the same number. These different fractions with the same value are called **equivalent fractions.** For example, $\frac{1}{2}$ has the same value as $\frac{2}{4}$ and $\frac{10}{20}$. To rewrite a fraction without changing its value, multiply or divide the numerator and the denominator by the same number.

EXAMPLE

$$\frac{1 \times 2}{2 \times 2} = \frac{2}{4}$$

$$\frac{1 \times 10}{2 \times 10} = \frac{10}{20}$$

Multiplying the numerator and denominator of a fraction by the same number does not change the value of the fraction because you are really multiplying the fraction by 1:

$$\frac{1 \times 2}{2 \times 2} = \frac{1}{2} \times \frac{2}{2} = \frac{1}{2} \times 1 = \frac{1}{2}$$

A fraction can be **simplified** by dividing its numerator and denominator by their greatest common factor. For example, let's simplify $\frac{60}{105}$. First, we'd factor 60 and 105:

$$60 = 2 \times 2 \times 3 \times 5$$

$$105 = 3 \times 5 \times 7$$

60 and 105 have the common factors 3 and 5, so their greatest common factor is $3 \times 5 = 15$. Therefore, we can simplify the fraction by dividing the numerator and denominator by 15:

$$\frac{60 \div 15}{105 \div 15} = \frac{4}{7}$$

OPERATIONS WITH FRACTIONS

You can only add or subtract two fractions when they have the same denominator—in other words, when they have a **common denominator**.

To add or subtract fractions with the same denominator, add or subtract the numerators and keep the denominator.

EXAMPLE

$$\frac{7}{9} - \frac{2}{9} = \frac{7-2}{9} = \frac{5}{9}$$

If the fractions have different denominators, you must convert them to equivalent fractions with the same denominator. Try using the least common multiple of the denominators.

EXAMPLE

Let's add $\frac{5}{6} + \frac{3}{8}$. Since the fractions have different denominators, the first step is to convert them to a common denominator. We'll use 24 because it is the least common multiple of 6 and 8:

$$\frac{5}{6} = \frac{5 \times 4}{6 \times 4} = \frac{20}{24}$$

$$\frac{3}{8} = \frac{3 \times 3}{8 \times 3} = \frac{9}{24}$$

Now that we have two fractions with a common denominator, we can add them:

$$\frac{20}{24} + \frac{9}{24} = \frac{29}{24}$$

To convert mixed numbers to improper fractions, add the integer to the fraction:

EXAMPLE

$$2\frac{1}{4} = 2 + \frac{1}{4} = \frac{2 \times 4}{1 \times 4} + \frac{1}{4} = \frac{8}{4} + \frac{1}{4} = \frac{9}{4}$$

You can multiply fractions without converting them to common denominators. Just multiply their numerators and denominators:

EXAMPLE

$$\frac{5 \times 7}{3 \times 8} = \frac{35}{24}$$

To divide by a fraction, multiply by its reciprocal. The **reciprocal** of a fraction is the fraction created when you flip the original numerator and denominator. For example, the reciprocal of $\frac{7}{10}$ is $\frac{10}{7}$. The reciprocal of 3 is the reciprocal of $\frac{3}{1}$, which is $\frac{1}{3}$.

EXAMPLE

To divide $\frac{7}{10}$ by 3, you need to multiply by the reciprocal of 3:

$$\frac{7}{10} \div 3 = \frac{7}{10} \times \frac{1}{3} = \frac{7}{30}$$

COMPLEX FRACTIONS

Complex fractions are fractions that have one or more fractions in their numerator and/or denominator.

EXAMPLE

$$\frac{2 - \frac{1}{2}}{3 + \frac{5}{6}}$$

To simplify a complex fraction, you can simplify the numerator and denominator and then divide. For example, to simplify the complex fraction above, you can first simplify the numerator:

$$2 - \frac{1}{2} \ = \ \frac{4}{2} - \frac{1}{2} \ = \ \frac{3}{2}$$

Then, you can simplify the denominator:

$$3 + \frac{5}{6} \ = \ \frac{18}{6} + \frac{5}{6} \ = \ \frac{23}{6}$$

And finally, you can divide the two fractions:

$$\frac{3}{2} \div \frac{23}{6} \ = \ \frac{3}{2} \times \frac{6}{23} \ = \ \frac{18}{46} \ = \ \frac{9}{23}$$

FRACTIONS AND DECIMALS

If you divide the numerator by the denominator, you can convert a fraction into an integer or a **decimal**, which is a way of representing a fraction out of 10.

EXAMPLE

$$\frac{3}{4} \ = \ 3 \div 4 \ = \ 0.75$$

Decimals can be easier to compare than fractions if the fractions have different denominators or different numerators. On the calculator section, you can use a calculator to convert fractions to decimals. For the no-calculator section, you should know the common fraction-decimal conversions:

$$\frac{1}{2} = .5 \qquad \frac{1}{3} = .\overline{3} \qquad \frac{2}{3} = .\overline{6} \qquad \frac{1}{4} = .25 \qquad \frac{3}{4} = .75$$

The horizontal bar over the decimal means that it repeats infinitely: $.\overline{3} = .33333\ldots$

RATIOS, PERCENTAGES, PROPORTIONS, AND RATES

PART 4

RATIOS

A **ratio** shows a relationship between two quantities. Ratios can be expressed as a fraction $\frac{1}{4}$, with a colon (1:4), or with the word "to": (1 to 4). Ratios can be converted like fractions by multiplying or dividing each quantity by the same number. For example, if a jar has 12 red marbles and 15 blue marbles, the ratio of red marbles to blue marbles would be $\frac{12}{15}$ or 12:15. This can be reduced to 4:5.

Notice that ratios are *not* a "part-to-whole" relationship like a fraction unless one quantity is the total. In our jar of marbles, there is a total of 27 marbles. Therefore, if we wanted to write the fraction of marbles that are red, we'd write $\frac{12}{27}$, *not* $\frac{12}{15}$.

Ratios can compare more than 2 quantities. For example, if a jar has 12 red marbles, 15 blue marbles, and 6 green marbles, the ratio of red to blue to green marbles is 12:15:6 or 4:5:2.

PERCENTAGES

A **percentage** is a ratio that compares a quantity to 100. For example, 20 is 80% of 25 because $\frac{20}{25} = \frac{80}{100}$.

To convert a percentage to a fraction, re-write it as a fraction of 100 and simplify.

$$45\% = \frac{45}{100} = \frac{9}{20}$$

To convert a percentage to a decimal, divide the percentage by 100:

EXAMPLE

$$45\% = .45$$

PROPORTIONS

A **proportion** is an equation stating that two fractions are equal. For example, the proportion $\frac{5}{15} = \frac{7}{21}$ shows that $\frac{5}{15}$ and $\frac{7}{21}$ are the same number. They are both multiples of $\frac{1}{3}$.

Proportions will often involve one or more variables. To solve these equations, you can **cross-multiply** by multiplying the numerator of each side by the denominator of the other: if $\frac{a}{b} = \frac{c}{d}$, then $ad = cb$.

EXAMPLE

If $\frac{4}{13} = \frac{x}{78}$, what is the value of x?

First, cross-multiply:

$$4(78) = 13x$$

Then, solve for x:

$$x = \frac{4(78)}{13} = 24$$

RATES

A **rate** is a fraction that shows the relationship between two quantities with different units. A rate is different than a ratio, which compares quantities within a certain category, like red marbles to blue marbles or boys to girls. Rates often use the word "per," as in cents per pound or miles per hour.

EXAMPLE

If Jane can read 10 pages in 25 minutes, how many minutes will it take her to read 35 pages?

First, let's say that x is the number of minutes it will take Jane to read 35 pages. We can then set up a proportion:

$$\frac{10 \text{ pages}}{25 \text{ minutes}} = \frac{35 \text{ pages}}{x \text{ minutes}}$$

Then, we can cross-multiply and solve for x:

$$10x = 25(35)$$

$$x = \frac{25(35)}{10} = 87.5$$

The correct answer is 87.5 minutes.

When solving problems involving rates, pay attention to the units in the question. The answer may be in different units than are given in the problem. To convert units, set up and solve a proportion between the different units.

EXAMPLE

If Juan is driving at 50 miles per hour, how many miles does he travel in 12 minutes?

First, set up a proportion to convert the rate to miles per minute:

$$\frac{50 \text{ miles}}{1 \text{ hour}} \times \frac{1 \text{ hour}}{60 \text{ minutes}} = \frac{5 \text{ miles}}{6 \text{ minutes}}$$

Then, find the distance travelled in 12 minutes:

$$\frac{5 \text{ miles}}{6 \text{ minutes}} = \frac{x \text{ miles}}{12 \text{ minutes}}$$

$$x = \frac{5(12)}{6} = 10 \text{ miles}$$

EXPONENTS AND RADICALS
PART 5

An exponent indicates that a number is being multiplied by itself a certain number of times. The number being multiplied is called the **base**. The raised digit is the **exponent**, and it tells you how many times a number is being multiplied by itself.

EXAMPLE

In the expression 3^5, 3 is the base and 5 is the exponent. This tells you that 3 is being multiplied by itself 5 times:

$$3^5 = 3 \times 3 \times 3 \times 3 \times 3$$

An exponent is also called a **power**. In the example above, we can say that 3^5 is the 5th power of 3.

In the equation $3^2 = 9$, 3 is the **square root** of 9, which we can also write as $\sqrt{9}$. This means that $3 \times 3 = 9$. The symbol we use for square roots $(\sqrt{})$ is called a **radical**. The number under the square root is called the **radicand**.

$\sqrt{9}$ is also the equivalent of $9^{\frac{1}{2}}$. The xth **root** of any number a is written as $a^{\frac{1}{x}}$ or $\sqrt[x]{a}$. For example, $\sqrt[4]{81} = 81^{\frac{1}{4}} = 3$ because $3^4 = 81$.

EXPONENT RULES

Here is a chart that shows some important rules for exponents and radicals. In this chart, a and b represent any number, and m and n represent any positive integers.

Exponent Rules	
Rule	Example
$a^1 = a$	$8^1 = 8$
$a^0 = 1$	$8^0 = 1$
$a^{-m} = \dfrac{1}{a^m}$	$8^{-2} = \dfrac{1}{8^2} = \dfrac{1}{64}$
$a^{\frac{1}{m}} = \sqrt[m]{a}$	$8^{\frac{1}{3}} = \sqrt[3]{8} = 2$
$a^m a^n = a^{m+n}$	$8^2 \times 8^3 = 8^{2+3} = 8^5 = 32768$
$\dfrac{a^m}{a^n} = a^{m-n}$	$\dfrac{8^3}{8^2} = 8^{3-2} = 8^1 = 8$
$(a^m)^n = a^{mn}$	$(8^2)^3 = 8^{2 \times 3} = 8^6 = 262144$
$a^m b^m = (ab)^m$	$8^3 \times 2^3 = (8 \times 2)^3 = 16^3 = 4096$
$\dfrac{a^m}{b^m} = \left(\dfrac{a}{b}\right)^m$	$\dfrac{8^3}{2^3} = \left(\dfrac{8}{2}\right)^3 = 4^3 = 64$
$a^{\frac{m}{n}} = \sqrt[n]{a^m}$	$8^{\frac{2}{3}} = \sqrt[3]{8^2} = \sqrt[3]{64} = 4$
$\sqrt{ab} = \sqrt{a} \times \sqrt{b}$	$\sqrt{16 \times 4} = \sqrt{16} \times \sqrt{4} = 4 \times 2 = 8$
$\sqrt{\dfrac{a}{b}} = \dfrac{\sqrt{a}}{\sqrt{b}}$	$\sqrt{\dfrac{16}{4}} = \dfrac{\sqrt{16}}{\sqrt{4}} = \dfrac{4}{2} = 2$

In the expression $\sqrt[m]{a}$, if m is even, a must be positive to give a real result. Otherwise the result is expressed as a complex number, a concept that is explained in Section 7 of this chapter.

Remember to use the correct order of operations when you are working with expressions with exponents and roots. First, do all operations inside parentheses. Then simplify all exponents and roots before multiplying, dividing, adding, or subtracting.

SCIENTIFIC NOTATION

PART 6

PLACE VALUES

Each digit in a decimal has a **place value**, which refers to where the digit is located in the number. In the number 123, 1 is in the hundreds place, 2 is in the tens place, and 3 is in the ones or units place. Digits to the right of the decimal point also have place values. In the number 0.45, 4 is in the tenths place and 5 is in the hundredths place.

Each place value represents a power of 10. Places to the left of the decimal point are products of 10 to a positive integer, while places to the right of the decimal point are products of 10 to a negative integer.

EXAMPLE

$$123.45 \ = \ 1 \times 10^2 + 2 \times 10^1 + 3 \times 10^0 + 4 \times 10^{-1} + 5 \times 10^{-2}$$

You can also write 123.45 as the product of a single decimal and a power of 10:

$$123.45 \ = \ 1.2345 \times 10^2$$

SCIENTIFIC NOTATION

Place values and powers of 10 are useful for writing very large or very small numbers in a shorter form called scientific notation. **Scientific notation** displays a number as a product of a decimal and a power of 10.

To convert a number to scientific notation, re-write the number as the product of the non-zero digits and the power of ten of the digit occupying the largest position. For example, the largest non-zero digit in 7,100,000 is 7, which is in the millionths place (10^6). $7,100,000 \div 10^6 = 7.1$, so $7,100,000 = 7.1 \times 10^6$.

You can write very small numbers as a product of ten to a negative exponent. For example, the largest non-zero digit in 0.000003409 is the 3 in the millionths place (10^{-6}). $0.000003409 \div 10^{-6} = 3.409$, so $0.000003409 = 3.409 \times 10^{-6}$.

Notice that a number in scientific notation always consists of a decimal whose largest digit is in the ones place multiplied by a power of ten. Large numbers greater than 1 or negative numbers less than -1 are positive powers of 10. Numbers between -1 and 1 are negative powers of 10.

OPERATIONS WITH SCIENTIFIC NOTATION

If two or more numbers have the same power of ten, you can add or subtract them by adding or subtracting the decimals:

EXAMPLE

$$5.4 \times 10^8 - 2.93 \times 10^8 \ = \ (5.4 - 2.93) \times 10^8 \ = \ 2.47 \times 10^8$$

If the result is larger than or equal to 10 or smaller than 1, you must adjust the power of ten so that the decimal has one digit to the left of the decimal point.

EXAMPLE

What is the sum of 7.2×10^{-3} and 5.5×10^{-3}?

First, you add the decimals:

$$7.2 \times 10^{-3} + 5.5 \times 10^{-3} \ = \ 12.7 \times 10^{-3}$$

Then, you convert this result to correct scientific notation. Divide the decimal by 10 and multiply the 10^{-3} by 10:

$$12.7 \times 10^{-3} \ = \ 1.27 \times 10^{-2}$$

If the numbers are multiplied by different powers of 10, you must convert them to standard notation to add or subtract them. Then perform the arithmetic and convert them back to scientific notation.

To multiply numbers in scientific notation, multiply the decimals and add the exponents on the powers of 10. To divide numbers in scientific notation, divide the decimals and subtract the exponents on the powers of 10. Make sure the result is in correct scientific notation.

EXAMPLE

What is $(2.5 \times 10^{13}) \times (6.8 \times 10^{-5})$?

First, multiply the decimals:

$$2.5 \times 6.8 = 17$$

Then, add the exponents:

$$10^{13} \times 10^{-5} = 10^{13 - 5} = 10^8$$

The product is therefore $17 \times 10^8 = 1.7 \times 10^9$.

FUNDAMENTAL MATH PRACTICE SET

PART 7

1. What are the prime factors of 825?

2. List all the factors of 306.

3. Find the least common multiple of 28, 56, and 70.

4. Find the greatest common factor and least common multiple of 1,950 and 1,365.

5. $6\left(3^2 - 8 \times 2\right) + 1 =$

6. $2 \times \left(3^2 + 1\right) \div 5 =$

7. Evaluate the expression:

$$\frac{9}{16} - \frac{6}{3} \times \frac{1}{4}$$

8. Evaluate the expression:

$$\frac{2 + \dfrac{8}{14}}{5 - \dfrac{2}{7}}$$

9. If a farm has 12 horses, 8 cows, and 20 chickens, what fraction of these animals are cows?

10. If $\dfrac{4}{5} = \dfrac{24}{x}$, what is the value of x?

11. Sally got 85% of the questions on a test correct. If she got 3 questions wrong, how many questions did the test contain?

12. If a store sells packages of 6 bagels and produces 126 bagels per day, how many packages of bagels does the store produce in 3 days?

13. Brian can walk 5 laps in 8 minutes. At this pace, how many full laps can he walk in 23 minutes?

14. $(7-3)^{\frac{1}{2}} - 6 \times 2 =$

15. $2^5 \times 4^2 =$

16. $6^2 \times 6^{-3} \div 6^{\frac{1}{5}} =$

17. Simplify the following expression:

$$\sqrt{720x^5}$$

18. Rewrite the following expression without a radical sign:

$$\sqrt[3]{225y^7}$$

19. $\left(9.4 \times 10^{-15}\right) \times \left(3.0 \times 10^{31}\right) =$

20. If $1.6 \times 10^5 + x = 4.46 \times 10^6$, what is the value of x? Write your response in scientific notation.

Answers: Fundamental Math Practice Set

1. 3, 5, 5, 11

2. 1, 2, 3, 6, 9, 17, 18, 34, 51, 102, 153, 306

3. 280

4. GCF: 195 LCM: 13,650

5. −41

6. 4

7. $\dfrac{1}{16}$

8. $\dfrac{6}{11}$

9. $\dfrac{1}{5}$

10. 30

11. 20

12. 63

13. 14

14. −10

15. 2^9 or 512

16. $6^{-\frac{6}{5}}$

17. $12x^2\sqrt{5x}$

18. $15^{\frac{2}{3}}y^{\frac{7}{3}}$

19. 2.82×10^{17}

20. 4.3×10^{6}

HEART OF ALGEBRA

The **Heart of Algebra** questions on the SAT test your fundamental algebra skills. Algebra is one of the most important "languages" of math. You use letters, numbers, and signs to represent information and perform operations. The language of algebra allows you to create a mathematical model for real world situations.

On the new SAT, a solid understanding of algebra will be very important. Out of the 58 questions on the Math Test, 19 will involve the Heart of Algebra topics explained in this section. You will not only need to recognize and understand concepts of algebra but also to apply them in order to analyze, solve, and create equations.

In this section, you will learn how to use algebra to analyze, solve, and create linear equations and inequalities, solve systems of equations, and apply these methods to real world situations.

The concepts covered in this section are:

- Algebraic Expressions
- Linear Equations
- Inequalities
- Absolute Value
- Functions
- Interpreting Equations
- Graphing Equations and Inequalities

ALGEBRAIC EXPRESSIONS
PART 1

An algebraic **expression** is a mathematical "phrase" containing numbers, variables, and operations. A **variable** stands for an unknown number, and is usually represented by a letter. Any letter—x, y, z, N, A—can be used to represent a number that is unknown. The opposite of a variable is a **constant**, which is an unchanging number in an expression.

An algebraic expression is made up of **terms**, which are variables or numbers multiplied together. When a number is right in front of a variable, it means the variable is being multiplied by that number. This number is called the **coefficient**.

Coefficient $\longrightarrow$ $9x$ $\longleftarrow$ Variable

Term

When a variable does not have a written coefficient, it has a coefficient of one. The term x is the same as $1x$.

Any expression with one or more terms is called a **polynomial**. An expression with one term only, like the one above, is called a **monomial**. The expression $4x + 6$ has two terms and is called a **binomial**.

LIKE TERMS

You can simplify an algebraic expression by adding or subtracting like terms. **Like terms** have the same variable and are raised to the same power. For example, $4x$ and $6x$ are like terms. However, $3y$ and $3x$ are not like terms because they contain two different variables.

To add or subtract like terms, add or subtract their coefficients:

$$5x + 6x = 11x$$

If you have more than one term, add or subtract the like terms, and leave any remaining terms as they are.

EXAMPLE

Add $(P + Q + 6)$ and $(2P - 4)$.

The two sets of like terms are P and $2P$, and 6 and -4. Add these like terms together, and leave Q as it is:

$$P + Q + 6 + 2P - 4 \;=\;$$

$$(P + 2P) + (6 - 4) + Q \;=\;$$

$$3P + Q + 2$$

DISTRIBUTIVE PROPERTY

You can also simplify expressions by multiplying and dividing. To multiply or divide like terms, multiply or divide their coefficients:

$$4x \div 2x \;=\; 2$$

The distributive property can help you multiply and divide expressions with more than one term. Remember that according to the **distributive property**, multiplying a number by a sum of two other numbers in parentheses is the same as multiplying it by each number separately and then adding:

$$a\,(b + c) \;=\; ab + ac$$

$$6\,(x + 2y) \;=\; 6x + 12y$$

The distributive property also works for division. Dividing a sum of two numbers by another number is the same as dividing each number separately and then adding:

$$\frac{b+c}{a} = \frac{b}{a} + \frac{c}{a}$$

$$\frac{2x+3y}{5} = \frac{2x}{5} + \frac{3y}{5}$$

FACTORING

Factoring is the opposite of distributing. You can factor out numbers or variables from expressions. When **factoring** an expression, find the greatest common factor that all of your terms have in common. Then, work backwards to take this factor out of your expression.

EXAMPLE

$$5x + 5y - 10$$

The greatest common factor is 5, so you can factor it out of each term in the expression. Factoring out 5 from $5x$ gives you x, 5 from $5y$ gives you y, and 5 from 10 gives you 2:

$$5x + 5y - 10 = 5(x + y - 2)$$

You can always check that you have factored correctly by distributing and checking that your answer matches the original expression.

PART 1 PRACTICE: ALGEBRAIC EXPRESSIONS

For questions 1-3, simplify the expressions by combining like terms.

1. $x + 3x =$

2. $17 - 6h - 23 + 2h =$

3. $6x - 2y - x + 5y =$

For questions 4-6, use the distributive property to multiply or divide the expressions.

4. $3(x + 12) =$

5. $(3g + 9) \div 3 =$

6. $2\left(a - \dfrac{a}{2} + 3b\right) =$

7. What is the greatest common factor of both terms in the expression $3x + 12y$?

8. What is the result when 2 is factored out of the expression $6x - 10y$?

9. Factor the expression $4x + 16 - 2y$.

10. Factor the expression $3y - 15xy + 21x$.

Answers: Algebraic Expressions

1. $4x$
2. $-4h - 6$
3. $5x + 3y$
4. $3x + 36$
5. $g + 3$
6. $2a - a + 6b$
7. 3
8. $3x - 5y$
9. $2(2x + 8 - y)$
10. $3(y - 5xy + 7x)$

LINEAR EQUATIONS
PART 2

An algebraic **equation** tells you that two expressions are equal to each other.

EXAMPLE

You can use an equation to say that $9x$ is equal to 36:

$$9x = 36$$

Often, you will be asked to solve an algebraic equation. If you are asked to "solve for x," you need to find a value for x that makes the equation true. For the equation above, you may know right away that $x = 4$ because $9 \times 4 = 36$.

MANIPULATING EQUATIONS

For more complicated algebraic equations, you may not be able to figure out the answer in your head. You will need to use a method to manipulate the equation and solve for the unknown variable. Your goal is always to **isolate** your variable—to get it by itself on one side of the equation. To do this, you can work backwards to "undo" all of the operations that are being performed on your variable until you can get it by itself.

There's one important rule to remember when working with equations: whatever you do to one side of the equation, you must also do to the other! If you violate this rule, the two sides of your equation will no longer be equal.

EXAMPLE

You know the equation 4 = 4 is a true statement. However, if you add a number to one side of the equation but not to the other, the two sides are no longer equal:

$$4 + 2 \neq 4$$

You need to add the same number to both sides of the equation so they remain equal:

$$4 + 2 = 4 + 2$$

Let's see how this works with the following algebraic equation:

$$3x - 2 = 13$$

On the left side of the equation, x is being multiplied by 3, and 2 is being subtracted from the product. You need to "undo" each of these operations by adding numbers to and dividing numbers from both sides of your equation. First, deal with the operations that don't involve the variable. In this case, you can undo the subtraction by adding 2 to each side:

$$3x - 2 + 2 = 13 + 2$$

$$3x = 15$$

Then, undo the multiplication by dividing each side by 3:

$$\frac{3x}{3} = \frac{15}{3}$$

$$x = 5$$

What if the equation has variables on both sides? First, get all of the variables onto one side of the equation and combine like terms. Then, isolate the variable like you just did above.

EXAMPLE

$$5a - 7 = 2a - 1$$

First, get all of your variables on one side of the equation by subtracting $2a$ from each side and combining like terms:

$$5a - 2a - 7 = 2a - 2a - 1$$

$$3a - 7 = -1$$

Then, undo the subtraction by adding 7 to each side:

$$3a - 7 + 7 = -1 + 7$$

$$3a = 6$$

And finally, undo the multiplication by dividing each side by 3:

$$\frac{3a}{3} = \frac{6}{3}$$

$$a = 2$$

To test if you got the right answer, you can plug this number back into the original equation:

$$5a - 7 = 2a - 1$$

$$5 \times 2 - 7 = 2 \times 2 - 1$$

$$10 - 7 = 4 - 1$$

$$3 = 3$$

More Complicated Equations

Some equations will look much more complicated than the ones above. Don't let this scare you! You will always use the same process for solving linear equations with one variable. Work carefully through each step. Get your variable on one side and then undo the operations.

Example

$$\frac{5(x + 7)}{4} = \frac{100 - 5x}{5}$$

You can see there are a lot of operations in this equation. You need to get the variable (x) on one side, but you'll have to do some other operations first. First, cross-multiply and use the distributive property:

$$(5 \times 5)(x + 7) = 4(100 - 5x)$$

$$25x + 175 = 400 - 20x$$

Then, undo the operations to get your variable on one side of the equation and your constant on the other side:

$$25x + 175 + 20x = 400 - 20x + 20x$$

$$45x + 175 = 400$$

$$45x + 175 - 175 = 400 - 175$$

$$45x = 225$$

Finally, divide by 45 to completely solve for x.

$$\frac{45x}{45} = \frac{225}{45}$$

$$x = 5$$

EQUATIONS WITH TWO VARIABLES

Sometimes you will see an equation that has two different variables in it, such as $y = 2x + 6$. You will not be able to find an exact number for x or y without more information, as we will see in Part 5. However, you can solve for one variable *in terms of* the other. This means that your answer will still contain a variable.

To solve for one variable in terms of the other, use the same steps as for single-variable equations and treat the second variable as if it were a number. For the equation above, let's solve for x in terms of y.

Because you're solving for x, you need to get x by itself. Start by subtracting 6 from both sides, and then divide by 2:

$$y = 2x + 6$$

$$y - 6 = 2x + 6 - 6$$

$$\frac{y - 6}{2} = \frac{2x}{2}$$

$$\frac{y - 6}{2} = x$$

$\dfrac{y - 6}{2}$ is how you would represent x in terms of y.

You may also be asked to use an equation to solve for another algebraic expression.

EXAMPLE

If $6x + 2y = 24$, what is the value of $3x + y$?

At first it might seem like you cannot find the answer without solving for x and y individually. Luckily, there is another way. We are looking for $3x + y$, not x or y alone. Look closely at the left side of the equation. You may notice that $6x + 2y$ divided by 2 gives you

$3x + y$—the exact expression we are looking for! Therefore, divide both sides of the equation by 2:

$$\frac{6x}{2} + \frac{2y}{2} = \frac{24}{2}$$

$$3x + y = 12$$

$3x + y$ is equal to 12.

PART 2 PRACTICE: LINEAR EQUATIONS

1. If $a + 20 = 5$, what is a?

2. If $3x - 5 = 7$, what is x?

3. If $2x + 8 = 14$, what is x?

4. If $6x + 7 = 12x - 11$, what is x?

For questions 5-8, solve for x in terms of y.

5. $3y = 5x$

6. $2(x + 3) = y + 6$

7. $\frac{1}{3x} = \frac{4}{7y}$

8. $y = \frac{2(x + 10)}{3}$

9. If $5j + z = 3$, what is $2z$ in terms of j?

10. If $\frac{2c}{3} + \frac{4d}{12} = 4$, what is $6c$ in terms of d?

ANSWERS: LINEAR EQUATIONS

1. -15
2. 4
3. 3
4. 3
5. $x = \dfrac{3y}{5}$
6. $x = \dfrac{y}{2}$
7. $x = \dfrac{7y}{12}$
8. $x = \dfrac{3y}{2} - 10$
9. $6 - 10j$
10. $36 - 3d$

INEQUALITIES

PART 3

An **inequality** is a mathematical statement comparing two unequal quantities. Inequalities can be represented with these symbols:

Inequality Symbols	
>	greater than
<	less than
≥	greater than or equal to
≤	less than or equal to

An algebraic inequality states that a certain algebraic expression is greater than or less than another quantity. For example, $x < 3$ means "an unknown quantity, x, is less than 3." There are many possible solutions for this inequality. x might equal 1, 2, 0.5, –4, –6, 0, or any other number that is less than three.

To solve a more complex inequality, treat it like an equation— manipulate the inequality to isolate your variable. You'll end up with a range of solutions that can satisfy the inequality.

EXAMPLE

$$4x \geq 24$$

Isolate your variable by dividing both sides by 4:

$$\frac{4x}{4} \geq \frac{24}{4}$$

$$x \geq 6$$

If $4x$ is greater than or equal to 24, then x can be any value greater than or equal to 6.

RULES FOR INEQUALITIES

Just as with an equation, you can add or subtract the same number from both sides of an inequality and the inequality will be **preserved** (the inequality symbol will stay the same).

EXAMPLE

$$x + 3 > 7$$

To solve, subtract 3 from both sides of the inequality:

$$x + 3 - 3 > 7 - 3$$

$$x > 4$$

You have to be more careful when multiplying or dividing. Multiplying or dividing both sides of an inequality by a positive number preserves the inequality, but multiplying or dividing by a negative number *reverses* the inequality. When you multiply or divide by a negative number, you have to flip the sign. Consider the true inequality $7 > 2$. You can multiply both sides of this inequality by a positive number, and the inequality is still true:

$$7 \times 4 > 2 \times 4$$

$$28 > 8$$

However, if you multiply both sides by a negative number, you get a false result:

$$7 \times (-4) > 2 \times (-4)$$

$$-28 > -8$$

Wrong!

Therefore, you need to reverse the inequality when multiplying or dividing by a negative number:

$$7 \times (-4) \ < \ 2 \times (-4)$$

$$-28 \ < \ -8$$

EXAMPLE

Let's try a more complex example:

$$-4x + 1 \ > \ 3$$

First, undo the addition by subtracting 1 from both sides:

$$-4x + 1 - 1 \ > \ 3 - 1$$

$$-4x \ > \ 2$$

Then, undo the multiplication by dividing both sides by -4. Remember to reverse the inequality sign because you are dividing by a negative number!

$$\frac{-4x}{-4} \ < \ \frac{2}{-4}$$

$$x \ < \ -\frac{1}{2}$$

Now you know x can be any number less than $-\frac{1}{2}$. You can check your solution by picking a possible value for x and plugging it back into the original inequality. Let's try -1:

$$-4x + 1 \ > \ 3$$

$$(-4 \times (-1)) + 1 \ > \ 3$$

$$4 + 1 \ > \ 3$$

$$5 \ > \ 3$$

Because 5 is greater than 3, you know your solution was correct.

INEQUALITIES ON A NUMBER LINE

Algebraic inequalities are sometimes shown using lines, line segments, and circles on a number line. A shaded line segment represents all of the possible solutions for the inequality. Circles show whether numbers at the end of a line segment are part of the solution set. If a circle is shaded in completely, it means the number is included in the solution set: it is a possible solution for the inequality. If a circle is unshaded, it means the number is excluded from the solution set: it is not a possible solution for the inequality.

For example, the number line below shows the possible solutions for $x > 1$:

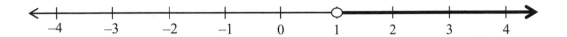

All numbers greater than 1 are possible solutions for this inequality, so a shaded line extends to the right of 1. The number 1 is not a possible solution for this inequality, so there is an unshaded circle over the number 1.

EXAMPLE

What inequality is represented by the number line below?

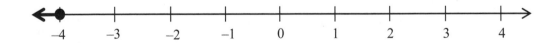

The shaded line segment to the left of –4 means that all numbers less than or equal to –4 are possible solutions for this inequality. The shaded circle over –4 means that –4 is a possible solution for this inequality. The inequality would therefore be written as:

$$x \leq -4$$

Inequalities with Two Variables

Sometimes you will see an inequality that has two different variables in it, such as $y < -4x - 5$. Just like you saw with equations in Part 2, you will not be able to find an exact number for x or y without more information. You can, however, solve for x in terms of y. Follow the same steps as you did for equations, but remember to be careful of the inequality sign.

For the inequality above, let's see how you would solve for x in terms of y. Start by adding 5 to both sides, then divide by -4 and reverse the inequality sign.

$$y < -4x - 5$$

$$y + 5 < -4x - 5 + 5$$

$$\frac{y+5}{-4} > \frac{-4x}{-4}$$

$$\frac{y+5}{-4} > x$$

Part 3 Practice: Inequalities

1. What happens when you divide both sides of an inequality by a negative number?

For questions 2-3, write an inequality that corresponds with the diagram:

2.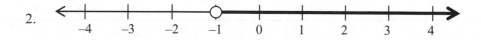

3.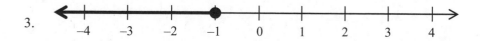

4. If $N < 15$, what is a possible value for N?

5. If $3 < a < 13$, what is NOT a possible value for a?

6. If $23 \leq 7x + 2 \leq 37$, what is a possible value for x?

For questions 7-8, solve for x.

7. $7x \geq 21$

8. $3x + 7 \leq x + 1$

9. If $-2a + 10 > 4b$, what is a in terms of b?

10. If $12d - 3c \leq 45$, what is c in terms of d?

Answers: Inequalities

1. You flip the sign of the inequality.

2. $x > -1$

3. $x \leq -1$

4. Any value less than 15

5. Any value greater than 13 or less than 3

6. Any value less or equal to 5 and greater than or equal to 3

7. $x \geq 3$

8. $x \leq -3$

9. $a < -2b + 5$

10. $c \geq 4d - 15$

Absolute Value
Part 4

The **absolute value** of a number is its distance away from zero on a number line. To represent the absolute value of a quantity, you write two vertical bars around the quantity.

Example

|−5| represents the absolute value of −5, or the distance between −5 and zero on a number line. −5 is 5 units away from zero, so its absolute value is 5:

$$|{-}5| \ = \ 5$$

The absolute value of any number or expression will always be a positive number or zero.

Example

What is |4 − 7|?

This question is asking you to find the absolute value of the expression 4 − 7. First, you need to solve for the quantity within the absolute value bars:

$$|4 - 7| \ = \ |{-}3|$$

Now, you need to find the absolute value of −3. −3 is 3 units away from zero, so its absolute value is 3:

$$|{-}3| \ = \ 3$$

Equations with Absolute Value

On the SAT, you may need to solve an absolute value equation using algebra. Here is an important rule to remember:

$$\text{If } |x| = a, \text{ then } x = a \text{ or } x = -a.$$

Example

If $|x| = 4$, then what values are possible for x?

This question is asking you to find any values of x that have an absolute value of 4. You know that 4 is a possible value. However, the value -4 is also possible. Think about it: both of these numbers are 4 units away from zero on the number line. Therefore, they both have an absolute value of 4.

$$\text{If } |x| = 4, \text{ then } x = 4 \text{ or } x = -4.$$

Example

If $|x - 5| = 4$, what are the possible values for x?

You know that both 4 and -4 have an absolute value of 4. Therefore, the quantity $x - 5$ could either be equal to 4 or -4. You can set up two equations and solve each separately to find the two possible values of x:

$$x - 5 = 4 \qquad x - 5 = -4$$

$$x = 9 \qquad\qquad x = 1$$

You have two solutions: $x = 1$ or $x = 9$.

ABSOLUTE VALUE INEQUALITIES

You may also need to solve an absolute value inequality on the SAT. Here are two rules for absolute value inequalities:

$$\text{If } |x| < a, \text{ then } -a < x < a.$$
$$\text{If } |x| > a, \text{ then } x < -a \text{ or } x > a.$$

EXAMPLE

If $|x| \leq 3$, then what values are possible for x?

The inequality tells you that the distance between x and 0 is less than or equal to 3. All numbers between -3 and 3, including -3 and 3, have a distance from zero that is 3 units or less. If you were to graph the range of solutions for this inequality on a number line, it would look like this:

Therefore:

$$\text{If } |x| \leq 3, \text{ then } -3 \leq x \leq 3.$$

You can always check your answer by making sure that a value from your solution set makes the original inequality true. -2 is a value from your solution set. Is $|-2| \leq 3$? The absolute value of -2 is 2, and 2 is certainly less than 3.

$$|-2| \leq 3$$

$$2 \leq 3$$

EXAMPLE

What values for x satisfy the inequality $|x - 2| + 1 > 3$?

First, you need to get the inequality by itself. To do that, subtract 1 from each side:

$$|x - 2| + 1 - 1 \; > \; 3 - 1$$

$$|x - 2| \; > \; 2$$

You know that all quantities less than –2 and greater than 2 have an absolute value greater than 2. Remember, when using the greater than sign to solve for an absolute value inequality, you need to set up two inequalities and solve:

$$x - 2 \; > \; 2 \qquad x - 2 \; < \; -2$$

$$x \; > \; 4 \qquad\qquad x \; < \; 0$$

The values of x that satisfy the inequality $|x - 2| > 2$ are any values greater than 4 or less than 0. In other words, they are any values more than 2 units away from 2 on the number line.

PART 4 PRACTICE: ABSOLUTE VALUE

1. $|7 - 6| =$

2. $|-3| =$

3. $|2 - 7| =$

For questions 4-7, find all possible values of a.

4. $|a - 3| = 2$

5. $-|a - 5| = -2$

6. $\left|\dfrac{5a}{3}\right| = 10$

7. $\dfrac{|7a - 2|}{3} + 5 = 9$

For questions 8-10, solve for b.

8. $-|b - 3| < -5$

9. $|b - 11| \geq 7$

10. $|-3b + 5| \leq 23$

Answers: Absolute Value

1. 1

2. 3

3. 5

4. $a = 1$ or 5

5. $a = 3$ or 7

6. $a = \pm 6$

7. $a = 2$ or $-\dfrac{10}{7}$

8. $b < -2, b > 8$

9. $b \leq 4, b \geq 18$

10. $-6 \leq b \leq \dfrac{28}{3}$

SYSTEMS OF EQUATIONS AND INEQUALITIES

PART 5

A **system of equations** is a group of equations that share like terms. On the SAT, you may see systems of two equations. Even though you now have to deal with two equations instead of one, systems of equations are actually very useful things! If you have two equations and two variables, you can use both equations to find the value of x and y.

EXAMPLE

$$x + y = 3$$
$$2x - y = 12$$

You can use two methods to solve this system of equations: substitution and elimination.

SUBSTITUTION

The **substitution method** allows you to solve for one variable at a time by substituting an equivalent equation for one variable. First, choose a variable to isolate in either equation. Let's try isolating y in the first equation. To isolate y, subtract x from both sides of the equation:

$$x + y - x = 3 - x$$

$$y = 3 - x$$

You now know that y is equal to the value of $3 - x$. Now, substitute this value into the second equation by writing $3 - x$ instead of y:

$$2x - y = 12$$

$$2x - (3 - x) \;=\; 12$$

Now you have a single equation with only one variable, so you can solve this equation for x:

$$2x - (3 - x) \;=\; 12$$

$$3x - 3 \;=\; 12$$

$$3x \;=\; 15$$

$$x \;=\; 5$$

Now that you know that $x = 5$, you can plug this value of x into either of the original two equations to solve for y. Let's plug this into the first equation:

$$x + y \;=\; 3$$

$$5 + y \;=\; 3$$

$$y \;=\; -2$$

You've found that $x = 5$ and $y = -2$. You can check that you've solved this system of equations correctly by plugging these values back into the original two equations and verifying that they are true:

$$\checkmark \quad 5 + (-2) \;=\; 3$$

$$\checkmark \quad 2 \times 5 - (-2) \;=\; 12$$

ELIMINATION

You can also solve this system of equations using the elimination method. The **elimination method** allows you to cancel variables by adding or subtracting the two equations. In the example above, if you add the two equations together, the ys will cancel each other out:

$$x + y = 3$$
$$+ \quad 2x - y = 12$$
$$3x \quad\quad = 15$$

You now have one single equation in which you can solve for x:

$$3x = 15$$

$$x = 5$$

Then, you can plug this value for x back into one of the two original equations to solve for y, following the same steps you used above.

$$x + y = 3$$

$$5 + y = 3$$

$$y = -2$$

How do you know when to use substitution and when to use elimination? If one of the equations involves variables without coefficients (like $x + y = 3$) or could be easily simplified by dividing (like $2x + 2y = 8$), then substitution may be easier. However, some systems of equations are more effectively solved using elimination, even if they don't look like it at first. You may have to transform equations in order to use elimination.

TRANSFORMING EQUATIONS

Some systems of equations don't seem like they can be solved using elimination at first.

EXAMPLE

$$6x + 3y = 18$$
$$2x + 5y = 14$$

You can transform one of the equations so that you can use elimination to solve the equations. To **transform** an equation, you multiply or divide both sides of the equation by the same number. Since you want to be able to eliminate one variable, you should choose a number that will change your equation so that it can be easily added to or subtracted from the other equation.

In the example above, you can transform the second equation by multiplying both sides by 3. Why? Because multiplying the equation by 3 gives you $6x + 15y = 42$. You can now use subtraction to eliminate the $6x$'s.

$$
\begin{array}{rcl}
6x + 3y & = & 18 \\
- \quad (6x + 15y & = & 42) \\
\hline
-12y & = & -24
\end{array}
$$

$$\frac{-12y}{-12} = \frac{-24}{-12}$$

$$y = 2$$

Now plug y into one of the original equations to solve for x:

$$6x + 3(2) = 18$$

$$6x + 6 = 18$$

$$6x = 12$$

$$x = 2$$

SYSTEMS OF INEQUALITIES

On the SAT, you may also see **systems of inequalities**. You may be asked to solve for values of x that satisfy both inequalities.

EXAMPLE

$$7x \geq 21$$

$$2x < 10$$

In order to find the values of x that would satisfy both inequalities, you need to solve each inequality, determine if there is any overlap, and create a range of possible values. For the example above, first solve each inequality individually:

$$\frac{7x}{7} \geq \frac{21}{7}$$

$$x \geq 3$$

$$\frac{2x}{2} < \frac{10}{2}$$

$$x < 5$$

In order for a value of x to satisfy both inequalities, x must be greater than or equal to 3, but also less than 5. Therefore, you can write a range of values that represents the possible solutions to both inequalities:

$$3 \leq x < 5$$

You can check your answer by plugging in a value of x from your solution set into both equations. Let's try 4:

$$7(4) \geq 21$$

$$28 \geq 21$$

$$2(4) < 10$$

$$8 < 10$$

PART 5 PRACTICE: SYSTEMS OF EQUATIONS AND INEQUALITIES

In questions 1-5, solve for both variables.

1. $5x = 5$
   $x + y = 5$

2. $2m = 3$
   $4m + n = 10$

3. $5p - 2q = 16$
   $4p + q = 5$

4. $2a + b = 21$
   $3a + 3b = 36$

5. $4r - 6s = 16$
   $5r + 4s = -3$

In questions 6-10, solve for x in the system of inequalities.

6. $7x \geq 21$
   $x < 36$

7. $x - 4 > 8$
   $3x \leq 39$

8. $16 \leq 4x < 24$
   $5x + 5 > 30$

9. $7x + 2 \leq 37$
   $\frac{x}{4} > 1$

10. $4x + 13 < 1$
    $2x - 4 \leq 4x + 6$

ANSWERS: SYSTEMS OF EQUATIONS AND INEQUALITIES

1. $x = 1,\ y = 4$

2. $m = \dfrac{3}{2},\ n = 4$

3. $p = 2,\ q = -3$

4. $a = 9,\ b = 3$

5. $r = 1,\ s = -2$

6. $3 \le x < 36$

7. $12 < x \le 13$

8. $5 < x < 6$

9. $4 < x \le 5$

10. $-5 \le x < -3$

LINEAR FUNCTIONS
PART 6

A **function** is a relationship between inputs and outputs. A function shows how an "input" value is transformed into an "output" value. The input, x, will produce an output, $f(x)$, according to the rules of the function. The notation $f(x)$ is read as "f of x." Functions are most often referred to by f, but you may also see other letters like g, h, or A.

FUNCTION NOTATION

For linear functions, the notation $f(x)$ is another way of representing the y-value in a function. For example, $f(x) = 2x - 3$ is the same thing as $y = 2x - 3$.

The function $f(x) = 2x - 3$ means that for any input x, the function assigns it the output $2x - 3$. Therefore:

$$f(2) = 2(2) - 3$$

$$f(2) = 1$$

This is how you **evaluate** a function—just replace the variable in the function with the given input value and solve. What if $x = a + b$?

$$f(a + b) = 2(a + b) - 3$$

$$f(a + b) = 2a + 2b - 3$$

The chart below represents the input (x) and output ($f(x)$) values for the function $f(x) = 2x - 3$. You can see how the function acts as a rule for what happens to the input to generate the output. For each input, you multiply it by 2 and then subtract 3.

$f(x)$	−1	1	3	5
x	1	2	3	4

The following graph also represents $f(x) = 2x - 3$. Because the graph is a line, we call this a linear function. We will talk about how to graph linear functions in Part 8, but you can use this graph to visualize what the function means. You can see that when the input (x) is at 2, the output (y) is at 1—just like we found when we were evaluating the function.

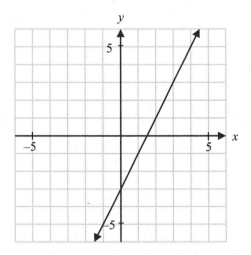

DOMAIN AND RANGE

Every linear function has a domain and range. The **domain** is the set of all values for which the function generates an output. The **range** is the set of all values that could be the output of the function.

$$\text{Domain} \implies \text{Function} \implies \text{Range}$$

Often, the domain of a linear function is "all real numbers." This is because most linear equations can use any input and still be defined. For example, in the function $f(x) = -2x - 3$, you'll get an output for any real number that you plug in for x. The exception is a function that produces a vertical line, which only has one possible x value.

The range of a linear function is also typically "all real numbers." Most lines can extend infinitely in both directions, so there are no limits to the range of y values that can be generated. The exception is a function that produces a horizontal line, which only has one possible y value.

COMBINING FUNCTIONS

On the SAT, you might see functions combined through a notation like $f(g(x))$. This notation means that you need to take the output of $g(x)$, and use it as the input of $f(x)$. You would read this as "f of g of x."

EXAMPLE

If $f(x) = 3x - 4$ and $g(x) = 8x$, what is the value of $(f(g(\frac{1}{2}))$?

Start by working from the inside out. First, find $g(\frac{1}{2})$. Then, use that answer and plug it into $f(x)$:

$$g\left(\frac{1}{2}\right) = 8\left(\frac{1}{2}\right) = 4$$

$$f(4) = 3(4) - 4 = 8$$

There are many other things to learn about functions, such as how to graph and transform them. We will cover these topics in Part 8.

PART 6 PRACTICE: LINEAR FUNCTIONS

1. If $f(x) = 2x$, what is $f(9)$?

2. If $h(x) = 5x + 3$, what is $h(2)$?

3. If $g(x) = \dfrac{30}{x} + 5$, what is $g(10)$?

4. If $j(x) = 6x + 5$, what is $j(3)$?

5. What is the domain of $f(x) = 3x - 2$?

6. What is the range of $f(x) = 6$?

7. What is the range of $g(x) = |x - 3| - 2$?

8. If $f(x) = 2x$ and $g(x) = x + 5$, what is the value of $f(3) + g(3)$?

9. If $g(x) = 5x$ and $h(x) = x - 5$, what is the value of $g(h(5))$?

10. If $f(x) = x + 9$ and $g(x) = \frac{x}{4}$, what is the value of $f(g(8))$?

11. If $f(x) = \frac{x}{2} + 10$ and $g(x) = \frac{2x}{5} + 4$, what is the value of $g(f(10))$?

Answers: Linear Functions

1. 18
2. 13
3. 8
4. 23
5. All real numbers
6. 6
7. All real numbers greater than or equal to –2
8. 14
9. 0
10. 11
11. 10

INTERPRETING EQUATIONS
PART 7

In the previous parts of this section, you learned how to work with the "vocabulary" of the language of algebra. For example, you learned how to solve linear equations and inequalities and perform operations on functions. Now, you need to learn how to interpret the vocabulary and create your own "sentences" with linear equations. In this part, we will discuss what the different parts of linear equations mean and how to use them in word problems.

VARIABLES AND CONSTANTS

In Part 1, you learned that both variables and constants represent values in algebraic expressions. The difference is that constants represent values that can't change, while variables represent values that can change.

EXAMPLE

Jeannie's phone company charges her a flat rate of $20 per month plus $0.20 per minute of call time. If Jeannie places 120 minutes of calls in January, how much will her phone company charge her for that month?

You can use an equation to solve this problem. Jeannie is charged $20 per month—this is a flat rate, so it is unchanging. She is also charged an unchanging rate of $0.20 per minute. Therefore, $20 and $0.20 are constants. What will determine how much Jeannie's phone company charges her? How many minutes of call time she uses. That is a variable, which you could decide to call m. You are looking for her total monthly charge, which you could call c. Using these variables, you could write the equation:

$$c = 0.20m + 20$$

This means that Jeannie's monthly phone bill is found by multiplying her total minutes by $0.20 and adding $20. Jeannie places 120 minutes of calls in January, so you can plug in 120 for m:

$$c = 0.20 \times 120 + 20 = 44$$

Jeannie's phone company will charge her $44 for the month of January.

TRANSLATING FROM WORDS TO MATH

As you've seen in the examples above, to solve any word problem on the SAT, all you have to do is "translate" the words in the problem into letters and operations. Here is a chart you can use to translate between words and math:

Words	Meaning
Is, was, will be, has	Equals ($=$)
More, older, total, increased by, exceeds, gained, further, greater, sum	Addition ($+$)
Fewer, younger, less, decreased by, gave away, lost, difference	Subtraction ($-$)
Of, each, product	Multiplication ($\times$)
For, per, out of, quotient	Division ($\div$)
At least	Greater than or equal to ($\geq$)
At most	Less than or equal to ($\leq$)
What, how many	Variable (x, y, etc.)

EXAMPLE

The total of Jake's and Amy's ages is 17. If A is Amy's current age, which expression represents Jake's age in 3 years, in terms of A?

The question tells you that A stands for Amy's current age. If you let J stand for Jake's current age, then you can use addition to represent the total of their ages right now:

$$J + A = 17$$

Then, you can isolate J to find an expression for Jake's age right now:

$$J + A = 17$$

$$J = 17 - A$$

However, the question isn't asking you for Jake's age right now—you need to find his age 3 years from now. Translating into math, you need to find the value of $J + 3$. To do this, add 3 to both sides of your equation:

$$J = 17 - A$$

$$J + 3 = 17 - A + 3$$

$$J + 3 = 20 - A$$

The expression $20 - A$ represents Jake's age three years from now.

INTERPRETING ABSOLUTE VALUE

You may also need to translate a word problem into an absolute value equation.

EXAMPLE

A candle factory has machines that cut wax into candles. Each candle is supposed to be 6 inches long. If a candle differs from this length by more than 0.25 inches, it will be rejected. What absolute value inequality represents the lengths of the products that will be rejected?

Candles will be rejected if they are 0.25 inches greater or less than the goal of 6 inches. This means any candles greater than 6.25 inches or less than 5.75 inches will be rejected. You can use an absolute value inequality to represent all values that are more than 0.25 units away from 6 on a number line:

$$|x - 6| > 0.25$$

The absolute value sign works here because it allows you to take into account candles that are greater than the goal size and also those less than the goal size. The amount that the candles can differ from is on the right side of the inequality. The absolute value expression on the left represents the difference between the size of any candle and the goal size.

To check that your inequality is correct, solve for x using the rules you learned in Part 5:

$$x - 6 \ > \ 0.25 \qquad\qquad x - 6 \ < \ -0.25$$

$$x \ > \ 6.25 \qquad\qquad x \ < \ 5.75$$

Your inequality generated all values greater than 6.25 and less than 5.75. You know that these are the lengths of candles that will be rejected, so your inequality is correct.

CREATING A SYSTEM OF EQUATIONS

Some word problems will require you to create a system of equations.

EXAMPLE

In a school cafeteria, students can either buy sandwiches or salads for lunch. Sandwiches cost $5.50 and salads cost $5.00. On one day, a total of 557 lunches were served for a total of $3036. Which set of equations could be used to solve for the number of sandwiches, x, and the number of salads, y, served that day?

The question tells you that the total number of lunches served was 557, so the sum of sandwiches (x) and salads (y) must be 557:

$$x + y \ = \ 557$$

You also know that the total cost was $3036. Sandwiches cost $5.50, so the cost of all the sandwiches would be $5.50 multiplied by the number of sandwiches purchased (5.50x$). Similarly, the cost of all the salads would be $5.00 multiplied by the number of salads purchased (5.00y$). The total cost is the sum of the sandwich cost and the salad cost:

$$5.50x + 5y \ = \ 3036$$

You have now found a system of equations that would allow you to solve for x and y:

$$x + y \ = \ 557$$

$$5.50x + 5y \ = \ 3036$$

PART 7 PRACTICE: INTERPRETING EQUATIONS

1. Irene runs two miles every morning. What equation could she write to find out how many days it would take to run 26 miles? What would be the variable in the equation?

2. Wendy has $10 and receives an additional $10 per week for her allowance. If she doesn't spend any of her money, what equation can you write for how much money, m, she will have at the end of w weeks?

3. Joy is selling cupcakes for $5 each. Write an expression to represent the amount of money Joy earns from selling c cupcakes.

4. When 6 is subtracted from four times a number L, the result is 26. Write an equation that represents this statement.

5. Krystal gives Jessica a number. Jessica triples it and divides the result by 2. If she ends up with the number 9, what number did Krystal give her?

6. The students in Mr. Brown's class are an average of 1.6 meters tall. The tallest student is 1.8 meters, and the shortest student is 1.4 meters. Write an absolute value inequality that represents all possible heights, h, of the students in Mr. Brown's class.

7. If a certain medication is exposed to a temperature less than $55°$ or greater than $85°$, it must be discarded. Write an absolute value inequality that represents all possible temperatures, x, at which the medication must be discarded.

8. Adult tickets for an event are $10 each and student tickets are $8 each. The ticket office has sold 77 tickets totaling $686. What system of equations can you write to solve for the number of adult tickets, a, and student tickets, s, sold?

9. Suzy has $4.95 worth of quarters and dimes. If she has 27 coins in total, what system of equations represented the number of quarters (q) and dimes (d) Suzy has?

10. There are 15 total cows and chickens on a farm. If the total number of legs for these animals equals 42, how many cows are on the farm?

ANSWERS: INTERPRETING EQUATIONS

1. $2d = 26$. Number of days (d) is the variable. Any letter could be used to represent this variable—we've just picked d for convenience.

2. $m = \$10 + \$10w$

3. $5c$ dollars

4. $4L - 6 = 26$

5. 6

6. $|h - 1.6| \leq 0.2$

7. $|x - 70| > 15$

8. $a + s = 77$

    $10a + 8s = 686$

9. $4.95 = 0.25q + 0.1d$

    $27 = q + d$

10. 6

GRAPHING EQUATIONS

PART 8

In the previous parts of this section, you learned how to solve equations, inequalities, absolute values, and systems of equations algebraically. While knowing how to solve these types of problems algebraically is essential, you also need to know how to solve them graphically on the SAT Math Test.

GRAPHING LINEAR EQUATIONS

Linear equations can be graphed as lines on a coordinate plane. Some equations represent horizontal or vertical lines.

- The equation of a **horizontal line** is $y = b$, where b represents the point where the line crosses the y-axis.
- The equation of a **vertical line** is $x = a$, where a represents the point where the line crosses the x-axis.

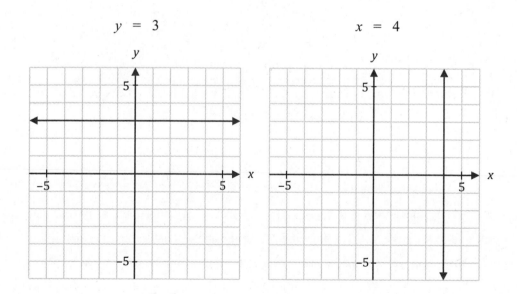

$$y = 3 \qquad\qquad x = 4$$

You can also graph equations with two variables. The **standard equation** of a line can be represented as:

$$y = mx + b$$

Each part of this equation tells you something about how the line looks on the graph. The letter *m* represents the **slope**—how steep the line is. The letter *b* represents the **y-intercept**—the point where the line crosses the *y*-axis. Here is the graph of the line $y = 2x + 6$.

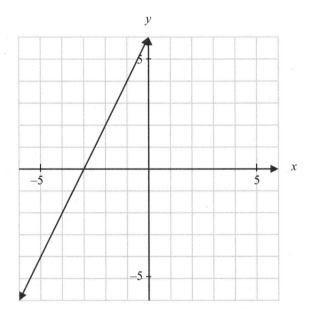

You can see that the line crosses the *y*-axis at 6. The equation also tells you that the slope of the line is 2. Let's see what that means.

SLOPE

The **slope** of a line tells you how steep it is—in other words, how quickly *y* is increasing for every unit that *x* increases. The equation of the line above tells us that the slope is 2. If you look at the graph, you can also see that *y* increases 2 units for every unit that *x* increases.

The SAT won't always give you the equation for a line. You might need to find the slope of a line using a graph. Choose any two points on the line and plug their coordinates into the slope formula. If the first point has the coordinates (x_1, y_1) and the second point has the coordinates (x_2, y_2), the slope formula tells you:

$$m = \frac{y_2 - y_1}{x_2 - x_1}$$

You might have also learned the slope formula as "rise over run." The "rise" between two points is the same thing as the difference between their two y-coordinates, and the "run" is the difference between their two x-coordinates. Therefore, "rise over run" is the same as the formula above.

Let's test this formula by plugging in some points from the line graphed above. You can see that the line contains the points $(-3,0)$ and $(0,6)$. If you plug in these values for the formula for slope, you get:

$$m = \frac{y_2 - y_1}{x_2 - x_1} = \frac{6 - 0}{0 - (-3)} = \frac{6}{3} = 2$$

This formula tells us that the slope of the line is 2.

Here are a few important facts about slope:

- Vertical lines have undefined slopes.
- Horizontal lines have a slope of 0.
- A slope is positive if the line goes up from left to right.
- A slope is negative if the line goes down from left to right.
- Parallel lines have the same slope.
- The product of the slopes of two perpendicular lines is −1.

Let's talk a little bit more about that last point. The product of the slopes of two perpendicular lines is −1. To find the slope of a perpendicular line, flip the fraction to find the reciprocal, and then reverse the sign. For example, a line perpendicular to $y = -\frac{3}{4}x + 7$ will have a slope of $\frac{4}{3}$.

GRAPHING INEQUALITIES

Graphing inequalities is similar to graphing equations. Start by graphing the inequality as if it were a linear equation. Use a solid line for $\leq$ or $\geq$, and a dashed line for $<$ or $>$. Then, shade in the solution area. For "greater than" inequalities, shade above the line. For "less than" inequalities, shade below the line.

EXAMPLE

$$y \leq \frac{1}{2}x + 3$$

Start by graphing the line $y = \frac{1}{2}x + 3$. The line crosses the y-axis at 3. The slope of the line is $\frac{1}{2}$, so y increases 1 unit for every 2 units that x increases. Because the inequality uses the symbol $\leq$, you'll want to graph a solid line:

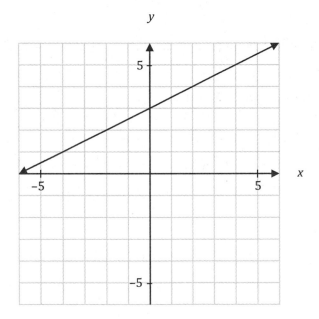

Next, shade in the solution area. Because this is a "less than" inequality, shade below the line.

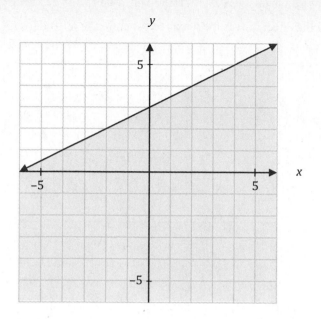

GRAPHING ABSOLUTE VALUES

In order to graph absolute values, you want to recall what the absolute value means. The absolute value of a number is its distance away from zero on a number line. Here is the graph of $y = 3x$:

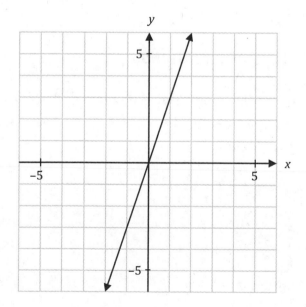

What about the graph of $y = |3x|$? For every positive value of x, the graph will stay the same. However, for negative values of x, the absolute value will be positive—so the left side of the graph needs to have positive values for y. This graph will keep the right side of the graph the same, but will reflect it over the y-axis to generate the left side:

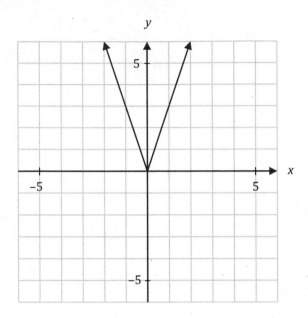

Absolute-value equations often give you a graph that looks like the "V" shape above. If you are given a graph like this on the SAT, the equation that it represents is probably an absolute value.

GRAPHING SYSTEMS OF EQUATIONS

In Part 5, you learned how to solve systems of equations algebraically. You can also solve systems of equations graphically. To solve a system of two equations, graph the lines and find the point where they cross.

EXAMPLE

$$2x - 3y = 6$$

$$4x = 12 - 4y$$

Start by rearranging each equation to get y by itself:

$$y = \frac{2}{3}x - 2$$

$$y = -x + 3$$

Now, graph each line using the slopes and y-intercepts:

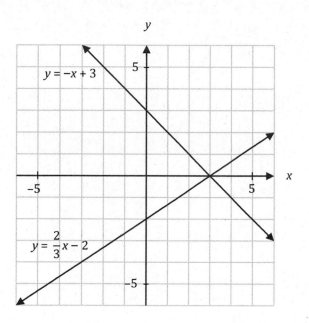

The lines cross at the point $(3, 0)$, so the solution for the system of equations is $x = 3$, $y = 0$. You can always check your answer by plugging in the values into original equations and confirming that they are both true.

GRAPHING FUNCTIONS

Linear functions are graphed just like linear equations. You simply treat $f(x)$ as your y variable. Therefore, the graph of $f(x) = -2x - 3$ is the same as the graph of $y = -2x - 3$:

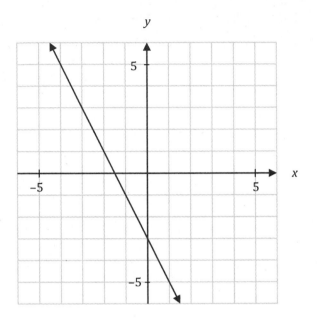

Some questions on the SAT will require you to create or recognize the transformation of a linear function. If you start with the function $f(x) = ax$, you can shift the function vertically b units by adding b to the right side of the function:

$$f(x) = ax + b$$

If b is positive, the function shifts b units up. If b is negative, the function shifts b units down.

The graphs below show the function $f(x) = 2x$ and the same function shifted 3 units up:

$f(x) = 2x$

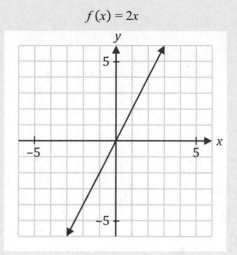

$f(x) = 2x + 3$

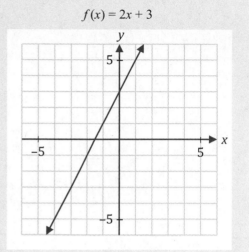

If you start with the function $f(x) = ax$, you can shift the function horizontally b units by taking the function of $x + b$:

$$f(x + b) \;=\; a(x + b)$$

If b is positive, the function shifts b units to the left. If b is negative, the function shifts b units to the right.

The graphs below show the function $f(x) = 2x$ and the same function shifted 1 unit to the left:

$f(x) = 2x$

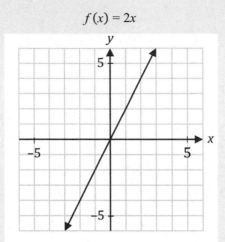

$f(x + 1) = 2(x + 1)$

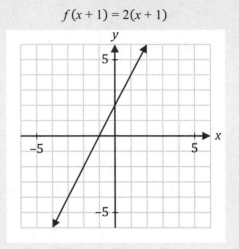

If you start with the function $f(x) = ax$, you can stretch the function by multiplying it by b:

$$b \times f(x) = b \times ax$$

For a linear function, this means the slope of the line is multiplied by b.

EXAMPLE

The graphs below show the function $f(x) = 2x$ and the same function stretched by a factor of 3:

$f(x) = 2x$

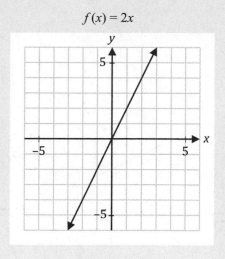

$3f(x) = 3 \times 2x$

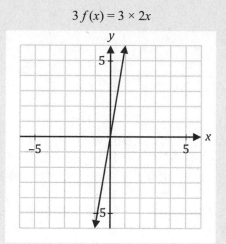

To reflect a function about the x-axis, multiply the whole function by -1.

EXAMPLE

The graphs below show the function $f(x) = \frac{1}{2}x + 1$ and the same function reflected about the x-axis:

$$f(x) = \frac{1}{2}x + 1$$

$$-f(x) = -\left(\frac{1}{2}x + 1\right)$$

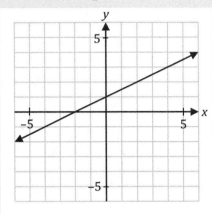
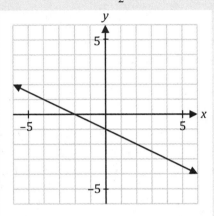

To reflect a function about the y-axis, take the function of $-x$.

EXAMPLE

The graphs below show the function $f(x) = \frac{1}{2}x + 1$ and the same function reflected about the y-axis:

$$f(x) = \frac{1}{2}x + 1$$

$$f(-x) = -\frac{1}{2}x + 1$$

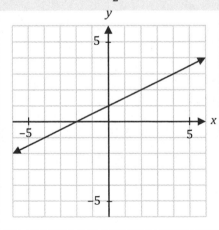
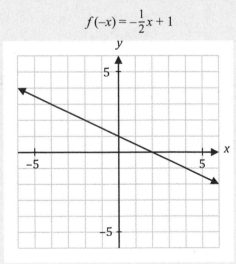

PART 8 PRACTICE: GRAPHING EQUATIONS

For questions 1-5, graph the equation or inequality on the coordinate grid provided.

1. $y = 3$

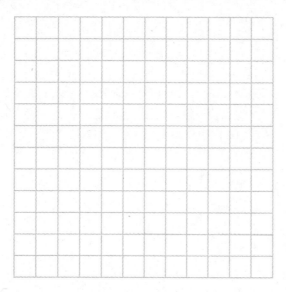

2. $y = \dfrac{x}{2} - 3$

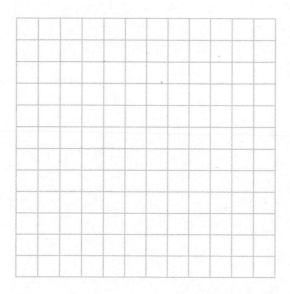

3. $y = |2x - 2|$

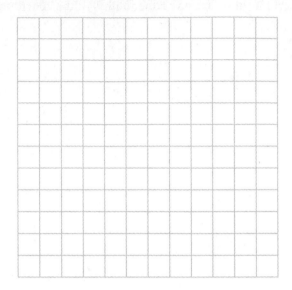

4. $y \geq |x + 3| - 2$

5. What is the slope of the equation $10x + 2y = 3$?

6. Line L has an equation of $3 - 5x = 2y$. If Line M is drawn perpendicular to Line L, what is the slope of Line M?

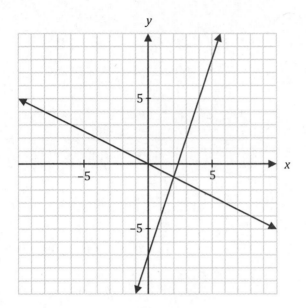

7. Based on the graph above, find the point where the two lines intersect.

For questions 8-9, graph the result of the function after applying the given transformation.

8.   Reflect the function below over the *y* axis:

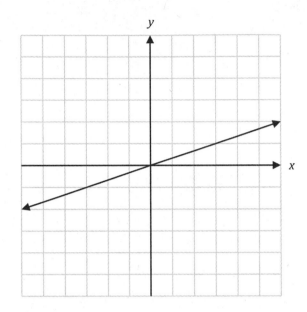

9.   Translate the function below 3 units up:

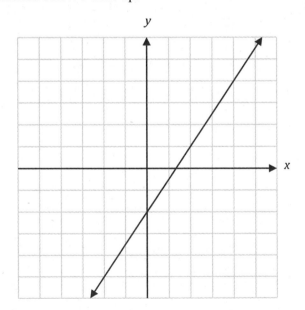

Answers: Graphing Equations

1.

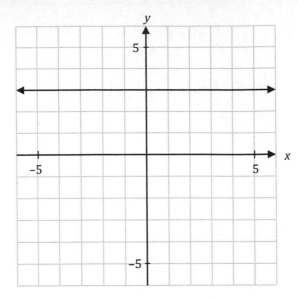

2.

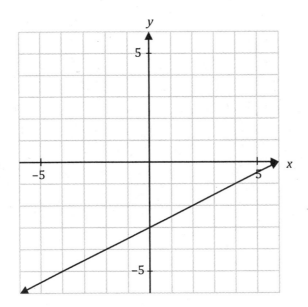

3.

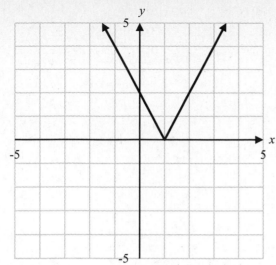

4.

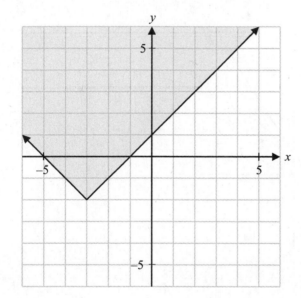

5. −5

6. $\dfrac{2}{5}$

7. (2, −1)

8.

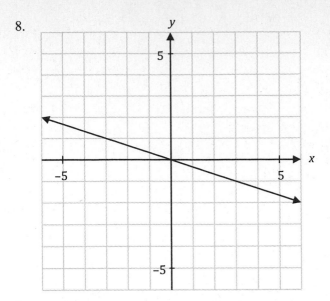

9.

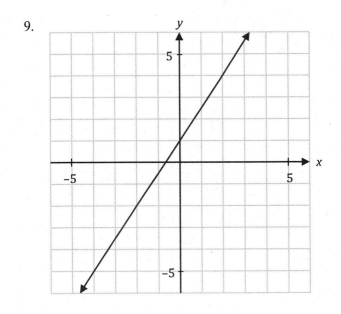

PRACTICE SET

In this part, you will find 30 SAT-style questions to practice the Heart of Algebra topics you learned in this section. Check your answers with the answer key that follows. For any question that you get wrong, identify the topic of the question, and then review the part of this section that covers that topic.

$$5 + 6(2 - 7) - 10 = x(4 - 10) + 1$$

1. In the equation above, what is the value of x?

   (A)   2

   (B)   6

   (C)   −6

   (D)   −2

2. If $5y + 6x = x$, which of the following must be equal to $15y + 15x$?

   (A) 0

   (B) 10

   (C) 10y

   (D) 10$y + 5$

3. For which of the following values of x will $5x + 14$ be greater than 30?

   (A) 1

   (B) 2

   (C) 3

   (D) 4

4. Roger orders tires to be delivered to his truck company. Each tire costs $30, plus a sales tax of 10%. The tire company also charges a flat rate $5 for each delivery. Which of the following expressions represents the total cost of ordering x tires, in dollars?

(A) $0.1(30x) + 5$

(B) $1.1(30x) + 5$

(C) $0.1x + (30)(5)$

(D) $1.1x + (30)(5)$

5. If $m = \dfrac{5k}{3}$, what is $4k$ in terms of m?

(A) $\dfrac{3m}{4}$

(B) $\dfrac{4m}{3}$

(C) $\dfrac{12m}{5}$

(D) $\dfrac{5m}{12}$

$f(x)$	-2	1	4
x	-3	-1	1

6. Based on the table above, which of the following equations could represent $f(x)$?

(A) $f(x) = 2x + 1$

(B) $f(x) = \dfrac{3}{2}x + \dfrac{5}{2}$

(C) $f(x) = x + \dfrac{1}{2}$

(D) $f(x) = \dfrac{2x + 1}{3x + 2}$

7. Which of the following equations is a line that is parallel to $6x + 5y = 10$?

(A) $y = -\frac{4}{5}x - \frac{9}{10}$

(B) $y = \frac{5}{6}x - \frac{5}{12}$

(C) $y = -\frac{6}{5}x + \frac{1}{2}$

(D) $y = -\frac{4}{5} + \frac{13}{10}$

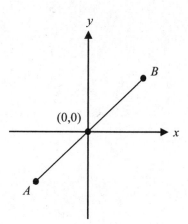

8. The coordinates of point B in the figure above are (c, d), where $c > d$. Which of the following could be the slope of $\overline{AB}$?

(A) $-\frac{1}{2}$

(B) 0

(C) $\frac{3}{4}$

(D) $\frac{4}{3}$

9. Kevin can paint an entire wall in p minutes. Which of the following expressions correctly represents the number of walls that Kevin can paint in 7 minutes?

(A) $7 + p$

(B) $\dfrac{p}{7}$

(C) $\dfrac{7}{p}$

(D) $1 + 7p$

10. The lines $4y = 2x + 6$ and $2y = -x + 7$ intersect at coordinates (j, k) in the xy-plane. What is the value of j?

(A) -3

(B) -2

(C) 2

(D) 3

$$2k + 3n < 2k$$

11. Based on the inequality above, which of the following must be true?

(A) $k > \dfrac{2}{3}n$

(B) $k = 0$

(C) $n < 0$

(D) $n > \dfrac{3}{2}$

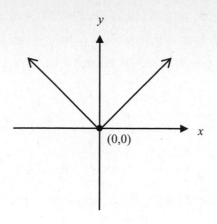

(0,0)

12. The graph of $y = |x|$ is shown above. Which of the following graphs represents $y = 3|x - 2| - 1$?

(A)

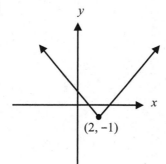

(2, −1)

(B)

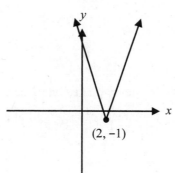

(2, −1)

(C)

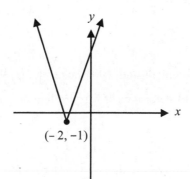

(−2, −1)

(D)

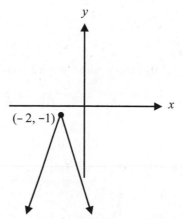

(−2, −1)

13. Truck A is moving at 10 miles per hour, and Truck B is moving at 12 miles per hour in the same direction. If Truck A is initially 40 miles ahead of Truck B, how many hours will it take for Truck B to catch up to Truck A?

(A)   5
(B)   10
(C)   15
(D)   20

14. If $|2x - 4| \leq 6$, which of the following inequalities represents the possible values of x?

(A) $-1 \leq x \leq 5$

(B) $1 \leq x \leq 5$

(C) $-5 \leq x \leq -1$

(D) $-5 \leq x \leq 1$

15. In the xy-plane, line l passes through the points $(1, 4)$ and $(5, 16)$. What is the y-intercept of the graph of line l?

(A) -3

(B) -1

(C) 1

(D) 3

16. A factory must produce rods between 60 and 100 inches long. Which of the following inequalities can be used to determine if a rod's length l satisfies these criteria?

(A) $|l - 20| < 80$

(B) $|l - 60| < 100$

(C) $|l - 80| < 20$

(D) $|l - 100| < 60$

$$f(x) = 2x + 6$$

17. $f(x)$ is defined above. If $2f(k) = 24$, what is the value of $f(3k)$?

    (A)   12

    (B)   24

    (C)   36

    (D)   48

18. Steve's truck uses one liter of gas for every 6 kilometers travelled. Steve started with 60 liters of gas in his truck and drove at an average speed of 100 kilometers per hour. Which of the following functions represents the liters of gas remaining in the truck's gas tank after x hours of driving?

    (A) $f(x) = \dfrac{60 - 100}{6}x$

    (B) $f(x) = 60 - \dfrac{100}{6}x$

    (C) $f(x) = 60 - \dfrac{6}{100}x$

    (D) $f(x) = 60 - 100x$

19. Line k passes through the point $(0, 0)$ and is perpendicular to the line $y = -2x + 5$. If the two lines intersect at the point (a, b), what is the value of b?

    (A)   1

    (B)   2

    (C)   3

    (D)   4

20. If $x < 0$ and $y > -1$, which of the following must be true?

   (A) $\dfrac{x}{y} > 0$

   (B) $|x| + |y| > 0$

   (C) $x < y$

   (D) $\dfrac{|x + y|}{x} > 0$

GRID-INS

21. If $g(x) = 3x$ and $h(x) = 4x + 7$, what is the value of $g(h(5))$?

22. A line passes through the points $(-9, 0)$, $(0, 6)$, and $(6, a)$. What is the value of a?

23. A company ordered $400 worth of muffins. Bran muffins cost $2 each and blueberry muffins cost $4 each. If the company ordered twice as many blueberry muffins as bran muffins, how many muffins were ordered in total?

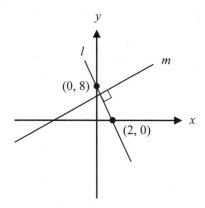

24. In the xy-coordinate plane above, line l is perpendicular to line m. What is the slope of line m?

25. Tom and Jerry start at the same point on a circular 7500m track. Tom runs at a speed of 1m/s and Jerry runs at a speed of 3m/s in the opposite direction. How long, in seconds, will it take them to meet?

$$y = x - \frac{200}{15}$$

$$2x = 3y$$

26. Based on the system of equations above, what is the value of x?

27. If $2x - 4z = -2x$, what is the value of $\frac{2z}{x}$?

Item	Price
Graphing Calculator	$50
Scientific Calculator	$30

28. The table above shows the prices for graphing and scientific calculators at a store. If the store sold 64 calculators for a total of $2340, how many scientific calculators were sold?

$$\frac{y}{4} + \frac{x}{2} = 1$$

$$y - 2 = 2x$$

29. Based on the system of equations above, what is the value of $4x$?

30. If $\frac{6x + 2y}{3y} = \frac{6}{5}$, what is the value of $\frac{x}{y}$?

PRACTICE SET ANSWERS

1. B
2. A
3. D
4. B
5. C
6. B
7. C
8. C
9. C
10. C
11. C
12. B
13. D
14. A
15. C
16. C
17. B
18. B
19. A
20. B
21. 81
22. 10
23. 120
24. $\dfrac{1}{4}$
25. 1875
26. 40
27. 2
28. 43
29. 2
30. $\dfrac{4}{15}$

SECTION 5
PASSPORT TO ADVANCED MATH

The **Passport to Advanced Math** questions cover important topics for college-level math, focusing on expressions, equations, and functions. There will be sixteen Passport to Advanced Math questions on the Math Test: seven in the Calculator Section and nine in the No Calculator Section. In this section, we'll go over the following topics:

- Polynomial expressions
- Factoring polynomials
- Quadratic equations
- Quadratic functions and their graphs
- Advanced equations
- Applications of functions

POLYNOMIAL EXPRESSIONS
PART 1

A **polynomial** is an expression that is a sum of one or more terms. Each **term** consists of one or more variables multiplied by a coefficient. Coefficients can be negative, so don't be surprised if you see a minus sign in a polynomial—that just means there's a term with a negative coefficient.

Here are some examples of polynomials:

$$5x^2$$
$$3x^3 + 2xy - y$$
$$-3x^2 + 6x - 7$$

Polynomials are classified by the number of terms they have when they are expressed in their simplest form. A **monomial** has one term, a **binomial** has two terms and a **trinomial** has three. $3x + 2$ is a binomial, because it has two terms. $x^2 - 4x + 2$ is a trinomial, because it has three terms.

Polynomials are also classified by their degree. The **degree** of a term is the sum of the exponents of its variables. The **degree of a polynomial** is the same as its the highest degree term. For example, $x^2 + 3$ is a second-degree polynomial because its highest exponent is 2. The expression $x^3 + x^2 + 2x + 1$ is a third-degree polynomial because its highest exponent is 3.

Certain polynomials have special names determined by their degree:

Degree	Name	Example
0	Constant	5
1	Linear	$x + 7$
2	Quadratic	$x^2 + 9$
3	Cubic	$2x^3 + 19x^2 - 6x + 13$

Just like regular numbers, polynomials can be added, subtracted, multiplied, and divided. Next up, we'll cover how to add, subtract, and multiply polynomials, as well as some techniques for basic division.

ADDING POLYNOMIALS

To add two polynomials, you need to combine the like terms. **Like terms** have the same variables raised to the same powers. So $5x^3y^2z$ and $7x^3y^2z$ are like terms because each term has x cubed, y squared, and z. However, $5x^3y^2z$ and $7xyz$ are not like terms, because although they have the same variables, the variables are not raised to the same powers.

EXAMPLE

Let's say you want to find the sum of $3m^2 + 2m + 6$ and $m - 9$. You can join them with a plus sign:

$$3m^2 + 2m + 6 + m - 9$$

Then, put like terms next to each other. Remember to pay attention to the signs!

$$3m^2 + 2m + m + 6 - 9$$

Finally, add and subtract the like terms, including the constants:

$$3m^2 + 3m - 3$$

SUBTRACTING POLYNOMIALS

Subtracting polynomials is very similar to adding them: join the expressions and combine like terms. However, with subtraction, you first have to take care of the signs.

EXAMPLE

What is the value of $4p^3 + 6p^2 - 8p + 11$ minus $3p^3 - 2p^2 + 12p - 3$?

Just like with addition, you'll need to join the terms. With subtraction, however, you need to put the second term in parentheses:

$$4p^3 + 6p^2 - 8p + 11 - (3p^3 - 2p^2 + 12p - 3)$$

Then, distribute the negative sign across the parentheses:

$$4p^3 + 6p^2 - 8p + 11 - 3p^3 + 2p^2 - 12p + 3$$

Now you're ready to combine like terms for your result:

$$p^3 + 8p^2 - 20p + 14$$

MULTIPLYING POLYNOMIALS

To multiply two monomials, use exponent rules.

EXAMPLE

$$5x^3y^5z^2 \times 2x^6y^8z$$

Remember that when you multiply two expressions with the same base, you can add their exponents. Don't forget to multiply the coefficients!

$$5x^3y^5z^2 \times 2x^6y^8z = 10x^{3+6}y^{5+8}z^{2+1}$$

Once you do the arithmetic, you're left with:

$$10x^9y^{13}z^3$$

When you multiply polynomials with more terms, you will need to use the Distributive Property, which we talked about in Section 4, Part 1. Take a moment to review the Distributive Property, and then look at this example:

EXAMPLE

$$2x(x+3)$$

Using the Distributive Property, you can rewrite the expression like this:

$$2x \times x + 2x \times 3$$

Then, simplify to get your solution:

$$2x^2 + 6x$$

When you're multiplying more than one polynomial with multiple terms, the idea is the same: use the Distributive Property and simplify. You just have to make sure you've multiplied every term in one polynomial by every term in the other. Luckily, for multiplying two binomials, there's an easy way to keep everything straight. The **FOIL method** tells you to multiply the **F**irst terms, the **O**uter terms, the **I**nner terms, and the **L**ast terms. Always remember to combine like terms when you've finished.

EXAMPLE

$$(x+3)(2x+5)$$

You need to multiply both terms in the first binomial by both terms in the second, like this:

$$(x+3)(2x+5)$$

The FOIL method makes this simple. Multiply together the *first* terms in the parentheses (x and $2x$), then the *outer* terms (x and 5), then the *inner* terms (3 and $2x$), and finally the *last* terms (3 and 5):

$$(x \times 2x) + (x \times 5) + (3 \times 2x) + (3 \times 5)$$

Then, simplify and combine like terms:

$$2x^2 + 5x + 6x + 15$$

$$2x^2 + 11x + 15$$

DIVIDING POLYNOMIALS

To divide polynomials, you can use the same techniques you learned for factoring expressions.

EXAMPLE

$$\frac{2x^3 + 4x^2 - 6x}{2x}$$

This operation is asking you to divide each term of the polynomial by $2x$. Remember that dividing two expressions with the same base means you can divide the coefficients and subtract the exponents:

$$\frac{2}{2}x^{3-1} + \frac{4}{2}x^{2-1} - \frac{6}{2}x^{1-1}$$

Carry out that arithmetic, and simplify the coefficients where you can:

$$x^2 + 2x - 3$$

Don't worry if the number you're dividing the coefficients by isn't a common factor. It's fine to leave coefficients as fractions in lowest terms.

PART 1 PRACTICE: POLYNOMIALS

1. Add $x^3 + 2x - 6$ and $4x^3 - 5x + 9$.

2. Find the sum of $m^4 + 4m^3 - m^2 + 17m - 2$ and $3m^4 - m^3 - 2m^2 + 3m - 8$.

3. Find the value of $3x + 16$ minus $x + 8$.

4. Subtract $10x - 10$ from $4x + 7$.

5. $12m^2n^7 \times 5m^{10}n^3 =$

6. $(x - 7)(x + 3) =$

7. $(2x + 5)(x - 11) =$

8. $\dfrac{5x^2 + 10x - 15}{5} =$

9. What is $100x^4 + 44x^2$ divided by $4x^2$?

10. $\dfrac{3x^4 + 36x^3 - 12x^2}{-3x} =$

Answer Key: Polynomials

1. $5x^3 - 3x + 3$

2. $4m^4 + 3m^3 - 3m^2 + 20m - 10$

3. $2x + 8$

4. $-6x + 17$

5. $60m^{12}n^{10}$

6. $x^2 - 4x - 21$

7. $2x^2 - 17x - 55$

8. $x^2 + 2x - 3$

9. $25x^2 + 11$

10. $-x^3 - 12x^2 + 4x$

FACTORING POLYNOMIALS
PART 2

In the previous section you learned how to multiply polynomials. With multiplication, you start with two or more factors and find their product. Remember from Section 4 that factoring is the opposite of multiplication: you start with a product and find its factors. In this section, we'll build on what you learned in Section 4 and discuss how to factor quadratic and cubic polynomials. Here's what it looks like:

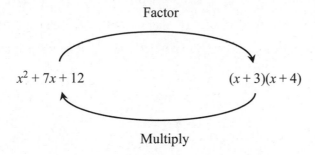

Factor

$$x^2 + 7x + 12 \qquad (x+3)(x+4)$$

Multiply

FACTORING QUADRATIC TRINOMIALS

Remember that a quadratic expression has a degree, or highest power, of two, and a trinomial is a polynomial with three terms. Therefore, a quadratic trinomial is a second-degree polynomial with three terms. You can write a general expression for quadratic trinomials like this:

$$ax^2 + bx + c$$

In this form, a is the coefficient of x^2, b is the coefficient of x, and c is the constant. So in the quadratic trinomial $x^2 + 2x - 8$, $a = 1$, $b = 2$, and $c = -8$. Quadratic trinomials where $a = 1$ are a little simpler to factor, so we'll take this one as our first example. To fully factor it, we want to write it as two binomials multiplied together, like this:

$$(x + m)(x + n)$$

How do we find m and n? Well, we can multiply these two binomials using FOIL, and then simplify:

$$x^2 + nx + mx + mn = x^2 + (n + m)x + mn$$

By comparing this to our general expression for quadratic trinomials above, we can see that two things must be true:

$$n + m = b$$
$$m \times n = c$$

In other words, to find m and n, we need to find two numbers that have a sum of b and a product of c. For the trinomial $x^2 + 2x - 8$, that means we're looking for two numbers that add up to 2 and multiply together to -8. First, let's see what numbers multiply to -8:

$$-1 \times 8 = -8$$
$$-8 \times 1 = -8$$
$$-2 \times 4 = -8$$
$$-4 \times 2 = -8$$

Which pair of numbers has a sum of 2? Only -2 and 4:

$$-2 + 4 = 2$$

Therefore, our two constants are -2 and 4. To plug them into our binomials, we add them to x:

$$\left(x + (-2)\right)(x + 4) = (x - 2)(x + 4)$$

We can then check that we have factored correctly by using FOIL to multiply the two binomials:

$$(x - 2)(x + 4) = x^2 + 4x - 2x - 8 = x^2 + 2x - 8$$

Because multiplying leads to the expression we started out with, we know we have factored correctly.

FACTORING WITH DIFFERENT VALUES

Now you know how to factor a quadratic trinomial when a — the coefficient of the quadratic term — is equal to 1. But what if a is equal to another number? First, check whether you can factor this number out of the entire expression.

EXAMPLE

$$5x^2 + 15x + 10$$

Did you notice that every term has a common factor of 5? That means you can start by pulling 5 out of the entire expression:

$$5x^2 + 15x + 10 = 5(x^2 + 3x + 2)$$

Now you can use the method you've just learned to factor the quadratic expression in parentheses. You're looking for two numbers have a product of 2 and a sum of 3. The numbers 1 and 2 fit those requirements:

$$5(x^2 + 3x + 2) = 5(x + 1)(x + 2)$$

You can tell that you've factored correctly because when you multiply these binomials together using **FOIL**, you get the trinomial you were trying to factor:

$$5(x + 1)(x + 2) = 5(x^2 + 3x + 2) = 5x^2 + 15x + 10$$

However, what happens when you can't factor out a from the entire expression? This time, one or both of the x's in the binomials will have a coefficient, marked here by p and q:

$$ax^2 + bx + c = (px + m)(qx + n)$$

We need a few things to happen:

1. $p \times q = a$
2. $m \times n = c$
3. $p \times n + m \times q = b$

$$3x^2 - 5x - 2$$

p and q will multiply to 3 so their values will be 1 and 3. (If a is negative, first factor -1 out of the equation.) Therefore, you know the two binomials will look something like this:

$$3x^2 - 5x - 2 = (3x + m)(x + n)$$

To find m and n, you need values that will multiply to -2. There are two sets of possible values: 1 and -2 or -1 and 2. Which of these values should you pick so that $3 \times n + m \times 1 = -5$? The only option is 1 and -2, because $3 \times -2 + 1 \times 1 = -5$. Therefore, the two binomials must be:

$$(3x + 1)(x - 2)$$

FACTORING A DIFFERENCE OF SQUARES

Expressions that consist of subtracting one perfect square from another, such as $x^2 - 25$, are called a **difference of squares**. Recognizing when a polynomial is a difference of squares will come in handy, because these expressions all factor according to a simple formula:

$$a^2 - b^2 = (a + b)(a - b)$$

Here are some examples:

$$x^2 - 4 = (x + 2)(x - 2)$$
$$x^2 - 64 = (x + 8)(x - 8)$$
$$x^2 - y^2 = (x + y)(x - y)$$
$$x^4 - y^4 = (x^2 + y^2)(x^2 - y^2)$$

But wait – notice that in our last example, the second factor is also a difference of squares! We can factor that, too:

$$x^4 - y^4 = (x^2 + y^2)(x + y)(x - y)$$

Factoring a Sum or Difference of Cubes

There are also special formulas for factoring a sum or difference of cubes:

$$a^3 + b^3 = (a + b)(a^2 - ab + b^2)$$
$$a^3 - b^3 = (a - b)(a^2 + ab + b^2)$$

These two formulas look very similar – in fact, the only differences are in the signs. To keep the signs straight, think **SOAP**: "same, opposite, always positive." The first sign is the same as the one in the original expression, the second sign is the opposite, and the last sign is always a plus sign.

Here are some examples:

$$x^3 + 8 = (x + 2)(x^2 - 2x + 4)$$
$$x^3 - 27 = (x - 3)(x^2 + 3x + 9)$$
$$x^6 - 64 = (x^2 - 4)(x^4 + 4x^2 + 16)$$

Did you catch that the first factor in our last example is a difference of squares? You can use the difference of squares formula to further simplify:

$$x^6 - 64 = (x + 2)(x - 2)(x^4 + 4x^2 + 16)$$

Using Factoring to Simplify Rational Equations

On the SAT, you won't have to do complicated division with polynomials. However, you may be asked to look at a rational expression involving polynomials and simplify. In Part 1, you learned about how to do some basic division with polynomials. Your new factoring skills will allow you to divide polynomials with multiple terms in the denominator.

Example

$$\frac{x^2 + 3x + 2}{x + 2}$$

The denominator is a linear expression and can't be factored. However, the numerator is a quadratic trinomial, which you can factor:

$$x^2 + 3x + 2 = (x + 1)(x + 2)$$

Substituting that into the original expression, you can quickly see that one of those factors is a common factor with the denominator:

$$\frac{(x + 1)(x + 2)}{x + 2}$$

As with any rational expression, cancel common factors to simplify:

$$\frac{(x + 1)(x \cancel{+} 2)}{x \cancel{+} 2} = x + 1$$

EXAMPLE

$$\frac{x^2 + 7x + 12}{x^2 - 9}$$

In this case, both polynomials can be factored (notice that the denominator is a difference of squares):

$$\frac{(x + 3)(x + 4)}{(x + 3)(x - 3)}$$

After cancelling out the common factor $(x + 3)$, you're left with:

$$\frac{x + 4}{x - 3}$$

This can't be simplified any further, so you're all done!

PART 2 PRACTICE: FACTORING POLYNOMIALS

Factor the following polynomials.

1. $x^2 - 11x - 12$

2. $x^2 - 9x + 18$

3. $2x^2 + 27x + 70$

4. $-9x^2 + 22x + 15$

5. $4x^2 - 4x - 120$

6. $4x^2 + 10x + 4$

7. $x^2 - 100$

8. $8x^3 + 27$

9. $x^3 - 125$

10. $x^8 - 64$

Answers: Factoring Polynomials

1. $(x - 12)(x + 1)$

2. $(x - 3)(x - 6)$

3. $(x + 10)(2x + 7)$

4. $-(9x + 5)(x - 3)$

5. $4(x - 6)(x + 5)$

6. $2(2x + 1)(x + 2)$

7. $(x + 10)(x - 10)$

8. $(2x + 3)(4x^2 - 6x + 9)$

9. $(x - 5)(x^2 + 5x + 25)$

10. $(x^4 + 8)(x^4 - 8)$

QUADRATIC EQUATIONS
PART 3

Quadratic equations are equations with one variable raised to the second degree. Here's an example:

$$x^2 + 10x + 21 = 0$$

To solve quadratic equations, you can use what you've learned about factoring quadratic polynomials. How? Take look at the quadratic equation above, and factor the left side:

$$x^2 + 10x + 21 = 0$$

$$(x + 3)(x + 7) = 0$$

On the left side, you now have two factors that have a product of zero. For two numbers to have a product of zero, at least one of them has to be equal to zero. In this equation, there are two ways for that to be true:

$$x + 3 = 0 \qquad\qquad x + 7 = 0$$

$$x = -3 \qquad\qquad x = -7$$

Therefore, this quadratic equation has two possible solutions: $x = -3$ or $x = -7$. These values are known as the **roots** of the equation.

EXAMPLE

$$2x^2 + 21x + 40 = 13$$

Notice that unlike our first example, this equation is not set up so that one side is equal to zero. You have to gather all your terms on one side. In this case, subtract 13 from both sides to get zero on the right side of the equation:

$$2x^2 + 21x + 27 = 0$$

Now you are ready to factor the left side:

$$(2x + 3)(x + 9) = 0$$

Then, set each factor equal to zero in order to solve for x:

$$2x + 3 = 0 \qquad\qquad x + 9 = 0$$

$$x = -\frac{3}{2} \qquad\qquad x = -9$$

The two roots of the quadratic equation are $-\frac{3}{2}$ and -9.

WORD PROBLEMS WITH QUADRATIC EQUATIONS

On the SAT, you may need to solve word problems using quadratic equations.

EXAMPLE

Patricia throws a tennis ball out of her window. The height h of the ball at time t is given by $h = -t^2 - t + 20$. At what time does the tennis ball fall to the ground?

The height of something is how far away it is from the ground. That means that when the tennis ball falls to the ground, its height (h) is zero. You can substitute 0 for h in the equation:

$$-t^2 - t + 20 = 0$$

Now that you have a quadratic equation, you can factor it to find the roots. Notice that right now, the coefficient of the quadratic term, t^2, is -1. Factoring would be simpler if that coefficient were 1. Since any number multiplied by zero equals zero, you can multiply both sides by -1 to get:

$$t^2 + t - 20 = 0$$

Now you have a quadratic polynomial that's easier to factor:

$$(t+5)(t-4) = 0$$

You've solved the equation: $t = -5$ or $t = 4$. However, remember that you're not just solving an equation this time; you're answering a word problem. The ball can't fall to the ground twice, so you need to figure out which one of your solutions makes sense for the problem.

This problem is asking you to find a particular time after Patricia throws the ball. Since you know that time is never negative, you can look at your solutions and realize that $t = -5$ doesn't make sense. This makes it an **extraneous solution**: a solution that works mathematically but doesn't make logical sense. This leaves you with only one solution: the tennis ball falls to the ground when $t = 4$.

THE QUADRATIC FORMULA

Not all quadratic equations can be easily solved by factoring. For quadratic equations that can't be easily factored using the methods we've covered, you can use the Quadratic Formula. The **Quadratic Formula** states that if you have a quadratic equation in the form:

$$ax^2 + bx + c = 0$$

You can solve for x using this formula:

$$x = \frac{-b \pm \sqrt{b^2 - 4ac}}{2a}$$

EXAMPLE

Solve for x in the equation:

$$x^2 + 17x + 72 = 0$$

In this equation, $a = 1$, $b = 17$, and $c = 72$. Putting these values into the Quadratic Formula gives you:

$$x = \frac{-17 \pm \sqrt{17^2 - 4(1)(72)}}{2(1)}$$

After this, it's just a matter of remembering your orders of operation to simplify:

$$x = \frac{-17 \pm \sqrt{289 - 288}}{2}$$

$$x = \frac{-17 \pm \sqrt{1}}{2}$$

$$x = \frac{-17 \pm 1}{2}$$

That $\pm$ sign is read as "plus or minus," and it means you need to both add those terms and subtract them. Doing so gives you:

$$x = \frac{-16}{2} \quad \text{or} \quad x = \frac{-18}{2}$$

Simplify those fractions for your final solutions:

$$x = -8 \quad \text{or} \quad x = -9$$

The two roots for the quadratic equation are –9 and –8. Take note that while we used the quadratic formula, this equation can also be solved by the factoring technique (try it!).

IRRATIONAL AND NONEXISTENT SOLUTIONS

There are two types of quadratic equations that the Quadratic Formula is especially useful for. The first is quadratic equations with irrational solutions. Take this equation:

$$x^2 + 5x - 7 = 0$$

Applying the Quadratic Formula gives you:

$$x = \frac{-(5) \pm \sqrt{(5)^2 - 4(1)(-7)}}{2(1)}$$

$$x = \frac{-5 \pm \sqrt{25 + 28}}{2}$$

$$x = \frac{-5 \pm \sqrt{53}}{2}$$

This one couldn't be solved by factoring because its roots are irrational, so you needed to use the Quadratic Formula.

The other kind of quadratic equation, the Quadratic Formula, is especially useful for quadratic equations with *no* solutions.

EXAMPLE

$$x^2 + x + 2 = 0$$

Look what happens when you try to apply the Quadratic Formula:

$$x = \frac{-1 \pm \sqrt{1^2 - 4(1)(2)}}{2(1)}$$

$$x = \frac{-1 \pm \sqrt{1-8}}{2}$$

$$x = \frac{-1 \pm \sqrt{-7}}{2}$$

Wait a minute! You can't take the square root of a negative number. That means there is **no solution**: the expression cannot be factored, and there are no values of x that will make the equation true. A quadratic equation will always have zero, one, or two roots, and you can use the Quadratic Formula to figure out how many it has.

PART 3 PRACTICE: QUADRATIC EQUATION

Solve the following quadratic equations. If there is no solution, write "no solution."

1. $x^2 - 4x - 21 = 0$

2. $4x^2 - 12x + 8 = 0$

3. $2x^2 - 24x + 72 = 0$

4. $x^2 - 10x = 0$

5. $3x^2 + 25x + 42 = 0$

6. $3x^2 - 2x = 5$

7. $24x^2 - 70x + 49 = 7x$

8. $9x^2 + 12x = -4$

9. $2x^2 + x + 13 = 0$

10. $x^2 + 2x + 3 = 0$

Answers: Quadratic Equation

1. $x = -3$ or $x = 7$

2. $x = 1$ or $x = 2$

3. $x = 6$

4. $x = 0$ or $x = 10$

5. $x = -6$ or $x = -\dfrac{7}{3}$

6. $x = -1$ or $x = \dfrac{5}{3}$

7. $x = \dfrac{7}{8}$ or $x = \dfrac{7}{3}$

8. $x = -\dfrac{2}{3}$

9. No solution

10. No solution

QUADRATIC FUNCTIONS
PART 4

In Section 4, you learned that a **function** is a formula that turns every "input" value into an "output" value. So far, we've talked about linear functions. Now you're going to learn about **quadratic functions**, which are functions with a variable raised to the second power. Like linear functions, quadratic functions can either be written with the function notation $f(x)$, or with a second variable like y:

$$f(x) \;=\; ax^2 + bx + c$$

$$y \;=\; ax^2 + bx + c$$

GRAPHING QUADRATIC FUNCTIONS

To graph quadratic functions, let's begin with the simplest quadratic function:

$$f(x) \;=\; x^2$$

To start graphing this quadratic function, you can create a chart with some input and output values:

x	$f(x)$
−3	9
−2	4
−1	1
0	0
1	1
2	4
3	9

Then, you can plot these points on a graph:

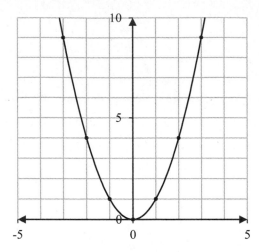

The type of curve created by graphing quadratic functions is called a **parabola**. Parabolas can move up or down, be wider or narrower, or flip upside down, but they will always retain this basic shape.

Notice that the parabola above is symmetric about the y-axis. All parabolas are symmetric about a vertical line drawn through their **vertex**, which is the highest or lowest point. To find the x-coordinate of the vertex of any parabola, you can use the following formula:

$$\text{vertex} \ = \ \frac{-b}{2a}$$

In the function above, b is equal to zero, so the vertex has the x-coordinate 0. If you plug $x = 0$ into the function, you can find the y-coordinate of the vertex: $f(x) = 0^2 = 0$. Therefore, the parabola's vertex is located at (0, 0)—which you can see on the graph.

What if we had the function $f(x) = x^2 + 4x$? In this case, $b = 4$, so the x-coordinate of the vertex would be $\frac{-b}{2a} = \frac{-4}{2 \times 1} = -2$. You can plug this x value into the function to find the y-coordinate: $f(x) = (-2)^2 + 4 \times (-2) = -4$. Therefore, the vertex is located at the point (−2, −4).

TRANSFORMATIONS OF QUADRATIC FUNCTIONS

Like we saw in Section 4, manipulating a function will move or stretch the graph of the function on the coordinate plane.

If you add a constant to a quadratic function, this moves its vertex up or down. Adding a positive constant moves the vertex up, and adding a negative constant moves the vertex down. For example, if you add 5 to the function $f(x) = x^2$, you'll shift the vertex of the parabola up by 5 units. If you subtract 7, you'll shift the vertex of the parabola down by 7 units:

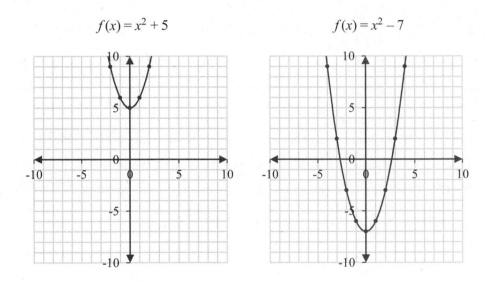

$$f(x) = x^2 + 5 \qquad\qquad\qquad f(x) = x^2 - 7$$

Instead of being located at (0, 0), the vertex of the function $f(x) = x^2 + 5$ is located at (0, 5). The vertex of the function $f(x) = x^2 - 7$ is located at (0, –7).

Just like with linear functions, you can shift a parabola left or right by taking the function of x plus a constant. Adding a positive constant shifts the parabola's vertex to the left, and adding a negative constant shifts the parabola's vertex to the right. For example, if you take the function of $(x + 2)$, you'll shift the vertex of the parabola left by 2 units. If you take the function of $(x - 1)$, you'll shift the vertex of the parabola right by 1 unit:

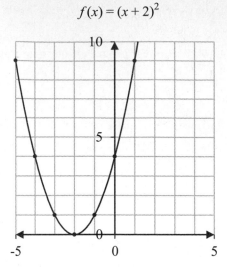

$$f(x) = (x + 2)^2$$

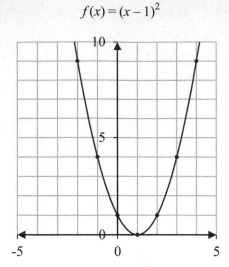

$$f(x) = (x - 1)^2$$

The vertex of the function $f(x) = (x + 2)^2$ is located at $(-2, 0)$. The vertex of the function $f(x) = (x - 1)^2$ is located at $(1, 0)$.

You can "stretch" a quadratic function by changing the value for a. If a is bigger than 1, you'll end up with a narrower parabola. If a is a fraction between 0 and 1, you'll end up with a wider parabola. For example, the function $f(x) = 2x^2$ is stretched so it is narrower, and the function $f(x) = \frac{1}{2}x^2$ is stretched so it is wider:

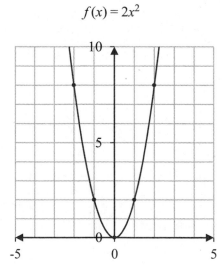

$$f(x) = 2x^2$$

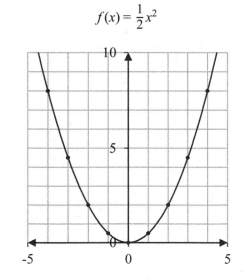

$$f(x) = \frac{1}{2}x^2$$

Finally, what about a negative constant? If *a* is equal to a negative number, the parabola flips upside down. In other words, it's reflected about the *x*-axis:

$$f(x) = -x^2$$

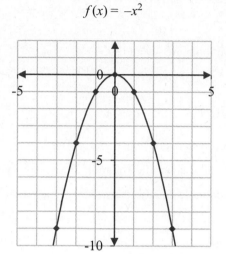

FINDING *X*− INTERCEPTS

A parabola's ***x*-intercepts** are the points where the parabola meets the *x*-axis. A parabola can have zero, one, or two *x*-intercepts. The *y*-coordinate for any point on the *x*-axis is always zero, so the coordinates for the *x*-intercepts are *x* values of the quadratic function that will make *y* equal to 0.

You already know how to find the values of *x* that will make a quadratic function equal to 0 – this is the same as finding the roots of any quadratic equation! Just set the quadratic function equal to zero, and then factor it into two binomials.

EXAMPLE

$$f(x) \ = \ 6x^2 - 19x - 36$$

First, set this function equal to zero. Then, use the method you learned in Part 3 to factor and solve for *x*:

$$6x^2 - 19x - 36 \ = \ 0$$

$$(3x + 4)(2x - 9) \ = \ 0$$

$$3x + 4 = 0 \qquad\qquad 2x - 9 = 0$$

$$x = -\frac{4}{3} \qquad\qquad x = \frac{9}{2}$$

The x-intercepts of this parabola are $-\frac{4}{3}$ and $\frac{9}{2}$.

SYSTEMS OF EQUATIONS

On the SAT, you might see systems of linear and quadratic equations. Since a linear equation represents a line and a quadratic equation represents a parabola, the solution to a system of a linear and a quadratic equation represents where that line and that parabola meet.

Systems of linear and quadratic equations can have zero, one, or two solutions. If there are no solutions, the line and the parabola do not intersect at all. If there is only one solution, the line is **tangent** to the parabola, touching it at exactly one point. If there are two solutions, the line intersects the parabola at two points.

To solve a system of equations consisting of one quadratic equation and one linear equation, you'll use substitution, just like with systems of linear equations.

EXAMPLE

$$y + 30 = x^2 + 3x$$

$$y - 5x = 90$$

In order to substitute, you need to first solve for y in terms of x. Add $5x$ to both sides of the second equation:

$$y - 5x = 90$$

$$y = 5x + 90$$

Plug this value for y into the first equation:

$$y + 30 = x^2 + 3x$$

$$5x + 90 + 30 = x^2 + 3x$$

Then, solve this equation. Add and subtract like terms until one side is equal to zero:

$$5x + 90 + 30 = x^2 + 3x$$

$$x^2 - 2x - 120 = 0$$

Now you just need to use one of your strategies for solving quadratic equations. This one factors to:

$$(x + 10)(x - 12) = 0$$

$$x = -10 \quad \text{or} \quad x = 12$$

You're not done yet! You need to solve for both variables. Substitute these x values into either equation to find the corresponding y values. Both equations will give you the same values, so pick the easiest one to handle – usually the linear equation. Plug both x values into this equation:

$$y = 5(-10) + 90 \qquad\qquad y = 5(12) + 90$$

$$y = 40 \qquad\qquad\qquad\quad y = 150$$

The parabola and the line intersect at two points: $(-10, 40)$ and $(12, 150)$.

PART 4 PRACTICE: QUADRATIC FUNCTIONS

For questions 1–2, find the vertex of the function.

1. $f(x) = x^2 - 8x - 22$

2. $f(x) = -2x^2 + 20x - 4$

For questions 3–6, match the following functions to their corresponding graph.

3. $f(x) = -2x^2 - 5$

4. $f(x) = (x + 7)^2 - 5$

5. $f(x) = (x - 3)^2$

6. $f(x) = x^2 - 3$

(A)

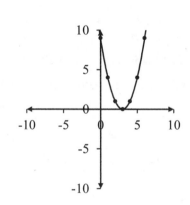

(B)

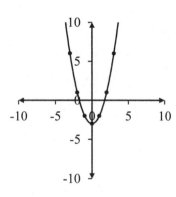

(C)

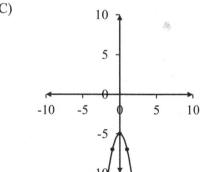

(D)

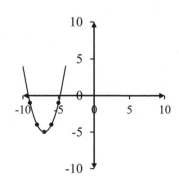

For questions 7–8, find the x-intercept(s) of the function.

7. $f(x) = x^2 - 7x + 10$

8. $f(x) = x^2 - 14x + 49$

For questions 9–10, find the points where the parabola and line intersect in the xy-plane.

9. $y = x^2$ and $y = 5x + 14$

10. $y = x^2 + 10x$ and $y = 3x$

Answers: Quadratic Functions

1. (4, –38)

2. (5, 46)

3. C

4. D

5. A

6. B

7. 2 and 5

8. 7

9. $(x, y) = (-2, 4)$ and $(x, y) = (7, 49)$

10. $(x, y) = (-7, -21)$ and $(x, y) = (0, 0)$

ADVANCED EQUATIONS
PART 5

In this section, you'll learn about some more kinds of equations you might see on the SAT: exponential equations, rational equations, and radical equations.

EXPONENTIAL EQUATIONS

In an **exponential equation**, the variable you are solving for is part of an exponent.

EXAMPLE

$$2^x = 8$$

One way of putting this equation into words is, "2 raised to what power equals 8?" If you don't know off the top of your head, you can use trial and error:

$$2^1 = 2$$

$$2^2 = 4$$

$$2^3 = 8$$

Since $2^x = 8$ and $2^3 = 8$, you know that $x = 3$.

EXAMPLE

Sometimes the exponent will be a little more complicated:

$$4^{2x-6} = 16$$

You know that $16 = 4^2$. Replacing 16 with 4^2 in the equation gives you:

$$4^{2x-6} = 4^2$$

Since the bases are the same, using exponent rules you know that the exponents must also be the same. You can write an equation using only the exponents to solve for x:

$$2x - 6 \ = \ 2$$

$$x \ = \ 4$$

It's a good idea to check your work by plugging the value you found for x in to the original equation:

$$4^{2(4)-6} \ = \ 4^{8-6} \ = \ 4^2 \ = \ 16$$

Since this gives you the same value, you know that x is equal to 4.

RATIONAL EQUATIONS

A **rational equation** is one in which one or more terms are in the form of a fraction.

EXAMPLE

$$\frac{x}{3} = \frac{1}{5}$$

You can cross-multiply to solve for x:

$$5 \times x \ = \ 1 \times 3$$

$$x \ = \ \frac{3}{5}$$

Now let's try something a little more complicated:

$$\frac{1}{x+1} = \frac{2}{3x}$$

The idea is the same. You simply cross multiply and divide to solve for x:

$$3x \times 1 = (x+1) \times 2$$

$$3x = 2x + 2$$

$$x = 2$$

You have solved for x, and determined that it is equal to 2. But you're not quite done. When dealing with rational equations, you have to check that the solution was allowed by the original equation, which had some restrictions.

Restrictions are rules that limit the values that your variable is allowed to take. In the original equation, x can't be equal to negative 1 or 0 because this would mean you are dividing by zero. However, it isn't an issue if x is equal to 2 – this isn't one of the restrictions of the equation. Therefore, you can now confidently say that $x = 2$.

RADICAL EQUATIONS

A **radical equation** is an equation where the variable is inside a radical.

EXAMPLE

$$\sqrt{x} = 5$$

To solve this equation, you need to square both sides:

$$\sqrt{x}^2 = 5^2$$

$$x = 25$$

You have determined that x is equal to 25.

What if the equation is a little more complicated?

EXAMPLE

$$2\sqrt{x+8} - 4 = x + 1$$

Squaring both sides right away would lead to something very messy and unproductive. To save time and hassle, first isolate the radical by adding 4 to both sides:

$$2\sqrt{x+8} = x + 5$$

Now you can square both sides:

$$\left(2\sqrt{x+8}\right)^2 = (x+5)^2$$

$$4(x+8) = x^2 + 10x + 25$$

$$4x + 32 = x^2 + 10x + 25$$

Move everything to one side and combine like terms. Then, solve by factoring:

$$4x + 32 = x^2 + 10x + 25$$

$$x^2 + 6x - 7 = 0$$

$$(x+7)(x-1) = 0$$

$$x = -7 \quad \text{or} \quad x = 1$$

You have found that x is equal to -7 or 1, but you are not quite done. Squaring both sides of an equation can introduce extraneous solutions, so you need to check whether your value for x is a real solution of the equation. You can do this by plugging the solutions into both sides of the original equation and seeing if they match. Start with $x = -7$:

$$2\sqrt{-7 + 8} - 4 = -7 + 1$$

$$2 - 4 = -6$$

$$-2 = -6$$

Wrong!

Since the two sides are not equal, $x = -7$ is an extraneous solution. You have found that your solution for x doesn't include -7.

The fact that you ruled out one solution as extraneous doesn't necessarily mean the other solution is valid, so make sure to repeat the check with $x = 1$:

$$2\sqrt{1 + 8} - 4 = 1 + 1$$

$$2 \times 3 - 4 = 2$$

$$2 = 2$$

In this case, the two sides of the original equation match, so you can say that $x = 1$. This is the only solution for your equation.

PART 5 PRACTICE: ADVANCED EQUATIONS

Solve the following equations for x.

1. $2^x = 64$

2. $2^x = 16^{x-3}$

3. $\dfrac{17}{2} = \dfrac{x}{4}$

4. $\dfrac{x-2}{6} = \dfrac{x}{12}$

5. $\dfrac{5}{x} = \dfrac{4}{x-1}$

6. $\dfrac{1}{x-1} = \dfrac{x}{x+3}$

7. $\sqrt{x} = 6$

8. $\sqrt{-x} = 9$

9. $\sqrt{2(x+15)} = 6$

10. $\sqrt{3x-5} = x-3$

Answers: Advanced Equations

1. $x = 6$
2. $x = 4$
3. $x = 34$
4. $x = 4$
5. $x = 5$
6. $x = -1$ or $x = 3$
7. $x = 36$
8. $x = -81$
9. $x = 3$
10. $x = 7$

APPLICATIONS OF FUNCTIONS

PART 6

The functions discussed in this chapter have several real-world applications. In this section you'll get a look at applications that you might see on the SAT.

ZEROES AND INTERCEPTS

Recall that the zeroes of a function are the places where its graph intercepts the x-axis. This can also be used in real-world applications.

EXAMPLE

Juana throws a paper airplane. Its height h above the ground at time t seconds is given by $h = -t^2 + 3t + 10$. At what time does it fall to the ground?

When the airplane falls to the ground, you know that its height above the ground is zero. Since you know that $h = 0$, you can write the function as:

$$0 = -t^2 + 3t + 10$$

Now you're back in familiar territory. Factoring will give you:

$$0 = (t + 2)(t - 5)$$

As an equation, this has the solutions $t = -2$ or $t = 5$. However, you're looking for a specific time, and you know that a real quantity such as time can never be negative. This means that you know that the paper airplane hits the ground at $t = 5$ seconds.

OTHER PROBLEMS WITH QUADRATICS

The SAT may also ask you to find particular points in a function that show you understand its structure. Let's use the same paper airplane to solve a different problem:

EXAMPLE

Juana throws a paper airplane. Its height h above the ground at time t seconds is given by $h = -t^2 + 3t + 10$. At what time is its height the same as the height at which Juana threw it?

To solve this problem, you need to understand that when Juana threw the airplane, its time t was 0. You can find its height by plugging that value in for t:

$$h = -(0^2) + 3(0) + 10$$

$$h = 10$$

Now you want to find the other value of t that gives h a value of 10, which you can do by setting h equal to 10 and factoring.

$$10 = -t^2 + 3t + 10$$

$$0 = -t^2 + 3t + 10 - 10$$

$$0 = -t^2 + 3t$$

$$0 = (-t)(t - 3)$$

Factoring reveals that $t = 0$ or $t = 3$. In this case, you know that $t = 0$ when Juana threw the airplane, which means we want the other value. The airplane reaches the same height it was thrown from when $t = 3$.

EXPONENTIAL GROWTH

One common use of exponential functions is to model the growth of particular populations. **Exponential growth** occurs when a quantity increases by the same factor over a particular period of time.

EXAMPLE

A colony of bacteria that begins with 100 specimens doubles in size every hour. What function models the colony's rate of growth?

If the colony begins with 100 specimens, the equation after it has doubled in size can be given by:

$$y = 100 \times 2$$

That's the number that will double in the next hour, meaning that after two hours, the number of bacteria will be:

$$y = 100 \times 2 \times 2$$

Following this pattern, you can see that you are multiplying the original number by increasing powers of 2. You can create a general function for this that looks like this:

$$y = 100 \times 2^x$$

Where x stands for the number of hours the bacteria have been multiplying.

Exponential functions create graphs that look like this:

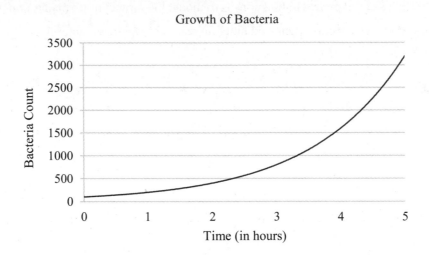

Growth of Bacteria

Exponential curves look similar to one half of a parabola. They're smooth curves that curve up slowly at first and become increasingly steep. They also don't reverse direction; one end is always going up and the other is always going down. If you see this shape on the SAT you'll know it represents exponential growth.

EQUATION COMPARISON

Linear, quadratic, and exponential functions can all be used to model situations. Here is a table and a graph comparing examples of the first few values of each of these types:

x	Linear: $y = 3x + 5$	Quadratic: $y = x^2 + 5$	Exponential: $y = 2^x + 4$
0	5	5	5
1	8	6	6
2	11	9	8
3	14	14	12
4	17	21	20
5	20	30	36

Notice that the linear function grows the fastest at the start, and the quadratic function catches up first. But, by the end, the exponential function is both the biggest and growing the fastest. The following graph shows the comparison of these three equation types:

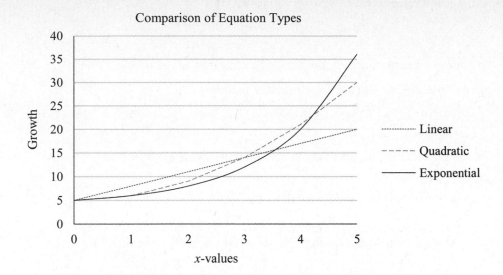

Comparison of Equation Types

Part 6 Practice: Applications of Functions

1. The volume V of a basin of water, in liters at time t, is given by the equation $V = t^2 - 24t + 144$. Time is measured in seconds. How many seconds will it take for the basin to be empty?

Questions 2–3 refer to the following situation.

A watchmaker finds that the revenue in thousands of dollars, R, which she makes on watches is related to the price in dollars of the watches, p, according to the equation:

$$R = -p^2 + 9p - 20$$

2. What is the lowest whole dollar amount she can charge without losing money?

3. What is the highest whole dollar amount she can charge without losing money?

Questions 4–6 refer to the following situation.

Paul throws a book straight up in the air. The height h of the book at time t is given by $h = -t^2 + 3t + 4$, where h is measured in meters.

4. How far from the floor was Paul holding the book when he threw it?

5. At what time does the book fall to the floor?

6. At what time does it reach the same height from which he threw it?

Questions 7–9 refer to the following situation:

Every year for the past ten years, the population of bats in a nearby mountain range has been 1.2 larger than it was the year before.

7. If there were originally 40 bats, what is the function that models this pattern?

8. How many bats are there now? Round to the nearest integer.

9. If this pattern continues, how many bats will there be in 9 years? Round to the nearest integer.

10. A fountain shoots water up to 25 feet into the air. If the water takes 5 seconds to fall back to the ground from its highest point, write a function that models the water's height h at time t.

ANSWERS: APPLICATIONS OF FUNCTIONS

1. 12

2. $4

3. $5

4. 4 meters

5. 4 seconds

6. 3 seconds

7. 40×1.2^t

8. 248

9. 1,278

10. $h = -t^2 + 10t$

PRACTICE SET

In this part, you'll find 30 SAT-style questions to practice the Passport to Advanced Math topics you learned in this section. Check your answers with the answer key that follows. For any question that you get wrong, identify the topic of the question, and then review the part of this section that covers that topic.

1. What is the sum of $x^2 + 8x + 3$ and $x^2 - 7x + 5$?

   (A) $x^2 + 15x - 8$

   (B) $x^2 + 15x + 2$

   (C) $2x^2 + x + 8$

   (D) $2x^2 - x + 2$

2. If $x^2 - 6x + 9 = 0$, what is the value of x?

   (A) 2

   (B) 3

   (C) 6

   (D) 9

$$x^2 + 24 = 28$$

3. For the equation above, what is the value of x^4?

   (A) 4

   (B) 8

   (C) 16

   (D) 64

4. At time $t = 0$, Steven kicks a soccer ball. The equation for the height of the soccer ball above the ground is $h = t^2 - 6t$. How many seconds does it take for the ball fall back to the ground?

(A) 3

(B) 4

(C) 5

(D) 6

$$f(x) = x^2 + 1$$

5. For the function above, what is the value of $f(f(3))$?

(A) 81

(B) 82

(C) 100

(D) 101

6. If $2^4 \times 8^x = 2^{16}$, what is the value of x?

(A) 2

(B) 4

(C) 8

(D) 16

7. What is the value of x for the equation $2x^2 + 16x = -32$?

(A) −4

(B) −2

(C) 4

(D) 8

8. Outdoor temperature, in degrees Fahrenheit, is measured from 8:00 PM to 8:00 AM the next day. The temperature T was related to the number of hours after 8:00 PM, h, according to the equation $T = h^2 - 12h + 46$. At what time was the temperature 10 degrees Fahrenheit?

(A) 12:00 AM

(B) 2:00 AM

(C) 4:00 AM

(D) 6:00 AM

Day	Number of Bacteria
0	300
1	600
2	1200
3	2400
4	4800
5	9600

9. A biologist is growing a colony of bacteria. The table above summarizes the daily number of bacteria in the colony. Which expression represents the number of bacteria in the colony after x days?

(A) 300×2^x

(B) 2^x

(C) $x^2 + 300$

(D) 600^x

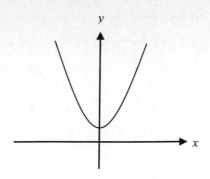

10. Which equation corresponds to the graph above?

(A) $y = 2x + 2$

(B) $y = x^2 + 2$

(C) $y = x^2 - 2$

(D) $y = (x + 2)(x - 2)$

11. How many times does the graph of $y = 4x^2 - 16x - 20$ intersect the graph of $y = 5x + 6$ in the xy-plane?

(A) 0

(B) 1

(C) 2

(D) 3

$$y = (x - 4)^2 + 9$$
$$y = 2x$$

12. Two equations are given above. What is the value of x?

(A) 4

(B) 5

(C) 6

(D) 9

13. If $f(x) = x^2 + 7$ and $g(x) = -f(x) + 3$, what is $g(4)$?

(A) 26

(B) 19

(C) −1

(D) −20

14. How many times do the equations $y = 3x^2 - 4x + 3$ and $y = 2x$ intersect in the xy-plane?

(A) 0

(B) 1

(C) 2

(D) 3

15. If b and c are positive integers, which of the graphs below represents
$y = -x^2 - 2bx - b^2 + c$?

(A)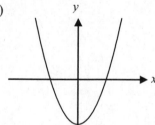

(C)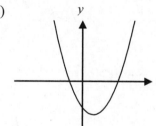

(B)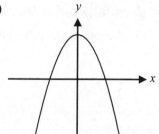

(D)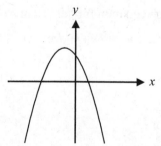

16. Natalie has found that she gets the highest grade after studying for 10 hours. If her model is quadratic and predicts a grade of zero for $0h$ and $20h$, what is a possible equation for the number of hours spent studying, t, and the grade, g?

(A) $g = t - 20$

(B) $g = -t(t - 20)$

(C) $g = -(t - 20)$

(D) $g = t(t - 20)$

$$\frac{x^2 - 9}{x^2 + 6x + 9}$$

17. Which of the following expressions is equal to the expression above?

(A) $\dfrac{x + 3}{x - 3}$

(B) $\dfrac{x - 3}{x + 3}$

(C) $\dfrac{1}{x + 3}$

(D) $\dfrac{9}{x - 3}$

$$h = -(t - 5)^2 + 3$$

18. The equation for the height h of a toy rocket above the top of its launch platform at time t is shown above. At what time will the rocket attain its maximum height?

(A) 3

(B) 5

(C) 8

(D) 10

$$\frac{x^2 - 2x - 15}{x + 3} = 0$$

19. Which of the following answers represents the solution for x in the equation above?

   (A) 5
   (B) 0
   (C) –3
   (D) –5

20. If the expression $\frac{x^2 + 2x - 3}{x^2 + 3}$ is equal to $\frac{A}{x^2 + 3} - 1$, what is A in terms of x?

   (A) $x + 4$
   (B) $x^2 + 3$
   (C) $2x^2 + x$
   (D) $2x^2 + 2x$

GRID-INS

21. John can run 20 meters in 8 seconds. Sheryl is twice as fast as John, and Barry is twice as fast as Sheryl. How many seconds does it take Barry to run 200 meters?

$$\sqrt{x + 1} - 5 = x - c$$

22. If the values of x in the equation above are 0 or -1, what is the value of c?

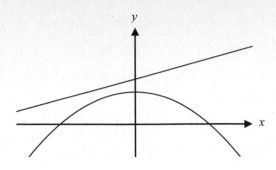

23. A linear and a quadratic equation are graphed above. How many solutions are there for the two equations?

$$y = 2x - 2$$
$$z = 2x^2 - 2x$$

24. For the system of equations above, if $z - y = 0$, what is the value for x?

25. What is the product of the values of x, in the equation $(2x + 10)(x - 2) = -20$?

$$f(x) = \frac{x^3 - 3x^2 + 4x + 4}{x + 1}$$

26. Based on the function above, what is the value for $f(-2)$?

27. If $2x^2 - 7x + 6 = 0$, what is the sum of the solutions for x?

$$x^2 + px + q = 0$$

28. If the only solution for x in the equation above is 5, what is the value of $p + q$?

29. The owner of a store has found that the weekly profit D in dollars for a certain product is given by $D = -p^2 + 12p - 35$, where p is the product's price, in dollars. What integer dollar value for p would result in a profit for the store?

$$\frac{6}{x+4} + 1 = \frac{6}{x+1}$$

30. If $x > 0$, what is the value of x in the equation above?

ANSWER KEY

1. C
2. B
3. C
4. D
5. D
6. B
7. A
8. B
9. A
10. B
11. C
12. B
13. D
14. B
15. D
16. B
17. B
18. B
19. A
20. D
21. 20
22. 4
23. 0
24. 1
25. 0
26. 24
27. 7/2
28. 15
29. 6
30. 2

SECTION 6
PROBLEM SOLVING AND DATA ANALYSIS

In this section, we'll talk about measurements and conversions of quantities between different units. You will learn how to read different types of diagrams as well as how to interpret and analyze data.

We will cover the following topics:

- Measurements and Units
- Properties of Data
- Ratios, Rates, and Proportions
- Statistics and Probability
- Modeling and Evidence Data
- Using Data

MEASUREMENT AND UNITS
PART 1

You use **units** in many aspects of daily life. The distance you travel to school, the time you spend studying, and the price of this book are all described in terms of units. Units like miles, feet, and meters are units of distance. Seconds, days, and years are units of time. Dollars and cents are units of money. A dozen is a unit that refers to a group of 12 things.

There are two systems of units frequently used to measure mass, length, and volume. The imperial system is used frequently in the United States. The following table summarizes common units in imperial units of measurement:

Weight	Length	Volume
Ounce	Inch	Cup
Pound: 16 ounces	Foot: 12 inches	Pint: 2 cups
Ton: 2000 pounds	Yard: 3 feet	Quart: 2 pints (4 cups)
	Mile: 1760 yards (5280 feet)	Gallon: 4 quarts (16 cups)

The **metric system** is commonly used internationally and in the scientific community. In the metric system, mass is measured in grams (g), length is measured in meters (m), and volume is measured in liters (l).

The metric system uses prefixes, or different word beginnings, to indicate multiples of 10. These prefixes can be combined with any of the units (grams, meters, or liters). Each prefix has a short form that is combined with the unit abbreviation. The following table summarizes the metric system:

Factor	Prefix	Short Form
1000	Kilo	k
100	Hecto	h
10	Deca	D
0.1	Deci	d
0.01	Centi	c
0.001	Milli	m

For example, a kilogram (kg) is 1,000 grams, a centimeter (cm) is 0.01 meters, and a milliliter (ml) is 0.001 liters.

Here's a quick way to remember the correct order of prefixes. If you write out the prefix abbreviations from biggest to smallest, you'll get:

$$k \quad h \quad D \quad d \quad c \quad m$$

A common phrase to remember this order is **K**ing **H**enry **D**ied **D**rinking **C**hocolate **M**ilk.

CONVERSIONS

Some problems on the SAT will require you to convert between different units. To do this, set up a ratio between the two units so that the numerator and the denominator are equal. For example, let's look at converting kilometers (km) to meters (m). Since 1 km = 1,000 m, the ratio of meters to kilometers is:

$$\frac{1{,}000 \text{ m}}{1 \text{ km}}$$

This can also be written as a ratio of kilometers to meters:

$$\frac{1{,}000 \text{ m}}{1 \text{ km}} = \frac{1 \text{ km}}{1{,}000 \text{ m}}$$

The ratio between two units is called a **conversion factor**. Conversion factors are always equal to 1 because the numerator is equal to the denominator.

To convert a measurement into a different value, multiply it by the conversion factor with the desired units on top and the current units on the bottom. For example, to convert 16 kilometers you would use the following equation:

$$\frac{16 \text{ km}}{1} \times \frac{1,000 \text{ m}}{1 \text{ km}} = 16,000 \text{ m}$$

When you multiply a measurement by a conversion factor, the old units cancel out in the numerator and denominator. You are left with the new units:

$$\frac{16 \cancel{\text{ km}}}{1} \times \frac{1,000 \text{ m}}{1 \cancel{\text{ km}}} = 16,000 \text{ m}$$

Always check that the units cancel out correctly. You should be able to cancel out all units in the conversion except for the units of the answer.

You may also have to convert between units in different systems on the SAT. The SAT problems will give you the necessary conversion factors.

EXAMPLE

How many centimeters are in half a mile? (1 mile is equal to 1.6 kilometers.)

This problem requires multiple conversions. First, convert 0.5 miles to kilometers:

$$0.5 \text{ miles} \times \frac{1.6 \text{ km}}{1 \text{ mile}} = 0.8 \text{ km}$$

Now convert 0.8 kilometers to centimeters. It may be easiest to convert first to meters, then centimeters like this:

$$0.8 \text{ km} \times \frac{1,000 \text{ m}}{1 \text{ km}} \times \frac{100 \text{ cm}}{1 \text{ m}} = 80,000 \text{ cm}$$

Half a mile is equal to 80,000 centimeters.

COMPOUND UNITS

A car's speedometer measures its speed in miles per hour and kilometers per hour. Gas mileage is measured in miles per gallon. These quantities have **compound units**, or units that combine multiple measurements. Speed depends on measurements of both distance and time. Gas mileage depends on measurements of distance and volume of gas consumed.

When you use or convert compound measurements, pay extra attention to the units of quantities and answers. Convert one unit at a time. For example, speed is always distance divided by time. When you convert speed using different units, check that the new units are also distance over time.

EXAMPLE

What is 15 m/s in km/hr?

You can solve this using the same conversion method you practiced earlier:

$$\frac{15 \text{ m}}{\text{s}} \times \frac{1 \text{ km}}{1{,}000 \text{ m}} \times \frac{60 \text{ s}}{1 \text{ min}} \times \frac{60 \text{ min}}{1 \text{ hr}} = \frac{54 \text{ km}}{\text{hr}}$$

15 m/s is equal to 54 km/hr. Both m/s and km/hr are correct units of speed because they are units of distance over time.

WORD PROBLEMS

Units and measurement often come up in SAT word problems. Some of the problems will involve conversions and compound units. Most of the problems that you will solve will be either distance and rate problems, or geometry and measurement problems. Here is an example of a geometry and measurement problem:

EXAMPLE

A wooden cube has a side length of 20 cm. Its density is 0.65 g/cm³. What is the mass of the block in kilograms? (Density is equal to mass divided by volume.)

Your first step is finding the volume of the block. The volume of a cube is equal to its side length cubed, so the volume of the block is equal to:

$$\text{volume} = (20 \text{ cm})^3 = 8{,}000 \text{ cm}^3$$

Now you can find the mass of the block through the density formula in the question. You can re-arrange that formula in order to solve for mass:

$$\text{density} = \frac{\text{mass}}{\text{volume}}$$

$$\text{mass} = \text{density} \times \text{volume}$$

Just plug in the values that you have for density and volume:

$$mass = \frac{0.65\text{g}}{\text{cm}^3} \times 8{,}000 \text{ cm}^3 = 5{,}200 \text{ g}$$

Now you have calculated that the mass of the block is 5,200 grams. The last step is converting the mass of the block from grams to kilograms:

$$5{,}200 \text{ g} \times \frac{1 \text{ kg}}{1{,}000 \text{ g}} = 5.2 \text{ kg}$$

The mass of the block is 5.2 kg.

EXAMPLE

Now let's take a look at a speed and distance problem:

A train travels from Toronto to Hamilton, a distance of 72 km. The train travels at an average speed of 36 km/hr. How many hours did the trip take?

To solve this problem, all you need to use is the average speed as a conversion factor:

$$72 \text{ km} \times \frac{1 \text{ hr}}{36 \text{ km}} = 2 \text{ hours}$$

Since the kilometer units cancel, you are left with your answer of 2 hours.

Here is an important formula to remember when answering speed and distance questions:

$$\text{distance} = \text{rate} \times \text{time}$$

You could also solve the question above using this formula. Just plug in 72 km for distance and 42 km/hr for rate, and then solve for time:

$$72 \text{ km} = 36 \text{ km/hr} \times \text{time}$$

$$\text{time} = \frac{72 \text{ km}}{36 \text{ km/hr}} = 2 \text{ hours}$$

Using this formula, you get the same answer: the trip took 2 hours.

PART 1 PRACTICE: MEASUREMENT AND UNITS

1. How many milliliters are in 0.65 liters?

2. How many millimeters are there in 18 kilometers?

3. How many inches are there in 2.4 yards?

4. How many seconds are there in 0.8 hours?

5. Mr. and Mrs. Liu are covering their living room floor with tiles. The tiles they are using cost $5 per square foot. If the room is 10 feet by 12 feet, how much will they spend on tiles?

6. Tyler went for a 20 km bike ride. If he rode for an hour and 20 minutes, what was his average speed in kilometers per hour?

7. To train for an upcoming 10 km race, Mariam ran 5 km to the post office and back. If it took her 25 minutes to run there and 30 minutes to run back, what was her average pace over her whole run, in minutes per kilometer?

8. Alex drove 6 miles from his house to the grocery store at an average speed of 22 mph. On the way back, Alex drove this same distance at an average speed of 33 mph. What was his average speed for the round trip?

9. The density of iron is 7.87 g/cm³. What is the mass, in grams, of a block of iron with dimensions of 3 cm by 5 cm by 6 cm?

10. The density of silver is 10.5 g/cm³. The density of gold is 19.3 g/cm³. What volume of gold, rounded to the nearest tenth of a cubic centimeter, has the same mass as 100 cm³ of silver?

ANSWER KEY: MEASUREMENTS AND UNITS

1. 650

2. 18,000,000

3. 86.4

4. 2,880

5. $600

6. 15 km/hour

7. 5.5 min/km

8. 26.4 mph

9. 708.3 g

10. 54.4 cm^3

PROPERTIES OF DATA

PART 2

Data sets are not very useful unless you know how to interpret them. In order to draw conclusions about sets of data, you need to be able to determine the range, mean, median, mode, and standard deviation of data sets. You'll also need to be able to interpret data presented visually in a chart or a graph. Let's look at these concepts and how to use them.

RANGE

The **range** of a set of data is the difference between its biggest and smallest values. All data in a set of data fall within the set's range. To find the range of any set of data, put the data in numerical order and subtract the smallest from the biggest value.

EXAMPLE

Dmitri's History Quiz Scores				
Quiz 1	Quiz 2	Quiz 3	Quiz 4	Quiz 5
87	83	94	87	90

What is the range of Dmitri's quiz scores in the chart above?

To find the range of these scores, let's first put them in numerical order:

$$83, 87, 87, 90, 94$$

Dmitri's lowest score was 83 and his highest was 94, so his range is the difference between these two:

$$\text{Range} = 94 - 83 = 11$$

Dmitri's scores fall within a range of 11 points.

MEAN

The **mean** of a set of data is the same as its **average**—it represents a typical value in a data set. To calculate the mean or average of a set of data, add up all of the data values and divide by the total number of data points:

$$\text{Mean} = \frac{\text{Sum of data values}}{\text{Total number of values}}$$

EXAMPLE

What is the mean of Dmitri's quiz scores from the previous chart?

First add up all his scores. Then divide by the number of quizzes:

$$\frac{87 + 83 + 94 + 87 + 90}{5} = \frac{441}{5} = 88.2$$

Dmitri's average score is 88.2.

MEDIAN

The **median** refers to the value that is exactly in the middle of a set of data. To find the median, put all of the data in numerical order and locate the middle number.

EXAMPLE

What is the median of Dmitri's quiz scores?

Put the scores in numerical order:

$$83, 87, 87, 90, 94$$

The middle number in this data set is 87, so Dmitri's median history quiz score is 87.

What if your data set has an even number of values, so there is no middle number? In this case, the median is the average of the two numbers closest to the middle.

Dmitri is able to score a 99 on his sixth history quiz. What is the median of his new set of scores?

The data set will now be:

$$83, 87, 87, 90, 94, 99$$

There is no number in the middle of this set of data, but the two numbers closest to the middle are 87 and 90. To find the median, take the average of these two numbers:

$$\frac{87 + 90}{2} = 88.5$$

The average of 87 and 90 is 88.5, so 88.5 would be the median of Dmitri's six quiz scores.

MODE

The **mode** of a set of data refers to the value that occurs most frequently. A set of data can have one or more modes if there are one or more numbers that occur more frequently than any other number. A set of data may have no mode if all values occur the same number of times.

EXAMPLE

Dmitri and his classmates received the following scores on their last history quiz: 91, 88, 94, 90, 82, 79, 84, 94, 85, 88, 93, 97, 92, 80, 96. Identify the mode or modes in this data set.

The answer to this question is easiest to find out if we put the data in numerical order:

$$79, 80, 82, 84, 85, 88, 88, 90, 91, 92, 93, 94, 94, 96, 97$$

Both 88 and 94 occur two times, and the rest of the values only occur once. Therefore, 88 and 94 are the two modes of these quiz scores.

STANDARD DEVIATION

Standard deviation measures how much the values in a set of data vary from its mean. The greater the standard deviation, the farther the data points are from the mean. For example, take a look at these two lists of data:

List A: 1, 2, 3, 10, 17, 18, 19

List B: 7, 8, 9, 10, 11, 12, 13

Although these two lists both have a mean of 10, List A has a higher standard deviation because the points are more spread out.

Standard deviation can be found with the following expression, where m is the mean of the data set, n is the number of data points, and each value of x represents an individual data point:

$$\sqrt{\frac{(x_1 - m)^2 + (x_2 - m)^2 + (x_3 - m)^2 + \dots + (x_n - m)^2}{n}}$$

To use this formula, first square the difference between each data point and the mean. Then, add together these squares, divide by the number of data points, and take the square root of the result.

EXAMPLE

What is the standard deviation of the data set {1, 3, 6, 8, 12}?

First, calculate the mean:

$$m = \frac{1 + 3 + 6 + 8 + 12}{5}$$

$$m = 6$$

For each data point, find its difference from the mean, square this difference, and add together the squares:

$$(1-6)^2 + (3-6)^2 + (6-6)^2 + (8-6)^2 + (12-6)^2$$
$$= 25 + 9 + 0 + 4 + 36$$
$$= 74$$

Then, take the average of the differences by dividing the sum by the number of data points:

$$\frac{74}{5} = 14.8$$

And finally, take the square root:

$$\sqrt{14.8} \approx 3.85$$

The standard deviation of this data set is about 3.85.

You can also say that a data point is a certain number of standard deviations away from the mean. For example, let's look at the first number in the data set above—the number 1. The mean of the data set is 6, so 1 is 5 units away from the mean. In order to express this difference in terms of standard deviations, just divide by the standard deviation of the data set, which is 3.85:

$$\frac{5}{3.85} \approx 1.3$$

1 is approximately 1.3 standard deviations from the mean.

CHARTS

One way to make properties of data easy to see is to display them as a chart or graph. When you see a problem with a chart or graph, examine it carefully to make sure you understand it. Ask yourself the following questions:

- What is the main purpose of this chart or graph?
- What is being measured?
- What is the **scale**, or what units are being used?

Let's use these questions to analyze the chart below:

Population by Town, 1960-2000			
	Population (in thousands)		
Town	1960	1980	2000
Cedarville	72	83	104
Franklin	80	82	73
Pine Ridge	121	136	143

- What is the main purpose of this chart or graph? From the title, you can tell that the chart above shows the population of several towns from 1960 to 2000.
- What is being measured? The chart is comparing the population of these three different towns (Cedarville, Franklin, and Pine Ridge) at three different dates (1960, 1980, and 2000).
- What is the scale, or what units are being used? The numbers give the population of each town for each year. Notice that the data is represented "in thousands."

Now that you are familiar with this data in chart format, let's take a look at how it might be represented in different types of graphs. The most common types of graphs on the SAT include pie charts, bar graphs, line graphs, and histograms.

PIE CHARTS

A **pie chart** compares different sections of data as fractions out of a whole. A circle represents the total amount, and differently sized sections of that circle represent parts out of the total amount. A legend or labels on the chart will explain what data each section represents.

Let's look again at the populations of Cedarville, Franklin, and Pine Ridge in 1960. Here is a representation of the data as a pie chart:

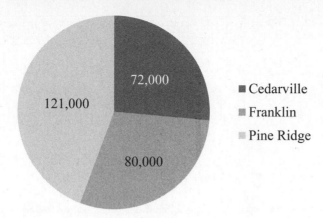

Population Breakdown by Town in 1960

- Cedarville
- Franklin
- Pine Ridge

The title of this graph tells you that you are looking at the population of the three towns in 1960. The legend tells you that each of the slices in this pie chart represents a town, and the entire pie chart represents the total population of all three towns. The data labels for each slice also tell you exactly how many people lived in each town.

You can also estimate the relative proportion of residents by looking at the sizes of their slices in the pie chart. You can tell that slightly more than a quarter of the people lived in Cedarville, slightly less than a third lived in Franklin, and slightly less than half lived in Pine Ridge.

BAR GRAPHS

A **bar graph** uses bars of different lengths to visually compare different sizes of data. Bar graphs represent data along two axes using vertical or horizontal bars. If a bar graph uses differently colored or patterned bars, the legend will explain what other variables these colors or patterns represent.

The data from the chart we saw earlier can be represented in a bar graph:

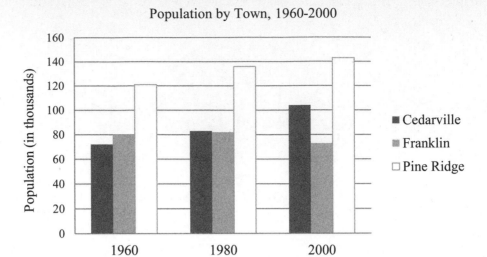

Population by Town, 1960-2000

In this graph, the legend tells you that the different-colored bars represent different towns. These are grouped together at each date along the horizontal axis. The vertical axis displays what is being measured: population. Again, you are told that the units are in thousands.

Because numbers are given in thousands, each tick mark along the vertical axis represents 20,000 people. With these tick marks, you can tell that the population of Pine Ridge in 1960 was about 120,000, and by 1980 it had grown by about 15,000. You can also tell that the populations of Cedarville and Franklin were relatively similar in 1960 and 1980, but they differed by about 30,000 people in 2000.

LINE GRAPHS

A **line graph** uses a line or several lines to visually represent changes in amounts, usually over time. Like bar graphs, line graphs also represent data along two axes. The horizontal x-axis displays different dates or time periods, and the vertical y-axis displays the amounts being measured.

Here is the population data for Cedarville, Franklin, and Pine Ridge as a line graph:

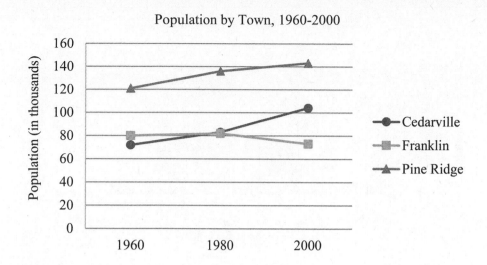

Population by Town, 1960-2000

The legend tells you that each line on this graph represents the population of a different town. Just like our bar graph, the scale of the *y*-axis tells us that each tick mark represents 20,000 people.

Because this graph displays a line across the whole time period, you can use the graph to make estimates about population at specific years. For example, you don't know the exact population of Pine Ridge in 1970, but by looking at the middle of the line drawn from 1960 to 1980, you can estimate that the population was around 130,000. You can also use the slopes of line segments to determine the rate of change between two data points.

HISTOGRAMS

A **histogram** is a graphical distribution of data, grouped together by values or ranges of values. By grouping the data together, a histogram displays the **frequency** of those groupings, which is the number of times those values or ranges occurred in the data set. A histogram is another tool that allows you to graphically calculate specific statistical information such as range, mean, median, and mode. Furthermore, the graphical representation of data often allows you to quickly find or estimate some of this information without calculation.

Here is an example of a histogram:

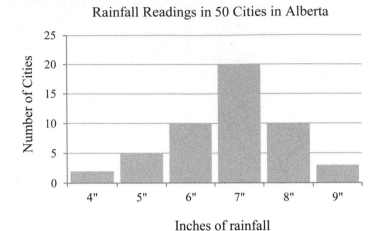

Rainfall Readings in 50 Cities in Alberta

The x-axis displays the different rainfall readings (in inches) that were recorded. The y-axis displays the number of cities that recorded each reading. This information tells you the frequency with which each reading occurred. For example, the graph shows that 20 cities recorded 7" of rainfall, but only about 2 cities recorded 4" of rainfall.

It is easy to find the mode and the range of the data from the histogram. 7" was the most frequent value recorded, so 7 is the mode of this data. To find the range of this data, subtract the smallest rainfall reading (4") from the largest (9"): $9 - 4 = 5$. The range of the data is 5.

You can use the histogram to calculate the mean. First, you need to multiply each grouping by its frequency and add those products together:

$$(4 \times 2) + (5 \times 5) + (6 \times 10) + (7 \times 20) + (8 \times 10) + (9 \times 3) = 340$$

You can find the total number of readings in the graph by adding together all of the frequencies for each rainfall reading:

$$2 + 5 + 10 + 20 + 10 + 3 = 50$$

Finally, divide the sum of all of the data by the number of values:

$$\frac{340}{50} = 6.8$$

The mean rainfall reading in this data is 6.8 inches.

You can also find the median from the histogram. Because the median is the middle number in a data set, you need to find which rainfall reading would represent the middle number if all 50 readings were arranged in order from least to greatest. Because you have 50 readings, the middle number would be the average of the 25th and 26th readings.

Which group on the histogram would contain the 25th reading? To find this, start adding up the frequencies of each grouping, from left to right, and stop when you get above 25. There were 2 readings of 4", 5 readings of 5", and 10 readings of 6". This is 17 readings total, which is still less than 25. However, there were 20 readings of 7", which brings you to 37 readings total. Therefore, the 25th and 26th readings must both be in the 7" group. You can conclude that the median rainfall reading is 7".

PART 2 PRACTICE: PROPERTIES OF DATA

1. A set of five numbers had an average of 14. When two of these numbers were removed, the remaining three numbers had an average of 13. What was the sum of the two numbers that were removed?

2. William measured the heights of his five friends in inches. His results were 60, 62, 63, 66, and 69. What is the standard deviation of the heights of his friends, to the nearest hundredth of an inch?

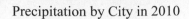

Precipitation by City in 2010

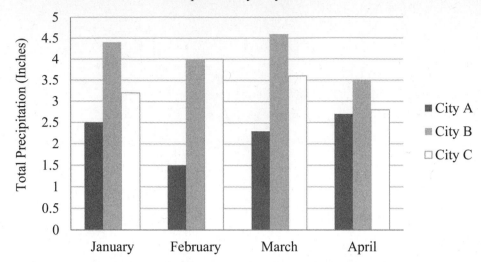

3. According to the graph above, during which month did City B experience about twice as much precipitation as City A?

Survey of 200 Students' Favorite Sports

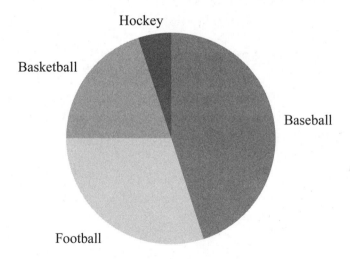

4. According to the diagram above, approximately how many surveyed students reported either hockey or basketball as their favorite sport?

For questions 5 and 6, refer to the following graph.

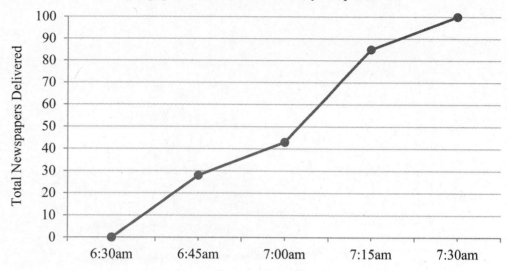

Newspapers Delivered on Anthony's Paper Route

5. Which of the following is the best estimate for the number of newspapers that Anthony delivered between 7:15 and 7:30am?

(A) 15
(B) 45
(C) 75
(D) 100

6. Over which 15-minute time period did Anthony deliver newspapers at the fastest rate?

(A) 6:30am – 6:45am
(B) 6:45am – 7:00am
(C) 7:00am – 7:15am
(D) 7:15am – 7:30am

For questions 7-9, refer to the following information.

The histogram below shows the test scores of students in a writing class.

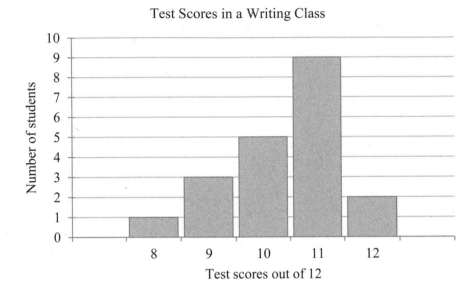

7. What is the median test score?

8. What is the mode of this data set?

9. What is the mean of the test scores?

Highway Repair Costs by County in 2011		
County	Highway Repair Costs	Miles of Highway in County
Pinellas	$45,000	300
Hillsborough	$169,000	1,300
Glendale	$81,000	450

10. Pinellas County wants to reduce the amount of money it spends repairing each mile of highway. If Pinellas County had repaired its highways at the same repair cost per mile as Hillsborough County in the chart above, how much money, in dollars, would Pinellas County have saved in 2011?

Answers: Properties of Data

1. 31
2. 3.16
3. March
4. 100
5. A
6. C
7. 11
8. 11
9. 10.4
10. $6000

RATIOS, PERCENTAGES, PROPORTIONS, AND RATES

Ratios, percentages, proportions, and rates compare two or more quantities, either by comparing parts to a whole or by representing a relationship between the quantities. In Section 3, we covered some basic properties of these topics. However, some of the problems involving these topics on the SAT will require more steps or more complex algebra than the examples in Section 3. Let's see what this looks like.

FRACTIONS AND PROPORTIONS

Word problems with fractions and proportions will often require you to multiply a number by a proportion or to find an equivalent proportion. To find a fraction of a number, multiply the number by the fraction:

$$\frac{3}{8} \text{ of } 24 = \frac{3}{8} \times 24 = 9$$

You can find equivalent proportions by setting them equal to each other. For example, if 12 is $\frac{3}{4}$ of x, you can find x by setting up the equivalent proportions:

$$\frac{12}{x} = \frac{3}{4}$$

Which you can solve by cross-multiplying:

$$3x = 4 \times 12$$
$$x = 16$$

Here is an example of a word problem involving fractions and proportions:

> Four friends eat a whole pizza. Shelley had $\frac{1}{5}$th of the pizza, Ming had 4 slices, Lily had 3 slices, and Adam had 1 slice. How many slices did Shelley have?

To find the number of slices that Shelley had, you first need to find the total number of slices in the pizza. The four friends ate the whole pizza and Shelley ate $\frac{1}{5}$th, so Ming, Lily, and Adam must have eaten $1 - \frac{1}{5} = \frac{4}{5}$ of the pizza. This means that $4 + 3 + 1 = 8$ slices make up $\frac{4}{5}$ of the pizza. You can write this as a proportion:

$$\frac{8 \text{ slices}}{\text{Total slices}} = \frac{4}{5}$$

Then, cross-multiply to find the total slices in the pizza:

$$40 \text{ slices} = 4 \times \text{Total slices}$$
$$\text{Total slices} = 10$$

Now, you can calculate the number of slices that Shelley ate by setting up a proportion and cross-multiplying:

$$\frac{\text{Shelley's slices}}{10 \text{ total slices}} = \frac{1}{5}$$
$$5 \times \text{Shelley's slices} = 10$$
$$\text{Shelley's slices} = 2$$

Shelley ate 2 slices of pizza.

RATIOS

Ratio problems will involve applying ratios to quantities or finding ratios from quantities. It is important to remember that ratios are different than fractions or proportions: they compare a part to a part instead of a part to a whole. To find the whole, add all of the parts. For example, the ratio 2:5:3 has a whole of $2 + 5 + 3 = 10$.

Remember that you can convert ratios to fractions. Each part of the ratio becomes a numerator, and the denominator is the whole. If your ratio is 1:3:6, for example, the denominator will be $1 + 3 + 6 = 10$ and the fractions would be $\frac{1}{10}$, $\frac{3}{10}$, and $\frac{6}{10}$.

It may help to use variables when working with ratios. If you know the total quantity that the ratio describes, you can write it as the sum of each part multiplied by a variable.

Here is an example of a solution that uses a variable:

> The measures of the two acute angles of a right triangle have the ratio 11:4. What is the difference between the two angle measures?

To solve this problem, you need to recall some geometric properties of triangles. First, the sum of the angle measures in a triangle is 180°. Since this is a right triangle, one of those angles is 90°, so the remaining acute angles must have a sum of $180° - 90° = 90°$.

You also know that one angle measure is equal to 11 times an integer, and the second angle measure is equal to 4 times the same integer. If you call the unknown integer x, you could represent the two angle measures as which $11x$ and $4x$. Because you know that the two angles add to $90°$, you can set up an equation to solve for x:

$$11x + 4x = 90°$$
$$15x = 90°$$
$$x = \frac{90°}{15}$$
$$x = 6°$$

Now, you can plug the value of x back into your expressions for each angle measure: $11x = 66°$ and $4x = 24°$. The question asks for the difference between these two angle measures:

$$66° - 24° = 42°$$

Your answer is 42 degrees.

PERCENTAGES

These word problems will give you a mix of percentages and quantities. If you have to find a percent of a whole number, like 12% of 4, multiply the percentage by the whole: $4 \times 0.12 = 0.48$.

If you are given a quantity that is a percent of a whole, divide the quantity by the percentage to get the whole. For example, if 3 is 5% of x, then $x = \dfrac{3}{0.05} = 60$.

Here is an example of a word problem with percentages:

> Two sweaters have the same original price. Then, one sweater is marked up 20% and the other is put on sale for 20% off. The difference between the new prices is $9.60. What was the original price of each sweater?

Let's say that p represent the original price of each sweater. The marked-up price of the first sweater is 20% greater, so you could represent this by $1.2p$. The sale price of the second sweater is 20% less, so you could present this by $0.8p$. You know that the difference between these prices is $9.60, so you can set up an equation to solve for p:

$$1.2p - 0.8p = 9.60$$

$$0.4p = 9.60$$

$$p = \frac{9.60}{0.4}$$

$$p = 24$$

The original price of each sweater was $24.

RATES

Rate problems come up frequently on the SAT. Remember that rates compare two related quantities, like distance and time. You can often set up rate problems as equivalent proportions. Be sure to write the proportions so that the two rates have the same units, and make sure that your answer is in the correct units as well.

Here is an example of a rate problem that is solved using proportions:

> Paola is training for a 10 km race. She can run 5 miles in 36 minutes. If she keeps this pace, what will her race time be? (1 mile is equal to approximately 1.6 kilometers)

First you should find Paola's pace in minutes per mile:

$$\frac{36 \text{ min}}{5 \text{ miles}} = \frac{7.2 \text{ min}}{\text{mile}}$$

Since the length of the race is in kilometers, you need to convert the pace to minutes per kilometer:

$$\frac{7.2 \text{ min}}{\text{mile}} \times \frac{1 \text{ mile}}{1.6 \text{ km}} = \frac{4.5 \text{ min}}{\text{km}}$$

Finally, to find the time it would take Paola to run 10 km, multiply her pace in minutes per km by the distance of the race:

$$10 \text{ km} \times \frac{4.5 \text{ min}}{\text{km}} = 45 \text{ min}$$

Paola's race time would be 45 minutes.

For some rate problems, you will have to combine rates. To combine rates, first make sure that they have the same units. Then add them together in their fraction form with a common denominator. The units of the new rate will be the same as the units of each individual rate.

Here is an example of a combined rate problem:

Rachel can grade 5 tests in 6 minutes and Sebastian can grade 2 tests in 3 minutes. Rachel and Sebastian have 21 tests to grade. If they work together, how long will it take them to grade the tests?

First, you need to find the rate at which Rachel and Sebastian can grade tests separately. Divide the number of tests by the number of minutes: Rachel's rate is $\frac{5}{6}$ tests/min and Sebastian's rate is $\frac{2}{3}$ tests/min. Then, to find their combined rate, you need to add the two rates:

$$\frac{5}{6} + \frac{2}{3} = \frac{5}{6} + \frac{4}{6} = \frac{9}{6} = 1.5$$

Rachel and Sebastian have a combined rate of 1.5 tests per minute. Now you can use this rate to find the time it would take Rachel and Sebastian to grade the 21 tests. Remember to flip the rate so that the unit "tests" cancels:

$$21 \text{ tests} \times \frac{1 \text{ min}}{1.5 \text{ tests}} = 14 \text{ min}$$

It will take Rachel and Sebastian 14 minutes to grade the tests if they work together.

Part 3 Practice: Ratios, Percentages, Proportions, and Rates

1. A jar of buttons contains purple and black buttons. The ratio of purple to black buttons is 4:7. If 5 red buttons are added for every 4 purple buttons that are in the jar, what fraction of the buttons will be purple?

2. The ratio of the width to the height of a rectangle is $x:y$. When the width is doubled and the height is tripled, the rectangle becomes a square. What is x in terms of y?

3. Antony buys an $80 guitar on sale for 10% off. He pays 8% sales tax on the reduced price. How much does Antony pay for the guitar?

4. What percent of 0.1 kilometers is 500 millimeters?

5. A factory produces nails and screws. 4% of the nails produced are defective, and 6% of the screws are defective. If nails and screws are produced in a ratio of 5:3, what percent of the total nails and screws produced are defective?

6. A store sells CDs at 20% off the displayed price. The store buys copies of a CD for $12 each. If the store owner wants to make a 10% profit on the CDs, what price should she list for each CD?

7. If $2x = 5y$ and $4y = 3z$, what is the ratio of x to z?

8. Antja scored the following percentages of correct answers on her first, second, third, and fourth math quizzes: 85, 93, 81, 97. Each quiz had 20% more questions than the previous quiz. What percent of the total number of questions did Antja get correct? Round to the nearest percent.

9. Mark's car has a gas mileage of 36 miles per gallon. Gas costs $2.40 per gallon. How much will Mark pay for gas if he drives 120 miles?

10. Lily and Arjun are filing papers. Lily can file 2 papers every 15 seconds. Together, Lily and Arjun can file 1 paper every 4 seconds. How many minutes would it take Arjun, working alone, to file 21 papers?

Answers: Ratios, Percentages, Proportions, and Rates

1. $\dfrac{1}{4}$

2. $x = 1.5y$

3. $77.76

4. 0.5%

5. 4.75%

6. $16.50

7. 15:8

8. 90%

9. $8.00

10. 3 minutes

PROBABILITY AND STATISTICS
PART 4

If you've ever used a weather forecast or looked up the chance that your favorite sports team will win a game, you have used **probability**. Probability describes how likely something is to happen. On the SAT, you will use probability to solve word problems and problems involving data in charts or graphs. First, let's look at some important terms.

A **set** is a group of things, often numbers. Each number or thing in a set is called an **element**. Sets are often written inside brackets, like this: {–3, 0, 2, 6.6, 100}.

A useful tool for working with sets of numbers is the **Venn diagram**. A Venn diagram uses overlapping circles that demonstrate relationships between sets of numbers. Here is an example of a Venn diagram of two sets:

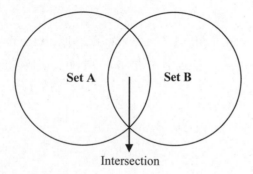

Intersection

Each set is represented by a circle. If the sets share elements, those elements go in the portion of the Venn diagram where the circles overlap: this portion is called the **intersection** of the sets.

If you combine all the numbers in the Venn diagram, you will get the union of the sets. The **union** of two or more sets contains all the elements of all the sets.

At Forestview High School, 60 students are taking math, science, or both. If 50 of these students are taking math and 30 students are taking science, how many are taking both?

You may have noticed that $50 + 30$ is more than 60. This reminds us that some students are taking both math and science, so they are counted in both categories. These students represent the intersection of the two sets. Let's represent the intersection with the variable x. Our Venn Diagram then looks like this:

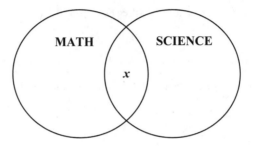

Since 50 students are taking math, you know that the total students in the "MATH" circle must be 50. Since there are x students overlapping both circles, the students only taking "MATH" is $50 - x$ because:

$$x + (50 - x) = 50$$

Notice that 50 are all the students in "MATH", and that this number also includes the students in both "MATH and SCIENCE" (your x variable).

In the same way, the number of students only taking "SCIENCE" is $30 - x$. Our updated Venn diagram is:

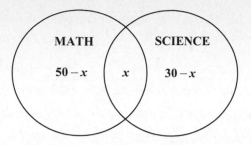

You know that the total number of students is 60. Since this number represents the union of the two sets, it equals the number of students in the three areas:

$$(50 - x) + x + (30 - x) = 60$$

Now you can solve for x:

$$80 - x = 60$$
$$x = 20$$

You have found that the number of students taking both math and science is 20.

THE COUNTING PRINCIPLE

Another type of counting question asks you to come up with the number of possibilities for a given situation. Listing these possibilities can be long and tedious, but luckily there are ways to count them quickly.

The **Counting Principle** tells us how to find the number of possibilities for completing two or more tasks. To find the number of ways you can complete these tasks together, you multiply together the number of ways you can complete each task individually.

EXAMPLE

Christy has two scarves and three hats. She wants to pick one scarf and one hat to wear. How many different combinations of one scarf and one hat could she pick?

Christy is trying to complete two tasks: her first task is to pick a scarf, and her second task is to pick a hat. Christy has 2 ways to complete her first task because she has two scarves she could pick. She has 3 ways to complete her second task because there are three hats she could pick.

To find the number of ways to complete both tasks using the Counting Principle, you multiply the number of ways Christy could complete the first task (2) by the number of ways she could complete the second task (3):

$$\text{number of hats} \times \text{number of scarves} = 2 \times 3 = 6$$

There are 6 different combinations of hats and scarves Christy could choose.

Why does this work? You can diagram this by showing that Christy has two scarves, and that for each scarf she could choose three different hats:

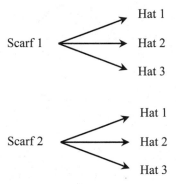

There are two scarf choices and three hat choices for each scarf, so there are $2 \times 3 = 6$ combinations in total.

PERMUTATIONS

Counting problems also require you to think about order. In some cases, the order of the tasks matters. For example, order certainly matters in the result of a race. A series of tasks for which order matters is called a **permutation**.

EXAMPLE

How many different three-digit numbers can you write using the digits 1, 2, and 3, without repeating any digits?

This question involves permutations because the order in which the digits are arranged matters. The number 123 is not the same as 213 or 231. Here are all of the permutations involving these three digits:

123	213	312
132	231	321

There are 6 different numbers possible.

You can quickly find the answer using the Counting Principle. You have 3 choices for the first digit. Because you can't repeat any digits, you have 2 choices left for the second digit, and one choice for the third digit. Multiplying your choices together you get $3 \times 2 \times 1 = 6$ choices. This is the same answer as you found using the table.

Some questions will ask for permutations that are smaller than the number of elements in the set. In other words, the number of slots may be smaller than the number of objects to arrange.

EXAMPLE

To determine the 1st, 2nd, and 3rd prize of a lottery drawing, three tickets are selected one at a time from a pool of 50 total tickets, with no repeats allowed. How many ways can the 3 tickets be selected?

This is a permutation question because the order matters: selecting person A for the 1st prize and person B for the 3rd prize is different than selecting person B for the 1st prize and person A for the 3rd prize.

Since the lottery only has 3 prizes, you only need to find the possible permutations for the 3 prize winners, not for all entries in the lottery. You need to select one 1st, 2nd, and 3rd place winner.

$$50 \times 49 \times 48 = 117{,}600$$

3 tickets can be selected in 117,600 ways.

The problems on the SAT will *not* require you to memorize or use any formulas for permutations or combinations. You will always be able to solve counting or probability problems by writing out the possibilities or by using the Counting Principle.

COMBINATIONS

In some counting problems, order doesn't matter because the result is the same regardless of how objects are arranged. For instance, if you are picking fruit to go in a basket, it doesn't matter whether you pick an apple first and an orange second, or an orange first and an apple second—the contents of your basket will remain the same. A group of events where the order doesn't matter is called a **combination**.

EXAMPLE

Jeff, Annie, Marie, and Tom are members of a soccer team. In how many ways can their coach choose two of them to be midfielders?

If the order that the players were chosen mattered, then you would have the following 12 possibilities:

Jeff and Annie	Jeff and Marie	Jeff and Tom
Annie and Jeff	Annie and Marie	Annie and Tom
Marie and Jeff	Marie and Annie	Marie and Tom
Tom and Jeff	Tom and Annie	Tom and Marie

In this example, however, it doesn't matter in what order the players are chosen:

Jeff and Annie = Annie and Jeff

This is the same for any of the players. You can, therefore, cross out all of the duplicate possibilities on the table:

Jeff and Annie	Jeff and Marie	Jeff and Tom
~~Annie and Jeff~~	Annie and Marie	Annie and Tom
~~Marie and Jeff~~	~~Marie and Annie~~	Marie and Tom
~~Tom and Jeff~~	~~Tom and Annie~~	~~Tom and Marie~~

Because order doesn't matter, there are only 6 ways that the coach could choose two players to be midfielders. Notice that if you treated this combination problem as a permutation problem, you would overcount by a factor of 2.

You can find the number of combinations from the number of permutations for the same event. First, find the number of permutations for that event. For example, if the coach wanted to select three players, there are $4 \times 3 \times 2 = 24$ permutations of 4 players in 3 slots.

Next, find the number of ways that each combination of objects can be arranged. If the coach picks Jeff, Annie, and Marie, they can be arranged in $3 \times 2 \times 1 = 6$ ways.

Finally, divide the number of permutations by the number of ways each combination can be arranged in permutations. This will give you the number of combinations:

$$\frac{24}{6} = 4 \text{ combinations}$$

EXAMPLE

Michael has 10 friends that he wishes to invite to his birthday party, but his parents have told him that he can only invite 6. How many different groups of 6 friends can Michael invite?

Michael has 6 friends to invite, so let's start by drawing 6 slots:

$$\underline{} \times \underline{} \times \underline{} \times \underline{} \times \underline{} \times \underline{}$$

Assuming that order mattered, Michael would have 10 friends possible for his first choice, 9 for his second, 8 for his third, and so on. You would fill out the slots like this:

$$\underline{10} \times \underline{9} \times \underline{8} \times \underline{7} \times \underline{6} \times \underline{5}$$

There are $10 \times 9 \times 8 \times 7 \times 6 \times 5$ permutations of 6 out of Michael's 10 friends.

Since order doesn't matter, you need to divide by the number of ways the 6 friends can be arranged:

$$\frac{10 \times 9 \times 8 \times 7 \times 6 \times 5}{6 \times 5 \times 4 \times 3 \times 2 \times 1} = \frac{10 \times 9 \times 8 \times 7}{4 \times 3 \times 2} = \frac{5,040}{24} = 210$$

Michael has 210 combinations of 6 friends he could choose.

PROBABILITY

Probability is the likelihood that something will happen. Scientists and mathematicians can make educated predictions about the future by analyzing data and using the principles of probability. For example, weather forecasters use probability to predict the chance of rain tomorrow, and medical researchers use probability to predict people's chance of developing heart disease or lung cancer.

The formula to calculate probability is:

$$\text{Probability} = \frac{\text{Number of ways to get a certain outcome}}{\text{Number of possible outcomes}}$$

Let's take a look at a common SAT probability question:

EXAMPLE

What is the probability of rolling an even number on a six-sided number cube, with faces numbered 1 through 6?

With a six-sided number cube, there is an equal chance that you will roll any of the numbers from 1 through 6. Therefore, there are six possible outcomes. To find the probability of rolling an even number, you divide the number of even-number outcomes (3) by the number of possible outcomes (6):

$$\text{Probability of rolling an even number} = \frac{3}{6} = \frac{1}{2}$$

The probability of rolling an even number is $\frac{1}{2}$. You can also state this as a decimal (0.5) or as a percent (50%).

EXAMPLE

Some problems will give you a probability and ask you to solve for numbers:

A jar contains 40 jellybeans. The probability of choosing a red jellybean is $\frac{1}{4}$. How many red jellybeans are in the jar?

The question tells us that there is a $\frac{1}{4}$ or 25% probability of choosing a red jellybean. You're told that the number of total jellybeans is 40. Let's write the probability of choosing a red jellybean using our formula:

$$\text{Probability of choosing a red jellybean} = \frac{\text{Number of red jellybeans}}{40} = \frac{1}{4}$$

Now all you need to do is solve by cross-multiplying your proportion:

$$\frac{x}{40} = \frac{1}{4}$$

$$40 = 4x$$

$$x = 10$$

The number of red jellybeans in the jar is equal to 10.

UNDERSTANDING PROBABILITY

Probabilities are written as fractions or decimals between 0 and 1, or as percentages between 0% and 100%. The lower the probability, the less likely an event is to occur. The higher the probability, the more likely an event is to occur.

A probability of 0 means an event is impossible and will never occur.

What is the probability of rolling a 7 on a six-sided number cube, with faces numbered 1 through 6?

There are six possible outcomes, but the number cube does not have the number 7. Therefore, there are zero ways to roll an outcome of 7. If you plug this into our formula, you get:

$$\text{Probability of rolling a } 7 = \frac{0}{6} = 0$$

The probability of rolling a 7 is 0, so there is a no chance that you will roll a 7. This event is impossible.

On the other hand, a probability of 1 or 100% means that an event is absolutely certain to happen.

EXAMPLE

What is the probability of rolling a positive number on a six-sided number cube, with faces numbered 1 through 6?

There are six possible outcomes, and all six of these numbers are positive numbers. Therefore, there are also six ways to get a positive number outcome:

$$\text{Probability of rolling a positive number} = \frac{6}{6} = 1$$

The probability of rolling a positive number is 1, so this event is always going to happen. Since a probability of 1 means an event will always happen, you will never get a probability greater than 1 or 100%.

If you know the probability of getting a certain outcome, you can also calculate the probability of *not* getting that outcome. These two possibilities are called **complementary events**. If you add the probabilities of complementary events, you will get 1. This means that every outcome will be one of the two complementary events.

> What is the probability of not rolling the number 4 on a six-sided number cube, with faces numbered 1 through 6?

Rolling the number 4 and not rolling the number 4 are complementary events. Since the probability of rolling a 4 is $\frac{1}{6}$, the probability of *not* rolling a 4 is:

$$1 - \frac{1}{6} = \frac{5}{6}$$

You have a $\frac{5}{6}$ chance of not rolling the number 4, but of rolling any of the other possible numbers (1, 2, 3, 5, or 6).

Two events are **mutually exclusive** if it is impossible for both of them to happen at the same time. For example, if you roll once on a six-sided number cube, with faces numbered 1 through 6, it is impossible to roll both the number 5 and the number 3. You can either roll one number or the other. Complementary events are always mutually exclusive.

You can find the chance of one event *or* another event occurring by adding together their individual probabilities:

EXAMPLE

> What is the probability of rolling either a 5 or a 3 on a six-sided number cube, with faces numbered 1 through 6?

The probability of rolling a 5 on a six-sided number cube is $\frac{1}{6}$ and the probability of rolling a 3 is also $\frac{1}{6}$. To find your chances of rolling a 5 or a 3, add their probabilities together:

$$\text{Probability of rolling 5 or 3} = \frac{1}{6} + \frac{1}{6} = \frac{1}{3}$$

If you add together the probabilities of all of the possible mutually-exclusive outcomes of an event, you will get the number 1. For example, there is probability of 1 that you will roll a 1, 2, 3, 4, 5, or 6 on a six-sided number cube, with faces numbered 1 through 6.

CONDITIONAL PROBABILITY

Conditional probability is the probability that an event occurs given that another event has already occurred. Questions dealing with conditional probability are often phrased as, "What is the probability of P *given that* X is true?"

Since you are dealing with multiple events, you need to figure out what relationship the events have to each other.

If two events are **independent**, the first event does not affect the probability of the second event. For instance, if you were to roll two six-sided number cubes, with faces numbered 1 through 6, your chance of rolling an even number on one cube does not affect your chance of rolling an even number on the second cube. For each cube, you have a $\frac{1}{2}$ probability of rolling an even number.

If two events are independent, you can find the chance of *both* occurring by multiplying together their individual probabilities:

EXAMPLE

What is the probability of rolling two even numbers on one roll of two six-sided number cubes, with faces numbered 1 through 6?

The probability of rolling an even number for the first number cube is $\frac{1}{2}$, and the probability of rolling an even number on the second number cube is also $\frac{1}{2}$:

$$\text{Probability of rolling an even number on both number cubes} = \frac{1}{2} \times \frac{1}{2} = \frac{1}{4}$$

You have a $\frac{1}{4}$ or 25% chance of rolling an even number on both number cubes.

Why does this work? Let's try diagramming all of the possible outcomes on a table. The table shows all of the different pairs of numbers that you could roll on the two number cubes, with the even pairs shaded:

1 and 1	1 and 2	1 and 3	1 and 4	1 and 5	1 and 6
2 and 1	2 and 2	2 and 3	2 and 4	2 and 5	2 and 6
3 and 1	3 and 2	3 and 3	3 and 4	3 and 5	3 and 6
4 and 1	4 and 2	4 and 3	4 and 4	4 and 5	4 and 6
5 and 1	5 and 2	5 and 3	5 and 4	5 and 5	5 and 6
6 and 1	6 and 2	6 and 3	6 and 4	6 and 5	6 and 6

There are 9 possible outcomes that give us two even numbers. The probability is equal to 9 possible outcomes divided by 36 total outcomes:

$$\frac{9}{36} = \frac{1}{4}$$

This result matches the answer you got through multiplication.

Events are **dependent** if one event affects the probability of the other event occurring. If two events are dependent, you need to figure out what happens to the probability of the second event after the first one has taken place:

EXAMPLE

Janice picked cards randomly from a standard 52-card deck. She picked her first card and then set it aside, without replacing it, before drawing her second card. What is the probability that both cards were kings?

The probability for the first card is easy: there are 52 cards in the deck and 4 of them are kings, so Janice has a $\frac{4}{52}$ or $\frac{1}{13}$ chance of picking a king for her first card.

However, now that she has removed one card, the number of cards in the deck has changed. She now has only 51 cards in her deck. If her first card was a king, there are only 3 kings left. Therefore, the probability that her second card will also be a king is $\frac{3}{51}$.

You've figured out the probability of the first event, and how the probability of the second event will be affected if the first event takes place. You can now multiply these probabilities together to find the probability of both events occurring:

$$\text{Probability of picking two kings} = \frac{1}{13} \times \frac{3}{51} = \frac{3}{663} = \frac{1}{221}$$

If Janice is drawing two cards one at a time, without putting her first card back in the deck, the probability that she will pick two kings is 1 out of 221.

GEOMETRIC PROBABILITY

Some SAT questions ask you to calculate the probability of something occurring in a specific region of a geometric figure. In this case, the "number of ways to get a certain outcome" is equal to the area of the specific region, and the "number of possible outcomes" is equal to the area of the whole figure:

$$\text{Probability of something happening in a region} = \frac{\text{Area of specific region}}{\text{Area of whole figure}}$$

This type of question often involves throwing an object, such as a dart, at a surface, such as a dartboard. The larger the target, the higher the probability that a dart will hit it.

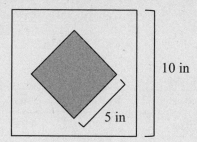

The diagram above shows a square board with a shaded square in the middle. What is the chance that a small coin thrown completely at random onto the board will land in the shaded region?

To find this probability you first need to find the area of the shaded square and then divide it by the area of the whole figure. The shaded square has a side length of 5 inches, so its area is 25 square inches. The whole board is a square with a side length of 10 inches, so its area is 100 square inches. Therefore, the probability of our coin landing in the shaded region is:

$$\text{Probability of landing in the shaded region} = \frac{25}{100} = \frac{1}{4}$$

There is a $\frac{1}{4}$ or 25% chance that our coin, thrown at random onto the board, will land in the shaded square.

ANALYZING TWO-WAY TABLES

Conditional probability may also be used to analyze two-way tables.

EXAMPLE

	Classical	Rock	Pop	Total
9th grade	50	21	39	110
10th grade	63	22	20	105
11th grade	3	90	19	112
12th grade	47	12	44	103
Total	163	145	122	430

The table above summarizes students' preferences for music. If one student out of 430 students surveyed, is randomly selected, what is the probability that the student is in the 9th grade?

This is a regular probability question. There are 110 9th graders out of 430 total students, so the probability that the student is in the 9th grade is $\frac{110}{430}$, or $\frac{11}{43}$, or approximately 26%.

EXAMPLE

A more complicated question for the same table is:

What is the probability that a student prefers rock music given that he or she is in the 11th grade?

This is a conditional probability question, since you are only looking at the students in 11th grade. There are 90 students who prefer rock music out of the 112 students in 11th grade, so the probability is $\frac{90}{112} = \frac{45}{56}$, or approximately 80%.

Making Predictions

You can use samples of data to make predictions about larger populations or groups. The accuracy of these estimates depends on properties of the sample data such as size and selection process. You will discuss how to evaluate sample data in Part 6.

In order to make an estimate for a population from sample data, you treat the sample data as proportional to the entire population. This allows us to use proportions and percentages to make estimates for the whole population.

Example

A city surveyed residents about their opinion on a proposed policy. The results are summarized in the chart below:

	For the Policy	Against the Policy	Total
Male	126	42	168
Female	81	69	150
Total	207	111	318

The city has a population of 12,000 female residents and 13,000 male residents. Based on the survey results, how many female residents would the city predict to support the policy?

The question asks for the number of female residents who are "for" the policy. The survey found that 81/150=54% of the women surveyed supported the policy. Multiply the percent of women supporting the policy in the survey by the total number of female residents in the city:

$$12,000 \times 0.54 = 6,480$$

Our estimate is that around 6,480 of the female residents support the policy.

PART 4 PRACTICE: PROBABILITY AND STATISTICS

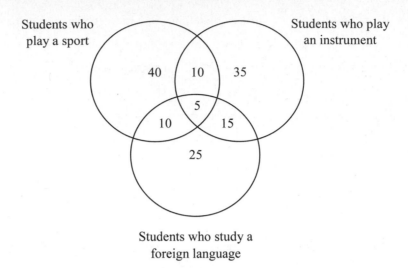

Students who play a sport

Students who play an instrument

40   10   35

5

10   15

25

Students who study a foreign language

1. According to the Venn Diagram above, how many students play a sport and play an instrument, but do not study a foreign language?

2. 100 students were surveyed about the musical instruments they play. 52 play the piano, 30 play the violin, and 24 play neither. How many play both piano and violin?

3. There are 20 lottery tickets available. If there is a 1st and a 2nd place winner, how many different ways can the winners be chosen?

4. Susan is buying groceries. She needs to buy 4 different fruits to fill her basket. There are 10 different types of fruit available. How many different baskets of fruit are possible?

5. Mr. Johnson's class has 12 boys and 14 girls. If Mr. Johnson picks one student at random from the class, what is the probability that he will pick a boy?

6. A standard deck of cards has 4 kings, 4 queens, 4 jacks, and 40 other cards. If Carol picks a card at random from this standard deck, what is the probability that she will NOT pick a king, queen, or jack?

7. Brian rolls two six-sided number cubes, each numbered 1-6. What is the probability that the sum of their numbers is greater than 9?

8. In the United States, about 40% of people will be diagnosed with cancer in their lifetime. If two people are randomly chosen from the United States, what is the percent probability that both of them will be diagnosed with cancer in their lifetime?

9. In the figure above, the radius of the larger circle is twice as large as the radius of the grey circle. The diameter of the grey circle is 16 inches. If a marble is thrown at the figure, what is the probability that it hits the grey circle?

For questions 10 and 11, refer to the table below.

Repairs During the Year 2010 by Car Color			
Car Color	Repaired	Not repaired	Total
Silver	397	305	702
Red	322	226	548
Total	719	531	1250

10. Based on the table above, what is the percent probability that a car is silver given that it underwent a repair in 2010?

11. There were a total of 3000 red cars in 2010. Based on the table above, approximately how many red cars would be expected to have been repaired in 2010?

ANSWER KEY: PROBABILITY AND STATISTICS

1. 10 students

2. 6 students

3. 380

4. 210

5. $\dfrac{6}{13}$

6. $\dfrac{10}{13}$

7. $\dfrac{1}{6}$

8. 16%

9. $\dfrac{1}{4}$

10. $\dfrac{397}{719} \approx 55.2\%$

11. ~1,763 red cars

MODELING DATA

PART 5

When scientists or researchers collect data, they look for relationships between different variables. For example, imagine Mario is running a lemonade stand. He wants to know if there is a relationship between the temperature and the amount of lemonade he sells. He collects the following information over a series of days:

Average Temperature (°F)	Cups Sold
76	19
89	54
68	12
82	25
91	61
74	23
84	41

One way to find trends in data is to create a scatterplot. A **scatterplot** is a graph of two variables compared against each other; these types of graphs are commonly found on the SAT. It is the most common means of analysis because you can visually see patterns, or **trends** of data. Here is a scatterplot of Mario's data:

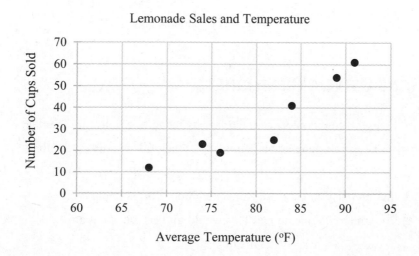

From this scatterplot, you can see that the number of cups of lemonade sold tended to be higher on days with a higher temperature. The trend is not a perfect line or curve, but you can estimate an equation that will approximate this data: this is called **modeling data**. Modeling data allows us to find an equation for the relationship between two pieces of information and to make estimates or predictions.

To model the data from Mario's lemonade stand, you first need to decide what type of curve best models the relationship between the temperature and the number of cups sold. This relationship could be linear, quadratic, polynomial, or exponential. The data in Mario's scatterplot appears to follow a linear trend.

Now you need to draw a trend line or a line of best fit. **A trend line** or **line of best fit** is a line that best approximates all the scatterplot data. It should be as close to *all* the points as possible, but it does not have to pass through all – or any – of the actual data points. The line of best fit of Mario's data is:

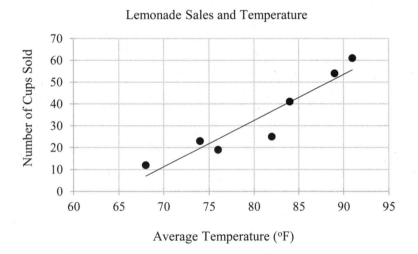

ESTIMATING USING A TREND LINE

You can estimate the equation of the trend line by using two points on the line. Make sure you do *not* use the experimental data points unless they fall exactly on the line!

Pick values that are easy to estimate from the graph. For example, you could use (70,12) and (90,54) from the trend line above. This would give us the equation:

$$y = 2.1x - 135$$

In this equation, y represents the number of cups sold and x is the temperature. If you wanted to predict how many cups of lemonade would be sold if the temperature were 80°F, for example, you would plug 80 into the formula:

$$\text{Cups Sold} = 2.1 \times 80 - 135 = 33$$

Based off of your line of best fit, you could estimate that 33 cups would be sold at an average temperature of 80°F. You can similarly predict all temperatures within the range of 68° to 91° this way.

The SAT may also include quadratic or exponential prediction models.

EXAMPLE

Motorcycle manufacturers are measuring the acceleration of a new motorcycle. They record the cumulative distance traveled in intervals of one second. Their data is plotted on the graph below:

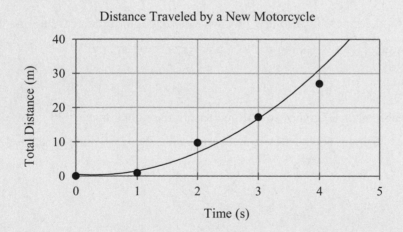

Distance Traveled by a New Motorcycle

Based on the trend line, how many seconds would it take for the new motorcycle to travel 10 meters? (Round to the nearest tenth of a second.)

You need to find the point where the trend line reaches 10 meters. This occurs at the second tick mark after 2 seconds. Since there are 5 tick marks between each second, each tick mark represents 0.2 seconds. Therefore, the time it takes for the motorcycle to reach 10 meters is about 2.4 seconds.

EXAMPLE

A researcher collects data on a mass of a radioactive material at different times and displays the results in the scatterplot below:

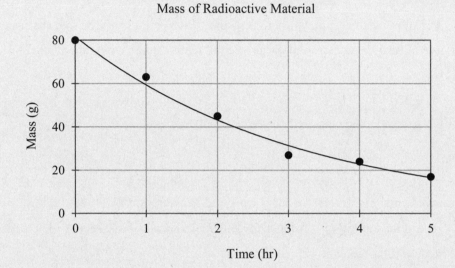

Mass of Radioactive Material

Based on the graph, how long will it take the material to decrease to one quarter of its original mass? (Round to the nearest quarter of an hour.)

The original mass is 80 grams, so one quarter of the original mass is 20 grams. The trend line reaches 20 grams about half way between 4 and 5 hours, so our estimate is 4.5 hours.

PART 5 PRACTICE: MODELING DATA

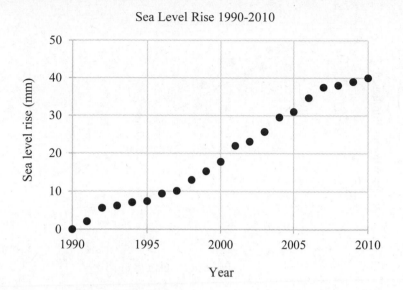

Sea Level Rise 1990-2010

1. On average, how much did the sea level rise per year between 1990 and 2010? Round to the nearest millimeter.

Temperature (°C)	Reaction Time (s)
20	13.5
24	11
28	7.9
32	3.6
36	2.1
40	1.3

2. A chemist measures the reaction time of an experiment at different temperatures. The results are summarized in the chart above. If this data is displayed as a scatter plot, will the slope of the trend line be positive, negative, or zero?

For questions 3 and 4, refer to the following graph.

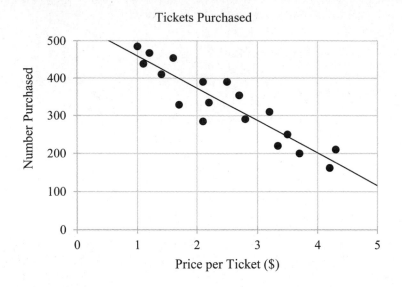

3. Based on the data above, how many tickets would you expect to be purchased if the price is $2.50?

4. Estimate the total money made from selling tickets at $4.00 each.

For questions 5 and 6, refer to the following graph.

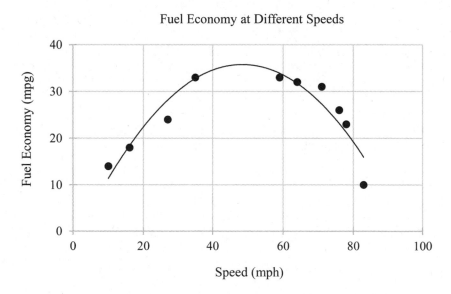

A group of researchers collects data on the fuel economy of a car at different speeds. The fuel economy is measured in miles per gallon (mpg) and speed is measured in miles per hour (mph). The data are displayed in the graph above.

5. What is the best estimate for the maximum fuel economy of this car?

6. The car has a fuel economy of 18 mpg at a speed of 18 mph. At which other speed should the car have the same fuel economy?

For questions 7 and 8, refer to the following graph.

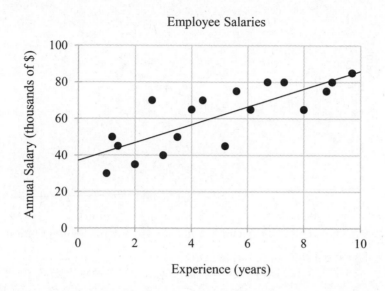

The graph above shows data collected on employees' salaries and experience. The data is modelled as a linear relationship where *e* is the employee's experience in years and *S* is their annual salary in thousands of dollars.

7. Estimate the salary of an employee with 4 years of experience.

8. Write an equation that estimates the trend line, using the variables *e* and *S*.

For questions 9 and 10, refer to the graph below.

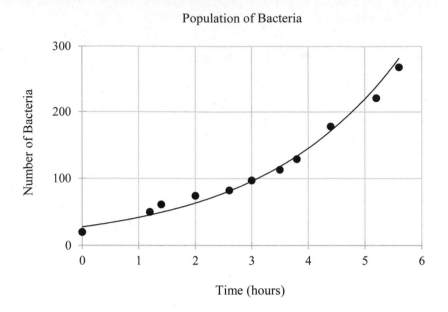

Population of Bacteria

A biologist is growing a culture of bacteria in his lab. He records the population at different times and displays the data in the chart above.

9. The original population is 20 bacteria. Based on the trend line above, how many hours should it take the population to grow to ten times its original size? Express your answer to the nearest tenth of an hour.

10. Based on the trend line above, how many hours does it take for the population at 1 hour to double? Express your answer to the nearest tenth of an hour.

ANSWERS: MODELING DATA

1. 2 mm
2. Negative
3. 325
4. $800
5. 36 mpg
6. 80 mph < answer < 82 mph
7. $56,000 to $58,000
8. $S = ae + b$ where $4 < a < 6$ and $33 < b < 40$
9. 4.8 hours or 4h 46m
10. 1.6 hours or 1h 36m

USING DATA AS EVIDENCE

PART 6

In Section 6, we've covered many topics related to data analysis. In this part, you'll learn how these topics will appear on the SAT. Data analysis questions will test your ability to read different types of charts and graphs, interpret data and trends, make conclusions and predictions from data sets, and analyze data.

READING CHARTS AND GRAPHS

To solve any data analysis problem, you must first make sure that you understand the purpose of the graph. Ask yourself which quantities are being measured and compared, and know the scale and units of those quantities. Make sure that you are familiar with the types of charts and graphs introduced in Part 2.

EXAMPLE

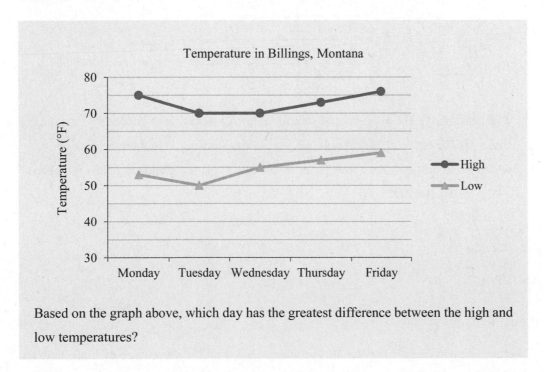

Based on the graph above, which day has the greatest difference between the high and low temperatures?

To solve the problem, you need to look at the graph and compare the high and low temperatures for each day. Monday and Tuesday have the widest gap between the high and low temperatures, so we should compare those more closely. There is a difference of about 22° between Monday's temperatures and only a 20° difference between Tuesday's temperatures, so the answer is Monday.

INTERPRETING DATA

In some cases, you will need to use data in the chart or graph to find information that is not part of the data you are given. You will have to do calculations with the data you are given or make estimates and predictions based on data or trends.

Some of these questions might ask you to use data from a sample group to make predictions for a larger population. For these problems, you can use fractions or percentages to compare the sample group to the larger population.

EXAMPLE

GPA of Graduating Students	
GPA	Number of Students
3.5-4.0	25
3.0-3.4	37
2.5-2.9	24
2.0-2.4	14

The chart above shows a random sample of GPAs from a high school's graduating students. The entire graduating class contains 600 students. Based on the data above, which is the best estimate for the number of students in the graduating class who had a GPA of 3 or higher?

(A) 62
(B) 150
(C) 222
(D) 372

We can use percentages to solve this problem. First, find the percentage of students in the sample who had a GPA of 3.0 or higher. This is 25 + 37 students out of 100 total students, so 62%. Now, multiply this percentage by the number of students in the graduating class:

$$600 \times 0.62 = 372 \text{ students}$$

The best estimate for the number of students in the graduating class who had a GPA of 3 or higher is 372 so (D) is the correct answer.

You may also be asked to model data or to use a model to make predictions. The scatterplot is often used in these types of questions; you could be asked, for example, to estimate the slope or to find the function that best models the data. These problems will look like the examples and practice exercises in Part 5.

EXAMPLE

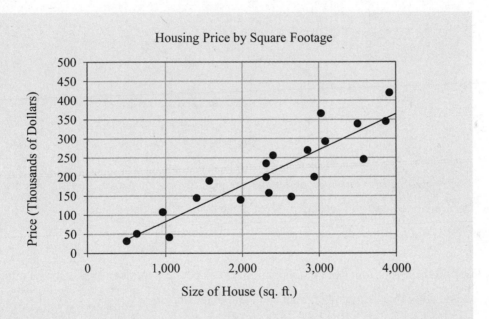

The graph above is a scatterplot of the size and price of houses. Based on the trend line, which of the following is the best estimate for the price per square foot of a 2,000 sq. ft. house?

(A) 10
(B) 70
(C) 90
(D) 180

Since the question asks us to use the trend line, find the price that corresponds to 2,000 sq. ft. on the trend line. This is approximately 180 thousand dollars. Make sure to check your units – $180 will give a much different answer than $180,000! To find price per sq. ft., divide $180,000 by 2,000 sq. ft. to get 90, which is choice (C).

Data analysis questions will ask you to find or compare the mean, median, mode, range, or standard deviation of data sets. These problems might include raw data sets, tables of values, or bar graphs, so you should be familiar with finding statistical quantities from these types of graphics.

EXAMPLE

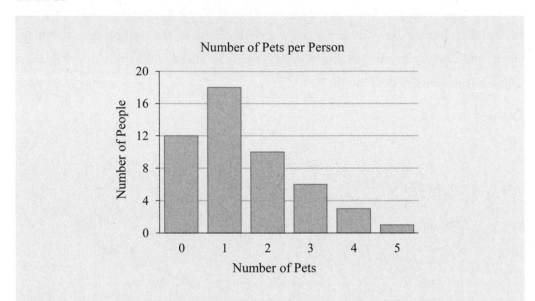

Fifty people are surveyed about the number of pets they own and the results are summarized in the chart above. What is the mean of the data?

To find the mean from a bar graph, multiply each possible number of pets by the number of people who own that number, then add them together:

$$(0 \times 12) + (1 \times 18) + (2 \times 10) + (3 \times 6) + (4 \times 3) + (5 \times 1) = 73$$

This is the total number of pets owned by the 50 people. Now divide by the number of people, 50, to find the mean:

$$\frac{73}{50} = 1.46$$

The mean is 1.46.

DATA COLLECTION METHODS

The goal of data collection is to get data that accurately reflects the entire population. When a question on the SAT asks you to evaluate a data collection method, consider factors like how participants are selected, the size of the data set, and the characteristics of the larger population to which you are comparing your sample.

In order to be accurate, your data must reflect the entire population that you are studying.

Consider the map below:

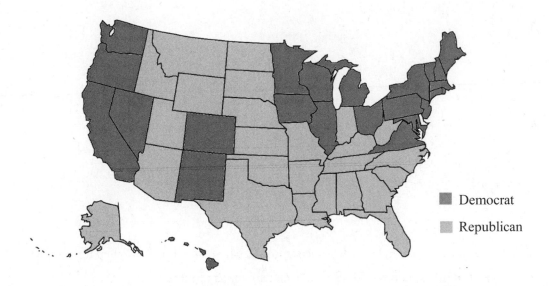

Democrat
Republican

If you only surveyed people from the northeast, you would get very different results than if you only surveyed people from southern states. Neither group would give you results that reflect the political preference of all U.S. residents.

The *type* of data that you are collecting also determines what makes a good sample. A sample group that includes only college students, for example, is a great sample group if you are studying college students. It is not, however, a good sample group to represent the entire population of the U.S.

When evaluating a sample selection, consider how well it represents the entire population and how that may affect results.

The *size* of the sample also affects the accuracy of data. If you only collect a few data points, they will not reflect the entire population as well as many data points.

Imagine you are rolling a six-sided number cube numbered 1 through 6 and recording the results. You would expect each number to be rolled about $\frac{1}{6}$ or 17% of the time. If you only rolled the cube 5 times, your data would look something like this:

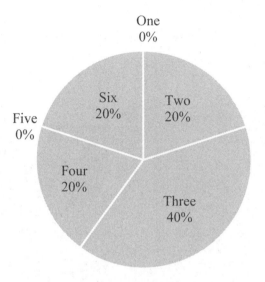

This data is not very accurate because the sample size is so small. If you rolled the number cube 50 or 100 times, you would get results that are much more accurate:

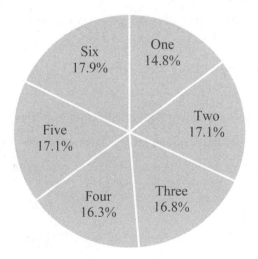

This principle is true for all kinds of data collection: the bigger the sample size, the better the chance it will give accurate results.

MEASURING ERROR

Researchers can estimate the accuracy of their data with a margin of error or a confidence interval. You will not have to calculate margins of error or confidence intervals on the SAT, but you need to understand what these mean and know how to use them to analyze data.

A **margin of error** measures how well a sample group represents the entire population. Consider the chart below:

Pre-Election Survey	
Candidate	Percent of Votes (± 3%)
Jones	28%
Liu	37%
Albini	35%

The chart gives a margin of error of 3%. This means that the actual percentages may vary as much as 3% in either direction. Jones could have anywhere between 25% and 31% of the votes. Liu's range is 34% to 40% and Albini's range is 32% to 38%. These ranges are called **confidence intervals**.

The margin of error affects how we analyze the data. Notice that Liu has 2% more of the votes than Albini. However, the margin of error tells us that the percentages can vary up to 3%. This means that Liu could actually have 34% of the votes or Albini could have 38% of the votes, which would put Albini in the lead. A good rule is that if the difference between two numbers or percentages is smaller than the margin of error, you cannot conclude that one is greater or smaller than the other.

Margins of error and confidence intervals can also be represented visually on a graph. Confidence intervals are shown as vertical bars like the ones in the following graph.

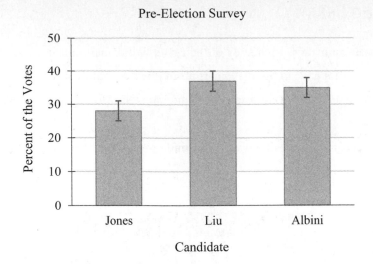

Pre-Election Survey

Since the margin of error is 3%, each confidence interval extends 3% above and below the measured percentage. You can see that the confidence intervals for Liu and Albini overlap, which tells you that you don't know for sure which candidate has a larger percentage of votes.

Part 6 Practice: Using Data as Evidence

Questions 1 and 2 refer to the following graph.

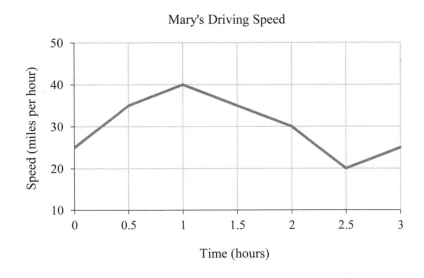

Mary's Driving Speed

1. What is the difference between Mary's fastest and slowest speed over the three-hour period?

2. How many miles did Mary cover between hours 1 and 2?

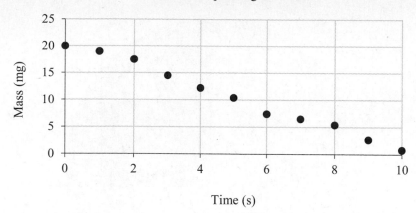

Susanne conducts an experiment in which she heats a solid to its boiling point so that it evaporates. She records the mass of the remaining solid every second. The plot above shows her resulting data.

3. The data is modeled as the linear function $M = 20 + at$, where M is the mass of the substance in milligrams, t is time in seconds, and a is a constant. What integer is the best estimate for a?

Length of English Papers

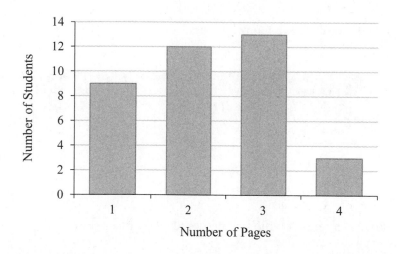

4. The histogram above shows the length of 37 students' English papers. What is the median paper length?

College Expenses

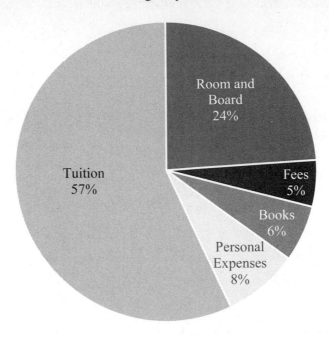

5. The chart above is a summary of Malik's expenditures for his first year in college.

    If Malik's total expenditure for the year is $30,000, how much more did Malik spend on tuition than on the other categories combined?

Questions 6 and 7 refer to the following data.

November Sales Report		
Store	Price of Product	Number Sold
A	$99	15
B	$85	21
C	$110	18

The chart above is a report on the sale of a product by three stores.

6. What is the difference in sales between Store A and Store B?

7. The product costs $80 for the stores to purchase. If this is the stores' only cost, what is the profit from the product's sales at all three stores?

Product	Average Rating	Standard Deviation
A	4	0.43
B	3	0.76

8. Customers rate two products on a scale of 1-5. The chart above summarizes statistics from these reviews. Which of the following statements can you conclude from the information given?

(A) More customers rated Product B than Product A.
(B) All of the ratings for Product A were a 3, 4, or 5.
(C) The ratings for Product B were more varied than for Product A.
(D) The range of the ratings for Product B is larger than that for Product A.

Questions 9 and 10 refer to the following graph.

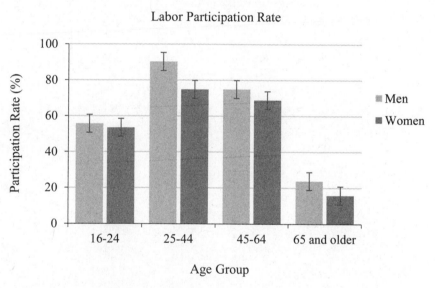

9. Which of the following conclusions can you make from the graph above?

(A) A higher percentage of men ages 16-24 work than women age 16-24.
(B) Between 70% and 80% of women ages 25-44 work.
(C) The margin of error is ±10%.
(D) There are more men aged 65 or older than women aged 65 or older.

10. 200 men ages 25-44 who took the original survey are selected for a second survey. Incorporating margin of error, what are the maximum and minimum number of men that you would expect to work in this age group?

Answers: Using Data as Evidence

1. 20 mph
2. 35
3. –2
4. 2
5. $4200
6. $300
7. $930
8. C
9. B
10. Minimum of 170 men and maximum of 190 men

PART 7: PRACTICE SET

In this part, you'll find 30 SAT-style questions to practice the Problem Solving and Data Analysis topics you learned in this section. Check your answers with the answer key that follows. For any question that you get wrong, identify the topic of the question, and then review the part of this section that covers that topic.

1. A machine can cut 36 sheets of tin in 30 minutes. How many sheets of tin can it cut in two hours?

   (A) 144
   (B) 72
   (C) 36
   (D) 18

2. Wallace ran 100 meters in 12 seconds at a track meet. What was Wallace's speed, in kilometers per hour?

   (A) 30
   (B) 24
   (C) 20
   (D) 15

Questions 3-4 refer to the following information:

Ms. Lu released the grades for a recent math test. The results for four students are shown in the table below.

Student	Grade
Stacy	87
Ahmed	68
Satoshi	76
Mark	71

3. What is the average grade for these four students?

   (A) 73.5
   (B) 75.5
   (C) 80.3
   (D) 81.8

4. What is the median grade for these four students?

(A) 73.5
(B) 75.5
(C) 80.3
(D) 81.8

5. Betty has 24 coins in her purse. If she has a 1/6 chance of randomly selecting a nickel, how many nickels are in her purse?

(A) 1
(B) 4
(C) 6
(D) 12

6. Kareem is driving home at 50 miles per hour. Approximately how many miles will he travel in 10 minutes?

(A) 5
(B) 8
(C) 10
(D) 12

Diego's Budget

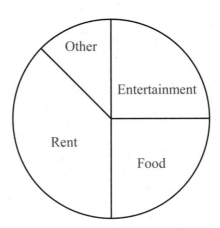

7. If Diego spends $350 on food each month, according to the diagram above, about how much does Diego spend on rent each month?

(A) $175
(B) $470
(C) $525
(D) $700

8. If Trey can plant 25 trees in 1 hour and 15 minutes, how many trees can he plant in 2 hours?

(A) 30
(B) 34
(C) 40
(D) 50

Size of Mr. Sanchez's Chemistry Class

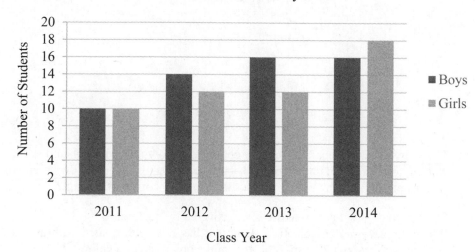

9. Using the graph above, what is the ratio of the average number of boys to the average number of girls in Mr. Sanchez's class each year?

(A) 56:52
(B) 52:56
(C) 14:13
(D) 13:14

10. If there are 36 inches in a yard, and approximately 0.39 inches in a centimeter, approximately how many centimeters are in a yard?

(A) 0.39
(B) 2.6
(C) 14.0
(D) 92.3

11. Alex drove 20 km to work at a speed of 80 km/hour. On the way back, he drove at a speed of 60 km/hour. What was his average speed for the round trip?

(A)   60 km/h
(B) 68.6 km/h
(C)   70 km/h
(D)   80 km/h

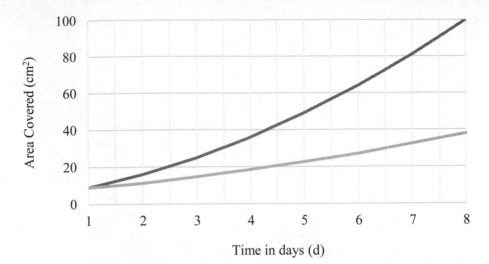

Bacteria Growth

12. The growth of two separate bacterial colonies is shown in the graph above. Antibiotics were used on one of the bacteria colonies in order to slow its growth. According to the graph, which of the following is a correct statement?

(A) At time $d = 8$, both areas are 100% covered by bacteria.
(B) At time $d = 7$, the bacteria colony that has not been treated with antibiotics occupies about 2.5 times the area of the other bacteria colony.
(C) At time $d = 4$, the bacteria colony that has been treated with antibiotics occupies about 2 times the area of the other bacteria colony.
(D) At time $d = 1$, there are no bacteria in the testing environment.

13. If the ratio of x to y is 5 to 3 and the ratio of y to z is 7 to 3, what is the ratio of z to x?

(A) $\dfrac{35}{9}$

(B) $\dfrac{5}{3}$

(C) $\dfrac{3}{5}$

(D) $\dfrac{9}{35}$

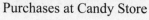
Purchases at Candy Store

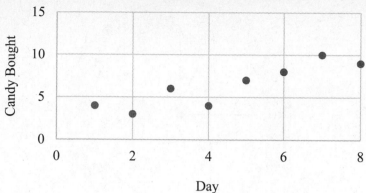

14. The amount of candy bought each day at a candy store is plotted on the scatter plot above. If a line of best fit were drawn through the data in the scatter plot, what would be the direction of the slope of the line?

(A) Positive
(B) Negative
(C) Random
(D) Zero

15. The density of gold is 19.3 g/cm^3. What is the mass of a block of gold with dimensions of 7 cm by 4 cm by 3 cm, to the nearest hundredth of a gram? (Density is mass divided by volume.)

(A) 1621.20
(B)   19.30
(C)   4.35
(D)   0.23

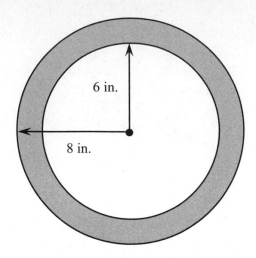

16. The radius of the dart board above is 8 inches, and the radius of the inner circle is 6 inches. If Chen randomly throws a dart and it lands on the dart board, what is the approximate probability that it lands in the shaded ring?

(A) 25%
(B) 44%
(C) 56%
(D) 75%

17. Phil has 5 chocolate chip cookies, 6 peanut butter cookies, and 3 sugar cookies in a jar. He randomly selects two cookies from the jar, one after the other, without putting them back. What is the probability that Phil selects two sugar cookies?

(A) $\dfrac{1}{7}$

(B) $\dfrac{3}{14}$

(C) $\dfrac{3}{91}$

(D) $\dfrac{3}{98}$

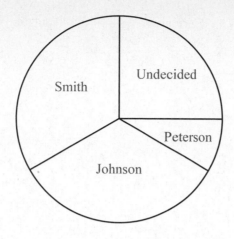

18. The results of a poll of 100 voters for an election are shown above. The voters were asked which candidate they would vote for. The sample of 100 voters was randomly selected from the entire voting population. If the whole population consists of 500 voters, approximately how many voters could be expected to vote for Smith?

(A) 25
(B) 33
(C) 125
(D) 167

19. A data set has a standard deviation equal to 4. If each data value in the data set is multiplied by 6, which of the following statement is true?

(A) The standard deviation of the data set increases.
(B) The standard deviation of the data set stays the same.
(C) The standard deviation of the data set decreases.
(D) It is impossible to determine with the information given.

Fungus Growth			
Time	1h	2h	3h
Fungus Area	4 cm^2	16 cm^2	64 cm^2

20. Fungus A grows at a linear rate and Fungus B grows at an exponential rate. Which fungus is most likely represented in the table above?

(A) Fungus A
(B) Fungus B
(C) Both Fungus A and B
(D) Neither Fungus A nor B

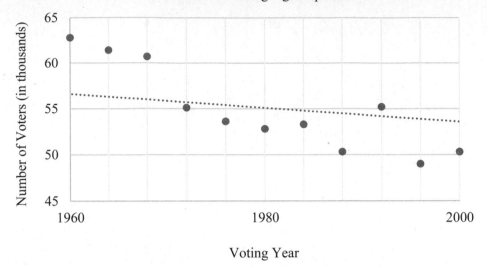

Turnout of Voting Age Population

21. The scatterplot above shows the number of voters who voted in a municipal election from the year 1960 to 2000. Based on the line of best fit drawn, what is the closest estimate to the percent decrease in voters from 1960 to 2000?

(A) 0.1%
(B) 0.7%
(C) 5.4%
(D) 19.3%

Questions 22-23 refer to the following information.

A survey was conducted in a small city, asking whether the city's residents prefer dogs or cats. The table below displays a summary of the survey results.

	Dog Preference	Cat Preference	Total
Male 18- to 35-year-olds	10,342	6,436	16,788
Female 18- to 35-year-olds	8,358	8,734	17,092
Male 36-years old and older	11,345	5,249	16,594
Female 36-years old and older	9,426	7,246	16,672
Total	39,471	27,665	67,146

22. According to the table above, what is the group that least prefers dogs?

(A) Male 18- to 35-year-olds
(B) Female 18- to 35-year-olds
(C) Male 36- to 65-year-olds
(D) Female 36- to 65-year-olds

23. 500 residents who prefer cats were selected at random and asked to specify if they prefer long- or short-haired cats. 25.6% said they prefer long-haired cats. The results were true 19 times out of 20 with a margin of error of 4.2%. Using the data from the follow-up survey and the initial survey, which of the following is an accurate statement?

(A) 95% of the city's population prefers short-haired cats.
(B) The number of city residents who prefer short-haired cats is most likely between 5,920 and 8,244.
(C) The number of city residents who prefer short-haired cats is exactly 7,082.
(D) The number of female city residents who prefer long-haired cats is greater than the number of male city residents who prefer long-haired cats.

24. The average of five numbers is 45. If four of the numbers are 20, 19, 48, and 65, what is the fifth number?

(A) 38
(B) 42
(C) 45
(D) 73

GRID-INS

25. The mean age of the 13 employees of a bakery is 43. When a new employee is hired, the mean age decreases to 41. How old is the new employee?

26. It takes Darion 45 minutes to unpack 10 bags of groceries. His wife and son unpack groceries at the same rate. If his wife and son help Darion, how many minutes will it take the three of them to unpack 10 bags of groceries?

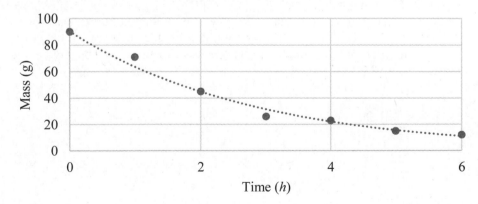

Mass of Radioactive Material

27. The half-life is the point at which radioactive material has degraded to half its original mass. According to the graph above, what is the half-life, in hours, of the radioactive material?

28. Antonella has 5 different T-shirts that she can hand out to 3 different people. If each person gets only 1 T-shirt, how many different combinations of T-shirts are possible?

29. Enrique wants to buy a new bike. In the bike store near his home, there are three mountain bikes for every two road bikes, and two hybrid bikes for every road bike.

Part 1: If there are 34 road bikes, how many hybrid and mountain bikes are at the bike store?

Part 2: The bike store sells 110 bikes per month. Survey results from the area around the bike store indicate that 400 of 1000 people who are looking to purchase a bike want to buy a road bike. Given this data, how many road bikes should the store purchase for the next month in order to keep 34 road bikes in stock?

30. The table below shows the prices of burritos at a restaurant.

Costs of Burritos by Type	
Type	Price
Chicken	$7.00
Beef	$7.25
Vegetable	$6.50

Part 1: Pablo eats 3 chicken and 2 beef burritos, Johan eats 3 beef and 3 vegetable burritos, and Stacy eats 1 chicken and 5 vegetable burritos. On average, how much, in dollars, did Pablo, Johan, and Stacy each spend on burritos? (Round your answer to the nearest dollar.)

Part 2: The burrito restaurant offers a weekly unlimited burrito card for $65. If Xiao eats only beef burritos, how many burritos does he needs to eat during the week in order for the unlimited card to be less expensive than buying the burritos individually?

ANSWERS

1. A
2. A
3. B
4. A
5. B
6. B
7. C
8. C
9. C
10. D
11. B
12. B
13. D
14. A
15. A
16. B
17. C
18. D
19. A
20. B
21. C
22. B
23. B
24. D
25. 15
26. 15
27. 2
28. 60
29. 119, 44
30. 39, 9

SECTION 7

ADDITIONAL TOPICS

The **Additional Topics** questions on the SAT test various advanced topics in geometry, trigonometry, and complex numbers. Although a variety of topics fall under this content area, Additional Topics questions make up the smallest portion of the Math Test. You'll only see 6 total questions on these topics: 2-4 in the Calculator Section and 2-4 in the No-Calculator Section.

In this section, we will cover the following material tested in the Additional Topics questions:

- Introductory Geometry
- Right Triangles
- Radians and Degrees
- Circles
- Complex Numbers

INTRODUCTORY GEOMETRY
PART 1

The SAT Math sections will include a small number of questions on geometry. In Part 1, we'll discuss some basic concepts relating to geometric shapes.

All geometric shapes have **dimensions**, or distances you can measure. Shapes with one dimension, like simple lines, can only be measured by length. Two dimensional shapes can be measured two ways, by length and width. Shapes in three dimensions can be measured three ways—by height, length, and width. We'll start by discussing lines, and then we'll talk about two- and three-dimensional shapes.

LINES

A **line** is a straight, one-dimensional object: it has infinite length but no width. Using any two points, you can draw exactly one line that stretches in both directions forever. For instance, between the points A and B below, you can draw the line $\overleftrightarrow{AB}$. You name a line by drawing a horizontal bar with two arrows over the letters for two points on the line.

A **line segment** is a portion of a line with a finite length. The two ends of a line segment are called **endpoints**. To name a line segment, identify two points on the line, and draw a horizontal bar with arrows above the letters for those two points. For instance, in the figure below, the points M and N are the endpoints of the line segment $\overline{MN}$.

The point that divides a line segment into two equal pieces is called its **midpoint**. In the figure below, the point Q is the midpoint of the line segment $\overline{PR}$.

Because Q is the midpoint, it divides the segment into two equal pieces. Therefore, you know that $PQ = QR$.

ANGLES

An **angle** is formed when two lines or line segments intersect. Angles are measured in degrees from 0° to 360°, which represents the angle of a full circle. Angles are classified according to their degree measurements:

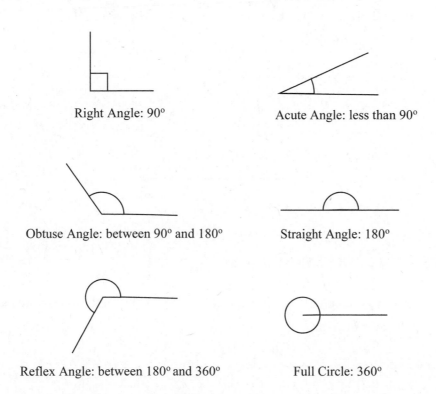

Right Angle: 90°

Acute Angle: less than 90°

Obtuse Angle: between 90° and 180°

Straight Angle: 180°

Reflex Angle: between 180° and 360°

Full Circle: 360°

Pairs of angles can also be classified by comparing their degree measurements. **Complementary** angles are a pair of angles that add up to 90°. **Supplementary** angles are a pair of angles that add up to 180°. **Congruent** angles are a pair of angles that have equal measures.

Complementary Angles   Supplementary Angles

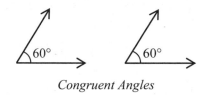

Congruent Angles

A line that **bisects** an angle divides it into two equal parts. In the figure below, line $\overleftrightarrow{BD}$ bisects $\angle ABC$ and divides it into two congruent angles, $\angle ABD$ and $\angle DBC$:

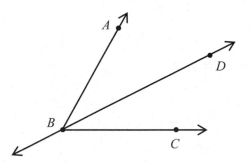

Intersecting Lines and Angles

Two lines are **perpendicular** if they intersect to form a right angle. If two lines are **parallel**, then they will never intersect.

Perpendicular Lines   Parallel Lines

When one line intersects with another line, they form two sets of **vertical angles**. Vertical angles are congruent. In the figure below, $a = d$ and $b = c$.

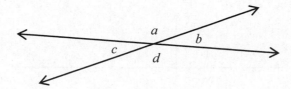

If a third line (a **transversal**) intersects a pair of parallel lines, it forms eight angles:

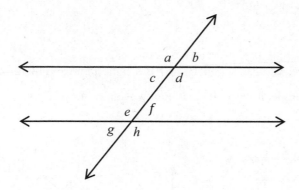

Here are some properties of transversals:

- The pairs of **corresponding angles** are congruent: $a = e$, $b = f$, $c = g$, and $d = h$.
- The pairs of **alternate interior angles** are congruent: $c = f$ and $d = e$.
- The pairs of **alternate exterior angles** are congruent: $a = h$ and $b = g$.
- The pairs of **same side interior angles** are supplementary: $c + e = 180°$ and $d + f = 180°$.

EXAMPLE

In the figure below, line *m* and line *n* are parallel, and line *p* bisects ∠*RST*. What is the value of *x*?

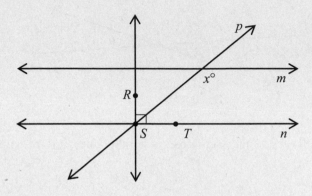

Based on the figure, you can see that ∠*RST* is a right angle and therefore measures 90°. If line *p* bisects this angle, it must divide it into two angles measuring 45° each. You can label these on the figure:

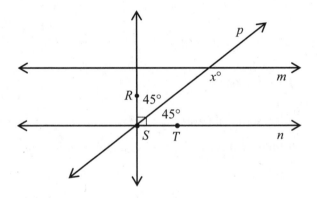

Because line *p* intersects two parallel lines, you know that pairs of same-side interior angles are supplementary. Therefore, you know that *x*° and 45° must add to equal 180°. You can write an algebraic equation and solve for *x*:

$$x + 45 = 180$$

$$x + 45 - 45 = 180 - 45$$

$$x = 135$$

POLYGONS

A **polygon** is a two-dimensional shape with straight sides. Polygons are named for the number of their sides:

Types of Polygons	
Name	Number of Sides
Triangle	3
Quadrilateral	4
Pentagon	5
Hexagon	6
Heptagon	7
Octagon	8

A **vertex** of a polygon is a point where two sides meet. An **interior angle** of a polygon is an angle on the inside of the polygon formed by the intersection of two sides. A **regular polygon** has sides that are all the same length and interior angles that are all the same measure.

To calculate the interior angles of any polygon with n sides, use the following formula:

$$\text{Sum of interior angles} = 180(n - 2)$$

Using this formula, the sum of the interior angles in a hexagon is $180(6 - 2) = 720°$.

Like with congruent angles, two polygons are **congruent** if they have the same size and shape. Congruent polygons have an equal number of sides, equal lengths of corresponding sides, and equal measures of corresponding interior angles. For example, the quadrilaterals below are congruent because they are identical in shape and in size. One just happens to be rotated.

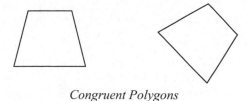

Congruent Polygons

Two polygons are **similar** if they have the same shape, but not the same size. Similar polygons have an equal number of sides, equal measures of corresponding interior angles, and proportional lengths of corresponding sides. For example, the two triangles below are similar because their angles are the same and their sides maintain the same ratio of 3:4:5. However, the triangle on the right is twice as large as the triangle on the left.

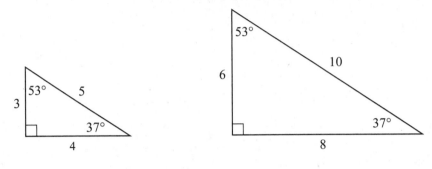

Similar Polygons

The **perimeter** of the polygon is the distance around the polygon. To find any polygon's perimeter, add up the lengths of its sides. For example, the triangles above have perimeters of $3 + 4 + 5 = 12$ and $6 + 8 + 10 = 24$.

The **area** of any polygon is the total space inside a polygon's perimeter. Area is always expressed in terms of square units, such as square inches (in^2) or square centimeters (cm^2). Because polygons can have different numbers of sides, each type of polygon has its own formula for calculating area. Continuing reading to learn about the areas of triangles and quadrilaterals, as well as other special properties of these polygons.

TRIANGLES

A **triangle** is a polygon with exactly three sides. The interior angles of a triangle add to 180°.

Triangles can be categorized according to their sides and angles:

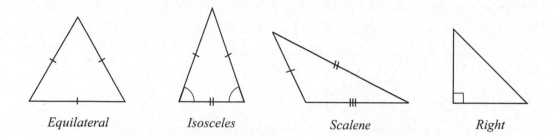

Equilateral   *Isosceles*   *Scalene*   *Right*

- In an **equilateral** triangle, all three sides are the same length and each angle is 60°.
- In an **isosceles** triangle, two of the sides are the same length and the two angles opposite them are congruent.
- In a **scalene** triangle, all three sides are different lengths and all three angles are different measures.
- In a **right** triangle, two sides of the triangle are perpendicular, creating a right angle.

To find the area of a triangle, multiply its base by its height, which is a line segment perpendicular to the base. Then, divide by two:

$$\text{Area of a triangle} = \frac{\text{base} \times \text{height}}{2}$$

The triangle to the right has a base of 8 units and a height of 6 units, so it has an area of 24 square units:

$$\text{area} = \frac{8 \times 6}{2} = 24$$

In Part 2, we'll talk about some more special properties of triangles.

QUADRILATERALS

A **quadrilateral** is a polygon with exactly four sides. The interior angles of a quadrilateral add to 360°. Here are some types of quadrilaterals.

A **parallelogram** is a quadrilateral with two sets of parallel sides. The opposite sides of a parallelogram have equal lengths. The area of a parallelogram is equal to its base multiplied by its height, or a line segment drawn perpendicular to its base. For example, the parallelogram to the right has an area of 60 square units.

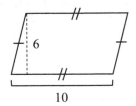

$$\text{Area} = \text{base} \times \text{height} = 6 \times 10 = 60$$

A **rectangle** is a parallelogram with four right angles. Like all parallelograms, the opposite sides of a rectangle are parallel and have equal lengths. The area of a rectangle is equal to its length multiplied by its width. For example, the rectangle to the right has an area of 35 square units:

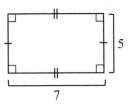

$$\text{Area} = \text{length} \times \text{width} = 5 \times 7 = 35$$

A **square** is a rectangle with four equal sides. A square is a regular quadrilateral because all sides are the same length and all angles are the same measure (90°). The area of a square is equal to the length of one of its sides squared. For example, the square to the right has an area of 9 square units:

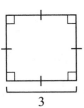

$$\text{Area} = \text{side}^2 = 3^2 = 9$$

A **trapezoid** is a quadrilateral with only one set of parallel sides. These parallel sides are called the trapezoid's bases. The area of a trapezoid is equal to the sum of its bases divided by two, multiplied by its height. For example, the trapezoid to the right has an area of 28 square units:

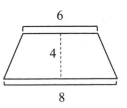

$$\text{Area} = \frac{(\text{base 1} + \text{base 2}) \times \text{height}}{2} = \frac{(6 + 8) \times 4}{2} = 28$$

CIRCLES

A **circle** is a two-dimensional figure made up of points that are all the same distance from its center. The line segment drawn from the center of the circle to any point on the circle is called a **radius** (plural: radii). All possible radii of a circle are the same length.

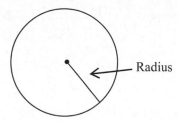

The **diameter** of a circle is a line segment that connects two points on the circle and passes through the center. The length of the diameter of a circle is equal to twice the length of its radius. All diameters of a circle are the same length.

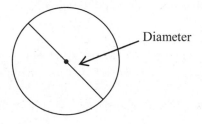

$$\text{diameter} = 2 \times \text{radius}$$

The **circumference** of a circle is the distance around the circle. It can be found by multiplying the diameter by π (**pi**), a special number equal to approximately 3.14:

$$\text{circumference} = \text{diameter} \times \pi$$

Because π is a non-repeating, non-ending decimal number (3.1415927…), you often leave the symbol π as it is when calculating the circumference or area of a circle. Answers on the SAT will be left in terms of π or will give a number (usually 3.14) for π to use for calculations. This gives a more accurate answer than rounding a lengthy decimal number.

To find the **area** of a circle, multiply π by the circle's radius squared:

$$\text{area} = \pi \times \text{radius}^2$$

What is the circumference and area of the circle below?

To calculate the circumference, use the radius of 4 to find the diameter and then multiply by π:

$$\text{circumference} \;=\; \text{diameter} \times \pi \;=\; (2 \times 4) \times \pi \;=\; 8\pi$$

To calculate the area, square the radius and multiply by π:

$$\text{area} \;=\; \pi \times \text{radius}^2 \;=\; \pi \times 4^2 \;=\; 16\pi$$

The circumference of the circle is 8π units, and its area is 16π units squared.

In Part 4, we'll talk about some more special properties of circles.

PRISMS

A prism is a type of **solid,** or a three-dimensional shape. A **prism** is a solid with two congruent polygons, called **bases,** joined by perpendicular rectangles. Each exterior surface of a prism is called a **face,** the lines where these faces intersect are called **edges,** and the points where these edges intersect are called **vertices** (singular: vertex).

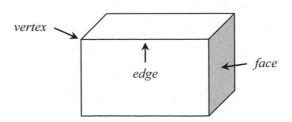

Prisms are named for the shape of their bases. The prism above is a **rectangular prism** because it has a rectangular base—in other words, it's a box.

The volume of a prism is the space contained within the prism. To find the volume of a rectangular prism, multiply its length by its width by its height. For example, the prism to the right has a volume of 40 units cubed:

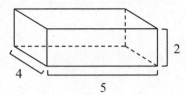

$$\text{Volume} \ = \ \text{length} \times \text{width} \times \text{height} \ = \ 5 \times 4 \times 2 \ = \ 40$$

A rectangular prism whose edges are all the same length is called a cube. The volume of a cube is equal to the length of one of its edges cubed. For example, the cube to the right has a volume of 64 units cubed:

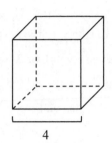

$$\text{Volume} \ = \ \text{edge}^3 \ = \ 4^3 \ = \ 64$$

The volume of any other type of prism can be found by multiplying the area of one of its bases by its length, or the edge perpendicular to its bases. For example, the triangular prism to the right has a volume of 150 cubed units:

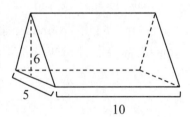

$$\text{Volume} \ = \ \text{base} \times \text{length} \ = \ \frac{6 \times 5}{2} \times 10 \ = \ 150$$

The surface area of any prism can be found by adding together the areas of its faces.

The figure below shows the dimensions of a cardboard box. If there are no overlapping sides, how many square inches of cardboard are needed to make this box?

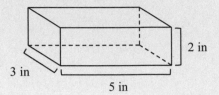

3 in

5 in

2 in

This question is asking you to find the surface area of a rectangular prism with a height of 2 inches, a width of 3 inches, and a length of 5 inches. To find how many square inches of cardboard make up the exterior of the box, you need to find the area of each rectangular face and then add these areas together.

The top and bottom faces each have an area of 5 in × 3 in = 15 in². The front and back faces each have an area of 5 in × 2 in = 10 in². The left and right faces each have an area of 3 in × 2 in = 6 in². To find the total surface area of the box, add together the areas of each of these faces:

$$\left(2 \times 15 \text{ in}^2\right) + \left(2 \times 10 \text{ in}^2\right) + \left(2 \times 6 \text{ in}^2\right) = 62 \text{ in}^2$$

If you wanted to build this box, you would need 62 in² of cardboard.

CYLINDERS

A **cylinder** is like a prism, but its base is a circle instead of a polygon. A cylinder is formed by two circular bases connected by a perpendicular curved surface:

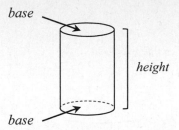

base

height

base

To find the surface area of a cylinder, imagine that the cylinder was sliced along its height and "unfolded" on a flat surface. You would then have two circular bases and one rectangle that normally wraps around the bases. To find the surface area of the cylinder, you need to add up the areas of the bases and the area of this rectangle.

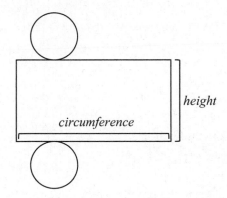

height

circumference

This rectangle has a length that is equal to the circumference of one of the bases, and a width that is equal to the height of the cylinder. Therefore, to find the area of this rectangle, you would multiply the cylinder's circumference by its height. You would then add this number to the area of the two bases to find the total surface area of the cylinder:

$$\text{Surface area} = (\text{area of bases}) + (\text{circumference} \times \text{height})$$

EXAMPLE

Find the surface area of the cylinder below.

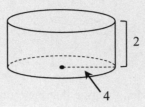

First, find the area of the bases:

$$\text{Area of each base} = \pi \times 4^2 = 16\pi$$

Then, find the circumference:

$$\text{Circumference} = 2 \times \pi \times 4 = 8\pi$$

Finally, add the area of the bases to the product of the circumference and the height:

$$\text{Surface area} = (\text{area of bases}) + (\text{circumference} \times \text{height})$$

$$= (2 \times 16\pi) + (8\pi \times 2)$$

$$= 32\pi + 16\pi = 48\pi$$

The total surface area of the cylinder is 48π square units.

The volume of a cylinder is equal to the area of its base multiplied by its height. The area of the cylinder's base is equal to pi times the radius of the cylinder squared, so you can use the formula below to find the volume of any cylinder:

$$\text{Volume} = \pi \times \text{radius}^2 \times \text{height}$$

What is the volume of the cylinder below?

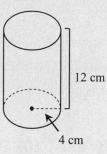

12 cm

4 cm

First, find the area of the cylinder's base, and then multiply by its height:

$$\text{Volume} = \pi \times \text{radius}^2 \times \text{height}$$

$$= \pi \times 4^2 \times 12$$

$$= \pi \times 16 \times 12 = 192\pi$$

The volume of the cylinder is 192π cubic centimeters.

SPHERES

A **sphere** is like a three-dimensional circle: the surface of the sphere is a collection of points that are all the same distance away from the center. As in a circle, the line segment drawn from the center to a point on the sphere's surface is called the sphere's radius, and all radii of a sphere are equal lengths.

The volume of a sphere is equal to $\frac{4}{3}$ pi times its radius cubed. For example, the sphere to the right has a volume of $\frac{32}{3}$ pi units cubed:

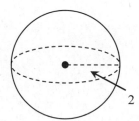

2

$$\text{volume} = \frac{4}{3}\pi r^3 = \frac{4}{3}\pi \times 2^3 = \frac{4}{3}\pi \times 8 = \frac{32}{3}\pi$$

You'll never have to memorize this formula on the SAT. The test will always give you the formula for the volume of a sphere if you need it in order to solve a problem.

In this part, we reviewed some properties of lines, angles, quadrilaterals, triangles, and circles. We also reviewed some properties of solids, including prisms, cylinders, and spheres. During the rest of the section, we'll build on these simple concepts in order to solve some of the more complex Additional Topics questions on the SAT.

PART 1 PRACTICE: INTRODUCTORY GEOMETRY

1. In the figure below, R is the midpoint of $\overline{QS}$. If $QR = 6$, what is the length of $\overline{QS}$?

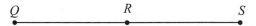

2. In the figure below, angles ABC and CBD are complementary. If $\angle CBD$ measures 70°, what is the measure of $\angle ABC$?

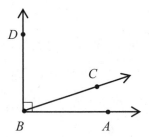

3. If the area of a square is 81 m², what is the length of one of the square's sides?

4. What is the area of the polygon shown below?

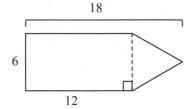

5. What is the area of the circle below?

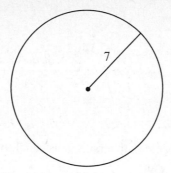

6. If the area of a circle is 64π, what is its diameter?

7. What is the surface area of the rectangular prism below?

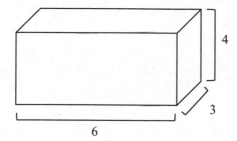

8. What is the volume of the triangular prism below?

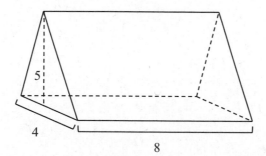

9. What is the volume of the cylinder below?

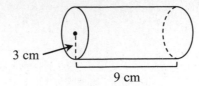

3 cm

9 cm

10. The volume of a sphere with a radius r is equal to $\frac{4}{3}\pi r^3$. If the volume of a sphere is 36π, what is its radius?

ANSWERS: INTRODUCTORY GEOMETRY

1. 12
2. 20°
3. 9 m
4. 90
5. 49π
6. 16
7. 108
8. 80
9. 81π cm^2
10. 3

RIGHT TRIANGLES

PART 2

In the last section, we discussed some basic properties of triangles: their side lengths, perimeters, and areas. In this section we will look at right triangles and see how you can use their special properties to find angles and lengths.

ANGLES OF RIGHT TRIANGLES

In a **right triangle**, one of the angles is always 90°. As we discussed in the last section, the angles of any triangle add to 180°. Therefore, the sum of the two acute angles of a right triangle is always equal to $180 - 90 = 90°$. You can use this information to find unknown angles in a right triangle.

EXAMPLE

Find the value of the angle x.

Because this is a right triangle, you know that the sum of the two acute angles is 90°. You can write an equation to solve for x:

$$20° + x = 90°$$

$$x = 90° - 20° = 70°$$

The angle x is 70°.

PYTHAGOREAN THEOREM

We've seen one way of finding a missing angle of a right triangle. Now we are going to look at how to find a missing side length of a right triangle.

The sides of a right triangle have special names. The **hypotenuse** of a right triangle is the side opposite the right angle, and the other two sides of a right triangle are called its **legs**. The Pythagorean Theorem gives us a formula to solve for the side lengths of a right triangle. According to the **Pythagorean Theorem**, if a and b are the lengths of the triangle's legs and c is the length of its hypotenuse, then a squared plus b squared equals c squared.

This is the Pythagorean Theorem:

$$a^2 + b^2 = c^2$$

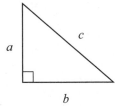

EXAMPLE

What is the value of x in the figure below?

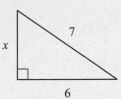

To find the length of the missing side, plug the lengths of the two sides given into the Pythagorean Theorem and solve for x. The sum of the lengths of our two sides squared ($x^2 + 6^2$) is equal to the length of the hypotenuse squared (7^2):

$$x^2 + 6^2 = 7^2$$

$$x^2 + 36 = 49$$

$$x^2 = 13$$

$$x = \sqrt{13}$$

13 isn't a perfect square, so you can't simplify this expression further. For calculator grid-in questions on the SAT, you may occasionally be asked to calculate this as $x = 3.61$. Most often, however, you will find a multiple-choice answer in the form of $x = \sqrt{13}$.

SPECIAL TRIANGLES

While the Pythagorean Theorem can help you find the sides of a right triangle, many triangles don't need so much calculation. The SAT is full of **special triangles**—triangles whose three side lengths have fixed ratios. These include 3-4-5 triangles, 5-12-13 triangles, 30-60-90 triangles, and 45-45-90 triangles. Recognizing a special triangle reduces the time you need to calculate the missing sides.

3-4-5 and 5-12-13 triangles are named for the ratios of their side lengths. **3-4-5 triangles** have side lengths in the ratio of 3:4:5, and **5-12-13 triangles** have side lengths in the ratio of 5:12:13.

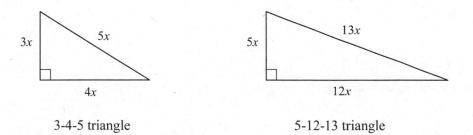

3-4-5 triangle   5-12-13 triangle

For these triangles, x can be any number, and the side ratios will remain the same. For example, if $x = 3$, then the sides of the 3-4-5 triangle would be 9, 12, and 15—but they're still in a 3:4:5 ratio.

Find the missing side of the triangle below:

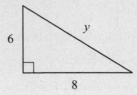

This is a right triangle whose sides have a common factor of 2. You can re-write the side lengths as multiples of 2:

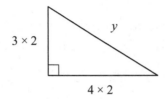

Now you see that these sides are in the ratio of 3:4, and you can use your knowledge of the 3-4-5 special triangle to calculate the missing side. If the lengths of the two legs are 3×2 and 4×2, then the length of the hypotenuse must be 5×2:

$$y = 5 \times 2 = 10$$

The missing side is equal to 10.

30-60-90 triangles and 45-45-90 triangles are named for their angles. **30-60-90 triangles** have angles measured 30°, 60°, and 90°, and side lengths in a ratio of $1:\sqrt{3}:2$. **45-45-90 triangles** have angles measured 45°, 45°, and 90°, and side lengths in a ratio of $1:1:\sqrt{2}$.

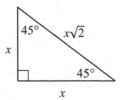

45-45-90 triangle

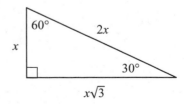

30-60-90 triangle

What are the values of *x* and *y* in the triangle below?

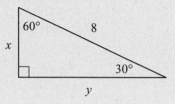

Using what you know about 30-60-90 triangles, you can easily find *x* and *y*. You know that *x* is half of the value of the hypotenuse because it is located opposite the 30 degree angle:

$$x = 8 \div 2 = 4$$

Now that you have the value of *x*, you can find *y* by multiplying *x* by $\sqrt{3}$:

$$y = 4 \times \sqrt{3} = 4\sqrt{3}$$

Knowing the value of just one side and one angle (other than the right angle) of a 30-60-90 triangle allows you to find the values for all three sides!

TRIGONOMETRY

Trigonometry is a more specialized type of math that deals with relationships between sides and angles in right triangles. In addition to using the Pythagorean Theorem and special triangle ratios, you can use trigonometry to calculate the length of sides in right triangles.

In trigonometry, the relationships between sides and angles of right triangles can be written as ratios with specific names. The three ratios you will find on the SAT are sine (abbreviated sin), cosine (abbreviated cos), and tangent (abbreviated tan).

You can find the **sine** of an angle by dividing the length of the side opposite the angle by the length of the triangle's hypotenuse. You can find the **cosine** by dividing the length of the side adjacent to the angle by the length of the hypotenuse. You can find the **tangent** by dividing the length of the opposite side by the length of the adjacent side. These ratios are summarized in the following formulas, where x stands for the measure of any angle in the triangle:

$$\sin(x) = \frac{\text{opposite}}{\text{hypotenuse}}$$

$$\cos(x) = \frac{\text{adjacent}}{\text{hypotenuse}}$$

$$\tan(x) = \frac{\text{opposite}}{\text{adjacent}}$$

In order to help you remember these ratios, it can be useful to think of the acronym **SOHCAHTOA**:

Sine	$\dfrac{\text{Opposite}}{\text{Hypotenuse}}$
Cosine	$\dfrac{\text{Adjacent}}{\text{Hypotenuse}}$
Tangent	$\dfrac{\text{Opposite}}{\text{Adjacent}}$

EXAMPLE

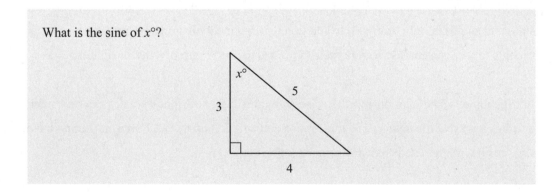

What is the sine of $x°$?

In order to calculate the sine for angle x in this triangle, first locate the side opposite to $x°$. The opposite side has a length of 4. Then, plug this value into the formula for sine:

$$\sin(x°) = \frac{\text{opposite}}{\text{hypotenuse}} = \frac{4}{5}$$

The sine of $x°$ is $\frac{4}{5}$.

You can use your knowledge of sine, cosine, and tangent to solve for the length of one of the sides of a triangle. For example, let's look at the following question:

EXAMPLE

In the triangle below, what is the value of B?

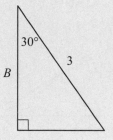

In this triangle, you know the measure of an angle and the length of the hypotenuse. You need to find the length of the side adjacent to the angle. "**SOHCAHTOA**" reminds us that the cosine of an angle compares the adjacent side with the hypotenuse. You can plug the values from the triangle into the cosine ratio formula:

$$\cos(x) = \frac{\text{adjacent}}{\text{hypotenuse}}$$

$$\cos(30°) = \frac{B}{3}$$

Then, you can solve for B:

$$B = \cos(30°) \times 3$$

Using trigonometry, you have determined that the length of B is equal to $\cos(30°) \times 3$. On the SAT, the answer will normally remain in this format. You will not be required to memorize trigonometric values such as $\cos(30°)$.

Before you leave this chapter, make sure that you understand how to find the missing angles and sides of right triangles using the Pythagorean Theorem and trigonometry. Also remember that many questions on the SAT use special right triangles. By memorizing just a few of their ratios and angles, you will save a lot of time and avoid many complex calculations!

PART 2 PRACTICE: RIGHT TRIANGLES

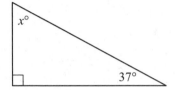

1. Find the value of x in the triangle above.

2. If you know two side lengths of a right triangle, what other information can you calculate?

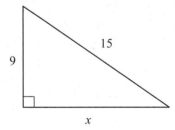

3. What is the value of x in the triangle above?

4. Tim constructed an isosceles right triangle with a hypotenuse of $\sqrt{8}$ in. Each of the triangle's legs is how many inches long?

5. What is the hypotenuse of a right-angled triangle whose legs measure 6cm and 8cm?

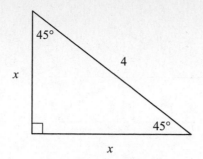

6. What is the value of *x* in the triangle above?

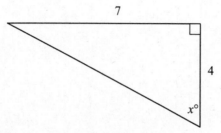

7. For the triangle above, label the hypotenuse and the sides adjacent and opposite to angle *y*.

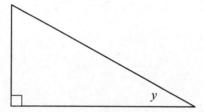

8. What is the tangent of *x*° in the triangle above?

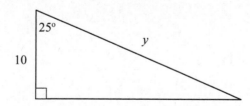

9. What is the value of *y* in the triangle above? Leave your answer in terms of sine, cosine, or tangent.

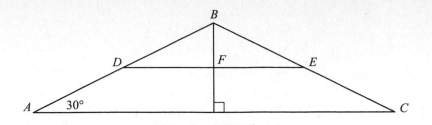

10. In the figure above, $AB = BC = 10$, and $\overline{DE}$ is parallel to $\overline{AC}$. If $BE = \frac{1}{2}BC$, what is the length of $\overline{BF}$?

ANSWER KEY: RIGHT TRIANGLES

1. 53°

2. You can calculate the length of the remaining side. You can also always calculate the angles if you are given two sides of a right triangle.

3. 12

4. 2 in

5. 10 cm

6. $2\sqrt{2}$

7.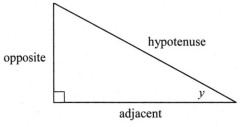

8. $\dfrac{7}{4}$

9. $\dfrac{10}{\cos(25)}$

10. $\dfrac{5}{2}$ or 2.5

RADIANS AND THE UNIT CIRCLE

MEASURING ANGLES

So far, we have been measuring angles in lines and polygons by using degrees. Angles can also be measured in another unit called radians. A **radian** is a unit that measures an angle as a part of a circle. Radians are expressed in the unit pi (π).

There are 2π radians in a circle, or full rotation. Since both 2π radians and 360° are equal to a full rotation, $360° = 2\pi$ radians. You can divide both sides by 2 to get the following equation:

$$180° = \pi \text{ radians}$$

You can use this equation to convert between degrees and radians.

EXAMPLE

What is 270° in radians?

You know that there are π radians in 180°, so you can convert from degrees to radians by multiplying by the conversion factor $\dfrac{\pi}{180°}$:

$$270° \times \frac{\pi \text{ radians}}{180°} = \frac{3\pi}{2} \text{ radians}$$

Here is a table of common angles in degrees and radians:

Degrees	Radians
30°	$\pi/6$
45°	$\pi/4$
60°	$\pi/3$
90°	$\pi/2$
180°	π
270°	$3\pi/2$
360°	2π

THE UNIT CIRCLE

On the SAT, you'll often see questions involving radians and trigonometry. You can solve these questions using a special circle called the unit circle. The **unit circle** is a circle drawn on the x-y plane, centered at $(0, 0)$, with a radius of 1 unit:

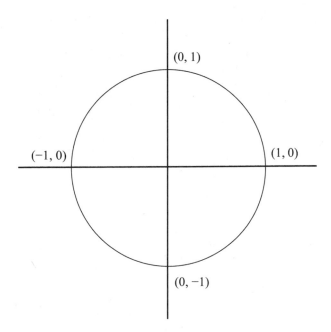

In the unit circle, angles and radians are calculated counterclockwise from the point $(1, 0)$. For example, the angle formed between point $(1, 0)$ and $(0, 1)$ is 90° or $\frac{\pi}{2}$ radians. The angle formed between point $(1, 0)$ and $(0, -1)$ is 270° or $\frac{3\pi}{2}$ radians.

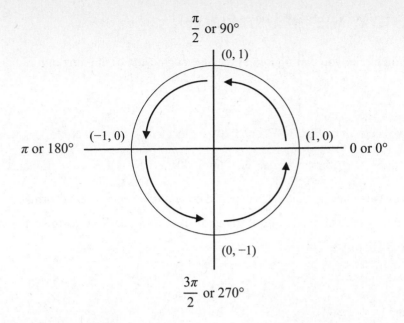

As you move counterclockwise around the unit circle, you can divide it into four quadrants. A **quadrant** is one quarter of the circle. In the diagram below, the labels I, II, III and IV show you the first, second, third, and fourth quadrants.

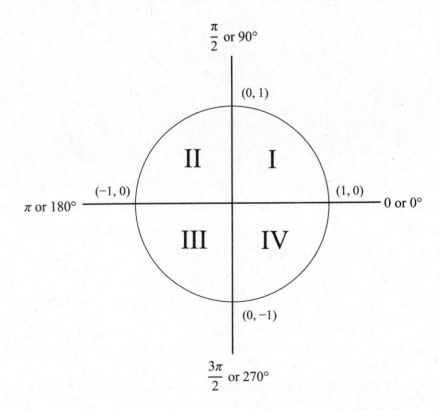

Trigonometry and the Unit Circle

Using the unit circle, you can figure out the sine and cosine of any angle in radians. Let's see how.

So far, we've seen where 90°, 180°, and 270° are located on the unit circle. But what if you wanted to draw a different angle, like 60°? 60° is the same as $\dfrac{\pi}{3}$ radians. Moving counterclockwise from the point (1, 0), you'd draw a line segment that forms a 60° angle with the x-axis. You can make a right triangle with this angle by drawing a line segment down to the x-axis:

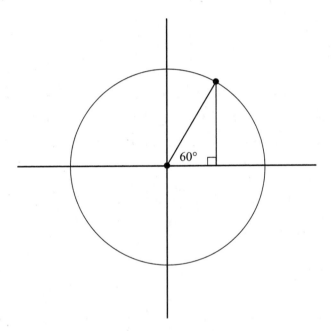

Because you know that the unit circle has a radius of 1, the hypotenuse of the right triangle must be equal to 1. From Part 2, you also know that a right triangle with a 60° angle is a type of special right triangle—a 30-60-90 triangle. Using the formula for the side lengths of 30-60-90 triangles, you can figure out that the lengths of the two sides must be equal to $\dfrac{1}{2}$ and $\dfrac{\sqrt{3}}{2}$.

You can then figure out the point where the right triangle intersects the unit circle. It is $\dfrac{\sqrt{3}}{2}$ units above the x-axis and $\dfrac{1}{2}$ units to the right of the y-axis, so it must be located at point $\left(\dfrac{1}{2}, \dfrac{\sqrt{3}}{2}\right)$:

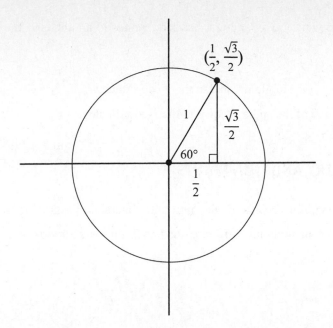

Even though you can calculate the coordinates of this point using 30-60-90 triangles, you actually won't have to do this on the SAT. If you're asked a question about a point on the unit circle, you'll be given its coordinates.

Now that you have all of the side lengths for your right triangle, you can calculate the sine and cosine of 60°, or $\frac{\pi}{3}$ radians. Remember that $\sin(x) = \frac{\text{opposite}}{\text{hypotenuse}}$ and that $\cos(x) = \frac{\text{adjacent}}{\text{hypotenuse}}$. The hypotenuse of the triangle has a length of 1, the side opposite to the 60° angle has a length of $\frac{\sqrt{3}}{2}$, and the side adjacent to the 60° angle has a length of $\frac{1}{2}$. You just have to plug these values into the trigonometric ratios:

$$\sin(60) = \frac{\text{opposite}}{1} = \frac{\sqrt{3}}{2}$$

$$\cos(60) = \frac{\text{adjacent}}{1} = \frac{1}{2}$$

Remember that the point formed by 60° on the unit circle has the coordinates $(\frac{1}{2}, \frac{\sqrt{3}}{2})$. The sine of 60° is $\frac{\sqrt{3}}{2}$, which is the y-coordinate of that point. The cosine of 60° is $\frac{1}{2}$, which is the x-coordinate of that point.

Therefore, when you're given a point that corresponds to an angle on the unit circle, you know that:

- The sine of the angle is equal to the y-coordinate.
- The cosine of the angle is equal to the x-coordinate.

TRIGONOMETRY AND QUADRANTS

Remember that the unit circle is divided into four quadrants. What if we wanted to find the sine and cosine of an angle in a different quadrant? Let's take a look at the angle 120°, or $\frac{2\pi}{3}$ radians:

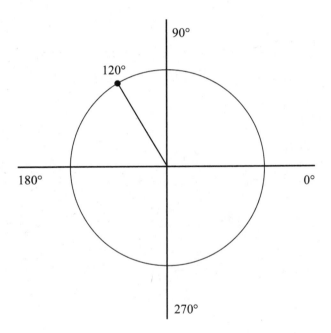

If you draw a line from this point to the x-axis, you'll form another 30-60-90 triangle with side lengths $\frac{1}{2}$ and $\frac{\sqrt{3}}{2}$. The point where this angle intersects the unit circle is $\frac{\sqrt{3}}{2}$ units above the x-axis and $\frac{1}{2}$ units to the left of the y-axis, so it must have the coordinates $(-\frac{1}{2}, \frac{\sqrt{3}}{2})$:

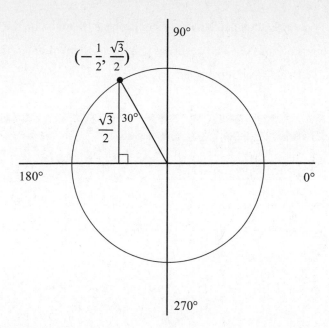

Remember that, for any point corresponding to an angle on the unit circle, the sine of the angle is equal to the y-coordinate and the cosine of the angle is equal to the x-coordinate.

Because $120°$ has the coordinates $(-\frac{1}{2}, \frac{\sqrt{3}}{2})$ on the unit circle, you know that:

$$\sin(120°) \text{ equals the } y\text{-coordinate: } \frac{\sqrt{3}}{2}$$

$$\cos(120°) \text{ equals the } x\text{-coordinate: } -\frac{1}{2}$$

In the first quadrant, you saw that both the sine and cosine were positive. Now that you've drawn an angle in the second quadrant, the sine is still positive but the cosine is negative. This is because all of the points in the second quadrant have positive y-coordinates but negative x-coordinates.

While the SAT will not ask you to calculate the coordinates of points on the unit circle, you need to know the signs of both sine and cosine as you move counterclockwise along the unit circle. Here is a table to help you remember:

Signs of Sine and Cosine around the Unit Circle				
	Quadrant I	Quadrant II	Quadrant III	Quadrant IV
sine	+	+	-	-
cosine	+	-	-	+

EXAMPLE

$$\cos(x) = \frac{\sqrt{2}}{2}$$

Which of the following could be a value for x, in radians?

(A) $\dfrac{\pi}{4}$

(B) $\dfrac{3\pi}{4}$

(C) $\dfrac{6\pi}{5}$

(D) $\dfrac{5\pi}{4}$

First, notice that the cosine of the angle is a positive number. Using the unit circle, you know that cosines are only positive for angles in the first or fourth quadrant, where all points have positive x-coordinates. Next, take a look at the answer options, and draw these angles on the unit circle:

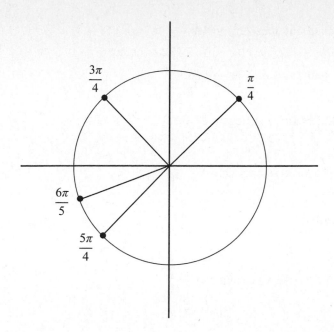

You can see that $\dfrac{3\pi}{4}$ is located in the second quadrant, and $\dfrac{5\pi}{4}$ and $\dfrac{6\pi}{5}$ are located in the third quadrant. You know that cosine is negative in the second and third quadrants, so these angles can't possibly have a cosine equal to $\dfrac{\sqrt{2}}{2}$. Therefore, you can eliminate answer choices (B), (C), and (D).

Since $\dfrac{\pi}{4}$ is located in the first quadrant, we know that its cosine is positive. Therefore, (A) is the only possible answer choice that could have a cosine equal to $\dfrac{\sqrt{2}}{2}$. The correct answer is (A).

PART 3 PRACTICE: RADIANS AND THE UNIT CIRCLE

1. Convert 3π radians into degrees

2. Convert $\pi/6$ radians into degrees.

3. Convert $300°$ into radians.

4. Which quadrant does $\dfrac{\pi}{4}$ fall into?

5. Which quadrant does 228° fall into?

6. Which quadrant does 179° fall into?

7. Is $\cos(32°)$ positive or negative?

8. Is $\cos(\frac{5\pi}{6})$ positive or negative?

9. Is $\sin(\frac{4\pi}{3})$ positive or negative?

10. Is $\cos(317°)$ positive or negative?

ANSWERS: RADIANS AND THE UNIT CIRCLE

1. $540°$

2. $30°$

3. $\dfrac{5\pi}{3}$

4. Quadrant I

5. Quadrant III

6. Quadrant II

7. Positive

8. Negative

9. Negative

10. Positive

CIRCLES
PART 4

In Part 1, we discussed how to find the area and circumference of a circle using the circle's radius and diameter. In this part, we'll talk about different parts of circles, and we'll discuss how to find the perimeters and areas of sections within a circle.

CHORDS

A **chord** is a line segment that connects two different points on the circumference of a circle.

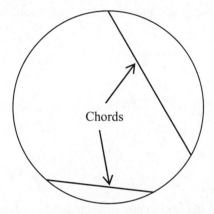

Chords

In order to find the length of a chord, you will need to know the circle's radius (r) and the distance from the chord to the center of the circle (d). You can plug these values into the following formula for chord length:

$$\text{Chord length} = 2\sqrt{r^2 - d^2}$$

You might notice that this formula looks very similar to the Pythagorean Theorem. This is because you can derive this formula by using a right triangle. Half of the chord is one leg of the triangle, so in order to find the whole chord, you multiply the leg by two. Can you figure out how to get the rest of the formula from the Pythagorean Theorem? Hint: the radius of the circle is the hypotenuse of the right triangle.

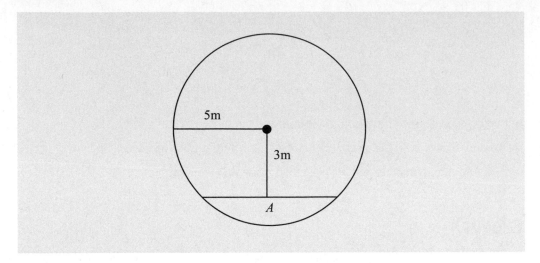

The circle has a radius of 5 m, and chord A is 3 m from the center of the circle. To find the length of chord A, plug these values into the formula for chord length:

$$2\sqrt{(5)^2 - (3)^2} \;=\; 2\sqrt{16} \;=\; 8$$

The length of the chord is 8 m.

ARCS

An **arc** is a portion of the circumference of a circle. You can think of the arc as being "enclosed" by two radii:

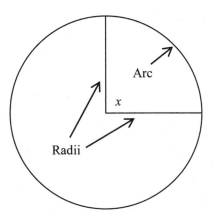

Each arc corresponds to the angle formed between the two radii. The arc in the diagram above corresponds to the angle x.

Arc length is the measure of distance along an arc. The ratio of the arc length to the circumference of the circle is equal to the ratio of the arc angle to the angle of the entire circle, which is 2π radians or $360°$.

To calculate the arc length for an arc angle x, use the following proportions:

$$\frac{\text{Arc Length}}{\text{Circumference}} = \frac{x°}{360°} \qquad \frac{\text{Arc Length}}{\text{Circumference}} = \frac{x \text{ radians}}{2\pi \text{ radians}}$$

EXAMPLE

What is the arc length for a circle with a radius of 3 and an arc angle of $120°$?

First, calculate the circumference of the circle:

$$\text{Circumference} = 2\pi r = 2\pi \times 3 = 6\pi$$

Then, set up the proportion to solve for arc length:

$$\frac{\text{Arc Length}}{\text{Circumference}} = \frac{x°}{360°}$$

$$\frac{\text{Arc Length}}{6\pi} = \frac{120°}{360°}$$

$$\text{Arc Length} = 6\pi \times \frac{120°}{360°} = 2\pi$$

The arc length is 2π.

If the arc angle x is in radians, you can manipulate the arc length proportion above to create a very simple formula for arc length. Here's the proportion again:

$$\frac{\text{Arc Length}}{\text{Circumference}} = \frac{x}{2\pi}$$

First, plug in $2\pi r$ for the circumference, and then simplify:

$$\frac{\text{Arc Length}}{2\pi r} = \frac{x}{2\pi}$$

$$= 2\pi r \times \frac{x}{2\pi}$$

$$= r \times x$$

The length of an arc is equal to the radius of the circle multiplied by the arc angle in radians. To solve the example question above, you could also convert 120° into radians and multiply by the radius. 120° is equal to $\frac{2\pi}{3}$ radians, and the radius is 3, so the arc length is equal to:

$$r \times x = 3 \times \frac{2\pi}{3} = 2\pi$$

SECTORS

A **sector** is the area enclosed by two radii and the arc that they create. Think of a sector as a slice from a circular pizza.

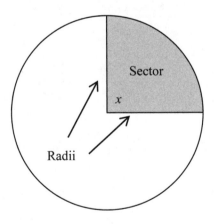

The area of a sector is also determined by the angle x between the two radii. The ratio of the sector area to the area of the circle is equal to the ratio of the sector angle to the angle of the entire circle. To calculate the sector area for a sector angle x, use the following proportions:

$$\frac{\text{Sector Area}}{\text{Circle Area}} = \frac{x°}{360°} \qquad \frac{\text{Sector Area}}{\text{Circle Area}} = \frac{x \text{ radians}}{2\pi \text{ radians}}$$

What is the area of a sector with an angle of 120° and a radius of 3?

First, calculate the area of the circle:

$$\text{Circle Area} = \pi r^2 = \pi \times 3^2 = 9\pi$$

Then, set up the proportion to solve for sector area:

$$\frac{\text{Sector Area}}{\text{Circle Area}} = \frac{x°}{360°}$$

$$\frac{\text{Sector Area}}{9\pi} = \frac{120°}{360°}$$

$$\text{Sector Area} = 9\pi \times \frac{120°}{360°} = 3\pi$$

The area of the sector is 3π.

GRAPHING CIRCLES

Circles can be graphed on the xy-plane. On the SAT, you will need to know the equation of a circle on the xy-plane. You will also need to know how to find the circle's center and radius from its equation or its graph. If you know the central point of the circle and another point on the circumference, you can find the radius of the circle.

The figure below shows a circle with a center at point (a, b). The point (x, y) is found on the circumference of the circle. You can connect these two points with a radius of the circle, and draw a right triangle:

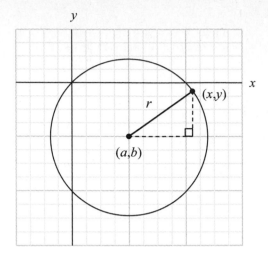

The hypotenuse of this right triangle is the radius of the circle, r. The base of the triangle is equal to the difference between the two x-coordinates of the points: $x - a$. The height of the triangle is equal to the difference between the two y-coordinates: $y - b$.

To set up an equation that describes the relationship between the radius and the two points, you can plug in the lengths for the sides of the triangle into the Pythagorean Theorem:

$$(x - a)^2 + (y - b)^2 \ = \ r^2$$

This is the standard form for the equation of a circle. This equation tells you that the circle has its center at point (a, b) and a radius with length r.

EXAMPLE

The equation of a circle is defined by the equation $(x - 2)^2 + (y + 1)^2 = 144$. What are the center and radius of this circle?

In order to find the center and radius of this circle, you'll need to rewrite its equation so it looks like the formula above:

$$(x - 2)^2 + (y - (-1))^2 \ = \ 12^2$$

Now that the equation is in standard form, you can see that $a = 2$, $b = -1$, and $r = 12$. Therefore, the circle's center is located at $(2, -1)$, and the circle's radius is 12.

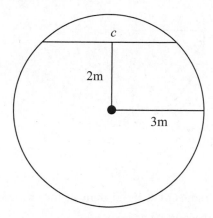

1. On the diagram above, what is the length of chord *c*?

2. A chord is located 12 ft from the center of a circle. If the chord is 10 ft long, what is the radius of a circle?

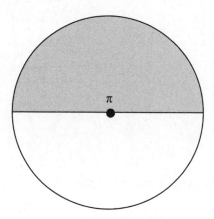

3. The circle above has a diameter of 20. If the angle of the shaded area is π radians, what is the length of the corresponding arc?

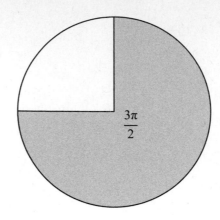

4. The circle above has a radius of 4. If the angle of the shaded area is $\frac{3\pi}{2}$ radians, what is the length of the corresponding arc?

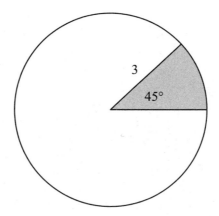

5. If the angle of the shaded area in the circle above is 45°, what is the length of the corresponding arc?

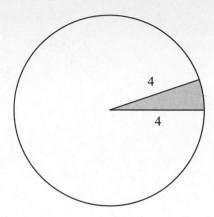

6. The shaded sector in the circle above makes up $\dfrac{1}{16}$ of the total area of the circle. What is the area of the shaded sector?

7. A circle has a diameter of 1 m. Sector Z of the circle has an area of 0.5 m². What is the value of the sector angle, in radians, that corresponds to Sector Z?

8. What are the center and radius of a circle on the xy-plane described by the equation $x^2 + y^2 = 1$?

9. What are the center and radius of a circle on the xy-plane described by the equation $(x - 1)^2 + (y + 1)^2 = 9$?

10. A circle has radius of 5 units and is centered at point (–1, 17). What is the equation that describes this circle?

Answer Key: Circles

1. $2\sqrt{5}$ m

2. 13 ft

3. 10π

4. 6π

5. $\dfrac{3\pi}{4}$

6. π

7. 4 radians

8. Center: $(0, 0)$. Radius: 1

9. Center: $(1, -1)$. Radius: 3

10. $(x + 1)^2 + (y - 17)^2 = 25$

COMPLEX NUMBERS
PART 5

So far, we have discussed the properties of real numbers, or any number that can be found on a number line. In this part, we'll see what numbers lie beyond the real numbers. These include imaginary and complex numbers, which use the symbol *i* and follow special rules.

IMAGINARY NUMBERS

Normally, it is impossible to take the square root of a negative number. Even when you square a negative number, you end up with a positive result. Therefore, there isn't a way to work backwards and find a real number that is the square root of a negative number.

However, sometimes it is helpful to "imagine" that we can take the square root of a negative number and use this in our calculations. We can do this by introducing the unit *i*, which is equal to the square root of −1:

$$i^2 = -1$$

$$i = \sqrt{-1}$$

Because a number like *i* does not exist in the set of real numbers, we call it an **imaginary number**. In equations and calculations that involve imaginary numbers, we can use *i* as a placeholder for $\sqrt{-1}$.

SIMPLIFYING EXPRESSIONS WITH *i*

In an expression that involves imaginary numbers, you can simplify the square root of any negative number by using *i*.

EXAMPLE

Simplify $\dfrac{\sqrt{-16}}{2}$ in terms of i.

First, re-write the square root as the product of two square roots:

$$\frac{\sqrt{-16}}{2} = \frac{\sqrt{-1} \times \sqrt{16}}{2}$$

Then, plug in i for $\sqrt{-1}$ and simplify:

$$\frac{\sqrt{-1} \times \sqrt{16}}{2} = \frac{i \times \sqrt{16}}{2} = \frac{4i}{2} = 2i$$

Your final answer is $2i$.

We know that the square of i is -1, but now let's look at what happens when we raise i to another exponent. For example, what happens when you take the cube of i? You can substitute $\sqrt{-1}$ for i in order to work out the equation:

$$i^3 = \left(\sqrt{-1}\right)^3$$

$$i^3 = \sqrt{-1} \times \sqrt{-1} \times \sqrt{-1}$$

$$i^3 = -1 \times \sqrt{-1}$$

$$i^3 = -1 \times i$$

$$i^3 = -i$$

The square of i is -1, but the cube of i is $-i$.

Here is a chart showing the values of i raised to some other exponents:

$i^0 = 1$
$i^1 = i$
$i^2 = -1$
$i^3 = -i$
$i^4 = 1$

Using this table, you can determine the value of i raised to any other power.

EXAMPLE

Let's see how to figure out the value of i^5.

You know that $i^4 = 1$ and $i^5 = i^4 \times i$. Plugging in these values, you can write:

$$i^5 = 1 \times i = i$$

Therefore, i^5 is the same thing as i, or $\sqrt{-1}$.

COMPLEX NUMBERS

A **complex number** is the sum of a real number and an imaginary number. Complex numbers are normally written in the form $a + bi$, where a is the real component and bi is the imaginary component. For example, $4 + 2i$ is a complex number with a real component, 4, and an imaginary component, $2i$.

On the SAT, you'll need to know how to simplify expressions with complex numbers by adding, subtracting, and multiplying. These operations are simple if you treat the imaginary variable i like any other variable in an algebraic expression.

To add or subtract expressions with complex numbers, first group together like terms—that is, group real numbers together and group imaginary numbers together. Then, add or subtract the real numbers, and add or subtract the imaginary numbers.

EXAMPLE

$$(3 + 5i) + (2 + 3i)$$

First, group together the real numbers and the imaginary numbers:

$$3 + 5i + 2 + 3i = (3 + 2) + (5i + 3i)$$

Then, add the like terms:

$$(3 + 2) + (5i + 3i) = 5 + 8i$$

The final answer is $5 + 8i$.

Multiplying complex numbers is similar to multiplying binomials: use the FOIL method to multiply all of the components in the complex numbers. The only difference is that you'll need to simplify i raised to any power greater than 1. See Section 5 for a review of the FOIL method.

EXAMPLE

$$(3 + 4i)(6 + 2i)$$

Use the FOIL method to multiply out the two binomials:

$$(3 - 4i)(6 + 2i) = 18 + 6i - 24i - 8i^2$$

Then, combine like terms:

$$18 + 6i - 24i - 8i^2 = -8i^2 - 18i + 18$$

Notice that you have i^2 in the answer. Because $i^2 = -1$, you can plug -1 into the answer in place of i^2:

$$-8(-1) - 18i + 18 \ = \ 8 - 18i + 18$$

Finally, combine like terms again:

$$26 - 18i$$

The final simplified answer is $26 - 18i$.

PART 5 PRACTICE: COMPLEX NUMBERS

1. Write $\sqrt{-64}$ in terms of i.

2. Write $8\sqrt{-49}$ in terms of i.

3. $\dfrac{5\sqrt{-4}}{2i} =$

4. $5i^3 =$

5. $i^7 =$

6. $(8 + 2i) + (2 + 8i) =$

7. $(1 + i) + (7 - i) =$

8. $(49 - 3i) - (48 + 2i) =$

9. $(1 + i) \times (1 + i) =$

10. $(3 + 3i) \times (4 - 4i) =$

ANSWER KEY: COMPLEX NUMBERS

1. $8i$

2. $56i$

3. 5

4. $-5i$

5. $-i$

6. $10 + 10i$

7. 8

8. $1 - 5i$

9. $2i$

10. 24

PRACTICE SET
PART 6

In this part, you'll find 30 SAT-style questions to practice the Additional Topics in Math subject matter that you learned in this section. Check your answers with the answer key that follows. For any question that you get wrong, identify the topic of the question, and then review the part of this section that covers that topic.

1. What is the area of a circle with a diameter of 6?

    (A) 6π
    (B) 9π
    (C) 18π
    (D) 36π

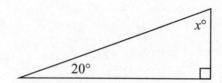

2. In the figure above, what is the value of x?

    (A)   70
    (B)   80
    (C)   110
    (D)   160

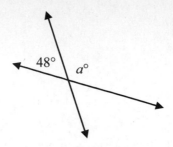

3. What is the value of *a* in the figure above?

    (A)   42

    (B)   48

    (C)   90

    (D)   132

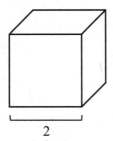

2

4. What is the surface area of the cube above?

    (A)   4

    (B)   12

    (C)   18

    (D)   24

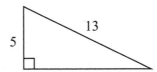

5. The triangle above has an area of 30. What is its perimeter?

    (A)   12

    (B)   18

    (C)   24

    (D)   30

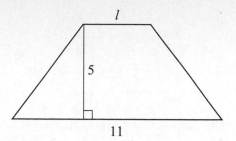

6. The trapezoid above has an area of 35. What is *l*?

   (A) 1

   (B) 2

   (C) 3

   (D) 4

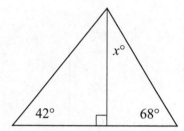

7. In the diagram above, what is the value of *x*?

   (A) 22

   (B) 48

   (C) 70

   (D) 72

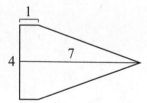

8. The diagram above is a top view of a paper airplane. What is the surface area of the top of the plane?

   (A) 8

   (B) 12

   (C) 16

   (D) 28

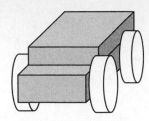

9. The wheels on the toy car above are cylinders. The face of each wheel has an area of 80 mm² and each wheel is 5 mm thick. What is the combined volume of the four wheels, in mm³?

(A)   400

(B)   800

(C) 1,200

(D) 1,600

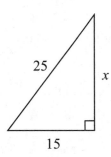

10. In the above diagram, what is the value of x?

(A) 18

(B) 20

(C) 22

(D) 24

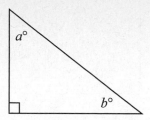

11. If $a \neq b$, which of the following is equivalent to cos (a)?

    (A) sin (a)

    (B) sin (b)

    (C) tan (a)

    (D) cos (b)

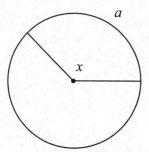

12. The circle above has a radius of 6. Angle x forms arc a. If the measure of angle x in degrees is 120°, what is the length of arc a?

    (A) 2π

    (B) 4π

    (C) 6π

    (D) 12π

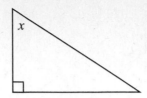

13. If $\sin(x) = \frac{4}{5}$, what is $\cos(x)$?

(A) $\frac{1}{5}$

(B) $\frac{3}{5}$

(C) $\frac{3}{4}$

(D) $\frac{4}{3}$

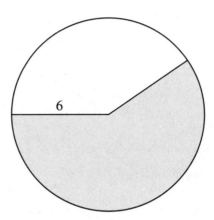

14. The circle above has a radius of 6. If the shaded region has an area of 24π, what is the arc length of the shaded region?

(A) 4π

(B) 8π

(C) 9π

(D) 12π

15. The imaginary number i is defined such that $i^2 = -1$. Which of the following expressions is equivalent to $\sqrt{-9}$?

(A) $3i$

(B) $3i^2$

(C) $9i$

(D) $9i^2$

16. A circle on the xy-plane has its center at $(0, 0)$ and a radius of 4. Which of the following points lies on the circumference of the circle?

(A) $(2, 2)$

(B) $\left(2, 2\sqrt{3}\right)$

(C) $\left(2\sqrt{3}, 2\sqrt{3}\right)$

(D) $(4, 2)$

$$\cos \frac{\pi}{3} = \cos \frac{x\pi}{3}$$

17. Which of the following values of x completes the equation above?

(A) -1

(B) 0

(C) 2

(D) 3

18. The imaginary number i is defined such that $i^2 = -1$. What is the sum of $4 + 7i$ and $-3 - 4i$?

(A) $1 + 3i$

(B) $-1 + 3i$

(C) $7 - 3i$

(D) $7 + 11i$

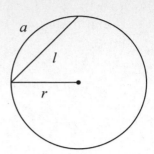

19. The circle above has a radius r. Arc a has a length of $\frac{\pi r}{2}$. What is l, the length of the chord, in terms of r?

(A) r

(B) $\sqrt{2}r$

(C) $2r$

(D) πr

$$\sin\left(\frac{3\pi}{2}\right)$$

20. Which of the following is equal to the expression above?

(A) $\sin\left(\frac{\pi}{2}\right)$

(B) $\sin\left(\frac{3\pi}{4}\right)$

(C) $\sin(3\pi)$

(D) $\sin\left(\frac{7\pi}{2}\right)$

GRID-INS

21. A circle has a circumference of 16π. What is its radius?

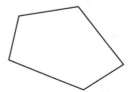

22. The diagram above shows an irregular pentagon. What is the sum of its interior angles, in degrees?

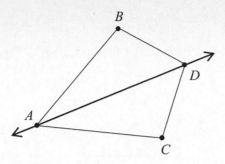

23. In the diagram above, $\overline{AD}$ bisects $\angle BAC$ and $\angle BDC$. $\angle BAC = 50°$ and $\angle BDC = 110°$. What is the measure of $\angle ABD$, in degrees?

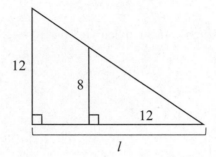

24. In the diagram above, what is the length l?

25. A cylindrical can of soup has a volume of 45π cubic inches and a height of 5 inches. What is the radius of one of its faces, in inches?

26. What is the value of $\sqrt{-4} \times \sqrt{-4} \times \sqrt{-9} \times \sqrt{-16}$?

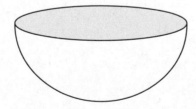

27. A bowl is in the shape of half a sphere with a diameter of 6 inches. If the bowl is completely filled with water, it fits πw cubic inches of water. What is w? (The volume V of a sphere with a radius of r is given by $V = \frac{4}{3}\pi r^3$).

28. If $\cos(x) = -\dfrac{3}{4}$, what is the value for $\cos(x + \pi)$?

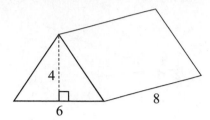

29. A regular triangular prism is shown above. What is the surface area of the prism?

$$(2 - i) \times (1 - 2i) = p - 5i$$

30. The imaginary number i is defined such that $i^2 = -1$. What value of p satisfies the equation above?

Answer Key: Part 6 Practice Set

1. B
2. A
3. D
4. D
5. D
6. C
7. A
8. C
9. D
10. B
11. B
12. B
13. B
14. B
15. A
16. B
17. A
18. A
19. B
20. D
21. 8
22. 540
23. 100
24. 18
25. 3
26. 48
27. 18
28. $\frac{3}{4}$
29. 152
30. 0

SAT Math Practice Test (Calculator)

Time – 55 minutes
38 Questions

Download and print an answer sheet available at ivyglobal.com/study.

Notes

1. Choose the best answer choice of those provided. Be sure to fill in the corresponding circle on your answer sheet.
2. You may use a calculator on this section.
3. If a problem includes a figure and does not state that the figure is NOT to scale, you may assume the figure provides a correct representation of the information in the problem.
4. The domain of any function f is the set of all real numbers x for which $f(x)$ is a real number, unless otherwise stated.

Reference

$A = \frac{1}{2}bh$ $a^2 + b^2 = c^2$ Special Triangles $V = \frac{1}{3}lwh$ $V = \frac{1}{3}\pi r^2 h$

$A = lw$ $V = lwh$ $V = \pi r^2 h$ $A = \pi r^2$ \quad $C = 2\pi r$ $V = \frac{4}{3}\pi r^3$

- There are 360° in a circle.
- The sum of the angles in a triangle is 180°.
- The number of radians of arc of a circle is 2π.

---

1. A biochemist is counting the number of cells in a sample using a square grid. If he counts 15 cells in one square, which of the following is the best estimate for the total number of cells in n squares?

(A) $\dfrac{15}{n}$

(B) $15n$

(C) $225n$

(D) $15n^2$

2. Which graph could represent the function $y = -2x + 1$?

(A)   (B)

(C)   (D)

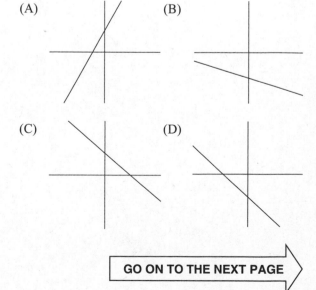

GO ON TO THE NEXT PAGE

3. If $f(x) = \dfrac{1000}{x - 20}$, what is $f(10)$?

(A) −100
(B) −102
(C) −120
(D) −1200

$$y = 0.75x + 10$$

4. In the equation above, what is the value of x if y is equal to 10?

(A)   0
(B)   7.5
(C)   10
(D)   17.5

5. There are 6 blue marbles, 3 yellow marbles, and 4 red marbles in a jar. John randomly draws 2 marbles without replacing them. What is the probability that both of these marbles are blue?

(A) $\dfrac{30}{169}$

(B) $\dfrac{3}{13}$

(C) $\dfrac{5}{26}$

(D) $\dfrac{12}{13}$

$$10x - 2y + 3 = 11$$

$$y = 5x - 4$$

6. Which of the following describes the solution set for the system of equations above?

(A) There are zero solutions.
(B) There is one solution.
(C) There are two solutions.
(D) There are infinite solutions.

GO ON TO THE NEXT PAGE

7. If $(x + 20)^2 = (70 - x)^2$, what is the value of x?

(A)   5
(B) 25
(C) 45
(D) 90

9. Which of the following is equal to $(3x - 5)^2$?

(A) $9x^2 - 25$
(B) $9x^2 - 15x + 25$
(C) $9x^2 - 30x - 25$
(D) $9x^2 - 30x + 25$

Distance Travelled

8. The scatterplot above shows the cumulative distances travelled by two truck drivers over a 10-hour period. What is the difference between the average speeds of the two drivers over this time period?

(A) 10 miles per hour
(B) 20 miles per hour
(C) 30 miles per hour
(D) 50 miles per hour

10. The element palladium has a density of 12 g/cm^3. What is the volume in cubic centimeters of 2.4 kilograms of palladium? (Density is equal to mass divided by volume.)

(A)   0.2 cm^3
(B)   28.8 cm^3
(C)   200 cm^3
(D)   2880 cm^3

GO ON TO THE NEXT PAGE

M □ □ □ □ □ □ M
Unapproved reproduction or distribution
of any portion of this material is unlawful.

11. If $1.5x + 2y = 58$ and $x + y = 34$, what is the value of x?

(A) 10
(B) 20
(C) 30
(D) 58

---

12. A group of scientists in an observatory catch, tag, and then release 50 butterflies. The next day, they catch 100 butterflies and observe that 10 of them are tagged. Which of the following is the best estimate for the total number of butterflies at the observatory?

(A) 140
(B) 150
(C) 200
(D) 500

13. If $a^7 \times a^x = (a^2)^4$, what is the value of x?

(A) -1

(B) 1

(C) $\dfrac{6}{7}$

(D) $\dfrac{8}{7}$

	Cheetah	Seahorse
Average Speed	70 km/hr	1.5 cm/min
Top Speed	120 km/hr	2.5 cm/min

14. How many times faster is the top speed of a cheetah than the top speed of a seahorse, according to the table above?

(A) 48
(B) 800
(C) 80,000
(D) 480,000

GO ON TO THE NEXT PAGE

$$2x = x^2 - 8$$

15. Which of the following could be a value for x in the equation above?

(A) −4
(B)   0
(C)   2
(D)   4

16. What is the distance between the points $(-2, 5)$ and $(5, 12)$ in the xy-plane?

(A)   7
(B) $7\sqrt{2}$
(C) $\sqrt{58}$
(D)   14

17. A chemist has an experiment that requires a solution made of 80 µL of hydrochloric acid and 10 mg of magnesium oxide. If the chemist uses 300 mg of magnesium oxide, how many milliliters of the hydrochloric acid solution does she need? (1 L = 1,000,000 µL).

(A)   2.4 mL
(B)   24 mL
(C)   240 mL
(D)   2,400 mL

18. A car is travelling at an average speed of 50 miles per hour, and the distance from its starting point to its destination is 600 miles. Which function models the remaining distance, in miles, to be travelled after t hours of travel?

(A) $f(t) = 12t$
(B) $f(t) = 50t$
(C) $f(t) = 600 + 50t$
(D) $f(t) = 600 - 50t$

GO ON TO THE NEXT PAGE

$$4y > 3x - 5$$

19. Which of the following points in the *xy*-plane could be a solution to the inequality above?

(A) $(-1, -5)$
(B) $(-1, -2)$
(C) $(1, -2)$
(D) $(3, 2)$

---

20. Stacey's recipe can bake 42 cookies with one gallon of milk. Milk costs $2.40 per gallon. How many cookies can Stacey bake with $10 worth of milk?

(A) 100 cookies
(B) 125 cookies
(C) 150 cookies
(D) 175 cookies

$$f(x) = 2x - 10$$
$$g(x) = \frac{x}{3} + 1$$

21. What is the value of $g(f(23))$?

(A) $\dfrac{22}{3}$

(B) $\dfrac{26}{3}$

(C) 12

(D) 13

	In Favor	Not in Favor	Total
Non-drivers	20	10	30
Drivers	12	20	32
Total	32	30	62

22. A random group of people were surveyed about their opinion on building a new bridge in their city, and the results are shown above. If there are a total of 700 people in the city, which of the following is the best estimate for the total number of people in the city who would be in favor of building the new bridge?

(A) 263
(B) 350
(C) 361
(D) 467

GO ON TO THE NEXT PAGE

$$x^2 - y^2 = 9$$

$$x - y = 1$$

23. In the system of equations above, what is the value of $x + y$?

(A)   4
(B)   8
(C)   9
(D)   10

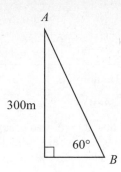

25. What is the shortest distance between Points A and B in the figure above?

(A) $\dfrac{200\sqrt{3}}{3}$ m

(B) $100\sqrt{3}$ m

(C) $200\sqrt{3}$ m

(D)   400 m

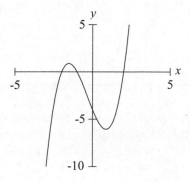

24. The function graphed above is defined by the function $f(x) = (x + 2)(x - 2)(x + a)$. What is the value of a?

(A)   −1
(B)   0
(C)   1
(D)   2

$$f(x) = (x + 7)(x - 2)^2$$

26. For what values of x is $f(x)$ positive?

(A) $x < -2$
(B) $x < 7$
(C) $x < -7, x > 2$
(D) $x > -7$

GO ON TO THE NEXT PAGE

	Group A	Group B
Standard Deviation	2.0	3.0
Number of Data Points	50	100

27. The standard deviation of two groups of data is summarized the table above. Which of the following statements is true?

(A) Group A has a smaller standard deviation than Group B because there are fewer data points.
(B) The difference in standard deviation between the two groups is not statistically significant.
(C) The data points of Group B are farther from their mean on average than the data points of Group A.
(D) Group B's data points have a larger range than Group A's data points.

28. If $i^2 = -1$, what is the value of $(2i + 2)(2i - 4)$?

(A) -12
(B) $-4i - 12$
(C) -8
(D) $-4i - 8$

Questions 29 and 30 refer to the following information.

Gross domestic product (GDP) is a measure of the value of goods and services produced in a year. GDP per capita is an area's GDP divided by its population.

GDP of a City

Year	GDP	GDP per capita
1990	$120 million	$32,000
2000	$135 million	$30,000
2010	$147 million	$28,000

29. According to the table above, what was the city's population in the year 2000?

(A) 3,000 people
(B) 4,500 people
(C) 22,222 people
(D) 45,000 people

30. What was the city's percent increase in population between 1990 and 2010?

(A) 1.67%
(B) 16.67%
(C) 30.00%
(D) 40.00%

GO ON TO THE NEXT PAGE

GRID-INS

$$y + 3x < 10$$

31. If $x = 2$, what is a positive value of y that satisfies the inequality above?

32. Phone Plan A charges a flat rate of $20 per month plus 40 cents per minute. Phone Plan B charges $10 plus 50 cents per minute. If Tess uses the same number of minutes each month, she pays the same amount of money on either plan. How many minutes does Tess use each month?

33. If $\dfrac{p}{3} - 5 = \dfrac{q}{4}$, what is the value of $4p - 3q$?

34. Adam, Bella, Carlos, Diana, and Eric run a race. If Carlos and Diana finish in the first two places and there are no ties, what is the total number of possible outcomes of the race?

GO ON TO THE NEXT PAGE

$$\frac{10 - (m - 2)}{4} = \frac{3(m + 6)}{8}$$

35. In the equation above, what is the value of m?

36. A farmer is creating a rectangular fenced-in pasture for his cattle that is twice as long as it is wide. Fencing costs $4 per meter. If the whole fence costs $2,400, how many meters is the pasture's longest side?

Annual Income	Tax Rate
$1 to $30,000	10%
$30,001 to $70,000	14%
$70,001 to $100,000	20%
$100,001 or over	25%

Questions 37 and 38 refer to the following information.

Many countries use progressive tax systems for income like the one summarized in the chart above. Using this chart, a person making $50,000 per year would be taxed at 10% for their first $30,000 and 14% for their next $20,000.

37. Liu makes $75,000 per year. According to the progressive system in the chart above, how much income tax would Liu pay per year, in dollars?

38. In Kristof's country, he pays a fixed tax of 14% on his entire income. Kristof makes $80,000 per year. How much more yearly income tax would Kristof pay in his country than in a country that uses the progressive system in the chart above?

STOP

If you complete the problem set before time elapses, you may review your responses for this section.

Do not view or begin working on any other sections.

ANSWER KEY:

1. B
2. C
3. A
4. A
5. C
6. D
7. B
8. A
9. D
10. C
11. B
12. D
13. B
14. C
15. D
16. B
17. A
18. D
19. D
20. D
21. D
22. C
23. C
24. C
25. C
26. D
27. C
28. B
29. B
30. D
31. $0 < y < 4$
32. 100
33. 60

34. 12

35. 1.2 or 6/5

36. 200

37. 9600

38. 600

Full explanations available at ivyglobal.com/study

SAT Math Practice Test (No-calculator)

Time – 25 minutes
20 Questions

Download and print an answer sheet available at ivyglobal.com/study.

Notes

1. Choose the best answer choice of those provided. Be sure to fill in the corresponding circle on your answer sheet.
2. You may NOT use a calculator on this section.
3. If a problem includes a figure and does not state that the figure is NOT to scale, you may assume the figure provides a correct representation of the information in the problem.
4. The domain of any function f is the set of all real numbers x for which $f(x)$ is a real number, unless otherwise stated.

Reference

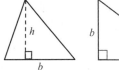

$A = \frac{1}{2}bh$

$a^2 + b^2 = c^2$

Special Triangles

$V = \frac{1}{3}lwh$

$V = \frac{1}{3}\pi r^2 h$

$A = lw$

$V = lwh$

$V = \pi r^2 h$

$A = \pi r^2$
$C = 2\pi r$

$V = \frac{4}{3}\pi r^3$

- There are 360° in a circle.
- The sum of the angles in a triangle is 180°.
- The number of radians of arc of a circle is 2π.

$$50x > -20$$

1. Which of the following represents all values of x that satisfy the inequality above?

(A)

(B)

(C)
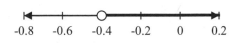

(D)

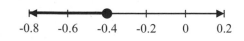

2. John runs three laps around a 400 m track at a constant speed. If it takes John 10 minutes to run all three laps, what is his speed in meters per second?

(A) 1
(B) 2
(C) 3
(D) 10

GO ON TO THE NEXT PAGE

3. If $m - 2 = \dfrac{x}{5}$, what is the value of $10x$ in terms of m?

   (A) $10m - 20$
   (B) $10m - 2$
   (C) $50m - 100$
   (D) $50m - 2$

x	$f(x)$
10	70
15	60
20	50

4. The table above shows values for the linear function $f(x)$. What is $f(30)$?

   (A) 25
   (B) 30
   (C) 35
   (D) 40

5. Armin is leasing a car. He pays $2,000 for the first month and $400 for every month after the first. If Armin has $20,000 to spend, for how many months can he lease the car?

   (A)   5
   (B) 10
   (C) 46
   (D) 50

$$2y - x = 12$$
$$4x + y = 12$$

6. Based on the system of equations above, what is the value of $x + y$?

   (A)   6
   (B)   8
   (C) 12
   (D) 24

GO ON TO THE NEXT PAGE

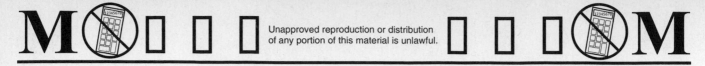

Brick Type	Price Per Brick
Type A	$3
Type B	$5

7. The price of two different types of bricks is shown in the chart above. The number of bricks predicted to be sold, b, varies according to the price per brick, p, according to the equation $b = -150p + 950$. How many Type A bricks are predicted to be sold?

(A) 150
(B) 200
(C) 500
(D) 950

8. If $2x^2 - 9x - 5 = 0$ and $x > 0$, what is the value of x?

(A) $\dfrac{1}{2}$

(B) 1

(C) 2

(D) 5

9. Jocelyn bought a new computer 2 years ago for $1000. If the computer's value decreased by 10% each year, how much is it now worth?

(A) $1000
(B) $900
(C) $810
(D) $800

10. If a and b are the two x-intercepts of the graph of $y = x^2 - 36$, and $a > b$, what is the value of $\dfrac{a}{b}$?

(A) -1
(B) 0
(C) 1
(D) 6

GO ON TO THE NEXT PAGE

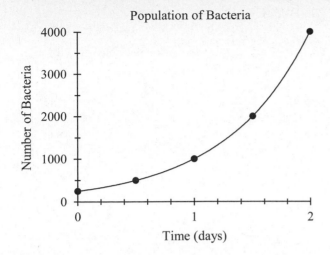

Population of Bacteria

11. A biologist is growing a colony of bacteria that doubles every 12 hours, as shown in the graph above. There were initially 250 bacteria in the colony. Which equation correctly models number of bacteria N as a function of time t, measured in days since the population began growing?

(A) $N = 500 \times t^{12}$
(B) $N = 250 \times 2^{t/2}$
(C) $N = 250 \times 2^{t}$
(D) $N = 250 \times 2^{2t}$

$$\sqrt{2x - 5} = x - 2$$

12. Which of the following describes the solution set of the equation above?

(A) There are no real solutions.
(B) There is one real solution.
(C) There are two real solutions.
(D) There are three real solutions.

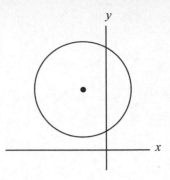

13. A circle with radius 6 is centered at $(-3, 7)$ as shown above. What is the circle's equation?

(A) $(x + 3)^2 + (y - 7)^2 = 36$
(B) $(x - 3)^2 + (y + 7)^2 = 36$
(C) $(x + 3)^2 + (y - 7)^2 = 6$
(D) $(x - 3)^2 + (y + 7)^2 = 6$

14. What is the least common multiple of $p^5 q^8 r$ and $p^6 q^4 r^2$?

(A) $p^5 q^4$
(B) $p^5 q^4 r$
(C) $p^6 q^8 r^2$
(D) $p^{11} q^{12} r^3$

GO ON TO THE NEXT PAGE

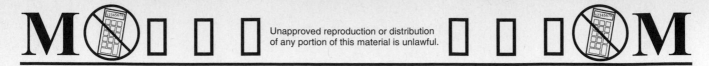
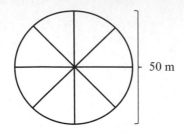

50 m

15. The figure above shows a wheel with a diameter of
50 m. If one full revolution of the wheel takes 3
minutes, what is the average speed of a point on the
outer edge of the wheel, in meters per second?

(A) $\dfrac{5\pi}{36}$

(B) $\dfrac{5\pi}{18}$

(C) $\dfrac{25\pi}{3}$

(D) $\dfrac{50\pi}{3}$

GRID-INS

16. If $1 < x + \dfrac{1}{3} < 2$, what is one possible value for $3x$?

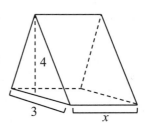

4

3   x

17. The volume of a triangular prism is equal to the area
of one of its triangular bases multiplied by its length.
If the triangular prism above has a volume of 36,
what is the value of x?

GO ON TO THE NEXT PAGE

18. In the xy–plane, lines m and n are perpendicular. Line m is represented by the equation $y = 3x - 1$. If line n contains the points $(2,0)$ and $(0, k)$, what is the value of k?

$$\frac{10}{x-2} - \frac{5}{x+1} = \frac{5}{2}$$

20. What is a positive value of x that satisfies the equation above?

19. Wei throws a ball to Sam. The height of the ball is given by the function $h(t) = -t^2 + 4t + 1.5$, where h is the height in meters and t is the time in seconds. If the ball has a height of 1.5 meters when Sam catches it, for how many seconds was the ball in the air?

STOP

If you complete the problem set before time elapses, you may review your responses for this section.

Do not view or begin working on any other sections.

ANSWER KEY

1. A
2. B
3. C
4. B
5. C
6. B
7. C
8. D
9. C
10. A
11. D
12. B
13. A
14. C
15. B
16. $2 < 3x < 5$
17. 6
18. 2/3, .666, or .667
19. 4
20. 5

Chapter 6
Practice Tests

TAKING PRACTICE TESTS

In this chapter, you'll find two full-length practice tests to help you prepare for the new SAT. Each test has been designed to reflect the College Board's specifications for the 2016 redesigned exam. In these practice tests, you'll encounter the same format, content, and difficulty that you'll experience when you take your actual SAT exam.

If you take these tests just as if they were the actual SAT, you'll get a chance to practice applying all of your test-taking strategies under a time limit. You'll be able to figure out how to pace yourself and how to avoid making mistakes under pressure. And if you take each test in one four-hour sitting, you'll build your stamina so your actual SAT exam won't feel so long!

In order to get these benefits, however, you'll need to simulate a real testing environment. Sit at a desk in a quiet location free of distractions—no TV, computers, phones, music, or noise—and clear your desk of all materials except pencils, erasers, and a calculator. Use the calculator you plan to use on the actual SAT (see Chapter 1 for a list of acceptable calculators). Remember that you can only use your calculator on the Calculator Section of the Math Test. Don't take out any rulers, protractors, dictionaries, or other aids—you can't use them on the SAT.

Work through each test using the timing guidelines below. Use a stopwatch to time yourself for each section. You might see the sections in a different order on your actual SAT test date, but the amount of time per section will always be the same:

Section	Subject	Time Limit
1	Reading	65 minutes
2	Math (No-Calculator)	25 minutes
5 minute break		
3	Writing	35 minutes
4	Math (Calculator)	55 minutes
5 minute break		
5	Essay	50 minutes

As you go, enter your answers into the answer sheets provided. You can tear out or photocopy the answer sheets to make this easier or download and print answer keys from our website. Use a pencil to shade in the appropriate bubble for each question and write your essay on the lined pages. Pay attention to the section and question numbers on the answer sheet to avoid entering your answers in the wrong place.

When your time is up, put down your pencil immediately. You won't be given any extra time on your test day, so make sure you finish entering all of your answers before time is called. (Note: If you have a diagnosed learning disability, you may qualify for extra time or additional accommodations on the SAT. Speak with your guidance counselor to learn more.)

When you are finished, check your answers against the answer keys provided. Then, score your exam using the directions at the end of this chapter. Look over each question you answered incorrectly and see if you can figure out where you went wrong. If you have trouble figuring out a question, you can view a full set of answer explanations at http://ivyglobal.com/study.

Use your results to determine what areas to continue studying before your actual SAT test date. Take note of the types of questions you tend to get wrong more frequently, and review the parts of this book where those question types are covered. If you learn from your mistakes on these practice tests, you're less likely to make the same mistakes on your actual test date.

All ready? Take a deep breath, set your stopwatch, and get started!

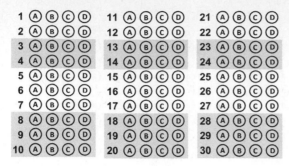

IMPORTANT: USE A NO. 2 PENCIL. WRITE INSIDE THE BORDERS.

Continue on next page.

Continue on next page.

SECTION 1

Time – 65 minutes

52 Questions

Turn to Section 1 of your answer sheet to answer the questions in this section.

Directions: For these questions, determine the solution to each question presented and choose the best answer choice of those provided. Be sure to fill in the respective circle on your answer sheet.

Questions 1-11 are based on the following passage.

Ask people how they feel about getting older, and they will probably reply in the same vein as Maurice Chevalier: "Old age isn't so bad when you consider the alternative."
Line
Stiffening joints, weakening muscles, fading eyesight and the
5   clouding of memory, coupled with the modern world's careless contempt for the old, seem a fearful prospect—better than death, perhaps, but not much. Yet mankind is wrong to dread aging. Life is not a long slow decline from sunlit uplands towards the valley of death. It is, rather, a U-bend.

10   When people start out on adult life, they are, on average, pretty cheerful. Things go downhill from youth to middle age until they reach a nadir commonly known as the mid-life crisis. So far, so familiar. The surprising part happens after that. Although as people move towards old age they lose
15   things they treasure—vitality, mental sharpness and looks— they also gain what people spend their lives pursuing: happiness.

This curious finding has emerged from a new branch of economics that seeks a more satisfactory measure than
20   money of human well-being. Conventional economics uses money as a proxy for utility—the dismal way in which the discipline talks about happiness. But some economists, unconvinced that there is a direct relationship between money and well-being, have decided to go to the nub of the
25   matter and measure happiness itself.

Ask a bunch of 30-year-olds and another of 70-year-olds (as Peter Ubel, of the Sanford School of Public Policy at Duke University, did with two colleagues, Heather Lacey and Dylan Smith, in 2006) which group they think is likely
30   to be happier, and both lots point to the 30-year-olds. Ask them to rate their own well-being, and the 70-year-olds are the happier bunch. The academics quoted lyrics written by Pete Townshend of The Who when he was 20: "Things they do look awful cold / Hope I die before I get old". They

35   pointed out that Mr. Townshend, having passed his 60th birthday, was writing a blog that glowed with good humor.

Mr. Townshend may have thought of himself as a youthful radical, but this view is ancient and conventional. The "seven ages of man"—the dominant image of the life-
40   course in the 16th and 17th centuries—was almost invariably conceived as a rise in stature and contentedness to middle age, followed by a sharp decline towards the grave. Inverting the rise and fall is a recent idea. "A few of us noticed the U-bend in the early 1990s," says Andrew Oswald, professor of
45   economics at Warwick Business School. "We ran a conference about it, but nobody came."

Since then, interest in the U-bend has been growing. Its effect on happiness is significant. It appears all over the world. David Blanchflower, professor of economics at
50   Dartmouth College, and Mr. Oswald looked at the figures for 72 countries. The nadir varies among countries—Ukrainians, at the top of the range, are at their most miserable at 62, and Swiss, at the bottom, at 35—but in the great majority of countries people are at their unhappiest in their 40s and early
55   50s. The global average is 46.

GO ON TO THE NEXT PAGE

Minimum Happiness Across Countries

The age of minimum happiness records the age during their adult lives at which people report being the least happy.

Country Name	Age of Minimum Happiness
All countries	46.1
Australia	40.2
Brazil	36.6
Canada	54.0
France	61.9
Mexico	41.4
Puerto Rico	35.6
Ukraine	62.1
United States	40.1

Adapted from David G. Blanchflower, Andrew J. Oswald, "Is Well-Being U-Shaped over the Life Cycle?" (September 2007). IZA Discussion Paper No. 3075. Available at SSRN: http://ssrn.com/abstract=1026895

1. The primary purpose of the passage is to

   (A) explain a phenomenon observed by economists.
   (B) discuss the findings of a group of economists.
   (C) explore competing measures of happiness.
   (D) relate an interesting anecdote about happiness and aging.

2. The author would most likely agree with which of the following statements?

   (A) Conventional economic measures of happiness are unsatisfactory.
   (B) The "seven ages of man" can still describe the lives of some seniors.
   (C) Conventional economists have not previously been interested in happiness.
   (D) The trend of happiness increasing in old age means people will no longer fear aging.

3. Which choice provides the best evidence for the answer to the previous question?

   (A) Lines 8-9 ("Life is ... death")
   (B) Lines 14-17 ("Although as ... happiness")
   (C) Lines 20-22 ("Conventional economics ... happiness")
   (D) Lines 30-32 ("Ask ... happier bunch")

4. The passage suggests that the conventional view of aging as "a slow decline" from a happy youth to a depressing old-age is

   (A) precisely the opposite of the truth in most cases.
   (B) basically correct about life through middle age, but not old age.
   (C) usually correct, but with a few notable exceptions.
   (D) accurate with respect to the elderly, but not the young.

5. As used in line 2, "vein" most nearly means

   (A) style.
   (B) humor.
   (C) strain.
   (D) streak.

6. The Duke University academics in the passage mostly likely referred to Pete Townshend (line 33) in order to

   (A) support the idea that most 70-year-olds underestimate their happiness.
   (B) exemplify a typical contrast between our expectations and experiences of aging.
   (C) suggest that most seniors are happier than they expected to be as they aged.
   (D) explain why a conventional view has often been perceived as radical.

7. Which choice provides the best evidence for the answer to the previous question?

   (A) Lines 1-3 ("Ask ... the alternative.")
   (B) Lines 22-25 ("But some ... itself.")
   (C) Lines 34-36 ("They ... good humor.")
   (D) Lines 37-38 ("Mr. Townshend ... conventional.")

8. The author refers to the "seven ages of man" (line 39) primarily in order to

   (A) highlight how the definition of happiness has changed over time.
   (B) suggest that some of our attitudes about aging have a basis in history.
   (C) contrast an earlier view of happiness and aging with the one introduced in the passage.
   (D) emphasize that numerous models exist for predicting happiness during various life stages.

GO ON TO THE NEXT PAGE ⟩

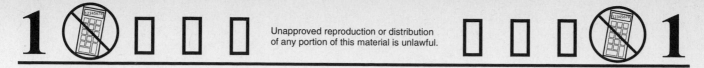

1

Unapproved reproduction or distribution
of any portion of this material is unlawful.

1

9. As used in line 51, "nadir" most nearly means

   (A) abyss.
   (B) low point.
   (C) zero.
   (D) bedrock.

10. It can reasonably be inferred from the passage that

   (A) most Ukrainians are happier at 70 than at 62.
   (B) most Ukrainians are at their happiest in their 70s.
   (C) few Ukrainians are as happy as the Swiss.
   (D) Ukrainian 35-year-olds are happier than Swiss 35-year-olds.

11. It can reasonably be inferred from the passage and chart that

   (A) The countries with the happiest citizens also tend to have the earliest ages of minimum happiness.
   (B) Brazilians tend to be happiest around the age of 36.6, while Mexicans are not at their happiest until 41.4.
   (C) Australians and Americans experience roughly the same levels of unhappiness during adulthood.
   (D) After the age of 54, Canadians tend to become happier, while the French tend to become less happy.

GO ON TO THE NEXT PAGE

Questions 12-21 are based on the following passage.

The following is adapted from a speech given by President Dwight D. Eisenhower in 1953. Eisenhower was addressing the General Assembly of the United Nations.

I feel impelled to speak today in a language that in a sense is new–one which I, who have spent so much of my life in the military profession, would have preferred never to
Line use. That new language is the language of atomic warfare.
5   The atomic age has moved forward at such a pace that every citizen of the world should have some comprehension, at least in comparative terms, of the extent of this development of the utmost significance to every one of us. Clearly, if the peoples of the world are to conduct an
10 intelligent search for peace, they must be armed with the significant facts of today's existence. Atomic bombs today are more than 25 times as powerful as the weapons with which the atomic age dawned, while hydrogen weapons are in the ranges of millions of tons of TNT equivalent. Today,
15 the United States' stockpile of atomic weapons, which, of course, increases daily, exceeds by many times the explosive equivalent of the total of all bombs and all shells that came from every plane and every gun in every theatre of war in all of the years of World War II.
20   But the dread secret, and the fearful engines of atomic might, are not ours alone. In the first place, the secret is possessed by our friends and allies, Great Britain and Canada, whose scientific genius made a tremendous contribution to our original discoveries, and the designs of
25 atomic bombs. The secret is also known by the Soviet Union. The Soviet Union has informed us that, over recent years, it has devoted extensive resources to atomic weapons. During this period, the Soviet Union has exploded a series of atomic devices, including at least one involving thermo-nuclear
30 reactions.
       If at one time the United States possessed what might have been called a monopoly of atomic power, that monopoly ceased to exist several years ago. Therefore, although our earlier start has permitted us to accumulate
35 what is today a great quantitative advantage, the atomic realities of today comprehend two facts of even greater significance.
       First, the knowledge now possessed by several nations will eventually be shared by others—possibly all others.
40 Second, even a vast superiority in numbers of weapons, and a consequent capability of devastating retaliation, is no preventive, of itself, against the fearful material damage and

toll of human lives that would be inflicted by surprise aggression.
45   The free world, at least dimly aware of these facts, has naturally embarked on a large program of warning and defense systems. That program will be accelerated and expanded. But let no one think that the expenditure of vast sums for weapons and systems of defense can guarantee
50 absolute safety for the cities and citizens of any nation. The awful arithmetic of the atomic bomb does not permit of any such easy solution. Even against the most powerful defense, an aggressor in possession of the effective minimum number of atomic bombs for a surprise attack could probably place a
55 sufficient number of his bombs on the chosen targets to cause hideous damage.
       Surely no sane member of the human race could discover victory in such desolation. Could anyone wish his name to be coupled by history with such human degradation and
60 destruction? Occasional pages of history do record the faces of the "Great Destroyers" but the whole book of history reveals mankind's never-ending quest for peace. It is with the book of history, and not with isolated pages, that the United States will ever wish to be identified. My country wants to be
65 constructive, not destructive. It wants agreements, not wars, among nations. It wants itself to live in freedom, and in the confidence that the people of every other nation enjoy equally the right of choosing their own way of life.
       So my country's purpose is to help us move out of the
70 dark chamber of horrors into the light, to find a way by which the minds of men, the hopes of men, the souls of men everywhere, can move forward toward peace and happiness and well being.

12. The passage primarily focuses on which of the following characteristics of atomic warfare?

    (A) The serious threat it poses to the future of humanity
    (B) Its application to new situations in warfare
    (C) How recently it became available to Western nation
    (D) Its advantages over other types of warfare

13. Which choice provides the best evidence for the answer to the previous question?

    (A) Lines 11-14 ("Atomic … TNT equivalent")
    (B) Lines 31-33 ("If at … years ago")
    (C) Lines 52-56 ("Even against … hideous damage")
    (D) Lines 66-68 ("It wants … of life")

GO ON TO THE NEXT PAGE

14. Eisenhower's tone is best described as

    (A) apologetic.
    (B) exhilarated.
    (C) concerned.
    (D) cynical.

15. The passage most strongly suggests that Eisenhower would wish to pursue which of the following?

    (A) Expansion of the United States' nuclear weapons production
    (B) Using the United States' understanding about nuclear processes to generate energy
    (C) Agreements between the United States and other countries to limit nuclear weapons usage
    (D) The sharing of United States nuclear weapons expertise with other countries

16. Which choice provides the best evidence for the answer to the previous question?

    (A) Lines 38-39 ("First … all others")
    (B) Lines 45-47 ("The … defense systems")
    (C) Lines 48-50 ("But let … nation")
    (D) Lines 65-66 ("It wants … among nations")

17. The main rhetorical effect of lines 14-19 is to

    (A) emphasize the unprecedented power of atomic weapons.
    (B) explain how numerous the weapons of World War II were.
    (C) provide background information on other types of weaponry.
    (D) suggest that atomic weapons function in similar ways to older types of arms.

18. As used in line 42, "material" most nearly means

    (A) physical.
    (B) essential.
    (C) relevant.
    (D) worldly.

19. As used in line 59, "coupled" most nearly means

    (A) compounded.
    (B) fused.
    (C) married.
    (D) joined.

20. Eisenhower refers to "the book of history" (line 63) in order to

    (A) suggest that the United States wishes to be associated with seeking peace rather than destruction.
    (B) argue that through the choices it makes the United States is able to shape history.
    (C) imply that the United States will seek compromises with other nations to avoid atomic warfare.
    (D) show that the United States identifies strongly with the history of warfare.

21. The final paragraph primarily serves to

    (A) contradict Eisenhower's earlier statements about peace.
    (B) offer a concrete strategy for avoiding warfare.
    (C) suggest how Eisenhower wishes the United States to proceed.
    (D) encourage other countries to cooperate with the United States.

GO ON TO THE NEXT PAGE

Questions 22-32 are based on the following passage.

A novelist scrawling away in a notebook in seclusion may not seem to have much in common with an NBA player doing a reverse layup on a basketball court before a screaming crowd. But if you could peer inside their heads, you might see some striking similarities in how their brains were churning.

That's one of the implications of new research on the neuroscience of creative writing. For the first time, neuroscientists have used fMRI scanners to track the brain activity of both experienced and novice writers as they sat down—or, in this case, lay down—to turn out a piece of fiction. The researchers, led by Martin Lotze of the University of Greifswald in Germany, observed a broad network of regions in the brain working together as people produced their stories. But there were notable differences between the two groups of subjects. The inner workings of the professionally trained writers in the bunch, the scientists argue, showed some similarities to people who are skilled at other complex actions, like music or sports.

To begin, Dr. Lotze asked 28 volunteers to simply copy some text, giving him a baseline reading of their brain activity during writing. Next, he showed his volunteers a few lines from a short story and asked them to continue it in their own words. The volunteers could brainstorm for a minute, and then write creatively for a little over two minutes. Some regions of the brain became active only during the creative process, but not while copying, the researchers found. During the brainstorming sessions, some vision-processing regions of volunteers became active. It's possible that they were, in effect, seeing the scenes they wanted to write.

Other regions became active when the volunteers started jotting down their stories. Dr. Lotze suspects that one of them, the hippocampus, was retrieving factual information that the volunteers could use. One region near the front of the brain, known to be crucial for holding several pieces of information in mind at once, became active as well. Juggling several characters and plot lines may put special demands on it.

But Dr. Lotze also recognized a big limit of the study: His subjects had no previous experience in creative writing. Would the brains of full-time writers respond differently? To find out, he and his colleagues went to another German university, the University of Hildesheim, which runs a highly competitive creative writing program. The scientists recruited 20 writers there (their average age was 25). Dr Lotze and his colleagues had them take the same tests and then compared their performance with the novices'.

As the scientists report in a new study in the journal NeuroImage, the brains of expert writers appeared to work differently, even before they set pen to paper. During brainstorming, the novice writers activated their visual centers. By contrast, the brains of expert writers showed more activity in regions involved in speech. "I think both groups are using different strategies," Dr. Lotze said. It's possible that the novices are watching their stories like a film inside their heads, while the writers are narrating it with an inner voice.

When the two groups started to write, another set of differences emerged. Deep inside the brains of expert writers, a region called the caudate nucleus became active. In the novices, the caudate nucleus was quiet. The caudate nucleus is a familiar part of the brain for scientists like Dr. Lotze who study expertise. It plays an essential role in the skill that comes with practice, including activities like board games.

When we first start learning a skill—be it playing a piano or playing basketball—we use a lot of conscious effort. With practice, those actions become more automatic. The caudate nucleus and nearby regions start to coordinate the brain's activity as this shift happens. "I was really happy to see this," said Ronald T. Kellogg, a psychologist who studies writing at Saint Louis University. "You don't want to see this as an analog to what James Joyce was doing in Dublin. But to see that they were able to get clean results with this, I think that's a major step right there." But Steven Pinker, a Harvard psychologist, was skeptical that the experiments could provide a clear picture of creativity. "It's a messy comparison," he said.

GO ON TO THE NEXT PAGE

Difference in Activation of Brain Regions during Creative Writing

Non-experts   Expert Writers

■ Region 1: Associated with language and verbal comprehension.

■ Region 2: Associeted with visual processing.

■ Region 3: Associated with language and short-term memory.

□ Region 4: Associated with visual processing.

□ Region 5: Associated with motor control and automatic skills.

The graph above shows the difference in activation of certain areas of the brain between expert writers and non-experts during creative writing. The direction of the bar shows which group showed greater activation; experts (right), or non-experts (left). The length of the bar shows the size of the difference.

Based on data from K. Erhard, F. Kessler, N. Neumann, H.-J. Ortheil, M. Lotze, "Professional training in creative writing is associated with enhanced fronto-striatal activity in literary text continuation task." NeuroImage 100 (2014).

22. The stance the author takes in the passage is best described as that of

(A) an interested observer.

(B) an excited colleague.

(C) a skeptical rival scientist.

(D) a concerned creative writer.

23. The passage most strongly suggests that

(A) writers draw on their own knowledge when creating fiction.

(B) most people may not realize that creative writing is a learnable skill.

(C) it is important for all neuroscience studies to include both experts and novices.

(D) all expert writers employ the same approach to writing.

24. Which choice provides the best evidence for the answer to the previous question?

(A) Lines 32-34 ("Dr. … could use")

(B) Lines 54-57 ("It's possible … voice")

(C) Lines 59-61 ("Deep inside … active")

(D) Lines 66-67 ("When … conscious effort")

25. As used in line 6, "churning" most nearly means

(A) producing.

(B) working.

(C) proceeding.

(D) spinning.

26. The first paragraph primarily serves to

(A) make a surprising comparison that the rest of the passage will explain.

(B) lay out a hypothesis that the passage will prove to be false.

(C) describe a question that has long puzzled researchers.

(D) prove that a surprising comparison is indeed true.

27. Based on the passage, which choice best describes the relationship between novice and expert writers?

(A) Novices' brains are less active than experts' brains during writing.

(B) Novices' brains are more active than experts' brains during writing.

(C) Novices' behavior is less automatic than experts' behavior during writing.

(D) Novices' behavior is less intense than experts' behavior during writing.

GO ON TO THE NEXT PAGE

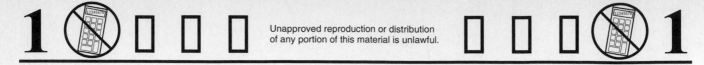

28. Which choice provides the best evidence for the answer to the previous question?

(A) Lines 4-6 ("But if ... churning")
(B) Lines 12-15 ("The researchers ... their stories")
(C) Lines 25-27 ("Some ... researchers found")
(D) Line 68 ("With practice ... automatic")

29. It can reasonably be inferred from the passage that

(A) the hippocampus plays a role in memory.
(B) the caudate nucleus grows larger as people learn more skills.
(C) experts in any field are less likely to rely on their visual centers when writing creatively.
(D) most skills activate only a single area of the brain.

30. As used in line 69, "coordinate" most nearly means

(A) match.
(B) organize.
(C) correlate.
(D) negotiate.

31. The passage most strongly suggests that Steven Pinker would agree with which of the following statements?

(A) It is impossible for neuroscientists to truly study creativity.
(B) Dr. Lotze's results may not support the broad conclusions discussed in the passage.
(C) The caudate nucleus does not become more active in the brains of expert writers.
(D) Writing is not a skill that can be easily improved.

32. Based on information from the passage and graph, the brain region labeled "Region 5" on the graph is most likely to include which of the following parts of the brain?

(A) The hippocampus
(B) The visual centers
(C) The speech centers
(D) The caudate nucleus

GO ON TO THE NEXT PAGE

Questions 33-42 are based on the following passage.

It is a most extraordinary thing, but I never read a patent medicine advertisement without being impelled to the conclusion that I am suffering from the particular disease therein dealt with in its most virulent form. The diagnosis seems in every case to correspond exactly with all the sensations that I have ever felt.

I remember going to the British Museum one day to read up the treatment for some slight ailment of which I had a touch—hay fever, I fancy it was. I got down the book, and read all I came to read; and then, in an unthinking moment, I idly turned the leaves, and began to indolently study diseases, generally. I forget which was the first distemper I plunged into – some fearful, devastating scourge, I know— and, before I had glanced half down the list of "premonitory symptoms," it was borne in upon me that I had fairly got it.

I sat for awhile, frozen with horror; and then, in the listlessness of despair, I again turned over the pages. I came to typhoid fever—read the symptoms—discovered that I had typhoid fever, must have had it for months without knowing it—wondered what else I had got; turned up St. Vitus's Dance—found, as I expected, that I had that too,—began to get interested in my case, and determined to sift it to the bottom, and so started alphabetically – read up ague, and learnt that I was sickening for it, and that the acute stage would commence in about another fortnight. Bright's disease, I was relieved to find, I had only in a modified form, and, so far as that was concerned, I might live for years. Cholera I had, with severe complications; and diphtheria I seemed to have been born with. I plodded conscientiously through the twenty-six letters, and the only malady I could conclude I had not got was housemaid's knee.

I felt rather hurt about this at first; it seemed somehow to be a sort of slight. Why hadn't I got housemaid's knee? Why this invidious reservation? After a while, however, less grasping feelings prevailed. I reflected that I had every other known malady in the pharmacology, and I grew less selfish, and determined to do without housemaid's knee. Gout, in its most malignant stage, it would appear, had seized me without my being aware of it; and zymosis I had evidently been suffering with from boyhood. There were no more diseases after zymosis, so I concluded there was nothing else the matter with me.

I sat and pondered. I thought what an interesting case I must be from a medical point of view, what an acquisition I should be to a class! Students would have no need to "walk the hospitals," if they had me. I was a hospital in myself. All they need do would be to walk round me, and, after that, take their diploma.

Then I wondered how long I had to live. I tried to examine myself. I felt my pulse. I could not at first feel any pulse at all. Then, all of a sudden, it seemed to start off. I pulled out my watch and timed it. I made it a hundred and forty-seven to the minute. I tried to feel my heart. I could not feel my heart. It had stopped beating. I have since been induced to come to the opinion that it must have been there all the time, and must have been beating, but I cannot account for it. I patted myself all over my front, from what I call my waist up to my head, and I went a bit round each side, and a little way up the back. But I could not feel or hear anything. I tried to look at my tongue. I stuck it out as far as ever it would go, and I shut one eye, and tried to examine it with the other. I could only see the tip, and the only thing that I could gain from that was to feel more certain than before that I had scarlet fever.

I had walked into that reading-room a happy, healthy man. I crawled out a decrepit wreck.

33. The primary purpose of the passage is to

(A) persuade the reader by using a personal story as evidence.
(B) frighten the reader with a chilling anecdote.
(C) entertain the reader with a story about false beliefs.
(D) describe the symptoms of several common diseases.

34. The passage most strongly suggests that the narrator's self-diagnoses of disease are based on

(A) his tendency to be swayed by what he reads.
(B) changes to his health that he had observed.
(C) careful examination by medical professionals.
(D) his rigorous study of medicine.

GO ON TO THE NEXT PAGE ▷

1 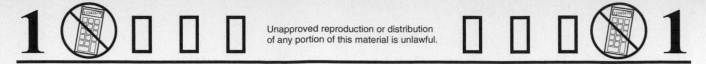 1

Unapproved reproduction or distribution
of any portion of this material is unlawful.

35. Which choice provides the best evidence for the answer to the previous question?

(A) Lines 1-4 ("It is ... virulent form")
(B) Lines 43-45 ("I thought ... a class")
(C) Lines 57-59 ("I patted ... the back")
(D) Lines 62-64 ("I ... scarlet fever")

36. The tone of the passage can best be described as

(A) reflective.
(B) panicked.
(C) apologetic.
(D) humorous.

37. It can reasonably be inferred from the passage that the narrator

(A) somewhat enjoys believing he has many illnesses.
(B) is likely to seek medical treatment for his many ailments.
(C) has a great respect for the practice of medicine.
(D) frequently visits the British Museum.

38. Which choice provides the best evidence for the answer to the previous question?

(A) Lines 7-9 ("I remember ... it was")
(B) Lines 28-29 ("Cholera ... born with")
(C) Lines 35-37 ("I reflected ... housemaid's knee")
(D) Lines 60-62 ("I stuck ... the other")

39. As used in line 29, "plodded" most nearly means

(A) stumbled.
(B) blundered.
(C) worked.
(D) strived.

40. As used in line 33, "slight" most nearly means

(A) indignity.
(B) criticism.
(C) outrage.
(D) shame.

41. The statement "I was a hospital in myself" (line 46) suggests that the narrator

(A) suffered from nearly as many diseases as can be found in an entire hospital.
(B) had knowledge of so many illnesses that he could run a hospital.
(C) was a breeding ground for illness, just like a hospital.
(D) was typical of patients found in hospitals of the time.

42. The last two lines (65-66) primarily serve to

(A) summarize the transformation that the narrator recounts during the passage.
(B) suggest that the narrator was permanently changed by his visit to the British Museum.
(C) emphasize the severity of the author's many illnesses.
(D) demonstrate that the narrator's experience in the British Museum was unusual for him.

GO ON TO THE NEXT PAGE

Questions 43-52 are based on the following passage.

Passage 1

Glover's Reef, about 28 miles from the coast of Belize, is one of the only true atolls in the Atlantic Ocean. It is also the site of Belize's largest "no-take" marine reserve, a 17,500-
Line acre zone where all types of fishing are prohibited. The no-
5 take zone makes up about 20 percent of the wider 87,000-acre Marine Protected Area here. Within 75 percent of the reserve, some types of fishing are allowed, although there are restrictions on the type of gear that can be used.

According to scientists here, the marine reserve at
10 Glover's Reef offers a test case for the viability of similar reserves around the world. They are now hoping to apply some of the conservation strategies here to make other places succeed. "I think Glover's Reef is a model of hope," says Ellen K. Pikitch, a marine biologist at the Stony Brook
15 University School of Marine and Atmospheric Sciences. Dr. Pikitch runs the Institute for Ocean Conservation Science, an organization seeking wider protection for sharks worldwide. She said that the effort at Glover's "shows that marine reserves, even small marine reserves, can work. I think it's
20 very transportable, this concept."

Dr. Pikitch, a self-professed "shark fanatic," has other reasons to be hopeful. She leads the largest shark population study in the Caribbean here at Glover's Reef, now in its 10th year. Shark populations here have remained stable, while
25 others around the world are in severe decline.

The sharks are an integral part of a healthy reef. Along with other top predators they help keep barracuda populations in check, which is important because barracuda consume algae grazers like parrotfish that prevent runaway
30 algae growth from choking the corals.

There are still significant challenges. Enforcement remains a problem. The Wildlife Conservation Society shares its home on Middle Caye with an outpost of the Belize Fisheries Department. The department employs four
35 rangers here whose job is to patrol the reef and catch fishermen who violate the fishing ban or who poach undersized conch and spiny lobster outside the no-take zone.

Dr. Pikitch acknowledges that the problems facing reefs here are significant, but she remains optimistic that new
40 information, including data from her shark study, will increase awareness and prompt action to protect reefs. "We are losing coral reefs at an astounding rate," she said. "It's like death by a thousand cuts. So when you have a success like this in a coral ecosystem you say, 'Wow this is great.'"

Passage 2

45 One of the few bright spots in the struggle to protect the world's fragile oceans has been the rapidly increasing number of "marine protected areas," places where fishing is limited or banned and where, presumably, depleted species can recover by simply being left to themselves. The benefits
50 of hands-off environmental protection may seem self-evident. But creating a preserve and rebuilding a healthy ecosystem are not necessarily the same thing. A recent study published in Nature found that, more often than not, marine protected areas don't work as well as they could.

55 Researchers with the University of Tasmania studied 87 marine protected areas in 40 countries worldwide, and found that 59 percent of the areas were no better off than areas where fishing was allowed. The reasons for failure varied, but they boiled down to this: Not all marine protected areas
60 are alike. Some allow fishing; others forbid it. Some are managed well; others are managed badly. Some are relatively intact; others have been left barren by generations of overfishing.

The researchers identified five essential characteristics of
65 the most successful marine protected areas: These areas were designated "no take" (allowing no fishing whatsoever), their rules were well enforced, they were more than 10 years old, they were bigger than 100 square kilometers, and they were isolated by deep water or sand. Compared with regular fished
70 areas, the areas that had four or five of those attributes had a far richer variety of species, five times the biomass of large fish and 14 times the biomass of sharks, which are indicators of ecological health.

Most underachieving marine sanctuaries had only one or
75 two of these magic factors, and thus "were not ecologically distinguishable from fished sites." The four sanctuaries lucky enough to have all five characteristics were isolated areas in the oceans off Costa Rica, Colombia, New Zealand and Australia. The "coral triangle" of Southeast Asia also got
80 high marks, but it did not have as great an array of large species as its more isolated counterparts.

GO ON TO THE NEXT PAGE

43. Both passages make use of which kind of evidence?

(A) Statistical evidence about fish populations
(B) Data on the ecological health of various protected sites
(C) Information about marine predator populations
(D) A summary of recently published scientific research

44. Compared to Passage 2, Passage 1 is

(A) narrower in its focus.
(B) more persuasive in tone.
(C) less adamant about its conclusion.
(D) more complex in its reasoning.

45. Passage 1 discusses the difficulty of ensuring which of the essential characteristics of marine protected areas discussed in Passage 2?

(A) Having areas designated "no-take"
(B) Proper enforcement of the rules
(C) Being isolated by deep water
(D) Placing restrictions on what fishing gear can be used

46. As used in line 20, "transportable" most nearly means

(A) addressable.
(B) transmittable.
(C) easily moved.
(D) transferable.

47. Which of the following situations is most analogous to the role of sharks presented in lines 26-30?

(A) Bears contribute to healthy ecosystems by consuming unwanted human trash, which benefits other species.
(B) Bears contribute to healthy ecosystems only when their populations are kept low so they do not excessively hunt other animals.
(C) Bears contribute to healthy ecosystems by keeping salmon populations under control, which ensures that smaller fish can survive.
(D) Bears damage healthy ecosystems by over-fishing salmon populations, which prevents salmon from controlling smaller fish populations.

48. Based on information from Passage 2, we can conclude that designating a reef as a marine protected area

(A) is the only way to safeguard the variety of fish species inhabiting the reef.
(B) has no effect unless the marine protected area covers more than 100 square kilometers.
(C) is less effective than other methods of protecting marine ecosystems.
(D) can be an effective method of protecting fish populations if certain standards are met.

49. Which choice provides the best evidence for the correct answer to the previous question?

(A) Lines 45-49 ("One of ... to themselves")
(B) Lines 58-60 ("The reasons ... are alike")
(C) Lines 69-73 ("Compared with ... health")
(D) Lines 76-79 ("The four ... Australia")

50. The author of Passage 2 would most likely agree with which of the following?

(A) Marine protected areas are a poor approach to marine conservation and not worth pursuing.
(B) It is necessary to protect the oceans, but marine protected areas are effective only if certain standards are met.
(C) Even when they meet rigorous standards, marine protected areas are not the best method for protecting marine species.
(D) Ocean health cannot be improved by a hands-on approach, so marine protected areas are ineffective.

51. Which choice provides the best evidence for the answer to the previous question?

(A) Lines 52-54 ("A recent ... they could")
(B) Lines 55-58 ("Researchers with ... allowed")
(C) Lines 74-76 ("Most ... fished sites")
(D) Lines 79-81 ("The ... isolated counterparts")

52. As used in line 62, "intact" most nearly means

(A) solid.
(B) faultless.
(C) unspoiled.
(D) complete.

STOP

If you finish early, you may review your responses for this section.
Do not view or begin working on any other sections.

Acknowledgements for this Section

The passages in this section were adapted from the following sources:

The Economist, "The U-Bend of Life." © 2014 *The Economist Newspaper Limited*. Originally published December 16, 2010.

Dwight D. Eisenhower, "Address Before the General Assembly of the United Nations on Peaceful Uses of Atomic Energy." New York City, December 8, 1953.

Jerome K. Jerome, "Three Men in a Boat."

Carl Zimmer, "This Is Your Brain on Writing." © 2014 by *The New York Times Company*. Originally published June 20, 2014.

Erik Olsen, "Protected Reef Offers Model for Conservation." © 2010 by *The New York Times Company*. Originally published April, 2010.

The New York Times Editorial Board, "To Save Fish and Birds." © 2014 by *The New York Times Company*. Originally published February, 2014.

SECTION 2
Time – 25 minutes
20 Questions

Turn to Section 2 of your answer sheet to answer the questions in this section.

Notes

1. Choose the best answer choice of those provided. Be sure to fill in the corresponding circle on your answer sheet.

2. You may NOT use a calculator on this section.

3. If a problem includes a figure and does not state that the figure is NOT to scale, you may assume the figure provides a correct representation of the information in the problem.

4. The domain of any function f is the set of all real numbers x for which $f(x)$ is a real number, unless otherwise stated.

Reference

$$A = \frac{1}{2} bh$$

$$a^2 + b^2 = c^2$$

Special Triangles

$$V = \frac{1}{3} lwh$$
$$V = \frac{1}{3}\pi r^2 h$$

$$A = lw$$

$$V = lwh$$

$$V = \pi r^2 h$$

$$A = \pi r^2$$
$$C = 2\pi r$$

$$V = \frac{4}{3}\pi r^3$$

- There are 360° in a circle.
- The sum of the angles in a triangle is 180°.
- The number of radians of arc of a circle is 2π.

---

1. What is the difference when $-3 + 3x$ is subtracted from $4 - x$?

(A) $7 + 2x$
(B) $1 + 2x$
(C) $7 - 4x$
(D) $1 - 4x$

2. One coin is randomly selected from a bag of 132 coins. If there is a 1 in 12 probability that a dime is selected, how many dimes are in the bag?

(A) 1
(B) 12
(C) 11
(D) 132

GO ON TO THE NEXT PAGE

2

2

3. If k is a positive integer greater than 2, which of the following could be a graph of $y = \dfrac{kx}{2}$?

(A)

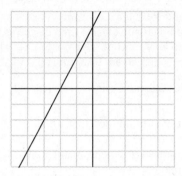

(B)

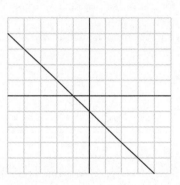

(C)

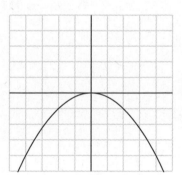

(D)

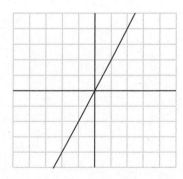

4. If the ratio of x to y is 4:5 and the ratio of y to z is 1:2, what is the ratio of x to z?

(A) 1:4
(B) 4:1
(C) 2:5
(D) 5:2

5. A car lease costs a flat fee of $1000 plus a monthly charge of $100. A 5% tax is applied to the monthly rate. Which of the following expressions represents the total cost, in dollars, if the car is leased for m months?

(A) $1.05\,(100m) + 1000$
(B) $1.05\,(100m + 1000)$
(C) $(100 + 0.05m) + 1000$
(D) $1.05\,(100 + 1000)\,m$

GO ON TO THE NEXT PAGE

$$x^2 + y^2 = 25$$

$$y = -2x$$

6. In the system of equations above, what is the value of x^2 ?

(A) -25
(B) $\sqrt{5}$
(C) 5
(D) 20

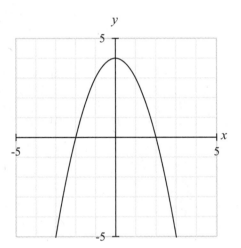

7. If p represents the product of the x-intercepts in the graph above, what is the value of $\dfrac{p}{6}$?

(A) 2

(B) $\dfrac{2}{3}$

(C) $-\dfrac{1}{3}$

(D) $-\dfrac{2}{3}$

$$\frac{1}{x} + \frac{3}{x} = p$$

8. Daphne and Velma have 1 minute to eat as many pies as they can. Daphne can eat three times as many pies per minute as Velma. If the equation above represents the situation described, where p is the total pies eaten, which does the expression $\dfrac{3}{x}$ represent?

(A) The time, in minutes, that it will take Daphne to eat all the pies.
(B) The portion of the pies that Daphne will eat in 1 minute.
(C) The portion of the pies that Velma will eat in 1 minute.
(D) The time, in minutes, that it will take Daphne to eat 1 pie.

9. If $-\dfrac{5}{3} < -2x - 1 < \dfrac{1}{5}$, what is one possible value of $4x + 2$?

(A) -1
(B) 0
(C) 4
(D) 5

GO ON TO THE NEXT PAGE

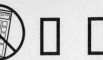
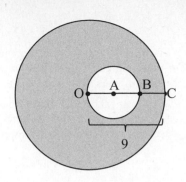

9

10. Circle O in the diagram above has a radius of 9, which is divided into 3 equal segments: $\overline{OA}$, $\overline{AB}$, and $\overline{BC}$. Circle A's diameter is $\overline{OB}$. What is the area of the shaded region, in terms of π?

(A)   6
(B)   36
(C)   72
(D)   81

$$\frac{1}{4}x - \frac{y}{2} = 4$$

$$ax - 2y = 16$$

11. If the system of equations above has infinite solutions, what is the value of a?

(A)   1

(B) $\frac{3}{2}$

(C) $\frac{1}{4}$

(D)   3

12. Fred's motorcycle runs for 1 hour on one gallon of gas. The motorcycle's gas tank starts with 12 gallons of gas and Fred travels at a constant speed. Which of the following functions models the number of gallons of gas remaining in the tank t hours after the trip begins?

(A) $f(t) = \frac{t}{12}$
(B) $f(t) = t$
(C) $f(t) = t - 12$
(D) $f(t) = 12 - t$

13. If $\dfrac{2x^2}{x-1} = \dfrac{2}{x-1} + A$, what is A in terms of x?

(A) $2x - 2$
(B) $2x + 2$
(C) $2x^2$
(D) $2x^2 - 2$

GO ON TO THE NEXT PAGE

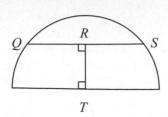

Q   R   S

T

14. The semicircle above has a diameter of 2. If the length of $\overline{RT}$ is $\frac{1}{2}$, what is the length of the chord $\overline{QS}$?

(A) $\frac{\sqrt{2}}{2}$

(B) $\frac{\sqrt{3}}{2}$

(C) $\sqrt{3}$

(D) 2

---

15. If $0 < x < \frac{\pi}{2}$, what is the value of $\cos(x + \pi)$?

(A) $-\frac{\cos x}{2}$

(B) $-\cos x$

(C) $\frac{\cos x}{2}$

(D) $\cos x$

GRID-INS

16. If the product of three different positive integers is 48 and the sum of these integers is less than 13, what is the largest of these numbers?

---

17. If $n^{2+x} = 125$ and $n^0 = x$, what is the value of n?

GO ON TO THE NEXT PAGE

$$10 = |x - 4|$$

18. What is the greatest possible integer that satisfies the equation above?

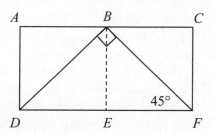

19. In the diagram above, $2 \times BE = DF$, and $BF = \sqrt{2}$. What is the perimeter of rectangle $ACFD$?

20. If $\dfrac{1}{4}x + \dfrac{1}{5}y = 6$, what is the value of $5x + 4y$?

STOP

If you complete the problem set before time elapses, you may review your responses for this section.

Do not view or begin working on any other sections.

3  3

Unapproved reproduction or distribution
of any portion of this material is unlawful.

SECTION 3
Time – 35 minutes
44 Questions

Turn to Section 3 of your answer sheet to answer the questions in this section.

Directions: For these questions, determine the solution to each question presented and choose the best answer choice of those provided. Be sure to fill in the respective circle on your answer sheet.

Questions 1-11 are based on the following passage.

Decoding Honey Bee Dance Language

If you look inside a bustling honey bee hive, you may see a single bee dancing wildly among a crowd. On the honey bee "dancefloor," other bees gather around to watch and **1** imitate the dancing bee. After a few minutes of matching the movements, the bees leave the hive and all take flight in the same direction. The dancing bee has just communicated the location of an abundant food source to the other bees. Scientists have studied the dances of **2** honey bees and the scientists then determined that honey bees readily communicate reliable food sources to each other by dancing.

How does this process work? First, honey bees called "scouts" go out to find flowers rich with the bees' main source of energy—nectar. When a scout finds a promising location of **3** nectar, they return to the hive to "perform" for the other bees. The scout dances in quick and deliberate circuits. Forager bees dance behind the scout, "practicing" the dance until they learn its meaning. The foragers then leave to seek out the nectar and bring it back to the hive.

[1] Researchers studying the dance patterns and reactions of honey bees suggest that there is, in fact, meaning in the dances of the bees. [2] When a nectar source is closer than fifty meters from the hive, scouts perform a "round dance." [3] When the food is farther than seventy-five meters from the hive, scouts perform a "waggle dance." [4] The waggle dance consists of elaborate "figure eight" circuits. [5] The number of dance circuits per fifteen seconds signals how far the nectar source is **4** from the hive; the angle of the dance tells the forager bees the direction they should fly. [6] For instance, if the nectar source is in the opposite direction from the sun, the bee **5** will perform at least 180 circuits. The circuits signal important information about the location of food to the rest of the hive. **6**

Both the forager bees **7** and the scout plays important roles in the process of collecting nectar. Scouts must find the best locations for nectar. Scouts must also be cautious of sites with damaged flowers or deceased bees, as these may be signs of predators. **8** The foragers watch and imitate the dance. Then the foragers use the cues from the scouts to locate the site and return with nectar for the hive.

9 Because bees have small brains relative to humans, they can convey complex and vital information to each other through their dances. Scientists suggest that the bees "understand" the dance because it **10** illicits a uniform response from the viewers; most forager bees fly to the location encoded in the dance. In this way, honey bees use these dances as **11** tools for both to navigate and communication.

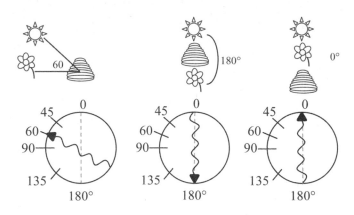

The figure above illustrates the waggle dances performed based on the location of the nectar source (flowers) in relation to the hive and the sun.

GO ON TO THE NEXT PAGE

1. (A) NO CHANGE
   (B) impersonate
   (C) mock
   (D) duplicate

2. (A) NO CHANGE
   (B) honey bees; and then the scientists determined
   (C) honey bees and have determined
   (D) honey bees then determining

3. (A) NO CHANGE
   (B) nectar; they return
   (C) nectar; it returns
   (D) nectar, it returns

4. (A) NO CHANGE
   (B) from the hive the angle of the dance
   (C) from the hive: the angle of the dance
   (D) from the hive, the angle of the dance

5. Which choice completes the sentence with accurate information based on the graph?

   (A) NO CHANGE
   (B) will perform the dance at a 180° angle.
   (C) will perform the dance at a 60° angle.
   (D) will perform no circuits.

6. For the sake of the cohesion of this paragraph, sentence [7] should be placed

   (A) where it is now
   (B) after sentence 2
   (C) before sentence 1
   (D) before sentence 5

7. (A) NO CHANGE
   (B) and the scout play important
   (C) and the scout were playing important
   (D) and the scout was playing important

8. (A) NO CHANGE
   (B) The foragers watch and imitate the dance and they
   (C) The foragers both watch and imitate the dance, and then they
   (D) After watching and imitating the dance, the foragers

9. (A) NO CHANGE
   (B) Although bees have small brains
   (C) Without their small brains
   (D) Accordingly, bees have small brains

10. (A) NO CHANGE
    (B) elicits
    (C) illuminates
    (D) excises

11. (A) NO CHANGE
    (B) tools to both navigate
    (C) tools for both navigation
    (D) tools to be used for both navigation

GO ON TO THE NEXT PAGE

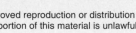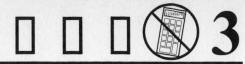
Questions 12-22 are based on the following passage.

Maya Angelou: A Voice for Caged Birds

At President Bill Clinton's inauguration, Maya Angelou stands at the podium to recite a poem just as she did when she was a young girl in church. As a child, [12] too nervous to complete her reading in front of her congregation. Now on stage in front of the world, [13] however, Angelou does not resemble that frightened girl at all. She reads "On the Pulse of Morning," a poem she composed that proposes inclusion, change, and progress as America's goals. It is easy to see how her life and journey [14] has not only influenced her work but also embodied the change and progress for which she calls. Passion and courage are evident in her performance, not fear or anxiety. She speaks with a strong voice—a voice that has long touched generations of listeners.

[1] Angelou faced a difficult childhood. [2] She and her brother, Bailey, were raised for a period of time with their grandmother [15] in Arkansas. [3] It was here that Angelou experienced the devastating effects of racism firsthand. [4] Yet from her grandmother's example she also learned how to be resilient. [5] In her autobiographical work, *I Know Why the Caged Bird Sings*, Angelou describes herself as an insecure young girl. [6] She notes that her awkward looks brought on ridicule, and she felt she did not fit in with her peers. [16]

[17] Angelou first tried her hand at singing and dancing, touring Europe and releasing a musical album. During this time, she gained a sense of confidence and a set of valuable mentors and collaborators. With the help of these connections, she wrote and produced a documentary series and began work on *I Know Why the Caged Bird Sings*. Finally able to shake the insecurities [18] of her youth, Maya Angelou had found her voice.

Angelou put her voice to use throughout the rest of her life [19] by composing and producing; acting and writing. [20] Both her poetry and also her prose were widely acclaimed, and her script for the film Georgia, Georgia was nominated for a Pulitzer Prize. Much of Angelou's success has been attributed to her ability to connect with her audience through vivid imagery, [21] instigating powerful emotions from her listeners.

In "On the Pulse of Morning," Angelou encourages Americans to have courage to live each day with hope. She [22] invites them to move forward with her into the light of the morning. On stage at the inauguration, she is not a caged bird or a shy little girl; she is a songbird whose melodies

echo through television cables and touch hearts across the nation.

12. (A) NO CHANGE
    (B) too nervous to complete reading
    (C) she was too nervous, completing her reading
    (D) she was too nervous to complete her reading

13. (A) NO CHANGE
    (B) for instance
    (C) therefore
    (D) moreover

14. (A) NO CHANGE
    (B) has influenced
    (C) have not only influenced
    (D) have influenced

15. Which choice most effectively combines the sentences at the underlined portion?

    (A) in Arkansas, and she experienced
    (B) in Arkansas, here Angelou experienced
    (C) in Arkansas, where Angelou experienced
    (D) experiencing in Arkansas

16. Which choice, inserted between sentences 3 and 4, would most improve the focus of the paragraph?

    (A) Angelou's later work would be influenced by her experience in Arkansas.
    (B) For example, the white dentist in the town refused to treat her because of her skin color.
    (C) However, she grew very close with her grandmother during this period.
    (D) Her brother, Bailey, also experienced disturbing incidents of overt racism.

17. Which sentence, inserted here, would most effectively establish the main topic of the passage?

    (A) Angelou was a pioneer for African American women in film.
    (B) Angelou was the recipient of many honors and awards for her work in the arts.
    (C) *I Know Why the Caged Bird Sings* was the first work in Angelou's autobiographical series.
    (D) Angleou's life changed when she began discovering her creativity.

GO ON TO THE NEXT PAGE

18. (A) NO CHANGE
    (B) she had experienced as a youth, her voice was found.
    (C) of her youth, her voice was found.
    (D) of her youth; Maya Angelou had found her voice.

19. (A) NO CHANGE
    (B) by composing; producing; acting and writing.
    (C) by composing, producing, acting, and writing.
    (D) by composing and producing; and acting and writing.

20. (A) NO CHANGE
    (B) Her poetry and prose were widely acclaimed,
    (C) Her poetry, and also her prose, were acclaimed,
    (D) Both her poetry but also her prose were widely acclaimed,

21. (A) NO CHANGE
    (B) infuriating
    (C) agitating
    (D) evoking

22. (A) NO CHANGE
    (B) invites themselves
    (C) invites him or her
    (D) invited them

GO ON TO THE NEXT PAGE

3 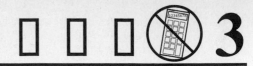 **3**

Unapproved reproduction or distribution
of any portion of this material is unlawful.

Questions 23-33 are based on the following passage.

Living the Wild Life

Many branches of science are devoted to preserving, protecting, 23 and the study of animals and their habitats. For example, biologists and environmentalists may make observations and collect data 24 in order that they might determine the effects of temperature increase on rainforest wildlife. However, these scientists cannot do their work alone. They often employ 25 assistants to help them carry out their projects. These are called wildlife technicians. By assisting scientists who study animals and their relationships to the Earth, wildlife technicians enjoy a rewarding career working with both humans and animals.

Wildlife technicians have a variety of responsibilities. Most often, they work directly with animals or natural resources. Wildlife technicians are responsible for observing animals and collecting data for use in research. Sometimes they collect data 26 by tagging and observing animals; other times, they collect samples or follow trails to determine patterns. Some wildlife technicians are able to perform hands-on work, such as caring for injured animals or restoring areas that have been disturbed or destroyed. Technicians may also use or create maps to help scientists understand patterns of weather or animal migration.

Once they collect data, wildlife technicians then input the data into computer databases to be used as inventories for further research. They may also create reports, develop hypotheses, and make suggestions based on 27 his or her observations. 28 Thus, some wildlife technicians are able to utilize their knowledge of science, math, and statistics to uncover valuable information about environments and the animals that live on earth.

29 Many wildlife technicians work in nature parks or nature centers, but others work in harsh and 30 reserved environments, such as the isolated lands of the tundra. In some of these environments, wildlife technicians may encounter uncomfortable weather or dangerous conditions.

[1] Wildlife technicians need a two-year degree to get started, but many 31 chose to pursue a bachelor's degree to obtain the benefits of a more advanced degree.[2] Wildlife technicians study in numerous areas, including biology, ecology, forestry, and zoology. [3] Wildlife technicians need to be skilled in science, math, and computer technology as well as be comfortable working with animals. [4] Some students develop a focus area in a particular topic, such as aquatic life or resource conservation. [5] They might join nature or outdoors clubs or volunteer at local zoos or arboretums. 32

Wildlife technicians, because they devote their lives to helping animals and the Earth, 33 feels good about their career. For nature lovers, the position of a wildlife technician offers an exciting and satisfying career.

23. (A) NO CHANGE
    (B) and the study of animals and they're habitats.
    (C) and studying animals and their habitats.
    (D) and to study animals and their habitats.

24. (A) NO CHANGE
    (B) in order that they might determine the affects
    (C) to determine the affects
    (D) to determine the effects

25. (A) NO CHANGE
    (B) assistants to help them carry out projects. They are also known as wildlife technicians.
    (C) assistants, helping them carry out projects, called wildlife technicians.
    (D) assistants, called wildlife technicians, to help them carry out their projects.

26. (A) NO CHANGE
    (B) by tagging and observing animals, other times, they collect
    (C) through the use of tagging and observation of animals; other times, they collect
    (D) to tag and observe animals, and other times, they collect

27. (A) NO CHANGE
    (B) their
    (C) they're
    (D) his or hers

28. (A) NO CHANGE
    (B) However,
    (C) Unfortunately,
    (D) Although

GO ON TO THE NEXT PAGE

29. Which sentence, inserted here, would most effectively establish the main topic of the paragraph?

 (A) Wildlife technicians need several skills to perform their difficult tasks.
 (B) Some wildlife technicians need to drive large trucks in order to travel.
 (C) The life of a wildlife technician is not always easy.
 (D) Wildlife technicians are able to work with a variety of animal species.

30. (A) NO CHANGE
 (B) improbable
 (C) diffident
 (D) remote

31. (A) NO CHANGE
 (B) choose to pursue
 (C) choosing to pursue
 (D) will have chosen to pursue

32. Which choice, inserted between sentences 4 and 5, would most improve the cohesion of the paragraph?

 (A) Fisheries management is another popular focus area.
 (B) Some wildlife technicians are experts in other professional areas as well.
 (C) Many experienced wildlife technicians gain certifications in CPR and emergency response.
 (D) Many aspiring wildlife technicians get involved in relevant extracurricular activities.

33. (A) NO CHANGE
 (B) feels good about his or her career
 (C) feel good about their career
 (D) feel good about his or her career

GO ON TO THE NEXT PAGE

Questions 34-44 are based on the following passage.

Children of the Industrial Revolution

Imagine this is your daily routine. You wake up at 5:00 A.M. and walk to your job at a coal mine. There you spend fourteen hours in a mine shaft, breaking and collecting rock. At the end of the day, you receive ten cents and return home. Before going to sleep, **34** it is required that the money be put in a jar for family expenses.

This was the routine of many children during the Industrial Revolution. The Industrial Revolution marked a dramatic change in the way goods were produced and manufactured, making the processes quicker and easier. **35** Since the gains in efficiency were great, the extreme use of child labor has cast a dark shadow of disgrace on the Industrial Revolution.

Before the Industrial Revolution, many children did work. Some children completed tasks at home or assisted with a family farm or business. Other children became apprentices, assistants to workers who would teach them a trade in exchange for labor. **36**

However, during the Industrial Revolution, the role of the child in the labor force changed dramatically. Young children were allowed to work in many industries, including coal mines, textile mills, tobacco factories, and sweatshops. In fact, children were often the preferred type of employee. Children's pay **37** was much less than adults even when they produced the same amount of work. Additionally, children could perform some tasks that **38** adults could not. They replaced spinning bobs and reached into small compartments under running machines.

Many accounts of child labor investigations describe horrific and deplorable working conditions. In mills and factories, children were forced to use dangerous equipment. After working more than twelve hours per day, **39** many fatigued children were injured by the machinery. Many child laborers also faced cruel treatment by their supervisors. Children had always received discipline at home, but employers took extreme measures **40** to ensure that the working of the children was happening efficiently.

One of the most dangerous jobs for **41** children were coal mining. Not only did they face the immediate danger of working underground with heavy machinery, but they also risked later damage to their lungs and skin. During the mining process, coal dust and poisonous gases were released and inhaled. Because mining was so dangerous, boys had to be **42** at least of age fourteen years old to work

underground. However, some parents would create fake birth certificates to allow their young boys to work in the mines.

Overall, the conditions during the Industrial Revolution were unacceptable for children. Children were missing out on education and **43** worked in dangerous situations. The increase in productivity did not **44** validate the harms caused to child laborers.

34. Which choice is most consistent with the rest of this passage?

   (A) NO CHANGE
   (B) you were asked to put the money in the jar for family expenses.
   (C) the money is put in a jar for family expenses.
   (D) you put the money into a jar set aside for family expenses.

35. (A) NO CHANGE
   (B) Although
   (C) As a result
   (D) Additionally,

36. Which choice, inserted here, would provide the best transition between the paragraphs?

   (A) The Industrial Revolution would rapidly alter the working lives of adults and children.
   (B) In those days, the function of child labor was to assist the family and build skills.
   (C) Many rural families were self-sustaining, in part due to their children's efforts in the home.
   (D) During the Industrial Revolution, agrarian societies were transformed into leaders of industry.

37. (A) NO CHANGE
   (B) was much fewer than adults
   (C) were much less than adults
   (D) was much less than adults' pay

GO ON TO THE NEXT PAGE

3 3

Unapproved reproduction or distribution
of any portion of this material is unlawful.

38. Which choice most effectively combines the sentences at the underlined portion?

(A) adults could not, they replaced spinning bobs and reached into small compartments under running machines.

(B) adults could not; for example, replacing spinning bobs or reaching into small compartments under running machines.

(C) adults could not, such as replacing spinning bobs or reaching into small compartments under running machines.

(D) adults could not; replacing spinning bobs or reaching into small compartments under running machines.

39. (A) NO CHANGE

(B) and being fatigued, many children were injured by the machinery.

(C) the machinery injured many fatigued children.

(D) the machinery injured many of the children who were fatigued.

40. (A) NO CHANGE

(B) to ensure that the working of the children was efficiently being done.

(C) in order to ensure that the children's work was being done efficiently.

(D) to ensure that the children were working efficiently.

41. (A) NO CHANGE

(B) children being

(C) children was

(D) children are

42. (A) NO CHANGE

(B) at least fourteen years old to work

(C) at least fourteen years of age, working

(D) at least age fourteen, working

43. (A) NO CHANGE

(B) had worked

(C) were working

(D) had been working

44. (A) NO CHANGE

(B) justify

(C) rate

(D) corroborate

STOP

If you complete the problem set before time elapses, you may review your responses for this section.

Do not view or begin working on any other sections.

SECTION 4

Time – 55 minutes
38 Questions

Turn to Section 4 of your answer sheet to answer the questions in this section.

Notes

1. Choose the best answer choice of those provided. Be sure to fill in the corresponding circle on your answer sheet.
2. You may use a calculator on this section.
3. If a problem includes a figure and does not state that the figure is NOT to scale, you may assume the figure provides a correct representation of the information in the problem.
4. The domain of any function f is the set of all real numbers x for which $f(x)$ is a real number, unless otherwise stated.

Reference

$A = \frac{1}{2}bh$ $a^2 + b^2 = c^2$ Special Triangles $V = \frac{1}{3}lwh$ $V = \frac{1}{3}\pi r^2 h$

$A = lw$ $V = lwh$ $V = \pi r^2 h$ $A = \pi r^2$ $V = \frac{4}{3}\pi r^3$
$C = 2\pi r$

- There are 360° in a circle.
- The sum of the angles in a triangle is 180°.
- The number of radians of arc of a circle is 2π.

Peter	Rita	Juan	Isabella	Ming
19	8	9	7	2

1. The table above shows the number of magazines purchased by a group of students during the month of July. What was the average number of magazines purchased per student?

(A) 8
(B) 9
(C) 17
(D) 45

2. How much smaller is $p - 3$ than $p + 4$?

(A) 1
(B) 3
(C) 6
(D) 7

GO ON TO THE NEXT PAGE

3. The population of Manchester increased by 12.1% between 1990 and 1999, and then decreased by 5.0% between 1999 and 2009. Between 1990 and 2009, Manchester's population changed by approximately which of the following percentages?

(A) 6.5%
(B) 7.1%
(C) 16.1%
(D) 17.7%

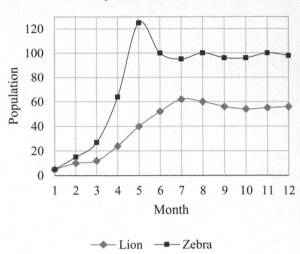

Populations of Lions and Zebras

4. A set of numbers contains 3, 4, 5, 7, 8, and 11. What is the median of this set?

(A) 3
(B) 5
(C) 6
(D) 7

5. Researchers measured the populations of lions and zebras every month during a one-year period. The population data is fit to a curve, as shown above. Which of the following is a correct interpretation of the data?

(A) At the 2nd month, the population of lions and zebras is the same.
(B) At the 7th month, the populations of lions and zebras were the closest.
(C) At the 4th month, there were about 3 times more zebras than lions.
(D) At the 1st month, the population of lions and zebras was zero.

6. The sum of 3 consecutive integers is 900. What is the value of the largest of these integers?

(A) 299
(B) 300
(C) 301
(D) 900

GO ON TO THE NEXT PAGE

7. If $4^{2y} = 256$, then $y =$

(A) 4
(B) 3
(C) 2
(D) 1

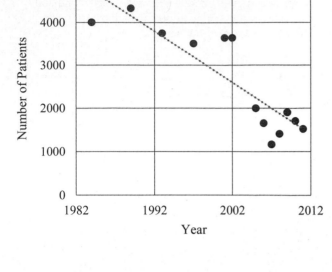

9. The scatterplot above shows the number of patients treated for chicken pox in a hospital from 1984 to 2011. Based on the line of best fit in the diagram, which of the following values is closest to the average yearly decrease in the number of chicken pox patients?

(A)   27
(B)   45
(C)   120
(D)   500

8. What is the slope of the line that connects the points $(2, 5)$ and $(-\frac{10}{3}, 1)$?

(A) $-\frac{2}{9}$

(B) $\frac{2}{9}$

(C) $\frac{3}{4}$

(D) $\frac{4}{3}$

10. Jack purchases a 1.2kg steak from the grocery store. The steak costs $10/kg before tax, and an additional 6% tax is charged. If Jack gives the cashier $15, how much change should he receive?

(A) $2.20
(B) $2.28
(C) $2.30
(D) $4.59

GO ON TO THE NEXT PAGE

11. What is the value of x in the equation $\dfrac{2x-1}{3} = 7x - 1$?

(A) $x = \dfrac{1}{21}$

(B) $x = \dfrac{1}{19}$

(C) $x = \dfrac{2}{19}$

(D) $x = \dfrac{5}{19}$

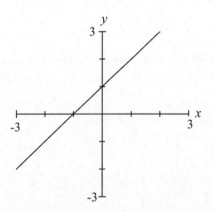

12. The figure above shows the graph of $y = mx + b$. If the slope of this line were doubled, what would be the value for y at $x = 2$?

(A)   2
(B)   3
(C)   5
(D)   6

13. The average of four test scores is 70. After a fifth test score is added, the new average is 80. What is the value of the fifth test score?

(A)   75
(B)   80
(C)   100
(D)   120

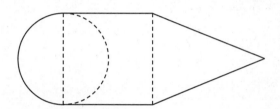

14. What is the perimeter of the figure outlined by the solid line if the area of the square shown in the middle is 36 and the perimeter of the triangle is 24?

(A)   32
(B) $24 + 3\pi$
(C) $24 + 6\pi$
(D) $30 + 3\pi$

GO ON TO THE NEXT PAGE

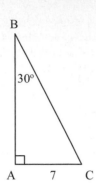

15. In the figure above, what is the length of $\overline{BC}$?

(A) 7
(B) 10
(C) 14
(D) 21

16. If $x = -2$, what is the value of $|x^3| - x^2 - x$?

(A) −14
(B) −10
(C) 2
(D) 6

17. Carlos walks at a constant pace of 13 miles per x minutes. How many miles does he walk in 35 minutes, in terms of x?

(A) $455x$

(B) $\dfrac{455}{x}$

(C) $\dfrac{35}{13x}$

(D) $\dfrac{13}{35x}$

18. How many different ways can five different books be arranged on a bookshelf?

(A) 5
(B) 15
(C) 24
(D) 120

GO ON TO THE NEXT PAGE

Questions 19 and 20 refer to the following information.

A survey on cereal preference was conducted among a random sample of United States citizens in 2010. The table below displays a summary of the survey results.

| | Favorite Cereal Grain | | | |
	Corn	Oats	Other	Total
18 years or younger	3,401	2,305	2,532	8,238
19- to 44-years-olds	7,325	5,321	8,432	21,078
45- to 64-years-olds	5,643	3,423	9,647	18,713
Total	16,369	11,049	20,611	48,029

19. According to the table, which age group has the greatest percentage of people who prefer corn cereal?

   (A)   18 years or younger
   (B)   19- to 35-year-olds
   (C)   45- to 64-year-olds
   (D)   All the groups' percentages are equal

20. In 2010 there were 81 million 45- to 64-year-olds in the United States. If the sample in the table accurately reflects the rest of the population, what is the best estimate of the number of 45- to 64-year-olds in the United States who prefer oat cereal?

   (A)   13 million
   (B)   15 million
   (C)   32 million
   (D)   42 million

21. One film is 10.4 gigabytes in size. Stefan can download 5.4 megabytes per second. What is the maximum number of films that Stefan can download in 10 hours? (1 gigabyte equals 1,024 megabytes.)

   (A)   5
   (B)   10
   (C)   18
   (D) 189

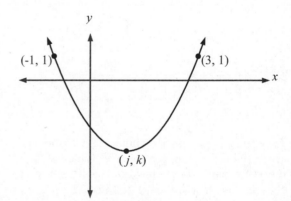

22. The curve above follows the equation $y = ax^2 + bx + c$. The vertex of the curve is located at (j, k). If $(-1, 1)$ and $(3, 1)$ are two points on the curve, what is the value of j?

   (A)   0
   (B)   0.5
   (C)   1
   (D)   1.5

GO ON TO THE NEXT PAGE

23. There is a 33% chance of rain in Boston and a 62% chance of rain in London. If weather conditions in London are independent of weather conditions in Boston, what is the approximate percent probability that it rains in both Boston and London?

(A) 13%
(B) 20%
(C) 71%
(D) 95%

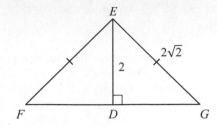

25. What is the area of the triangle *EFG* above?

(A) $\sqrt{2}$
(B) 4
(C) $4\sqrt{2}$
(D) 8

List 1	List 2
$-a, a, b$ and 118	$a, b,$ and 76

24. Two lists of variables and numbers are written in ascending order in the table above. Which of the following expressions represents the difference between the ranges of List 1 and List 2?

(A) $2a + 42$
(B) $a + 42$
(C) 42
(D) $a + 42$

26. The function $f(x)$ is defined by $f(x) = x^2 - 16$. In the *xy*-plane, the graph of $f(x)$ intersects with the *x*-axis at the points $(-4, 0)$, and $(c, 0)$. What is the value of *c*?

(A) −4
(B) 4
(C) 8
(D) 16

GO ON TO THE NEXT PAGE

27. Which expression is equivalent to $x^3y^3 - 64$?

(A) $(xy - 6)(x^2y^2 + 2xy + 12)$
(B) $(xy - 4)(x^2y^2 + 2xy + 12)$
(C) $(xy - 4)(x^2y^2 + 4xy + 16)$
(D) $(xy - 4)(2x^2y^2 + 4xy + 16)$

x	$f(x)$
-1	3
0	6
1	9
2	12

28. The table above contains values of the function $f(x) = 3x + c$. If $g(x) = -7x - 13$, what is the value $g(f(11))$?

(A) -20
(B) -90
(C) -286
(D) -496

29. The data in List A has a standard deviation of 10, and the data in List B has a standard deviation of 7. Which of the following statements is always true?

(A) The mean for List A is different than the mean for List B
(B) The data for List A varies less than the data for List B
(C) The data for List A varies more than the data for List B
(D) List A has more accurate data than List B

$$12x + 15y = 106$$

$$36x + 45y = 6z$$

30. In the system of equations above, which value of z would result in infinitely many solutions?

(A) 318
(B) 106
(C) 53
(D) 18

GO ON TO THE NEXT PAGE

GRID-INS

31. When three times a number is divided by 4, the result is 6. What is the number?

32. The density of lead is 11.3 g per cm^3. A lead pipe weighs 50 kg. What is the volume of the pipe, rounded to the nearest cubic centimeter? (Density is equal to mass/volume.)

33. If $-3 < -4x + 6 < -\frac{2}{3}$, what is a possible value of x?

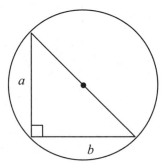

34. The circumference of the circle above is 20π. What is the value of $a^2 + b^2$?

GO ON TO THE NEXT PAGE

$$|x - 12| = 4$$

35. What is a value of x that satisfies the equation above?

36. If $x = 2^{2t} + 5$ and $y = t - 1$, what is the value of $x + y$ when $t = 1.5$?

Questions 37 and 38 refer to the following information.

Monique, a student traveling abroad, frequently uses her American debit card to make purchases. When she makes a purchase, the bank converts the purchase price at the daily foreign exchange rate and then charges a 3% fee on the converted cost.

Monique also converts cash from one currency to another at her bank. To convert cash into a different currency, her bank uses the daily foreign exchange rate and charges a 2.5% fee on the converted cost.

37. In Mexico, Monique used her debit card for a purchase that cost 235 pesos. The bank charged her card 18.62 U.S. dollars, including the 3% conversion fee. What foreign exchange rate, in Mexican pesos per U.S. dollar, did the bank use for Monique's purchase? Round your answer to the nearest whole number.

38. Before her trip, Monique asked her bank to convert 100 U.S. dollars into Mexican pesos. Monique did not spend any of these pesos during her trip, and she asked her bank to convert them back into U.S. dollars when she returned. If the daily foreign exchange rate stayed the same, how many U.S. dollars did Monique lose after these two conversions? Round your answer to the nearest whole number.

STOP

If you complete the problem set before time elapses, you may review your responses for this section.

Do not view or begin working on any other sections.

SECTION 5

Time – 50 minutes

Turn to Section 5 of your answer sheet to write your essay.

Important Reminders:

- You have 50 minutes to write your essay.
- A pencil is required for the essay. An essay written in ink will receive a score of zero.
- Do not write your essay in your test book. You will receive credit only for what you write on your answer sheet.
- Write legibly.

As you read the passage below, consider how Theresa Brown uses

- evidence, such as facts or examples, to support claims.
- reasoning to develop ideas and to connect claims and evidence.
- stylistic or persuasive elements, such as word choice or appeals to emotion, to add power to the ideas expressed.

Adapted from Theresa Brown, "When No One Is on Call." © 2013 by the New York Times Company. Originally published August 17, 2013.

We nurses all have stories—if we're lucky, it's just one—about the time we failed a patient. It's usually a problem of being too busy: too many cases, too many procedures to keep track of until one critical step, just one, slips through our frenetic fingers and someone gets hurt.

I saw it happen the first time while in nursing school. A patient needed an escalating dose of pain medicine. Her pain eased, but her breathing slowed and her oxygen level dropped. I told her nurse that the patient might need narcan, a reversing agent for opioids.

"Narcan?" The nurse didn't have time for that. Caring for eight patients on a busy medical-surgery floor meant that getting through the day's tasks took up all her time. Half an hour later, though, the patient needed an emergency team to revive her.

Bedside nurses are the hospital's front line, but we can't do the first-alert part of our jobs if there aren't enough of us on the floor. More demands for paperwork, along with increasing complexity of care, means the amount of time any one nurse has for all her patients is diminishing. And as hospitals face increasing financial pressure, nurse

staffing often takes a hit, because nurses make up the biggest portion of any hospital's labor costs.

For patients, though, the moral calculus of the nurses-for-money exchange doesn't add up. Pioneering work done by Linda H. Aiken at the University of Pennsylvania in 2002 showed that each extra patient a nurse had above an established nurse-patient ratio made it 7 percent more likely that one of the patients would die. She found that 20,000 people died a year because they were in hospitals with overworked nurses.

Research also shows that when floors are adequately staffed with bedside nurses, the number of patients injured by falls declines. Staff increases lead to decreases in hospital-acquired infections, which kill 100,000 patients every year.

The importance of sufficient nurse staffing is becoming irrefutable, so much so that the Registered Nurse Safe-Staffing Act of 2013 was recently introduced by Representatives Lois Capps, a Democrat from California and a nurse, and David Joyce, a Republican from Ohio. Concerns over money will determine whether this bill has even a chance at passing.

It's hard to do a definitive cost-benefit analysis of a variable as complicated as nurse staffing because health

GO ON TO THE NEXT PAGE ➡

care accounting systems are often byzantine. But data suggest that sufficient staffing can significantly reduce hospital costs.

Medicare penalizes hospitals for readmitting too many patients within 30 days of discharge, and a full nursing staff is one way to reduce readmissions. Having enough nurses increases patient-satisfaction scores, which also helps maintain Medicare reimbursement levels. Understaffing leads to burnout and nurses' quitting their jobs, both of which cost money in terms of absenteeism and training new staff. Finally, falls and infections have associated costs.

What this discussion of finances misses, though, is that having enough nurses is not just about dollars and cents. It's about limiting the suffering of human beings. When hospitals have insufficient nursing staffs, patients who would have gotten better can get hurt, or worse.

Several months ago I started a new job and a few weeks in, I heard my name being called. A patient getting a drug that can cause dangerous reactions was struggling to breathe. I hurried to her room, only to discover that I wasn't needed. The other nurses from the floor were already there, stopping the infusion, checking the patient's oxygen and drawing up the rescue medication. The patient was rattled, but there were enough nurses to respond, and in the end she was completely fine.

Now picture the same events in a different hospital, one that doesn't adequately staff, and this time the patient is you. As the drug drips in, you feel a malaise. You breathe deeply but can't quite get enough air. Your thinking becomes confused, your heart races. Terrified, you press the call light, you yell for help, but the too few nurses on the floor are spread thin and no one comes to help in time. A routine infusion ends with a call to a rapid-response team, a stay in intensive care, intubation, ventilation, death.

This kind of breakdown is not the nurses' fault, but the system's. We are not an elastic resource. We can be where we are needed, but only if there are enough of us.

Assignment: Write an essay in which you explain how Theresa Brown builds an argument to persuade her audience that hospitals must have sufficiently large nursing staffs. In your essay, analyze how Brown uses one or more of the features listed in the box above (or features of your own choice) to strengthen the logic and persuasiveness of her argument. Be sure that your analysis focuses on the most relevant features of the passage.

Your essay should not explain whether you agree with Brown's claims, but rather explain how Brown builds an argument to persuade her audience.

STOP

If you complete the problem set before time elapses, you may review your responses for this section.

Do not view or begin working on any other sections.

Answer Key (Practice Test 1)

Part 1: Reading

1. B	12. A	23. A	34. A	45. B
2. A	13. C	24. A	35. A	46. D
3. C	14. C	25. B	36. D	47. C
4. B	15. C	26. A	37. A	48. D
5. A	16. D	27. C	38. C	49. C
6. B	17. A	28. D	39. C	50. B
7. C	18. A	29. A	40. A	51. A
8. C	19. D	30. B	41. A	52. C
9. B	20. A	31. B	42. A	
10. A	21. C	32. D	43. C	
11. D	22. A	33. C	44. A	

Part 2: Math (no-calculator)

1. C	5. A	9. B	13. B	17. 5
2. C	6. C	10. C	14. C	18. 14
3. D	7. D	11. A	15. B	19. 6
4. C	8. B	12. D	16. 6	20. 120

Part 3: Writing

1. A	10. B	19. C	28. A	37. D
2. C	11. C	20. B	29. C	38. C
3. D	12. D	21. D	30. D	39. A
4. A	13. A	22. A	31. B	40. D
5. B	14. C	23. C	32. D	41. C
6. D	15. C	24. D	33. C	42. B
7. B	16. B	25. D	34. D	43. C
8. D	17. D	26. A	35. B	44. B
9. B	18. A	27. B	36. B	

PART 4: MATH (CALCULATOR)

1. B	9. C	17. B	25. B	33. $5/3 < x < 9/4$
2. D	10. B	18. D	26. B	34. 400
3. A	11. C	19. A	27. C	35. 8 or 16
4. C	12. C	20. B	28. C	36. 13.5
5. C	13. D	21. C	29. C	37. 13
6. C	14. D	22. C	30. C	38. 5
7. C	15. C	23. B	31. 8	
8. C	16. D	24. A	32. 4425	

Full explanations available at ivyglobal.com/study

SCORING YOUR TESTS

To score your tests, first use the answer key to mark each of your responses right or wrong. Then, calculate your **raw score** for each section by counting up the number of correct responses. Use the tables below to help you calculate your scores:

Raw Score: Practice Test 1

Section	# of Questions Correct
1. Reading	_____
2. Math: No-Calculator	_____
3. Writing	_____
4. Math: Calculator	_____

Raw Score for Reading (Section 1): _____

Raw Score for Writing (Section 3): _____

Raw Score for Math (Section 2 + 4): _____

SCALED SCORES

Once you have found your raw score for each section, convert it into an approximate **scaled test score** using the charts below. These charts provide an estimate for your SAT scaled scores based on your performance on each practice test. To find a scaled test score for each section, find the row in the Raw Score column which corresponds to your raw score for that section, then check the column for the section you are scoring in the same row. For example, if you had a raw score of 48 for reading, then your scaled reading test score would be 39. Keep in mind that these scaled scores are estimates only. Your actual SAT score will be scaled against the scores of all other high school students taking the test on your test date.

The scaled scores below have been adjusted for Edition 1.1 of this guide.

Raw Score	Math Scaled Score	Reading Scaled Score	Writing Scaled Score	Raw Score	Math Scaled Score	Reading Scaled Score	Writing Scaled Score
58	40			28	23	26	25
57	40			27	22	25	24
56	40			26	22	25	24
55	39			25	21	24	23
54	38			24	21	24	23
53	37			23	20	23	22
52	36	40		22	20	22	21
51	35	40		21	19	22	21
50	34	40		20	19	21	20
49	34	39		19	18	20	20
48	33	39		18	18	20	19
47	33	38		17	17	19	19
46	32	37		16	16	19	18
45	32	36		15	15	18	18
44	31	35	40	14	14	17	17
43	30	34	39	13	13	16	16
42	30	34	38	12	12	16	15
41	29	33	37	11	11	14	14
40	29	33	35	10	10	13	13
39	28	32	34	9	10	12	12
38	28	31	33	8	10	11	11
37	27	31	32	7	10	10	10
36	27	30	31	6	10	10	10
35	26	30	30	5	10	10	10
34	26	29	29	4	10	10	10
33	25	29	28	3	10	10	10
32	25	28	27	2	10	10	10
31	24	28	27	1	10	10	10
30	24	27	26	0	10	10	10
29	23	26	26				

Use the table below to record your scaled scores:

Scaled Scores	
	Practice Test 1
Scaled Score for Reading (Out of 40):	_____
Scaled Score for Writing (Out of 40):	_____
Scaled Score for Math (Out of 40):	_____

ESSAY SCORE

Review the essay scoring criteria in Chapter 4. Then, estimate your essay score by assigning your essay a score out of 1-4 in each scoring area, using the following charts as a guide. Have a trusted reader check your work.

Essay Score: Practice Test 1		
Scoring Area	Reader 1 Score (1-4)	Reader 2 Score (1-4)
Reading	_____	_____
Analysis	_____	_____
Writing	_____	_____

AREA SCORE CONVERSION

You can look up your area score out of 800 below. To find your overall score, combine your area score for Reading + Writing with your area score for Math to get your total score out of 1600.

READING + WRITING

Scaled Score	Area Score	Scaled Score	Area Score	Scaled Score	Area Score
80	760-800	59	550-630	39	350-430
79	750-800	58	540-620	38	340-420
78	740-800	57	530-610	37	330-410
77	730-800	56	520-600	36	320-400
76	720-800	55	510-590	35	310-390
75	710-790	54	500-580	34	300-380
74	700-780	53	490-570	33	290-370
73	690-770	52	480-560	32	280-360
72	680-760	51	470-550	31	270-350
71	670-750	50	460-540	30	260-340
70	660-740	49	450-530	29	250-330
69	650-730	48	440-520	28	240-320
68	640-720	47	430-510	27	230-310
67	630-710	46	420-500	26	220-300
66	620-700	45	410-490	25	210-290
65	610-690	44	400-480	24	200-280
64	600-680	43	390-470	23	200-270
63	590-670	42	380-460	22	200-260
62	580-660	41	370-450	21	200-250
61	570-650	40	360-440	20	200-240
60	560-640				

MATH

Scaled Score	Area Score	Total Points	Scaled Score
40	760-800	24	440-520
39	740-800	23	420-500
38	720-800	22	400-480
37	700-780	21	380-460
36	680-760	20	360-440
35	660-740	19	340-420
34	640-720	18	320-400
33	620-700	17	300-380
32	600-680	16	280-360
31	580-660	15	260-340
30	560-640	14	240-320
29	540-620	13	220-300
28	520-600	12	200-280
27	500-580	11	200-260
26	480-560	10	200-240
25	460-540		

Use the table below to record your area scores and to calculate your overall score:

	Reading + Writing Area Score	Math Area Score	Overall Score (400-1600)
Practice Test 1	_____ +	_____ =	_____

Cross-test scores and Subscores

Starting in 2016, the College Board will report a couple of new types of scores. In addition to receiving scores that show your performance on each section, in the areas of Math and English, and overall, you will also receive scores based on particular aspects of your performance within and across test sections.

You will receive **cross-test scores** for Analysis in Science and Analysis in History/Social Studies. The scores are based on your performance on questions in their respective subject domains across all sections of the exam. These scores will be reported on a scale of 10-40.

You will also receive **subscores** based on your performance on certain question types within each test section. Subscores will be reported on a scale of 1-15. There will be seven subscores, for the following areas:

- **Words in Context:** this subscore will be based on your performance on questions related to determining the meanings of words in the context of a passage in the English area.
- **Command of Evidence:** this subscore will be based on your performance on questions that ask you to identify the best evidence in the Reading and Writing tests.
- **Expression of Ideas:** this subscore will be based on your performance on questions that ask you to identify clear, stylistically appropriate choices in writing passages.
- **Standard English Conventions:** this subscore will be based on your performance on questions that ask you to identify and correct errors of grammar, punctuation, usage, and syntax in writing passages.
- **Heart of Algebra:** this subscore will be based on your performance on Math questions testing key concepts in Algebra.
- **Problem Solving and Data Analysis**: this subscore will be based on your performance on Math questions testing your ability to analyze sets of data, the meanings of units and quantities, and the properties of different objects and operations.
- **Passport to Advanced Math:** this subscore will be based on your performance on Math questions that test the skills you'll build on as you continue to learn more advanced math including rewriting expressions, solving quadratic equations, working with polynomials and radicals, and solving systems of equations.

As of our publication date, the College Board had not released detailed information on how these scores will be calculated.

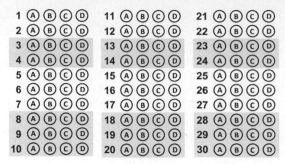

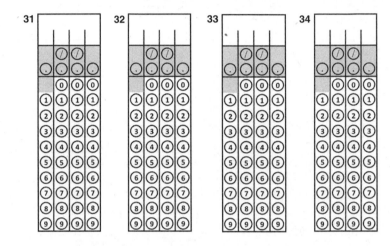

IMPORTANT: USE A NO. 2 PENCIL. WRITE INSIDE THE BORDERS.

Continue on next page.

Continue on next page.

SECTION 1

Time – 65 minutes

52 Questions

Turn to Section 1 of your answer sheet to answer the questions in this section.

Directions: For these questions, determine the solution to each question presented and choose the best answer choice of those provided. Be sure to fill in the respective circle on your answer sheet.

Questions 1-11 are based on the following passage.

Recycling bins overflow after the holidays, stuffed with gift wrapping and tangled Christmas-tree lights. Rarely does this junk earn a second thought. But where does it all go?
Line
5   Probably Asia, and particularly China, the largest importer of recycling from the rich world. Those broken lights, for example, may turn up in Guangdong province where factories salvage the copper wire and melt the stripped plastic into new slipper soles. China's thriving economy is desperate for stuff that consumers in America and elsewhere
10   carelessly throw away.

The multibillion-dollar recycling trade stands as "one of globalization's great, green successes," writes Adam Minter, an American journalist, in *Junkyard Planet*. It is also a largely unsung one, as under-appreciated as a rusty bike. The
15   industry turns over as much as $500 billion annually, and employs a huge number of people. After years spent travelling the junk heaps of the world, and a decade living in China, Mr. Minter is keen to give the scrap-dealers their due. Son of an American scrap-yard owner, he approaches the
20   industry with affectionate curiosity, marveling at the "groan and crunch" of machines that turn rubbish into usable goods.

When Mr. Minter first moved to Shanghai in 2002, the city had three subway lines; ten years later it boasts one of the world's largest systems, with 11 lines and 270 miles of
25   track. Building booms in the developing world, particularly in China, have caused an explosion of demand for steel, copper and other resources. Yet China lacks the raw materials it needs, so it imports the metal, often as scrap. This has pushed up prices; a pound of copper has risen from
30   60 cents in the late 1990s to nearly $3.40 today. Americans, meanwhile, have more scrap than they can handle. Known among scrap traders as the "Saudi Arabia of Scrap," the country lacks real demand for manufacturing materials. American labor costs are too high—and environmental

35   regulations too onerous—for it to be cost-effective to salvage most scrap anyway. For the savvy, fast-talking businessmen of the international scrap trade, this has created a profitable exchange. It has also driven the kind of innovation that diverts more junk from landfills.

40   For example, people now worry more about the afterlife of their mobile phones than their cars because of the invention of the motor shredder, which turns old vehicles into scrap metal. In 1970, at least 20 million rusting cars were abandoned across America. In 2012, America recycled
45   nearly 11.9 million cars. China, the world's biggest car buyer, has become the fastest growing market for shredders. America's trade deficit with China reinforces the two countries' relationship as recycling partners. Americans consume, and therefore dispose of, more goods than their
50   Chinese counterparts. And it is also often cheaper for American scrap-yards to send their goods to China than anywhere else in the world. This is because shipping companies hauling goods to America would rather not return to China empty, and so they offer discounts on what they call
55   their "back-hauls."

Whether Mr. Minter is accompanying a Chinese scrap buyer on a road trip through the American Midwest or trying to sell his old mobile phones in Guiyu, China's controversial electronic-waste recycling zone, he is an authorial, engaging
60   guide through the global trash trade. Dirty, dangerous, cheap to get into and not without romance, the junk business extracts value from what others see as worthless. Mr. Minter is not blind to the grim realities of the industry. Wen'an county in China, a place once known for its fertile soil, clear
65   streams and peach trees, was the "most polluted place" he ever visited because of its role in the plastics trade.

But any recrimination over these recycling practices is best directed at the rich world and at the increasingly wealthy Chinese who are beginning to match their wasteful,
70   spendthrift counterparts in the West. The recycling industry

GO ON TO THE NEXT PAGE

squeezes value from used goods, but nothing is 100% recyclable. The special chemistry of many products, such as iPhone touchscreens, means they cannot be recycled. Consumers should be more aware of what is harmful, and
75 companies should be nudged to design products that are easier to repair and recycle. In the meantime, a bit more appreciation might be spared for junkyards, without which "the world would be a dirtier and less interesting place."

United States Scrap Exports to China

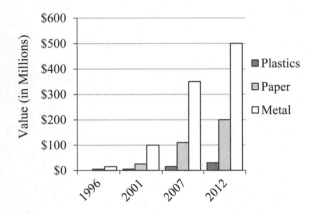

The above chart shows the amount of US scrap exports to China by value over time. Data from the United States International Trade Commission.

1. The main purpose of the passage can best be described as

   (A) describing the economic relationship between two countries.
   (B) criticizing the environmental policies of a major world power.
   (C) discussing the virtues of a valuable and growing industry.
   (D) expressing an opinion about the rising cost of certain metals.

2. It can be reasonably inferred from the passage that the author believes which one of the following claims about the global recycling industry?

   (A) Its economic importance has been over-emphasized.
   (B) Its impact on other industries is largely insignificant.
   (C) It disproportionately benefits already developed economies.
   (D) Its benefits are often not fully appreciated.

3. Which choice provides the best evidence for the answer to the previous question?

   (A) Lines 4-5 ("Probably … world")
   (B) Lines 13-14 ("It is … bike")
   (C) Lines 19-21 ("Son … goods")
   (D) Lines 25-27 ("Building … resources")

4. The author's attitude towards Adam Minter's book Junkyard Planet could best be described as

   (A) respectful and approving.
   (B) perplexed and reserved.
   (C) enthusiastic and worshipful.
   (D) detached and unimpressed.

5. As used in line 23, "boasts" most nearly means

   (A) gloats.
   (B) exaggerates.
   (C) brags.
   (D) features.

6. According to the passage, the rapid expansion of the global recycling trade in the past few decades has been caused mainly by

   (A) the depletion of natural resources in Asia through environmentally unsafe practices.
   (B) the increased demand for resources to sustain construction projects in the developing world.
   (C) the growing innovation in consumer goods that has caused products to become obsolete sooner.
   (D) the swiftly expanding Chinese population that has created a large new market for American goods.

GO ON TO THE NEXT PAGE

7. According to the passage, which of the following claims is true about American scrap metal?

    (A) The price of scrap metal has increased more since the late 1990s than ever before.
    (B) Scrap metal has been used in the past to construct subway lines in major American cities.
    (C) It is usually not profitable to recycle scrap metal in America.
    (D) Safety regulations prevent scrap metal from being recycled for domestic construction projects.

8. Which choice provides the best evidence for the answer to the previous question?

    (A) Lines 22-25 ("When … track")
    (B) Lines 29-30 ("This has … today")
    (C) Lines 34-36 ("American … anyway")
    (D) Lines 38-39 ("It has … landfills")

9. The purpose of the fourth paragraph (lines 40-55) can best be described as

    (A) providing evidence to support a claim made in an earlier paragraph.
    (B) defining terms that were introduced in an earlier paragraph.
    (C) describing a scenario that demonstrates a general rule.
    (D) articulating the disadvantages of a position that was advocated for in an earlier paragraph.

10. As it is used in line 62, "extracts" most nearly means

    (A) removes.
    (B) derives.
    (C) selects.
    (D) exacts.

11. Which one of the following claims is supported by the chart?

    (A) Total United States plastic exports to China reached 200 million tons in 2012.
    (B) From 1996 to 2012, the value of United States scrap metal exported to China was greater than the value of paper and plastic exports combined.
    (C) In 2001, China imported less than $50 million worth of scrap paper from around the world.
    (D) The United States exported a total of $500 million worth of scrap metal in 2012.

GO ON TO THE NEXT PAGE

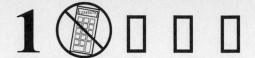
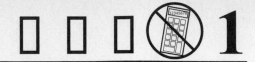
Questions 12-22 are based on the following passage.

Passage 1

Heart disease is the leading cause of death in the U.S., and people with higher cholesterol are at higher risk for heart attacks. There's good evidence that people who already have heart disease benefit from cholesterol-lowering medications,

Line
5   or statins. Among those people, statin treatment reduces risk of heart attack and may prolong life.

But what about healthy people with high cholesterol? Many doctors have taken the evidence from studies of people with heart disease and made a leap of logic: they've treated
10   millions of healthy people with statins to prevent heart disease.

But there's a serious problem with that logic. For most healthy people, data show that statins do not prevent heart disease, nor extend life or improve quality of life. And they
15   come with considerable side effects. That's why I don't recommend giving statins to healthy people, even those with higher cholesterol.

Despite research that has included tens of thousands of people, there is no evidence that taking statins prolongs life,
20   although cholesterol levels do decrease. Using the most optimistic projections, for every 100 healthy people who take statins for five years, one or two will avoid a heart attack. One will develop diabetes. But, on average, there is no evidence that the group taking statins will live any longer
25   than those who don't.

Some argue that clinical trials of statin use among healthy people haven't demonstrated a reduced mortality rate because each individual trial only follows patients for a few years— not long enough to show a reduction in mortality. Many
30   doctors, including me, believe that we need clinical trials that actually follow healthy people treated with statins for the long term to see if treatment really results in lower mortality. Statin proponents think such trials would be prohibitively expensive. That's a disappointing stance, considering the
35   billions that have already been spent on statin prescriptions and advertising.

Some statin supporters argue that even if the data don't support the benefits of statins in healthy people, they might help and can't hurt. But that's untenable, because statins
40   undeniably harm some people. Besides increasing the risk for developing diabetes, statins can cause memory loss, muscle weakness, stomach distress, and aches and pains. These aren't merely anecdotal results, as some critics assert; they're documented by recent studies.

Passage 2

45   We don't prescribe drugs to otherwise healthy people without rigorous scientific evidence. And, in this case, there is a mountain of high-quality scientific evidence.

Heart disease is an insidious process that takes decades to manifest itself. Risk factors for developing heart disease
50   often go unrecognized and undertreated until it's too late. So, the first manifestation of cardiovascular disease is often sudden cardiac death, heart attack or stroke—which may result in disability or death. A little late at that point to start prescribing statins.

55   Yet critics say we should wait until after a patient has gone through one of these life-shattering events before we prescribe a statin. It makes no sense that a medication that slows the progression of hardening of the arteries would be harmful the day or week before a heart attack, but helpful the
60   day or week after a heart attack.

The totality of the available biologic, observational and clinical-trial evidence strongly supports the selective use of statin therapy in adults demonstrated to be at high risk for heart disease. Studies have conclusively shown that statins
65   prolong life and reduce the risk of heart attack, stroke and death in patients with known heart disease. Similarly, they have been shown to do the same in patients without heart disease, but who are at high risk of developing heart disease.

For instance, a study of 6,600 Scottish men who hadn't
70   had heart attacks showed a decrease in mortality rates after five years with statin therapy. Likewise, the recent world-wide Jupiter study of men and women without prior heart disease showed statins significantly decreased the risk of death after two years in people with an average age of 66.

75   Critics raise a number of complaints about these studies —exaggerated, in my view—but many other large prevention trials of people with multiple risk factors have consistently shown reductions in total cardiovascular events of 30% to 40% with the use of a statin.

GO ON TO THE NEXT PAGE

12. The authors of both passages would most likely agree on which of the following statements?

    (A) Drugs should never be prescribed to healthy patients.
    (B) Past studies measuring the effects of statin use have been flawed.
    (C) Statins are effective at treating patients with heart disease.
    (D) Statins should only be prescribed after a patient has experienced a cardiovascular incident.

13. Which one of the following pieces of evidence is included in Passage 2 but not Passage 1?

    (A) A discussion of the side effects of cholesterol-lowering medication
    (B) Statistics from specific scientific studies
    (C) Information about the prevalence of statin use
    (D) An analysis of the financial costs of statin use

14. As used in line 28, "individual" most nearly means

    (A) peculiar.
    (B) personal.
    (C) secluded.
    (D) particular.

15. It can be reasonably inferred from Passage 1 that the author would most likely recommend statins for a patient

    (A) who is male and between the ages of 65 and 74.
    (B) who has an unusually high cholesterol level.
    (C) who is at a higher than average risk of having a heart attack.
    (D) who is already suffering from heart disease.

16. Which choice provides the best evidence for the answer to the previous question?

    (A) Lines 3-5 ("There's good … statins")
    (B) Lines 8-11 ("Many doctors … disease")
    (C) Lines 15-17 ("That's why … cholesterol")
    (D) Lines 29-32 ("Many … mortality")

17. According to Passage 1, which of the following best describes the relationship between statins and diabetes?

    (A) People with diabetes are not allowed to take statins.
    (B) People are more likely to develop diabetes when using statins.
    (C) Statins are often prescribed for the treatment of diabetes.
    (D) People are less likely to develop diabetes when using statins.

18. Which of the following best summarizes the position held by the author of Passage 2?

    (A) Since it is unethical to treat people for a disease they don't have, statins should be considered preventative medication and prescribed to anyone who wants them.
    (B) Since people with heart disease don't know they have it, doctors should prescribe statins to patients who might have or might develop heart disease.
    (C) Since statins are not known to prevent the development of heart disease, doctors should only prescribe them to patients at risk for diabetes.
    (D) Since doctors only prescribe medicines whose record of success is well-documented, patients should trust their doctors' recommendations.

19. The main rhetorical effect of lines 53-54 ("A little late… statins") is to

    (A) specify the correct moment for prescribing statins.
    (B) provide information about when the prescription of statins is most appropriate.
    (C) portray the opposing argument as nonsensical and dangerous.
    (D) convey a sense of regret about the preventable death of a patient.

20. As used in line 62, "selective" most nearly means

    (A) exacting.
    (B) choosy.
    (C) judicious.
    (D) exclusive.

GO ON TO THE NEXT PAGE

1 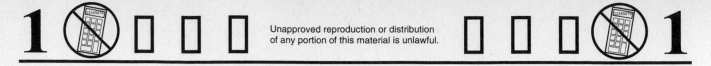 **1**

Unapproved reproduction or distribution
of any portion of this material is unlawful.

21. How would the author of Passage 2 most likely respond to the claim made in lines 26-29 ("Some ... mortality") of Passage 1?

(A) By asserting that certain studies have shown a reduction in mortality for healthy patients who use statins

(B) By agreeing that more studies need to be conducted that follow patients for longer periods of time

(C) By suggesting that scientists should examine the quality of life of statin users rather than just the risk of death

(D) By arguing that following patients for only one year is enough to prove reduced mortality in healthy patients who use statins

22. Which choice provides the best evidence for the answer to the previous question?

(A) Lines 49-50 ("Risk ... late")
(B) Lines 57-60 ("It makes ... attack")
(C) Lines 64-66 ("Studies ... disease")
(D) Lines 69-71 ("For instance ... therapy")

GO ON TO THE NEXT PAGE

Questions 23-32 are based on the following passage.

This passage is adapted from The Federalist Papers: No. 3. Originally published between 1787 and 1788, the Federalist Papers aimed to build support for ratification of the United States Constitution, which would unify the States under a national government. In this excerpt, John Jay addresses the "dangers from foreign force and influence."

The just causes of war, for the most part, arise either from violation of treaties or from direct violence. America has already formed treaties with no less than six foreign nations.
Line It is of high importance to the peace of America that she
5 observe the laws of nations towards all these powers, and to me it appears evident that this will be more perfectly and punctually done by one national government than it could be either by thirteen separate States or by three or four distinct confederacies. For this opinion various reasons may be
10 assigned.

The prospect of present loss or advantage may often tempt the governing party in one or two States to swerve from good faith and justice; but those temptations, not reaching the other States, and consequently having little or
15 no influence on the national government, the temptation will be fruitless, and good faith and justice be preserved. The case of the treaty of peace with Britain adds great weight to this reasoning.

If even the governing party in a State should be disposed
20 to resist such temptations, yet as such temptations may, and commonly do, result from circumstances peculiar to the State, and may affect a great number of the inhabitants, the governing party may not always be able, if willing, to prevent the injustice meditated, or to punish the aggressors.
25 But the national government, not being affected by those local circumstances, will neither be induced to commit the wrong themselves, nor want power or inclination to prevent or punish its commission by others.

So far, therefore, as either designed or accidental
30 violations of treaties and the laws of nations afford just causes of war, they are less to be apprehended under one general government than under several lesser ones, and in that respect the former most favors the safety of the people.

As to those just causes of war which proceed from direct
35 and unlawful violence, it appears equally clear to me that one good national government affords vastly more security against dangers of that sort than can be derived from any other quarter.

Because such violences are more frequently caused by
40 the passions and interests of a part than of the whole; of one or two States than of the Union. Not a single Indian war has yet been occasioned by aggressions of the present federal government, feeble as it is; but there are several instances of Indian hostilities having been provoked by the improper
45 conduct of individual States, who, either unable or unwilling to restrain or punish offenses, have given occasion to the slaughter of many innocent inhabitants.

Besides, it is well known that acknowledgments, explanations, and compensations are often accepted as
50 satisfactory from a strong united nation, which would be rejected as unsatisfactory if offered by a State or confederacy of little consideration or power.

In the year 1685, the state of Genoa having offended Louis XIV., endeavored to appease him. He demanded that
55 they should send their Doge, or chief magistrate, accompanied by four of their senators, to France, to ask his pardon and receive his terms. They were obliged to submit to it for the sake of peace. Would he on any occasion either have demanded or have received the like humiliation from
60 Spain, or Britain, or any other powerful nation?

23. The main purpose of the passage can best be described as

(A) illustrating how a united government should operate.
(B) proposing a new form of government.
(C) explaining some of the benefits of united government.
(D) recounting the recent history of the United States.

24. Which of the following describes the overall structure of this passage?

(A) A collection of loosely associated thoughts on a common theme
(B) A criticism of a system followed by a series of accusations
(C) A statement of a position followed by a number of arguments in support of that position
(D) A list of problems and step-by-step solutions to those problems

GO ON TO THE NEXT PAGE

1 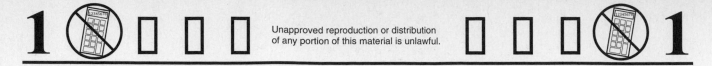 1

Unapproved reproduction or distribution
of any portion of this material is unlawful.

25. According to Jay, which of the following would most likely constitute a "just cause" of war?

    (A) A country seeks to expand its borders.
    (B) Treaty negotiations between two countries are stalled by one side's refusal to compromise.
    (C) One country discovers that its neighbor has been producing weapons and training troops.
    (D) A country repeatedly violates the terms of a treaty that it has signed.

26. As used in line 8, "distinct" most nearly means

    (A) separate.
    (B) prominent.
    (C) unmistakable.
    (D) precise.

27. As used in line 11, "prospect" most nearly means

    (A) hope.
    (B) candidate.
    (C) view.
    (D) possibility.

28. In lines 11-13, Jay raises the concern that individual states, if left to their own devices, might

    (A) behave improperly towards other nations for their own short-term gain.
    (B) allow their citizens to over-indulge in pleasurable activities.
    (C) start practicing a different religion from the rest of the union.
    (D) attack other nations without the consent of the national government.

29. Jay believes that "one general government" is less likely than "several lesser ones" to provoke a war (line 31-32) because

    (A) it is less likely to catch and punish foreign criminals.
    (B) it is less likely to break its treaties with other nations.
    (C) it is more likely to keep its people safe, happy, and obedient.
    (D) it will not be able to fund as many foreign wars.

30. Which of the following choices provides the best evidence for the answer to the previous question?

    (A) Lines 1-3 ("The ... nations")
    (B) Lines 29-33 ("So far ... people")
    (C) Lines 48-52 ("Besides ... power")
    (D) Lines 57-60 ("They ... nation")

31. In the sixth paragraph (lines 39-47), Jay implies that the federal government has not provoked conflicts with the Native Americans because

    (A) it is much weaker than they are and would suffer serious casualties in the case of war.
    (B) it is unwilling to punish its citizens for their inappropriate behavior.
    (C) such conflicts arise from local concerns that are not important to the nation as a whole.
    (D) such conflicts are best resolved on the local level without federal interference.

32. The final paragraph (lines 53-60) serves to

    (A) support the claim in the previous paragraph with a historical example.
    (B) direct the reader's attention to the United States' relationship with France.
    (C) predict what will happen to the United States if Jay's proposals are not acted upon.
    (D) illustrate how much superior the United States are to Genoa.

GO ON TO THE NEXT PAGE

1 **1**

Questions 33-42 are based on the following passage

What would you give for a retinal chip that let you see in the dark or for a next-generation cochlear implant that let you hear any conversation in a noisy restaurant, no matter
Line how loud? Or for a memory chip, wired directly into your
5 brain's hippocampus, that gave you perfect recall of everything you read? Or for an implanted interface with the Internet that automatically translated a clearly articulated silent thought ("the French sun king") into an online search that digested the relevant Wikipedia page and projected a
10 summary directly into your brain?

Science fiction? Perhaps not for very much longer. Brain implants today are where laser eye surgery was several decades ago. They are not risk-free and make sense only for a narrowly defined set of patients—but they are a sign of
15 things to come. Unlike pacemakers, dental crowns or implantable insulin pumps, neuroprosthetics—devices that restore or supplement the mind's capacities with electronics inserted directly into the nervous system—change how we perceive the world and move through it. For better or worse,
20 these devices become part of who we are.

Neuroprosthetics aren't new. They have been around commercially for three decades, in the form of the cochlear implants used in the ears (the outer reaches of the nervous system) of more than 300,000 hearing-impaired people
25 around the world. Last year, the Food and Drug Administration approved the first retinal implant, made by the company Second Sight. Both technologies exploit the same principle: an external device, either a microphone or a video camera, captures sounds or images and processes
30 them, using the results to drive a set of electrodes that stimulate either the auditory or the optic nerve, approximating the naturally occurring output from the ear or the eye.

Another type of now-common implant, used by
35 thousands of Parkinson's patients around the world, sends electrical pulses deep into the brain proper, activating some of the pathways involved in motor control. A thin electrode is inserted into the brain through a small opening in the skull; it is connected by a wire that runs to a battery pack
40 underneath the skin. The effect is to reduce or even eliminate the tremors and rigid movement that are such prominent symptoms of Parkinson's (though, unfortunately, the device doesn't halt the progression of the disease itself). Experimental trials are now under way to test the efficacy of
45 such "deep brain stimulation" for treating other disorders as well.

Electrical stimulation can also improve some forms of memory, as the neurosurgeon Itzhak Fried and his colleagues at the University of California, Los Angeles, showed in a
50 2012 article in the New England Journal of Medicine. Using a setup akin to a videogame, seven patients were taught to navigate a virtual city environment with a joystick, picking up passengers and delivering them to specific stores. Appropriate electrical stimulation to the brain during the
55 game increased their speed and accuracy in accomplishing the task.

But not all brain implants work by directly stimulating the brain. Some work instead by reading the brain's signals —to interpret, for example, the intentions of a paralyzed
60 user. Eventually, neuroprosthetic systems might try to do both, reading a user's desires, performing an action like a Web search and then sending the results directly back to the brain.

How a Cochlear Implant Works

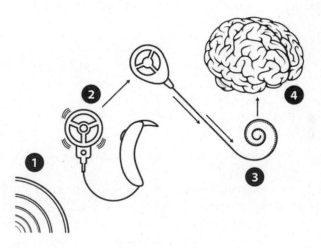

1 Microphone receives sound from environment

2 Transmitter sends signal to implanted receiver

3 Electrode array stimulates aural nerve

4 Brain receives and interprets signal from nerve

Adapted from National Institutes of Health, "Cochlear Implants."

33. Which one of the following best describes the overall structure of the passage?

(A) Disparate facts are joined by a central story.
(B) A common misconception is explained and refuted.
(C) Speculation about the future is supported with examples.
(D) An experiment is discussed to support a prediction.

34. The series of questions in lines 1-10 ("what would … your brain") serves mainly to

(A) demonstrate the incredible advances that have been achieved by a new technology.
(B) prompt readers to consider the potential value of hypothetical technologies.
(C) suggest that technologies that most of us desire will soon be available.
(D) challenge readers to consider the true costs of future advances in technology.

35. As used in line 14, "defined" most nearly means

(A) explained.
(B) interpreted.
(C) characterized.
(D) delineated.

36. Which of the following statements is supported by the passage?

(A) Neuroprosthetics are used exclusively to treat brain disorders.
(B) Retinal implants are currently used by nearly 300,000 people.
(C) Cochlear implants represent a significant improvement over pacemakers.
(D) Neuroprosthetics alter the way in which patients experience the world.

37. It can be reasonably inferred from the passage that cochlear and retinal implants

(A) took a long time to become approved by the Food and Drug Administration.
(B) attempt to recreate the sensations experienced by the average person.
(C) allow the user to see or hear just as well as someone who does not need these implants.
(D) are as safe and effective as laser eye surgery.

38. Which choice provides the best evidence for the answer to the previous question?

(A) Lines 11-13 ("Brain … ago")
(B) Lines 15-19 ("Unlike … through it")
(C) Lines 21-25 ("They have … world")
(D) Lines 28-33 ("An external … eye")

39. As used in line 27, "exploit" most nearly means

(A) harness.
(B) abuse.
(C) deceive.
(D) contrive.

40. Information provided by the passage suggests that electrical stimulation of parts of the nervous system

(A) is currently being used around the world to cure patients with Parkinson's disease.
(B) could soon become a part of commercially available video games.
(C) may have the potential to alleviate the symptoms of patients living with a variety of medical conditions.
(D) has been shown to improve memory in seven out of every ten patients.

41. Which choice provides the best evidence for the answer to the previous question?

(A) Lines 34-37 ("Another … control")
(B) Lines 44-46 ("Experimental … well")
(C) Lines 54-56 ("Appropriate … task")
(D) Lines 58-60 ("Some work … user")

GO ON TO THE NEXT PAGE

42. Based on information from the passage and graphic, which of the following best describes how a cochlear implant works?

(A) The aural nerve is replaced by an implanted electrode, which receives signals from a microphone.

(B) An implanted microphone sends a signal directly to the brain.

(C) A microphone responds to signals from the brain by sending and receiving sound through a series of transmitters.

(D) An implanted electrode receives signals from a microphone, and sends signals to the brain through the aural nerve.

GO ON TO THE NEXT PAGE

Questions 43-52 are based on the following passage.

My travelling companion was a "Free Trader," whose name was Spear—a tall, stoop-shouldered man with heavy eyebrows and a shaggy, drooping moustache. The way we met was amusing. It happened in a certain frontier town. His first question was as to whether I was single. His second, as to whether my time was my own. Then he slowly looked me over from head to foot. He seemed to be measuring my stature and strength and to be noting the color of my eyes and hair.

Narrowing his vision, he scrutinized me more carefully than before, for now he seemed to be reading my character— if not my soul. Then, smiling, he blurted out:

"Come, be my guest for a couple of weeks. Will you?"

I laughed.

He frowned. But on realizing that my mirth was caused only by surprise, he smiled again and let flow a vivid description of a place he called Spearhead. It was the home of the northern fur trade. It was the center of a great timber region. It was the heart of a vast fertile belt that was rapidly becoming the greatest of all farming districts. It virtually stood over the very vault that contained the richest veins of mineral to be found in the whole Dominion—at least that's what he said—and he also assured me that the Government had realized it too, for was it not going to hew a provincial highway clean through the forest to Spearhead? Was it not going to build a fleet of steamers to ply upon the lakes and rivers in that section? And was it not going to build a line of railroad to the town itself? In fact, he also impressed upon me that Spearhead was a town created for young men who were not averse to becoming wealthy in whatever line of business they might choose. It seemed that great riches were already there and had but to be lifted. Would I go?

But when I explained that although I was single, and quite free, I was not a businessman, he became crestfallen, but presently revived enough to exclaim:

"Well, what are you?"

"An artist," I replied.

"Oh, I see! Well … we need an artist very badly. You'll have the field all to yourself in Spearhead. Besides, your pictures of the fur trade and of pioneer life would eventually become historical and bring you no end of wealth. You had better come. Better decide right away, or some other artist chap will get ahead of you."

But when I further explained that I was going to spend the winter in the wilderness, that I had already written to the Hudson's Bay Factor at Fort Consolation and that he was expecting me, Spear gloated:

"Bully boy!" and slapping me on the shoulder, he chuckled: "Why, my town is just across the lake from Fort Consolation. A mere five-mile paddle, old chap, and remember, I extend to you the freedom of Spearhead in the name of its future mayor. And, man alive, I'm leaving for there tomorrow morning in a big four-fathom birch bark. Be my guest. It won't cost you a farthing, and we'll make the trip together."

I gladly accepted. Free Trader Spear was a character, and I afterward learned that he was an Oxford University man, who, having failed, left for Canada, entered the service of the Hudson's Bay Company, and had finally been moved to Fort Consolation where he served seven years, learned the fur-trade business, and resigned to become a "free trader", as all fur traders are called who carry on business in opposition to "The Great Company." We were eight days upon the trip, but, strange to say, during each day's travel toward Spearhead, his conversation in reference to that thriving town made it appear to grow smaller and smaller, until at last it actually dwindled down to such a point, that, about sunset on the day we were to arrive, he turned to me and casually remarked:

"Presently you'll see Fort Consolation and the Ojibwa village beyond. Spearhead is just across the lake, and by the bye, my boy, I forgot to tell you that Spearhead is just my log shack. But it's a nice little place, and you'll like it when you pay us a visit."

43. Which of the following provides the most reasonable summary of the passage?

(A) A businessman receives a rare financial opportunity that he finds impossible to pass up.
(B) An explorer undertakes a journey that he later regrets.
(C) A well-educated fur trader attempts to succeed independently.
(D) A man is persuaded into undertaking a trip under false pretenses.

GO ON TO THE NEXT PAGE

1 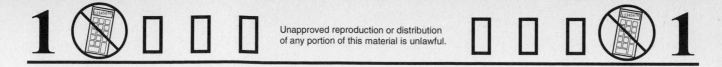 **1**

Unapproved reproduction or distribution of any portion of this material is unlawful.

44. Spear's tone throughout the passage can best be described as

    (A) eager insistence.
    (B) reluctant acceptance.
    (C) zealous conviction.
    (D) restrained confidence.

45. The suggestion that Spear was reading the narrator's soul (lines 11-12) serves to

    (A) highlight Spear's mystical inclinations.
    (B) emphasize the intensity of Spear's visual inspection.
    (C) imply that the narrator has something to hide.
    (D) illustrate Spear's ability to judge the character of a stranger.

46. As used in line 21, "richest" most nearly means

    (A) wealthiest.
    (B) most opulent.
    (C) most expensive.
    (D) most bountiful.

47. Which of the following does Spear assure the narrator that he will gain if he comes to Spearhead?

    (A) The opportunity to make a great deal of money
    (B) A life of independence and adventure
    (C) The reputation of one who opposes The Great Company
    (D) A tranquility which could not be found in other cities

48. Which choice provides the best evidence for the answer to the previous question?

    (A) Lines 19-20 ("It was … districts")
    (B) Lines 39-41 ("Besides … wealth")
    (C) Lines 50-52 ("A mere … mayor")
    (D) Lines 63-66 ("We were … smaller")

49. As used in line 51, "extend" most nearly means

    (A) expand.
    (B) increase.
    (C) proffer.
    (D) exert.

50. Which of the following best describes the current relationship between Spear and the Hudson's Bay Company?

    (A) Spear trades in competition with the Hudson's Bay Company.
    (B) Spear lives in subservience to the Hudson's Bay Company.
    (C) The Hudson's Bay Company is pointedly disinterested in Spear's activities.
    (D) The Hudson's Bay Company appreciates the efforts of free traders like Spear.

51. Which choice provides the best evidence for the answer to the previous question?

    (A) Lines 1-3 ("My travelling … moustache")
    (B) Lines 17-18 ("It was … fur trade")
    (C) Lines 33-36 ("But when … are you")
    (D) Lines 61-63 ("and resigned … Company")

52. The final paragraph of the passage (lines 70-74) serves mainly to

    (A) describe the town of Spearhead in detail.
    (B) expose the true intentions of the narrator's companion.
    (C) reveal how the narrator was deceived by his companion.
    (D) indicate the precise location of the narrator's destination.

STOP

If you finish early, you may review your responses for this section.
Do not view or begin working on any other sections.

Acknowledgements for this Section

The passages in this section were adapted from the following sources:

Adam Minter, "Plastic Arts: What Really Happens to Human Junk." © 2014 by *The Economist Newspaper Limited*.

Robert S. Blumenthal, Rita Redberg, "Should Healthy People Take Cholesterol Drugs to Prevent Heart Disease?" © 2014 by *The Wall Street Journal*.

John Jay, "Concerning Dangers From Foreign Force and Influence." Originally published in the *Independent Journal*, November 3, 1787.

Gary Marcus, Christof Koch, "The Future of Brain Implants." © 2014 by *The Wall Street Journal*. Originally published March 14, 2014.

Arthur Hendry Howard Heming, "The Drama of The Forests." First published 1921.

SECTION 2

Time – 25 minutes
20 Questions

Turn to Section 2 of your answer sheet to answer the questions in this section.

Notes

1. Choose the best answer choice of those provided. Be sure to fill in the corresponding circle on your answer sheet.
2. You may NOT use a calculator on this section.
3. If a problem includes a figure and does not state that the figure is NOT to scale, you may assume the figure provides a correct representation of the information in the problem.
4. The domain of any function f is the set of all real numbers x for which $f(x)$ is a real number, unless otherwise stated.

Reference

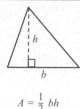
$A = \frac{1}{2}bh$

$a^2 + b^2 = c^2$

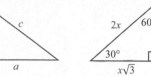
Special Triangles

 $V = \frac{1}{3}lwh$

 $V = \frac{1}{3}\pi r^2 h$

$A = lw$

 $V = lwh$

 $V = \pi r^2 h$

 $A = \pi r^2$
$C = 2\pi r$

 $V = \frac{4}{3}\pi r^3$

- There are 360° in a circle.
- The sum of the angles in a triangle is 180°.
- The number of radians of arc of a circle is 2π.

---

1. Which of the following represents the solution set to the inequality $1 \le -2x + 3$?

(A)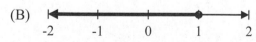
  -2   -1   0   1   2

(B)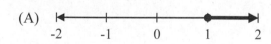
  -2   -1   0   1   2

(C)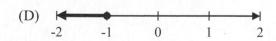
  -2   -1   0   1   2

(D)
  -2   -1   0   1   2

2. The chemical formula for water is H_2O, which indicates that each molecule of water contains two hydrogen atoms and one oxygen atom. A cup of water contains approximately 2.4×10^{25} hydrogen and oxygen atoms combined. How many of these atoms are hydrogen atoms?

(A) 8×10^{24}
(B) 1.6×10^{25}
(C) 2.4×10^{25}
(D) 4.8×10^{25}

GO ON TO THE NEXT PAGE

$$3x \geq y - 1$$

3. Which of the following ordered pairs is NOT a solution to the inequality above?

(A) $(-1, -4)$
(B) $(0, 0)$
(C) $(2, 7)$
(D) $(3, 11)$

4. A gas station charges \$3.39 per gallon of gas and a flat fee of \$2 per transaction. Which of the following graphs represents the cost of a transaction as a function of the number of gallons of gas purchased?

(A)

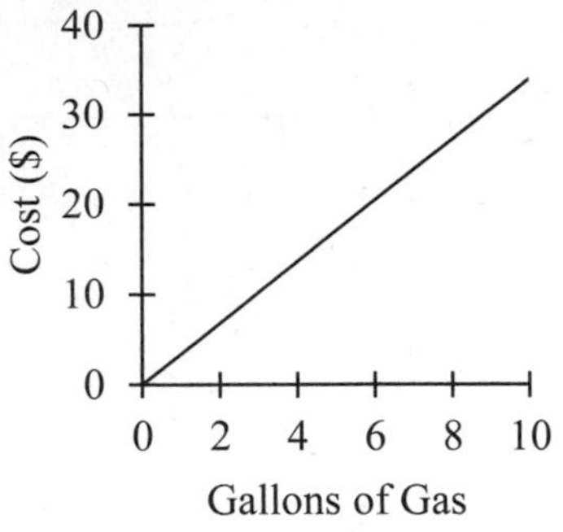

(B)

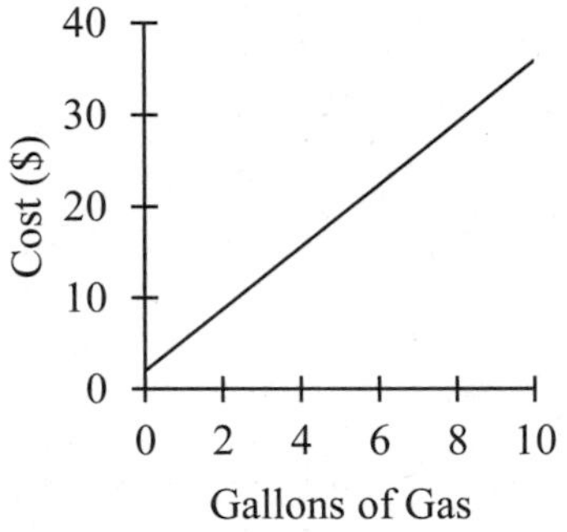

(C)

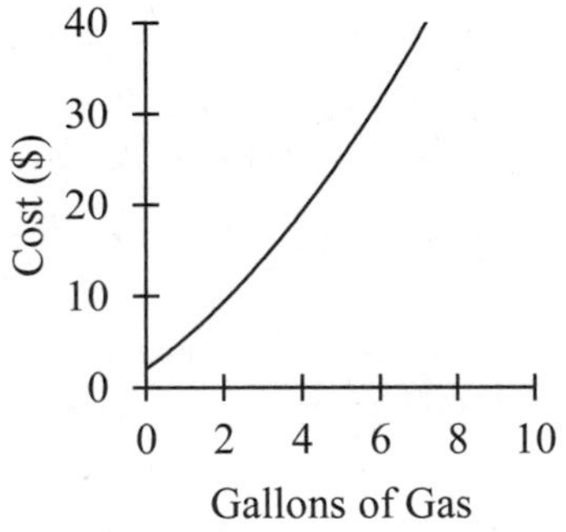

(D)

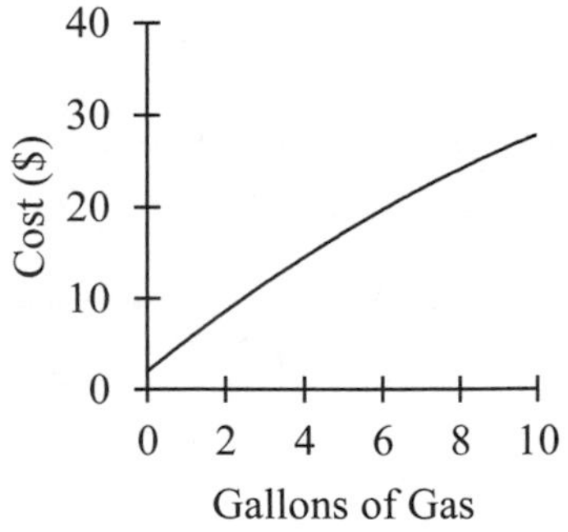

GO ON TO THE NEXT PAGE ➡

5. A fast food restaurant sells hot dogs for $1.00 each and hamburgers for $1.50 each. A group of 15 friends orders $20 worth of hot dogs and hamburgers. If every person in the group orders one item, how many hot dogs does the group order?

(A) 5
(B) 6
(C) 8
(D) 10

	Membership Fee	Locker Rental	Day Fee
Membership	$100	Free	Free
No Membership	None	$10	$7

7. The table above shows possible rates at a gym. Without a membership, customers pay a fee of $10 per month for a locker and $7 per visit. A membership includes a locker and unlimited visits for $100 per month. How many times per month must a customer go to the gym in order to benefit from purchasing a membership?

(A) 13
(B) 12
(C) 11
(D)   2

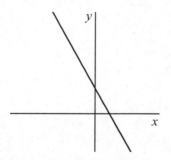

6. The graph above represents the function $y = mx + b$. Which of the following is a possible equation for x as a function of y?

(A) $x = my + b$

(B) $x = -my - b$

(C) $x = \dfrac{y - b}{m}$

(D) $x = \dfrac{-y - b}{m}$

8. Which of the following equations has exactly one real solution?

(A) $x^2 + 6x + 3 = 0$
(B) $2x^2 + 6x + 3 = 0$
(C) $3x^2 + 6x + 3 = 0$
(D) $4x^2 + 6x + 3 = 0$

GO ON TO THE NEXT PAGE

9. Andre is planning a field trip to a museum for his class of s students. He has \$200 to spend on tickets and meals, and each student gets one meal and one ticket. If tickets cost t dollars each, how much money can Andre spend on each meal?

(A) $200 + ts$ dollars

(B) $200 - ts$ dollars

(C) $\dfrac{200 + ts}{s}$ dollars

(D) $\dfrac{200 - ts}{s}$ dollars

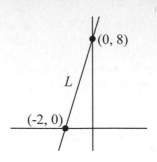

11. Which of the following equations describes a line that is perpendicular to line L above?

(A) $y = 4x + 8$

(B) $y = -4x + 8$

(C) $y = \dfrac{1}{4}x + 8$

(D) $y = -\dfrac{1}{4}x + 8$

---

10. All of these expressions are equivalent EXCEPT

(A) $2\sqrt{2x}$

(B) $\sqrt{8x}$

(C) $\sqrt[4]{16x^2}$

(D) $\sqrt[4]{4^2 \times 4x^2}$

---

12. If $f(x) = \dfrac{x+1}{3x}$ and $g(x) = 2x^2$, what is the value of $f(g(x))$?

(A) $\dfrac{2x^2 + 1}{6x^2}$

(B) $\dfrac{2y^2 + 1}{6y^2}$

(C) $\dfrac{2x^2 + 1}{3x}$

(D) $\dfrac{(x+1)(2y^2)}{3x}$

GO ON TO THE NEXT PAGE

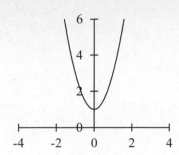

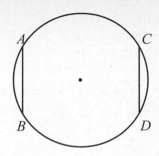

13. The graph above represents the function $f(x) = ax^2 + c$. The point $(2,6)$ is found on $f(x)$. If $g(x) = 2f(x)$ and $g(x)$ contains the point $(2, b)$, what is the value of b?

(A) 6
(B) 12
(C) 14
(D) 16

15. The circle above has a radius r and parallel chords $\overline{AB}$ and $\overline{CD}$. Each chord has a length of r. If a rectangle is formed by connecting the points $A, B, C,$ and D, what is the area of the rectangle?

(A) $r\sqrt{3}$
(B) $r\sqrt{5}$
(C) $r^2\sqrt{3}$
(D) $r^2\sqrt{5}$

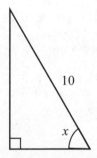

14. The diagram above shows a flag pole casting a shadow. The distance between the top of the flag pole and end of the shadow is 10. What is the difference between the height of the flag pole and the length of the shadow, in terms of x?

(A) $\sin(x) \times 10 - \cos(x) \times 10$

(B) $\dfrac{\sin(x)}{10} - \dfrac{\cos(x)}{10}$

(C) $\cos(x) \times 10 - \sin(x) \times 10$

(D) $\dfrac{\cos(x)}{10} - \dfrac{\sin(x)}{10}$

GRID-INS

16. Josh has $6.90 in quarters and nickels. If he has the same number of quarters and nickels, how many quarters does Josh have?

GO ON TO THE NEXT PAGE

$$y + 3 = 2x^2 - 5x$$
$$y - 3 = 6x$$
$$x > 0$$

17. What is a value of x that satisfies the system of equations above?

18. Carlos runs directly towards Xiao at 15 miles per hour. Xiao walks directly toward Carlos at 3 miles per hour. If they meet after 20 minutes, how far apart were they, in miles, before they started moving?

19. When the positive integer u is divided by 12, the remainder is 8. What is the remainder for the quotient $\dfrac{u + 10}{12}$?

$$2(a^3 + a^2 + 4a - 8) = 2a^3 + 4a^2 - 5a - 1$$

20. What is one possible value of a for the equation above?

STOP

If you finish early, you may review your responses for this section.
Do not view or begin working on any other sections.

SECTION 3
Time – 35 minutes
44 Questions

Turn to Section 3 of your answer sheet to answer the questions in this section.

Directions: For these questions, determine the solution to each question presented and choose the best answer choice of those provided. Be sure to fill in the respective circle on your answer sheet.

Questions 1-11 are based on the following passage.

Our culture tends to place high value on natural ability as a measure of our potential. We often praise our children more for their talent than for their effort or ambition. We exalt musical or athletic prodigies, whose early successes seem to promise great things for the future, in the sincere belief that we are encouraging them to pursue their potential. **1**

Social science research has indicated that to praise children **2** for their talent instead of his or her effort can cause them to feel constrained by their own perceived limits. An influential study by Stanford psychologist Carol Dweck identified the different effects of these two types of praise. Dweck and a colleague, Claudia Mueller, conducted a study with 128 children ranging in age from 10 to 12. Each child was given a set of moderately challenging puzzles. Regardless of their performance on the puzzles, all the children were told that they had done well. However, some children **3** were praised in that instance for their intelligence in particular, while others were praised for their effort.

After receiving this praise, each child was asked whether he or she wanted to continue working on fairly easy problems or to move on to harder ones that would be **4** educational; but might not make the student "look smart." When presented with this choice, the students who had been praised for their intelligence **5** tend to ask for the easier puzzles. Furthermore, when these children were later presented with harder puzzles, they reported feeling very discouraged if they could not complete them. Dweck and her colleagues believe these children felt that if solving puzzles meant they were smart, **6** failing to solve them would mean they were not smart. As a result, they avoided **7** risking failure. They were discouraged when they **8** espied it. The children who had been praised for effort, **9** on the same page, were more likely to seek out challenging but educational problems, and were less discouraged by failure.

Dweck's work has important implications for how parents and teachers interact with children—even very intelligent ones. In Dweck's study, students who performed very well on the first set of puzzles responded **10** to praise for they're intelligence in the same way as students who performed less well. This means that even students who do possess **11** awesome talents could be blocked from reaching their full potential by a fear of failure. Children should be taught that they are not constrained by a set of talents determined at birth, and that they have the opportunity to grow through practice, effort, and constructive failure.

1. Which choice, inserted here, most effectively transitions to the next paragraph?

   (A) Nevertheless, children should be shielded from knowledge of their own weaknesses.
   (B) Therefore, children should not be taught that they can overcome any obstacle through hard work and perseverance alone.
   (C) However, praising children for talent over effort may actually be stifling their development.
   (D) Accordingly, we should praise children for recognizing their own strengths and following them.

2. (A) NO CHANGE
   (B) for his or her talent instead of effort
   (C) for their talent instead of their effort
   (D) for his or her talent instead of their effort

3. (A) NO CHANGE
   (B) were praised for their intelligence
   (C) were praised and complimented for their intelligence
   (D) were praised in that instance for their intelligence

GO ON TO THE NEXT PAGE ⟹

3 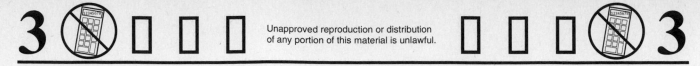 3

Unapproved reproduction or distribution
of any portion of this material is unlawful.

4. (A) NO CHANGE
    (B) educational but, might
    (C) educational, but might
    (D) educational. But might

5. (A) NO CHANGE
    (B) would have tended
    (C) will tend
    (D) tended

6. (A) NO CHANGE
    (B) fail to solve them
    (C) failure solving them
    (D) to fail to solve them

7. Which choice most effectively combines the sentences
    at the underlined portion?

    (A) risking failure; they were also observed to be
        discouraged
    (B) risking that they might fail, and also they were
        discouraged
    (C) risking failure and were discouraged
    (D) risking failure; they were discouraged

8. (A) NO CHANGE
    (B) intuited
    (C) imagined
    (D) encountered

9. (A) NO CHANGE
    (B) on the up-and-up
    (C) on the merits
    (D) on the other hand

10. (A) NO CHANGE
    (B) to praise for their intelligence
    (C) to praise for his or her intelligence
    (D) to their praise for his or her intelligence

11. Which choice is most consistent with the tone of the
    passage?

    (A) NO CHANGE
    (B) exceptional
    (C) unbelievable
    (D) superb

GO ON TO THE NEXT PAGE

Questions 12-22 are based on the following passage.

The United States has 35,000 museums. If you visit one of these museums, **12** <u>one can see</u> pieces of art, historical documents, or scientific models. What you may not **13** <u>see are</u> the many people who work behind the scenes to collect, restore, and improve the collections of museums. The **14** <u>professionals</u> that work for museums are responsible for restoring, preserving, and promoting the treasures that museums hold.

Overseeing the museum's historical archives are its archivists. Archivists take care of records and documents, such as letters, diaries, maps, films, and **15** <u>audio recordings and it is their job to preserve</u> these records so that they can be accessed by both researchers and the general public. To properly preserve documents and records, archivists need to have an understanding of their unique physical properties. An archivist may need to **16** <u>understand, for example, the</u> conditions necessary to safely store papyrus, vellum, paper, or film media. Some archivists also create electronic versions of documents so that the information can be easily distributed. Perhaps most importantly, archivists maintain digital databases that keep track of the documents in a museum and those that are being borrowed. Without this information, it would be impossible to keep track of these valuable pieces of history.

[1] **17** <u>While archivists care for documents in museums,</u> conservators care for objects. [2] The job of a conservator is to preserve and restore important objects. [3] Depending on the museum that they work for, conservators may encounter many different kinds of objects. **18** [4] Because they work with many different types of objects, conservators have to understand both history and chemistry. [5] They have to understand how different materials will **19** <u>decompress</u> over time and what chemicals will best preserve them during this process. [6] Conservators sometimes even use x-rays to determine the best way to protect or restore an aging object.

Conservators may also design replacements for missing parts of an object or create replicas for use in other museums. Some conservators become experts in a specific type of object or material. **20** <u>However,</u> some conservators specialize in restoring and preserving objects made of stone. Expert conservators may be asked to travel around the world in order to protect the world's supply of historical objects.

Most conservator and archivist positions require at least a Master's degree. **21** <u>Many museum professions require many years of study. Yet they are also highly rewarding</u>. Archivists and conservators continue to learn throughout

their life. They also have the satisfaction of knowing that their jobs help people of all ages learn about history, art, and **22** <u>the study of science</u>.

12. (A) NO CHANGE
    (B) one could see
    (C) you can see
    (D) someone could see

13. (A) NO CHANGE
    (B) be seeing is
    (C) see is
    (D) seeing are

14. Which choice best establishes the author's tone?

    (A) dedicated professionals
    (B) underachieving professionals
    (C) heroic professionals
    (D) mysterious professionals

15. (A) NO CHANGE
    (B) audio recordings, it is also their job to preserve
    (C) audio recordings: it is their job to preserve
    (D) audio recordings; it is their job to preserve

16. (A) NO CHANGE
    (B) understand; for example, the
    (C) understand, for example the
    (D) understand for example, the

17. Which choice establishes the best transition between paragraphs?

    (A) NO CHANGE
    (B) While most people think documents are more important than objects,
    (C) Even though archivists care only for documents,
    (D) Since archivists have complete control of documents,

GO ON TO THE NEXT PAGE →

18. Which choice, inserted here, most effectively adds support for sentence 3?

    (A) Conservators have to possess a broad range of skills and techniques to satisfy the requirements of their profession.
    (B) They also have to work with many different populations, including collectors and tourists.
    (C) A museum's collection might contain ivory carvings, bronze works, paintings, or even pieces of ancient buildings.
    (D) The objects that conservators work with are often expensive and precious.

19. (A) NO CHANGE
    (B) decompose
    (C) degenerate
    (D) renege

20. (A) NO CHANGE
    (B) On the other hand,
    (C) Therefore,
    (D) For instance,

21. Which choice most effectively combines the underlined sentences?

    (A) Many museum professionals studied for many years and they are therefore highly rewarded.
    (B) Although these professions require many years of study, they are also highly rewarding.
    (C) Requiring years of study, many professions calling for such degrees are highly rewarding.
    (D) Museum professions are often highly rewarding, but they require many years of study.

22. (A) NO CHANGE
    (B) studying science.
    (C) to study science.
    (D) science.

GO ON TO THE NEXT PAGE ⟹

Questions 23-33 are based on the following passage.

Individual practitioners of meditation have long touted its mental benefits, but [23] in recent decades it has now also been a subject of scientific interest—and the evidence suggests that the practice may actually promote brain health. Researchers have been conducting meditation studies since the 1950s, and it is now well-established that meditation can cause people to become more relaxed and that long-term practice can change the way that the brain works. In 2005, a group of scientists at Yale University conducted a study to investigate whether meditation might also [24] infect the physical growth and development of certain parts of the brain.

[1] Previous studies had demonstrated that the physical structures of the brain [25] are changed by tasks that repeatedly activate specific areas of the brain. [2] In other words, just as muscles grow or shrink in response to use or disuse, different parts of the brain can physically change in response to how they are used. [3] MRI scans reveal thickening of brain tissue in areas of the brain which have been [26] repeatedly activated over and over by stimulation. [4] These changes in brain structure are detectable through the use of magnetic resonance imaging, or MRI, which creates three-dimensional maps of the brain or other organs. [5] The Yale team hypothesized that regular meditation might cause similar thickening. [27]

[28] To confirm these findings, the Yale team designed a study to compare the brains of participants from two groups: a control group of non-meditators, and an experimental group of seasoned meditators. The researchers were most concerned with areas of the brain [29] associated with attention and sensory processing, which are activated during meditation. They designated these areas of the brain the "search area," and used MRI scans to map out differences in brain tissue thickness in the search area between [30] the meditators and the brain scans of non-meditators.

The team's results indicated that tissue in the search area was indeed [31] much less thick in meditators' brains than in non-meditators'. Furthermore, while older subjects tended to have thinner brain tissue in the search area, age differences were much less pronounced within the group of meditators. While the study did not follow participants [32] over time, suggesting that meditation may help to slow the thinning of brain tissue that takes place throughout the brain as people age.

The study did not determine whether the increased thickness was the result of larger [33] brain cells; new brain cells or the growth of blood vessels in the brain. However, any of these causes would be likely to improve brain function. That gives researchers some reason to believe that meditation may help to preserve healthy brain function.

Thickness of Brain Tissue in the Search Areas of Meditators and Non-meditators

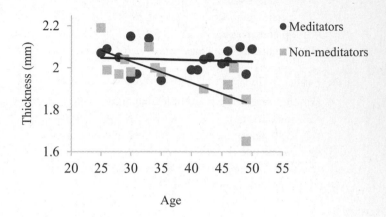

23. (A) NO CHANGE
    (B) in decades it has
    (C) in the most recent decades it has now also
    (D) in recent decades it has also

24. (A) NO CHANGE
    (B) affect
    (C) inflect
    (D) effect

25. (A) NO CHANGE
    (B) is changed by
    (C) have been changed by
    (D) are changing by

26. (A) NO CHANGE
    (B) activated again and again by repeated stimulation.
    (C) repeatedly activated by stimulation.
    (D) activated by stimulation.

27. For the sake of cohesion, sentence 4 should be placed

    (A) where it is now.
    (B) before sentence 1.
    (C) before sentence 3.
    (D) after sentence 4.

GO ON TO THE NEXT PAGE

28. Which option provides the best transition between paragraphs?

   (A) NO CHANGE
   (B) To verify this result,
   (C) To test this hypothesis,
   (D) To learn more about MRIs,

29. (A) NO CHANGE
   (B) complicit in
   (C) encouraged by
   (D) attentive to

30. (A) NO CHANGE
   (B) the brain image scans of meditators and non-meditators.
   (C) the brains of meditators and the brains of non-meditators.
   (D) the search areas of meditators versus those scans of non-meditators.

31. Which choice is most consistent with the information provided in the graphs?

   (A) NO CHANGE
   (B) thinner
   (C) thicker
   (D) older

32. (A) NO CHANGE
   (B) over time to suggest
   (C) over time it was suggested
   (D) over time, this suggests

33. (A) NO CHANGE
   (B) brain cells; new brain cells; or the growth
   (C) brain cells; new, brain cells, or the growth
   (D) brain cells, new brain cells, or the growth

Questions 34-44 are based on the following passage.

A lighted Christmas tree grows larger and larger until it fills half the stage. A pugnacious, many-headed mouse is [34] renounced in battle by a living doll. Twenty-foot windows open onto a landscape awhirl with snow.

Every year since 1954, George Balanchine's *The Nutcracker* has delighted the thousands of families who come—some once, some a few times, some annually—to see this hallmark work of American ballet. Choreographed by a Russian to Russian music based on a German story, *The Nutcracker* might not seem like an obvious candidate for the title of "great American ballet." However, both its origins and [35] its reception has marked it as essentially American.

Balanchine choreographed *The Nutcracker* for New York City Ballet, [36] the company he had founded, with Lincoln Kirstein six years earlier. Balanchine was Russian by birth, but [37] Kirstein was an American. Kirstein longed to bring ballet, which was chiefly performed in Europe, to an American audience. Kirstein's love of ballet was kindled when, as a child, he saw the Russian ballerina Anna Pavlova perform on tour in Boston. But much as he admired them, his hope was not merely to bring European artists to America: he wanted the art form itself to take root in his native soil.

[1] Kirstein first saw Balanchine's work in the late '20s in Paris, and he was impressed by [38] its physical vitality and modernism. [2] Balanchine's response, "but, first a school," suited Kirstein's ambitions perfectly. [3] In 1933, he invited the choreographer to move to the United States [39] and would found an American ballet company. [4] Before staging his ballets with dancers unschooled in European techniques, [40] the dancers needed training. [5] In 1934, Kirstein and Balanchine founded the School of American Ballet, where Balanchine taught a technique that combined elements of the European tradition with [41] backwards ideas of his own, many of them inspired by what he saw as the uniquely American qualities of his new ensemble. [42]

The pair's attempts at founding a professional company were interrupted by World War II, [43] but eventually reached their fruition with the event of the establishment of New York City Ballet in 1948. [44] *The Nutcracker* was not the first ballet Balanchine staged for his new company, it was his most ambitious project to date and the first to include students at the School of American Ballet onstage alongside adult dancers. *The Nutcracker* quickly became an American classic, performed annually not only by New York City Ballet but also by regional companies across the country.

34. (A) NO CHANGE
    (B) retreated
    (C) defeated
    (D) upended

35. (A) NO CHANGE
    (B) their reception have marked them
    (C) their reception has marked it
    (D) its reception have marked it

36. (A) NO CHANGE
    (B) the company he had founded with Lincoln Kirstein six years earlier.
    (C) the company, he had founded with Lincoln Kirstein, six years earlier.
    (D) the company he had, founded with Lincoln Kirstein six years earlier.

37. Which choice most effectively combines the sentences at the underlined portion?

    (A) Kirstein, as an American, longed
    (B) Kirstein was an American which longed
    (C) Kirstein was an American who longed
    (D) Kirstein, an American, that longed

38. (A) NO CHANGE
    (B) his
    (C) their
    (D) that

39. (A) NO CHANGE
    (B) and to found
    (C) and founding
    (D) and have founded

40. (A) NO CHANGE
    (B) the dancers needed to train.
    (C) Balanchine needed to train them.
    (D) they needed training.

41. Which choice is most consistent with the tone of the passage?

    (A) NO CHANGE
    (B) shocking
    (C) newfangled
    (D) fresh

GO ON TO THE NEXT PAGE

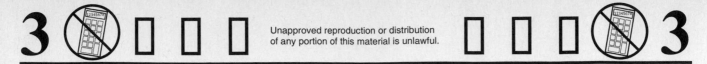
42. For the sake of the cohesion of this paragraph, sentence 2 should be placed

    (A) where it is now.

    (B) before sentence 1.

    (C) after sentence 3.

    (D) before sentence 5.

43. (A) NO CHANGE

    (B) but reached fruition eventually when New York City Ballet was established at last in 1948.

    (C) but finally reached fruition with the establishment of New York City Ballet in 1948.

    (D) but reached their eventual fruition, finally, with New York City Ballet's establishment in 1948.

44. (A) NO CHANGE

    (B) *The Nutcracker* was not the first ballet Balanchine staged for his new company, and it was

    (C) *The Nutcracker* was not the first ballet Balanchine staged for his new company, but rather it was

    (D) While *The Nutcracker* was not the first ballet Balanchine staged for his new company, it was

STOP

If you finish early, you may review your responses for this section.
Do not view or begin working on any other sections.

SECTION 4
Time – 55 minutes
38 Questions

Turn to Section 4 of your answer sheet to answer the questions in this section.

Notes

1. Choose the best answer choice of those provided. Be sure to fill in the corresponding circle on your answer sheet.

2. You may use a calculator on this section.

3. If a problem includes a figure and does not state that the figure is NOT to scale, you may assume the figure provides a correct representation of the information in the problem.

4. The domain of any function f is the set of all real numbers x for which $f(x)$ is a real number, unless otherwise stated.

Reference

$A = \frac{1}{2}bh$

$a^2 + b^2 = c^2$

Special Triangles

$V = \frac{1}{3}lwh$

$V = \frac{1}{3}\pi r^2 h$

$A = lw$

$V = lwh$

$V = \pi r^2 h$

$A = \pi r^2$
$C = 2\pi r$

$V = \frac{4}{3}\pi r^3$

- There are 360° in a circle.
- The sum of the angles in a triangle is 180°.
- The number of radians of arc of a circle is 2π.

---

1. If $2x - 6 = 4x + 4$, what is the value of x?

(A) −5
(B) −1
(C) 1
(D) 5

2. If a and b are both even integers, which of the following must be an odd integer?

I. $(a+1)(b+1)$
II. $(a+1)(b+2)$
III. $(a-1)(b+1)$

(A) I and II
(B) I and III
(C) II and III
(D) I, II, and III

GO ON TO THE NEXT PAGE

3. A tree is planted when it is 3 feet tall. If the tree's growth rate is linear, which of the following graphs could represent its yearly height?

(A)

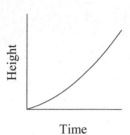

(B)

(C)

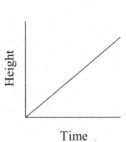

(D)

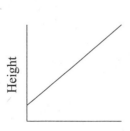

4. For how many pairs of positive integers (x, y) is $3x + y < 8$?

(A) One
(B) Three
(C) Five
(D) Seven

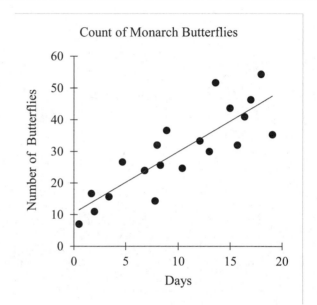

Count of Monarch Butterflies

5. The scatterplot above shows the number of Monarch butterflies over a three-week period. Based on the line of best fit, which of the following values is closest to the average daily increase in the number of Monarch butterflies?

(A) .5
(B) 2
(C) 10
(D) 40

GO ON TO THE NEXT PAGE

6. *a* is 8% of *b* and *b* is 150% greater than *c*. If *c* is 20, what is the value of *a*?

(A) 5
(B) 4
(C) 3
(D) 2

	Symptoms	No Symptoms
Vaccinated	216	1134
Not Vaccinated	584	336

7. A hospital collected data from patients who were exposed to a certain virus. The hospital recorded whether the patients had been vaccinated for the virus and whether they showed symptoms. The data is summarized in the chart above. What percentage of patients who showed symptoms had been vaccinated?

(A) 16%
(B) 27%
(C) 37%
(D) 73%

8. If $x \times 3 = \frac{1}{2} y$, what is $\frac{y}{3}$ in terms of x?

(A) $\frac{2}{3} x$

(B) x

(C) $\frac{3}{2} x$

(D) $2x$

$$p(x) = |2x - 5|$$

9. $p(2) + p(-2) =$

(A) −10
(B) −8
(C)   8
(D) 10

GO ON TO THE NEXT PAGE

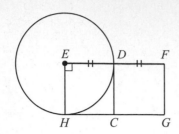

10. In the diagram above, the circumference of circle E is 6π. What is the area of rectangle *EFGH*?

(A) 3π
(B) 18
(C) 12π
(D) 24

11. What is the length of the line segment beginning at the point $(-2,3)$ and ending at the point $(1,7)$?

(A) 0.75
(B) 3.00
(C) 4.00
(D) 5.00

Questions 12 and 13 refer to the following information.

James conducted a survey in two of his classes about the number of languages his fellow students could speak fluently. The following charts show the results of his survey for each class.

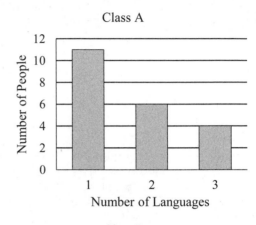

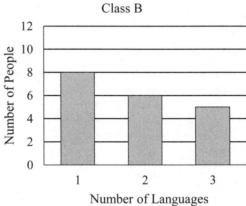

12. Approximately what percentage of students in Class A speak more than two languages?

(A) 14%
(B) 19%
(C) 29%
(D) 48%

GO ON TO THE NEXT PAGE

13. Which of the following statements correctly compares the medians and modes of the data from the two classes?

   (A) Class A has a smaller median than Class B. Class A and Class B have the same mode.
   (B) Class A has a larger median than Class B. Class A and Class B have the same mode.
   (C) Class A has the same median as Class B. Class A has a smaller mode than Class B.
   (D) Class A has the same median as Class B. Class A has a larger mode than Class B.

14. Which of the following is a NOT a factor of the expression $2x^2 + 2x - 12$?

   (A) 2
   (B) $(x - 2)$
   (C) $(x - 3)$
   (D) $(2x + 6)$

15. A car dealer buys a car from a manufacturer. The dealer increases the price of the car by 20% to $36,000. The dealer then decreases the price by 5% and sells the car. What is the dealer's total profit from the sale of the car?

   (A) $4,200
   (B) $6,000
   (C) $7,200
   (D) $9,000

$$\frac{4(x + 1) - 1}{3} = \frac{8 - (5 - x)}{5}$$

16. What is the value of x in the equation above?

   (A) $-\dfrac{24}{17}$

   (B) $-\dfrac{6}{17}$

   (C) $-\dfrac{24}{23}$

   (D) $-\dfrac{6}{23}$

GO ON TO THE NEXT PAGE

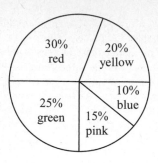

17. The circle graph above represents the distribution in sales of different colors of umbrellas for a department store in 2009. If the store sold 1800 umbrellas, how many red, yellow, and blue umbrellas were sold?

   (A)   540
   (B)   720
   (C)   1020
   (D)   1080

18. Which of the following expressions is NOT equal to $3\sqrt{32}$?

   (A) $12\sqrt{2}$
   (B) $6\sqrt{8}$
   (C) $4\sqrt{12}$
   (D) $\sqrt{288}$

19. Macey and Sam both have $100 in their bank accounts. Each year Macey's bank increases her balance by $10, and Sam's bank increases his balance by 10%. If Macey and Sam do not deposit or withdraw any money, what is the difference between Macey's balance and Sam's balance after 5 years?

   (A)   Macey's account will have $11.05 more than Sam's account.
   (B)   Macey's account will have the same balance as Sam's account.
   (C)   Macey's account will have $9.05 less than Sam's account.
   (D)   Macey's account will have $11.05 less than Sam's account.

20. For which of the following functions is $f(2) < f(-2)$?

   (A) $f(x) = \dfrac{3}{x}$

   (B) $f(x) = 3x^2 + 3$

   (C) $f(x) = 3 - x^3$

   (D) $f(x) = -3$

GO ON TO THE NEXT PAGE

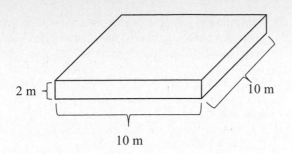

Count of Wolves in a Protected Wilderness Area	
Year	Count of Wolves
0	20
6	27
12	36

21. As shown above, a rectangular pool is 10 meters long and 10 meters wide, with a uniform depth of 2 meters. If a pump fills the pool at a rate of 55 gallons per minute, how many hours will it take to fill half of the pool? (1 cubic meter equals approximately 264 gallons.)

(A)   4
(B)   8
(C)   16
(D)   30

23. A group of scientists have reintroduced a species of wolf into a protected wilderness area and are measuring the population growth, as summarized in the table above. 20 wolves were initially released and data shows that the population increased at a rate of approximately 5% each year. Which of the following functions approximates the relationship between the wolf population, P, and time in years, t?

(A) $P = 20 + 0.05t$
(B) $P = 20 \times 1.05 \times t$
(C) $P = 20(0.05)^t$
(D) $P = 20(1.05)^t$

$$y - x = -3x$$

22. What is the value of $\dfrac{x}{y}$?

(A) $-\dfrac{1}{4}$

(B) $-\dfrac{1}{2}$

(C) -2

(D) -4

$$p = \dfrac{2q}{r^2}$$

24. If both q and r are divided by 2, what happens to the value of p in the equation above?

(A) p is halved.
(B) p is not changed.
(C) p is doubled.
(D) p is tripled.

GO ON TO THE NEXT PAGE

Questions 25 and 26 refer to the following information.

A survey was conducted to determine the types of vehicles owned by people in different age groups. The table below displays a summary of the survey results.

Car Type by Age

Age	SUV/ Minivan	Sedan/ Coupe	Truck	Electric/ Hybrid	None	Total
18 – 29	9,357	6,980	3,537	3,583	3,498	**26,955**
30 – 49	11,439	13,476	4,343	3,953	2,309	**35,520**
50 – 69	10,964	14,055	1,506	1,068	2,004	**29,597**
70+	7,033	15,610	680	792	5,377	**29,492**
Total	**38,793**	**50,121**	**10,066**	**9,396**	**13,188**	**121,564**

25. According to the table, which age group contained the smallest percentage of people who did not own a vehicle?

(A) 18 – 29
(B) 30 – 49
(C) 50 – 69
(D) 70+

26. According to the table, approximately what is the percent probability that the owner of a hybrid or electric car is 50 or more years old?

(A) 3%
(B) 11%
(C) 20%
(D) 24%

27. Which of the following is NOT a solution to the equation $\sin(x) = \sin^2(x)$?

(A) π

(B) $\dfrac{\pi}{2}$

(C) $-\dfrac{\pi}{2}$

(D) $-\pi$

GO ON TO THE NEXT PAGE

28. A construction worker uses a chain-link fence to completely enclose a rectangular area. The worker has 40 feet of fencing material. Which of the graphs below shows the total enclosed area as a function of the length of one side of the rectangle? (Note: Graphs not drawn to scale.)

(A)

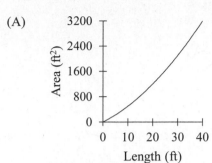

(B)

(C)

(D)

29. The imaginary number i is defined such that $i^2 = -1$. Which of the following expressions is equivalent to $(5 - i)(2 + 6i)$?

(A) $4 + 28i$
(B) $16 + 28i$
(C) $6 - 28i$
(D) $14 - 28i$

30. $\dfrac{9x^2}{3x + 1}$ is rewritten as $A + \dfrac{1}{3x + 1}$. What is A in terms of x?

(A) $3x - 1$
(B) $3x + 1$
(C) $9x - 1$
(D) $9x + 1$

GO ON TO THE NEXT PAGE

GRID-INS

31. A train travels at an average speed of 30 miles per hour. How many minutes will it take the train to travel 75 miles?

32. If $\dfrac{2}{5}$ of n is 48, what is $\dfrac{2}{3}$ of n?

$$f(x) = x^3 + 3x^2 - 6x + 14$$

33. What is the value of $f(-3)$?

34. Kavi takes two buses to get to work. Bus A has an average speed of 20 miles per hour, and Bus B has an average speed of 15 miles per hour. If Kavi takes Bus A for 3 miles and Bus B for 6 miles, how many minutes does Kavi spend on the two buses on his way to work?

GO ON TO THE NEXT PAGE

35. What is a positive value of a that satisfies the equation $\dfrac{12}{a-2} + \dfrac{5}{a+2} = 1$?

Top view of a box

36. A beverage company is designing boxes to contain cans of juice. The cans are right cylinders with a diameter of 3 inches and a height of 5 inches. The company is constructing boxes with a square base and a height of 5 inches to hold 9 cans packed as shown above. What volume of the box, to the nearest cubic inch, is NOT filled by the juice cans? (Use the approximation $\pi = 3.14$.)

Questions 37 and 38 refer to the following information.

Mia is graduating from college in four years. She took out a loan of $2,000 at the beginning of each year to pay part of her tuition and expenses. The annual interest rate for her loan is 4%, calculated on her total debt at the end of every year. Interest is added to her total debt for that year.

37. What is Mia's total debt with interest at the end of the fourth year? Round to the nearest dollar.

38. Suppose Mia does not borrow more money or pay off any of her debt for two years after graduating. Her interest continues to accrue at the same 4% yearly rate. At the beginning of her third year after graduating, Mia pays a lump sum of $8,000 towards her loan. After making that payment, how much debt does she still owe? Round to the nearest dollar.

STOP

If you complete the problem set before time elapses, you may review your responses for this section.

Do not view or begin working on any other sections.

5 5

Unapproved reproduction or distribution
of any portion of this material is unlawful.

SECTION 5
Time – 50 minutes

Turn to Section 5 of your answer sheet to write your essay.

Important Reminders:

- You have 50 minutes to write your essay.
- A pencil is required for the essay. An essay written in ink will receive a score of zero.
- Do not write your essay in your test book. You will receive credit only for what you write on your answer sheet.
- Write legibly.

As you read the passage below, consider how David Epstein uses

- evidence, such as facts or examples, to support claims.
- reasoning to develop ideas and to connect claims and evidence.
- stylistic or persuasive elements, such as word choice or appeals to emotion, to add power to the ideas expressed.

Adapted from David Epstein, "Sports Should Be Child's Play." © 2014 by the New York Times Company. Originally published June 10, 2014.

The national furor over concussions misses the primary scourge that is harming kids and damaging youth sports in America. The heightened pressure on child athletes to be, essentially, adult athletes has fostered an epidemic of hyperspecialization that is both dangerous and counterproductive.

Children are playing sports in too structured a manner too early in life on adult-size fields—i.e., too large for optimal skill development—and spending too much time in one sport. It can lead to serious injuries and, a growing body of sports science shows, a lesser ultimate level of athletic success. We should urge kids to avoid hyperspecialization and instead sample a variety of sports through at least age 12.

Nearly a third of youth athletes in a three-year longitudinal study led by Neeru Jayanthi, director of primary care sports medicine at Loyola University in Chicago, were highly specialized—they had quit multiple sports in order to focus on one for more than eight months a year — and another third weren't far behind. Even controlling for age and the total number of weekly hours in sports, kids in the study who were highly specialized had a 36 percent increased risk of suffering a serious overuse injury. Dr. Jayanthi saw kids with stress fractures in their backs, arms or legs; damage to elbow ligaments; and cracks in the cartilage in their joints.

Some young athletes now face surgeries befitting their grandparents. Young hockey goaltenders repeatedly practice butterfly style—which stresses the developing hip joint when the legs are splayed to block the bottom of the goal. The sports surgeon Marc Philippon, based in Vail, Colo., saw a 25-year-old goalie who already needed a hip replacement.

In the Loyola study, sport diversification had a protective effect. But in case health risks alone aren't reason enough for parents to ignore the siren call of specialization, diversification also provides performance benefits.

Kids who play multiple "attacking" sports, like basketball or field hockey, transfer learned motor and anticipatory skills—the unconscious ability to read bodies and game situations—to other sports. They take less time to master the sport they ultimately choose.

GO ON TO THE NEXT PAGE

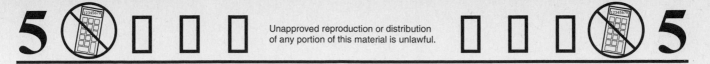

Several studies on skill acquisition now show that elite athletes generally practiced their sport less through their early teenage years and specialized only in the mid-to-late teenage years, while so-called sub-elites—those who never quite cracked the highest ranks—homed in on a single sport much sooner.

Data presented at the April meeting of the American Medical Society for Sports Medicine showed that varsity athletes at U.C.L.A.—many with full scholarships—specialized on average at age 15.4, whereas U.C.L.A. undergrads who played sports in high school, but did not make the intercollegiate level, specialized at 14.2.

We may prize the story of Tiger Woods, who demonstrated his swing at age 2 for Bob Hope. But the path of the two-time N.B.A. M.V.P. Steve Nash (who grew up playing soccer and didn't own a basketball until age 13) or the tennis star Roger Federer (whose parents encouraged him to play badminton, basketball and soccer) is actually the norm.

A Swedish study of sub-elite and elite tennis players—including five who ranked among the top 15 in the world—found that those who topped out as sub-elites dropped all other sports by age 11. Eventual elites developed in a "harmonious club environment without greater demands for success," and played multiple sports until age 14.

The sports science data support a "sampling period" through at least age 12. Mike Joyner, a Mayo Clinic physician and human performance expert, would add general physical literacy-building to the youth sports menu: perhaps using padded gymnastics gyms for parkour, which is essentially running, climbing or vaulting on any obstacle one can find.

In addition to athletic diversity, kids' sports should be kid-size. In Brazil, host of this month's World Cup, kids are weaned on "futsal," a lightly structured and miniaturized form of soccer. Futsal is played on tiny patches of grass or concrete or on indoor courts and typically by teams of five players. Players touch the ball up to five times as frequently as they do in traditional soccer, and the tighter playing area forces children to develop foot and decision-making skills under pressure.

A futsalization of youth sports generally would serve engagement, skill development and health.

Assignment: Write an essay in which you explain how David Epstein builds an argument to persuade his audience that kids should avoid specializing in a specific sport too early. In your essay, analyze how Epstein uses one or more of the features listed in the box above (or features of your own choice) to strengthen the logic and persuasiveness of his argument. Be sure that your analysis focuses on the most relevant features of the passage.

Your essay should not explain whether you agree with Epstein's claims, but rather explain how Epstein builds an argument to persuade his audience.

STOP

If you complete the problem set before time elapses, you may review your responses for this section.

Do not view or begin working on any other sections.

ANSWER KEY (PRACTICE TEST 2)

PART 1: READING

1. C	12. C	23. C	34. B	45. B
2. D	13. B	24. C	35. D	46. D
3. B	14. D	25. D	36. D	47. A
4. A	15. D	26. A	37. B	48. B
5. D	16. A	27. D	38. D	49. C
6. B	17. B	28. A	39. A	50. A
7. C	18. B	29. B	40. C	51. D
8. C	19. C	30. B	41. B	52. C
9. A	20. C	31. C	42. D	
10. B	21. A	32. A	43. D	
11. B	22. C	33. C	44. A	

PART 2: MATH (NO-CALCULATOR)

1. B	6. C	11. D	16. 23	20. 5 or 1.5
2. B	7. A	12. A	17. 6	or 3/2
3. D	8. C	13. B	18. 6	
4. B	9. D	14. A	19. 6	
5. A	10. C	15. C		

PART 3: WRITING

1. C	10. B	19. B	28. C	37. C
2. C	11. B	20. D	29. A	38. A
3. B	12. C	21. B	30. C	39. B
4. C	13. A	22. D	31. C	40. C
5. D	14. A	23. D	32. D	41. D
6. A	15. D	24. B	33. D	42. C
7. C	16. A	25. A	34. C	43. C
8. D	17. A	26. C	35. D	44. D
9. D	18. C	27. C	36. B	

Part 4: Math (calculator)

1. A	9. D	17. D	25. B	33. 32
2. B	10. B	18. C	26. C	34. 33
3. D	11. D	19. D	27. C	35. 18
4. C	12. B	20. C	28. D	36. 87
5. B	13. A	21. B	29. B	37. 8833
6. B	14. C	22. B	30. A	38. 1553 or
7. B	15. A	23. D	31. 150	1554
8. D	16. B	24. C	32. 80	

Full explanations available at ivyglobal.com/study

SCORING YOUR TESTS

To score your tests, first use the answer key to mark each of your responses right or wrong. Then, calculate your **raw score** for each section by counting up the number of correct responses. Use the tables below to help you calculate your scores:

Raw Score: Practice Test 2

Section	# of Questions Correct
1. Reading	_____
2. Math: No-Calculator	_____
3. Writing	_____
4. Math: Calculator	_____

Raw Score for Reading (Section 1): _____

Raw Score for Writing (Section 3): _____

Raw Score for Math (Section 2 + 4): _____

SCALED SCORES

Once you have found your raw score for each section, convert it into an approximate **scaled test score** using the charts below. These charts provide an estimate for your SAT scaled scores based on your performance on each practice test. To find a scaled test score for each section, find the row in the Raw Score column which corresponds to your raw score for that section, then check the column for the section you are scoring in the same row. For example, if you had a raw score of 48 for reading, then your scaled reading test score would be 39. Keep in mind that these scaled scores are estimates only. Your actual SAT score will be scaled against the scores of all other high school students taking the test on your test date.

The scaled scores below have been adjusted for Edition 1.1 of this guide.

Raw Score	Math Scaled Score	Reading Scaled Score	Writing Scaled Score	Raw Score	Math Scaled Score	Reading Scaled Score	Writing Scaled Score
58	40			28	23	26	25
57	40			27	22	25	24
56	40			26	22	25	24
55	39			25	21	24	23
54	38			24	21	24	23
53	37			23	20	23	22
52	36	40		22	20	22	21
51	35	40		21	19	22	21
50	34	40		20	19	21	20
49	34	39		19	18	20	20
48	33	39		18	18	20	19
47	33	38		17	17	19	19
46	32	37		16	16	19	18
45	32	36		15	15	18	18
44	31	35	40	14	14	17	17
43	30	34	39	13	13	16	16
42	30	34	38	12	12	16	15
41	29	33	37	11	11	14	14
40	29	33	35	10	10	13	13
39	28	32	34	9	10	12	12
38	28	31	33	8	10	11	11
37	27	31	32	7	10	10	10
36	27	30	31	6	10	10	10
35	26	30	30	5	10	10	10
34	26	29	29	4	10	10	10
33	25	29	28	3	10	10	10
32	25	28	27	2	10	10	10
31	24	28	27	1	10	10	10
30	24	27	26	0	10	10	10
29	23	26	26				

Use the table below to record your scaled scores:

Scaled Scores	
	Practice Test 2
Scaled Score for Reading (Out of 40):	_____
Scaled Score for Writing (Out of 40):	_____
Scaled Score for Math (Out of 40):	_____

ESSAY SCORE

Review the essay scoring criteria in Chapter 4. Then, estimate your essay score by assigning your essay a score out of 1-4 in each scoring area, using the following charts as a guide. Have a trusted reader check your work.

Essay Score: Practice Test 2		
Scoring Area	Reader 1 Score (1-4)	Reader 2 Score (1-4)
Reading	_____	_____
Analysis	_____	_____
Writing	_____	_____

AREA SCORE CONVERSION

You can look up your area score out of 800 below. To find your overall score, combine your area score for Reading + Writing with your area score for Math to get your total score out of 1600.

READING + WRITING

Scaled Score	Area Score	Scaled Score	Area Score	Scaled Score	Area Score
80	760-800	59	550-630	39	350-430
79	750-800	58	540-620	38	340-420
78	740-800	57	530-610	37	330-410
77	730-800	56	520-600	36	320-400
76	720-800	55	510-590	35	310-390
75	710-790	54	500-580	34	300-380
74	700-780	53	490-570	33	290-370
73	690-770	52	480-560	32	280-360
72	680-760	51	470-550	31	270-350
71	670-750	50	460-540	30	260-340
70	660-740	49	450-530	29	250-330
69	650-730	48	440-520	28	240-320
68	640-720	47	430-510	27	230-310
67	630-710	46	420-500	26	220-300
66	620-700	45	410-490	25	210-290
65	610-690	44	400-480	24	200-280
64	600-680	43	390-470	23	200-270
63	590-670	42	380-460	22	200-260
62	580-660	41	370-450	21	200-250
61	570-650	40	360-440	20	200-240
60	560-640				

MATH

Scaled Score	Area Score	Total Points	Scaled Score
40	760-800	24	440-520
39	740-800	23	420-500
38	720-800	22	400-480
37	700-780	21	380-460
36	680-760	20	360-440
35	660-740	19	340-420
34	640-720	18	320-400
33	620-700	17	300-380
32	600-680	16	280-360
31	580-660	15	260-340
30	560-640	14	240-320
29	540-620	13	220-300
28	520-600	12	200-280
27	500-580	11	200-260
26	480-560	10	200-240
25	460-540		

Use the table below to record your area scores and to calculate your overall score:

	Reading + Writing Area Score		Math Area Score		Overall Score (400-1600)
Practice Test 2	_____	+	_____	=	_____

CROSS-TEST SCORES AND SUBSCORES

Starting in 2016, the College Board will report a couple of new types of scores. In addition to receiving scores that show your performance on each section, in the areas of Math and English, and overall, you will also receive scores based on particular aspects of your performance within and across test sections.

You will receive **cross-test scores** for Analysis in Science and Analysis in History/Social Studies. The scores are based on your performance on questions in their respective subject domains across all sections of the exam. These scores will be reported on a scale of 10-40.

You will also receive **subscores** based on your performance on certain question types within each test section. Subscores will be reported on a scale of 1-15. There will be seven subscores, for the following areas:

- **Words in Context:** this subscore will be based on your performance on questions related to determining the meanings of words in the context of a passage in the English area.

- **Command of Evidence:** this subscore will be based on your performance on questions that ask you to identify the best evidence in the Reading and Writing tests.

- **Expression of Ideas:** this subscore will be based on your performance on questions that ask you to identify clear, stylistically appropriate choices in writing passages.

- **Standard English Conventions:** this subscore will be based on your performance on questions that ask you to identify and correct errors of grammar, punctuation, usage, and syntax in writing passages.

- **Heart of Algebra:** this subscore will be based on your performance on Math questions testing key concepts in Algebra.

- **Problem Solving and Data Analysis**: this subscore will be based on your performance on Math questions testing your ability to analyze sets of data, the meanings of units and quantities, and the properties of different objects and operations.

- **Passport to Advanced Math:** this subscore will be based on your performance on Math questions that test the skills you'll build on as you continue to learn more advanced math including rewriting expressions, solving quadratic equations, working with polynomials and radicals, and solving systems of equations.

As of our publication date, the College Board had not released detailed information on how these scores will be calculated.